The Anglicized words of Irish Placenames

The Anglicized words of Irish Placenames

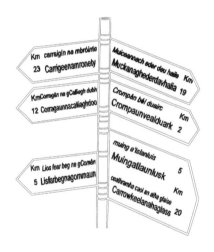

Tom Burnell

NONSUCH

First published 2006

Nonsuch Publishing
73 Lower Leeson Street
Dublin 2
Ireland
www.nonsuchireland.com

British Library Cataloguing in Publication Data.
A catalogue record for this book is available from the British Library.

ISBN 1 84588 505 8
ISBN-13 (from January 2007) 978 184588 505 2

Typesetting and origination by Tempus Publishing Limited
Printed in Great Britain

Contents

Introduction

In a broad sense this book is an Anglicized Irish place-name dictionary. It is not a book of Irish place-names *per se*, but a breakdown of the English forms of Irish wordings used in most Irish place-names.

I have collected all the available place-names in their Anglicized form and split them into their relevant word or words. Beside these I have added the corresponding Irish word or words followed by the English translation.

For every complete place name you find in this book there are 99 that are split in to their relevant wordings.

As a rule Anglicized place-names are based on the phonetic version of the Gaelic wording, however there are always exceptions.

The modern spelling of some places may differ somewhat since their meaning was recorded.

★ Should a place-name lose relevant letters if it were split, it is included in its entirety with the full translation beside it.

★ Bilingual and foreign wordings of Irish place-names are included (as found) with the translation.

★ Should differing versions (not mine) of a place-name translation exist, they are included as found.

★ English place-names of Irish locations are not generally included, eg Michaels field or Middle third, unless they are particularly interesting.

★ I do not offer my opinions nor translations; what you see is what I have found. However if a spelling might appear to be a typographical mistake, obvious error, a curious Anglicized/Irish variation or a questionable translation, (sic) is placed beside it.

★ When an Irish version of the place-name has two or more words, I have adopted the style of P W Joyce and separated the words with dashes.

★ When an Irish translation occurs without an explanation, it is noted 'not given' even though it may be obvious to all what that translation is. Almost all of these translations are from various forms of Na-Log-Ainmneacha.

★ Places beginning with '**Bally**' (*baile* in Irish) can mean a town, village, cluster of houses, townland, place, spot, homestead, enclosure, dwelling, residence, habitation, patrimony, settlement or situation. However another (but not the only) version of *baile* with the same meaning is the Anglicized word '**Ball**' and occurs mostly where family, clan or tribal names follow. Here are some examples;

Ballyine, *(Ball-Yine) baile-Uí-Eidhnigh,* Ó hÉidhnigh's (a family name) town. You would be forgiven if you assumed the Anglicisation was **Bally-ine.**

Ballycue, *(Ball-Ycue) baile-mic-Aodha,* Mackay or MacHugh, a family name and again it could mistakenly be assumed the Anglicisation was **Bally-cue.**

The same principle can <u>sometimes</u> apply to places beginning with **Anna, Annaghy, Arry, Ballyna,**

Bohery, Boola, Booly, Cappagh, Carricka, Carriga, Clasho, Clon, Clona, Cloney, Clony, Cloony, Cool, Coola, Cooly, Corry, Craggy, Crossy, Curragh, Curry, Derry, Drominy, Dromo, Farrana, Firo, Foily, Garrana, Garrauny, Garry, Glen, Gorteen, Gorty, Inchi, Inchy, Islandi, Kil, Kill, Killa, Killy, Killo, Kishy, Knocka, Knocky, Largy, Latty, Lemy, Lisma, Lissa, Lisso, Lissy, Meeny, Mona, Money, Mony, Rath, Ratho, Ringa, Templey, Terry, Tobery, Tooma, Toomy, Tullig, Tulligo, and *Tullo.*

All Anglicized family clan or tribal names found this way begin with the letters 'A' 'Y', 'O' or 'I' and are listed as such. A few of the longest place-names give the reader an insight into how most place-names are Anglicized:

* **Muckanaghederdavhalia** is split thus; Muckanagh-eder-dav-halia.
In Irish this place-name is:
Muiceannach-eder-dau-haile, and is split thus:
Muckanagh, *muiceannach, muiceanach:* a place of pigs, a pig feeding place or a piggery.
Eder, *eder, dir, eadar:* between.
Dav, *dau:* two.
Halia, *haile:* briny inlets.
Meaning the 'piggery between two briny inlets'.

* **Crompaunvealduark** is split thus: Crompaun-veal-duark.
In Irish this place-name is:
Crompán-bél-duairc, and is split thus:
Crompaun, *crompán:* a little creek.
Veal, *bél:* mouth.
Duark, *duairc:* surly.
Meaning the 'little creek of the surly mouth'.

* **Muingatlaunlusk** is split thus: Muing-a tlaunlusk.
In Irish this place-name is: *muing-a'tslanluis.*
Muing, *muing, muinga:* a sedgy place or a morass.
Atlaunlusk, *a'tslanluis:* the rib grass.
Meaning the 'sedgy place of the rib grass'.

* **Carrowkeelanahaglass** is split thus: carrow-keel-an-aha-glass.
In Irish this place-name is: *ceathramha-caol-an-atha-glaise:*
Carrow, *ceathrú, ceathru, ceathramha, ceathramhadh:* a quarter of land.
Keel, *caol, caola, cael:* narrow/slender.
An, *an:* the word 'the'.
Aha, *átha, atha, ath:* a ford.
Glass, *ghlais, glaise, glas:* green or a green place.
Meaning the 'narrow quarter of the green ford'.

* **Corragaunnacalliaghdoo** is split thus: Corragaun-na-calliagh-doo
In Irish this place-name is: *Corragán-na-gCalliagh-dubh.*
Corragaun, *corragán:* rock.
Na, *na,* .....of the (plural)...
Calliaghdoo, *gCalliagh-dubh:* literally 'black hags' or cormorants.
Meaning the 'rock of the cormorants'.
A few more of the longest place-names and local names in Ireland;
Bawnhubbamaddereen, *bán-thobair-maidrín,* field of the well of the little dog.
Carrigeenamronety, *carraigín-na-mbróinte,* little rock of the mill stones.
Carrignanonshagh, *carraig-na-nÓinseach,* rock of the female idiots.

Glassillaunvealnacurra, glas-oileán-beal-na-cora, little green island of/at the mouth of the weir.
Lisfarbegnagommaun, Lios-fear-beg-na-gComán, fort of the little hurlers.
Surhanleanantawey, sruthán-léana-an-tSamhaidh, stream of the meadow of sorrel.
And finally the one that got away, that elusive Mayo place-name;
Cooneenashkirroogohifrinn, little harbour sliding to hell.

This book could not have been possible without the help of Bibliophile Phil Fitzgerald of Doon road, Cappaghmore who kindly allowed me access to his extensive library, the research section of the Tipperary County Library, Thurles, the internet, the unyielding devoted help of my daughter Kathlene Burnell and my devoted and significant better half Ruth Burnell.

I hope you enjoy using this book as much as I did creating it.

Tom Burnell
Holycross, County Tipperary, AD 2006
museumtom@hotmail.com

Placenames in
Alphabetical Order

A

A, *a', an, na,* the…, of the…

A, *áth, ath, átha, atha,* a ford.

Aarum, *Atharam,* not given.

Aarum, *eachdhroma, each-dhroma,* horses ridge.

Aas, *eas,* a cataract or waterfall.

Abarna, *abar-na…,* not given.

Abartagh, *abartach,* a place of mires or puddles.

Abba, *abbadh,* the abbot.

Abban, *Abbán,* St Abban.

Abbe, *mainister,* a monastery or abbey.

Abber, *abar,* a mire.

Abbera, *abar a'…,* mire of the…

Abbert, *abhar,* a marsh.

Abbert, *aidhbeirt, iodhbairt,* the offering.

Abbey, *mainister,* a monastery or abbey.

Abh, *abhainn, abhann,* a river.

Abhuish, *a'bus,* near.

Abington, *Mainister-Uathine/Uaithne, Mainistir-Uaithne,* Irish version of the anglicized Abbey of the territory, district of Owney (*Uathine*).

Aboclone, *atha-bocluana,* ford of the cow meadow.

Abogan, *Uí-Bhogáin, Ó Bogáin,* O'Boggan, a family name and means descendants of Bogáin.

Aboggan, *Uí-Bhogáin, Ó Bogáin,* O'Boggan, a family name.

Abon, *abhann,* a river.

Abounia, *Buaidhne,* St Buonia.

Aboy, *abha-buí,* yellow river.

Acahill, *Ó-gCathail,* not given.

Acantha, *áth-an-Chiontaigh,* not given.

Acanty, *Uí-Cainte,* O'Canty, a family name.

Acanver, *Mhic-Ainbhir,* MacKenvir, a family name.

Acarreagh, *an-tAcra-riabhach,* not given.

Acaw, *a'chátha,* of the chaff.

Accar, *accar,* the acre.

Ach, …*ach,* as an ending to a word can sometimes mean, a place of…. or abounding in…

Ach, *achadh,* a field.

Achaill, *Uí-Cathail,* Cahill, a male name.

Achill, *Acla, Acaill,* not given.

Achonry, *achadh-Conair/Chonaire/Conaire,* Conaire or Conary's (a male name) field.

Acknew, *a'cneamhach,* garlic producing place.

Acknew, *cneamh,* wild garlic.

Aclara, *A-Chlaraigh,* De Clare, a male name.

Aclare, *áth-an-chláir,* ford of the plain or plank.

Aclint, *baile-átha-claonta,* not given.

Acnav, *a'cneamhach,* of garlic producing place.

Acnav, *a'chneamha,* of the wild garlic/gentian.

Acody, *Iócoidigh,* McCody, a family name.

Acomb, *da-chon,* two hounds.

Acon, *dá-chon,* two hounds.

Aconnigan, *Uí-Chionagáin,* not given.

Acoose, *dhá-chuas,* two caves.

Acra, *acra, acre, tAcra,* an acre.

Acra, *acraí,* not given.

Acranareen, *crannarín,* little tree.

Acrena, *acra-an/na…,* not given.

Acres, *na-hAcraí,* not given.

Acro, *acra, acre,* an acre.

Acrow, *a'cró,* the hut.

Acton, named after the village of Iron Acton in Gloucestershire.

Ad, *fhada,* long.

Ada, *fhada,* long.

Adair, *Adhair, Adhar,* a personal or family name.

Adam, *Adaim,* not given.

Adamnan, *Adhamhnán,* Adam, Eunan, Adamnan, a male name

Adan, *eadan,* front.

Adan, *fheadain,* a brook or hill.

Adane, *an-eadain,* the hill front.

Adane, *an-fheadain,* the streamlet.

Adare, *áth/ath-dara,* the oak ford or the oak grove ford.

Adarrig, *ath-dearg,* red fort.

Add, *fhada,* long.

Adda, *fhada,* long.

Addan, *éadain,* not given.

Addan, *feadan, fheadáin, fheadain,* a brook.

Addane, *Ádáin, Ádán,* not given.

Addane, *eadan,* the hill brow.

Adder, *eadar,* not given.

Adder, *eadar-da…,* between two…

Adder, *eadardha, eadar,* central, centre, middle or a place between…

Addera, *eadardha, eadar,* a place between……

Addoge, *bhFeadóg, fheadóg,* plovers.

Addra, *idir-dha-átha,* between two fords.

Addragh, *eadarach, eadrach,* middle or central place.

Addri, *eadardha, eadar,* a place between……

Addron, *Eadruain,* Addruan, a personal or family name.

Adea, O'Dea, a family name.

Adeas, *Chéile-Dé,* the Culdees of Devenish (monastic reformers). Culdee means 'companion of God'.

Aden, *Aodán, Aodáin,* Aodán, a personal name.

Ader, *eadar, dir, eder,* between.

Aderavally, *eder-dha-bhaile,* between two townlands.

Aderry, *Uí-Doirid,* O'Derry, a family name.

Adh, *ath,* a ford.

Adie, *na-doibhche, na-doibhthe,* of the cauldron, vat or round deep hollow.

Adile, *an-daill,* dark, gloomy.

Admiran, *ard-mireann,* the height of the divisions.

Adoagh, *Aduaidh,* not given.

Adooey, *Uí-Dhubhthaigh,* not given.

Adoolig, *a'dubhlaidh,* of the dark, black or gloomy.

Adoon, *áth-an-dúin, ath-duin,* ford of the fort.

Adoun, *sodán,* prosperous.

Adra, *eadardha, eadar,* a place between……

Adra, *eadar-dhá…,* a place between two…

Adri, *eadardha, eadar,* a place between……

Adrivale, *eadar-falla,* between walls.

Adriville, *eadargóiln*(sic), centre holding.

Adrool, *eadarghabhal, eadar-gabhal,* between the (river) forks.

Adruel, *eadar-shruill,* middle stream.

Adruel, *eadrúill,* not given.

Adry, *eadarach,* the central place.

Adry, *eadradh,* middle.

Adustra, *a-dosthaire,* the swaggerer.

Aelig, *áoileach,* dung.

Aellaun, *aoilán,* pleasant.

Aengus, *Aonghasa,* Aonghus, Angus, the name of a medeval Fir-Bolg chief.

Afaddy, *áth-fada, athfada,* long ford.

Afaddy, *achadh-fada,* the long field.

Afeen, St Aiffen.

Afeen, *Uí-Fhinn,* O'Finn, a family name.

Aff, *Aife,* not given.

Aff, *ath,* a ford.

Aff, *dhamh, damh, daimh,* an ox or oxen.

Affane, *ath-mheadhoin/mheadhon,* middle ford.

Affane, *áth-mheáin/meáin,* not given.

Affering, *aifrinn,* a mass or offering.

Affick, *an-afóg,* not given.

Affoley, *athbuaile, ath-buaile,* ford of the booley or dairying place.

Afoore, cold lake.

Agalish, a Church.

Agall, *áth-Gall,* not given.

Agan, *Ágain,* not given.

Agan, *Eochagan,* a personal name.

Agan, *Uí-Agáin, Uí-hAgain,* O'Hagan, a family name.

Agannon, *Uí-Gheanainn,* not given.

Agenerick, *an-eanaigh,* the swamp.

Aggard, *agart,* a haggard.

Agh, *achadh,* a field.

Agh, *ath,* a ford.

Agh, *each,* a horse.

Agh, *….ach,* as an ending to a word can sometimes mean, a place of…. or abounding in…

Agha, *achadh,* a field.

Agha, *achadh-an…,* field of the…

Agha, *an-tÁth,* not given.

Agha, *áth, ath,* a ford.

Agha, *áth-an/a* , ford of the…

Aghada, *achadh-fhada/fada,* the long field.

Aghada, *áth-fhada,* the long ford.

Aghade, *áth-Fadhat, ath-Fadad,* Fadad's (a personal or a family name) ford.

Aghadoe, *achadh-da-abha,* field of the two rivers.

Aghadoe, *achadh-dá-éo,* field of the two yews.

Aghaga, *achadh-gath,* ford of arrows or spears.

Aghagan, *Uí-hEochagain,* O'Haghagan, a family name.

Aghagh, *achadh,* a field.

Aghalile, *áth-Ó-Líolaigh,* not given.

Aghalinane, *ath-Chuilneain,* Cullinane's (a personal or a family name) ford.

Aghalode, *ath-an-chaol-fhoid,* ford of the narrow strip.

Aghan, *achadh-na…,* field of the…

Aghan, *áthán, athán,* a small ford.

Aghan, *neachán,* bracken.

Aghana, *achadh-na…,* field of the…

Aghanach, *eachineach,* not given.

Aghanacliff, *achadh-na-cloiche,* not given.

Aghanacliff, *schadh*(sic)*-na-cloiche,* field of the stones.

Aghanagh, *eachineach,* not given.

Aghancon, *achadh-cinn-chon,* not given.

Aghanish, *each-inis,* horse island.

Aghanloo, *áth-Lú, Lú's,* (a personal or family name) ford.

Agharra, *achadh-chara,* field of the weir.

Agharroo, *achadh-chara,* field of the weir.

Agharrow, *achadh-chara,* field of the weir.

Aghavas, *achadh-an-Mheasa,* not given.

Aghavea, *achadh-beithe,* field of birch.

Aghen, *achadh-an/na…,* field of the…

Agher, *achadh-ar…,* field on….

Agher, *achadhra,* a flat place, a plain.

Agher, *achair, chor, char,* as an ending to a word, a place of…. or abounding in…

Agher, *achair,* space.

Agher, *eachair,* horse/s.

Agher, *eachar, eachair,* entangled woods.

Aghera, *achadhra,* a flat place or a plain.

Aghera, *eachaire,* not given.

Aghern, *ath/áth-an-chairn,* the cairn fort.

Agherton, *achadh-an-tóin,* field on the low lying land or field on the low ground.

Agherty, *Uí-Fhachartaigh,* O'Faherty, a family name.

Aghery, *eachraí,* horses.

Aghery, *Eachtra,* not given.

Aghills, *eochaille,* yew woods.

Aghills, *hAcaillí, h-aichli,* hills or mounds.

Aghills, *hAcaillí,* not given.

Aghilly, *eochaille,* yew woods.

Aghin, *achaidh-an…, achadh-an/a'…,* the field of the …

Aghin, *áth-an…,* ford of the…

Aghinagh, *achadh-Aghnach,* Aghnach's (a personal or a family name) field.

Aghinagh, *achadh-Fhíonach/Aoineach,* not given.

Aghinis, *each-inis,* horse island.

Aghivey, *áth-Geimhidh,* not given.

Aghla, *eachla,* a stable or enclosure for horses.

Aghleam, *each-léim, eachléim,* horse leap.

Aghlin, *eachlann, eachlainne,* horse stables or horse enclosures.

Aghlis, a Church.

Aghlish, *hEaglaise, eaglais,* a Church.

Aghlisk, *eachlaisc,* a horse stable or enclosure.

Aghna, *achadh-na…,* field of the…

Aghna, *áth/átha-na…,* ford of the…

Aghnacue, *achadh-Mhic-Aodha*(sic), not given.

Aghnadargan, *achadh-dearg-mhónaidh,* field of the red bog.

Aghnaha, *achadh-na-aith,* field of the kiln.

Aghnahaha, *achadh-na-aith,* field of the kiln.

Aghnahaia, *achadh-na-aith,* field of the kiln.

Aghnameal, *achadh-cúile-Méala,* not given.

Aghnashalvy, *eachaire-Sealbha*(sic), not given.

Aghne, *áth-na…,* ford of the…

Agho, *achadh,* a field.

Aghody, *áth-Odach,* not given.

Aghoo, *achadh,* a field.

Aghoos, from *achadh,* fields.

Aghoos, *na-hEachú,* not given.

Aghort, *athghort,* not given.

Aghowle, *achadh-abhall,* apple tree field.

Aghra, *an-tAcra,* not given.

Aghra, *eachra,* horses.

Aghragh, *an-tAtharach,* not given.

Aghta, *ochta, ucht,* breast or hill breast.

Aghty, *Aitheachta,* Plebeians.

Aghullaghy, *achadh-thulcha*(sic), field of the

Aghy, *achadh,* a field or fields.

Aghy, *achaidh,* not given.

Aghy, *Eachaidh,* not given.

Aghy, *Eachdhach,* Eochy, a male name.

Aghy, the slough.

Agivey, *ath-geimhe,* the roaring water ford.

Aglass, *Eaglaise,* a Church.

Agleash, *Eaglais,* a Church.

Aglish, *Eaglais, Eaglaise,* a Church.

Aglisha, *Eaglaise,* a Church.

Agna, *eag-na…,* not given.

Agnaha, *eanach-na-hÁithe,* not given.

Agnee, *Uí-Ghniomha,* O'Gneeve or Agnew, a family name.

Agny, *Fachtna,* St Faghna.

Agola, *áth-gobhlach,* ford of the fork.

Agonagh, *O'gCuana,* O'Cooney, a family name.

Agonagh, *Ó-gCuanach,* not given.

Agonnell, *na-gConall,* of the Connells, a family name.

Agower, *a'ghamhair,* a winter stream.

Agower, *ath-gabhar,* goats ford.

Agra, *eachra,* a place for horses.

Agran, *átha-grean,* ford of the gravel.

Agroom, *dha-dhrom,* two ridges.

Aguinneen, *achadh-cooinin,* rabbit field.

Agunna, *a-ghunna,* the gun.

Aguse, *giumhas, ghiumhais,* fir.

Ah, *achadh* a field.

Ah, *áth, ath,* the ford.

Aha, *achadh…,* field of the…

Aha, *átha, atha, ath,* the ford.

Aha, *áth-an…,* ford of the…

Aha, *fhaithche,* a green.

Ahadagh, *áth-an-dá-each,* ford of the two horses.

Ahaga, *áth-an-ghá,* ford of the fight/arrow.

Ahagan, *Eathagáin,* Gahagan, a family name.

Ahair, *dhá-eithiar,* two air demons.

Ahair, *dhá-Thiar/Eithiar,* two demons.

Ahaire, *da-ethair,* two air demons/spirits.

Ahalarick, *ath-a'Lairge,* ford the river 'Lairge'.

Ahalia, *an-tSáile,* the salt water.

Ahamilla, *achadh-da-mhaol,* field of the two hills.

Ahan, *áthán,* not given.

Ahana, *áthán-na…,* little ford of the…,

Ahane, *athán, áthán, atháin, átháin, athain, ahaun,* small ford.

Ahane, *Athán,* little Church.

Ahara, *Eathara,* Eachar, a male name.

Aharagh, *atha-riabhach,* grey ford.

Aharna, *a-chárthain,* quicken trees, mountain ash or rowan trees.

Aharney, *áth-Charna,* ford of the heap.

Aharney, *áth-airne,* not given.

Ahascragh, *áth-eascrach, ath-eiscir,* ford of the sandhill.

Ahascragh, *áth-eascrach,* ford of the gravel ridge.

Ahascragh, *ath-eascrach-Chuain,* ford of St Cuan's sandhill.

Ahaun, *an-tÁthán/áthán/athán,* the small ford.

Ahaun, *Athán,* little Church(sic).

Ahavan, *Ui-Thaobhain,* O'Teevan, a personal or family name.

Ahavil, *abhaill,* an orchard.

Ahea, *achaidh,* a field.

Ahean, *dhá-én,* two birds.

Aheen, *aithín,* the little ford.

Aheen, *Eithín,* St Eheen.

Aheena, *h-aoine, aeine,* Friday.

Aheesha, *a-H-íse,* De Hyze, a family name.

Aheesha, *an-Hísigh,* not given.

Ahena, *h-aoine, aeine,* Friday.

Ahenny, *athán,* a small ford.

Ahenny, *áth-Eine,* not given.

Ahenny, *áth-theine/thine,* ford of fire or ford of the fire.

Aher, *an-Athar,* the father.

Aher, *ath-ar…,* ford on …

Ahera, *h-uidhre,* a dark bog stream.

Aherla, *eatharla,* not given.

Aherla, *eatharlach,* a valley.

Aherla, *eatharlach,* the hollow.

Aherlow, *eatharlach,* the valley.

Aherlow, *eatharlaí, eatharla,* not given.

Ahidelake, *achadh-an-da-leig,* field of the two flagstones.

Ahil, *aichil,* high ground or a rise of ground.

Ahil, *aith-choill,* second growth of wood.

Ahil, *eochaill,* yew wood.

Ahill, *Eothuile,* Eothuil, (name of a deciple of St Finbar).

Ahilla, *aith-choille,* new wood growth.

Ahilly, *a'choiligh,* of the grouse cock.

Ahimma, *ath-ime,* ford of the dam.

Ahinny, *aithine,* a fire brand.

Ahinny, *ath-tine,* ford of the fire.

Ahit, *…a'-chait,* of the cat.

Ahleen, *aillín,* a little cliff.

Ahna, *áth-na…,* ford of the…

Ahoe, *an-cheo,* the mist.

Ahoe, *an-cheóidh,* not given.

Ahoe, *na-hUamha,* of the cave.

Ahoghill, *áth-eóchaille/eochaille,* the yew tree ford.

Ahone, *na-hUamhan,* cave or grotto.

Ahony, *a'chonaidh,* of the firewood.

Ahose, *an-chuais,* the caves.

Ahy, *achaidh,* a field.

Ahy, *fhaithihe, fhaithche,* a green or a playing field.

Aidamee, *áirde-Midhe,* Midhe's (a personal or family name) height.

Aidamee, *árda-Mí,* not given.

Aighan, little play green.

Aighe, *Áighe,* not given.

Aighe, *faithche,* an exercise green.

Ailech, *grianán-Ailigh,* not given.

Aill, *aill,* a cliff.

Aill, *áill,* a hillside or a rock.

Aille, *aille,* cliffs.

Aille, *an-aill,* a cliff.

Aille, *na-hAille,* not given.

Ailleen, *aill-an….* cliff of the…

Aillena, *aille-na,* the cliff of…

Aine, *Aine,* not given.

Ainhagh, *ainbhtheth, anfuth,* the storm.

Ainy, *Áine, Aine,* Áine, Ainy, a celebrated banshee.

Air, Aire, *ár,* the slaughter.

Air, *fheir,* grass.

Aird, *ard,* high, height, a height or a hill.

Akea, *Mhic-Aodha,* son of Aodha or Hugh.

Akeevin, *Uí-Chiabháin,* not given.

Akela, *aicheala,* the eagle.

Akelly, *Uí-Cheallaigh,* not given.

Akenny, *Uí-Chionaoith,* Ó Cionaoith, a family name.

Akeo, *an-cheóidh,* not given.

Akey, *an-chaoith,* not given.

Akey, *cael, caol,* narrow.

Akin, *'ic-Chuinn,* Mac Quinn, a personal or family name.

Akinny, *aiteanach,* a place of gorse.

Akip, *ath-a'chip,* ford of the trunk.

Ala, *Ala,* Ala, a personal name and the founder of the Church of in Mayo.

Alagagh, *ealagach,* noble.

Alaghan, Allaghan, a personal or family name.

Alan, *elainn,* beautiful.

Alane, *oileáin,* not given.

Alaun, *oileain,* island.

Alaw, *a-lagha,* of the hill.

Alay, *na-laegh,* the calves.

Alban, *al-bán,* white rock.

Alban, *albanaigh,* a Scotsman.

Albanagh, *albanagh, albanach,* a Scotsman.

Albany, *Albanach, Albanaigh,* a Scotchman.

Aldragh, *geal-darach,* white oak.

Aldragh, *ghalracht,* not given.

Aldreen, *geal-draoighin,* white blackthorn.

Aldron, *Allaráin,* not given.

Alea, *Aedha,* Aedh or Hugh.

Alean, *liath,* grey.

Aleen, *aillín,* not given.

Aleen, *an/a -lín,* of the flax.

Aleenaghan, *Uí-Líonachain,* O'Leenahan or Lenahan, a family name.

Aleenaun, lake of filling or flowing.

Aleva, *an-tSléibhe,* not given.

Alewnaghta, *leamhnachta,* new milk.

Algan, *Uí-hEalgain,* O'Halligan, a family name.

Alia, *aille,* pleasant.

Alicky, *ath-lice,* flagstone ford.

Alin, *a'lin,* the pool or pond.

Aline, *a'Laighin,* the Leinsterman.

Aline, *a -lín,* the flax.

Aline, *aluinn,* delightful.

Aline, *oileán,* an island.

Aline, *Ó-Laighin,* not given.

Aline, *Uí-Leighin,* Ó Leighin, a family name.

Aline, *Uí-Leighin, Uí-Laighin,* O'Lyne or Lyons, a family name and means the descendants of Laighin.

Aline, *Uí-Liathain,* O'Lehane, a family name.

Aling, *a'lin,* the pool, pond.

Aling, *álainn,* not given.

Alisk, *álairg*(sic), *álaisg,* not given.

Alk, *fhalc,* floods.

Alkill, *aillchoill,* not given.

All, *áil,* a pig litter.

All, *aill,* a cliff.

Alla, aill-an…, aille a'…, cliff of the…

Alla, aille, a cliff, a slope, a hillside or a rock.

Alla, Ala, not given.

Alla, eala, swan/s.

Alla, Ealla, O'Hally a family name.

Alla, gheala, white or bright.

Allaban, Albain, Scotland.

Allaban, O'Hallaban, a family name.

Allagesh, an-log-glas, not given.

Allagh, Eala, not given.

Allaghan, Allacháin, not given.

Allaghtan, Fhalachtán, not given.

Allahee, alachaí, not given.

Allan, Áluinn, Dallain, Dallán, a male name.

Allateenoe, áit-an-tí-nua, site of the new house.

Allavoe, Albhú, not given.

Allavoe, Alloway, an old English personal name.

Alleen, aillín, a little cliff.

Allege, alla, a cliff.

Allen, ailín, slope or declivity.

Allen, aillín, a little cliff.

Allen, Aillinn, Aillinne, Aininn, Almhaine, not given.

Allen, Aillion, Aileann, not given.

Allen, Álainn, áluinn, álainn, beautiful.

Allen, all-an…, rock of the…

Allen, Almhain, Almhan, Alúine, a personal or family name.

Allen, tSalainn, salt.

Allenagh, ailleanach, rocky.

Allengort, áth-longfoirt, not given.

Allig, ailigh, a rock, a shoulder or rocky.

Allig, eallaig, eallaigh, cattle.

Allihies, ailichí, aill-achadh, cliff fields.

Allihies, na-hAilichí/hAillithí, not given.

Allinan, Uí-Áilíonáin, not given.

Allinan, Uí-hEallanain, O'Hallinan, a family name.

Allistragh, eileastrach, not given.

Allistragh, tAileastrach, a place of wild irises.

Allo, abhainn-ealla, not given.

Allogla, nGallóglach, gallowglasses or heavy-armed foot soldiers.

Alloly, Ailiolla, Alioll, a very old Irish personal name.

Allon, Fhallamhain, not given.

Allow, Ealla, not given.

Allow, Uí-Eala, O'Hally, a family name.

Allua, Lua, Luadh, Lua, Flann Luadh, a male name.

Ally, abhlaigh, apple trees.

Ally, aille, aill, a cliff or a rock.

Ally, alla, a cliff.

Ally, Uí-Ealla, O'Hally a family name.

Ally, Uí-Fhailbhe, O'Falvey, a personal or family name.

Allyduff, aille-duibhe, black cliff.

Aloan, Ó-Luáin, not given.

Aloan, Ua-Luain, O'Loane, a family name.

Aloan, Ui-Luin, O'Loan, a personal or family name.

Aloe, a-luaidhe, of the lead.

Aloe, an-lóigh, not given.

Aloe, Dalua, St Dalua, Do-Lua or Mo-Lua.

Alogurt, a'-lubhgoirt, the herb-garden.

Aloo, an-lao, the calf.

Aloona, Ma-Lún, Maloon, a male name.

Alp, alp, ailp, a mass or lump.

Alree, Eilíl, Alicia, a female name.

Alsmeed, Alsmeed, not given.

Alt, allt(sic), not given.

Alt, Alta, alt, ailt, a height, cliff, hill, gorge, precipice, ravine, glenside/s or a steep glenside.

Alta, ailt/alt-an/a'… cliff or glenside of…

Alta, ailt/alt-an…, height of the…

Alta, Ealta, not given.

Alta, Fháltaigh, not given.

Altacaille, glen of swans.

Altan, alltain, a small precipice.

Altan, alltán, Aldain, not given.

Altan, altan, altán, little height or hillside.

Altan, ealtan, flocks.

Altanagh, knots.

Altans, from altán, little hillsides.

Altar, altóir, altar.

Altarichard, alt-tighe-Ricaird, the glen-cliff of Richards house.

Altart Glebe, táite-an-hAltórach, not given.

Altavilla, tulaigh(sic), not given.

Altenach, altanach, precipices or cliffs.

Altenagh, altanach, not given.

Alternan, alt-Fharannáin/Fharannain, St Farannan/Forannan's height or cliff.

Altin, alt-an…, glenside of the…

Altishane, *alt-a'tSiodhain,* glen(sic) of the fairy fort.

Altna, *alt-na...,* hillside or height of the...

Alto, high.

Alton, *Alltáin,* not given.

Alton, *Altúin,* Altoun, not given.

Altore, *altóir,* altar.

Alts, from *alt,* heights.

Alts, *na-hAillt,* not given.

Alty, *aillte, altaighe,* the cliff.

Alty, *ailte,* the height.

Alty, *alltaí,* not given.

Alty, *ealta,* bird flocks.

Altyrickard, *alt-tighe-Ricaird,* the glen-cliff of Richards house.

Aluinn, *Fhloin,* Flann, a male name.

Alva, *albha,* heights.

Alvy, *Ailbhe,* Ailbhe, a personal name and can be either male or female.

Alwy, *ealbha,* the herd.

Amadan, *amadáin,* a fool.

Amadane, *amadáin,* a fool.

Amadaun, *amadáin,* a fool.

Amagh, *amach,* outer.

Amaile, *Uí-Mail,* Decendants of Mal, a personal or family name.

Aman, *Iomdhain,* not given.

Aman, *Uí-Meáin,* O'Meane, a family name.

Amase, *Emase, Masg,* Masg, a male name.

Amase, *Masc,* Mac, a personal or family name.

Amaun, *iomáin,* hurling.

Amber, *umair, an-umair,* the narrow channel or trough.

Amber, *umar, amar, amuir,* a trough shape or hollow.

Ambrogue, *Phiombróg,* not given.

Ameen, *Áimín,* not given.

Amer, *umar, amar, amuir,* a trough shape or hollow.

Amery, *iomaire,* a hill-ridge.

Amery, *Lamhraí,* St Lamhrach.

Amery, *Lamraigh,* St Lamrach.

Amh, *damh,* the ox, oxen.

Amicklon, *Uí-Milchon,* O'Milchon, a family name.

Amine, *ladhrann,* forks.

Ammer, *umar, amar, amuir,* a trough shape or hollow.

Amodawn, *amadáin,* a fool.

Amogan, *áth-Mhongáin,* not given.

Amon, *Ioman,* Ioman, a personal name.

Amon, *Iomgain,* the name of an ancient chief.

Amona, *Oighe-Mughaine,* the virgin named 'Mughain'.

Amongam, *áth-Mhongáin,* Mongán's (a personal or family name) ford.

Amoyne, *Ó-Muáin,* not given.

Amry, *aimhreidh,* uneven.

An, *an,* the word 'the'.

An, *ín, án,* (as a word ending) little.

Ana, *abhann-na/an...,* river of the...

Ana, *Ana,* Anna, a female name.

Ana, *áth/ath-na...,* ford of the...

Ana, marsh.

Anaar, the slaughter.

Anad, *Fhanaid,* St Athnad.

Anaddan, *an-fheadain,* the streamlet.

Anadrich, *an-árd-ruis,* the high wood.

Anaff, *an-ndamh,* the oxen.

Anagh, *abhnach,* marshy.

Anagh, *an-eich, na-nEach, an-nEach/neach,* the horse.

Anagh, *eannaigh, eanagh, eanaigh,* the marsh or bog.

Anagh, *na-nEach,* the horses.

Anaghta, *an-ochta,* the hill-breast.

Anahan, *Onchon,* Onchú, the name of a Church founder in Limerick.

Anahy, *Anfa,* not given.

Anahy, *eanaighthe,* swampy.

Anair, *an-áir,* not given.

Anair, *an-fheir,* the grass.

Anair, the slaughter.

Anairy, *an-aodhaire,* the shepherd.

Anal, *an-fháil,* not given.

Anallig, *an-ailigh,* a stone fort.

Anally, *an-eallaigh,* the cattle.

Analta, *an-Fháltaigh, an-Fáltach,* not given.

Anam, *anma,* the soul.

Anam, ghosts.

Anama, *anma,* the soul.

Anamer, *an-umair,* the narrow channel or trough.

Anammer, *an-umair,* the narrow channel or trough.

Anana, *an-eanaigh,* not given.

Anane, *an-néan,* the birds.

Ananny, *an-eanaigh,* the marsh.

Ananta, *na-neannta,* the nettles.

Ananty, *na-neanta,* the nettles.

Anaon, *an-én,* the birds.

Anare, *an-áir/air,* the slaughter.

Anarget, *an-airgead,* the silver.

Anarig, *an-araig-laochraidh,* the conflict of heroes.

Anarm, *an-airm,* of the army or armies.

Anaroo, *an-arbha,* the corn.

Anarra, *an-earraigh,* springtime.

Anarrig, *an-earraigh,* springtime.

Anarry, *an-earrach,* the spring (season).

Anash, *an-fáis,* a sapling.

Anasig, *an-easaigh,* a cataract.

Anass, *an-easa,* the cataract or water cascade.

Anaugh, *Anna, Áine,* Hannah, a female name.

Anaul, *an-fháil,* not given.

Anaul, *an-fhail,* the hedge.

Anav, *na-dhamh/nDamh,* the oxen.

Anay, *an-fheá,* not given.

Anay, *an-fheadha,* the rush (plant).

Anbally, *an-bhaile,* great town(sic).

Anchor, *Anchaire, Ancaire,* belonging to the Anchorite.

Anchor, *ancoire,* the hermit.

Ancory, *ancoire,* the hermit.

Andreen, *Aindrín,* Aindrin, not given.

Andrew, *Aindrín,* not given.

Andrew, *Andriais,* Andrew, a male name.

Androe, *Lándrúir,* Lander, Loundire, a family name.

Anea, *an-eich, an-neach,* the horse.

Anea, *an-fheadha,* the wood.

Anea, *an-fhia,* not given.

Anea, *an-fhiaidh,* the deer.

Aneady, *an-éide,* the clothes or cloth.

Aneag, *an-fhiadhaigh,* the hunt.

Aneag, *an-fhiaigh,* the deer.

Aneag, *an-fhiaigh,* the hunting.

Aneagh, *an-fiach,* the raven.

Aneagh, *Ó-nÉitheach,* not given.

Aneague, *an-fhiadhaig,* the hunting.

Anealy, *Chionnfhaolaidh,* Cionnfhaoladh, a personal or family name.

Anean, *an-én,* the birds.

Aneane, *an-n-ean, an-néan,* the birds.

Aneanvrick, *an-aein-bhric,* the one trout.

Anear, *an-fhéir,* the grass.

Anearagh, *Aniarthach,* not given.

Aneare, *an-fhéir,* the grass.

Anearla, *an-Iarla,* the Earl.

Aneary, *an-aodhaire,* not given.

Aneary, *an-aoire/aoirí, n-aedhaire,* of the shepherd.

Aneasy, *na-Déise/nDéise,* not given.

Anee, *an-fhéich,* not given.

Anee, *an-fheiche/fhiaigh,* the raven.

Anee, *an-fhia/fhiaigh,* the deer.

Aneea, *an-fhiaidh/fhia,* the deer.

Aneel, *an-aeil,* the lime.

Aneel, *an-aoil,* not given.

Aneelig, *an-aoilig,* manure.

Aneen, *Áithín,* little Anthony (a male name).

Aneen, *Fhinghín,* Fineen, a personal or family name.

Aneena, *an-aoine,* of the fasting.

Aneena, *an-aonaigh,* not given.

Aneena, *an-fhíona,* the wine.

Aneena, *an-iongnadh,* not given.

Aneer, *an-fhir,* the testing.

Aneer, *aniar,* western.

Aneer, *inbhir,* the river mouth.

Aneer, *Uí-nDoighre,* O'Deery, a family name.

Anees, *eanach,* marshes.

Aneese, *Aeneas,* Angus (a Clan name).

Aneese, *Aonghusa,* not given.

Aneha, *an-fheiche,* the raven.

Aneig, *an-fhiag,* the raven.

Aneigh, *an-eich, an-neach,* the horse.

Aneigh, *an-fhiaigh, an-fhiaidh, an-fiadh, an-fhia, an-feidh,* the deer.

Anelo, *an-éaloidh,*(sic) escaping.

Anena, *an-aonaigh,* the fair, cattle fair or market.

Anena, *an-éanach,* marshy land.

Aneneen, *an-éinin,* the little bird.

Anenig, *an-aonaigh,* the meeting, assembly or fair.

Aneny, *Ó-nÉanna,* not given.

Aneny, *an-eanaigh,* the marsh.

Anery, *an-aoire, aodhaire,* the shepherd.

Aness, *an-easa,* the waterfall.

Aness, the weasel.

Anewry, *an-iubhraigh,* the yew.

Anewry, *an-aoire,* the shephard.

Anewy, *an-fhiodhbhaidhe,* the wood.

Aney, *Aine, Áine,* Aine or St Anne.

Aney, *eanaigh,* bog.

Aney, *éanaigh,* watery.

Aney, *eidhnech, eidhnigh,* a place of ivy.

Aney, *Éine,* not given.

Aney, *mhaine,* a thicket.

Aney, *Mhaine,* Maine, a personal or family name.

Anga, *eanga,* a recess, angle or crevice.

Angal, *Aingil,* the angel.

Angal, *Cheangail,* Ceangal, a pesons name.

Angan, *Iomgháin, Iomghain,* Imgan or Iomghán, a male name.

Angan, the stronghold.

Angel, *Aingil,* the angel.

Angin, *aingin, na-n-éan,* the birds.

Angle, *aingil,* the angel.

Angle, *Aingle,* Aingeal, a personal or family name.

Angliham, *gort-an-chalaidh,* not given.

Anglode, *Anglóid,* not given.

Anglore, the noisy ford.

Ango, *eanga,* a crevice.

Angram, *abhann-ghorm,* blue river.

Angram, *eang-ghorm,* blue border.

Angus, *tírs-Aonghuisa,* Angus's (a male name) district.

Anhid, *aithnid,* not given.

Ania, *Áine,* a female name.

Aniddan, *an-fheadain,* the streamlet.

Aniddane, *an-fheadain,* the streamlet.

Anie, *an-eich,* the horse.

Anieran, the iron.

Anierin, *iarainn, aniárann,* the iron.

Anierna, *an-iarna,* the hank or skein of thread.

Anig, *eanach, eanaigh,* a marsh.

Anillar, *an-iolair,* not given.

Aniller, *an-iolair, fhiolair,* the eagles.

Anilt, *ailt,* a cliff.

Anim, *an-ime,* the butter.

Anima, *anama, anma,* the soul.

Anima, *an-ime,* the butter.

Animma, *an-im,* butter lake.

Animod, *an-iomaid,* the crowd or multitude.

Animud, *an-adhmaid/adhmuid,* the timber.

Animy, anama, not given.

Animy, *an-im,* the butter.

Anin, *aithinn,* not given.

Anine, *…an-ainneadh,* …of the patience.

Anine, *an-adhain,* the caldron.

Anine, *an-adhainn,* coltsfoot (plant).

Anine, *an-adhainn,* pan shaped.

Anine, *an-eidhin, an-eighinn,* the ivy.

Anine, *an-oighin,* not given.

Anine, *an-oighinn,* the marshy stream or river source.

Anioo, *an-nAeú,* not given.

Anira, *oighre,* the heir.

Anish, *Aenghuis,* Aenghus, a personal or family name.

Anish, *an-ois,* the fawn/s.

Anishery, *an-oisire,* the oyster.

Anisk, *an-uisce/uisge,* of the water.

Aniska, *an-uisge,* of the water.

Anisky, *an-uisge, an-uisce,* of the water.

Ankail, *eing-caol,* a narrow strip.

Anker, *Ancaire,* Ancorite, a personal or family name.

Anketel, *Anketel(sic)* , not given.

Anley, *Fhainle,* Ainle, a personal or family name.

Anly, *Uí-Ainly,* Hanly, a family name.

Ann, *Anna, Aine, Ana,* Anna, a female name.

Anna, *áth/ath-na….*the ford of …

Anna, *eanaig, eanaigh, eanach, eanagh,* a marsh, moor or cut out bog.

Anna, *Eanna,* not given.

Anna, horses.

Annacatty, *eanach-Gaitín,* not given.

Annaclone, *eanach-Luain,* marsh of the hunch-like hill.

Annaduff, *Aine-duibhe,* dark haired Anna, a female name.

Annagary, *anagaire,* not given.

Annagh, *abhnach,* marshy.

Annagh, *éanach,* a marsh.

Annagh, *annagh,* lowland, townland and sometimes field.

Annagh, *an-tEanach,* not given.

Annagh, *an-tEanach,* not given.

Annagh, *eanach, eanaigh, eanagh,* a morass, a marsh a moor or cut out bog.

Annaghanmoney, *eanach-re-móin*(sic), not given.

Annaghean, *eanach-Éan,* not given.

Annagherrig, *eanach-Ó-nEirg,* not given.

Annaghervy, *eanach-Airmhígh,* not given.

Annaghma, *eanach-magh…,* marsh of the plain of …

Annaghs, *na-hEanaigh,* not given.

Annaghs, *eanacha,* marshes.

Annaghvacky, *eanach-an-bhacaigh,* not given.

Annaghy, *eanachaidhe,* marshes.

Annaghybane, *eanach-Aodha-bán,* not given.

Annaghyduff, *eanach-Aodha-dubh,* not given.

Annahagh, *annahaia,* kiln ford.

Annahagh, *eanach-átha,* not given.

Annalee, *abhainn-eanach-lao,* river of the calf's marsh.

Annalore, *áth-an-lobhair,* not given.

Annaly, *Anghaile,* named after the great grandfather of Fergail.

Annan, *Uí-hAnnain,* O'Hannon, a family name

Annay, *eanaighe, eanaighe,* a marsh.

Annayalla, *eanaigh-gheala,* bright marshes.

Anne, *Aine,* Anne, a female name.

Anne, *Anna,* Anna, a female name.

Annee, *an-fhiaigha, an-bhfiach,* the raven.

Annees, *eanaighe,* marshes.

Anneeter, *rinn-an-íochtair,* not given.

Anner, *abhainn-fhuar,* cold water river.

Anner, *an-dobhar, Dobur, Annúir,* the water.

Anner, *annúir, hAnnúire,* not given.

Anney, *Aine, Áine,* Aine or St Anne.

Annfield, *gort-na-hAbhann,* field of the river.

Annies, *na-hEanaigh/hEanaighe,* not given.

Annig, *eanaigh,* a marsh.

Annin, *Ainthinne,* St Ainthinn/Anhin, the virgin Saint.

Annin, *Aithnín,* not given.

Annon, *Eoghan,* a personal name.

Annor, *abhain-uair,* cold river.

Anny, *abhainn,* a river.

Anny, *Aine,* Ainey or Aine, a female name.

Anny, *Ana,* Ana, a female name.

Anny, *eanach, eanaigh, eanaighe, eanagh,* a marsh, bog or cut out bog.

Anny, *eanaigh,* a moor.

Anny, *eanaighe, eanaighe,* a marsh.

Anny, *Éine, Sheanaigh,* not given.

Anny, *Fhainche,* St Fainche, the 6th century virgin Saint.

Anny, *fhine,* a district.

Anny, *na-hEanaigh,* not given.

Annyeeb, *eanach-Chíbe,* not given.

Anoar, *an-n-deoir,* of the drops.

Anode, *an-fhóid,* of the sod or soil.

Anoe, *an-iuir, an-éo/eo,* yew.

Anog, *fheannóg, fheannóige,* scaldcrow/s.

Anoge, *na-nÓg,* not given.

Anoher, *an-fhothair,* the forest.

Anone, *an-eóin,* the bird.

Anone, *inneona,* the anvil.

Anoo, *an-umha,* the lead (metal).

Anooag, *na-nDubhóg,* not given.

Anooan, *na-nuain,* lambs.

Anoon, *an-uain,* the lamb.

Anora, *an-fhothraigh,* not given.

Anoran, *an-Fhuaráin/uaráin,* not given.

Anore, *an-fheoir/fhoghmhair,* not given.

Anore, *an-fhóghmhair,* the harvest.

Anore, *an-fhobhair,* the well.

Anore, *an-fhóghair/fhóghóir,* harvest, gold or golden furze blossom.

Anore, *an-oir/óir,* the gold.

Anore, *an-uabhair,* the pride.

Anore, *an-uir,* wet or boggy.

Anoul, *nAbhall, n-abhall,* apples.

Anoul, *na-ubhall,* the apples.

Anour, *an-úir/iúbhair,* yew.

Anowra, *an-odhra,* reddish.

Anrahan, *Uí-Anracháin,* Ó hAnracháin or O'Hanrahan, a family name.

Anritta, *anratacha,* a bleach green for home made linens.

Anster, *Anstair, Anstar,* not given.

Antean, *an-tsiadhean,* the fairy mount.

Antee, *an-tí,* the marking(sic).

Anteean, *an-tSidheáin,* not given.

Anthony, *Fhiontan, Fhionntain,* not given.

Antin, *Antuin,* Anthony, a male name.

Antin, *Fhiontain,* not given.

Antonish, lucky.

Antrim, *aontroim, aontraim, oentrebh, an-troim,* one house/tribe or holding.

Antrim, *aontroim, aontroma,* soditary farm.

Anua, *an-uaighe,* the grave.

Anuddy, *an-Udaigh,* Hoode, a family name.

Anuddy, *an-Odaigh,* not given.

Anuish, *an-Ois,* not given.

Anully, *Fhionnghuala,* St Finola.

Anully, *an-ula,* not given.

Anummer, *an-umair,* the narrow channel or trough.

Anure, *an-Iúir/iobhair/iubhair,* the yew tree.

Anush, *ois,* a doe.

Anuss, *na-n-os, an-n-os,* the fawns.

Anvey, *an-bheith,* a birch tree.

Anveyerg, *an-bheitheach-dhearg,* not given.

Anvy, *Ainbhe,* Ainbhe, a personal name.

Anvy, *ainbhthith, ainbhtheth, anfuth,* the storm.

Any, *Áine,* Áine, a womans name.

Any, *eanaigh,* marshes.

Anylan, *an-oileain,* the island.

Aphort, *athphort,* not given.

Aplau, *a'phlaigh,* of the plague.

Aplawy, *a'phlaigh,* of the plague.

Appogue, *Molappog,* St Molappog/Lappog.

Appy, *an-Apadh,* the Abbot.

Apreagaun, (a lake) *a'phreachain,* periwinkle lake.

Ar, *airthir,* eastern.

Ar, *ar,* on.

Ar, *ár,* the slaughter.

Ar, *ard,* a height.

Ara, *a'rath,* of the fort.

Ara, *Ara, Arann,* an-ancient territory.

Ara, *Ára,* not given.

Ara, *athrach,* boat-shaped.

Ara, *bearach,* heifers.

Ara, *Uí-hEaghra,* O'Hara, a family name.

Arabela, *Arabeile,* not given.

Arable, *earbaill,* not given.

Aradotia, *na-Réidhe-dóighte,* not given.

Aragh, *abhrach,* a hill-brow.

Aragh, *agrach,* weird or airy.

Aragh, *athrach,* boat-shaped.

Aragh, *Oireach,* not given.

Araghan, Araghan or Harrahan, a personal or family name.

Araght, *Adrochtae,* Adrochta, a personal or family name and a founder of a Church in Sligo.

Araght, *Athracht, Athrachta,* St Athracht/Attracta, the virgin Saint.

Araglin, *Airglinn,* not given.

Arah, *a'rath,* of the fort.

Araheen, *'ic Raithín,* Mac Craithin, a family name.

Araheen, *Airchinn,* not given.

Aralt, Aralt or Harold, a male name.

Aran, (island and islands), *Árainn,* arched back, ridges or ridge island/s.

Aran, (island), *árainn, ára,* kidney/arch shaped.

Aran, *fhearann,* land.

Arane, *uarain,* the cold spring.

Araw, *a'-raith,* the fort.

Arbatt, *ard-Bata,* not given.

Arboe, *ard/árd/aird-bó,* promontory or height of the cow/s.

Archer, *Áirséaraigh,* not given.

Arclintagh, *ard-cluainte,* not given.

Ard, *aird,* a point or promontory.

Ard, *an-tArd,* not given.

Ard, *ard,* height of the…

Ard, *ard,* high, height, a height or a hill.

Ard, *Eraird,* a male name.

Arda, *arda,* heights or hills.

Arda, *árdachadh, ardachaidh,* the high field.

Arda, *ard-an/a'…* height of the …

Ardagh, *árd-a'…,* height of the…

Ardagh, *ard-achadh,* height of the field.

Ardagh, *ardachaidh, ardach, ardachadh, ard-achadh,* the high field.

Ardaghy, *ardachadh, ard-achadh,* the high field.

Ardakillin, (lake) *cairrgín*(sic), not given.

Ardaloo, *ard-Lú,* not given.

Ardaloo, *ard-leamhach,* height of the elms.

Ardamee, *ard-Mídhe,* the height or Mede, a male name.

Ardamine, *árd-Ladhrann,* height of the fork.

Ardan, *an-tArdán,* the high place.

Ardan, *Ardáin,* not given.

Ardan, *ardán,* little height or little hill.

Ardan, *Uí-Ardain,* O'Hardan or Harden, a family name.

Ardandra, *árdandra,* elevated ground.

Ardane, *an-tArdán,* not given.

Ardane, *ardín, ardán,* little height.

Ardane, *athán, ardín,* little height or hill.

Ardaneer, *ard-inbhir,* not given.

Ardara, *ard-an-rátha, ard-a'raith,* height of the fort.

Ardaragh, *ard-darach,* height of the oaks.

Ardarawinny, *ard-Daire-fhine,* height of the race of Daire.

Ardaun, *an-tArdán,* not given.

Ardaun, *athán*(sic), little height or hill.

Ardclinis, *ard-clon-easa,* sloping height of the waterfall(sic).

Ardea, *ard-Aodha,* Hugh's/Aodh's (a male name) height.

Ardea, *ard-fhia,* height of the deer.

Ardeash, *ard-éis,* height of the track.

Ardee, *baile-átha-Fhirdhia, baile-atha-Fhirdia, ath-Fhirdia,* Ferdias ford.

Ardee, *baile-atha-Fhirdia,* town of Ferdias ford.

Ardeen, *an-tAirdín, ardín, áirdín,* the little height.

Ardeen, *ardín,* little ford(sic).

Ardeenloun, *ard-Uí-Anluin, árd-Uí-h-Annlúan,* O'Hanlon's (a personal or family name) height.

Ardees, *ardaigh,* heights.

Ardell, Ardill, a personal or family name.

Arden, *ardín,* little hill or height.

Arderra, *ardaire,* not given.

Arderra, *ard-doire,* the high oak wood/grove.

Arderrow, *ard-dearmhagh,* high oak plain.

Ardfield, *ard-Ó-bhFicheallaigh,* not given.

Ardgroom, *áth-dhrom,* not given.

Ardgroom, *dhá-dhrom,*(sic) two ridges.

Ardillan, *ard-oilean,* high island.

Ardin, *ard-na/an...* hill of the...

Ardlaraghan, *ard-rathain*(sic), not given.

Ardle, *ardghail,* not given.

Ardle, *ardghall,* a high standing stone(sic).

Ardmaghbrague, *ard-Macha-breug,* the 'false' Armagh.

Ardna, *ardán,* not given.

Ardna, *ard-na...,* hill or height of the...

Ardneev, *Árdnaoimh,* the Archsaint.

Ardobireen, *ard-an-bhirín,* not given.

Ardoilen, *ard-oilean,* high island.

Ardolough, *árd-gulach,* hill of the charcoals.

Ardonan, *ard-Donáin,* Donan's (a personal or family name) height.

Ardoohy, *ard-Dubhaigh*(sic), Duffy's (a personal or family name.

Ardowling, *árdabhla,* height of the orchard.

Ardoyne, *Ard-Eoin/Eoghan,* Owen's (a male name) height.

Ardra, *ard-raithe/rátha,* not given.

Ardra, *ard-rath,* high fort.

Ardragh, *ard-rath,* high fort.

Ardrah, *ard-rath,* high fort.

Ardraw, *ard-rath,* high fort.

Ardress, *árd-dreasa,* height of the brambles.

Ardress, *ard-rois,* the high wood.

Ardrish, *ard-dorais,* (of) the high door.

Ardrish, *an-fhardorais,* the outer door.

Ardrish, *ard-ros,* the high wod.

Ardristan, *ard-dristean,* height of the brake.

Ardroe, *aird-rua,* red point.

Ardrum, *ard-druim,* high ridge.

Ardry, *Airdrí,* not given.

Ards, *áird, aird,* the point, peninsula or promontory.

Ards, *aird-Uladh,* promontory of the Ulstermen.

Ards, *an-ardaidh,* not given.

Ards, *hAirde,* the promontory.

Ards, heights.

Ardtry, high chief.

Ardue, *ard-Aodha,* Hugh's (a male name) height.

Ardue, *ard-Odhbha,* not given.

Ardun, *an-tArd-Donn,* not given.

Ardy, *árda,* high.

Are, *áir, air, ár,* the slaughter.

Area, *aimhréidh, aimhreidh,* rough or rugged.

Aready, *Uí-Riada,* O'Reidy, a family name.

Areague, *aimhreidh,* the rough plain.

Aree, *a'fraoich,* of the heath or heather.

Aree, *Áirí,* not given.

Aree, *an-Rí,* (of the) King.

Areema, *na-hImríme,* not given.

Arg, chests or coffers.

Arga, *Fhearga,* St Fearga.

Argadaun, *Uí-Argadain,* O'Hargadan, now known as Hardiman, a family name.

Argal, *airheann,* plunder.

Argan, *airgeann,* plundering.

Argan, *argan,* not given.

Argate, *airgid,* silver.

Arget, *airgead, airgid,* silver or money.

Arget, *airgid,* silver.

Argid, *airgid, airgead,* silver or money.

Argideen, *airgidín,* silver, silvery river.

Argit, *airgead,* silver.

Argit, *airgit,* silver or money.

Argle, *Uí-Ardghail,* O'Ardgal or O'Hargal, a family name.

Arglo, *arglach,* not given.

Argus, *Feargus, Fhearghuis,* Fergus, a male name.

Argy, *cairge, cargi, carriage,* a rock or rocky.

Arhen, *Airine,* St Arina.

Ariff, *aireamh,* arable land.

Ariff, *aireamh,* ploughmen.

Ariffe, *aireamh,* arable.

Arig, *earrach,* spring.

Arigg, *airg,* the chest.

Arigid, *airgead,* silver.

Arigna, *airgne,* sweeping away.

Arigna, *airgnigh,* the destroyer.

Arigna, *airhgneach,* despoiling.

Arigna, *arigna,* rapid.

Arigna, the destroying river.

Arignagh, *airgne,* sweeping away.

Aris, *an-rois,* not given.

Aris, *áruis,* on or beside the dwelling house.

Aris, *fhiabhrais,* fever.

Aris, *fhiaris,* crookedness.

Arive, *noireamh,* ploughmen.

Ark, *orc, arc,* pigs or young pigs.

Arkan, *Uí-Arcain,* Harkin or O'Harkin, a family name.

Arkane, *archon,* a watchdog.

Arkane, *orcain,* wild majoram.

Arkane, *orchain,* a piglet.

Arkane, *Uí-Arcain,* O'Harkan, Harkin or Harkan, a family name.

Arkeen, *Aircín,* not given.

Arkin, *Aircean,* not given.

Arkin, *Earcáin, Earcain,* Earcán or Earcain, a male name.

Arkin, *Earcáin, Ercain,* Earcan, Erkan or Harkan, a personal or family name.

Arkin, Harkin or O'Harkan, a family name.

Arkin, *Uí-Earcáin,* not given.

Arklow, *arklo,* Danish, Norse for the meadow of Arknel. The ancient name for Arklow was *tóchar-mór,* the great causeway, also known by *an-tInbhear-mór, an-inbhir-mhóir,* the big estuary.

Arla, *árlaidh,* slaughter.

Arlands, *arlianne,* stretches of good land in the midst of mountain or moor.

Arlands, *na-hArlanna,* not given.

Arles, *achadh-arghlais,* not given.

Arles, *ardleasa, ardlios, aird-leasa,* high fort or high ring fort.

Arless, *ardlios, ardlios,* high fort.

Arless, *arghlais,* not given.

Arley, *airle,* council meetings.

Arley, *airle,* the council (meetings).

Arm, *Airim,* Airem, an ancient chief.

Arm, *arma,* the weapon/s or army.

Armagh, *ard-Macha,* (Queen) Macha's height, It has also been suggested that 'macha' should mean a plain or land cleared for agriculture.

Armagh, *ard-Mhacha,* not given.

Armaghbrague, Armaghbreague, *ard-Macha-breug,* the 'false' Armagh.

Armon, Haremon or Harman, a personal or family name.

Armoy, *oirthear-maí, airthear-maighe/muighe,* east plain, eastern end of the plain or east of the plain.

Arn, *airne,* sloes.

Arnaghan, *airneachan,* a place of sloe bushes or sloes.

Arnane, *Narnáin,* Arannan, a family name.

Arneen, *airne,* blackthorn, sloes.

Arneen, *airnín,* not given.

Arnet, *Arnoid,* Harnet or Arnott, a family name.

Arney, *airne, áirne, airneach, arnaidhe, áirneadh,* sloe/s.

Arney, *Athairne,* Atharney's (a male name) fort.

Arney, *Éirne,* not given.

Arney, *Eithirne,* Eithirne, a personal or family name.

Arney, *fhearna, Earnan,* not given.

Arnot, *Arnoid,* Harnet or Arnott, a family name

Arny, *airne, airneach,* sloes.

Arny, *arna,* not given.

Aroan, *an-Róin,* the seal.

Aroe, *arubha,* rue.

Arogan, *Uí-Rógáin,* not given.

Arold, Araltaigh, not given.

Aronanig, *a-Ronáinaigh,* belonging to Ronayne (a personal or family name).

Aroo, *aradh,* a ridged hill.

Aroon, *Eireamhóin, Eir-Eam-Hone,* Irwin or Erwin, a male name.

Aroon, *Eireamhoin,* Irwin, a male name.

Aroon, *Eireamhón,* Eremon, Irwin or Harmon, a male name.

Aroon, *Urumhan,* Irvine, a family name.

Arosta, *A'Roistigh,* Roche, a family name.

Arough, *a-ratha,* of the fort.

Arr, *ártha,* well cultivated land.

Arra, *Ára, Ara,* an ancient district/ territory.

Arra, *arbha,* corn.

Arra, *earra,* a boundary.

Arra, *earraigh,* springtime.

Arra, ploughed land or a marsh.

Arragan, *argana,* plundering.

Arragh, *arrach, arach,* a ploughed/tilled field.

Arraght, *arraght, arracht,* an apparition.

Arraglen, *airghleann,* not given.

Arraher, *arrachair, arachair,* ploughing or tillage.

Arran, *arainn,* bread.

Arran, *fhearann, fearann, fhearainn,* land, ploughland or townland.

Arran, *Uí-Áráin, Uí-Áráin,* O'Aran, a family name.

Arranagh, *Aránach,* not given.

Arranaun, *a'rannain,* the cry of the deer.

Arreely, *fhearáile,* not given.

Arrell, *Fhearghail,* not given.

Arrell, *Fhearghaill,* Farrell or O'Farrell a family name.

Arrell, *Oirill,* not given.

Arret, *Airt,* Art, a male name.

Arrible, *earbaill,* not given.

Arrig, *aithrigheach,* a penitent.

Arrigal, *airegal,* a habitation or hermitage.

Arrigan, *aragain,* conflicts.

Arrigan, *argain,* plunder.

Arrigle, *an-tEaragal, airgeala, aireagal,* not given.

Arrilly, *Fhearaíle,* not given.

Arrilly, *Fhearghaile,* Farrelly, a family name.

Arrit, *Airid,* not given.

Arroge, *Ghearroige,* Garroge, a female name.

Arroo, *aradh,* a ladder.

Arroo, *arbhar,* corn.

Arroor, *arbhair,* not given.

Arroor, *arbhar,* corn.

Arrow, *an-rabhaidh,* not given.

Arrow, *arbha, arbhach, arbhar,* corn.

Arrow, *choradh,* a weir.

Arry, *aedhaire,* the shepherd.

Arry, *airbhre,* oak grove.

Arry, *áirí,* shielding.

Arry, *airighe,* sentinels.

Arry, *fharaidh,* not given.

Arryheernabin, *earra-thíre-na-binne,* not given.

Art, *Airt,* Art, a male name.

Art, *ard,* a height.

Art, *Art,* Arthur, a male name.

Art, *fhearta,* not given.

Arta, *arda,* heights.

Arta, *fhearta, fertach,* a place of graves.

Arta, *fhearta, fherta,* the grave.

Artagh, *fheartach, airteach,* not given.

Artana, *ardtamhnach,* the high mound(sic).

Artane, *árd-Aidhin,* Aidhean's (a personal or family name) height.

Artane, *fheartain,* a little vault or trench.

Artella, *Uí-Artghaile,* O'Hartley, a family name.

Artery, *Airtrí,* not given.

Arthur, *Airt,* not given.

Arthur, *Árthúir,* a male name.

Arti, *árd/ard-an…,* height or hill of the…

Arti, *art-tighe…,* height of the house of…

Arti, *ard-te*(sic)*-Domhnaigh,* height of Downeys (a personal or family name) house.

Artigan, *Artagáin,* not given.

Artiteige, *ard-tighe-Taidhg,* height or hill of Tighe's (a male name) house.

Artna, *ard-na…,* not given.

Artney, *airneadeach,* blackthorns.

Artney, *Uí-Airtinne,* O'Hartney, a family name.

Artonagh, *ard-tonach,* high quagmire or marsh.

Artoney, *ard-tamhnaí,* not given.

Artragh, *Artrach,* not given.

Artrea, *ard-Trea,* Trea's (a personal or family name) height.

Artry, *Atraí,* not given.

Arty, *Eachartaigh,* Arty, a persons name.

Arty, *Fhaghartaigh,* Fagahtagh, (the name of a race of people).

Arudda, (lake) *Roda,* not given.

Arulla, *Arúla,* not given.

Arum, *athrainn, atharum,* not given.

Arum, *eachdhroma,* horses ridge.

Arundel, *achadh-Dunlaing,* Dowling's (a personal or a family name) field.

Arush, *an-rois,* not given.

Arva, *arbha,* corn.

Arva, *árdmhaigh,* not given.

Arvagh, *armhach, ármhach,* the battlefield or place of the slaughter.

Arvey, *Fhormhaí,* not given.

Arwa, *abhair,* not given.

Arwa, *arbhar,* corn.

Ary, *aimhréidh,* crooked.

Ary, *airbhre,* oak grove.

Ary, *airí,* a milking place.

Ary, *Araide,* Araid, a personal or family name.

Asa, *Ásaigh,* not given.

Ascaud, *na-scád,* the slaughter.

Ascra, *eascrach,* a sand hill.

Ascragh, *eascrach, eascragh,* a sand hill or sand ridge.

Asdee, *easa-duibhe,* the dark waterfall.

Ash, *ais, aiss,* a hill.

Ash, *easa,* not given.

Ashandra, *a-sean-ratha,* of the old fort.

Ashbourne, *Cill-Dhéaghláin,* not given.

Ashea, *Uí-Aisí,* Ó hAisí, a family name.

Ashea, *Uí-Aisiath,* O'Hasset or Hasset, a family name.

Ashee, *Ausaille,* St. Ausaille or Auxilus.

Ashee, *Eisidhe,* not given.

Ashee, *Úsaill,* Úsaile, a personal or family name and a founder of a Church in Longford.

Asheea, *Ua-Asia,* O'Hassett, a family name.

Ashel, *asail,* not given.

Asheroe, *eas-ruadh,* red waterfall or cataract.

Asig, *Ásaigh,* not given.

Asig, *fhásaig,* wilderness.

Ask, *easca, eas,* a cataract, waterfall.

Aska, *easca,* a bog or a bog channel(sic).

Aska, *easca, eascach, eascach,* a water channel.

Aska, *easga,* wetland.

Aska, *na-sceiche,* little thorn bushes.

Askana, *easca-na…,* bog of the…

Askeaton, *eas-cead-tinne,* cataract (waterfall) of a hundred fires.

Askeaton, *ess-Geibtine, eas-Géitine, eas-Gephtine,* Géitine, Géitin or Gephtine's (a male name) cataract or waterfall.

Askerlough, *eascarlaigh,* place of the cascade.

Askey, *eascaigh,* the quagmire.

Askill, *ascaill, ascal,* the armpit, angle or corner.

Askill, *ascaill,* the corner.

Askillaun, *ascalán,* little angle.

Askin, *eascann,* a quagmire.

Askin, *easgainn,* the eel.

Askin, *sheascan, easgann, h-eascon,* eels.

Askintinny, *easca-an-tsionnaigh,* marsh, watercourse of the fox.

Aslaun, *easlán,* sick people.

Aslee, *na-slighe,* of the road.

Aslishen, *atha-slisean,* ford of beetles.

Asnagh, *easnach,* ribbed, furrowed or trenched land.

Asnet, *Osnata,* Osnat, the virgin Saint Osnat (a male name). It means 'little fawn'.

Aspic, *easpuig,* a bishop.

Aspick, *easboig, espuig, easpaig, easpuig, easpug,* a bishop.

Aspickoen, *easpog-Eóin,* not given.

Aspictarvin, *easpog-Tairbhin,* not given.

Aspig, *easpaigh,* a bishop.

Aspil, *Aspol,* not given.

Aspuck, *Easpuic,* a Bishop.

Aspucke, *Easpog, Easpoc,* a Bishop.

Aspug, *Easpuig,* a bishop.

Aspugbrone, *Easpog/Easpuig-Bróin,* Bishop Bron/Bronus.

Aspuglonan, *Easpog-Fhlannain,* St Flannan, second Bishop of Killaloe.

Aspuglonane, *Easpog, Easpuig-Fhlannán/Fhlannáin,* Bishop Flannan.

Aspy, *Easpaig, 'easboig*(sic), *Easpog, Easpoc,* a Bishop.

Ass, *eas, ess, easa,* a waterfall on a river, a fall in a river, a rapid or a cataract.

Assa, *eas, ess, easa,* a waterfall on a river, a fall in a river, a rapid or a cataract.

Assaan, *Asáin, Chasáin,* not given.

Assagh, *assig,* a waterfall.

Assaly, *ath-saile,* ford of the brine.

Assan, *easán,* a little waterfall on a river, a little fall in a river, a little rapid or a little cataract.

Assan, *Easain,* Easan, a personal or family name.

Assaroe, *eas-Aedha-ruaidh*, red Aedh's (a male name) waterfall.

Assaun, *easán*, a little waterfall on a river, a little fall in a river, a little rapid or a little cataract.

Assayroo, *eas-Ruaidh*, Hugh's waterfall.

Assel, a fall or stumble.

Assel, *Aisil*, Aisil, a personal or family name.

Assel, *Asail*, Asal, a personal name.

Assel, *iseal*, low.

Assel, *tuisil, eiseal*, not given.

Asser, *easair*, not given.

Asseragh, St Lassar.

Asses, *easa*, cataracts or water cascades.

Asset, Hasset, a personal or family name.

Assey, *ath-sidhe*, Sidhe's (a male name) ford.

Assey, *eas, easa*, waterfall.

Assig, *easach, easaig, easaigh*, a cataract or waterfall.

Assil, *assal*, territory lying around a hill.

Assolas, *ath-solais*, ford of light.

Assolus, *áth-solais*, ford of light.

Assroo, *eas-Ruaidh*, Hugh's(sic) waterfall.

Assy, *eas, ess, easa*, a waterfall on a river, a fall in a river, a rapid or a cataract.

Assy, *easaigh*, not given.

Ast, *Aiste*, not given.

Asta, *an-fhosta*, the encampment.

Asta, *fhasta*, a prison.

Asta, *Sheasta*, Seasta, Sheasta, a personal or family name.

Asta, *sheasta*, upright.

Asta, *thasta*, the rumour.

Astee, *easa/eas-duibhe*, the dark waterfall.

Astee, *eas-Daoi*, not given.

Aster, *aistir*, the journey.

Astia, *Aiste*, not given.

Astig, *astaigh*, level.

Astrish, *easrais*, not given.

At, *áth, ath*, a ford.

Ataha, *a'tsaithe*, the swarm or the bees.

Atalia, *a'tsaile*, of the brine.

Atallin, *a't-salainn*, salty.

Atan, *a'tsean, a'tseana…*, of the old….

Atane, *a't-séin*, of prosperity.

Atane, *a'tSiain*, the foxglove.

Ataniheen, *a't-seannaichín*, of the little fox.

Ataniheen, *a't-sonnaichín*, of the little bulwark or palisade.

Atar, *a-tSearraigh*, (of the) colt.

Atarriff, *a'tairbh*, of the bull.

Atatee, *áit-an-tí*, not given.

Atavy, *an/a'/-tSamhaidh*, the sorrel.

Atawy, *a'tsamhaidh*, the sorrel.

Atedaun, *an-tSéideáin*, not given.

Atee, *a'-tighe*, of the house.

Atehy, *a'-teithe*, the flight.

Ath, *áth, tÁth, ath*, a ford.

Athaleen, *a'tsailin*, the little sea inlet.

Athalia, *an-tSáile*, not given.

Athboy, *áth-buidhe-tlachtga*, the yellow ford of 'Tlachtga' which was a hill name. The hill is now known as the Hill of Ward.

Athboy, *baile-átha-buí*, not given.

Athea, *an-tSléibhe*, of the mountain.

Athea, *ath/Áth-an-tSléibhe, ath-a'tsleibhe*, ford of the mountain.

Atheawn, *a sideán*, a fairy mount.

Athen, *aiteann*, gorse.

Athenry, *áth-an-Ríogh*, ford of the kings.

Athenry, *ath-na-riogh*, ford of the kings.

Athnid, the 'ath' ford of the 'neid' birds nest.

Athnid, *áth-nid*, not given.

Athou, *a'tsamhaidh*, the sorrel.

Athy, *ath-I/Í*, Ae's (an 11 century Munster Chief) ford.

Athy, *Baile-Átha-Í*, not given.

Atin, *aitinn*, furze.

Atinagh, *an-tSnáimh*, not given.

Atinny, *an/a'-tsionnaigh*, of the fox.

Atlaunlusk, *a'tslanluis*, the rib grass.

Atlea, *an-tSliabh, a't-sléibh*, of the mountain.

Atlea, *an-tSléibhe*, not given.

Atloura, *ath-slabhra*, ford of the chain.

Atluggera, *an-tSlogaire*, not given.

Atna, *an-t-Snamha, a'tSnamha*, of the swimming.

Atnagh, *an-tSnáimh*, not given.

Atnaw, *a'tsnamha*, of the swimming.

Atoo, *a'tsamhaidh*, the sorrel.

Atoor, *a'-tuair*, the bleach-green or pasture.

Atorick, *an-Tóraic*, not given.

Atrave, *a'tsnamha*, of the swimming.

Atray, *otraigh*, dung or an otter.

Atta, *ait-an/a'…*the site/location of…

Atta, *áit-tí-a'…*the site/location of the house of…

Attanagh, *áth-tanaí,* the shallow ford.

Attanagh, *áth-tSeanach, Sheanach,* not given.

Attatantee, *áit-an-tSeantí/tSean-tighe, ait-a'tsean-tighe,* the site/location of the old house.

Attateenoe, *ait-a'tighe-nua,* site of the new house.

Attee, *ait-tighe,* site of the house.

Attetmore(sic)**,** *áit-an-tí-mhóir,* site of the big house.

Atten, *aitinn, aiteann,* furze.

Atti, *áit-tighe/tí…,* the site or location of the house of….

Attiaghygrana, *ait-tighe-Chongrana,* site of Cugrana's (a personal or a family name) house.

Attical, *áit-tí-Chathail,* the site of Cathal's (a male name) house.

Attimon, *ait-tighe-tSiomoin,* site of Simons house.

Attin, *aitin, aitinn, aiteann,* furze or gorse.

Attin, *aitinne,* not given.

Attin, *áit-tí-an…,* not given.

Attina, *aiteann,* furze.

Attina, *aitinne,* not given.

Attinadague, *ait-tige-na-dTadhg,* site of the house of the Teiges or Timothys, (male names).

Attinadague, *allt*(sic)*-na-dTadhg,* not given.

Atty, *áit-ti/tighe….* the site or location of the house of…

Atty, *áit-tighe,* the house site.

Attybrick, *áit-tí-bric,* not given.

Attybrick, *ait-tighe-bríc,* site of the speckled house.

Attychraan, *áit-tí-Uí-Chorráin,* not given.

Attymas, *áth-tighe-an-Mheasaigh,* not given.

Attymass, *áth-tí-Uí-Mheasaigh,* the location of the house of Ó Measagh, a family name.

Attymon, *áth-Tiomáin,* Tiomán's (a personal or family name) ford.

Attymon, *áth-tSíomoin,* not given.

Atyclogh, *a'-tighe-cloch,* …of the stone house.

Au, *abha,* river.

Au, *áth,* a ford.

Aubane, *abha-bhan,* white river.

Auburn, named after the poem 'The deserted village' by Oliver Goldsmith, the Irish name is *achadh-na-gréine,* field of the sun.

Aubwee, *an-tÁth-buí,* not given.

Augeris, *eachrais,* the way or passage.

Augh, *achadh* a field.

Augh, *each,* a horse.

Augh, *each, eich,* a horse.

Augh, muddy ground.

Augh, *tÁth, áth, ath,* a ford.

Augha, *achadh,* a field.

Augha, *achadh-an…,* field of the…

Augha, *áth-a…,* ford of…

Augha, *áth-an…,* ford of the…

Aughalin, *áith*(sic)*-Liní,* not given.

Aughall, *áth-Cál,* not given.

Aughall, *eochaill, eo-choill,* the yew wood.

Aughan, *achadh-an…,* field of the…

Aughan, *Uí-Eachaidhen,* O'Haughian, a family name.

Aughane, *athan,* little ford.

Augher, *achair,* not given.

Augher, *eachar, eacharadh,* a field or enclosure for horses or cattle.

Augher, *eochair,* a border or verge.

Augher, *eochair,* the border.

Aughera, *eacharadh,* a field or enclosure for horses or cattle.

Augheris, *eachrais,* the way, passage or wood of the horse.

Augheris, *eachros,* not given.

Augherna, *eochair-na…,* not given.

Aughil, *eochaill, eo-choill,* the yew wood.

Aughils, *eochaille,* yew woods.

Aughin, *achadh-an…,* field of the…

Aughine, *achadh-adhainn,* field of the round hollow.

Aughinis, *eich-inis, eachinis,* island of the horse.

Aughlis, *achlais,* not given.

Aughlis, *hEachlaisce,* the whip.

Aughlish, *each-laisc,* horse enclosure.

Aughna, *achadh-na…,* field of the…

Aughna, *áth/ath-na…,* the ford of the…

Aughna, *Uí-Fhiachna,* Fenton or Fiachna, a personal or family name.

Aughrim, *eachdhroim, eachroim, eich-dhruim, eachdhruim,* the hill ridge of the horse/s.

Aughrim, *áth-tirim,* dry ford.

Aughrim, *each-druim, eachdhroma, eachdhruim-Uí-Bhroin, eachdhruim-Uí-Cheallaigh,* not given.

Aughriman, *eichdruman,* the hill little ridge of the horse/s.

Aughris, *eachros,* promontory/peninsula of the horse.

Aught, *ucht,* the hill breast.

Aughtanny, *ochtú-an-fhia,* the eighth of the deer.

Aughter, *uachtair, uachtar,* upper.

Aughty, *Eachtgha, Eachtgha,* a personal or family name.

Aughty, *Echtghe, Echtghe,* a male name.

Aughullen, *achadh chuilinn,* field of holly.

Aughvallydeag, *áth-bhéal-átha-ghéag,* not given.

Augullies, *na-hAgalla,* not given.

Aulin, *Ailinne,* not given.

Aulin, *áluinn, alainn,* beautiful.

Ault, *alt,* a height.

Aultagh, *alltach,* a wild place or wilderness.

Aun, *ín, án,* little.

Auna, *áth/ath-na...,* ford of the...

Aurd, *árd,* high, height.

Auskurra, *áth-Scortha,* not given.

Auskurra, *áth-Scurraidh,* Scurry's or Scuire's (a personal or family name) ford.

Av, *damh,* the ox or oxen.

Ava, *a-mheadha,* (of the) mead.

Avad, *an-bháda,* the boat.

Avaghon, *mheitheáin,* not given.

Avaha, *mhacha,* cattle field.

Avahly, *a'baile,* of the town.

Avain, *a-bháin,* the green field.

Aval, *abhal, abhall, abhaille, abhaill,* an orchard.

Avan, *abhann,* a river.

Avanty, *Mantagh,* a male name.

Avar, *bh-fear,* men.

Avare, *a'Mhaoir,* a steward or overseer.

Avaroon, *a'Bharuin,* the Baron.

Avarra, *aimhreidh,* rough or complicated.

Avarrella, *a-bharraille,* of the barrel.

Avarrodig, *a'Bharoidigh,* belonging to the Barrets, a family name.

Avarry, *Uí-Bhearraigh,* O'Berry, a family name.

Avas, *easa,* a waterfall.

Avas, *mheasa,* fruit or nuts.

Avatta, *na-bhata,* the stakes.

Avaul, *dha-bhall,* two spots.

Avea, *bhFiadh,* deer.

Avean, *b-Fiann,* the Fianna.

Aveela, *a'-mhíle,* of the soldier.

Aveenoge, *Dha-bhFinog,* St Dabhinog, Winnoc.

Aveeragh, *Uí-bhFiachrach,* the tribe of Hy Fiachrach.

Avehir, *an-iubhar,* yew.

Avelin, *O'Havlin,* a family name.

Avenoge, *Dha-bhFinog,* St Dabhinog/Winnoc.

Averty, *abhartach,* of the dwarf.

Averty, *Abhartaigh,* Averty or Haverty, a family name.

Avery, *aimhréidh,* not given.

Avery, *aimhreidh,* rough or complicated.

Avie, *a'maighe, an-muigh,* a plain.

Avie, *na-bh-fiagh,* deer.

Avil, *Ábhail, Fhábhail,* not given.

Avil, *abhaill,* apple trees.

Avil, *abhal, abhaille, abhaill,* an orchard.

Avil, *abhall,* apples.

Avill, *Aoibhill, Aoibhill,* a female name.

Avill, *haibhle,* the orchard.

Avin, *a-bhinn,* a pointed hill.

Avin, *O'bhFinn,* O'Finn a family name.

Avinally, *abhann-shailigh,* river of willows or sallies.

Avine, *O'bhFinn,* (of the) O'Finn/s, a family name.

Avinoge, *Dha-bhFinog,* St Dabhinog/Winnoc.

Avinoge, *Momhéanóg, Mobhinóg,* not given.

Avirane, *Uí-Bhearain,* Bearan, (name of the son of Loingseach mór).

Avirra, *a'mhire,* of the madness.

Avish, *éibhis, eibhis,* a mountain meadow.

Avisha, *éibhis-an,* mountain meadow of the...

Avisteen, *Aibhistín,* Augustine, a male name.

Avoca, *abhóca,* from Ptolemy's *Oboka* (not given). It was formerly *an-droichead-nua,* the new bridge.

Avoca, *tráigh-dá-abhainn,* not given.

Avoe, *an-bhó,* the cow.

Avoe, *an-bhotha,* the (monastic) cell.

Avoe, *Uí-Bhuaigh,* not given.

Avon, *abhainn,* a river.

Avon, *amhain,* not given.

Avonea, *abhann Aodha,* Aodh's/Hugh's river.

Avory, *aborraigh,* borage.

Avoughalla, *Uí-Bhuachall,* O'Buachalla, a family name.

Avrea, *aimhreidh,* rough or complicated.

Avrick, *…a'-bhruic,* of the badger.

Avy, *abhaigh, abhaich,* a dwarf.

Aw, *abh, abha,* a stream or a river.

Aw, *átha, áth, atha, ath,* a ford.

Award, *a'bhaird,* the bard or poet.

Award, *Bháird,* Ward, a personal or family name.

Awardy, *a'bharda,* a ward or guard.

Awark, *amharc, amhairc,* prospect or view.

Awas, *amhais,* soldiers.

Awas, *amhus, amhas,* a hired soldier.

Awee, *a'mhuighe,* of the plain.

Aweer, *a'-mhaoir,* of the steward.

Awfund, *ath-fionn,* white ford.

Awill, *abhaill,* the orchard.

Awla, *abhla,* apple or orchard.

Awlan, *Áthláin, Athláin,* Awlan, a personal or family name.

Awleen, *an-aillín,* little cliff.

Awley, *Amhalghaidh,* Amhalghaidh, a personal or family name.

Awley, *Amhlaidh, Amhlaibh,* not given.

Awley, *Amhlaoidh,* Auliff, a personal or family name.

Awley, *Náile,* St Náile.

Awling, *áluinn,* beautiful.

Awly, *Amhalgaidh, Amalgaidh,* Amhalgadh, the name of an ancient King.

Awn, *bán,* white.

Awnaun, *Adhamhnain,* St Awnaun, Adamnan.

Awoddy, *a'-bhodaigh,* a churl.

Ayellowin, *ghealbhain,* the sparrow.

Ayelvin, *ghealbhain,* the sparrow.

Ayle, *áill,* a steep hillside.

Ayle, *aille, aill,* a cliff, slope, declivity or precipice.

Aylea, *áill-an…,* steep hill near…

Ayne, *eidhinn,* ivy.

Aynog, *éanach,* where birds congregate(sic).

Ayoosy, *giumhas, ghiumhais,* fir.

B

Baah, *Bágha,* not given.

Baan, *bán,* white.

Babe, *Bhábaigh,* not given.

Babeswood, *coille-na-bhábaigh,* not given.

Baccal, *bhachaigh,* the cripple.

Back, *baic,* inclining, a bend, winding or crook.

Back, *bhaic,* a bend.

Back, *breac,* speckled.

Backa, *bacach,* a cripple or invalid.

Backagh, *bacach,* Cripples or beggars.

Backey, *bacaigh,* a cripple or a beggar.

Backey, *baice,* a river bend, angle or a hollow.

Backode, *an-bhocóid,* not given.

Bacon, *Phiacáin,* O'Peakin, a family name.

Bad, *bád,* the boat.

Baggan, *Becan,* a personal or family name.

Baggot (Carrickbaggot), *an-bhaóidigh, not given.*

Bagh, *beith, bheitheach,* birch trees.

Bagh, *bheacha,* bees.

Baghran, *báchrán,* bogbean also known as bogbine, its latin name is *Menyanthes trifoliate.*

Baghran, *boithreáin,* dried cow dung (for burning).

Bah, *beithe,* birches.

Baha, *Beatha,* Bith, the name of a pre-deluvian colonist.

Baha, *Beithí, beathach, bheithigh,* not given.

Baha, *bheathach, bheatha, beithe,* birch.

Bahagh, *beathacha,* not given.

Bahagh, *beitigh, beitheach,* birches, birch land.

Bahagha, *na-beathacha,* not given.

Bahagher, *beannchar, beannchain*(sic), not given.

Bahaghs, *na-beathacha,* not given.

Bahaha, *beathacha, beitheah,* birch lands or birches.

Bahalla, *bachallach,* of the crosier.

Bahana, *beathanna,* not given.

Bahana, *beithéanach, beathacha, beitheah,* birch lands or birches.

Baher, *bother,* a road.

Bahernaugh, *beatharnach,* not given.

Bahy, a kiln.

Bailey, a fortress.

Bailie, *Báilleach,* not given.

Baills, *baile,* a town, townland.

Bainin, *báinín,* white tweed.

Bakeen, *béicín,* a little haggard or field in front of a dwelling.

Bal, *baile, baile-na…* see **Bally**.

Bal, *ball,* a spot.

Bal, *balla,* a wall.

Bala, *beal-ath,* the ford mouth.

Balalley, *baile-Mac-Amhlaibh,* not given.

Baleen, *baile-Fhinn/Uí-Fhinn,* not given.

Balief, *baile-Aoidh/Aodha,* Hugh's town.

Balief, *baile-Ífe,* not given.

Balier, *bhiolair,* water cresses.

Balin, *baile,* a town, townland.

Balin, *baile-an…,* town of the…

Ball, *baile,* this can mean a town, townland, place, spot, homestead, enclosure, residence, habitation or situation. Please see the note on Bally in the introduction.

Ball, *béal,* a ford.

Ball, spots.

Balla, *balla,* a wall or walls.

Balla, *balla,* a well or spring.

Balla, *bealach,* not given.

Balla, *beilagh,* fire of fires.

Balla, *bel-atha…* ford mouth of…

Balla, *bhaile, baile,* a town, townland or homestead.

Balla, *ball-álainn,* not given.

Ballad, *béalaid,* a pass.

Balladean, *bealach-a'da-én,* pass of the two birds.

Balladian, *bealach-an-dá-éan,* pass of the two birds.

Balladian, *béal-átha-an-daingin,* not given.

Ballady, *beal-atha-duibhe,* mouth of the black ford.

Ballagh, *bealach,* the road, path, way, route, passage or pass.

Ballagh, *bealach,* an ancient pathway.

Ballagh, *béal-atha-an…,* mouth of the ford of the…

Ballagh, *bhallacha,* spotted.

Ballagha, *béal/beal-átha-an…,* mouth of the ford by the…

Ballagha, *bealach-a…,* pass of the…

Ballagha, *bealach-an…,* way or road to or of the…

Ballaghalare, *bealach-lair,* middle road.

Ballaghan, *baile-Lagáin,* not given.

Ballaghan, *bhaile-Uí-Ágain,* homestead of Ó Ágain, family name.

Ballagharea, *bealach-an-Chairr-Fhiaidh,* not given.

Ballaghcullia, *bel-coille,* the mouth of the wood.

Ballaghkeen, *an-bealach*(sic), not given.

Ballaghkeen, *béal-átha-caoin,* beautiful ford mouth.

Ballaghna, *bealach-na…,* not given.

Ballaghoge, *bealach-óg,* the little roadway.

Ballahy, *bealach,* the path.

Ballallog, *baile-Alog,* not given.

Ballaghoge, *bealach-óg,* not given.

Ballan, *baile-an…,* town/homestead of the…

Ballan, *Balán,* not given.

Ballana, *béal-átha-na…,* ford mouth of the…

Ballard, *baile-ard,* high homestead.

Ballard, *baile-árd-tíghe-goill,* high town/town of the height of the Englishmans house.

Ballaverty, *baile-Uí-Laibheartaigh,* not given.

Ballbbeg,(sic) *baile-beag,* small town.

Ballea, *baile-Aodha/Aodh,* Hugh's or Aodh's (a male name) town.

Balleally, *baile-Uí-Eilighe,* O'Healy's (a family name) town.

Ballee, *baile-atha,* the town of the ford.

Ballee, *béalghach,* not given.

Balleeghan, *baile-aighidh-chaein/chaoin, baile aghaidh-chaoin,* town of the beautiful face or surface.

Balleek, *baile-liag,* not given.

Balleek, *bél-leice,* ford mouth of the flagstone.

Balleen, *baile-Fhinn/Uí-Fhinn,* homestead of O'Finn, family name.

Balleen, *baile-Uí-Fhinn,* town of Finn (a personal or family name.

Balleen, *bailéin*(sic) little townland.

Balleen, *baile-Uí-Eidhin, baile-Eidhin,* not given.

Balleen, *bailín,* little town or homestead.

Balleven, *baile-Aoibhin,* Evan's (a personal or family name) homestead.

Balli, *baile,* town.

Balli, *bel-atha,* ford mouth of…

Ballic, Ballick, *baile-Mhic…,* town/townland of the son of…

Ballickmoyler, *baile-Mhic/Mic-Mhaoilir/Maol-mhuire,* not given.

Ballicknahee, *baile-Mhic-na-hOíche/hOidhche,* not given.

Balliggan, *baile-Uí-Uiginn,* not given.

Ballilogue, *baile-Uilleog,* not given.

Ballilogue, *'baile-Uí-Mhaoil, Laodhóg'*(sic), O'Logue's (a personal or family name) homestead.

Ballin *baile-an/na…,* town/townland or homestead of the…

Ballin, *béal-átha-an/na…, beal-atha-na…,* fordmouth of the….

Ballina, (on Shannon) *béal-áth-na-Boróimhe,* not given.

Ballina, *baile-an/na…,* (see bally) of the…

Ballina, *baile-an-átha,* town of the ford.

Ballina, *baile-na…,* town/townland of the…

Ballina, *baile-Uí-Einigh,* Heany's (a family name) homestead.

Ballina, *béal-an-fheadha,* not given.

Ballina, *beal-átha, béal-an-átha, béal/beal-an-atha,* the mouth of the ford.

Ballina, *buaile-na…,* milking place of the…

Ballinab, *baile-an-aba,* not given.

Ballinafad, *béal-an-átha-fada,* mouth of the long ford.

Ballinagh, *béal-átha-na-nEach/nEich,* ford mouth of the horse.

Ballinaha, *béal-an-atha/átha,* the mouth of the ford.

Ballinaha, *bel-an-atha,* mouth of the ford.

Ballinamara, *béal-átha-na-marbh,* not given.

Ballinameen, *béal-an-átha-mín,* the smooth ford mouth.

Ballinamore, *béal-an-átha-mhóir,* mouth of the big ford.

Ballinduff, *baile-an-dubh,* town of the dark complexioned man.

Balline, *baile-Fhaghain,* Faghan's town.

Ballinea, *béal-an-átha,* the ford mouth.

Ballineen, *béal-áth/beal-ath-Fhingín,* mouth of Finin's or Finneen's, (a male name) ford.

Ballineen, *béal-átha-Fhinín, not given.*

Balliniry, *baile-an-oighre,* town of the heir.

Balliniry, *bhaile-an-oidhre,* not given.

Ballinla, *baile-an-Lea,* not given.

Ballinloughane, *baile-Uí-Gheileachain,* O'Geelahan's town.

Ballinran, *baile-doine-an-ghlaisne,* not given.

Ballinree, *baile-an-fraeigh,* town of the heather.

Ballinree, *baile-an-Righ,* town of the King.

Ballinrig, *baile-an-luig,* the town of the hollow.

Ballinroe, *an-mullán*(sic)*-rua,* not given.

Ballinskelligs, *baile-inis-sceilg,* not given.

Ballintee, *baile-an-Tiúigh,* Tew's (a personal or family name) homestead.

Ballintoppan, *mullach-an-tSopáin*(sic)*,* not given.

Ballintra, *béal-átha-an-tSratha,* not given.

Ballinunty, *baile- an-fhantaigh,* not given.

Ballinure, *baile-an-Iúir,* town of the yew.

Ballinurra, *baile-an-Noraigh,* Norris's (a personal or family name) homestead.

Ballinva, *baile-an-Bháthaigh,* not given.

Ballinva, *baile-an-Bhádhaigh,* de-Bathe's or Bath's (family names) homestead.

Ballinvir, *baile-an-bhioraigh,* not given.

Ballinvir, *baile-an-bhiorra,* town of the watery place.

Balliny, *baile-na-oi,* sheep pasturage(sic).

Balliny, *baile-Uí-hEinig,* O'Heany or O'Heeny, a family name.

Balliogan, *baile-Uí-Eochagáin,* not given.

Ballis, *baile, bhaile,* town.

Ballisodare, *baile-easa-dara,* homestead of the waterfall of the oak.

Ballitore, *béal-átha/atha-an-tuair, bel-atha-a'tuair,* ford mouth of the bleach green.

Ballon, *Balana, Balanna,* not given.

Ballon, *Uí-Ballain,* named after the tribe of Ui-Ballein.

Balloo, *baile/bail'-Lugha, bail'-Lúgh,* Lugh or Lewy's (a personal or a family name) town or townland.

Balloor, *baile-úr,* new town.

Ballough, *bail' locha,* town of the lake.

Ballough, *bealach,* a way, road, route or pass.

Balloughdalla, *bail'locha-Dalla,* town of Lough dalla, (*da-ela,* two swans).

Balloughkeen, *baile-achadh-chaoin/chaein,* town of the beautiful field.

Ballug, *bail'luig,* town of the hollow.

Ballug, *baile-Luig,* not given.

Ballure, *baile-úr,* new town.

Bally, *baile,* this can mean a town, village, cluster of houses, townland, place, spot, homestead, enclosure, dwelling, residence, habitation, patrimony, settlement or situation. Please see note on Bally in the introduction.

Bally, *bealach,* the road or pass.

Bally, *beal-átha/atha, béal-átha...* ford mouth of...

Bally, *buaile,* a booley or dairying place.

Ballya, *baile-atha,* town of the ford.

Ballyagran, *baile-átha-grean,* not given.

Ballyan, *baile-Uí-Éidhin,* not given.

Ballyane, *baile-Uí-Éidhin,* Ó hÉidhin's (a family name) town.

Ballyanrahan, *baile-Uí-Anracháin,* not given.

Ballyarr, *béal-áth-dhaire,* not given.

Ballyarrell, *corr-na-seisc,* not given.

Ballyashea, *baile-Uí-Aisí,* not given.

Ballyatty, *béal-átha-Eitigh,* not given.

Ballybay, *béal-átha/áth-beithe, bel-atha-beithe,* ford mouth of the birch.

Ballybeggane, *baile-Uí-Bheagáin,* not given.

Ballybloun, *baile-Mhic-Giolla-na-bh-Flann,* Mac Gillanavlann's (a family name) town.

Ballybo, *baile-boithe...* town of the hut of... or town of ......'s hut.

Ballybo, *baile-mbo,* cowland.

Ballybobaneen, *baile-mbo-báinín,* townland or cowland of the white flannel.

Ballybodonnell, *baile-boithe-Dhomhnaill,* town of Donal's (a male name) booth, hut or tent.

Ballybofey, *bealach-Féich/Fheich,* Fiach's pass or road.

Ballyboggan, *baile-Uí-Bhogáin,* O'Boggan's town.

Ballyboy, *baile-átha-buí,* homestead of the yellow ford.

Ballyboys, *baile-átha-buí,* not given.

Ballybrick, *baile-Mhic-Giolla Bhric,* Mac Gilbrick's or Mac Gillavrick's town.

Ballybricken, *baile-Bhreacáin/Bhricín, Teampull-Breacna,* not given.

Ballybrooney, *beal-atha-Bhronaigh,* ford mouth of the Broney/Brony.

Ballybrowney, *beal-atha-Bhronaigh,* ford mouth of the Broney/Brony.

Ballybruncullen(sic), *buaile-chromuillean,* not given.

Ballyburly, *baile-an-Bhuirléigh,* not given.

Ballyburly, *brú-molt,* not given.

Ballycahill, (Tipp) *Bealach-Achaille,* the pass of 'achall', (a rock in a high strategic place).

Ballycapple, *baile-locha-Capaill*(sci), not given.

Ballyconra, *béal-átha-Conrátha,* not given.

Ballyconra, *béal-átha-Chonaire,* Conaire's (a personal or family name) ford(sic).

Ballyconra, *béal-átha-Chonra,* Conra's (a personal or family name) ford mouth.

Ballyconra, *baile-Chonaire,* Conaire's (a personal or family name) town.

Ballycroy, *baile-fhoidh-cruaiche, baile-an-cruaich,* not given.

Ballycue, *baile-mic-Aodha,* Mackay or MacHugh's (a family name) town.

Ballycullen, *baile-Uí-Choiléin,* not given.

Ballycullen, *druim-Earc,* not given.

Ballyda, *baile-Dhaith,* David's (a male name) homestead.

Ballydaly, *doire-na-nGall,* not given.

Ballydavid, *baile-Dáithí,* not given.

Ballydoorlis, *béal-átha-durlais, beal-atha-durlios,* ford (mouth?) of the strong fort.

Ballyea, *baile-Aodha,* not given.

Ballyea, *baile-Uí-Aodha,* O'Hea's (a personal or family name) homestead.

Ballyea, *baile-Uí-Aodha/Aédha,* Ó hAodha's or O'Hea's town.

Ballyea, *Baile-Uí-Fhiaigh,* town of O'Fay, a family name.

Ballyeafy, *baile-Uí-Éafaigh,* not given.

Ballyeafy, *Uí-hEimhthigh,* O'Heaphy's (a family name.) town.

Ballyealan, *Baile-Uí-Fhaoláin,* O'Felan or O'Phelan, a family name.

Ballyfinboy River, *an-inithe,* not given.

Ballyfinnane, (Kerry), *beal-ath-Fionnain,* the ford or ford-mouth of Finnan.

Ballygarries, *bealaigh-gearra, bealoch gearr,* short passes or short roads.

Ballygraigue, *baile-Graife*(sic), not given.

Ballyhackamore, *an-bealach-áthchomair,* not given.

Ballyhally, *buoly-halagh,* dirty or miry dairying place.

Ballyhay, *bealach-átha,* road of the ford.

Ballyhea, *béalach-átha,* not given.

Ballyhealy, *bealach-áth-an-iubhair,* not given.

Ballyhee, *baile-Uí-Shidhe,* O'Hee's (a family name) town.

Ballyheen, *béal-átha-Hín,* not given.

Ballyheens, *Beilchín,* not given.

Ballyheens, *Bellithín,* the ancient tree of St Itin.

Ballyhenry, *corrán*(sic), not given.

Ballyhenry, *baile-an-Hanraígh,* not given.

Ballyhigh, *baile-Sheóin-de-hÁé,* not given.

Ballyhisky, *bealach-uisce,* road of the water.

Ballyhooley, *Baile-Átha-ubhla,* homestead of the apple-tree ford.

Ballyhoura Mountains, *an-sliabh-riabhach*(sic), not given.

Ballyina, *beal-átha-na...,* ford mouth of the...

Ballyinn, *baile-Fhinn,* Finn's (a personal or family name) homestead.

Ballyiine, *baile-Uí-hEidhin,* town of O'Hyne, a family name.

Ballyin, *baile-Fhinn,* not given.

Ballyine, *baile-Uí-Eidhnigh,* Ó hÉidhnigh's (a family name) town.

Ballyine, *baile-Uí-Eighin,* Hynes, a family name.

Ballyinn, *baile-Fhinn,* Finn's (a personal or family name) homestead.

Ballykilcross, *baile-giolla-chroise,* not given.

Ballykilmurry, *Baile-Uí-Mhuirithe*(sic), not given.

Ballylahan, *baile-atha-leathain,* town of the broad ford.

Ballylannidy, *baile-lann-Síada,* Sheeda's patrimony(sic).

Ballylease, *baile-lias,* hill ridge of the huts(sic).

Ballylusky, *baile-locha-loiscthe*(sic), not given.

Ballylusky, *baile-lusca,* the place of the vault.

Ballymac, (Shillelogher parish) *baile-Mhic-Dhaith,* Mac David, a family name.

Ballymack, *baile-Mac-Cua,* town of the sons of Cua, a personal or family name.

Ballymack, *baile-Mhic-Dháith,* not given.

Ballymagree, *baile-dhá-ghraí*(sic), not given.

Ballymalis, *béal-átha-Málais,* Málais (a personal or family name) ford mouth.

Ballymaloogh, *bhaile-na-mBulbhach,* not given.

Ballymona, *baile-an-mhóinín/mhóinin*(sic), not given.

Ballymore, *baile-mhóir/mhór,* the big town.

Ballymoreagh, *an-baile-riabhach,* not given.

Ballymot, *baile-an-adhmaid,* place of the timber.

Ballymureen, *baile-Amoraoin,* not given.

Ballyn, *baile-na/n...,* town of the ..., town of...

Ballyna, *baile-an*(sic)..., not given.

Ballyna, *baile-na..., bail'-na...,* town of the ...

Ballyna, *béal-átha-na...,* ford mouth of the...

Ballyna, *buaile-na...,* booley (dairying place) of the...

Ballyna, *baile-na...,* home of the...

Ballynabwee, *baile-an-atha-buidhe,* the town of the yellow ford.

Ballynagh, *bail'-na-neach,* town of the horses.

Ballynagh, *baile-an-átha,* not given.

Ballynahagh, *baile-Ó-nEachach,* not given.

Ballynakill, *baile-Mhic-Coiligh*(sic), not given.

Ballynakill, *baile-na-coille,* town of the wood.

Ballynalina, *baile-na-Laighneach,* Lynach's(sic) homestead.

Ballynamannin, *beul*(sic)*-atha-naMainín,* mouth of Mannins ford(sic)

Ballynamona, *baile-na-móna,* not given.

Ballynamona, *baile-na-nUaithneach*(sic), not given.

Ballynamorahan(sic), *baile-Uí-Mhoracháin,* not given.

Ballynastangford, *currach-beithe*(sic), not given.

Ballynaveen, *baile-Uí-Chnáimhín,* not given.

Ballynavin, *baile-Uí-Chnáimhín,* not given.

Ballynevin, *baile-Uí-Chnáimhín,* not given

Ballynote, *baile-an-fhóta,* place of invading or storming.

Ballyonan, *baile-Uí-Mhaonáin,* not given.

Ballyportry, *baile-pórtraithe,* Hogstown(sic).

Ballyrahan, *baile-Bhracham*(sic), not given.

Ballyre, *bail'-ladhair,* town of the river fork.

Ballyrea, *baile-riabhach,* grey town.

Ballyseedy, *bailte*(sic)*-Uí-Síoda,* not given.

Ballyslavin, *baile-an-lábáin*(sic), not given.

Ballytober, *baile-na-dtri-dtobar,* town of the three springs.

Ballyvally, *baile-Uí-Mháille,* not given.

Ballyvoghane, *baille-bothán-clan-Cinneíde*(sic), tract of the Kennedy clan.

Balnamore, *béal-an-átha-móir,* ther big ford mouth.

Balrathboyne, *baile-na-rátha*(sic), not given.

Balriggin, *baile-Uiginn,* not given.

Balrisk, town of the marsh.

Balt, *bailt,* welt or excrescence.

Balt, *bailte,* townlands.

Balteagh, *bailte-Fhiach,* Fee's (a personal or a family name) townlands.

Balteagh, *baile-da-fhiach,* town of the two ravens.

Balteen, *bailtin, bailtín, baltín,* little town, small holding or homestead.

Baltimore, *baile-tigh-mór, baile-an-tighe-mór, baile-na-tighe-mór,* place/town of the big house. The older name was *dún-na-séad,* fort of the jewels.

Baltin, *bealltaine,* a first of May day druidic festival.

Balting, *bealltaine,* a first of May day druidic festival.

Balting, *Bealtaine,* May.

Baltinglas, *bal-teach-na-glass,* town of the grey houses.

Baltinglas, *beal-tine-glas,* the fire of Beal's (a male name) mysteries.

Baltinglass, *bealach-Chon-Ghlais, Mainistir-an-bhealaigh,* not given.

Baltinglass, *bealach-Conglais/Chonglais/Conglais,* the road, way route or pass of Cúglas, Cuglas, a male name and means greyhound. He was the son of King Don Desa of Leinster.

Balty, *bailte,* towns, townlands.

Balwoges, *balbhóg,* soft land or ground that does not make any sound when walked upon.

Balyna, *bealach-an-fheadha,* not given.

Ban, *bán,* a green field or pasture land.

Ban, *ban, mBan,* a woman.

Ban, *bán,* white.

Ban, *beann,* a peak.

Ban, *beann,* the horn, pointed hill or pointed rock.

Bana, *bán/ban-a'...,* lealand of the...

Banad, *beannaid,* not given.

Banada, *beann-fhada, beannada,* not given.

Banada, *muine-na-fede,* thicket of the stream.

Banada, the long gable.

Banagh, *albanach,* a Scotsman.

Banagh, *Baghaineach,* land of Boghaine, grandson of Niall of the nine hostages.

Banagh, *báinigh, Boghaine,* not given.

Banagh, *beannach,* hilly.

Banagher, *beannchair,* pointed hills.

Banagher, *beannchaire,* a place of pointed hills.

Banagher, *beannchar, beannchor,* a pointed or peaked hill.

Banagher, *beannchar,* abounding in peaks.

Banaha, *beannuighthe,* blessed.

Banaha, *Beretheirt, Berehert,* a personal or family name.

Banane, *Bannon,* a personal or family name.

Banane, *Buinneáin,* not given.

Banard, *beann-ard,* the high peak.

Banaun, *Uí-Bhanain,* O'Bannon, a family name.

Banaway, *bin-buidhe,* yellow peak.

Banawn, *bonnán,* not given.

Bancha, *báinseach, bainseac, bainseach,* a level place or a pasture.

Bandan, *bandan,* not given.

Bandon, *banndan,* not given.

Bandon, from *banna,* goddess.

Bane, *báine,* the white cow.

Bane, *bán,* lea ground or pasture land.

Bane, *baine, ban,* waste or untilled land.

Bane, *bán,* white, whitish.

Bane, *bhadhuin,* an enclosure or cow-keep.

Bane, *Boghaine,* not given.

Banew, *bheannuighthe, beannughadh,* a blessing or salutation.

Bangan, *beangán,* not given.

Bangor, *baingear,* a pointed hill.

Bangor, *beannchar,* a peaked hill.

Bangor, *beannchar,* pointed arrangement(sic).

Bangor, *beannchor, bennchoir, mBeannchair,* horns, a place of gables or pointed rocks/hills.

Bangort, *bánghort,* not given.

Bania, *báine,* the white cow.

Baniff, pigs(sic).

Bank, *bannc,* a river bank or turf bank.

Bann, (the river) *an-Banna,* the Goddess and *an-bhanna,* not given.

Banna, *bheannach, banna,* not given.

Banna, *beanna,* hill peaks.

Banna, *beanna-a'...,* peak of the...

Banna, *beannaithe, beannuighthe,* a blessing or blessed.

Bannad, *Beannaid,* not given.

Bannag, *bánóg,* a field.

Bannagh, *banabh,* the Abbess.

Bannagh, *bannach,* a fox.

Bannagh, *beannach,* full of 'bens' or pinnacles.

Bannagh, *beannach,* pinnacled or gabled.

Bannagh, *bheannach, bhannach,* not given.

Bannagher, *beannchor,* horns, pointed hill/s or rocks.

Bannakey, *bán-na-cae,* foot of the quagmire.

Bannamore, *an-bábhun-mór,* not given.

Bannan, *Banán,* not given.

Bannan, *beannáin,* the little pinnacle.

Bannan, *Uí-Bhanain, Banain,* O'Bannon, a family name.

Banne, *Bhanain,* O'Bannon, a family name.

Banne, *bheanaigh,* blessed.

Bannif, *bainbh,* a suckling pig.

Bannin, *bheanáin,* not given.

Bannivane, Banivan, not given.

Bannive, *bainbh,* a suckling pig.

Bannix, *mBanog, mBánóg, bánóg,* little green fields or little lea fields.

Bannoo, *ban-uath,* female ghosts.

Bannow, *banbh,* a bonnive or young suckling pigs.

Bannow, *beannaighte,* blessed.

Bannow, *bun-abha,* bottom of the river.

Bannow, *carraig-an-bhainbh,* not given.

Bannow, *cuan-an-bhainbh,* harbour, bay of the bonnive or suckling pig.

Bannus, *bánach,* lea land.

Banny, *beannúighthe,* a blessing.

Banny, *bhainne, bainne,* milk.

Banny, *bainigh,* the white cow(sic).

Banny, *buinnighe,* oozing water or a watery surface.

Banoge, *bánóg, bánóige, bánoige,* little lea field or a grassy field.

Banoge, *bhánóg,* not given.

Banogue, *bánog,* a courtyard.

Banragh, *bánrach,* lea land.

Banragh, *bhánrainn,* not given.

Banree, *bann-raighe,* an enclosure or pound.

Banree, *bann-rioghan,* a queen.

Banse, *an-bansa,* not given.

Bansh, *báinseach,* grassy plain.

Bansha, *báinseach,* a sheep walk.

Bansha, *báinseach, an-bháinseach,* the grassy spot.

Bansha, *báinseach, báinsighe, bainseac, bainseach, bháinsigh, bhainséach, bhainseach,* a level grassy place, a small tract of lea ground, grassy land, a pasture or a grassy plain.

Bansha, *báinseach,* green(sic).

Bansha, *na-báinsí,* not given.

Banshagh, *báinseach,* a level grassy place.

Banshee, *báinseach,* a level grassy place.

Banshy, *báinseach,* grassy plain.

Banteer, *bántir, bántír,* white/fair country or land.

Bantierna, *baintighearana, baintighearna, ...*of the lady or ladies.

Bantis, *báinseach,* a pasture.

Bantis, *báinseach, bainseac, bainseach,* a level place or a pasture.

Bantis, *bánta,* green fields.

Bantree, *baintrighe,* the widow.

Bantree, *ban-draoi, the* sorceress.

Bantry Bay, *imbhear-na-mBarc,* ships harbour.

Bantry, *bain-treabhaighe,* a widow.

Bantry, *baintreabhaighe,* not given.

Bantry, *baintrighe,* the widow.

Bantry, *ban-draoi, the* sorceress.

Bantry, *Beanntraí, Beanntraighe,* the race or descendants of Beann, a personal or family name.

Bantry, *beanntraighe-Laighean,* not given.

Bantry, *Beannt-Righe,* Beannt's (a 9th century chief) territory.

Bantry, *Beantraighe,* Beann's (a personal or a family name) strand.

Bantry, *bheanntraighe,* not given.

Bar, *bairr, barr,* top, height or summit.

Bar, *Bharraigh,* Barry, a male name.

Bar, *Bharraigh,* de Barra, a family name.

Bara, *báire,* the winning goal.

Bara, *Beara, Beara,* a male name.

Bara, *beara,* the point.

Barabona, *bóthar-an-bhainne,* not given.

Baragh, *bearach,* not given.

Baragh, *bearrthach,* shorn, grazed or bare.

Baralty, *barr-alltaí,* not given.

Baran, shorn, grazed or bare.

Baran, *barr-an...,* crop of...(sic)

Bard, *bard, bárd,* a bard or poet.

Bardan, *O'Bardan,* a family name.

Bardinch, *barr-Duínse,* not given.

Bareen, *bairghín,* 'creeping crow foot', a plant name.

Barfort, *Bharfoird,* Barford, a personal or family name.

Bargy, *Uí-Bairche,* a family name.

Barheen, *barrithín,* little hilltop.

Barlom, *bairr-loim,* bare hilltop.

Barmeath, *bearna-Mheá,* not given.

Barn, *an-Bharúnaigh,* not given.

Barn, *bearn, beárna,* a gap or pass.

Barna, *barr,* the top or summit.

Barna, *barr-na...,* the top of ...

Barna, *barr-na...,* hill top(sic) of the...

Barna, *bearna,* a gap.

Barna, *bearna-Chlaí-Chosnaigh, bearna-Laoighre,* not given.

Barna, *beárnan,* a gap.

Barna, *bearna-na*, top of the…

Barnacole, *bearna-Niocóil*, Nichol's (a personal or family name) gap.

Barnagh, *báirneach*, limpets.

Barnagh, *bearnách*, dilapidated(sic).

Barnagh, *bhearnach*, *bearnach*, a gap or gapped.

Barnagh, *mBáirneach*, not given.

Barnan, *barr-na*…, not given.

Barnan, *bearna/barna-an*… gap of the…

Barnan, *bearnán*, *bearnan*, a gap.

Barnana, *beárna-na*…, gap of the…

Barnanang, *barna-na-nEang*, not given.

Barnane, *bearnán*, the little gap.

Barnard, *bearna-ard*, the high gap.

Barnay, *bearna*, a gap.

Barne, *bearna*, a gap.

Barnes, *bearnas*, *barnas*, a gap.

Barnet, *bearnait*, not given.

Barnet, from *bearna*, a gap.

Barney, *bearna*, a gap.

Barnis, *bearnas*, a gap.

Barnish, *béarnaise*, *béarnais*, *bearnas*, a gap.

Barnog, *bairneach*, *báirneóg*, limpet/s.

Barnora, *beárna-fhuardha*, the cooling gap.

Barnora, *bearna-uartha*, not given.

Baroule, *baramhail*, a person of common sense or good judgement.

Barny, *bearna*, not given.

Baroul, *baramhal*, judgement.

Barr, *barr*, the top, summit of…….

Barra, *barr*, the top.

Barra, *Barra*, St Finbarr.

Barra, *barra*, the top or summit.

Barra, *barr-a'*…, top, summit of the …….

Barra, *beara*, water.

Barra, *bearacháin*, heifers.

Barra, St Barra.

Barrack, *Balraic*, *Balrac*, a personal or family name.

Barrack, *Baroc*, *Bhalraic*, *Bheairic*, not given.

Barrack, *Baroc*, not given.

Barrack, *Bharóg*, *Bearóg*, St Berach or St Baróg/Bearóg.

Barrack, *Bharróg*, little Barra, a personal or family name.

Barrackton, *gleann-Chiotáin*, not given.

Barracum, *Bearchain*, St Berchan.

Barragh, *barrach*, top land or upland.

Barragh, *bearrach*, not given.

Barragh, *bearthach*, a bare town.

Barrahan, *Barrachain*, *Bearchain*, St Berchane/Berchan.

Barrahane, *Barrachain*, *Bearchain*, St Berchane/Berchan.

Barrahane, *Bhearcháin*, not given.

Barran, *bearna*, a gap.

Barran, *barran*, a small summit or hillock.

Barran, from *barr*, little summit.

Barrana, *barra-na*…, summit of the…

Barrana, *barr-na*…, hilltop of the…

Barranagh, *bearanach*, not given.

Barranagh, *bearránach*, *bearánach*, pointed hills.

Barranaghs, *barr-eanach*(sic), not given.

Barraree, *Barra-Riadha*, not given.

Barravane, *Bharraigh*, the fair Barry, a personal or family name.

Barravey, *barra-beithe*, summit of the birch.

Barravie, *barr-an-mhaí*, *barr-a'-mhuighe*, top of the plain.

Barreel, *barr-aoil*, hilltop of lime.

Barreen, *bairghín*, a circular piece of cake.

Barrees, *barraidhe*, *barraí*, hilltops or pinnacles.

Barren, *Barrain*, Barran or Barron, a personal or family name.

Barretts, *Báróidigh*, *Báróideacha*, not given.

Barrevagh, *barr-riabhach*, grey summit.

Barrigone, *Bairrgeoin*, not given.

Barro, *beara*, *biorra*, water.

Barron, *Barráin*, *Bharfionn*, *Bhairrfhinn*, St Barrán, Barron, Baurrain or Baurinn. The name means fair haired.

Barron, *Bharúin*, Barron, a personal or family name.

Barron, *Bharún*, *Bharráin*, *Bharúnaigh*, *Barrainn*, *Bhárrain*, not given.

Barron, *Biorán*, Birrin, a personal name.

Barron, *mBiorának*, sprats.

Barroo, *bár-ruadh*, *barr-ruadh*, red top.

Barrow, *bearbha*, *an-bhearú/bearrbha*, not given.

Barrow, *barra*, the top.

Barrow, *bearamha*, not given.

Barrow, *beirigh*, boiling.

Barrow, *ceann-beara*, not given.

Barry, *an-Bharraigh*, the Barries, male names or family names.

Barry, *an-Bharraigh*, the 'de-Barra's' a family name.

Barry, *baile,* town, townland.
Barry, *Barra,* Barra or St Finbar. The name means fair haired.
Barry, *Barra,* St Barr/Finbar.
Barry, *Barraigh,* not given.
Barry, *Bearaigh, Bearach,* St Bearach or Barry a male name.
Barry, *bearraidh,* a closely-grazed place.
Barry, *borraidhe,* ridges.
Barrymaiden, *Bara-Méidin,* St Barry and St Medin.
Barrymeaden, *Bhairméidín,* not given.
Barryroe, *barraidhe-ruadha,* red hilltops.
Barson, *bPearsann,* parish priests.
Bartagh, *beartach,* faggots.
Bartlemy, *tobar-Pártnán/Pártnáin,* not given.
Bartoose, *beartús,* a gathering or hoarding.
Bartragh, *beartrach,* a sandbank.
Bartragh, *beartrach-buidhe,* not given.
Bartrauve, *bar-Thráú,* not given.
Bartraw, *beartrach,* a sandbank.
Bash, *Bhais,* not given.
Baskin, *baiscinn,* a place of trees.
Baskin, *Bascinn,* Baskin, a male name and a tribe.
Baskinagh, *baiscinnach,* abounding in trees.
Baslick, *baisleac,* a Basilica or Church.
Baslickane, *baisleacán,* a little Basilica.
Baste, *bPiast,* enchanted serpents or worms.
Basty, *bPáiste, páiste,* children. A place where unbaptised children were interred.
Bate, *bhaid, bháid,* a boat.
Batteen, *bhaitín,* little sticks.
Batter, *bhathair,* not given.
Batter, *bóthar, bhóthair, bothir, bothyr(sic),* a road.
Battog, *Báiteoige,* not given.
Battog, *báitheach,* drowned or mashy.
Bauck, *bác,* a bend or angle.
Baul, *baile,* a town, townland.
Baul, *ball,* a spot, spots or portions.
Baultina, *bealltaine,* a first of May day druidic festival.
Baulting, *bealltaine,* a place where sports were held.
Baun, *bán, bána,* white, whitish.

Baun, *bhán, bán, badhun,* a field, an enclosure, a cow-keep, a field or fortress for cattle.
Bauna, *bán-an...* lea ground of the...
Bauna, *bán-na/a'...* lea-ground, field of the...
Baunan, *ban-an...,* bawn of the...
Baunan, Bannan, a personal or family name.
Bauneen, *an-báinín, báinín,* the little bawn.
Baunemon, *bán-Éamainn,* not given.
Baunhubbamaddereen, *bán-thobair-an-mhaidrín,* the well bawn of the little fox. (compare **Bawnhubbamaddereen**).
Baunna, *bán-na...,* lea-ground/field of the...
Baunoge, *bánóg,* little field.
Baunoge, *bhánóg,* not given.
Baunragh, *bánrach,* abounding in green fields.
Baunshy, *báinseach,* grassy plain.
Baunta, *bánta,* fields.
Baunta, *bánta,* a bawn(sic).
Bauntana, *bánta-na...,* fields of the...
Baunteen, *an-báintín,* not given.
Baunteen, little green field.
Baur, *bár,* a hilltop.
Baur, *barr,* high ground or the top.
Baura, *bár-an...,* hill top of the...
Baura, *barr-a'....*top of....
Bauran, *barr-an....*top of the...
Bauravilla, *barr-achadh-a'bhile,* top of the field of the ancient tree.
Baurearagh, *barr-agrach,* weird or airy summit.
Baurna, *barr-na...,* not given.
Baurnagh, *báirneach,* limpets.
Bauroe, *bár-rúadh,* red hill top.
Bauteoge, *báitheach,* drowned or mashy.
Bauteogue, *báiteog,* a morass.
Bautia, *baidhte,* drowning.
Bautia, *báidhthe,* drowned.
Bautia, *báite,* not given.
Bauttagh, *báitheach,* drowned or mashy.
Bauville, *bobhaile,* cow's town.
Bavan, *bábhún,* not given.
Bavan, *bó-dhún, bádhún, badhun,* enclosure or fortress for cattle and sometimes land associated with a castle.
Bavin, *babhdhun,* not given.
Bawn, *badhun, bábhún,* an enclosure.

Bawn, *badhbhdhun, bádhún, badhun,* an enclosure, field or fortress for cattle, sometimes land associated with a castle.

Bawn, *bán,* a green field, lea land, untilled or uncropped grassland.

Bawn, *bán,* white, whitish.

Bawna, *bán-a'*… field of the…

Bawna, bán-na…, dry pasture land of the…

Bawnagh, *bánach,* lea land.

Bawnakee, *bán-an-chaoith,* not given.

Bawnalassa, *bán-a'leása,* i.e. fortified(sic).

Bawnataafe, *bábhún-an-táthaigh,* not given.

Bawncross, *bán-mór*(sic), not given.

Bawnea, *ban-Aodha,* Aodh's or Hugh's (male names) land.

Bawnhubbamaddereen, *bán-thobair-maidrín,* field of the well of the little dog.

Bawnmedrum, *badbhdún-muighe-droma,* bawn or castle of the ridge of the plain.

Bawnoge, *bánóg,* little lea field.

Bawnoge, *na-bánóga,* little green fields or lea fields.

Bawnoges, *bánóga, mBánóg,* little green fields or lea fields.

Bawnt, *bánta,* fields.

Bawnta, *bánta,* fields.

Bawntard, *na-bánta-aird,* not given.

Bay, *béal, beal,* mouth.

Bay, *beithe, beith,* birch.

Bay, *bháthaigh,* not given.

Baylet, *Bealait,* not given.

Baylet, *bélat,* a pass, road or crossroad.

Baylin, *béilinn,* not given.

Baynanagh, *Beangánach,* not given.

Baysrath, *ráth-an-Bhádaigh,* Bath's or de-Bath's (a personal or family name) rath.

Beabus, *Béabas, Béabus,* not given.

Beacanty, *Beagnatan,* not given.

Beacanty, *Becnata,* St Becnat.

Beach, *traigh,* a strand.

Beacon, *Beacain, Beacan,* a personal or family name.

Beacon, *Beacán, Béacáin,* not given.

Beag, *beag, beaga,* small.

Beagh, *Beatha, Bith,* the name of an ancient hero and a pre deluvian colonist.

Beagh, *beithe, bheitheach, bheathaidh, beath-ach,* not given.

Beagh, *béite, beitigh, beitheach,* birches, birch land or birchy.

Beagha, *beith-aith,* birch wood of the ford.

Beagha, *bheitheach-Chatha,* not given.

Beagher, *buidheachair,* yellow clay.

Beagher, *buidheachar,* jaundice.

Beaghy, *an-bheitheach,* not given.

Beaghy, *beitigh, beitheach,* birches, birch land.

Beakeen, *beicín,* little field or haggard.

Beal, *béal,* a mouth, opening, gap, approach or access.

Beal, *beal,* mouth or entrance to a ford.

Beala, *beal-a…, beal-an…,* mouth or ford-mouth of the...

Beala, *béal-an…,* opening of the …

Beala, *béal-átha, beal-ath,* the ford mouth.

Beala, *béal-átha…,* ford mouth of the…

Bealad, *bealaid, bealad,* crossroads.

Bealad, *béalaid,* the pass.

Bealad, *beal-fhad,* long ford.

Bealad, *béil-fhada,* the long mouth.

Bealady, *beal-fhad,* long ford.

Bealaha, *béal-átha,* the ford mouth.

Bealahoe, *béil-átha-hÓa,* not given.

Bealana, *béal-áth/átha-na…,* not given.

Beale, *béala,* not given.

Bealick, *bealach-leachta,* route or pass of the grave mound.

Bealick, *beal-lice,* the flagstone ford.

Bealick, *beillic, beillice,* a cavern.

Bealin, *béal/béil-Linne, béilin,* not given.

Bealna, *béal-na…,* mouth of the…

Bealock, *beallach,* the way or passage.

Bealock, *béilic,* not given.

Bealy, *Béala,* not given.

Bealy, *béalaigh,* pass, mouth or opening.

Beama, *bhéama, béama,* a cut or blow.

Beamond, *béimeann,* not given.

Beany, *bhéine,* not given.

Bear, *Beara,* name of the wife of Conn of the hundred battles, and a Spanish Princess.

Bear, *Biúir,* not given.

Bear, from *bearr,* a place of short grass or a bare place.

Beara, *Beara,* name of the wife of Conn of the hundred battles, and a Spanish Princess.

Beara, *beara,* the point.

Bearchain, *Bearchain,* St Berchane.

Beare, *béarra,* not given.

Bearla, *béarla, bearla,* English language.

Bearn, *bearna,* a gap.

Bearna, *bearna, bearnas,* a gap.

Bearnagh, from *bearna,* a gap or gapped.

Bearney, *bearna,* not given.

Beasoon, *bPéasún,* pheasants.

Beasoon, *bPiasún,* not given.

Beast, *bPiast, a* serpent.

Beatin, *béitín,* burnt land.

Beatin, *bheítínn,* not given.

Beaufort, *lios-an-phuca,* not given.

Beaulieu, *béilinn,* not given.

Beauparc, *baile-Phaghain,* not given.

Beby(sic)*,* *bheithí,* not given.

Becan, *Phíocáin,* Becan or Pecan, the name of an early Irish saint.

Beclare, *béal-chláir,* mouth of the plain.

Bective, *Beicteach,* a 12th century daughter of Mellifont.

Bedlam, *bhealtaine,* Beltane, May, a place where May festivities were held.

Bee, *bidh,* food.

Bee, *buidhe,* yellow.

Beefan, *Bíofán,* the birch slope.

Beehane, *O'Biotháin,* O'Bihane, a family name.

Been, *binn,* a headland.

Been, *binn, beann,* a peak or pinnacle.

Beena, *beinn-a'...,* point or pinnacle of the...

Beenan, *binn-an...,* pinnacle or hill of the...

Beenbane, *an-bhinn-bháin,* not given.

Beenlea, *an-bhinn-liath,* not given.

Beeny, *beann,* a pinnacle.

Befflaght, *Beifleacht,* not given.

Beg, *beag, beaga, bheag,* small.

Beg, *beithe,* birch trees.

Began, *Beacán,* not given.

Begerin, *beig-Éire, beg-Eire,* little Ireland.

Begery, *beg-Eire,* little Ireland.

Begga, *bheaga,* little.

Beggan, *Beicce,* Becca, a female name.

Beggan, *Bheagáin, Beccan, Beagáin,* St Beagán/Beggan.

Beggan, *Uí-Beagain,* O'Beggan or Biggane, a family name.

Beggane, *Uí-Bheagáin,* Ó Beagáin, a family name.

Beggaun, *Beagain,* Beggan, a personal or family name.

Begh, *beag, beaga,* small.

Begh, *beithe,* birche trees or a birchy place.

Beglieve, *beagshliabh, beigshliabh,* not given.

Begly, *Uí-Beaglaoigh,* O'Begly, a family name.

Begnet, *Beagnatan,* not given.

Begnet, *Becnata,* St Becnat.

Begney, *beag-neimhe,* the small glebe.

Begrath, *beagráth,* not given.

Begs, *beag, beaga,* small.

Beha, *beith,* birches.

Beha, *bheitheach,* not given.

Beha, Bithe, a personal or family name.

Behagh, *beitigh, beitheach,* birches or birch land.

Behagh, *bheitheach,* not given.

Behaghane, *beitheachán,* little birch shrubbery or a little place of birch.

Behanagh, *beathacha, beitheah,* birch lands or birches.

Behanagh, *beithíneach,* not given.

Behaun, *brachan,* soft ground.

Behee, *beithe,* birch.

Beheen, from *beitheach,* birches, a birch grove.

Beheena, *beithineach,* a birch grove, a place of birches.

Beheenagh, from *beitheach,* birches or a birch grove.

Beheenaugh, *beithíneach,* a place of birches.

Behegh, *betheach,* birch.

Behenny, *bheithne,* birche wood.

Beheny, *beithne,* not given.

Beheny, *bheithne,* birches.

Behernagh, *beithearnach,* not given.

Behernagh, from *beitheach,* birches.

Beherny, *beithearnaighe,* birch.

Behy, *bheithigh, beithi, bheithí,* birches.

Behy, *beitheach,* birchen(sic).

Beigh, *beithe,* birches.

Beighra, *beithreach,* birches or birchy.

Beihy, *beithe,* not given.

Beilinn, *beilinn,* not given.

Beirn, *Beirn,* Bearn, not given.

Beirne, *Beirn,* Bearn, not given.

Bekan, *Béacán, Cill-Béacán,* not given.

Bekin, *peicin,* a small peak.

Bekin, *Picheain,* Pichan, a male name.

Bel, *baile,* town, townland or homestead.

Bel, *beal,* a ford(sic).

Bel, *béal,* a mouth, opening, entrance, approach or access.

Bel, *bel-ath,* the mouth of the ford.

Belaghy, *baile-Eachaidh,* townland of the horseman.

Belaghy, *beal-lathaighe,* a miry passage.

Belalt, *beal-ailt,* opening or entrance to the cliff or hillside.

Belan, *bioth-lann,* life for existence, reflection house.

Belan, *bithlann,* not given.

Belcoo, *béal-cú*(sic), mouth of the narrow neck of land.

Belfad, *béil-fhada,* log mouth.

Belfad, *béilfhada,* not given.

Belfast, *beal–feirste,* mouth of the sandbank.

Belgrove, *Cill-Bhochra,* not given.

Belhavel, *beal-Haibhil/Heibhil,* Haville's (a personal or family name) ford.

Belhavel, *claonloch,* not given.

Belix, *bealaigh, bealach,* passes or roads.

Bell, *béal,* a ford.

Bell, *béal, beal,* the mouth or the ford mouth(sic).

Bell, *bile,* the tree or the large, ancient or sacred tree.

Bella, *baile-an...,* town of the...

Bella, *béal/beal-an...,* the mouth, entrance or opening of ...

Bella, *bealach,* a road or pass.

Bella, *beal-atha, béal-áth, bel-ath,* the ford, ford mouth or ford mouth of the...

Bella, *beile, bile, bhile,* an ancient or sacred tree.

Bellafa, *beal-atha-feadha,* ford of the wood.

Bellaghy, *baile-Eachaidh,* Eochadh or Eochaidh's (a personal or family name) town or homestead.

Bellaghy, *béal-Lathaighe, bel-lathaigh,* mouth of the slough or mire.

Bellahan, *béal-átha-na...,* ford mouth of...

Bellaheen, *beilchín,* not given.

Bellaheen, *beilithín,* little (old) tree.

Bellahy, *béal-lathaí, beal-lathaigh,* mouth of the slough or mire.

Bellair, *baile-ard,* not given.

Bellair, *béal-léir,* not given.

Bellan, *béal-átha-an...,* ford mouth of the...

Bellana, *bealach-na...,* road or pass of the...

Bellana, *béal-an-átha, beal-atha,* the mouth of the ford.

Bellana, *béal-áth/átha-na..., beal-atha-na...,* the mouth of the ford of......

Bellanagh, *béal-átha-na-nEach,* ford mouth of the horses.

Bellanaman, *bealach-Neamhain,* not given.

Bellanamore, *béal-an-átha-mhóir,* mouth of the big ford.

Bellananagh, *béal-áth/átha-na-nEach,* ford mouth of the horses.

Bellananima, the ford of the soul.

Bellanarena, *baile-an-mhargaidh,* homestead, town of the market.

Bellantra, *bél-an-tsnamha,* ford of the swimming.

Bellarena, *baile-an-mhargaidh,* town of the market.

Bellarena, *béal-áth-Ríoghna,* not given.

Bellataleen, *bel-a'tsailin,* of the little sea inlet.

Bellaugh, *bel-lathaigh,* mouth of the slough or mire.

Bellaugh, *lathach,* a slough, puddle or miry spot.

Bellaveel, *bel-moil,* ford of the beast.

Bellaw, *béal-átha,* the ford mouth.

Bellaw, *bel-atha, béal átha,* the mouth of the ford.

Bellcotton, *láithreach-Minsí,* not given.

Belle, (Isle) *baile-Mhic-Maghnura,* not given.

Belle, (lake) *loch-Mhílis,* not given.

Belleek, *béal/beal/bél-leice,* mouth or ford mouth of the flagstone.

Belleeks, *béal-leice,* mouth of the flagstones.

Belleen, *beilín, beillín,* a large or ancient tree.

Belleen, *bilín,* not given.

Bellew, *Bheileogaigh,* Bellew, a personal or family name.

Bellew, *bile, beile,* the ancient or sacred tree.

Bellia, *bile, beile,* the ancient or sacred tree.

Bellina, *béal-an-átha, beil-an-atha,* mouth of the ford.

Belline, *baile-Uí-Fhinn,* not given.

Balline, *balla-Uí-Fhinn,* O'Finn's (a personal or family name) wall.

Bellinter, *baile-Fhinitir,* not given.

Bellmount, *cnoc-an-chloig, árd-an-chluig,* not given.

Bellmount, *árd-an-chluig ,ard-a-cloig,* height of the bell.

Bello, *beile, bile,* an ancient tree.

Bellough, *béal-Lathaí,* not given.

Bellow, from *bile,* the ancient tree.

Bellury, *baile-iubhraighe,* town of yews.

Bellevue, *baile-Ghoidir,* not given.

Belmont, *an-lios-dearg,* not given.

Belmont, *baile-na-graige,* the place of the hamlet.

Belmount, *baile-na-gráige, an-lios-dearg,* not given.

Belmullet, *béal-an-mhuirthead,* sea loop(sic).

Belmullet, *béal-an-Mhuirthid,* not given.

Belmullet, *beal-mullet,* mouth of the mullet.

Beloge, *bileoige,* a small sacred or ancient tree.

Belrose, *biolarach,* a place of watercress.

Beltany, *Bhealtaine, Bealltaine,* Beltane, a first of May day druidic festival.

Beltany, *bhealtaine, bealtaine,* a summer festival.

Beltichburne, *baile-Tichburne,* not given.

Beltra, *béal-trá,* not given.

Belvedere, *rathain,* not given.

Belvelly, *béal-an-bhealaigh,* end of the bealach(sic).

Belview, *drom-cuaigh,* not given.

Belville, *gartan,* not given.

Belvoir, *an-bhréadach,* not given.

Belvoir, *baile-mhaghair,* arable land(sic)

Ben, *beann, bhinn, beanna,* a mountain or hill peak or horn.

Bena, *beanna,* hill peaks.

Bena, *bheannach,* not given.

Benach, *beannach,* a pinnacle.

Benada, *caisleán-an-bheannada,* not given.

Benagh, *beannach,* full of bens or hill peaks.

Benagh, *beitheanach,* a place or birches.

Benbo, *beanna-bó/bo,* peaks, horns of the cow.

Benedin, *binn-Éidín,* not given.

Benfield, *gort-na-pónaire,* not given.

Bengour, *binn-odhar,* not given.

Bennan, *Beanán,* not given.

Bennan, *Bheanáin,* Beanán, a personal or family name.

Benneding, *bin-é-udain,* peak or pointed hill of the front.

Bennekerry, *beann-na-gCaorach,* peak of the sheep.

Bennekerry, *binn-an-choire,* not given.

Bennett, *Bheinéid,* Bennett, a personal or family name.

Benny, a peak.

Benone, *beann-Eoghain,* Owen's (a male name) peak.

Bens (the twelve). In Connemara, collectively they are known as *beanna-Beola.* Individually they are… *an-chailleach, binn-bhán, binn-Bhraoin, binn-breac, binn-breac. binn-chorr, binn-doire-chlár, binn-fraoigh, binn-gabhar, binn-glean-uisce, binn-leitrí,* and *meacanach.* They are also knows as the twelve pins.

Beo, *bó,* not given.

Beo, *mBeo, beo,* living beings.

Beola, *Beóla, Beola,* Beola, a male name.

Beoun, *beann,* a mountain or hill peak, horn, a pointed hill.

Beragh, *Bearach, Béarach,* not given.

Beragh, *biroach,* a place of peaks.

Beragh, *bearrthach,* shorn, grazed or bare.

Bercon, *Bearrcon,* not given.

Bercon, *Ó-mBearchon,* Úí Bhearchon, O'Bercon, a family name.

Bercon, *Ua-mBerchon,* O'Berchan, a family name.

Bere, *Bheartá,* Bear, a personal or family name.

Berehert, *Berchert,* St Berrihert, Beretchert.

Bern, *bearrtha,* close-cropped.

Bern, *Bheirn,* Bearn, a personal or family name.

Bern, *Bhirn, Baireann,* not given.

Berna, *bearna,* the gap.

Bernagh, *bearnach,* a gapped hill.

Bernagh, *bearnach,* gapped.

Berneens, *beirnínidhe,* little gaps or gapped hills.

Berneens, *biorrach*(sic), marshy fields.

Bernish, *béarnais,* the gap.

Berny, *barr,* the top or summit.

Berny, *bearna,* a gap between two mountains.

Berrihert, *Berchert,* St Berrihert.

Berrihert, *Breithcheart,* not given.

Berrin, *Bhirn,* not given.

Berrin, *Birran,* a personal or family name.

Berrings, *biorainn, bhiorainn, na-boirní,* not given.

Berrings, *boirinn,* a rocky place.

Berry, *bearaigh,* the heifer.

Berry, *Bhearaigh,* St Bearach.

Berry, *biorair,* watercress.

Berry, *m-biorai,* reeds.

Berry, *Uí-Bhearaigh,* O'Berry, a family name.

Bert, *beart,* not given.

Bert, *beirte,* two persons.

Berth, *beirt,* a pair.

Bertragh, *beartrach,* not given.

Bess, *beithi,* bitches(sic).

Bessbrook, Bess's brook, named after Elizabeth Pollock Nee Carlile of Newry. The original name was *an-sruthán,* the brook.

Bessbrook, *cloch-fhuaráin,* not given.

Bessy Bell (Mt), *sliabh-Togha/Truin,* not given.

Betagh, *Betach,* Betagh, a family name.

Betagh, *bhiathaigh, biataigh, biadhtaigh,* a hospitaller or keeper of a house of hospitality.

Betal, *béatáil,* burnt land.

Bettystown (bi-lingual), *baile-an-bhiataigh,* not given.

Bewley, *béal,* the mouth.

Bewley, *Bewley*(sic), not given.

Bhanogue, *bhanóige,* little bawn (field).

Bharnan, passage of the men at a gap(sic).

Bheag, *bheag,* little.

Bial, *beal,* mouth.

Biana, *Bóinne,* not given.

Bibe, *bPíob,* pipes.

Bidag, *bideóg,* dirks or daggers.

Biddyford, *baile-na-mBaintreach,* not given.

Bien, *bPian,* pains.

Bier, *Biúir,* not given.

Big-Bow-Meel, *bó-mhaol-mhór,* not given.

Bigge, little.

Biggeen, *beicín,* a small hill.

Bigger, *Bigir,* not given.

Biggil, *bigil,* watching.

Biggle, *bigil,* fasting.

Biggle, *bigile,* not given.

Bignian, *binneann,* not given.

Bignion, *beinnín, beannín,* little peak.

Biheel, *beith-choill,* wood of birches.

Bilberry, *carraig-na-bhFraochán, baile-na-bhFraochán, cnoc-na-nGabhar, fraoch-Oileán,* not given.

Bilboa River, *an-chlaoideach,* not given.

Bilboa, *béal-átha-bó, beal-atha-bo,* ford of the cow.

Bilboa, *bile-Buadha, bilbó, beil-bó, bhiolbó, biolbó,* not given.

Bile, *bhile, bil,* an ancient branchy tree.

Bill, *bile,* the ancient, large or sacred tree.

Billa, *bile,* the ancient tree.

Billaghan, *bileacháin,* little ancient tree.

Billary, *an-bhiolaraigh,* not given.

Billary, *biolarach, biolaraigh,* a place of watercress.

Billeady, *bile-Éadaí,* not given.

Biller, *bhiolair,* not given.

Biller, *biolair,* watercress.

Billeragh, *biolarach, biolaraigh,* a place of watercress.

Billis, *bile-easa,* not given.

Billis, *na-bilí/mBileadha,* trees, sacred trees or ancient/old trees.

Billises, *na-bili,* not given.

Billog, *billeóg,* coltsfoot or wood sorrel.

Billog, *billeóige,* a billhook.

Billy, *bhile, bile,* an ancient branchy tree.

Bin, *beann, beanna, binna, binne,* a mountain or hill peak, horn or pinnacle.

Bin, *bhinn, binn,* not given.

Binaby, *bin-buidhe,* yellow peak.

Binaby, *Binibe,* not given.

Binaghlon, *beann-each-labhra,* peak of the speaking horse.

Bine, *beann,* a mountain or hill peak, horn, pinnacle.

Bing, *beann,* a pinnacle.

Binganagh, *beanganach,* a branchy place.

Bingorms, *beanna/beann-gorma,* blue peaks.

Binis, *binnis,* melody or singing.

Binlettery, *binn-Dubhghlais,* not given.

Binn, *binn, beann,* a peak or pinnacle.

Binna, *beann, beanna, binna, binne,* a mountain, hill peak, horn or pinnacle.

Binna, *binn-an...,* peak of the...

Binnan, *binneáin,* a small peak.

Binnbrack, *binn-breac,* speckled hill.

Binnelly, *binn-aille,* peak of the cliff or slope.

Binnia, *binne,* a mountain or hill peak, horn or pinnacle.

Binnie, *beann, beanna, binna, binne,* a mountain or hill peak, horn, pinnacle.

Binnion, *beinnín, beannín,* little, low peak.

Binnis, *binnis,* melody.

Binny, *beann, beanna, binna, binne,* a mountain or hill peak, horn or pinnacle.

Bir, *bior,* not given.

Bircog, *biorcach, biorcóg,* a pointed hill shaped like a beehive.

Biree, *mBioraí,* reeds.

Birget, *Birget,* a personal or family name.

Birn, *Birn,* not given.

Birnaghs, *bearnach,* gapped (plural).

Biroge, *Bioróige,* not given.

Birr, *biorra,* water, stream, a watery place, spring wells or a low lying tongue of land.

Birra, *biorra,* water or stream.

Birra, *birra,* pointed hills.

Birragh, *biorach,* a hill pointed like a spit.

Birrane, *bhiorain,* a little point.

Birrane, *biorán,* the pin (shape).

Birrane, *biorrain,* strife.

Birrea, *mBiroar,* watercress.

Birreen, *birín,* not given.

Birreen, *birreen,* little pin or spit.

Birrinagh, *biríneach,* a place abounding in a particular type of coarse grass.

Bittern, *Beanain,* Benan, a personal or family name.

Bixy, *Bigsighe,* St Bigseach (the virgin).

Bla, *Bladhma,* Blaw, a male name.

Bla, *blatha,* flowers.

Bla, *bláthnach,* flowers, flowery.

Bla, *bleadhach,* milk.

Black, *an-blaic,* not given.

Black, *blac,* dark peaty soil.

Blacker, *Bhlaicear,* Blacker, a family name.

Blaffer, *bhlathmhar,* flowery.

Blagh, *bláiche, bleadhach,* milk.

Blagh, *bláiche, bleaghaighe,* buttermilk.

Blagh, *bláiche,* flowers.

Blagh, *bláthach,* flowery.

Blagh, *bláthnach,* flowers or flowery.

Blagh, *mBládach,* not given.

Blaha, *bláth,* the flower.

Blaha, *blátha,* flowers.

Blahee, *bláthaighe,* buttermilk.

Blahy, *bláiche,* not given.

Blahy, *bláthaigh, bláthach,* buttermilk.

Blain, *bléan,* a groin, a hollow.

Blake, *an-Bhlácaigh,* not given.

Blanchameen, *an-Bhlóinsiminígh,* not given.

Blanchameen, *Blainnsimín,* Flanchameen, Blanchameen or Blanchville, a family name.

Blanchameen, *Bhláthaimhínigh,* Blanchameen, a personal or family name.

Blanchard, *Bhlainséar,* Blanchard, a family name.

Blane, a curve or curved spot.

Blane, *Bhláin,* Bláin, a personal or family name.

Blane, *blaán,* not given.

Blane, *bléan,* not given.

Blane, *bléin,* a branching off creek.

Blaney, a curve or curved spot.

Blaney, *Blaney,* a personal or family name.

Blaney, *bléine, blean,* an inlet.

Blaney, *Bléine, Bléana,* not given.

Blaney, *bléinigh,* a creek.

Blaney, *bléinigh,* a tongue or narrow strip of land.

Blaney, from *bléin,* creeks.

Blaris, *bláras,* a field.

Blaris, *bláras, bláráis,* an exposed place or field.

Blares, Scottish Gaelic word for a moor.

Blarney, *an-bhlárna/bhlarna/blarna,* the small field.

Blarney, *bhlarna,* an exposed place or a small field.

Blarney, *na-blarnan,* not given.

Blasket, *blascaod,* not given.

Blaskets, now spelled *blascóid,* on old maps, *blaset, brasch, brascher,* meaning not given. In a ships record of 1597 it was named 'Yslas de Blasques' and that the natives there spoke Spanish (Basque?). It has also been suggested that its origin may be from the Norse word *brasker,* meaning a dangerous place.

Blath, *blaithe,* a hollow between hills.

Blaugh, *blaithe, bháthach, bláthnach,* flowers, flowery.

Blaugh, *bleadhach,* milk.

Blauha, *bláth,* flowers.

Blauhy, *bláthaighe,* buttermilk.

Blaw, *blathaigh,* flowery.

Bleach, *tuar,* not given.

Bleaght, *bleachta,* milk.

Blean, *bhléin,* not given.

Blean, *bléan,* a creek or a curved place.

Blean, *bléan,* a hollow, a tidal creek or an inlet.

Blean, *bleen,* a groin.

Bleana, *bléan-a'...,* inlet of the...

Bleana, *bleán-na...,* groin of the...

Bleanahouree, *baile-átha-na-hAbha-Riabhaí*(sic), not given.

Bleanish, creek island.

Bleanta, *bleanta,* low tongues of land or lions.

Bleantas, *bléantas,* not given.

Bleask, *bPlaosc,* skulls.

Bleask, *mBlaosg, bPléasc,* shells or sea shells.

Bleen, *blein,* a branching off creek.

Bleen, *bleing-áleen,* flax pits.

Blen, *bléan,* a hollow.

Blennerville, *cathair-Uí-Mhóráin,* not given.

Blessington, *baile-Choimín,* not given.

Blessington, *lios-na-mBeannacht,* font(sic) of the blessings.

Blety, *bleite,* grinding.

Blike, *blaithce,* flowers.

Bline, *Bhleidhin,* not given.

Bline, *Bhláin,* St Blaan.

Blisk, *bloisce,* noisy.

Blittog, *bliochtóg, bliochtog,* milk land or a milking place.

Blittoge, *bliotóg,* not given.

Blonic, *blainic,* land.

Blonog, *bhlonaige,* not given.

Blonog, *blonog,* lard, fat or suet.

Blood, *Blod,* Blod, a mans name.

Blood, *Uí-Bloid,* O'Blood, a family name.

Bloom, *Bládhma, Bladhma,* Bladhma or Bladh, the name of an ancient hero.

Bloom, *bladhma,* blaze.

Blough, *bloch,* round.

Bloun, *bhFlann,* not given.

Blowick, *Blathmhaic,* Blathmhac or Blowick a personal name.

Blue Ball (The), *an-phailís,* not given.

Bluid, *bluid,* a place of caves.

Blumick, *blonog,* lard.

Blunaga, *blonog,* lard.

Bo, *badh,* a recess.

Bo, *bó, bo, mbó, mBo,* cow/s.

Bo, *both,* a hut or tent.

Bo, *bothant,* a den.

Boa, *badhbha,* not given.

Boa, *bhugha,* glove.

Boagh, a hut.

Board, *buird,* a table.

Boardee, *bordaí,* verges.

Boarheeny, *na-bóithríní,* not given.

Boarty, *buartaigh,* a cattle shed.

Boat, *Beota,* not given.

Bobaunia, *bo-báine,* the white cow.

Bobigge, little cow.

Bobul, *bPobal,* not given.

Bobul, *bPobal,* congregation.

Bocarnagh, *both-cheatharnach,* hut of kerns or foot soldiers.

Bocarnagh, *buaic-chearnach,* the square pinnacle.

Bock, *an-bac,* not given.

Bock, *baic,* a bend.

Bock, *buaic,* a round hill.

Bocks, *an-bac, na-baic,* not given.

Bocombra, *buaic-iomaire,* the crown of the ridge.

Bodagh, *mBodach, bodaigh,* a churl, boorish plebeian people, a landlord or a bad mannered clown.

Bodal, *an-bhodail,* not given.

Bodal, *bothdáil, both-dáil,* assembly booth or hut.

Bodaly, *Bodaile,* not given.

Bodily, *both-dala,* hut of the assembly.

Bodaly, O'Daly's (a family name) hut.

Bodarra, *both-dara,* the oak hut.

Boden, *Baodain,* Baodan or Boden, a personal or family name.

Boden, *Bodún,* Boden, a family name.

Boden, *Buadáin,* not given.

Boden, *Uí-Bhuadain,* Bowden, Boden or O'Boden, a family name.

Boderg, *bo-dearg,* a red cow.

Boding, *buadainn,* the water-flag 'Sparganium-Natans'.

Bodony, *bothdomhnach,* not given.

Body, *Bodaigh,* not given.

Bodyke, *both-daoige,* not given.

Bodyke, *Lúbán-díge,* the winding dyke.

Boe, *bó, bo, bhó, mbó, mBo,* a cow or cows.

Boe, *Uí-Bhúath,* O'Boye, a family name.

Boer, *bothar,* a road.

Bofey, *bó-Fhéic,* not given.

Bofey, *bo-fiaich,* Fiachs (a male name) cows.

Bofey, *both,* tent, hut or booth.

Bofickil, *badh-fiada-choille,* recess of the wild wood.

Bofin, *bo-fin, finne, finde,* (the enchanted) white cow.

Bofin, *bó-finne,* the white cow.

Bofinny, *bó-finne,* the white cow.

Bog, *bog, moin,* a bog or boggy place.

Bog, *bog,* soft, bog or peat.

Bogagh, *bogán,* bog.

Bogagh, *bogach,* not given.

Bogan, O'Bogan, a family name.

Bogay, *both-Ghé/Gé,* not given.

Bogey, *bhogaigh,* bog or swamp.

Bogey, *Bóige,* not given.

Bogey, *Uí-Bhogaigh,* Buggy, a personal or family name.

Bogga, *bogach,* a soft boggy place.

Boggagh, *bogach,* bog, soft land or a boggy place.

Boggan, *bogán,* a little bog or soft land/soil, a boggy place.

Boggan, *Uí-Bhogáin,* Boggan, a family name.

Boggaun, *bhogain,* a quagmire.

Boggaun, *bogan, bogán,* a little bog, soft land or a boggy place.

Boggeragh, a soft boggy place.

Boggeragh, *bhograch, bograch, na–bograí,* not given.

Boggin, *bhogáin,* a bog or quagmire.

Boggin, *bhogain,* a small bog.

Boggoon, *bogán,* a quagmire.

Boggra, *bograch,* a marsh.

Boggy, *bogaigh, bogach,* bog, soft land or a boggy place.

Bogh, *bhoth, both,* a tent.

Bogha, *both-an...,* tent/hut of the...

Boghil, *bachaille, bachal, bachall,* a crozier.

Boghil, *mBuachaill, buachaill,* a boy or boys.

Boghilbo, *buachalla-bo,* cowboy.

Boghill, *buachaill,* a boy.

Boghilla, *bachaille,* a shepard.

Boghilla, *bachaille,* a crozier.

Boghlan, *buachalláin,* yellow ragweed.

Bogy, *bhogaigh,* bog.

Boh, *bhoth, botha,* a hut.

Boha, *boithe, botha,* a hut or tent.

Boha, *both-a...,* cabin of the...

Boha, *both-an...,* hut of...

Boha, *bhothog,* a booth.

Bohagh, *bothach,* a place of huts or booths.

Bohalas, *both-a'-leasa,* booth of the ancient fort.

Bohalas, *bothailios,* not given.

Bohalis, *both-a'-leasa,* booth of the ancient fort.

Bohan, *bothán,* little hut.

Bohar, *bóthar, bothair* a road.

Bohara, *bóthar-an...,* road of the...

Bohard, *an-bhoth-ard,* not given.

Boharkyle, *bóthar-caol,* narrow road.

Bohaun, *bothán,* little hut.

Boheh, *both-theith,* warm or cozy hut.

Boheny, *boithiní,* little huts.

Boher, *bóthar, bothair* a road.

Bohera, *bóthar-a'..., bóthar-an...,* road of the...

Boheradeel, *bordaíol,* not given.

Boherboyree, *ré-an-bhóthair-bhuí*(sic), not given.

Boherboyrea, *réith-an-bhothair-bhuidhe,* yellow road mountain plain(sic).

Bohereen, *bóithrín, bótharín,* a little road.

Boherna, *bóthar-na* , road of the...

Bohernarude, *barr*(sic)*-na-rúide,* not given.

Bohil Bregagh, *boughal-breige,* a standing stone named 'the false boy'.

Bohil, *beith-choill,* birch wood.

Bohil, *bhuachaill,* not given.

Bohil, *buachaill,* the boy.

Bohilbreaga, *boughal-breige,* a standing stone named 'the false boy'.

Bohill, *bachaill,* the shepherds crook.

Bohill, *bhuachaill,* the herdsman(sic).

Bohilla, *bhuachalla,* a cowboy.

Bohilla, *both-iughaile,* the hill of steep land.

Bohilla, *buachailleach,* not given.

Bohilly, *bothlaighe,* a hut location.

Bohilly, *buaile,* a booley or dairying place.

Bohilly, *mBouchaillidhe, mBuachaillidhe, mBuachailidh,* boys.

Bohilly, *mBuachaillí, buachaillidhe, buachaill,* boy/s.

Bohine, *Baeithin,* St Baeithin.

Boho, *botha,* huts or tents.

Boho, *both-Mhuinntir-Fialáin,* not given.

Bohoge, *bohóige, bothoige,* a hut.

Bohoge, *bothóg,* little hut.

Bohoge, *bothóighe,* not given.

Bohogy, *bohóg,* a hut.

Bohola, *both-Chomhla/Thóla,* not given.

Bohola, *both-ola,* hut/booth of drinking.

Bohoona, *both-Chuanna/Chuana,* Cuana's (a personal or a family name) booth.

Bohora, *both-Odhra,* Odhar's or Hoare's (a personal or a family name) booth.

Bohora, *both-Odhra,* Odran's (a personal or a family name) hut.

Bohullion, *both-chullinn,* hut of the holly.

Bohy, *boithe,* a hut or hunting booth.

Boice, *Bhuithín, Bhuithe, Buithe,* St. Buite, Buithin or Boethius, (a Bishop and abbot who died in 522).

Boihy, *beithighe,* birche trees.

Bointra, *baintreabhaighe,* a widow.

Bol, *bhuaile, bhualle, buaile,* a dairying place.

Bola, *Beola,* the name of an ancient chief.

Bola, *bhuaile, bhualle, buaile,* a dairying place.

Bola, *bhuaile, buaile,* a dairying place, a booley.

Bola, *bolach,* cattle.

Bola, *buaile,* a summer pasture.

Bolagh, *bealach,* not given.

Bolane, *an-beolán,* the small mouth.

Bolane, *Bhláin, Blaán,* not given.

Bolane, *Bholáin,* St Bolan, Bolán.

Bolart, *buaile-Airt,* not given.

Bolea, *both-liath,* grey hut.

Bolea, *buaile,* a dairying place or a booley.

Boleagh, *baile-Aodha,* Hugh's, Aodh's homestead.

Boley, *bhuaile, bhualle, buaile,* a dairying place.

Boley, *buaile,* a summer pasture.

Boleyna, *buaile-na...,* milking place of the...

Boleyneendorrish, *buaile-an-aen-dóras,* booley of the one door.

Boleytine, the sweathouse.

Bolg, *bolg,* sacks, bags.

Bolgan, *Bolcain,* St Bolcan.

Bolgan, *Bholgáin, Bolgan,* not given.

Bolgue, *bolg,* sacks, bags.

Bolie, *buaile,* a booley or milking place.

Bolies, *na-buailte/bhuailidh,* not given.

Bolin, *buaile-an...,* milking place of the...

Boling, *buaile-an/na...,* milking place of the...

Bolingbrook, *buaile-an-ghadhair,* not given.

Boll, *bhaile,* a town, townland.

Boll, *bPoll,* holes.

Bollagan, *bPollaghán,* not given.

Bollen, *bPollán,* hollows.

Bolling, *buaile,* a booley.

Bollis, *baile,* a townland.

Bollog, *bolg,* cows(sic).

Bologe, *bolg,* sacks.

Bologue, *bolg,* sacks or bags.

Bologue, *mBulóg, bológ,* bullocks.

Bologue, *mbulóg,* not given.

Boloooghera, *both-luacaire,* a hut in a rushy place.

Boloona, *ból-úana,* pasture of the lambs.

Boloona, *both-Lughna,* Loona's (a personal or a family name) booth.

Bolt, *buailte,* boolies or milking/dairying places.

Bolton, *Bóltan,* not given.

Bolton, *buailtín,* a small paddock(sic).

Boltown, *Tir-Pholla,* Bowles (a personal or a family name) district.

Bolug, *m-bolg,* caves or swellings.

Bolus, *Bhólais,* Bolas, a personal or family name.

Bolus, *Bólas,* not given.

Bomahas, *both-a'mais,* the hut or booth of the hollow.

Bon, *bun...,* foot of...

Bona, *bun-a'...,* bottom of...

Bona, *bun-an...,* not given.

Bona, *bun-na...,* mouth of the river...

Bonahum, *bhun-an-choim,* not given.

Bonalas, *bothailios,* not given.

Bonane, *Bhonáin, Bheanain,* St Benan/Benignus.

Bonane, *Bhonáin,* St Bonán/Bonan.

Bonane, *bunán, Buinneáin, bhuinneáin, Bonán,* not given.

Bonane, *bunán,* not given.

Bonarea, *bun-na-ré,* not given.

Bonatouk, *muine-an-tSeabhaic,* not given. Also known as by the name '**Monatouk**'.

Bonaun, *bunnán,* bitterns.

Boneham, *bun-a'choim,* bottom of the hollow.

Bonerea, *bun-a'reidh.* foot of the mountain flat.

Bonet, *an-bhuannad, buanaid,* the lasting river.

Boney, *bainne,* milk.

Boney, *Boinne,* Boinn, the name of a river Goddess.

Boney, *buinne,* a watery place.

Boniah, *bainneach,* milky.

Boniconlan, *muine-Uí-Chonalláin,* not given.

Bonnaha, *beanuighthe,* blessed.

Bonnane, *beannín,* little peak.

Bonneen, young pigs.

Bonnerbawn, *bunn-a'ghuirt-bháin,* bottom of the white ford.

Bonnets, *Bhoinéisigh,* not given.

Bonnets, *Bhoinéis,* Boney(s), a personal or family name.

Bonni, *muine,* a thicket.

Bonnia, *Buaidhne,* not given.

Bonniff, *bainbh, banbh,* young pig/s.

Bonniv, *bonna,* windy.

Bonniv, *bonnamh,* belonging to the tribe(sic).

Bonniv, *bonnan,* the wind.

Bonniveen, young pigs.

Bonny, *bainneach,* milky.

Bonny, *banbh,* young pigs.

Bonny, *buine,* stream or flood.

Bonny, *bun-an...,* not given.

Bony, *boinne,* not given.

Bony, *buine,* cows.

Bony, *buinne,* a watery place, a flow of water, a flood or a wave.

Boo, *Bú,* not given.

Boo, *bua, buadhach,* victory or victories.

Boo, *bugha,* hyacinth.

Booa, *bhugha,* foxglove.

Booa, *bua,* not given.

Booa, *buadha,* victory.

Boocaun, *buacán,* a pointed hill.

Boodan, *Mhuadáin,* not given.

Boodan, *Uí-Bhuadain,* O'Bodan, a family name.

Boodin, St Boodin.

Booey, *Buaí,* not given.

Booha, *botha,* huts or tents.

Book, *buac,* pinnacles or pointed hills.

Book, *buaic,* not given.

Bookalagh, *buacalach,* a place of pointed hills.

Bookaun, *buacán,* a pointed hill.

Bookeen, *buacín,* a pointed hill.

Bool, *buaile,* a milking or dairying place.

Boola, *bhuaile, bhualle, buaile,* a dairying place.

Boola, *buaile,* a cattle pen or milking yard.

Boola, *buaile-an...,* dairying place of the...

Boolack, *béal-leac,* opening, mouth of the flagstones.

Boolagh, *an-bhuaile,* not given.

Boolakeel, *buaile-Uí-Chuill,* not given.

Boolakiley, *buaile-Uí-Chadhla,* not given.

Boolan, *buaile-an...,*milking/dairying place of the...

Boolana, *bolán-na...,* the cow pasture at(sic)...

Boolana, *búaile/buaile-na/an...,* milking, dairying place of the...

Boolanunane, *buaile-Nuanáin,* Nunan's (a personal or a family name) booley.

Boolanunane, *buaile-Uí-Nuanáin,* not given.

Boolard, *buaile-ard,* the high booley or milking place.

Boolattin, *buaile-aitinn,* not given.

Booleen, *buailín, bualín,* little milking place.

Booley, *bhuaile, bhualle, buaile,* a dairying place.

Booley, *buailí,* a grazing and milking place.

Boolia, *buaile,* a dairying place.

Boolinarig, *buaile-na-nArg,* not given.

Boolteen, *buailtín,* not given.

Boolteenagh, *buailtíneach,* a place of little boolies or dairying places.

Boolteens, *na-buailtíní,* summer pastures.

Boolteeny, *buailtíní, buailtínídh,* little boolies or dairying places.

Booltheen, *buailtín,* little dairying place.

Booltiagh, *buailetighe,* milking places.

Booly, *buaile,* a summer pasture.

Boor, *buar,* not given.

Boora, *buaraí, búraighe,* not given.

Booragh, *buarach,* cow-land.

Boorawn, *buaran,* a field where oats were winnowed.

Boordan, *mBurdúnach,* not given.

Boorden, *Búrdáin,* Bourdan, a male name.

Boorhy, *buaidheartha,* contention, controversy.

Boorkagh, *mBurcach,* of the Burkes, a family/clan name.

Boory, *buarach,* cows.

Boory, *buaraí, búiridh,* not given.

Booter, *bhóthair, bóthar, bothir, bothyr*(sic), a road.

Bor, *bóthar,* a road.

Bora, *Bóra,* not given.

Boraghy, *barrachadh,* not given.

Boraghy, *barr-achaidh,* top of the field.

Boran, *boithréan,* dried cow dung.

Bord, *bórd,* a border or verge.

Borderreen, *bóthar-an-doirin,* not given.

Bore, *bodhar,* deaf.

Bore, *bodhar,* dull.

Bore, *bóthar, bothair, bóthair,* a road or pass.

Boreen, *bhuairchín, bairrín,* not given.

Boreen, *bóithrín, boithrín, bhoithrín,* little road.

Boreen, *buairthin,* little disturber.

Boreen, *O'Boirín,* O'Birren, a family name.

Boreena, *bóithrín-na...,* little road of the...

Borena, *bóthar-na...,* road of the...

Borheen, *bótharín, bóithrín, boithrín,* small road.

Borhen, *bóthairín,* little road.

Borim, *bo-dhruim,* cow ridge.

Borisk, *Bórais,* not given.

Borkill, *bórd-choill,* border wood.

Borna, *barr-na...,* top of the...

Borna, *bóthar-na...,* road of the....

Bornagh, *bóirinach,* a rocky place.

Bornagh, *boirneach,* rocky.

Borney, *boireann, boirne, borr-onn,* a rock, burren, a great stone or a rocky place.

Borniagh, *boirneach,* rocky.

Boro, *boromha,* not given.

Boro, *borumha,* cow tribute.

Borough, *boramha,* not given.

Borough, *burradh,* swelling up after rain.

Borragh, *bhorrach,* not given.

Borris, *bhuiríos, buríos, buirgheas, buirghes,* a burgage or borough.

Borrisnafarney, *buiríos/buirgheas-na-fearna,* not given.

Bortagh, *bPortagh,* turf banks.

Bortaun, *portán,* crabs.

Boscabell, *an-ráth-dhaingean,* not given.

Boshina, *bó-Sine,* not given.

Boskill, *Boscail,* not given.

Boston, *móinín-na-gCloigín, druim-na-doimhne, cúlbhaile-Uí-Ógáin, Bostún,* not given.

Both, *both,* a hut.

Bothoge, *bothóg,* a place of huts.

Bottera, *bPotaire,* potters.

Bough, *béithe,* birch or cows(sic).

Bough, *bhoth, both,* a hut, tent.

Bough, *bhothach,* not given.

Bough, *bocht,* poor.

Bough, *Uí-Boch,* O'Boch, a family name.

Bougha, *both-an...,* hut of the...

Boughal Breaga, *boughal-breige,* a standing stone named the false boy.

Boughal, *na-bachaille,* not given.

Boughan, *Uí-Bhuadhchain,* O'Boaghan, a family name.

Boughil, *buachaill,* a boy.

Boughil, *boghele, boughil, boughill, bua-choill,* not given.

Boughil, *bua-choill,* a shepherd or a boy.

Boughilbo, *buachaill-bó,* cow boy.

Boughill, *bachaill,* not given.

Boughlin, *bóchluana, bochluana,* a cow meadow.

Bought, *bocht,* poor.

Bouig, *Buadhaig,* Buadhach, a male name and means victorious.

Bouig, *Uí-Bhuadhaigh,* Bogue, a personal or family name.

Boul, *bPoll,* holes, pits, caves or hollows.

Boul, *bPoll, poul, poll,* a hole or holes.

Boula, *bhuaile, buaile,* a dairying place.

Boula, *buaile,* a summer pasture.

Boulaling, *buaile-Fhlainn,* Flann's retreat or booley (dairying place).

Boulea, *bhuaile, buaile,* a dairying place.

Boulen, *bhuaile-an,* the dairying place of the...

Boulia, *bhuaile, buaile,* a dairying place.

Boulic, *buailic,* a booley or dairying place.

Boulih, *buaile,* a booley.

Boulough, *buáileach,* full of boolies or dairying places.

Boulteen, *buailtíneach,* little milking fields.

Boulteen, *bualtín,* little milking field.

Boultra, *bualtrach,* mud mortar.

Boultry, *bualtraigh,* not given.
Boulty, *buailtínídh,* little boolies or dairying places.
Bounce, *bonsach,* rods.
Bounla, *bonlá,* bounla, not given.
Bour, *barr,* top.
Bour, *bodhar,* deaf.
Bourchim, *buirne, boirne,* burren, rocky lands.
Bourka, *buairce,* spancel.
Bourky, *buairce,* spancel.
Bourney, *boirinn,* not given.
Bourney, *Bourna,* St Baurchin.
Bourney, *buirne, boirne,* burren, rocky lands.
Bourney, *búirne, boirne,* rough rocky land/s.
Bov, *boh,* a hut.
Bovagh, *both-each,* not given.
Boveen, *both-mhín,* not given.
Boveva, *both-Fheadhbha,* not given.
Bovolcan, *both-Bolcain,* St Bolcan's hut or tent.
Bovroughaun, *both-Bhrochain,* not given.
Bow, *buaidh,* (secret) virtue.
Bowelk, *both-Bhoilc,* not given.
Bower, *bodhar,* echoless, deaf or silent.
Bower, *bodhar,* noisy or deafening.
Bower, *bother,* a road.
Bowler, *Bhúlaeraigh,* not given.
Boy, *bá, báighe,* a bay.
Boy, *baei, bhaoi,* the bear.
Boy, *Baoi,* Baoi, a personal or family name.
Boy, *Baoith,* Baoith, a personal or family name.
Boy, *beithe,* birch trees.
Boy, *bhmuighe,* a plain.
Boy, *buí, bhuí, buidhe,* yellow.
Boy, *Uí-Bhuídhe,* O'Boy, a family name.
Boya, *bo-teach,* cow house.
Boyagh, *bo-theach,* cow house.
Boyaghan, *buidheachán,* jaundice.
Boyger, *buidheachair,* yellowish water.
Boyheen, *Baoithín,* Baithen, a family or a personal name.
Boyheen, *búidhe,* gorse covered(sic).
Boyher, *bóithear,* a road.
Boyher, *buíochar,* not given.
Boyke, *Búacci,* not given.
Boyke, *Bucat,* Bucat, a personal or family name.
Boylagh, *Baoigheallach, Baeighellach,* O'Boyle's or Boyle's (Baeighill's) district.

Boylagh, *Baoigheallach,* territory of the descendants of Boyle.
Boylagh, *Baollaigh,* not given.
Boyland, *Uí-Bhaollain,* Ó Baollán, a personal or family name.
Boyle, *Buighill,* Boyle, a family name.
Boyle, *búille, búill, buill,* cow-river or pasture river.
Boyle, *Mainister-na-Búille,* monastery of the river Boyle.
Boyle, *Uí-Bhaoighill,* O'Boyle, a family name.
Boynagh, *buidh-eanach,* yellow marsh.
Boynagh, *bhuíonach, buíonach, not* given.
Boyne, *Baeithin,* St Baeithin.
Boyne, *Baoithín,* not given.
Boyne, *Boand,* an ancient goddess.
Boyne, *Boinne,* Boinn, a river Goddess, *bouinda, bououinda,* (Greek) and *buvinda* (Latin), cow-river, *Bóinne (bo-bhán), Boand,* the white cow goddess also *bhóinn,* the white cow.
Boyne, *bóinne,* not given.
Boyne, *Buaidhne,* not given.
Boyne, *Buaidhnighe,* not given.
Boyne, *Búinne,* Baethan, a personal or family name.
Boyne, *buinne, búinne,* surge, flood or stream.
Boyne, *mBuidhean,* crowds or troops.
Boyoga, *buidheóg,* jaundice.
Boyoge, *buidheóg,* jaundice.
Boyoge, *buidheoga,* yellow or jaundice.
Boyounagh, *bhuíonach, buíbheanach, buibheanach, buidheamhnach,* the yellow marsh.
Boyton, *Bhaightiúnaigh,* not given.
Bra, *brá,* a neck.
Bra, *breagh,* fine.
Braade, *an-bráid/bhráid,* the gorge.
Braade, *braghad,* a gorge or deeply cut glen.
Braccan, *Breacan, Brecan,* St Brecan (6th cent).
Braccas, *breacas,* speckled land.
Brack, *bhreac, breac,* speckled or speckled land.
Brack, *breac,* streaked soil(sic).
Brack, *Bhric, breach,* not given.
Brack, *breaca,* not given.

Brack, *Breacain,* Breacan, a personal or family name.

Brack, *mBreac, breac,* trout/s, (from 'breac' speckled skin).

Brackagh, *bhreacach,* not given.

Brackagh, *breacach, breacacha,* speckled or speckled land.

Brackahara, *brá-chathrach,* neck of the stone fort.

Brackaharagh, *breac-chathrach,* speckled land of the circular stone fort.

Brackan, *Breacáin, Bhreacán,* not given.

Brackan, *Breacán, Breacain,* not given.

Brackan, *Breacan,* Brecan or Brackan, a personal or family name.

Brackan, *breac-an...,* speckled land of the...

Brackan, St Brackan/Berchan.

Brackan, *Uí-Bhreacain,* O'Bracken or Bracken, a family name.

Brackane, *bhreacain,* striped or streaky.

Brackary, *breacaraidhe,* speckled land.

Bracken, *Bhreacain,* Brecan, a persons name.

Bracken, *Bracain,* not given.

Bracken, *na-mBreacan,* (of) the Brackens.

Bracken, *Uí-Bhreacain,* O'Bracken or Bracken, a family name.

Brackenagh, from *breac,* speckled.

Brackenen, from *breac,* speckled.

Brackernagh, from *breac,* speckled land.

Brackery, *breacaraidhe, bhreacraighe,* speckled land.

Brackey, *bracach,* not given.

Brackey, *breachmhaí, breac-raidhe,* not given.

Brackey, *bréamhaí,* the wolf plain.

Brackin, *breacain,* not given.

Brackin, *breacan,* a streaky soiled area.

Brackin, *breicín,* little spot of speckled land.

Bracklagh, *breaclach,* speckled or speckled place.

Bracklagh, *breaclach,* spotted or striped.

Bracklin, *breac-chluain,* speckled meadow.

Bracklin, *breach/breac-chluanach,* speckled town.

Bracklin, *breaclainn, breaclach,* not given.

Bracklone, *breac-chluain,* speckled meadow.

Brackloney, *breac-chluanach,* speckled meadow.

Brackloon, *an-bhreac-chluain, breac-chlu-anach/chluain,* speckled meadow.

Brackloonagh, *breac-chluanach,* speckled meadow.

Brackly, *bhreaclaigh,* not given.

Brackly, *breaclaigh,* the speckled place.

Bracklyn, *bhreaclainne, breaclainn,* the speckled meadow.

Bracklyn, *breaclainn,* the speckled place.

Brackna, *breacach-na...,* speckled land of the...

Brackna, *breacnach,* speckled.

Bracknagh, *bhreácanaigh, breacánach,* not given.

Bracknagh, *breacnach,* speckled land/place.

Bracks, *breac,* speckled or speckled land.

Bracky, *bhraice,* spotted.

Brackyle, *an-bhreac/breac-choille,* speckled wood.

Brad, *brághaid,* not given.

Brada, *Bhradaigh,* not given.

Brada, *bradach,* thieves.

Bradagh, *bradagh, bradach,* thieves.

Bradagh, *bráighdeach,* not given.

Bradan, *Bradain,* Braddan or Salmon, a family name.

Bradda, *bhradaig,* (of the) thief.

Braddagh, *bradach,* thievish or thieves.

Braddan, *Breatan,* not given.

Braddocks, from *braghad,* little gorges or deeply cut glens.

Braddocks, *na-bráideoga,* not given.

Braddon, *bradan, bradán,* salmon.

Brade, *brághad, braghad,* neck or gorge.

Brade, *na-Brád,* not given.

Bradican, Bradican, a personal or family name.

Brado, *bradaigh,* a thief.

Bradocks, *na-bráideoga,* not given.

Bradoge, *bhráighdeóg,* not given.

Bradoge, *bráideog,* the little throat.

Bradoge, from *braghad,* a little gorge or deeply cut glen.

Bradox, *bráideoga,* the little throats.

Bradox, *bráighdeóga,* not given.

Bradran, *Bhradaráin,* Bradarán, not given.

Brady, *bradach,* thieves.

Brae, *bhrae,* a hill.

Brag, *brágha,* a gorge.

Bragan, *Bragán,* Bragan, *bruighean,* not given.

Bragget, *bragóige, bragoide,* ale or beer.

Bragh, *Bhrácha, Brách,* St Brach.

Braghad, *bhraghaid,* neck land.

Braghan, *Bhearcháin, Berchaon,* St Berchan/Bearchain.

Braghan, *Brachán,* not given.

Braghy, *bhrachaidhe,* a maltster, from *braich,* malt.

Braghy, *brachaí,* not given.

Brague, *bréige, breug,* false or falsehood.

Brahallish, *braichlis,* malt or fermented grain.

Braher, *bhrathar, mBráthar, mBratar,* friar/s or monk/s or brothers.

Brahill, *Bhrotaill,* not given.

Brahy, *Bhrachaidhe,* Broughy, a personal or family name.

Braid, *bhraghad,* not given.

Braid, *braghad, braghaid,* a gorge or deeply cut glen.

Braid, *brághaid,* not given.

Braithar, *bhrathar, mBratar,* friars.

Brallaghan, *Uí-Bhrolchain,* O'Brollaghan, a family name.

Bran, *Bran,* Bran, a personal name.

Bran, *brean*(sic), *bran,* the raven.

Bran, *Brandubh,* Brandubh, the name of an ancient King of leinster. It means black raven.

Bran, *Uí-Bhrain,* O'Brin, a family name.

Branagan, *Uí-Bhranagain,* O'Branagan, a family name.

Branagh, *Bhreathnach,* not given.

Branagh, *branach,* ravens.

Branagh, *Breathnach,* Walsh, a family name.

Branagh, *mBreathnach,* Breatnaigh, not given.

Branagh, *na-mBreatnach,* not given.

Branar, *branar, branra*(sic), fallow land.

Brandaun, *Bhranndáin,* Brendan, a male name.

Brandaun, *Brandán,* not given.

Brandaun, *Breandán,* Brandon, a male name or St Brendan.

Brandon, *Bhréanain, Branndáin,* Bréanann, a personal or family name.

Brandon, *Breánainn, Bhreanainn,* St Brendan.

Brandon, *Cé-Bhréandainn,* not given.

Brandrum, *bréandroim, bréandruim,* not given.

Brandy, *bhrandy*(sic), brandy.

Brandy, *brannaí,* not given.

Brandy, *brannra,* the gibbet.

Brane, *braon,* drops, wet or oozy.

Brane, *bréan,* a evil odour.

Branigan, *Bhranagáin, Uí-Bhranagain,* O'Branagan, a family name.

Branks, *Branks,* a personal or family name.

Brannagh, *Breathnach,* a Briton, can also be Walsh, a personal or family name.

Brannagh, *Breathnach,* Walsh, a family name.

Brannan, *Bhreannain,* Brannan or Brennan, a personal or family name.

Brannan, *Braonáin,* not given.

Brannan, *Breannain,* Brennan, a personal or family name.

Brannan, *Uí-Bhranain,* O'Brennan, a family name, a family name.

Brannel, *Bhréanaill, Breanail,* St Brendan.

Branner, *branar, brannair,* fallow, ground.

Brannish, *Bhreathnais,* Brannagh or Walsh a family name.

Brannish, *bran-inis,* raven island.

Brannock (Island), *oileán-dá-Bhranóg,* not given.

Brannock, *Bhranóg,* not given.

Brannock, *Branoc,* a personal or family name.

Brannock, *Breathnach,* Walsh, a family name.

Branra, *branra,* fallow land.

Bransha, *bréansa,* stinking.

Brantry, *bréintre,* not given.

Braskelagh, *braiscealach,* not given.

Brasset, *Bhreasail,* Brassil, a family name.

Brassil, *Breasail,* a personal or family name and also the name of a 5th century chief.

Brassil, *Uí-Bhreasail,* O'Brassil or Brassil, a family name.

Brastle, *Breasail,* Brassil, a personal or family name.

Brat, *bratt,* mantles.

Bratar, *bhrathar, mBratar,* friars.

Brattan, *Bhreatan,* not given.

Brattan, *Bratain,* Bratan, a personal or family name.

Bratten, *Breatain,* Breatain, a personal or a family name.

Brattin, *mBreatan,* the Britons.

Brattoge, *Bratóige,* not given.

Brattonn, *Bretan,* Bretan a personal or family name.

Braud, *Bhrád,* not given.

Braugh, *Bhrácha,* not given.

Braughney, *Braichne,* Braichne, a personal or family name.

Brawny, *breaghmhaine,* not given.

Bray, (lough), *Bregha,* not given.

Bray, *bré,* a brae(sic).

Bray, *bré, breagh, brí,* a hill.

Bray, *Bréagán, brí-cualann,* not given.

Brazil, *Uí-Bhreasáil/Bhreasail,* O'Brassil, a family name.

Breadagh, *bréadagh, bréadach,* a gap or breach.

Bready, *bhréadach,* broken land.

Bready, *bhreadaigh, brédach,* broken land, ground.

Breaffy, *breachmhaighe,* the wolf-plain.

Breaga, *bhréige,* not given.

Breaga, *bréige,* false or falsehood.

Breagh, *breach, breach,* wolves or a place of wolves.

Breagh, *bréach,* not given.

Breagh, treacherous.

Breaghan, *Breacháin,* not given.

Breaghey, *breach-mhagh,* wolf plain.

Breaghmore, *bréachmhaighe*(sic), not given.

Breaghna, *breaghna,* a place of wolves.

Breagho, *bréachmhá,* from *breach,* a wolf, a place of wolves.

Breaghva, *bréachmhá* from *breach,* a wolf or a place of wolves.

Breaghwy, *bréachmhagh, bréachmhaighe, bréachmhá,* a wolf or a place of wolves.

Breaghwy, *bréachmhaigh,* the wolf plain.

Breaghwyan, *bréachmhagh-an...,* wolf plain or place of wolves of the...

Breaghy, *bréachmhá* from *breach,* a wolf or a place of wolves.

Breaghy, *breathmuigh,* wolf field.

Breagoge, *breagóg,* scarecrows.

Breague, *bréige,* false.

Breagy, *bhréige,* falsehood.

Breaka, *breaca,* speckled.

Brean, *Braen, Braon,* Breen, a personal name.

Brean, *breun, bréan, bhréan, bhréun,* stinking, putrid, foul or fetid.

Brean, Brian, a male name.

Breana, stinking spot.

Breanagh, stinking river.

Breane, *brean, bhréan,* stinking.

Breaninch, *bréininis,* not given.

Breanla, *Uí-Bhreanaill,* O'Brannall, a family name The modern form of this is Brabacy.

Breanriskculew, *breanruisc-choillead,* fetid moorland.

Breansha, *bhréinseach,* not given.

Breansha, *bréanseach,* stinking land.

Breanshagh, *bréanseach,* stinking land.

Breany, *bréanaidhe,* a fetid place, a slow flowing stream that becomes fetid.

Breany, *bréine,* a stench, fetid, stinking or an ill colour.

Brecagh-Burm, *breacach,* not given.

Brecan, *Bhreacain,* Breckan, a male name.

Brecaun, Brecan, a personal or family name.

Breck, *breac,* not given.

Breckagh, *breacach,* speckled land.

Breckan, *Brecan,* St Brecan.

Breckaun, *bPríochán,* crows.

Breckrie, *breacraighe,* not given.

Breda, *bréadaí, breda,* broken land.

Breda, *Bréadaí,* Breda, not given.

Breda, *briadaigh,* not given.

Bredach, *m-breadach,* narrow clefts or vallies.

Bredagh, *bhréadach, briadach, na-breadaí,* not given.

Bredagh, *bréadach,* a break, breach or gap.

Bredagh, *bréadach,* breaking, a breach, a cut or a narrow glen.

Bredagh, *brédach,* broken ground.

Bredagh, *m-breadach,* narrow clefts or vallies.

Bredane, *braghaideain,* a little neck or mountain pass.

Bredane, *braighdean,* prisoners.

Bredane, *Breadain,* Bredan, a personal or family name.

Bredon, *Bhrídeáin,* O'Bredon, a family name.

Bredon, *Ui-Bhrídeáin,* descendants of Bradan, the name of a Church founder in Tipperary.

Bree, *bhrí, brí,* a hill.

Bree, *brí,* brae(sic).

Bree, *Bri, Brighe, Bhríghe,* the Welsh virgin St Bree.

Bree, *Brioch,* St Brioch.

Bree, *brugh,* a farm.

Breed, *Bhrighde,* St Brigid or just Brigid.

Breeda, *bréadach,* a break.

Breeda, *Bhríde,* not given.

Breedage, broken land.

Breedeen, *Bhrídín,* not given.

Breedeen, *Bhrighdín,* little Brigit, a woman or a girls name.

Breedia, *Bhríde,* not given.

Breedia, *Bríde, Bhrighde,* St Brigit.

Breedin, *Bhrighdín,* little Brigit, a woman or a girls name.

Breedoge, *Bhrídeoige, Brídeóg,* not given.

Breedoge, *bráideog,* the little throat.

Breedoge, Brigit, a female name.

Breedy, *Bhríde,* Bríd, a womans name.

Breedy, *Bhríde, Brighde, Bhrighde,* Brigid or St Brigid.

Breegagh, *bréugach,* the living river.

Breeka, *brice, bhríce,* brick/s.

Breekins, *briocínidhe,* little badgers warren.

Breen, *Bhraoin,* Braon or Breen, a family or personal name.

Breen, *Bhriain, Braoin,* not given.

Breen, *Bhrian,* O'Brian, a family name.

Breen, *bhruin,* the breast.

Breen, *brí,* a hillside.

Breen, *bruighean, bruidhne,* a fairy mansion or an inn.

Breen, *brúion,* a fairy dwelling.

Breen, *Uí-Bhraoin,* Breen or O'Breen, a family name.

Breena, *braonacha,* dripping.

Breena, *bruighne, bruighean,* a mansion.

Breenagh, *brúine, bruighneach,* a fairy fort.

Breenagh, *na-bruíneacha, na-mBruíneach,* the fetid stream.

Breenaun, from *bruighean,* a little mansion.

Breenaun, *na-braonáin,* not given.

Breeny, *bruidhne,* mansions.

Breeny, *bruighne,* a fairy fort or palace.

Breeoge, *bruigheóg,* a little fort.

Breeole, *turlach-na-mbruigheol,* half dried lake of the cormorants.

Brees, from *bri,* hills.

Breesheen, *Buirísín,* not given.

Breffney, *breifne,* not given.

Breffy, *breachmhaighe,* a wolf plain.

Bregagh, *bhréaghach, bréagach,* not given.

Bregagh, *breige, breug,* treacherous, false, pseudo, not real, deceiver or the little liar.

Bregaun, *bréagán,* land of the treacherous stream.

Bregh, *breach,* wolves.

Bregoge, from *breug,* treacherous, false, deceiver or the little liar.

Brehaun, *brachán,* gruel or soft land.

Brehoge, *bréachóg,* not given.

Brehon, *mBreathamhain, mBreitheamhán,* Brehons or judges.

Brenaghan, Brennaghan, a personlal or family name.

Brenan, *braonán,* a droplet.

Brenan, *braonán,* an icicle or droplet.

Brenan, *bréanán,* not given.

Brenan, *brianán,* from *bréan,* stinking.

Brenan, *brianán,* from *brí,* a hill.

Brenan, St Brennan or Brendan, a male name.

Brenar, *bréanair,* not given.

Brenar, *branar,* fallow land.

Brennagh, *Breathnach,* Walsh, a family name.

Brennal, *Bhréanaill, Bhreanaill,* Bréanaill, Brendan or Brendanus, the name of a Church founder.

Brennan, *Bhréanainn,* not given.

Brennan, *Bhreanndain,* St Brendan.

Brennan, Brendan, a personal or family name.

Brennan, *Uí-Bhranain,* O'Brennan, a family name.

Brennan, *Uí-Bhraonáin,* Ó Braonáin, a family name.

Brenog, *brénóg,* a foul/fetid/lazy flowing stream.

Brenor, *branar, braenar,* fallow.

Brenor, *bréanair,* not given.

Brenter, *bréan-tír,* stinking district.

Bressal, *Bhreasail,* Brassil, a personal or family name.

Bressal, *Breasail,* not given.

Breteen, *britín,* a gentle breeze.

Brett, *briot,* not given.

Brew, *bhruaich, bruach, bruaighe,* boundary.

Brew, *brughaidh,* the keeper of a house of public hospitality. He would be known as a 'Brewy' or a 'Betagh'.

Bri, *brí,* a hill.

Brian, *Bhriain,* Brian, a male name.

Brian, *Braoin,* Braon, a personal or family name.

Brian, *Uí-Briain,* O'Brien, a family name.

Brican, *Bhricín,* Bricin, a personal or family name.

Brican, *Bhreacáin,* St Brecan.

Bricana, *breacánaigh,* speckled land.

Bricane, *Brecain,* St Bregan.

Bricane, *Brecan,* Breckan, a male name.

Bricaun, Brecan, a personal or family name.

Brick, (Taghnabrick), *brice,* the spotted cow.

Brick, *bhric,* trout.

Brick, *bhroic, bhrice,* not given.

Brick, *breac, bric,* speckled.

Brick, *bric,* speckled trout(sic).

Brick, *bric, broc, bríce, bruic, bhroic, bhruic,* badger/s.

Brick, *bric,* building brick.

Brick, *Bríc,* not given.

Brick, *Bruic,* Broc, a personal name.

Brick, *Uí-Bhruic,* O'Brick, a family name.

Bricka, *brice,* brick.

Bricka, *Bríce,* not given.

Bricka, *brice,* the speckled cow.

Brickagh, *broisceach,* broken ground.

Brickan, *Bhreacáin,* St Brecan.

Brickan, *Breccán,* St Breccaun.

Brickana, *bhroicneach,* not given.

Brickanagh, *breachánach,* not given.

Brickane, *Bhreacáin,* St Brecan.

Brickane, *bPríochán, bPréachán,* crows.

Brickane, Brecan or Breckan, a personal or family name.

Brickaun, *breac,* speckled.

Brickaun, *Breacain,* Brecan, a personal or family name.

Brickaun, *Breacán,* not given.

Brickeen, *bricín,* little trout (from '*breac*' speckled skin).

Brickeen, *bricín,* speckled place or speckled little spot.

Brickeens, *bricíní,* speckled little spots.

Brickeens, *na-broicíní,* badger warrens.

Bricken, *Bhricín,* Bricken, a personal or family name.

Bricken, *Bhriocáin,* Briocán, a personal or family name.

Bricken, *Bhreacáin,* Brocán, not given.

Brickendown, *Bricín*(sic), not given.

Brickendown, *Bricín-dúin,* speckled little hill of the fort.

Brickenough, *breac-eanach,* speckled bog, marsh or wet land.

Brickens, *na-broicíní,* badger warrens.

Brickey, *Bhroice, Bhrice,* not given.

Brickfirld, *baile-an-Bhaoilligh,* not given.

Brickland, *Bhricleann, Bricleann, Bricreann, Bricrenn,* Bricriu, a male name, a poets name and the name of an ancient chief.

Bricklieve, *bricshliabh, breic-shliabh,* speckled mountain.

Brickna, *Bricne,* Bricne, a personal or family name.

Brickoge, O'Brickoge, a family name.

Bridane, *broighdean,* little mountain rock.

Bridane, *brighdeán,* small mountain neck.

Bridaun, *braighdean,* place of the neck or gorge.

Briddane, *bradán,* salmon.

Bride, *Bhríd,* not given.

Bride, *Bhríde,* St Brigid/Bríd.

Bride, *Brighde, Bhrighde,* Brigit, a female name.

Bride, *Brighid,* a river named after a Celtic-Irish Goddess.

Brideswell, *tobar-Bríde,* not given.

Bridia, prisoners.

Brief, *bhreaghta,* playing.

Brien, *Bhriain,* Bran, an male name.

Brien, *Braen,* a personal or a family name, also O'Brien, O'Brian, a family name.

Brien, *Briain,* not given.

Brien, Broan or Brian, a male name.

Brien, *Uí-Bhriain, Briain,* O'Brien, a family name.

Briencan, *bruighean,* little fairy fort.

Brigane, *Uí-Breagáin, Breacain,* O'Bregan, Brecan, a personal or family name.

Briggan, *Brigín,* Brigin, a personal or family name.

Briggan, *Uí-Breagáin, Breacain,* O'Bregan, Brigan, Brecan, a personal or family name.

Brigh, *brí,* brae(sic).

Brigh, *bruigh,* lea land.

Bright, *breachtáin,* not given.

Brigown, *brí-gobhan,* hill of the smith.

Brika, *na-mBricí,* the bricks.

Brin, *Bhran,* Bran a personal or family name.

Brin, *Bhroin, Bhrain, Brain, Bruighne,* not given.

Brin, *Bran,* Brin, Bran or Byrne, a personal or family name.

Brin, *Broin,* Bron or Bran, a personal or family name.

Brin, *bun-na…,* bottom of the…

Brin, (Tullabrin) *Uí-Bhroin,* O'Brin, a personal or family name.

Brinagh, *brineach,* a place of coarse grass.

Brinlack, *bun-an-leaca, bréinleac,* not given.

Brinna, *Braonach, Bruithne,* not given.

Brinnia, *binne,* a summit.

Brinny, *boirne,* stony.

Brinoge, Brionoge or Breenoge, a personal or family name.

Briotas, *briotás,* a bretesche (military wooden roofed structure).

Brisca, *briosca,* brittle or easily tilled land.

Briscagh, *briosca,* brittle or easily tilled land.

Briscala, from *briosca,* brittle or easily tilled land.

Briscalagh, from *briosca,* brittle or easily tilled land.

Briscan, *brioscáin,* not given.

Briscan, *brioscan,* a parsnip like edible root.

Briscarnagh, *an-bhrioscarnach,* not given.

Briscaun, *brioscán, mBrioscán,* briscauns, a type of vegetable or succulent plant that grows near water and eaten like watercress.

Brisha, *brise,* not given.

Brisha, *briseadh,* a breach or cleft.

Brisha, *bruise,* debris left on a riverbank after floods.

Brishey, *briseadh,* a breach.

Brisk, *briosc,* brittle.

Briska, *bhroisceach, broisceach, bhruisce,* not given.

Briska, *brioscach, brisce,* brittle land.

Briska, *briosceach,* broken ground.

Briskagh, *broisceach*(sic), not given.

Briskalagh, *an-briosclagh,* not given.

Briskalagh, *briosclach,* fiable land.

Briskalagh, *briosclán,* a place of silverweed.

Briskill, *briosc-choill,* brittle wood.

Brisla, *brisle, brisleach,* broken up or uneven land.

Brisla, *brisleach,* a place of defeat.

Brislagh, *brisle, brisleach,* broken up or uneven land.

Brisny, *brisne,* a breach or gap.

Brist, *bhriste, bríste,* broken.

Brista, *briste, brista,* broken.

Bristan, *bristiann,* breached or broken.

Bristan, *Dristan*(sic), not given.

Bristy, *an-bhriste,* not given.

Bristy, *briste, brisde,* something broken.

Brit, *Bhriotaigh, Briotaigh,* Britt, a family name.

Brit, *bhriotaigh,* not given.

Brit, *brit, briot, breat,* speckled.

Britain, *Bretan,* Bretan a personal or family name.

Britain, *Britain,* Britan a personal or family name.

Britania, *leathcheathramha,* not given.

British, *briotas, briotás,* a wooden palisade.

Britt, *Bhriotaigh,* de-Brit, le-Bret/Brit, a family name

Britt, *Briotach, Bhriotaigh, Briotaigh,* Briotach or Britt, a family name.

Britta, *Bhriotaigh,* de-Brit, le-Bret/Brit, a family name

Brittain, *Bratán,* not given.

Brittain, *Breatain,* Britan, a personal or family name.

Brittain, *Breatan,* British or Welsh.

Brittain, *Briotáin,* St Briotan, Briotán, the name of a Church founder in Cork.

Brittan, *Bhriotáin,* not given.

Brittan, *Bretan,* Bretan a personal or family name.

Brittas, *bhriotáis,* not given.

Brittas, *briotais, briotás, briotas,* a palisade or brattice, (a temporary wooden fortification).

Brittas, *briotáis,* speckled.

Brittas, *briotas, briotás,* speckled land.

Brittas, *britas,* a bretescha(sic) or military wooden roofed structure.

Britway, *breachmhaí, breach-mhagh,* wolf plain.

Bro, *bro, brone,* a millstone or a quern.

Bro, *bró,* a handmill or quern.

Bro, *bro, brone,* a millstone.

Bro, *bró,* not given.

Bro, *bro,* the flood or gush.

Bro, *bruach,* a border.

Broad, *bradach,* sieves.

Broad, *brághad, braghad, braighid,* a neck, throat or gorge.

Broagh, *bruach,* a brink or margin.

Brocagh, *brocach,* not given.

Brocca, *brocach,* badgers.

Brochell, *bhrothaill,* not given.

Brock, *mBroc, broc,* badgers.

Brocka, *brocach,* badgers.

Brockagh, *an-bhrocach,* not given.

Brockagh, *brocach,* a place of badgers, a badger field or a badger warren.

Brockernagh, badger warren/s.

Brockernagh, *brocraigh*(sic), not given.

Brockey, *brocach,* badgers.

Brockish, from *brocach,* a place of badgers.

Brocklagh, a place of badgers, badger warren/s.

Brockles, *broc-lusca,* badger cave, den or warren.

Brockley, badger warren/s.

Brocklis, *broc-lusca,* badger cave, den or warren.

Brocklusk, *broc-lusca,* badger cave, den or warren.

Brockrah, *brocrach,* abounding in badger warrens.

Brockrah, *brocrach,* badger warren/s.

Brockry, *brocrach,* abounding in badger warrens.

Brocky, *brocach, brocaidhe,* the badger warren or fox cover.

Brocky, *brocaí,* not given.

Brodeen, *bróidín,* little corn island.

Broder, O'Brodar, a family name.

Brody, *Bhródaigh,* not given.

Brody, Brody or MacBrody, a personal or family name.

Brody, *Bróithe, Bróith,* a male name.

Brody, Bróithe, Brúide or Bruide, a personal or family name.

Brody, *Brot,* not given.

Brody, *Bruaideadha,* Brody, a personal or family name.

Brody, *Bruidín,* Mac-Brody, a family name.

Brody, *Mhic-Bhriuaidheadha,* MacBrody, a family name.

Broe, *breo,* signifies flame or fire but exact meaning uncertain.

Broga, a shoe.

Broga, *barróige,* not given.

Brogan, *Brógáin, Brogain,* St Brogan.

Brogan, *Brógán,* a personal or family name.

Brogan, *Uí-Bhrogain,* O'Brogan or Brogan, a family name.

Brogeen, *brogín,* little shoe.

Broghan, from *bruach,* a border or borders.

Broghan, *Uí-Bhruachain,* O'Broghan or Brohan, a family name.

Brogher, from *bruach,* a border or borders.

Broghin, *bruach-an…,* border of the…

Broghindrummin, *bruach-an-dromain, tam-hnach-raithinighe,* not given.

Broghlan, *Bhruachláin,* not given.

Brogue, *burróige, burróg,* black bog dye used for colouring wool.

Brogue, *mBróg,* not given.

Brogue, *mBarróg,* Boates, a personal or family name.

Brogue, *m-brog, bróg,* shoe/s.

Brohane, *Bruacháin,* not given.

Broher, *bhrathar,* the friar.

Broighter, *broghiochdar,* the lower fort.

Brolly, *Bhrolaigh,* Bradley, a male name.

Brolly, O'Brolly, a family name.

Bromhagan, *broghagan,* rushes.

Bronagh, *brónach,* abounding in mill stones or querns.

Brone, *bhróin,* lamentation.

Brone, *bro, brón, broín,* a mill stone, quern or hand mill.

Brone, *Brón, Bronus,* a male name.

Brone, *brón,* a champion or sad.

Brone, *Brónaigh, bruighne, bruighean,* not given.

Brone, marsh or flat.

Bronetore, *bhroinnteoraigh,* a quern-stone maker.

Broney, *Bronagh,* St Bronagh.

Broney, *Brónaí, Brónach,* St Brónach, Bronach, the virgin Saint.

Broney, *Brónaigh,* Bronach or Bronagh, a personal or family name.

Bronoge, *Bhreannóg,* not given.

Bronoge, *Bhronóig,* Brunnock, a personal or family name.

Bronoge, *Bronóg,* Brannock or Brannick, a family name.

Bronoge, *Moronoch,* St Moronoch.

Bronoge, *na-mBruthnóg,* the smelt furnace.

Broo, *brú,* not given.

Broo, *brugh,* a mansion, land or a farm.

Brood, *bhrúid,* ashes.

Brooey, *na-bruaí,* not given.

Brook, *broc,* badgers.

Brook, *Broc,* St Brock.

Brook, *buaic,* a round hill.

Brookley, *brugh,* the mansion, fort or Inn.

Brookley, *Brookley*(sic), not given.

Broom, *brúim,* the plant 'broom'.

Broona, Brown, a family name.

Brophy, *Uí-Bhróithe,* Ó Bróithe, Brophy, a family name.

Brosna, *brosnach, brusna,* brushwood or undergrowths fit for firewood.

Brosna, *mullach-ar*(sic)*-bhrosna/brosnacha, an-bhrosnach/brosnaí,* not given.

Brother, *Bruadar's,* belonging to Bruadar, a personal or family name.

Brothers, *Bruadar's,* belonging to Bruadar, a personal or family name.

Brough, *bruach,* a brink, bank or border.

Brough, *bruach,* a house or farm.

Brough, *bruach, brugh,* not given.

Broughal, *brothlach, brochaill,* not given.

Broughan, *brughachán,* on the hillface.

Broughan, from *bruach,* a little border.

Broughan, *Uí-Bhruachain,* O'Broghan or Brohan, a family name.

Broughane, from *bruach,* a little border.

Brougher, *bruach,* a border.

Broughill, a personal name.

Broughna, *bruach-na...,* bank of the...

Brow, *brugh,* a mansion or a fort.

Browley, *broghlae,* not given.

Browley, *brúgh-Lae,* Lea's (a personal or family name) fairy mansion.

Browley, *brugh-liath,* not given.

Brown, *Bhrunaigh, Bhrúnaigh, Brúnach,* Brown, a family name.

Brown, *Bhrúnaigh,* Brúnach, not given.

Brown, *Broin, Briuin,* St Brone.

Brown, *Brón,* not given.

Browne, *Bhrún, an-Bhrúnaigh,* not given.

Broydan, *broighdean,* little mountain rock.

Bru, *brú, brugha,* fort or a Palace.

Bru, *brugh,* a mansion, land or a farm.

Brucana, *breacanach,* speckled land.

Bruce, *brughas,* a farmhouse.

Bruchais, *bruachais,* not given.

Bruckana, *bhreachánach,* not given.

Brucken, from *broc,* a badger or badger warren.

Bruckless, *an-bhroclais,* the badger warren.

Bruckless, *an-broclas,* not given.

Bruckless, *broc-lusca,* badger cave, den or warren.

Brucklis, *broc-lusca,* badger cave, den or warren.

Brucky, *broca, brocaigh,* the badger warren.

Brufea, *Brú-Fí,* not given.

Bruff, (in Limerick) *an-brú, brugh,* shortened version of *brubh-na-leise/deise,* the mansion of the ancient territory of Deis beg.

Bruff, *an-Brú,* the abode

Bruff, *brú,* the palace or fort.

Bruff, *brugh,* a mansion, a fortified mansion, a fort or an Inn.

Bruff, *brugh-na-nDéire,* not given.

Brugh, *brugh,* the mansion.

Brughas, *brughachas, brúchais, bruachais, brughas,* a farm house.

Brughas, *brughais,* a dwelling or hill-fort.

Brughas, *brughas,* a mansion.

Bruis, *brí-Ois, ráth-Briúis,* not given.

Bruis, *brugh,* the mansion fort or inn.

Bruis, *brughas,* a farmhouse.

Bruis, *brús, brúg,* a fort.

Brulea, *brugh-liath,* grey hillock or district.

Bruna, *na-mBrianach,* of the O'Brien's, a family name.

Brunnock, *Uí-Bhronóig,* O'Bronoghue, a personal or family name.

Brunoge, *Bhreannóg,* not given.

Brunogue, *Bronóg,* Brannock or Brannick, a family name.

Bruree, *bru-Righ, brugh-Ríogh/Righ, brú-Rí, brunry, brughrigh,* the fort, palace or abode of the King.

Brusa, *an-Bhrúsaigh,* not given.

Brusa, *Uí-Bhrúsa,* O'Bruce, a personal or family name.

Bruscarnagh, *bruscarnach,* rubbish.

Bruse, Bruce or De Bruce, a personal or family name.

Bruse, *brughas,* a farmhouse or hill fort.

Bruse, *Brús,* Bruce, a personal or family name.

Brushes, *briseadh,* breaks or cracks.

Brusk, *brusc,* rubbish, a place of rubbish or refuse.

Bruslee, grey dust.

Brusna, *brosnaí,* the river Brosna, not given.

Brusna, *brosna, brusna,* small twigs or faggots.

Brusna, *brusna,* brushwood or under-growths fit for firewood.

Bryan, *Bhriain,* Brian, a male name.

Bryan, *bréan, Bhriain,* Brian, not given.

Bryan, *bruighean,* a fairy fort or a mansion.

Bryan, *na-mBrianach,* of the O'Brien's, a family name.

Brydane, *broighdean,* little mountain rock.

Bryol, *bruigheal,* cormorants.

Buany, *m-buannai,* soldiers.

Buccera, *bhocaire,* cake.

Buck, *Bhoic, Bhucoide,* not given.

Buck, *boc,* stags.

Buck, *bog,* bog.

Buck, *bPoc, buac,* not given.

Buck, *buic,* the stag.

Buckan, *mBocáin,* not given.

Buckode, *bocóid, bocáid,* a well defined piece/spot of land.

Buckode, *bogfhóid,* soft soil.

Buckree, *both-curaidhe,* soldiers hut, booth or tent.

Buckstown, *baile-Robac,* not given.

Bud, *both,* a hut or booth.

Bud, *both-a'…,* cattlehouse or hut of the…

Bud, *bun,* bottom.

Buddagh, *bodach,* churls.

Buddaghauns, (plural of) *bodacháin,* churls.

Buddoge, *bodóg,* the heifer.

Buddremeen, *both-a'dromin,* cattle house or hut of the small ridge.

Budogy, *bodóige,* the heifer.

Bue, *buí, bui, buidhe,* yellow.

Buf, *both,* a hut or tent.

Buffana, *both-mhanach,* monks hut or tent.

Buffanagh, *bofanach,* a place of thistles.

Buffanagh, *both-Mhanach,* not given.

Buffanna, *bofanach,* land full of thistles.

Buffanoky, *both-Bhunóice,* not given.

Buggan, *bogán, bogan,* soft land.

Buggane, *bogan, bogán,* bog or soft land.

Buggawn, *bogan, bogán,* bog or soft land.

Buggy, *Uí-Bhogaigh,* Buggy, a personal or family name.

Buine, *buinghe, buinne,* a stream.

Buinga, *buinne,* not given.

Bulbin, *Gulban, Gulbain, Ghulbain,* Gulban, a personal or family name.

Bulcan, *Bolcain,* St Bolcan.

Bulcane, *Bolcáin,* not given.

Bulcaun, *Bolcain,* St Bolcan.

Bulgaden, *Builgidín,* not given.

Bulgan, *Bolcain,* St Bolcan.

Bulgan, *Bolgan,* not given.

Bulgan, *Uí-Bholgain,* O'Bulgan, a family name.

Bulkaun, *bulcan,* middle land.

Bull, *bPoll,* holes.

Bullaun, *ballán,* a small round hill or a small patch.

Bullaun, *bollán, bullán,* a well in a rock.

Bullaun, *bulán,* a bullock.

Bullaunagh, *bullánach,* abounding in rock wells.

Bullen, *boillín,* not given.

Bullen, *buillín,* the loaf.

Bulleragh, *biolarach,* a place of watercress.

Bullig, *bhuilg,* sea swell or a sack.

Bullig, *boilg,* not given.

Bullig, *builg,* the sack.

Bulliga, *builge,* sea swell.

Bulligs, *bullóga,* knolls or humps.

Bullion, *bullain,* a large round stone or 'buttan'(sic).

Bullock, *bhulláin, blabhac,* not given.

Bullog, *bolg,* cows(sic).

Bullog, *bolg,* sack/s, bag/s.

Bullog, *bológ,* an ox.

Bulloga, *bullóige,* not given.

Bulloge, *bolg,* sacks, bags or bulges.

Bulloge, *bullóige, Bológ,* not given.

Bulloge, *bulóige,* skull or loaf.

Bullogue, *bolg,* bulges.

Bullogue, bolg, sacks or bags.

Bulrisk, town of the marsh.

Bumlin, buimlinn, not given.

Bun, bun, the bottom of something, bottom land, a foot hill or the mouth of a river.

Buna, bun-a…, hollow of the…

Buna, bun-an/a'…, the bottom of …, the mouth of a river, the bog-end or land-end.

Bunacham, bun-a'choim, bottom of the hollow.

Bunacum, bun-an-choim, not given.

Bunan, bun-an…, bottom or end of the…

Bunane, an-bunán, not given.

Bunaun, bunnán, bitterns.

Bunavie, bun-an-mhaí, not given.

Bunaw, bun-abha, mouth of the river.

Buncea, bun cae, bottom of the quagmire.

Bunclody, bun-Clóidí/Cladaighe, not given.

Bunduff, bun-Dubh, mouth of the river Duff.

Bunesca, bun-uisce, mouth of the river(sic).

Buninabber, bua-an-abair, not given.

Buninabber, end of the mire.

Bunion, Bhuinneánaigh, Bhuinneanaigh, Bunion or Bunyan, a personal or family name.

Bunkey, bun-Caoith, not given.

Bunlin, bunlinne, not given.

Bunn, bun, the bottom or base of something, can also be the mouth of a river or bottom land.

Bunna, both-na…, milking place on(sic)…

Bunna, bun-an/na…, bottom or bottom land of the…

Bunna, bun-an/na…, mouth of the… (river name).

Bunna, bun-na…, hollow of the(sic)…

Bunnaan, buineáin, Bunayne, a family name

Bunnagee, end or mouth of the river Gee.

Bunnan, bun-an…, foot, bottom, mouth or end of the…

Bunnan, bunnán, bitterns.

Bunnanilra, bun-an-ilraigh, mountain end of the eagle.

Bunnaton, bun-a'tonn, end of the waves.

Bunnaun, bunnán, bunnaun, bittern/s.

Bunnia, bainne, milk.

Bunnia, boinne, not given.

Bunnia, buinne, a stream.

Bunniff, bun-duibh, black bottom.

Bunniagh, buinneach, flooded.

Bunnion, Bhuinneánaigh, Buinneán or Bunnion, a personal or family name.

Bunnoe, bun-abha, mouth of the river.

Bunnow, bun-abha, bottom of the river.

Bunnow, bun-abhain, a place sloping to the river.

Bunny, bainne, milk.

Bunny, buine, a flood.

Bunny, buinne, a watery place, a flow of water, a stream, a flood or a wave.

Bunny, buinnighe, flowing water.

Bunny, bun a'…, end, bottom of the…

Bunny, muine, mhuine, a shrubbery or thicket.

Bunny, Munna, not given.

Bunoe, bun-abha, bottom, end or mouth of the river.

Bunone, bun'-abhann, mouth, end or source of the river.

Bunratty, the bottom of the river ratty (*raite*)

Bunree, bun-riaghaidh, river mouth of the executions.

Buntel, bPointeal, Payntle, a personal or family name.

Buogh, buadhach, victory or victories.

Bough, Buach, not given.

Buolick, buailic, bual-lic, not given.

Bur, bhurraigh, not given.

Bur, buídhe, yellow.

Burb, bhorb, bold or rough.

Burb, bhorb, borb, proud.

Burdautien, barr-Dóiteáin, not given.

Burden, Bhurdunaigh, Bhurdunaigh, Burden, a personal or family name.

Burden, Bhurdúnaigh, not given.

Bure, Biúir, not given.

Bure, buar, cows.

Burgagary lands, Burghaiste, not given.

Burgage, an-bhuirgeiseach, not given.

Burgage, buirghes, a borough.

Burgery, buidgeire, land of the Burgess (of Dungarvan).

Burgery, burgáiste, not given.

Burges, bhuirgéis, not given.

Burges, buirghiais, buirghes, a borough or burgage,

Burgess, *bhuirgéseach, buirghiais,* burgery or lands owned by the Burgesses.

Burgess, *buirghiais, buirghes,* a borough or burgage.

Burgess, *burgáiste,* not given.

Burgess, *tiobraid-an-bhuirghéiseach / Ciarán*(sic), not given.

Burke, *Burcach,* Burcach or Burke, a family name.

Burke, *na-Bhúrcach,* not given.

Burly, *Bhuirléigh,* not given.

Burly, Burly or Burleigh, a family name.

Burn, *Bhirn,* Birn, a personal or family name.

Burn, *Brian,* Brin and Byrne, male name.

Burn, rocky ground.

Burn, *Bruidhne,* not given.

Burn, of the spring (well).

Burncourt, *an-chúirt-dóite,* the burnt court. A location named after the burning of a house by Oliver Cromwell in 1649.

Burne, *bhairrinn,* not given.

Burne, *Brain,* Bran, a male name, and a name of a tribe.

Burnew, *boirne,* rocky lands.

Burney, *Bunne,* not given.

Burnfoot, *baile-idir-dá-abhainn, bun-na-hAbhann, ráth-an-Tóiteáin,* not given.

Burnfoot, *bun-an-hAbhann,* mouth of the river.

Burr, *bior,* not given.

Burr, *biorair,* watercress.

Burrane, *barrán, borran,* a low hill.

Burranure, *garran,* grove or shrubbery of yew trees(sic).

Burren, (river) *baireann-cliach,* not given.

Burren, *an-bhoirinn / bheirn,* not given.

Burren, *boireann, borronn,* a rock, rocks, a great stone or a rocky/stony place.

Burren, *boirinn, buithreann,* rocky, stony land.

Burris, *buirgheas, buirghes,* a borough.

Burrishoole, *buirgheas / buiríos-Umhaill,* the Borough of Umhaill/Umhall (an ancient territory).

Burrock, *burrúc,* mermaids.

Burrow, *coinicéar,* a rabbit warren.

Burry, *boirín,* rocky land.

Burry, *borraighe,* not given.

Burt, *Bhearaigh, Bearta,* not given.

Burth, *Bhuirt,* Burt, a personal or family name.

Burth, *Boirt,* not given.

Burth, *Murty, Mhuirt,* a personal or family name.

Burtlan, *bPoirtleann,* little banks or ports.

Burtown, *baile-bhiorra,* not given.

Bush, *Bhoisigh,* not given.

Bush, *Bhuiséir,* Busher, a personal or family name.

Bush, *bas,* flat land.

Bush, *Buas, Buaise,* (river) Bush, not given.

Bushtameen, *bas-Thóimín,* small Tom's(a male name) flat land.

Buska, *Bhoscaigh,* Fox, a family name.

Butler, Butler, a family name.

Buttevant, from *botavant, "Boutez en avard, an-avant, Boutes-en-avant",* (Norman French) family motto meaning to push forward. Irish names are *Cill-an-mallach,* Church of the summits(sic) and *Cill-na-Mollach,* not given.

Button, *Butúin,* not given.

Button, *botúin,* misfortune.

Buttry, *bPotairedh,* the potter.

Buy, *buidhe, bhuidhe,* yellow.

Buyher, *buidheachair,* yellow water.

Bwe, *bhuidhe,* yellow.

Bwee, *buidhe, bhuidhe,* yellow.

Bweeheen, (in Limerick) *Baeithin,* St Baithen.

Bweeheen, *Baoithín,* Baoithín, a personal or family name.

Bweeng, *na-mBoinn / boinn,* the swelling.

Byrne, *Bhriain,* not given.

Byrne, *Brain,* Bran or Byrne, a personal or family name.

Byrne, *Uí-Bhroin,* not given.

Byrneskill, *coill-Uí-Bhroin,* not given.

C

Ca, *cath, catha,* a battle.
Caban, *chaban,* cabins.
Cabban, *cabáin,* a cabin.
Cabbin, *cabáin,* a cabin.
Cabble, *capaill,* the horse.
Cabin, *cábán, cabáin,* a cabin.
Cabin, *Gobáin,* not given.
Caboon, *chabuin, cabún,* crowing hens or an ignorant man.
Cabra, *chabrach, cabrach, cabragh, cabra,* poor, bad, rough or unprofitable land.
Cabragh, *chabrach, cabragh, cabra, cabrach,* poor, bad, rough or unprofitable land.
Cabry, *cabra, cabragh,* bad, rough, unprofitable land.
Cabus, *Chábais,* not given.
Cabus, *Chabuis,* Cabus, a personal or family name.
Cack, *cac,* dirty.
Cacka, *coca,* a mound.
Cackanode, *cac-an-fhóid,* the dirty part of the sod or soil.
Cadaigh, a covenant.
Cadams, *Mhic-Adam,* MacAdam, a family name and means the son of the man called Adam.
Caddagh, *cadach,* not given.
Caddagh, *ceadach,* a flat topped hill.
Caddagh, *ceideach, ceide,* a smooth topped hillock.
Caddy, *cadaigh,* moss.
Caddy, *ceadach,* a flat topped hill.
Caddy, *chadaí,* not given.
Cadian, *céidín,* a hillock.
Cadian, from *ceide,* a little smooth topped hillock.
Cady, *ceideach, ceide,* a smooth topped hillock.

Caffe, *Chabha,* not given.
Cagh, *cogadh, cath, chata,* battle.
Caghan, *Cheachan,* not given.
Caghan, *leathan,* broad.
Caghan, *Uí-Cathain,* O'Cahan or O'Cane, a family name.
Cagher, *cathair,* not given.
Caghny, *Mhic-Eachain*(sic), not given.
Cagy, *caige,* jackdaws.
Cah, *caithe,* chaff.
Cah, *cath,* a battle.
Cah, *chatha,* not given.
Caha, (mountain) *cnoc-na-ceathain/ceachan,* showery mountain/hills.
Caha, *an-cheacha, ceacha,* not given.
Caha, *caithe, chátha,* winnowing, waste or chaff.
Caha, *cata,* a sheep fold.
Caha, *Cathane,* O'Cahan, a personal or family name.
Caha, *chatha, catha, cath,* the battle.
Cahalan, *Uí-Chathaláin, Chathalain,* O'Cahalan, a family name.
Cahan, *Cahan,* Cahan, a personal or family name.
Cahan, *ceachann,* a cliff, ledge or precipice.
Cahan, *ceathain,* the shower (rain).
Cahan, *Chatháin,* not given.
Cahan, *Ua-Cathain,* O'Kean, a family name.
Cahanagh, *Cathánach,* Kane's (a male name) place.
Cahane, *Cathain,* Cathan, Kane, a personal or family name.
Cahane, *Cathane,* O'Cahan, a personal or family name.
Cahane, *Uí-Chathain,* Keane a family name.
Cahane, *Uí-Chatháin,* Ó'Catháin, a family name.
Cahane, *Uí-Chathain,* O'Kane or Keane, a family name.
Caharagh, *cathrach,* a round stone fort.
Cahard, the high bog(sic).
Caharna, *cethearnach,* a lightly armed soldier.
Caharna, *cheatharnaigh,* ...of the cairn.
Cahaun, *cathadh,* fighting.
Cahee, *cáithe,* chaff.
Caheer, *Cathaoir,* Charles, a male name.

Caher, *cathair,* a residence surrounded by a high stone wall, a mansion or fortress.

Cahir (Island), *cathair-na-naomh,* city of the saints.

Caher, *cathair,* a round stone fort.

Caher, *cathaoir,* chair.

Caher, *cathrach, an-chathair,* not given.

Caher, *chathair, catharach,* a stone fort.

Cahera, *cathair,* as stone fort.

Cahera, *cathair-a'…,* stone fort of the…

Caher (Kilkeevin), *ceachair,* a bog.

Cahera, *chathraigh,* not given.

Caheragh, a stone fort or a chieftaincy.

Caheragh, *cathair, catherach, catharach, cathrach,* a round stone fort.

Caheragh, *cathair-an…,* the cahers by the…

Caheragh, *catharach,* caher-land.

Caheragh, *cathrach,* a stone fort or a place of stone forts.

Caheran, *cathair-an..,* stone fort of the…

Cahercon, *cathair-dha-chon,* round stone fort of the two hounds.

Cahercorcaun, *craig-Corcrain,* Corcran's rock.

Caherea, *cathair-Aodha/Aedha,* Hugh's (a male name) circular stone fortress.

Caherea, *cathair-Aodh,* residence of Aodh (a male name).

Cahereen, a small mansion.

Cahergh, *catharach,* a stone fort.

Caherhenryhoe, Henry's (a male name) caher-of-the-cave.

Caherhoe, *ceathramha,* quarters.

Caherhoereigh, *cheathrú/ceathramha-raibh-ach,* grey quarter.

Caherlly, *cathair-ailí,* not given.

Caherna, *cathair-na…,* round stone fort of the…

Cahernagh, *ceatharnach,* not given.

Cahernahallia, *ceathrú/ceathamhradh-na-hAille/haille,* quarter (land) of the cliff.

Cahernarry, *Carn*(sic)*-Fhearáigh,* not given.

Caheroe, *cathair,* a round stone fort.

Caherty, *cathair-n'tí…,* the caher of the-----house.

Cahill, *Achaille,* an old name for a rock in a high strategic place.

Cahill, *Chathail, Cathail,* not given.

Cahill, *Uí-Chathail,* Cahill, a family name.

Cahilroe, red haired Cahill, a male name.

Cahina, *caithne,* arbutus wood.

Cahir, *cathair,* a round stone fort.

Cahir, an-chathair, na-cathrach, not given.

Cahir, *Cathaoir,* Cahir, a personal or family name.

Cahirdague, *ceathairdeug,* fourteen.

Cahnicaun, *caithne,* arbutus wood.

Cahoge, *caitheóige,* not given.

Cahoge, *cathóige,* a skirmish or little battle.

Cahore, *rinn-cathóire, chathóir,* not given.

Cahrea, *cathair-a'…,* stone fort of the…

Cahy, *caithe,* chaff.

Cahy, *ceatha,* a bog cutting.

Cailagh, *gCailleach,* hags.

Cailly, hags.

Caim, *ceim, céim,* a narrow mountain pass, a step, a customary pass for animals or a roadway between rocks or hills.

Caime, *chéim, céim,* a gap.

Caimin, *Chaimín,* St Camin.

Cair, *Chéire,* not given.

Caird, *ceard,* an artificer.

Cairn, *chairn, cairn,* a monumental heap of stones.

Cairns, *carnaí,* grave heaps.

Cait, *chait,* a cat.

Cait, *chuit,* the wild cat.

Cake, *chaca,* not given.

Cal, *call,* hazel.

Cal, *cauld,* (Scottish) cold.

Cal, *cúil,* not given.

Calabber, *caladh-abair,* not given.

Calad, *caladh,* a landing place.

Calary, *calraighe,* not given.

Calary, *ceallárach, ceallamhnach,* a disused graveyard.

Calatrom, *calatuim,* not given.

Caldavnet, *Damhnat,* the Virgin Saint Dympna.

Caldragh, *cealldrach, cealdragh, cealdrach, ceallurach,* an old burying ground.

Caldragh, *cealtragh, ceallltrach,* a burial ground or graveyard.

Caldrim, *call-druim,* hazel ridge.

Cale, *Cathail,* Cathal a male name.

Cale, *chaol,* narrow.

Caledon, named after the Earls of Caledon. The Anglicized name was originally **Kenard,** *cinn-árd, cionn-aird,* the high head.

Calee, caillighe, hag.

Calf, Chatha, Caha/Caffa, a personal or family name.

Calf, Chátha, Cátha, not given.

Calga, calgach, a place of thorns.

Calga, cholgaigh, not given.

Calgy, Calgaigh, Calgach, a personal or family name.

Calhame, Calhaem(sic), not given.

Calkill, collchoille, hazel wood.

Call, Chathail, Cathail, Cahill, a personal or family name.

Call, coill, a wood.

Calla, cala, a marshy, wet meadow along a river that usually floods in winter or a landing place.

Calla, caladh, a riverside place, meadow, a water-meadow.

Calla, cealla, Churches.

Calla, chalaidh, not given.

Calla, Ua-Cealadh, O'Kelly, a family name.

Callagh, cala, marshy meadow.

Callagh, caladh, a ferry.

Callaghan, ceallachán, small place belonging to the Church.

Callaghan, Cheallachain, Ceallachán, Callaghan, a personal or family name.

Callaghan, Uí-Cheallachain, O'Callaghan, a family name.

Callaghane, Uí-Cheallacháin/Ceallachán, not given.

Callaha, caladh, chalatha, a landing place, embankment or wet meadow.

Callahy, calaith(sic), a harbour, embankment or landing place.

Callahy, calaithe, water-meadows.

Callan, caladh/ cala-an…, landing place or ferry of the…

Callan, chalainn, not given.

Callan, Calainn, named after the 8th cent-King Niall Cailne.

Callan, callainn, not given.

Callan, collán, callán, hazels.

Callan, Uí-Challáin, Ó Callain, a personal or family name.

Callan, Uí-Chaoláin, not given.

Callan, Uí-Chathalain, O'Cahalan, a family name.

Callas, calaidh, riverside patches.

Callaun, coll, coill, hazels.

Callcen, chailcin, not given.

Callee, chaillí, caillí, caillighe, a hag.

Calleen, chailín, caillín, a girl.

Callen, calainn, not given.

Calley, Cealladh, O'Kelly, a family name.

Calliagh, cailleach, Nuns.

Calliagh, caillí, the hag.

Calliagh, calliagh, a hag or hags.

Calliagh, chailleach, not given.

Calliaghdoo, gCalliagh-dubh, literally 'black hags' or cormorants.

Callick, cailc, chalk.

Callick, Challóg, Colga, not given.

Callidy, calloide, contention.

Calliff, cullach, wild boar.

Callis, cailíse, the chalice.

Calloughs, ceallachaigh, Church lands.

Callow, caladh, a holm(sic).

Callow, caladh, chalaidh, not given.

Callow, calbhach, a place of ridges(sic).

Callow, caltha, cala, a landing place or a marshy, wet meadow along a river that usually floods in winter.

Callow, caltha, wet meadows.

Callow, chala, cala, caladh, a riverside meadow, a ferry or a boat landing place.

Callow, tuath-an-chalaidh, not given.

Callowhill, collchoill, the hazel wood,

Callows, caltha, marshy meadows.

Callrick, calraic, hazels.

Callum, cala-lom, bare land.

Calluragh, cealdragh, ceallurach, an old burying ground.

Calluragh, ceallabhreach, a pagan place of burial.

Cally, caille, loss or damage.

Cally, cailléádh(sic), nuns.

Cally, caillí, caillighe, calliagh, a hag or hags.

Cally, caillige, wiches.

Cally, calaidh, the landing place for boats or a ferry.

Cally, calligh, callighe, caillighe, cailleach, a nun.

Cally, chaillí, not given.

Cally, Uí-Cheallaigh, O'Kelly, a family name.

Callybeara, caillighe-béarra, not given.

Callybeara, Chaillighe-Bheara, the name of a legendary lady.

Calmore, great hazel.

Calpin, *'ic-Ailpin,* Alpin or Halpin, a family name.

Calry, *Calraidhe,* the race (of people) of Cal, a male name.

Calry, *Chalraí, Calraighe,* not given.

Calteen, *Caitilín,* Catherine.

Calteraun, *caillterán,* a place of hazels.

Caltra, *cealdrach,* an old burying ground.

Caltra, *cealltrach,* not given.

Caltra, *Cealtchrach,* Cealtchair, an old pagan name.

Caltra, *cealtrach, chealtrach,* the burial ground.

Caltragh, *cealdragh, cealdrach, ceallurach,* an old burying ground or Churchyard.

Caltragh, *cealtrach,* a burial place.

Calvagh, *coill-bheithe,* the birch wood.

Calvy, *Calbhach,* Calvagh, a male name.

Cam, *chaim, caim, cam,* winding, crooked, a bend or curved.

Cama, *cam,* a bend or crooked.

Cama, *ceim-a'...,* pass of the ...

Camac, *camóg,* winding.

Camagh, *cam-mágh,* crooked glen.

Camalier, *camladhar, cam-ladhar,* crooked river fork.

Caman, *céim-an...,* not given.

Camara, *camra,* the sewer.

Camara, *cam-shrath,* crooked riverside land.

Camas, *camas,* bent, curved, winding or crooked.

Camas, *camus,* a bog, bend or a crooked place.

Camb, *caim, cam,* crooked.

Cambas, *camas,* bent, curved or crooked.

Camber, *cam-darach,* crooked oak.

Camble, *Comainn,* Coman, a personal or family name.

Camblin, *cam-ghlinn,* a winding valley.

Came, *ceim,* a pass.

Came, *céim,* step.

Came, *cam,* crooked.

Camea, *camaí,* not given.

Camea, *ceim-na...,* the step or pass of the...

Camena, *céim-na...,* track of the...

Cameron, *camshrón,* not given.

Cametringane, *céim-an-tSreangáin,* not given.

Camheen, *caimchín, caimthín,* any crooked little thing.

Camill, MacCathmaoil or Campbell, a family name.

Camin, *chaimín,* crooked hill.

Camin, *Chaimín,* St Camin.

Camira, *cam-eirghe,* crooked rising or rising grund.

Camla, *camla,* crooked hill.

Camla, *camloch,* not given.

Camlagh, *camlacha,* crooked hill of the lake.

Camleer, *cam-ladhar,* crooked river fork.

Camlin, *caim-lin,* crooked pond.

Camlin, *cam-líne,* crooked line.

Camlin, *cam-uillin,* crooked elbow.

Camlin, *chamlinn, chaimlinn,* not given.

Camline, *caimline,* crooked line or river.

Camline, *cruimm-ghlin, cruim-ghlinn,* crooked glen.

Camly, *camlaigh,* not given.

Camma, *camach,* curved or crooked places.

Cammadil, *chaimidil,* a winding stream.

Cammagh, *chamach, camacadh,* not given.

Cammanagh, *an-camanach,* not given.

Cammoge, *camóg,* winding stream.

Cammoge, *camóg,* winding.

Camog, *cam-óg,* little winding.

Camoge, *chamóg, camóg,* the crooked/winding stream.

Camolin, *cam-Eólaing/Eolaing,* Eolang's (a personal or family name) bend.

Camp, a fortress.

Camp, *an-cam,* not given.

Camp, *chamtha,* the camp.

Camp, *com,* a hollow.

Camphill, *cam-choill,* crooked wood.

Camphire, *caimthír, caimphír, chaimpíre, caimpír, chaimthíreach,* not given.

Camphire, *caimthir,* the irregular area.

Campile, *ceann-an-phuill,* head or point of the river 'Pill'.

Campile, *ceann-poil,* head of the creek.

Campile, *ceann-poill/puill,* not given.

Campion, *Chaimpion,* Caimpion, not given.

Camplagh, *camplach,* an encampment.

Campsey, *camaseach, camasaigh,* crooked (river, coastline) etc.

Campsie, camsa, camaseach, camasaigh, crooked (river, coastline) etc.

Campsie, camsain, meanders.

Cams, camac-Bhríde, not given.

Cams, camach, curved or crooked places.

Camucky, ceann-muice, pigs head.

Camus, camas, camus, chamais, a bog, bend or a crooked place.

Camusk, comaisg, mingling.

Camusk, cumaisc, not given.

Can, ceann, a head or hilltop.

Cana, ciuin, calm or quiet.

Canada, ceann-fhada, long head or hill.

Canadas, cheannadais, the chief fort.

Cananagh, gCanonach, canons.

Cananaun, ceanannán, not given.

Cananee, ceannanaighe, the cow with the white spot on its head.

Cananee, gCeanannaí, not given.

Canary, ceann-aedhaire, the shepherds head or hill.

Canauna, Canánaigh, Chanánaigh, the Canon.

Canavan, ceannbháin, bog-cotton.

Canavan, Uí-Cheannabháin, O'Canavan, a personal or family name.

Canavee, Ceanabhuidhe, Cannaway, a personal or family name.

Canavee, ceann-a'mhaighe, head of the plain.

Canavee, Cheannbhuí, Ceannmhuighe, not given.

Canbo, ceann-Bugha, Bugh's (a male name) head.

Canea, Ana, Anna, a female name.

Canew, Conway, a personal or family name

Canew, Uí-Chonnmhaí, Ó Connmhaí, a personal or family name.

Canfea, ceann-feadha, head of the wood.

Cangort(sic)*, camghort,* not given.

Cangy, ceangaí, not given.

Cankeel, ceann-caol, narrow hilltop.

Cann, ceann, a head.

Canna, ceann-na/a'..., head of the...

Cannagh, ceannach, head or hill.

Cannakill, Cill(sic)*-Mhic-Caille,* not given.

Cannan, ceinnfhinne, the white faced cow.

Cannan, Chonáin, Conán, a personal or family name.

Cannan, Uí-Chanainn, O'Cannon or Cannon, a family name.

Cannana, ceannaine, the white faced cow.

Cannana, ceannana, the spotted cow.

Cannaun, Conáin, Conán, a personal or family name.

Cannaver, ceannúir, not given.

Cannaway, ceann-a'mhaighe, head of the plain.

Cannawee, ceann-a'mhaighe, head of the plain.

Cannca, Ana, Anna, a female name.

Canneen, Cainín, not given.

Cannina, ceinnfhinne, the cow with a white spot on the forehead.

Cannon, Canainn, Canainn, a personal or family name.

Cannon, Canann, Canann, a personal or family name.

Cannon, Cannan, Conan or Kennan, a male name.

Cannon, Ceanann, a personal or family name.

Cannon, ceannaine, a bald faced hill.

Cannon, ceanon, ceannainne, ceinnfhion, ceannann, ceananaid, ceann-fhionn, cenn-fhionn, a cow with a white face or a white head, a cow with a white spot in the center of her forhead, spotted land or a spotted rock.

Cannon, Chanann, Cheanann, Cheanainn, not given.

Cannon, ceannain, white topped...

Cannon, cheannann, white headed.

Cannon, Chonáin, Conáin, Conan or St Conan.

Cannon, Conáin, Conani (Latin), Conan, the name of a Waterford Chieftain.

Cannon, Mhic-Ceannain, not given.

Cannon, Uí-Chanainn, O'Cannon or Cannon, a family name.

Cannon, Uí-Chuineain, Kinane, a family name.

Cannony, ceannainne, ceinnfhion, ceannann, chonáin, ceananaid, ceannfhionn, a white faced or spotted cow.

Cannor, Canar, a male name.

Cannor, Ceannúir, Ceannúr, a personal name.

Cannor, Ua-Conchobhair, O'Connor, a family name.

Cannovee, *ceannmhuighe,* not given.

Cannow, *ceann-abha,* head water or source or head of the river.

Cannower, *ceann-iubhair,* hill or head of the yew.

Cannucka, *cnucha,* not given.

Cannuigh, *ceannuighthe,* (of the) purchase.

Canny, *Caithne,* not given.

Canon, (Island) *inis-na-gCanánach,* not given.

Canon, *ceinnfhinn, ceannann,* spotted.

Canon, *ceinnfhinne,* the white faced cow.

Canon, *Chanann, Canann,* not given.

Canon, *gCanon,* canons.

Canony, *ceanainne,* not given.

Canony, *ceinnfionn,* a cow with a white face or a white head, a cow with a white spot in the center of her forhead.

Canovee, *ceann-an-mhuighe,* head of the plain.

Canrooska, *ceann-rusca,* summit of the marsh or bog.

Cant, *baile-Maol-Cainne,* O'Mulcanny's (a family name) residence.

Cant, *cainnt,* talking.

Cant, *cainnte,* controversy or dispute.

Cant, *Ciontach,* not given.

Canteen, *gainthiú,* sandy.

Cantra, *ceann-trá,* not given.

Canty, *cáinte,* dispraised places(sic).

Canty, *Cheantaigh,* not given.

Canty, *na-Cáintigh/cheantaigh,* not given.

Canty, *Uí-Chainte,* O'Canty, a family name.

Canuig, *ceannúigh, ceanbhaidh,* not given.

Canvan, *Uí-Cheannabhainn,* O'Canavan, a family name.

Canway, *ceann-a'mhaighe,* head of the plain.

Canway, *Conbhaidhe,* not given.

Cap, *caipigh, caipche,* not given.

Cap, *ceap,* a plot, a tillage plot.

Cap, *ceap,* a stake, stock or tree trunk.

Cap, from *ceap,* stakes.

Capanagh, *copanach,* abounding in dock leaves.

Capard, *ceap-ard,* high tree trunk or stake.

Capeen, *chaipín,* a little hood or cap.

Capel (Island), *oileán-na-gCapall, an-tOileán-so-amuigh,* not given.

Caplevane, *ceapaigh-an-leamháin,* not given.

Capewell, *tobar-an-chaipín,* not given.

Capna, *ceapa-na…,* plot of the…

Capogue, *ceapóg,* a little plot.

Capp, *ceap,* a plot, a tillage plot.

Cappa, *ceapa, cheapach, ceapach,* a plot of land, a tillage plot, a clearance plot, wood clearance or cutaway wood.

Cappa, *ceapaí,* not given.

Cappa, *ceap-an…,* not given.

Cappagh, *an-cheapóg/cheapaigh,* not given.

Cappagh, *ceapa, cheapach, ceapach,* a plot of land, land under cultivation or a tillage plot.

Cappagh, *ceapach,* clearance or cut away wood.

Cappagh, *ceapaí, ceapain,* little plots.

Cappagha, *ceapacha,* tillage plots.

Cappan, *ceapach/capach-an…,* clearance, tillage plot of the…

Cappana, *ceapach-na…,* clearing/clearance or plot of the…

Cappanilly, *capach-na-hÉileach,* not given.

Cappard, *ceapa-árd,* not given.

Cappass, *crochta-an-cheapaigh*(sic), not given.

Cappass, *ceapacha,* tillage plots.

Cappaugh, *ceapach,* a plot of land.

Cappauniac, *an-cheapach*(sic), not given.

Cappauniack, *ceapa-Uniac,* Uniac's (a personal or family name) plot.

Cappeen, *caipchin,* cleared wood or a hill crest.

Cappeen, *caipin, caipín,* the cap.

Cappel, *chapaill,* the horse.

Capper, *ceapach,* a plot (of land).

Capple, *capuill, gCapail, chapaill,* horse/s.

Capple, *capaill,* not given.

Cappo, *ceapa, ceapach, ceapain,* a tillage plot or just a plot of land.

Cappo, *ceapach,* a tillage plot.

Cappock, *an-Cheapógaigh,* not given.

Cappog, *an-cheapóg,* not given.

Cappog, *ceapa, ceapach, ceapain,* a plot of land.

Cappoge, *ceapa, ceapach, ceapain,* a plot of land.

Cappoge, *cheapóg, ceapóg,* not given.

Cappry, *cabragh,* roughland.

Cappul, *capaill, capuill, gCapail, chapail, chapaill,* horse/s.

Cappy, *ceapa, ceapaigh, ceapach, ceapain,* a plot of land or a tillage plot.

Cappy, *ceapaighe,* not given.

Cappyan, *ceapa-an…,* plot of the…

Cappyan, *ceapach-an…,* plot of the…

Cappyroe, *ceapach-Aodha-rua,* not given.

Capragh, *an-chabrach,* not given.

Capragh, *cabragh,* rubbish.

Capullagh, *Cabla,* not given.

Capullagh, from *capull,* horsey(sic).

Car, *cairr, chairr,* a rock, rocks or a rocky surface.

Car, *caraidh, cara,* not given.

Car, *carr,* a rock.

Car, *cárrthadh, cairthe,* a piller stone.

Car, *ceardcha, ceardhchan,* a forge or workshop.

Car, *ceathramh,* quarter (of land).

Car, *chairthe,* a standing stone.

Car, *Charthaigh, Cartach,* St Cartha, Carthach or Carthach, a persons name.

Car, *Charthaigh, Chartha, Carthaigh, chárthaighe,* not given.

Car, *Chathraigh, Cathrach,* not given.

Car, *chora, caradh,* a weir.

Car, *gCarr,* cars.

Car, *Uí-Carthaigh, O'Carthy, a family name.*

Cara, *caoirigh,* sheep.

Cara, *ceathra,* a quarry.

Cara, *chara, coradh, choraidh,* a weir.

Carabine, from *carbad,* chariot.

Caradh, *coradh, corra, cuarr,* a weir.

Caragh, *catharach,* a stone rampart or stone fort.

Caragh, *Carthach,* St Carthach.

Caragh, *charrthaigh, Catharach, chathach, Cárthaighe, Cárthaí, Chathrach, cathrach,* not given.

Caragh, *chárthaighe, cartaidhe,* rocky.

Caran, *caraun,* a rocky place.

Caran, *carran,* rocky land or a reaping hook.

Caran, *carrán,* rocky land.

Caran, *chairn,* a carn or grave monument.

Carana, *carn,* a monumental heap of stones.

Caranadoe, *caradh-na-dtuath,* weir of the (three) districts.

Caraun, a round abrupt hillock, a rocky hillock or a rocky place.

Caraun, *cárán, corrán,* not given.

Carbad, *carbad,* chariot.

Carbadagh, *carbadach, gCarbadach,* chariots.

Carban, *Carbain,* Carban a family name now called Corbett.

Carban, *Corbain, Carbáin,* not given.

Carbat, *carbait,* chariot.

Carbery, *Cairbre/Cairbre Aebhdh,* a son of Niall of the nine hostages.

Carbery, *Cairbrigh, Cairbre,* not given.

Carbery, *Ó-gCairbre/gCaibre,* O'Carbre, a family name.

Carbery, *Uí-Cáirbre,* O'Carbery, a family name.

Carbet, *carbad,* a jaw.

Carbine, *gCarbad,* not given.

Carbit, *carboid,* a chariot.

Carbry, Carbery, a personal or family name.

Carbry, *Chairbre,* Cairbre, a personal or family name.

Carbry, *Ó-gCairbre,* Uí Chairbre/ O'Cairbre, a family name.

Carbury, *Cairbre/Cairbre-Aebhdh,* a barony and the name of a son of Niall of the nine hostages.

Carbury, *Cairbre-Ó-gCiardha, Cairbre-dhroma-cliabh,* not given.

Carcair, *carcair,* a prison.

Carclunty, *ceathramhadh-cluainteach,* meadowy quarter.

Card, *ceard,* a smith, artificer or craftsman.

Card, *ceardcha,* the forge.

Card, *chearda,* not given.

Card, *gCeardcha,* forges or workshops.

Cardan, *Cárdáin,* a male name.

Cardan, *Cárdáin,* not given.

Cardeen, *cheardchain,* a small forge.

Cardon, *Cárdáin,* a male name.

Cardy, *gCeardacha,* forges.

Careen, *careen,* the little rock.

Careen, *chair-fhiadhín,* small wild deer.

Careen, *chairthín,* a pillar stone.

Careigh, *chairrfhiadh,* deer or a stag.

Carew, *ceathru, ceathramhadh, cheathrú,* a quarter of land.

Carey, (river) *cathraighe,* not given.

Carey, *carrtha,* the rock.

Carey, *cairthe,* a standing stone.

Carga, *cairge,* a rock.

Cargagh, *cairgeacha,* rocks or rocklands.

Cargagh, *carraig,* a rock or rocky.

Cargagh, *charraigeach,* not given.

Cargan, *cairgín, carraigín,* little rock.

Cargans, *cairrgin,* (with the English plural letter 's'), little rocks.

Cargin, *cairrgin,* not given.

Cargin, *carraigín,* little rock.

Cargy, *cairrge, carraige, carraig,* a rock.

Cargy, *cairrge,* rocks.

Cargy, *charraige,* not given.

Carha, *cairthe, chairthe,* a pillar stone.

Carha, *chartha, cartha,* not given.

Carhagh, *carrach,* rocky.

Carhan, *chartain, caorthann, carthan,* quicken trees, mountain ash, quicken trees or rowan trees.

Carhan, *charthainn,* a rowan tree plantation.

Carhanduff, *charna-duibh,* not given.

Carheen, *cairthín,* rocky land, a little stone fort or a stony ford.

Carheen, *caithrín,* not given.

Carheen, *cathairín,* a little caher.

Carheen, from *cairthín,* a little rock, rocky lands, little stone forts or stony fords.

Carheeny, *caithríní, cairthínidhe,* little rocks, rocky lands, little stone forts or stony fords.

Carheeny, *caithríní,* little stone forts.

Carhen, *carthann,* the rowan tree.

Carhoo, *ceathramhadh, ceathramha, an-ceathru,* a quarter of land.

Carhoo, *ceathrú-gharbh,* not given.

Carhoon, *ceathramhadh, ceathramha,* a quarter of land.

Carhoona, *ceathramha-na...,* quarter land of the...

Carhoona, *ceathramhna,* quarter acre plots or land quarters.

Carhoona, *ceathrúna,* not given.

Carhoonoe, new quarter.

Carhoway, *ceathrámhadh,* Hughs quarter.

Carhu, quarters.

Carhue, *ceathramhadh,* a quarter of land.

Carig, *carraig,* the rock.

Carigan, *carriage,* a rock.

Cark, *cearc, gCearc,* grouse, domestic hens or grouse hens.

Carker, *carcar, carcair,* prison.

Carker, *charcair, carcrach,* not given.

Carew, *an-cheathrú,* not given.

Carkey, *cairce,* oats.

Carkoge, *cearcóg,* grouse hens, a little hen or grouse hen.

Carks, *cearc* (with the English plural letter 's'), hens.

Carky, *chairce,* oats.

Carlan, Carlan, Carlin or Carolan, a personal or family name.

Carlan, *carlan,* rocky land.

Carland, *carrlann,* not given.

Carland, *Domhnach-carr,* Church on rocky land.

Carlin, *Caireallain,* Carlin or Carolan, a personal or family name.

Carling, *Cairlinn,* a male name.

Carlingford, *Cairlinn,* not given.

Carlingford, *cairlinn-fjórthr,* (Irish and Norse) hags bay. The previous name was *snamh-aighnech, snámh-each,* horses swimming ford.

Carlingford, *Kerling Fjorthr,* (Norse), the ford of the hag.

Carlow, *an-cheatharlach,* not given.

Carlow, *cathair-lach, catharlach,* city or fort of the lake or river.

Carlow, *ceatharlach, cheatharlaigh,* abounding in cattle.

Carlow, *cathair-lach,* fort of the lake or river.

Carlow, *ceatharlach, ceatharloch, cetherloch,* the quadruple lake or the four lakes.

Carlow, *ceithiorlach,* the quadruple lake.

Carman, *Cormáin,* not given.

Carmavy, *cairthe-muighe-bhó,* not given.

Carmavy, *carn-Méibhe,* Maeve's (a womans name) cairn.

Carn, *Cairnigh,* not given.

Carn, *carn,* a cairn-like hill.

Carn, *carn, chairn, charn, ghairn, carna, cairn,* a heap of stones usually an ancient monument, burial or grave-pile.

Carn, *ceithearn, ceitheirne,* lightly armed foot soldiers also called 'Kerns'.

Carna, *carna,* a monumental heap of stones.

Carna, *carna,* cairns or monumental heaps of stones.

Carna, *carnán,* a small mound.

Carna, *corr/cara-na...,* not given.

Carna, *carn-na...,* carn of the...

Carna, *carraig-na...,* rock of the...

Carnagarve, *carn-garbh,* not given.

Carnagh, carnach, a place of carns or heaps.

Carnaghagh, *carn-Eathach* Eochy's (a male name) 'carn' or monumental heap of stones or cairn of the kiln.

Carnaghan, *Mhic-Chearnachain,* MacKernaghan, a family name.

Carnahan, *Uí-Chearnachain,* Ó Cearnacháin, O'Carnahan or Kernahan, a family name.

Carnahaugh, *carn-Eathach,* Eochy's (a male name) 'carn' or monumental heap of stones or cairn of the kiln.

Carnaman, *cearnabhán,* hornets.

Carnan, *carnán, carnain, carnan,* a little monumental heap of stones.

Carnan, *charnáin, charnain, carnán,* a little carn, a heap or a monumental heap.

Carnane, *an-carnán,* the little heap.

Carnane, *carnan,* a monumental heap of stones.

Carnane, *charnáin,* not given.

Carnane, from *carn,* little carns.

Carnanee, *carnán-Aodha, carnan-Aedha,* Hugh's, Aodh's or Aedh's (a male name) little carn or monumental heap of stones/grave pile.

Carnaun, *carnán,* a little heap of stones or a high stony place.

Carnaun, from *carn,* a little carn or carns.

Carnave, *carn-naomh,* carn of the saints.

Carnave, *carn-cnámha,* the cairn of the bones.

Carnavy, *carn-Mhéabha,* Maeve carn.

Carne, *carna,* not given.

Carne, *chairn, cairn,* a monumental heap of stones.

Carnee, a limestone carn, a monumental heap of limestones.

Carneety, *carn-Fhaoite,* White's (a family name) carn.

Carnew, *carn-an-bhua,* the cairn of victory.

Carnew, *carn-bhuadha,* not given.

Carnew, *carn-Naoi,* Naoi's carn.

Carney, a cairn.

Carney, *cairne, carnaigh, Charnaí, Cearna, Carnaí, Cearnaigh,* not given.

Carney, *carn-Aedha/Aodha,* Aedh's, Aodh's or Hugh's (a male name) carn.

Carney, *Carnaigh,* a personal or family name.

Carney, *carnaigh,* a place of lumps.

Carney, Carney, a family name.

Carney, *Cearnach,* a personal or family name.

Carney, *cearnach,* victorious.

Carney, *cethern,* lightly armed foot soldiers.

Carney, *fearann-Uí-Chearnaigh,* not given.

Carney, *Uí-Chearnaigh/Catharnaigh,* Ó Cearnaigh or O'Carney, a family name.

Carney, *Uí-Cheithearnaigh/Chearnaigh,* Kearney or O'Kearney, a family name.

Carngarrow, *carn-garbhdhoire,* not given.

Carnhill, *gort*(sic)*-an-chairn,* not given.

Carnlough, *carnlach,* abounding in cairns.

Carnsore, *ceann-an-chairn,* headland of the cairn.

Carny, *camíath,* crooked land.

Carny, *Uí-Chearnaigh,* Ó Cearnaigh, a personal or family name.

Carolina, *corr-Leannáin,* not given.

Carpey, *Cairpthe,* not given.

Carr, a lone standing rock.

Carra, (lake) *ceara,* weir.

Carra, an ancient territory.

Carra, *cairthe, cairrthe,* a standing stone.

Carra, *cara,* the leg.

Carra, *cartha,* a rock or heap.

Carra, *carra,* stepping stones or a causeway.

Carra, *carrach,* a rough rugged place or a rocky place.

Carra, *carraic, charrach, charra,* rocky or rough surface.

Carra, *Ceara,* the name of a barony.

Carra, *ceathramhadh, ceathrú,* a quarter.

Carra, *ceathrú, ceathramha, ceathrún, charraigh, chatharaigh, cheathrú, cheathrúin,* not given.

Carra, *chairthe,* a pillar stone.

Carra, *chartha,* a rock.

Carra, *coraidh, caradh, cora, cara,* a weir or dam.

Carra, *corrach,* not given.

Carra, *garbh,* rough.

Carrabaun, Carban or Corban, a family name.

Carrag, a rock.
Carragaun, *carragán,* little rock.
Carragaun, *carragán,* rocky land.
Carrageen, *charraigín,* not given.
Carragh, *Caithreach, ceárach, charrach,* not given.
Carragh, *carach, carrach,* rough or scabby.
Carragh, *carach,* stones or hillocks.
Carragh, *carrach,* rough land.
Carragh, *carrach,* rough or rugged.
Carragh, crooked.
Carragh, *cathrach,* a circular stone fort.
Carragh, St. Carthach.
Carraghs, *cairrtheacha,* rocks or rocky land.
Carraghy, *carr-achaidh,* stony field.
Carrah, *carrach,* rough.
Carrahan, *carrachán,* rocky ground.
Carrahan, *carrachanh*(sic), rough ground.
Carrahane, *carrachán,* rocky ground.
Carraig, *cairrge, carraig,* a rock.
Carran, *cairn, carn,* a monumental heap of stones.
Carran, *charainn,* a rock pile.
Carran, *carn-an...,* not given.
Carran, *carrán, carran,* a reaping hook, stony or rocky land.
Carran, *chorráin, cruán, carann, chairn,* not given.
Carran, *chorráin,* an angle (of land).
Carran, *corrán,* uneven land.
Carran, *corrán, corran,* a curved mountain or shaped like a reaping hook.
Carran, *Uí-Carrain,* O'Carran, a family name.
Carrane, *Uí-Carrain,* O'Carran, a family name.
Carrane, *Uí-Chorráin,* Ó Corráin, a family name.
Carranroe, *an-chruan-rua*(sic), not given.
Carraun, *currán, carrán,* a reaping hook.
Carraun, *charrain, carran,* rocky land or a reaping hook.
Carraun, *chorráin,* not given.
Carravort, *garbhghort,* rough field.
Carrea, *chairrfhiaidh,* not given.
Carreen, *catharín, chaithrín, caithrín,* little caher or stone fort.
Carren, *Uí-Chairín,* not given.
Carrible, *charbaid,* the chariot.
Carrible, *charbaill,* not given.

Carrichue, *carraig-Aodha,* Aodh's or Hugh's (a mans name) rock.
Carrick, a corruption of *carra, caradh,* a weir.
Carrick, *carraig-an-ringce*(sic), not given.
Carrick, *charraig, charrig, cairrge, carraig,* a rock.
Carricka, *carraig,* rock.
Carricka, *carraig-an/a'...,* rock of the...
Carricka, *carraigheach, carraigeach,* a rocky place.
Carricka, *carraigigh,* not given.
Carrickallan, *carraig-Challáin,* not given.
Carrickan, *carraig-an...,* rock of the...
Carrickane, *carragán,* little rock.
Carrickaneagh, *carraig-Ó nEitheach,* not given.
Carrickeeny, *carraig-aonagh,* rock of the fair.
Carrickinab, *carraig-an-abbadh,* rock of the abbot.
Carrickittle, *carraig-Chiotal,* not given.
Carrick-on-Shannon, *cara/cora-droma-rúisc,* weir of the ridge of the bark(sic).
Carrickybegraly, *carraig-Uí-Mhic-Gréalaigh*(sic), not given.
Carrido, *caradog,* a welsh settler.
Carridoge, *caradog,* a Welsh settler.
Carridoge, *charadóg,* not given.
Carridogue, *caradog,* a Welsh settler.
Carrie, *caraidh,* the weir.
Carrig, *cairrge, carraic, carraig,* a rock.
Carrig, *carraig,* a rocky place.
Carrig, *charraig, charraige,* not given.
Carriga, *cairrge*(sic), *carrigaige*(sic), *carraige, carraig,* a rock.
Carriga, *carraig-a...,* rock of...
Carriga, *carraig-an...,* rock of the...
Carriga, *carriage,* rock/s.
Carrigagh, *charraigeach, carraigeach,* full of rocks or rocky land.
Carrigaloe, *carraig-an-lua,* not given.
Carrigan, *carraig-an...,* rock of the...
Carrigan, *charraigín, carraigeáin, carraigín,* little rock.
Carrigan, *carragán,* a hill composed of rock.
Carriganagh, *currach-an-feadha/fheadha,* marsh of the rush or rushes.
Carriganagh, *currach-an-fheá,* not given.

Carrigane, carrachan, rough land.

Carrigane, carraigín, a little rock or a small rocky place.

Carrigane, carrigáin, carragan, not given.

Carriganes, carragáin, little rocks (with the English plural letter 's').

Carrigans, an-carraigín, the little rock.

Carrigans, gaoth-an-chairrgín, not given.

Carrigans, na-carraigíní, not given.

Carrigart, ceathru-Fhiodhghoirt, quarter (a land measurment) of the wood of the field.

Carrigatna, carraig-an-tná, not given.

Carrigaun, carragán, charragáin, not given.

Carrigaun, carraigeán, carraigín, a small rocky place.

Carrigaun, carraigán, little rock.

Carrigawn, charrágáin, little rock/s.

Carrigeen, carraigín, a small rock or rocky place.

Carrageen, charraigín, not given.

Carrigeena, carraigín-na…, rock of the…

Carrigeenamronety, carraigín-na-mbróinte, little rock of the mill stones.

Carrigeenna, carraigín-na…, rock of the…

Carrigeeny, carraigini, carraigínidhe, little rocks or land of the little rocks.

Carrigeeveen, carriage-aoibhinn, beautiful rock.

Carrigenagh, carraigíneach, full of small rocks.

Carriggal, an-charraig-gheal, not given.

Carriglinneen, carraig-glinnín, not given.

Carrigna, carraig-na…, rock of the…

Carrignafoy, carraig-Neimhidh, carraig-an-eich-bhuidhe, not given.

Carrignanonshagh, carraig-na-nÓinseach, rock of the female idiots.

Carrigunane, carraig-Guináin, Guinan, a personal or family name.

Carrigy, carraige, cairrge, carraig, a rock.

Carrin, chairn, a cairn.

Carrive, ceathramhadh, ceathrama, ceathramha, a quarter.

Carrivetragh, ceathramha-iochtrach, lower quarter (of land).

Carrivetragh, cheathrú-Iochtarach, not given.

Carrogher, ceathramhadh-Ruaidhrí, Rory's quarter.

Carrogs, from *car*, little rocks.

Carroll, Carbhail, St Carbhail.

Carroll, Cearbhaill, not given.

Carroll, Cearúill, Carroll, a family name.

Carroll, Chearúill, Cearbhall, a personal or family name.

Carroll, Chearúill, Cearúill, a personal or family name.

Carroll, Uí-Chearúill/ Chearbhaill, Ua-Chearbhaill, O'Carroll, a family name.

Carron, Cairín, Carew, a male name.

Carron, Carann, Cáirthinn, Carainn, Charúin, not given.

Carron, carn, carron, a cairn or monumental heap of stones.

Carron, carráin, a hook or a reaping hook.

Carron, Charrúin, Carron, a personal or family name.

Carrona, carn-na…, not given.

Carronahyla, carn-na-hAidhle, carn of the adze.

Carrons, na-cairne, not given.

Carroon, Carrún, Charrún, Carew, a male name.

Carroona, Carúine, Carew, a personal or family name.

Carroona, Charrúnaigh, not given.

Carroons, na-cairne, the heaps.

Carrow, caradh, fishing-weirs.

Carrow, caraidh, coraidh, cora, cara, a weir.

Carrow, ceathramhadh, a townland(sic).

Carrow, ceathremhadh, a pasture.

Carrow, ceathrú, ceathru, ceathramha, ceathramhadh, a quarter of land.

Carrow, cheathrú, charaidh, charadh, not given.

Carrow, chora, caradh, not given.

Carrow, cora, a fish dam.

Carrow, gharbh, rough.

Carrowan, ceathramhadh-an…, a quarter or subdivision of land of the…

Carrowbarra, ceathrú-bhó-Bhearach, not given.

Carrowea, cheathrú/ceathramha-Aodha, Hugh's (a personal or a family name) quarter.

Carrowen, ceathramha-abhann, river quarter.

Carrowen, ceathramhadh-an…, quarter of the…

Carrowena, *ceathramhadh-oenach,* a fair green.

Carroweragh, *ceathramhadh-riabhac,* a brown division.

Carrowkeelanahaglass, *ceathramha-caol-an-atha-glaise,* narrow quarter of the green ford.

Carrown, *ceathramhadh/cheathrú/ceathru/ceathramha-'n/na…,* quarter land of the…

Carrown, *ceathrú-an…,* not given.

Carrowna, *ceathramha-na…,* quarter of the…

Carrownagh, *ceathramhnach,* land divided into quarters.

Carrownea, *ceathramha-an-fheadha,* quarter of the wood.

Carrownycleire, *ceathramhadh-na-Cleir,* property of the Clergy(sic).

Carru, *ceathrú, ceathramhadh,* a quarter (of land).

Carrueragh, *ceathrú-iartharach,* the western quarter.

Carry, crooked.

Carry, *cairthe,* a standing stone.

Carry, *carra, cora, coradh, choraidh,* a weir or dam.

Carry, *ceathrú, ceathramha,* a quarter.

Carry, *chairthe,* not given.

Carry, *currach,* a marsh.

Carry, *garrdha,* a garden.

Carryduff, *ceathrú-Aodha-Dhuibh,* not given.

Carsan, *casán,* not given.

Carsan, *cosán,* a path.

Cart, *cearda, ceardcha,* a workshop or forge.

Cart, *gCart,* carts.

Cart, *gCeart,* rights.

Cart, *na-ceárta,* not given.

Carta, *ceardcha,* a forge.

Carta, *ceárdchan,* a smithy.

Cartan, *ceardchan, ceardcan, ceardacht, ceardcha,* a forge.

Cartan, *ceártan,* not given.

Carte, *ceárta,* not given.

Carter, *cairte,* of the cart.

Cartha, *ceardtan,* a forge.

Carthage, *Carthaigh,* not given.

Carthy, *cairthe,* a pillar stone.

Carthy, *Cairtigh,* not given.

Cartin, *ceártan, ceártan,* a forge.

Cartlan, *Cartlann,* not given.

Carton, *baile-an-choirthe,* not given.

Carton, *Cartáin,* Carton, a personal name.

Carton, *cartún,* (Anglo-Norman) a quarter.

Carton, *cearda, ceardcha, ceardchan,* a workshop or forge.

Carton, *ceártan,* not given.

Carton, *Chartáin,* Cartan, a personal or family name.

Cartoor, *cartron,* a quarter of land.

Cartron, *cart,* a 4th part of a land division.

Cartron, *cartron,* quarter-land.

Cartron, *cartrún, cartún, cartramhan, chartrúin, an-leathchartúr,* not given.

Cartron, *cartúr(sic), ceathramhain,* and also an Anglo Norman/French word (*quarteron*) meaning a quarter of land.

Cartron, *chartrun,* Anglo Norman term for a measure of land between 60 and 160 acres.

Cartrona, *cartron-na…,* quarter-land of the…

Carty, *cairte,* a cart.

Carty, *cairthe,* a piller stone.

Carty, *Carhtach,* St Carthach.

Carty, *ceardcha,* a forge.

Carty, *Charthaich,* McCarthy, a family name.

Casarnagh, from *casar,* a place of paths.

Casaun, *casán,* a path.

Casaunna, *casán-na…,* path of the…

Cascan, *Chascain,* St Cascan.

Case, *catha,* a battle.

Casey, *Chathasach, Chathasaigh,* Casey, a family name.

Casey, from *ceis,* a little wickerwork causeway.

Casey, *Uí-Chathaisa,* the guard or sentinal(sic).

Casey, *Uí-Chathasaigh,* Ó Cathasaigh, a family name.

Cash, *caise,* noisy.

Cash, *cas,* twisted.

Cash, *ceis,* a wicker-causeway.

Cash, *Chais, Cais, Cas, Cass* a personal name and the name of a Church founder in Tipperary.

Cash, *Cais, Cass,* a personal or family name.

Cash, *Chaise,* not given.

Casha, *coise,* the foot or bottom land.

Cashan, *casán,* the path.

Cashaw, *cois-abha,* district along the river.

Casheen, *caise,* a stream

Casheen, *Caisín, Uí-Caisín,* O'Cashen, a family name.

Cashel, *caiseal, chaisil, cashel,* a circular stone fort.

Cashel, *caiseal,* heaps or clamps.

Cashel, *caisil,* a stone fort.

Cashel, *cias-ail,* rent rock.

Cashel, *cis-ail,* tribute rent.

Cashelin, *caiseal-Fhinn,* Finn, a personal or family name.

Cashelisky, *caise-liath-uisce,* butterwort stream.

Cashelisky, *caise-loiscthe,* burnt stream.

Cashelisky, *caise-luska,* stream of the cave.

Cashelna, *caiseal-na....,* the round stone fort of the...

Cashen, *gCosán,* path.

Cashen, *Uí-Caisín,* O'Cashen, a family name.

Cashin, *Chaisín,* not given.

Cashin, *Uí-Chaisín, Ó Caisín,* a personal or family name.

Cashin, *Caisin,* Caissin, a personal or family name.

Cashin, *Caisne,* Caisne, a personal or family name.

Cashl, *caiseal,* a stone fort.

Cashla, *caisle,* a stream.

Cashla, *chaisle,* not given.

Cashla, *chasla,* the inlet.

Cashla, *chasla,* the sea inlet.

Cashlagh, *caisleach,* stone forts.

Cashlan, *caisléan,* not given.

Cashlan, *chaisleáin, caislen* a castle.

Cashlane, *caisleán,* a castle.

Cashlane, *chaisleáin, caislen,* a castle.

Cashlaun, *chaisleáin, chaisleán, caisleáin, caislen,* a castle.

Cashlieve, *cas-sliabh,* twisted mountain.

Cashlings, *caislini,* not given.

Cask, *Caisc, Casca, Cásc,* easter.

Cask, *Cásca, Casc,* not given.

Cask, *cásg, cásc, caisc, cáisc,* Easter.

Caska, *cáisc,* Easter.

Caska, *Cásca,* easter.

Caskan, *Cascán,* not given.

Caskan, *Chascain,* St Cascan.

Caskin, *Cháiscín, Cáiscín,* the name of a Church founder in Limerick.

Caslagh, an inlet.

Caslagh, *caisleach,* stone forts.

Caslain, *caisleain,* a castle.

Caslan, *caisleáin,* a castle.

Caslan, *chaislín,* not given.

Caslanan, *caisleán-an...,* castle beside the....

Caslaugh, *caslach,* a creek.

Caslough, *caslach,* a creek.

Casorna, *caisbhearna,* not given.

Cass, *Cais,* not given.

Cass, *cas,* twisted.

Cassa, *ceasach,* a causeway.

Cassa, *chasa,* not given.

Cassagh, *ceasach,* a wickerwork causeway.

Cassagh, *ceasach,* a corduroy(sic) road.

Cassagh, *cheasach,* not given.

Cassagh, *gCeiseach,* causeways.

Cassan, *caisín,* not given.

Cassan, *cosán, casáin, chasáin,* a path or pathway.

Cassaun, *cosán,* a track.

Casses, *O'Casaig,* Cass, a family name.

Cassidy, *Uí-Caiside/Chaiside/Chaiside, Ó Caiside,* Cassidy or O'Cassidy, a family name and means the descendants of Caiside.

Casslagh, *caslach,* an inlet.

Casslagh, *caslach,* weak.

Casta, *Casta,* not given.

Caster, *castra,* conflagration.

Castle, *caiseal, cashel,* a circular stone fort.

Castle, *ceasail, chaisil, caisle, chaisleáin, caislean,* a castle.

Castle, *cos-a...,* the foot of...

Castleaffy, *caiseal-Laithmhe,* Laffy's (a family name) castle.

Castlebar, *Caislen-an-Barraich,* castle of the Barrys.

Castleblaney, *baile-an-lorgan,* not given.

Castleconor, *caislean-Mic-Chonchobhair,* Mac-Conor's (a personal or a family name) castle.

Castlecove, *an-siopa-dubh,* not given.

Castledermot, *Caisleán-díseart-Diarmada/ disert-Diarmada,* Castle of Dermot's or Diarmaid's (a mans name) hermitage.

Castledillon, *disert-Iolladhan,* Iolladhan's hermitage.

Castleforward, *cuil-Mhic-an-treoin,* recess of the son of the strong man.

Castlekeeran, *disert-Chiaran,* St Kieran's hermitage.

Castlering, *caisleán-Fhraing,* not given.

Castletownarra, *baile-an-chaisleáin,* not given.

Cat, *cait, cuit, cat,* a cat.

Cat, *chait,* a wild cat.

Cat, *cath,* a battle.

Cath, *cath,* a battle.

Cathair, *cathair,* a round stone fort.

Cathaleen, *cathailín,* a small gap.

Catherach, *cathrach,* the tribal city, (west Cork usage).

Catherine, *Ceathigheirn,* not given.

Catherine, *Chaitighearn,* St Caithighearn, a 6th century Bishop.

Cattan, *Chatáin, catán,* not given.

Cattan, *caitan,* cats.

Catteen, *caitín,* osier blossoms.

Catteen, *choitín,* cotton.

Catteens, *choitchínídhe,* commonages.

Cattry, *Catraighe,* not given.

Catty, *carrig,* rock.

Cau, *catha,* not given.

Caugh, *gadhach,* dangerous.

Caugher, *cathar,* a stone fort.

Cauhoo, *cathadh,* winnowing.

Caulfield, *Cathmhaoil,* Cawel, a personal or family name.

Cauly, Macauley, a family name.

Caum, *cám, cam,* winding, crooked, bent or curved.

Caumaglanna, *Chamghleanna,* not given.

Caummery, *cam-eirghe,* crooked hill.

Cauna, *cána,* tribute.

Cauneen, *cáinín,* little tribute.

Cauneen, *chainin,* not given.

Caunteens, from *cáintín,* little worthless spots of land.

Caura, *Cárthaigh,* not given.

Caura, *Chárthaigh,* Carthy, a personal or family name.

Cauran, *cáran, cárran,* rocky land.

Caurans, from *cáran, cárran,* rocky lands.

Caurha, *cáirt,* a large flat stone.

Caurhin, *cárthainn, chaorthainn,* quicken trees mountain ash or rowan trees.

Caushel, *chaisil,* a castle or stone fort.

Causk, *cásc, cásca, cásg, cáisc,* Easter.

Causkeen, *caiscin,* dried grain.

Cauteen, *caithtín,* a small winnowing sheet.

Cauteen, *an-coitín,* not given.

Cautheen, *coitchen, coitchionn,* a common or common land.

Cavan, *cabhain, cabhán, cabhan,* a round hill, a hollow or a round hollow place.

Cavan, *cabhan,* (from Drumcavan) a field.

Cavan, *Caomhan, Caemhan,* St Kevan.

Cavan, *chabháin, chabhán, Caomhán,* not given.

Cavan, *Cháomháin, Caemhain,* Caomhán or Kevan, a male name.

Cavan, *an-cabhán,* the four lakes(sic).

Cavana, *cabhán…, cabhan-na…* round hill of the…

Cavana, *cabhan-an…,* hollow of the…

Cavanagh, *cabhanach,* abounding in small hills.

Cavany, *cabhánach, cabhanach,* abounding in small hills.

Cave, *céibh,* long grass that grows in morasses.

Cavemount, *maol-locha,* not given.

Cavey, *ciabhach, ciabhaigh,* long grass that grows in morasses.

Cavil, *Cathmhaoil,* Caveel or Campbell, a personal or family name.

Caw, *cáth, cáith, cáithe, chátha, gcorr*(sic), chaff.

Caw, *cath, chatha, catha, cau,* battle.

Cawha, *catha,* battle.

Cawha, *catha,* seaspray.

Cawran, *carrán,* rocky land.

Caynty, *cáinte,* dispraised places(sic).

Cealldra, infants burial place.

Cealtra, *Cealtrach,* a personal or family name.

Cealtra, *Cealtrach,* Churches.

Cean, *ceann,* a head.

Ceanna, *ceann-an…,* hill top of the…

Cearmna, *Cearmna, Cearmna,* the name of an ancient Princess.

Cearta, a forge.

Ceary, *Chiadha,* O'Carey, a family name.

Ceera, *caoire, caor,* a lump or round mass.

Ceera, *chaor,* a big round hill.

Ceery, *Ciar,* a personal or family name.

Cel, *Cill,* a Church or a burying place.

Cella, *sailigh,* sallows.

Cellchattigern, *Chaitighearn,* St Caithighearn, a 6th century Bishop.

Chaff, *catha,* the battle.

Chaff, *cáithe,* not given.

Chair, *chathaoire,* not given.

Chaislaun, *chaisleán,* a castle.

Chala, *chaladh,* not given.

Challa, *an-chalaidh,* not given.

Challa, *cala, chaladh, chala,* a callow, wet meadow or landing place.

Challa, stone buildings.

Challow, *chalaidh,* not given.

Chally, *cala, chala,* a callow, wet meadow or landing place.

Chally, *chala, cala, caladh,* a ferry or a boat landing place.

Chamlough, *chamlocha,* the crooked lake.

Chamoyle, *chathmhaoil,* Caveel or Campbell, a personal or family name.

Chan, Cathan, a personal or family name.

Chanon, *gCanónach,* canons.

Chanonrock(sic), *carraig-na-gCanónach,* not given.

Chapel, *Séipéal, Seipeal,* a Chapel.

Chara, *carra,* a weir.

Charleville, *ráithín/ráth-lúisc, an-rath, baile-an-ghleantúnaigh,* not given.

Charley, *siarralach,* broom.

Charn, *cairn,* a heap of stones usually an ancient monument, burial or a grave-pile of stones.

Charnaun, *charnáin,* the little cairn.

Charra, *chairrthe,* the rock.

Charra, *chora, chartha,* not given.

Charroe, *ceathramhadh,* a quarter.

Charroo, *ceathramhadh,* a quarter.

Charry, *charaidh,* not given.

Charvey, *chearrbhaigh,* a gamester.

Charvy, *chearrbhaigh,* a gamester or gambler.

Chary, *choraidh, coradh, corra, cora, choradh,* a weir.

Chatsworth, *achadh-tiobrad,* not given.

Chaulig, *cháithlig, caithleach, caithlighe,* chaff.

Checkpoint, *loch-na-síge,* not given.

Chee, *chaoigh,* the half blind man.

Cheek, *síge,* a streak.

Cheek, *síge, sheega, sige,* fairies.

Cheesemount, *cnocán-na-Cáise,* not given.

Chemalter, *bun-cimeálta,* a type of bottom land.

Cheo, *cheoigh, ceo,* fog, mist or haze.

Chetwynd, *baile-an-ghalláin,* not given.

Chevy Chase, *doire-na-darach*(sic), not given.

Chiel, *chuill,* not given.

Chill, *choill,* not given.

Chill, *Cill,* a Church.

Chilla, *coille,* a wood.

Chilly, *Cille,* the Church.

Chirn, *crainn,* tree.

Chirn, *cruinn,* round.

Chluch, a building.

Choe, *chuach,* cuckoos.

Choe, *chuaiche,* a hollow.

Chole, *cheóil,* not given.

Cholea, *chuaille,* a pole or trunk.

Cholla, *chalaidh,* not given.

Cholly, *Chalbhaigh,* Calbhaigh or Calvagh, a personal or family name.

Chon, *chon,* hounds.

Chona, *chonaidh,* firewood.

Choney, *conna, chonaidh,* firewood.

Chonna, *chonaidh,* firewood.

Choosaun, *chuasáin,* a little cave.

Choosh, *cuas,* a cave.

Chor, *choradh,* a weir.

Chor, *gCorr,* cranes or herons.

Chorca, a marsh.

Chork, *chuirc,* a marsh.

Chorka, *choirce,* not given.

Chorran, *cor,* a round or stony hill.

Chorrib, *Chorb,* not given.

Chory, *chuaraidhe,* brogue makers.

Chory, *coire, choire,* a cauldren like pit or a hollow.

Chose, *chuais,* the cave.

Chree, heart shaped.

Chreena, *chríonaig,* firewood.

Chreer, *criathar,* sieves.

Chreest, *Chríost,* Jesus Christ.

Chreest, *Críost,* Jesus Christ.

Chrier, *chriathair,* soft bog.

Chrier, *chriathar,* sieves.

Chrin, *crann, crainn, chrainn,* a (great) tree.

Chrinn, *crann,* a tree.

Christal, *Mhic-Chriostamhail*, MacChrystal or Crystal's (a family name) town.

Christhamaun, *chros-Tomáin*, not given.

Chrock, *chnoc*, a hill.

Chrow, *chro, cro*, a glen.

Chrow, *cro*, a cattle hut.

Chuill, *chuill, coll*, hazel.

Chuit, *chait*, not given.

Chullia, *coille, choille*, a wood.

Chullion, *cullion, chuilinn, chuillion*, holly.

Chulter, *choltair*, not given.

Chulter, *coltar*, a plough-share.

Chuna, *chonaidh*, firewood.

Chunna, *chonaidh*, firewood.

Chunna, *chonnaidh*, not given.

Chunno, *chona*, firewood.

Chunny, *chonaidh*, firewood.

Churk, *coirce*, oats.

Churry, *currach*, a marsh.

Cil, *Cill*, a Church or a burying place.

Cill, *Cill*, a Church or a burying place.

Cilla, *Cille*, the Church.

Cille, *Cill*, a Church or a burying place.

Cillen, *cuillionn, cuileann*, holly.

Cilly, *Cille*, the Church.

Cincon, *Cinncon*, not given.

Cinowy, *ceann-a'mhuighe*, head of the plain.

Civeen, *Saidhbhín*, Sadhbh, a female name.

Civeen, *Saidhbhín*, little Sadhbh, a female name.

Cklin, *cluain*, a meadow, meadowland or boggy pasture.

Ckloon, *cluain*, a meadow, meadowland or boggy pasture.

Cla, *chladh, cladh*, a mound or a dyke or a raised clay dyke.

Claar, *chláir, clár*, a plain.

Clab, *clab*, a mouth, a wide mouth.

Clabby, *clabach*, not given.

Clabby, *clabaigh*, an open place.

Clack, *cloch*, a stone.

Clackaime, *cloch-chéim*, the stone pass.

Cladagh, *cladach*, land on the river margin.

Cladane, *chladáin*, not given.

Claddagh, *an-chlaedach*(sic), not given.

Claddagh, *cladach, clodach*, a sea shore, a flat stony beach, a bank (of earth), miry, slimy, dirty, filthy or a puddle.

Clade, *tSláid*(sic), not given.

Cladna, *cladach-na...*, not given.

Cladowen, *claí-Domhain*, not given.

Clady, *chladaigh, cladach*, the stony shore.

Clady, *cladach*, a shore.

Clady, *Claodaí, Clóidigh*, muddy, miry river, also a washing river.

Clady, land hard from trampling or a muddy place.

Clae, *Clae*, not given.

Clagan, *claigean*, a round, dry, hard or rocky hill.

Clageen, *craigín*, little rock.

Clagg, *craig*, land with a rocky surface.

Claggan, *claigeann, cloiginn, claigean*, a skull or a round, dry, hard or rocky hill.

Claggan, *cloigeann, chloigeann*, the head.

Claggan, *cloigean*, a bare headland or rocky round hill.

Claggan, *cloigne*, not given.

Claggan, headland.

Claggarnagh, *clogernach*, a round bell like or skull like hill or a place of round hills.

Clagnagh, *claignach*, full of skulls or round rocky hills.

Claha, *cleatha*, a pole or hurdle.

Claha, *cloiche*, stone.

Claha, *cleithe*, wattles.

Clahane, *clochán*, a stepping stone ford.

Clahaskeen, *glas-caoin*, formed from *cloc+clad+eascain*, beautiful green.

Clahernagh, *clochar, cloharach, cloithreach*, a stony place.

Claisa, *clais-an...*, trench/hollow of the...

Claise, *claise, clais*, a trench, dyke or furrow.

Claise, *claise, clais*, a trench, dyke or furrow.

Claisean, *clais-an...*, hollow of the...

Clamper, *chlampair*, dispute or controversy.

Clamph, *clamh*, lepers.

Clamy, *cladhmeith*, fences.

Clan, *chluain, cluain*, a meadow.

Clan, *clan*, children, descendants or race of....

Clan, *clan*, sons of...

Clan, *clann*, not given.

Clancy, *cluanaisighe*, a remote place.

Clandeboye, *clan-Aedha-buidhe, clan-Aodha-bhuí, clann-Aodha-buí*, descendants of yellow Hugh (a male name).

Clane, *claonadh*, the slope.

Clane, *cloanadh*, an inclined/slanted or false ford.

Clanickny, *cluain-Icne,* Icne's (a personal or a family name) meadow.

Clanickny, *lauin-Mhaicne,* not given.

Clankee, *clann-an-caoich,* descendants of the one eyed man.

Clann, *clan,* the clan or family.

Clannbryan, *Clainne-Briain,* Bryans clan or children.

Clanone, *clan-Eoghain,* Owen's (a male name) clan.

Clappy, *clapaigh,* not given.

Clar, *clar, chláir, chlair,* the plank, where a plank was used to ford a river etc.

Clar, *clár, cláir,* a plain or a level spot.

Clara, *chlaraigh, clárach, clarach, clar, clóirth-each,* a level place, level land or a plain.

Clara *(Vale of), clárach,* the wooden bridge.

Clara, *chláraigh,* not given.

Clara, *cláraidh,* a division of land.

Clara, *Cláraigh,* Clare, a female name.

Clarach, *clarach, claragh,* planks.

Claragh, *clar, clarach,* the plain or level land.

Claragh, *clár-áth,* ford of the river plain(sic).

Claraghy, *clárachadh,* not given.

Claran, *cláran,* a division.

Claranagh, *cláreanach,* the level marsh.

Clarary, *clarre,* the level tract.

Clare, *clair, cláir, chláir, clár, clar,* a level place, level land, a board, plank bridge or a plain.

Clare, *clar, chláir, chlair,* the plank, where a plank was used to ford a river etc.

Clare, *cláraigh,* not given.

Clare, *cléir, cléire,* the priest or clergy.

Clare, *cliara, chláraigh, clárach,* not given.

Clareen (Kilclareen), *Chléirín,* not given.

Clareen, *chláirín, cláirín, clarín,* little level place, a little board across a ford or a little plain.

Claremorris, *clár-chlainne/clainne-Muiris,* Plain of Morris's (a personal or family name) children.

Claress, *claras, clár-easa,* plain of the cascade (of water).

Claretrock, *Carraig-an-fhiona,* rock of the wine. The English version is Claret-Rock.

Clariana, *clár-Uí-Aille,* O'Halley's plain.

Clarig, *chlárig, clarach, chlaraig, chlaraigh,* a smooth, level or flat place, a plain, a plank/s to ford a dyke or river.

Clarig, *clárach,* a plain.

Clarin, *chláirín, chláirin,* a little plain.

Clarin, *clairin,* Clairin, a persons name.

Clarin, *clarin, chláirín, chlairín,* the little board or plank-bridge.

Clarina, *clár-Aidhne,* Aidhne,s (a personal name) plain or flat place.

Clarina, *clár-Aidhne,* Aidhne,s (a personal name) plank bridge.

Claris, *Chláiris,* Clarus or Claire, a personal name.

Claris, from *clar,* a plank bridge for crossing a river.

Clarish, *Cláiris,* Clarus, a male name.

Clash, *chlais, claise, clais,* a trench, dyke, hollow, vale, valley, ravine, glen, ditch, dry ditch, pit or deep furrow.

Clasha, *claise,* a trench.

Clasha, *claise-an/a'....,* trench of the...

Clasha, *clasa,* hollows or furrows.

Clasha, *glais-an..., glaise-an/a...,* not given.

Clasha, *glaise,* not given.

Clashawley, (river) *an-ghlais-alainn,* not given.

Clashawley, (river) *sruth-chlair-Amhlaoibh,* not given.

Clashe, *clais-an...,* not given.

Clasheen, *claisín,* a little hollow.

Clasheen, little trench.

Clasheen, *clairin*(sic), the small trench.

Clasheenan, *claisín-an...,* little trench/hollow of the...

Clasheleesha, *clais-Eilísigh,* not given.

Clashet, *claise,* a ravine.

Clashna, *clais/claise-na...,* trench of the...

Clashree, *chlais-Chria*(sic), not given.

Clashy, *claise,* the trench.

Class, *claise, clais,* a trench, dyke or furrow.

Classagh, *claisach,* trenches or furrows.

Classagh, *clasach,* a trench or trenches.

Classes, *claisach,* trenches.

Classes, *clasa, clasha,* hollows or vallies.

Claudy, *cládach,* not given.

Claudy, *clóideach, clóidigh,* muddy, miry river or the washing river.

Claughee, *clochach,* stony.

Claughy, *clochach,* stony.

Claur, *cláir,* the plank (for crossing a river or stream).

Claureen, *cláirín,* little plain.

Claureen, *clárín,* a small bridge of boards.

Claurig, *chláraigh,* planking.

Claurig, *clárach,* a board or level spot.

Clave, *chléibh,* wattle, wicker basket or creel.

Clave, *tSléibhe,* not given.

Claverty, *Mhic-Laithbheartaigh,* MacLaverty, a family name.

Clavlig, *chlamhlaig,* skeleton or bones.

Claw, *chladh, claidhe, cladh,* a mound or a dyke, a raised clay dyke.

Clay, *cléithe, cleithe,* a harrow, a hurdle or hurdles.

Clay, *cliath,* hurdles or harrow/s.

Clay, *tSleibhe,* a mountain.

Clayagh, *chlaíoch,* not given.

Clayagh, *cladach,* mounds or raparts.

Clea, *chlaidhe,* a hedge or ditch.

Clea, *chléithe,* not given.

Clea, *claidhe,* a fence.

Clea, *claimhe,* sheep mange.

Clea, *cleithe, cléithe,* a hurdle, a railing or a harrow.

Clea, *cloiche, claí,* not given.

Clea, *tSléibhe,* a mountain.

Cleady, *cladach, clodach,* can mean a flat stony beach, a bank (of earth). It can also mean miry, slimy, dirty, filthy or a puddle.

Cleagh, *cliath,* hurdles.

Clean, *claon,* sloping.

Clean, *claonach,* a sloping place.

Cleanglass, *an-chlaonghlais,* not given.

Clear, *Cléire,* clergy.

Clearagh, the presbytery.

Cleare, *cléire, gCléireach,* clergy.

Cleary, a family name.

Cleary, *Chléirigh, Cléirigh,* not given.

Cleary, *cleirig, clérech, cleire,* clergy or clergyman.

Cleary, *Uí-Cleirigh,* O'Cleary, a family name.

Cleave, *chlaidhimh,* the sword.

Cleave, *cléibh,* the breast.

Cleave, *tSléibhe*(sic), not given.

Cleaven, *ciabhán,* a cradle.

Cleaveragh, a place of baskets or hurdles.

Cleavery, a place of baskets or hurdles.

Clee, *cladh,* a mound, a dyke or a raised clay dyke.

Clee, *gCladh,* mounds.

Cleeagh, *cliath,* hurdles.

Cleedagh, a place of ditches.

Cleedagh, *cladach, clodach,* can mean a flat stony beach, a bank (of earth). It can also mean miry, slimy, dirty, filthy or a puddle.

Cleen, *claon, claen,* a slope or sloping.

Cleen, from *claen,* slopes.

Cleena, (Cork), *Clíodhna, Clíodna,* the name of a particular fairy Queen.

Cleena, *chlaoine,* slopes.

Cleena, *Cliodhna,* the name of a particular banshee.

Cleenagh, *claenach,* sloping.

Cleenagh, *claon-achadh,* sloping field.

Cleenaghan, *claon-achadh,* sloping field.

Cleenaghoo, *claon-achadh,* sloping field.

Cleenish, *claon/claen-inis,* sloping island.

Cleeny, from *claen,* slopes.

Cleevaun, *cliabháin, cliabhán,* a cradle.

Cleevaun, *cliabhain,* the basket.

Cleeve, *chliabh,* baskets.

Cleevragh, *cliabhrach, gCleavrach*(sic), baskets.

Cleffany, *cloitheamhnaidhe,* a stony place.

Cleg, *claigeann,* a skull or a round hill.

Clegarrow, *cladh-garbh,* rough dyke or mound.

Clegg, *claig,* a hollow.

Cleggan, *an-cloigean,* not given.

Cleggan, *claigeann, claigean,* a skull or a round/dry/hard or rocky hill.

Cleggan, *cloigeann,* the head or skull.

Cleghile, *cleachoill, cléithchoill,* not given.

Cleghile, *clét-choill,* wood of wattles or hurdles.

Clegna, *claignach,* full of skulls or round rocky hills.

Clegna, *cloigne,* round skull shaped hills.

Clegnagh, *claignach,* full of skulls or round rocky hills.

Cleha, *cliath, cléithe, cleithe,* hurdle/s,

Clehaun, *cliathán,* the breast or side.

Clehile, *clét-choill,* wood of wattles or hurdles.

Clehile, *cléithchoill,* not given.

Clehy, cleithe, a hurdle or fence.
Cleigh, cloch, cloiche, stone.
Cleigha, cloiche, the stone.
Cleighe, cliath, cleithe, hurdles.
Cleighille, cnamh-choill, wood of the bones.
Cleighragh, cloichreach, the stony place.
Cleighran, cloichreán, little stony place.
Cleighreen, cleithrín, stones.
Cleithe, cleithe, a hurdle.
Cleithe, cléithe, wattle.
Clement, Chleiméasaigh, not given.
Clemesig, Clemesig, Clema or Clemmesy, a male name.
Clen, chlaon, bent or diverted.
Clen, claen, a slope or sloping.
Clenagh, claenach, sloping.
Clenagh, cláonach, a sloping place.
Clenagh, claonachadh, not given.
Clenlough, claen-loch, sloping lake.
Clenlough, claon-loch, not given.
Clenor, claonabhar, cluain-odhar, dark grey meadow.
Clera, chléirigh, not given.
Clera, cleirig, cleire, clergy.
Cleragh, cliathrach, a hurdle passage.
Cleraghan, Uí-Chléireacháin, O'Clerihan, a family name.
Clerahan, baile-Uí-Chléireacháin, town of Ó Cléireacháin, a family name and means the descendants of Clerihan.
Cleran, cloichreán, little stony place.
Cleraun, Clothrann, Clothra, a personal or family name.
Clerhaun, cloichreán, little stony place.
Clerhawn, cloichreán, rocky ground.
Clerihan, O'Clerihan, a personal or family name.
Clerk, gCléireach, cleirig, cleire, clergy.
Clerragh, clochar, cloharach, cloithreach, a stony place.
Clerran, an-cloicheán, not given
Clerrann, cloichreán, little stony place.
Clery, cloichrigh, not given.
Clery, gCléireach, chléirigh, cleirig, cleire, the cleric or clergy.
Clery, Uí-Chléirigh, Ó Cléirigh, a personal or family name.
Clessy, chleasaí, not given.
Clessy, chleasaigh, the 'tricky' fellow or juggler.

Clevaghy, cliabh-achaidh, the basket field.
Clevan, chliabháin, not given.
Clevan, cliabhain, a cradle or hollow.
Clevane, cliabhain, basket or cradle shaped.
Clevane, cliabhán, a cradle.
Clevaun, chliabháin, not given.
Clevaun, cliabhán, a cradle or hollow.
Cleve, cliabh, not given.
Clevin, Chleimhín, chliabháin, not given.
Clevin, cléibhín, a small basket or crib.
Clew, (bay) *cuan-Mód,* not given.
Cliddaun, claideán, the muddy place.
Clief, cliabh, cleithe, cléithe, cleuthe, cliath, hurdles or wattles.
Clien, claon, inclining.
Clieve, cliabh, cleuthe, cliath, hurdles or wattles.
Clievragh, a place of baskets or hurdles.
Clifden (in Clare), *cosánatriomona,* the place of dry stepping stones.
Clifden, an-clochán, the little stone.
Clifden, chlocháin, clifden(sic), *ráth-Gharbháin,* not given.
Clifden, clochán, clochan, stepping stones or a beehive shaped stone house.
Cliff, chlaímh, not given.
Cliff, chliabh, baskets.
Cliff, chloidhimh, swords.
Cliff, cliath, hurdles.
Cliff, clíebh(sic), *cliabh,* baskets.
Cliff, cloiche, stones.
Cliff, cloiche, the rock.
Cliffe, chliabh, cliabh, baskets.
Clifferna, cliaifearna, chliaifearna, not given.
Clifferna, cliabharnach, a place of baskets.
Cliffoney, cliafuine, hurdled thicket.
Cliffony, cliafuine, cliathmhuine, hurdle shrubbery or thicket.
Cliffony, cloitheamhnaidhe, a stony place.
Cliffy, chlochach, stony.
Clifton, mullach-Imeanna, not given.
Clig, chluig, a bell.
Cline, calon, not given.
Cline, chlaoin, claen, a slope or sloping.
Clinis, claoin-inse, sloping island.
Clinoe, an-chlaí-nua, not given.
Clinta, cluainteach, meadow land.
Clintna, meadowland of the…
Clinty, cluainte, meadows or lawns.
Clione, chlaí-nua, new earthen fence.

Clittagh, *cleiteach,* plumes or feathers.

Cliven, *clibhín,* not given.

Clivore, *chlaí-mhóir,* not given.

Clivore, *claidhe-mhoír,* a large ditch or rampart.

Clivvy, *cluiché,* sports.

Clo, *an-chloch, cloch,* a rock or a stone building.

Clo, *cloch, clogh, cloiche,* a stone/s or a stone castle.

Cloan, *cluain, cluana,* a meadow or pasturage.

Clob, *chlob,* a swallow hole.

Clob, *clab,* the (open) mouth.

Clobbeen, *claibín,* little mouth.

Clobemon, *cloch-beimheann,* stone or stone castle of the blows or strokes.

Cloca, the cloak.

Cloch, *chlumhach,* long coarse grass.

Cloch, *cloch,* a stone.

Clochlowrish, *cloch-labhrais,* speaking stone.

Clochnach, the stony river.

Clocna, *cloch-na...,* rock of the...

Clocully, *cloch-a'-chlaidhe,* stone/stony place or stone castle of the dyke or mound.

Clocully, *cloch-a'chloidhe,* stone of the ditch.

Clocully, *cloch-Chullaí,* not given.

Clodagh, *cladach,* a stony river, stony land near a river.

Clodah, *cladach,* a stony strand or muddy river.

Clodah, *cloch-Dhaith,* David's (a male name) stone building.

Cloddagh, *cladach,* a flat stony beach.

Cloddagh, *cladach,* a stony strand or muddy river.

Clodia, *cloideach,* miry or muddy river.

Clodiagh, (river) *chlóideach,* not given.

Clodig, *chladaigh,* flat stony land or a stream channel.

Clodragh, *clodrach,* miry, slimy, dirty, filthy or a puddle.

Clodrum, *clochroim,* the stony ridge.

Clody, *Clóidí, Cladaighe* Clóideach, a river name, see **Clodia.**

Clody, *cloidighe,* not given.

Cloe, *cló,* of the impression.

Clog, *chloig,* a bell.

Clog, *chluig,* not given.

Clog, *clog, clocc,* a bell or bell-shaped hill.

Clogagh, *clogach,* a place of round shaped hills.

Clogaralt, *cloch-Ghearailt,* Gerald's/Garret's stone fortress.

Clogeen, *cloigín,* not given.

Clogga, *chlogach,* not given.

Clogga, *clocach,* stony.

Clogga, *cloga,* vetches.

Clogga, *clogach,* a place of small hills.

Cloggagh, *clogach,* a bell shaped hill.

Cloggan, *chlogáin,* the little bell.

Cloggarnagh, *clogernach,* a round bell like/ skull like hill or a place of round hills.

Cloggaun, a little round hill.

Cloggaun, *clochán,* a stony place.

Cloggeen, *cloigín,* the little bell.

Cloggy, *clogach,* a place of round shaped hills.

Cloggy, *clogai,* not given.

Clogh, *chloch, cloch, clogh, cloiche,* a stone/s, stony, a stone house or a castle.

Clogh, *cloch,* stones, a stone fortification or a 'castellated' stone building.

Clogh, *clochach, cloch,* stony.

Clogh, *cloch-muighe-leithid, chlochach, gCloch,* not given.

Clogh, *clumhach,* fleecy or fluffy.

Clogha, *chluiche,* the game.

Clogha, *cloch, cloiche,* not given.

Clogha, *clocha-a'...,* stone or stone castle of...

Clogha, *cloch-an...,* not given.

Clogha, *na-clocha,* the stones.

Clogha, the (remarkable) stone.

Cloghabrody, *cloch-an-Bhródaigh,* O'Brody's (a personal or family name) stone fortification.

Cloghagh, *chlochach,* stony.

Cloghagh, *clochach,* stones or stony.

Cloghagh, *na-cloiche,* not given.

Cloghaisty, *cloch-aiste,* the casting rock.

Cloghal, *chúlchoill,* not given.

Cloghala, *cloch-an-leá,* not given.

Cloghalea, *cloiche-liaithe,* grey stone.

Cloghan, *chlocháin, cloghan,* a stony spot or stepping stones.

Cloghan, *clocháin,* a stony ford.

Cloghan, *clochán,* a beehive shaped stone house.

Cloghan, *clochán, chlochain,* a row of stepping stones, a heap of stones, a stepping-stone ford, a stony place or an ancient circular stone house.

Cloghan, *cloch-an...,* not given.

Cloghana, *clochan-na..,* stone house of the...

Cloghana, *clochan-na..,* stony place or stepping stones of the...

Cloghanacody, *cloch-an-Mhonacóidigh,* not given.

Cloghanamina, *tulchán-an-Muimhneach*(sic), not given.

Cloghane, *chlocháin,* not given.

Cloghane, *clochán, clochan,* a stone building, a stony place or the ruins of a stone fort.

Cloghane, *clochán-an...,* cloghan of the...

Cloghane, *cloghan,* a ruin or a stony place.

Cloghane, *cloghan, clocháin, clochán,* a row of stepping stones.

Cloghaneanode, *clochán-an-fhóid,* cloghan of the sod.

Cloghaneely, *cloich-Cionnaola,* not given.

Cloghans, stepping stone fords.

Clogharaily, *cloch-an-ráiligh,* not given.

Cloghard, *cloch-árd,* not given.

Cloghaready, *cloch-an-Riadaigh,* not given.

Cloghaready, *cloch-Uí-Riada,* Oready's or O'Reidy's (a family name) stone castle.

Clogharinka, *cloch-an-ringce,* not given.

Clogharinka, *cloch-Fhrainc,* not given.

Clogharinka, *cloch-an-rinnce,* stone/stone building of the dancing.

Cloghas, *clogchás, clogas,* a square belfry.

Cloghast, *cloch-an-Chasta,* not given.

Cloghasty, *cloch-Hoiste,* not given.

Cloghatanny(sic), *tulchán-na-Bruíne,* not given.

Cloghateana, *cloch-an-tSeánaigh,* not given.

Cloghatrida, *cloch-an-Choitréadaigh,* not given.

Cloghaun, *chlocháin,* not given.

Cloghaun, *cloghan, clochán,* a row of stepping stones.

Cloghauna, *clochán-na...,* stepping stones by the...

Cloghboley, *clochbhuaile,* stone circle(sic).

Cloghe, *clogharnach, cloiche, cloichreán,* a stony place.

Clogheen, *chloichín,* a little stone fort.

Clogheen, *chloichín, cloichín,* a little stone, a little stone building, a castle or ruin.

Clogheen, *cloichín,* stony land.

Clogheen, *cloichín-an-mhargaidh,* not given.

Clogheen, *cloicín,* a little stone or stone house

Clogheen, *gCloichín,* little stones.

Clogheena, *cloichín-a ...,* stone castle of the...

Clogher, *chlochair, clochair, clochar, cloichir, clogher,* a stony place.

Clogher, *chlochair,* stones.

Clogher, *cloch-a'...,* the stone of...

Clogher, *clochár, clochar,* abounding in stones, a rocky, stony place, an assembly, a college, a ruin or a stone Church.

Clogher, *cloch-oir,* the golden stone.

Clogher, *cloichear, clochair, cluthair,* not given.

Clogher, *cluthmhar,* sheltered.

Clogher, *clochar, gClochar,* stone buildings.

Cloghera, *clochar, clochara, cloharach, cloith-reach,* a stony place.

Cloghera, *clogharnach, cloiche, cloichreán,* a stony place.

Clogherane, *an-cloichreán,* not given.

Clogherane, *chlochrain,* stepping stones.

Clogherane, *clogharnach, cloichrean,* a stony place.

Clogheraun, *cloichreán,* a stony place.

Cloghereen, *clochrín,* little stone.

Cloghereen, *cloichreán,* little stony place.

Clogherine, *cloichín,* a stony place or a stone building.

Clogherna, *clochar-na...,* not given.

Clogherna, *clogharnach,* the stony place.

Cloghernach, *clocharnach,* a stony place.

Cloghernagh, *an-chlocharnach,* not given.

Cloghernagh, *clogharnach, clochar, cloharach, cloithreach,* a stony place.

Cloghernal, *cloch-choirnéal,* the corner stone.

Cloghernane, stony.

Clogherny, *clocharnaigh, clochernach, clochar, cloharach, cloithreach,* a stony place.

Clogherowen, should be **Cloghercowan,** Cowan's (a family name) stony land.

Cloghessy, *Ua-Clochasadh,* O'Cloghessy, a family name.

Cloghfin, white stones.

Cloghila, *cloch-choill-an...,* not given.

Cloghineely, *cloch-Chinnfhaelaidh,* Kinfaela, Kineely's (a male name) stone.

Cloghna, *cloch-na....,* the stone or the stone castle of the...

Cloghnane, *chlochnain,* a stony place.

Cloghoge, *chlochóg,* not given.

Cloghoge, *clochóg,* a row of stepping stones, stony land or a little stone.

Cloghogle, *cloch-togbhala,* a raised or lifted stone or the covering flagstone of a cromlech.

Cloghore, *cloch/cloich-óir,* stone of gold.

Cloghoula, *clochbhuaile,* the stone circle(sic).

Cloghoula, *clochbhuaile,* the stony summer pasture(sic).

Cloghran, *clochrán,* a stony place.

Cloghran, *clochrán,* stepping stones.

Cloghran, *clogharnach, cloiche, cloichreán,* a stony place.

Cloghrane, *chloichréain,* not given.

Cloghrane, *cloichreán,* little stony place.

Cloghraun, a stony place.

Cloghrim, *clochdhroma,* a stony ridge.

Cloghspar, *cloch-a-spearra,* stone of the spear.

Cloghspar, *cloiche-speara,* not given.

Cloghultagh, *cloch-chodlatach*(sic), sleepy stone.

Cloghy, *cleithe,* a pole or wattle hut.

Cloghy, *cloch, clogh, cloiche,* a stone/s, stony, a castle or a stone building.

Cloghy, *clogharnach, cloiche, cloichreán,* a stony place.

Cloghy, *clochach,* stony.

Cloghy, *cloiche,* a remarkable stone.

Clogrennan, *cloch-grianáin,* not given.

Clogthogle, *cloch-togbhala,* a raised or lifted stone or the covering flagstone of a cromlech.

Clogy, *cloch, clogh, cloiche,* a stone/s, can sometimes mean a castle.

Cloha, *cleither,* hurdle.

Cloha, *cloiche,* a stone or stone cstle.

Clohalea, *cloiche-léithe/leithe,* the grey stone, rock or grey castle.

Clohamon, *cloch-Ámainn,* not given.

Clohanavowry, *cloch-na-bhFomharaigh,* (the old name for the Giants causeway), 'the stepping stones of the Femorians' (legendary Sea rovers).

Clohane, *Clocháin,* not given.

Clohaskin, *cloch-Sheascain,* not given.

Clohaskin, *glaise-easa-Caoin,* not given.

Clohassy, *Uí-Chlochasaigh,* Ó Clochasaigh, a family name.

Cloheen, *cloichín,* stony land.

Cloheen, *cloichín-na .,* stone castle of the...

Cloheen, little stones.

Cloheena, *cloch-adhnach,* stone of ivy.

Cloheena, *cloch-Aghnach,* Aghnach's (a personal or a family name) stone house.

Cloheena, *cloch-eidhnach,* flint stone.

Cloheena, *cloch-eidhneach,* not given.

Cloheena, *cloichíne, cloichinidhe,* small stone castles.

Cloheena, *cloichín-na ,* not given.

Cloher, *chloichir,* the stony place.

Cloher, *clochar,* stony ground.

Cloher, *clochain,* a stony pass.

Cloher, *cloichir, clochair, chlochair,* not given.

Cloher, *cluthar,* sheltered, shelter.

Cloher, *cluthmhar,* sheltered or cosy.

Clohernagh, *cloharach*(sic), *clocharnach,* not given.

Clohoga, *clochóg,* a stony place.

Clohoge, *chlochóg,* not given.

Clohoge, *clochóg,* a round stone or stony land.

Clohogue, *clochóg,* a round stone or stony land.

Clohy, *cloiche,* a (remarkable) stone or stone building.

Cloigh, *chlaí,* not given.

Cloigh, *cloiche,* the stone.

Cloka, *chlóca,* the cloak.

Cloka, *Chócaigh, Cócach,* not given.

Clolourish, *cloch-labhrais,* stone of speech.

Clomanta, *cloch-Mhantac,* not given.

Clomantagh, *chloch-Mhantach, cloch-Mhantaigh,* not given.

Clomatagh(sic), *cloch-mhanntach,* clefted rock.

Clon, *chluana,* not given.

Clon, *clann..., clan...,* the clan, family or descendants of...

Clon, *cluain,* a stone or stone house, a lawn, a lea field, grassland between two woods, boggy pasture but mostly a meadow or meadow-land.

Clona, *cluain,* meadow.

Clona, *cluana-na..., cluain-na...*clon (see clon) of the....

Clonacody, *cloch-an-Mhonacóidigh,* not given.

Clonad, *cluain-fhada,* the long meadow or a lawn.

Clonada, *cluain-a'-da...,* clon (see clon) of the two...

Clonada, *cluain-fhada,* the long pasture.

Clonagh (Kilclonagh), *Chluaine,* not given.

Clonagh, *cluain-each/eich,* meadow of the horse.

Clonagh, *cluana,* the meadow.

Clonagh, *cluanach,* meadows.

Clonagha, *cluanacha,* meadows.

Clonakenny, *cluain-Uí-Chionaoith,* not given.

Clonakilty, *cloch/cloich-na-coillte,* stone of the woods or stone fort of the woods.

Clonakilty, *cloch-na-coilltidh,* not given.

Clonakilty, *Clanna-Chaoilte,* Clans of Caoilte.

Clonalea, *cluain-lao,* not given.

Clonalis, *cluain-Álghas,* not given.

Clonamery, *cluain-Amaire,* Amaire's (a personal or family name) meadow. The older name for this parish was *pobal-an-Bharúin,* Baron (Fitzgerald's) parish.

Clonamicklon, *clauin-Ó-Míolchon,* not given.

Clonard, *cluain-ard,* high meadow.

Clonard, *cluain-Eraird,* Eraird's (a male name) meadow.

Clonard, *cluain-Ioraird,* Iorard's (a male name) meadow.

Clonaspoe, *cluain-lis-bó,* not given.

Clonavoe, *cluain-dá-bhó,* not given.

Clonbur, *an-fhairche,* not given.

Clonca, *cluain-catha,* meadow of battle.

Cloncath, *cluain-cath,* not given.

Cloncaun, *Cill-Fhionncháin,* not given.

Clonda, *cluain-dá/dhá...,* meadow of the two...

Clondouglas, *clainn-Diarmuda*(sic), not given.

Clone, *cluain-na...,* meadow of the...

Clone, *cluana, chluain, chluana, cluain,* meadow.

Clone, *cluain,* a meadow between two woods(sic)

Clonea, *cluain-fhia/fhiadh,* meadow of the deer.

Clonea, *clauin-eich,* meadow of the horse.

Clonea, *cluain-fhiadh-na-nDéireach,* not given.

Clonea, *cluain-fhiadh-Paorach,* not given.

Clonee, *cluain-Aodha,* Aodh's or Hugh's lawn.

Clonee, *cluain-fhiadh, fhiaidh,* plain or meadow of the deer.

Cloneen, *cluainín,* little meadow.

Cloneigh, *cluain-eich,* meadow of the horse.

Clonelly, *clann-Amhlaibh,* not given.

Clonely, *cluain-Eilighe,* Healy's meadow or lawn.

Clonely, *cluain-Éilí,* not given.

Clonenagh, *cluain-eidhneach,* not given.

Clonenagh, *cluain-eighneach,* meadow of ivy.

Clones, *cluain-eas,* meadow of the waterfall.

Clones, *cluain-Eois,* Eos's (a male name) meadow or a lawn.

Cloneska, *cluain-Eascann,* not given.

Cloney, *chluana, gCluainíní,* not given.

Cloney, *cluainidhe, cluain,* a meadow, pasture, meadowland or boggy pasture.

Cloney, *cluain-na...,* pasture of the...

Cloney, *cluana,* a field.

Cloney, *gCluainínidhe,* meadows.

Cloneygowny, *cluain-na-nGaibhne,* not given.

Clonhobert,(sic), *cluana-hObainn,* Hoban's (a personal or family name) meadow.

Clonhugh, *clann-Aodha,* descendants of Hugh, a mans name.

Cloniff, *cluain-duibh,* not given.

Clonin, *cluainín, cluanín,* a little meadow.

Clonis, *cluain,* a meadow, meadowland or boggy pasture.

Clonisboyle, *cluain-Eois-Buirgill,* Eos Boyles meadow.

Clonisboyle, *cluain-lios-Baoill,* not given.

Clonismullen, *cluain-lios-Muilinn,* not given.

Clonkirk, *cluain-Ciorcaill,* not given.

Clonlish, *claenghlais,* sloping streamlet.

Clonmellon, *Ráistín,* not given.

Clonnestin, *cluain-Oistin,* not given.

Clonoe, *cluain-eo,* meadow of yews.

Clonoghill, *cluain-achaill*(sic), not given.

Clonora, *cluain-odhartha,* grey lawn/boggy pasturage.

Clonree, *clochrigh,* the Kings stone.

Clonta, *cluain-dhá…,* meadow of the two…

Clonta, *cluainte,* meadows.

Clontagh, *cluainteach,* meadow land.

Clonteens, *cluaintínidhe,* meadows or meadow lands.

Clonterlough, cluain-Toirealaigh, not given.

Clontonkelly, *cluainte-na-coille,* meadows of the wood.

Clonty, *clauinte*(sic), *cluainte,* meadows or lawns.

Clony, *cluain-dá/dhá…,* meadow of the two…

Clony, *cluain-na…,* plain of the…

Clony, *cluana,* a meadow or an island.

Clony, *cluainí,* meadow lands.

Clonyn, *cluainín,* the little meadow.

Clood, *clúid,* the nook.

Cloom(sic)**,** *chluain,* not given.

Cloon, *chluain, cluana, cluain,* a meadow, pasture, meadowland, lawn, boggy pasture, an arable spot, fertile piece of land, a green arable spot surrounded or nearly surrounded by bog or marsh on one side and water on the other.

Cloon, *claon,* sloping.

Cloona, *cluaina*(sic), fields.

Cloona, *cluain-an/a'…,* meadow of the…

Cloona, *cluaine,* a watershed.

Cloona, *cluain-eanaigh,* not given.

Cloona, *cluain-na…,* pasture of the…

Cloona, *cluana,* a meadow.

Cloona, *cluanach,* meadows.

Cloonacauneen, *cluain-Mhic-Cáinín,* not given.

Cloonadea, O'Dea's (a family name) meadow.

Cloonadrum, *clauin-dhá-dhrom,* not given.

Cloonaduff, *cluain-eanaigh-dhubh,* not given.

Cloonagh, *cluain-each,* meadow of the horses.

Cloonagh, *cluanach, cluain,* a meadow, meadowland, boggy pasture.

Cloonagh, *cluanach,* full of cloons (bog islands).

Cloonaghlin, *clauin-eachlainn/eachlainne,* meadow of the horse stables or enclosures.

Cloonaheen, *cluain-Eichín,* not given.

Cloonalis, *cluain-atha-leasa,* meadow of the ford of the fort.

Cloonan, *cluain-an…,* meadow of the…

Cloonan, little meadow.

Cloonanaff, *cluain-na-ndamh,* meadow of the oxen.

Cloonanagh, *cluain-eanaigh/eanach,* not given.

Cloonanagh, *cluain-na-neach,* meadow of the horses.

Cloonaufill, *clauin-dha-phill,* meadow of the two horses.

Cloonavihony, *cluain-Mhic-Mhathghamhna,* MacMahon, a family name.

Cloonbur, *an-Fhairche*(sic), not given.

Cloondara, *cluain-dá-ráth,* meadow of the two forts.

Cloone, *cluain-Conmhaicne, cluain-an-éirc,* not given.

Cloone, *cluana, cluain,* a meadow, pasture, meadowland, boggy pasture.

Cloonee, *cluain-í,* meadow of the yew(sic).

Cloonee, *cluainí,* meadows.

Cloonee, *cluanaigh,* a meadow, pasture, meadowland or boggy pasture.

Clooneen, *cluainín,* little lawn or meadow.

Clooneena, *cluain-eadhneach,* ivy meadow.

Clooneenagh, *cluainin,* the little field(sic).

Clooneene, *cluainin, cluanín,* little lawn or meadow.

Clooneeny, *clauinínidhe,* little meadows.

Clooneigh, *cluain-eich,* meadow of the horse.

Cloonenagh, *chluain-eidhnech,* the retreat of the ivy.

Clooney, *cluanaidh, cluainidhe, chluana, chluanaidh, cluana, cluaine, cluain,* a meadow, pasture, meadowland or boggy pasture.

Clooniff, *cluain-duibh,* not given.

Cloonker, Kerr's or Carr's, (a personal or a family name) meadow.

Cloonmaghaura, *cluain-a'-chairrthe,* meadow of the pillarstone.

Cloonmee, *cluain-Midhe,* literally 'a meadow in County Westmeath'.

Cloonna, *cluain-na…,* meadow of the…

Cloonnagalleen, *cluain-Ó-gCoilín,* not given.

Cloonoan, *cluain-Dubhain,* Dubhan's (a personal or a family name) meadow.

Cloonoo, *cluain-uaighe,* a cave or grave.

Cloonshaghan, *clauinseachan,* abounding in little meadowlands.

Cloonshee, *cluain-riabhach,* fairy meadow(sic).

Cloont, *cluainte,* meadows or lawns.

Cloonta, *cloontha, chluanta,* lawn or meadow.

Cloonta, *cluainte,* meadows or lawns.

Cloontagh, *cluainteach,* having lawns or meadow land.

Cloonteen, *cluaintín,* little field(sic).

Cloonteen, *cluaintin, cluaintín,* little meadow.

Cloonteens, *cluaintínidhe,* little meadows.

Cloontia, *clauinte,* meadows.

Cloonties, *cluaninti*(sic), *cluantini,* meadows(sic).

Cloonties, *na-cluainte,* meadows or lawns.

Cloonty, *cluainte,* meadows or lawns.

Cloonty, *cluain-tí/tighe…,* the meadow of ….'s house.

Cloonty, *na-cluainte,* the plains.

Cloony, *cluain, chluana,* a meadow.

Cloony, *cluain-an…,* meadow of the…

Cloony, *cluaine,* a field.

Cloonyhea, O'Hea's (a family name) meadow.

Cloos, *chluais,* not given.

Cloos, *cluas,* the ear.

Cloosh, *cluas,* the ear.

Cloran, *clocharán, chlocharáin,* stepping stones.

Cloran, *cloichréan,* not given.

Cloran, *cloithreán, cloichreán,* little stony place.

Cloran, *chloichreáin, cloichrean,* a stony place.

Clorane, *cloichreán,* little stony place.

Cloranshea, *cloichreán-Uí-Shé,* not given.

Clorenawn, a burial place for unbaptised children.

Clorhane, *clochrán,* stepping stones.

Clorhane, *cloichreán,* little stony place.

Clorna, *cloichearnach,* not given.

Clornagh, *cloithearnach,* stony land.

Cloroge, *clotharóg,* little stony land.

Clos, *clais,* a trench.

Closdaw, *clais-Dáithi,* Davy's (a male name) trench.

Close, caves or hollows.

Close, *clos,* a yard, enclosure or narrow strip.

Close, *clós,* not given.

Closh, *clais,* a trench, furrow.

Closha, *claise,* the trench.

Closkelt, *cloch-scoilte,* cleft rock.

Clossagh, *an-chluasach,* not given.

Clossagh, *cluasach,* having ears.

Clothran, *Clothrann,* Clothra, a personal or family name.

Clottahina, *clot-áith/áithche,* sod of the fire kiln.

Clottahina, *clot-a-theine,* fire sod.

Clouch, *clochacha,* stony.

Clough, *chlumhach,* mossy.

Clough, *chlúmhach,* not given.

Clough, *cloch, clogh, cloiche,* stone/s, a castle or a stone fort or structure.

Clough, *cloch-machaire-Cat, cloch-dún-Eachdhach,* not given.

Cloughanmurry, *cloch-dhún-Muirigh,* stone castle of Murray's (a personal or family name) fort.

Cloughey, *clochaigh,* a stony place.

Cloughoge, *clochóg,* the little stone.

Cloughram, *cloch-ar-am,* the stony place.

Cloughrawn, *cloithréan,* a stony place or rocky land, stony or rocky bottom.

Cloughrim, *clochdhroma,* a stone/y ridge.

Cloughs, *clocha,* stones.

Cloughy, *chloiche,* stone.

Cloughy, *clochaigh, clochach,* stony or a stony place.

Cloun, *cluain,* a meadow.

Clounti, *cluainte,* meadows.

Clouracaun, *cloichrean,* a place of stones.

Cloustoge, *cluas-Damhóg,* not given.

Clovan, *Uí-Clumháin,* O'Clovan or Cluvan, a family name

Clovane, *chlumhain,* bog cotton.

Clovane, *cliabhain,* cradle shaped.

Clovane, *Uí-Chlúmháin/Chlumhain,* Coleman, a family name.

Clovaun, clomhán, dressing flax.

Clovers, na-Cleobhair, not given.

Clowney, chluana, a meadow

Clowney, cluanaí, meadows.

Clowney, cluainidhe, meadowland.

Clownings, cluainínidhe, little meadows.

Clowninny, cluain-Eithne, Eithne's (a personal or family name) meadows(sic).

Clownish, cluain-Eois, Eos's (a male name) meadow or a lawn.

Cloy, chlaidhe, cladh, an artificial mound, a dyke, a raised clay dyke or a rampart.

Cloy, claidhe, chlaí, a fence or fences.

Cloy, chloich, a stone.

Cloy, cloch, cloiche, a stone, stones or a (remarkable) stone.

Cloy, coithe(sic), the stone.

Cloydagh, cladach, clodach, a flat stony beach, a puddle, a bank (of earth), miry, slimy, dirty or filthy.

Cloyne, chaoin, smooth.

Cloyne, cluain, chluain, a meadow, pasture or park.

Cloyne, cluana, not given.

Cloyne, cluain-uamha, the meadow or a lawn of the cave.

Cloyragh, cloithreach, stony ground.

Cluan, cluan(sic)-*Amaire,* not given.

Clucka, cloigtheach, not given.

Clud, clod, sticky mud.

Cluddaun, clodán, a muddy place.

Cluen, cluain, a meadow.

Clug, chloig, not given.

Clug, chluig, clocc, clog, a bell or bells.

Clugga, an-Chloga/Chlogaidh/Chlogaigh, not given.

Clugga, na-chlogaigh, an-Clogach, not given.

Cluggin, chloigín, the bell.

Cluggin, chloiginn, headland.

Cluggin, chluiginn, cloigeann, skull or skull shaped.

Cluggin, clogan, chloigín, chlogain, the little bell.

Cluggin, cloigín, not given.

Cluggy, chlogaigh, a bell shaped hill.

Cluher, cluher, cluthar, sheltered or shelter.

Cluher, cluthair, shelter, sheltering.

Cluhir, cloichir, not given.

Cluhir, cluthair, sheltered.

Cluid, cluid, the nook.

Cluide, clued, the nook.

Cluide, clúide, not given.

Clun, cluain, a meadow.

Cluna, cluna, lawn, meadow or bog island.

Clunagh, cluain-each, not given.

Clunahill, cluain-Achaill, not given.

Cluntagh, cluainteach, having lawns or meadow land.

Clunty, cluainte, a meadow.

Cluntys, cluanta, meadows.

Clure, cluthar, sheltered or shelter.

Cluricane, luprachaun, luchorpán, leprechaun/s.

Cluttahina, cloch-dá-thine, not given.

Cluvane, chlumhain, the hairy man.

Cluvane, Uí-Chlúmháin/Chlumhain, Ó Clúmháin or Coleman, a family name.

Cly, cladh, a mound, a dyke or a raised clay dyke.

Cly, claí, clai, a rampart.

Clyda, cladach, clodach, miry, slimy, dirty, filthy, a flat stony beach, a bank (of earth) or a puddle.

Clydagh, a rocky place.

Clydagh, cladach, a flat stony shore or the muddy river.

Clydagh, cláideach, claodach, not given.

Clygeen, claidhgín, the little fence.

Clynagh, cladhnach, abounding in mounds or ramparts.

Clynan, cladhnán, a small dyke or rampart.

Clytagh, cladhtach, a place of dykes.

Clytagh, claoiteach, a place of ditches or mounds.

Cnag, cnag, a knob.

Cnappa, chnaipe, a lump or knob.

Cnav, chneamha, gentian or wild garlic.

Cnav, chreamha, not given.

Cnaw, chná, hazel nuts.

Cnaw, cnaoi, place producing nuts.

Cnegare, rabbit hill.

Cno, chneamha, wild garlic.

Cno, gCno, nuts.

Cnockaun, chnocáin, a hillock.

Co, chuach, a cuckoo.

Co, comhad, protection.

Co, cumha, not given.

Coa, a windy place.

Coa, comhad, protection.

Coa, *cuach*, a hollow.

Coad, *coíd*, brushwood.

Coad, *cómhad, comhad, comhfhod, cubhad*, a bed or grave.

Coagh, *comhthach*, not given.

Coagh, *cua*, acorns.

Coagh, *cuach*, a cup or a hollow.

Coagh, *cuach*, cuckoos.

Coagh, *cuaiche*, not given.

Coagh, *Cuaichi*, St Cuach.

Coaghan, *Chóchan*, not given.

Coaghan, *cuachán*, little cup or hollow.

Coaghen, *cuachen*, little cup or hollow.

Coaghen, *cuaichín*, not given.

Coam, *cam*, not given.

Coam, *chúim*, a hollow.

Coan, *Chuáin*, not given.

Coan, *cuan, chuain*, a harbour, haven, recess, curve, bend or winding.

Coardra, *Chordraeigh*, not given.

Coarlis, *cuar-lis*, the round fort.

Coasan, *cuasán*, little cave.

Cob, *cab, gab*, the mouth.

Cobane, *Gobáin*, Gobban, a personal or family name.

Cobbs, *cobbs*(sic), not given.

Cobh, *an-cóbh*, the cove or haven.

Cobh, *cóf*, not given.

Cobican, *Mhic-Oibícín*, not given.

Cocara, *cócaire*, the cook.

Cock, *Cóc, Choca, Cocha*, St Coca/Cocha.

Cocka, *chaca, coic*, excrement, ordour(sic) or a bad smell.

Cockan, *Chocáin, Coc, Cócca, Cockan*, the virgin St Coc/Cockan.

Cockan, *Chocain*, St Cocán.

Cockan, *Cocán*, not given.

Cocksoost, *cac-súist*, the dirty flail/s.

Cocksoost, *chacsúist*, not given.

Codd, *cod, cad, talamh-atá-lán-de-Chaonach*, not given.

Codd, *coda*, shares or allotments.

Cody, *cóide*, brushwood.

Coe, *chuach, cuach*, cuckoos.

Coe, *Có, Chó, Cóbhtha*, not given.

Coe, *coagh*, a round hollow.

Coff, *Uí-Chobhthaigh*, O'Coffey, a family name and a founder of Kileencoff Church in Mayo.

Coffey, *Cobhthaigh*, not given.

Coffey, *Uí-Cobhthaigh*, Coffey a family name.

Coffy, Coffagh, a personal or family name.

Coffy, Coffey, a family name.

Coffy, *Uí-Chobhthaigh*, O'Coffey, a family name.

Cogaile, *cuigéal*, distaffs or rocks.

Cogaile, *gCoigéal*, not given.

Cogaile, *gCuigéal*, distaffs.

Cogan, *Comhgán*, not given.

Coggal, *cogal*, cockles (corn-tares).

Coggal, *cogal*, tares (a weed) or cockles (corn-tares).

Coggal, *coigeal*, a distaff or a spinning camp.

Coggaula, *cogal*, cockles (corn-tares).

Coggaula, *coigeal*, a distaff.

Coggil, *chogaoil, cogal*, tares (a weed).

Coggrey, *cocríoch*, borderland.

Coggy, *chagaidh*, not given.

Coggy, *cogaidh*, battle.

Cogh, *catha*, a battle.

Cogh, *cuach*, cuckoos.

Coghalane, *chochallain*, the covering.

Coghill, *chochaill*, the net.

Coghill, *cochall*, fishing nets.

Coghill, *cochaill*, the cloak.

Coghlan, *Uí-Chochlain*, a family name.

Cogly, *Uí-Coigligh*, O'Quigley, a family name.

Cogram, *chograim*, whispering.

Cogran, *Cográn*, not given.

Cogue, *cogaidh*, war.

Coguish, *coguis, an-chógais*, not given.

Cogy, *Chóige*, St Chóige/Cóige/Coige, the name of a Church founder in Cavan.

Cogy, *Cóige*, not given.

Coh, *chatha*, not given.

Cohan, *Chuacháin, Cuacháin*, St Cuachan/Cuach.

Coheen, *cabhairín*, not given.

Coher, *Chathaoir*, not given.

Cohig, *chobhthaigh*, O'Cowhig, a family name.

Cohig, *choimhthigh*, a foreigner or stranger.

Cohig, *chomhthaigh*, not given.

Cohy, *cathaghadh*, a battle-field.

Coil, *choill*, a wood.

Coila, *coill-na...*, wood of the...

Coimirce, *coimirce,* not given.

Coin, *Caidhn,* not given.

Coin, *Choinn,* Conn, a personal name.

Coin, *gCadhan, cadhan,* a barnacle goose.

Coke, *Chóca, Cóc,* St Coca.

Cokery, *chócaire,* the cook.

Col, *coll,* hazel, a place of hazel.

Col, *cuil,* corner.

Cola, *comhla,* gates.

Colagh, *chómla,* the gate.

Colane, *Caláin,* Callan, a personal or family name.

Colane, *collain,* hazel.

Collan, *Chulláin,* Cullán, the name of a founder of Kilcollan Church.

Collane, *Collain,* Keolan, a personal or family name.

Coldragh, *cealldrach,* an old cemetery

Cole, *coll, coill,* hazels.

Cole, *cual,* faggots.

Cole, *cúil, cuil,* a nook or recess.

Colehill, *chúlchoill, cnoc-na-Góla,* not given.

Colehill, *collchoill,* hazel wood.

Coleman, *Cholmáin,* Colman, St Colman.

Coleraine, *cabhall-Riáin,* Ryans ruin.

Coleraine, *Coll-Rian,* not given.

Coleraine, *cúil-raithin,* recess of ferns.

Coleraine, *cúl-rathain,* not given.

Colgach, *calgach,* a prickly place.

Colgadh, *calagach,* the prickly place.

Colgagh, *calgach, colgach,* a thorny or prickly place.

Colgagh, *chalgach, cholgach,* not given.

Colgan, *Cholgáin,* St Colga (7th cent).

Colgan, *Cholgan,* St Colga/Colfa(sic).

Colgan, *Colgan,* not given.

Colgny, *colgnach, colgnaighe,* thorny.

Coll, *coll,* hazel, a place of hazel.

Colla, *chalaidh, caladh,* a pier, a ferry, a landing place or a wet meadow.

Colla, *chalaidh,* hard land(sic).

Colla, *chodla,* sleep.

Colla, *Cholla,* Colla, a personal or family name.

Colla, *cholla,* hard land.

Colla, *chollaigh,* a boar.

Colla, *coille,* a wood.

Colla, Collam, a personal or family name.

Collagan, *colgain,* thorn bushes.

Collagh, a boar.

Collagh, from *coll,* a place of hazels.

Collaire, *choiléir,* a quarry.

Collan, *Chlláin,* not given.

Collare, *choiléir,* not given.

Collare, *coiléir,* a quarry.

Collen, *coillín,* a little wood.

Coller, *coiléara,* a quarry.

Colli, *choiligh,* not given.

Collid, *challóide,* not given.

Collid, *collóide,* a wrangle on contention.

Colliers, *cailleach,* Nuns.

Collig, *choiligh,* woodcock.

Collig, *Chollaigh,* Coll, a family name.

Collig, *chollaigh,* the boar or wild boar.

Collig, *Colga,* not given.

Collig, *collaigh, chollaigh, chulloigh, chullaigh, cullaig,* a boar.

Colliga, *colgach,* a thorny place.

Colligan, *coilleagán, coilligeán,* hazel growing river.

Colligan, Colligan or Colgan, a personal or family name.

Colligan, *culligeain,* abounding in holly.

Colligane, *culligeain,* abounding in holly.

Colliher, *collachair, coll-choille,* hazel wood.

Collin, *Choillín, Chollāin,* not given.

Collin, Collin, a personal or family name.

Collin, *Uí-Coileain,* O'Collins or Collins, a family name.

Collina, *caladh-na...,* riverside meadow of the...

Collisteige, corner of Teige's (a male name) fort.

Colliton, *Uí-Codlatain/Coollatain,* O'Collatan, a family name now known as Colton.

Collive, *Cholbha,* not given.

Colliwee, *choiligh-bhuidhe,* not given.

Collog, *colg,* a straight bladed sword, a sharp spear, a dirk, a thorn or a thorn bush.

Collogher, *collachair,* hazelwood.

Collon, *callann,* not given.

Collon, *collann, collon,* hazels.

Collon, *cuilleann,* a place of holly.

Collon, *cuilleann,* the steep slope.

Colloo, *Chalbhaigh,* not given.

Colloo, *colba, colú,* a barrier.

Collooney, *cúil-mhúine/mhuine,* recess or nook of the thicket.

Colloony, *cúil-maoile*, the angle or recess of the bald or hornless cow.

Collop, *Cholpa*, Colpa, a personal or family name.

Collop, *cholpa*, the heifer.

Collop, *collop*, cattle.

Collop, *colpa*, heifer/s or cattle.

Collop, *colpha*, not given.

Collops, from *colpa*, a grazing place or herding place for cattle.

Collorus, *coll-ros*, hazel wood.

Collough, *coilleach*, a place of trees.

Collum, *colm, colum*, pigeons or doves.

Colly, *cheapchain*, a little green spot or denuded wood.

Colly, *chollaigh*, not given.

Colm, *Coilm*, Colm, a male name.

Colman, *Cholmáin*, St Colmán.

Colman, *Colmán, Colman*, a personal or family name.

Colman, *Cill-Cholmain*, not given.

Colman, *na-gColmán*, not given.

Colough, *colba, colú*, a barrier.

Colp, *cholpa*, a mature heifer.

Colp, *Colpa*, a male name.

Colpa, *colpach*, heifers.

Colpagh, *colpagh, colpa*, heifer/s.

Colpey, *cholpa*, heifers.

Colpy, *cholpa*, the steer or bullock.

Colpy, *colpa*, heifers.

Colt, *colt-cuileann*, not given.

Coltha, *Chuile*, Cuile, a personal or family name.

Coltig, *chobhlaigh*, the fleet.

Coltig, *chabhlaigh*, not given.

Colum, *colum*, a dove.

Columb, *Cholmai*, Colma, a persons name, possibly a Saint.

Columb, *Choluim*, Colum, a male name.

Columb, Colm, St Columb, St. Columba or Colman, a personal or family name.

Columb, *Colm*, St Columba.

Columb, *colm*, the wood pidgeon.

Columcille, *Colum-Cill*, St Columcille, his name means the Church of the dove.

Columkille, Colm, *Cholm-Cille*, Colm Cille, a Saints name.

Coly, *chuaille*, not given.

Coly, *cuaille*, the pole.

Com, *com, cam*, crooked.

Com, *com, cúm*, a hollow.

Comagh, *cam-mágh*, crooked plain.

Comaghy, *camachadh*, not given.

Comaghy, *com-achaidh*, crooked field.

Comain, *chomain*, a winding river.

Coman, *Chomáin*, St Comán.

Comane, *Damain*, St Daman.

Comaun, *com, cúmhach, cúm*, a hollow, dell or valley.

Comay, *Chomaigh*, Comey, a personal or family name.

Comb, *chon*, hounds.

Comb, *Coma*, not given.

Combe, *com, cúmhach, cúm*, a hollow, dell or valley.

Comber, Combra, *chomair, comar, chomar, cumar*, a confluence, joining of rivers.

Comenty, *Chomnaid, Coiminte*, not given.

Comer, *chomair, comar*, a confluence of rivers.

Comer, *chumair, chomair*, not given.

Comeragh, *chomaraigh*, not given.

Comeragh, *cumarach, comarach, chumaraigh*, confluences or a place of confluences.

Comertagh, *coimeartach*, not given.

Comhola, *comsheóla*, not given.

Comillane, *Comalán*, not given.

Comillane, *cum-Oileain*, hollow of the island.

Comin, *Chuimín*, Cuimín, a personal or family name and the founder of a Church in Offaly.

Comirce, *comairghe*, sanctuary.

Comisk, *Comaisc*, O'Comisk, a family name.

Comisk, *Cumaisc*, not given.

Comisk, *Uí-Cumascaigh*, O'Cummiskey, a family name.

Commadan, *Comadan*, not given.

Commade, *coimheada*, watching.

Commane, *coimead*, guarding, watching or outposts.

Commane, *Comáin*, not given.

Commane, *Uí-Chomain*, Cummins, a family name

Commane, *Uí-Chomain*, Cummins, a family name.

Commanealine, *comán-Laighean*, not given.

Commanes, little hollows.

Commanes, *na-comáin,* not given.

Commar, *comar,* a confluence of rivers.

Commaun, *com, cúmhach, cúm,* a hollow, dell or valley.

Commaun, *comán, comáin, camáin,* not given.

Commaun, *camán,* a winding glen.

Commaun, *cumán,* a little hollow.

Commaune, a little hollow.

Commauns, little hollows.

Commedagh, *coimhéideach, coimheada,* watching or guarding.

Commeen, *coimín,* a little valley.

Commeen, *coimín, choimín,* a common or common land.

Commeen, *commeen,* little valley.

Commeen, *cumin, coimín,* a little hollow.

Commeen, *coimin,* not given.

Commeen, from, *cúm,* little hollow.

Commeenlonagh, *achadh-na-manach,* not given.

Commera, *chamana,* seaweed.

Commera, *chamra,* not given.

Commock, *camóg,* a winding.

Commock, *dá-Chomóg,* not given.

Commoge, *camóg,* a winding or crooked place.

Commoge, *chamóg,* not given.

Commogue, *camog,* crooked little river.

Common, *Choimín, cumann,* not given.

Common, *cimíneacht, chimín,* commonage.

Common, *chomain, camán,* hurling or hurleys.

Common, *Chomáin,* Cummian, a personal or family name.

Common, *Chuimín,* Cuimín, St Comán, founder of a Church in Tipperary.

Common, *Comain,* St Coman or just Coman, a male name.

Common, *Uí-Chomain,* Cummins, a family name.

Common, *Uí-Chomáin,* Ó Comán, a family name.

Commons, *cimíneacht, coimín,* commonage.

Comock, *chamóg,* St Dácamog.

Comoge, *chamóg, camóg,* winding river.

Comoge, *chamóige,* not given.

Comortish, *chomórtais,* emulation.

Comortish, *cómórtus,* emulation, comparison or contention.

Comraghs, *na-comhracha,* not given.

Comroe, *cumrua, corca-Mrua,* not given.

Comroe, Modhruadh, a personal, tribal or family name.

Comy, *chomaigh,* not given.

Con, *ceann,* a head.

Con, *Choinn,* Conn, a personal or family name.

Con, *Chonnaidh, Cana,* Cana, not given.

Con, *coin, con,* a hound or hounds.

Con, *cuan,* a recess or bend.

Cona, *ceann-a'...,* not given.

Cona, *cuan-a'...,* bend or curve of...

Conaghan, Conaghan, a personal or family name.

Conagher, *conadhchair,* a place of firewood.

Conaghoo, *con-achaidh,* hound field.

Conaghra, *conach-réidh,* not given.

Conaghra, *conachra,* the dogs shrubbery.

Conaghy, *conachadh, con-achaidh,* hound field.

Conahy, *coin*(sic)*-achadh,* hound field.

Conair, *conair,* a path.

Conan, *coinín,* not given.

Conane, *Canáin,* not given.

Conane, *Chonáin, Conáin,* St Conan.

Conane, *Conáin,* Conan a male name.

Conarty, *conairte, conairt, cuanartaigh,* a pack of hounds.

Conaun, *Conáin, Conaun,* Conan, a personal or family name.

Conaun, *Conáin,* not given.

Conboy, *Mhic-Chonbuidhe,* Mac Conboy, a family name.

Concamoree, *cuan-cam-mhór,* the big crooked bend.

Concoose, *chon-cuais/chuais,* greyhound-cave.

Concra, *conchró,* not given.

Concra, *con-cro,* dog hut.

Concroe, *con-cro,* dog hut.

Condon, *Chondúnaigh,* not given.

Condon, *Chundúnaigh,* Condon, a personal or family name.

Condra, *Chonrach, Connrach,* not given.

Condra, *Conra, Conreach, Conrach,* Contra, a male name.

Condra, *conrach,* the path.

Condry, *con-doire/darach,* oak wood of the hounds.

Conduff, *Chonduibh,* Cuduff, a male name. It means black hound.

Conduff, *Conduibh,* not given.

Conduff, *con-duibhe,* the black hound.

Condy, *Chonda,* St Conda or St Conna.

Coneen, *coinín, choinín,* rabbits.

Coneera, *Conaorta,* not given.

Conegar, *coinicéar,* a rabbit warren.

Coneirn, *Coindeirin,* not given.

Conenagh, *acha-nAoineach,* Acha (a female name) of the fastings.

Cones, from *chuain,* a harbour or winding.

Coney, (island) *Oileán-na-gCoiníní, inis-maolchloiche,* not given.

Coney, (island) *Inis-Uí-Mhaolcluiche,* O'Mulclohy's (a family name) island.

Coney, *Oilean-na-gCuinigh,* Ilsand of the rabbits.

Coney, *coinín,* a rabbit or rabbit warren.

Coney, *conaidh, chonaidh,* firewood.

Coney, *connaidh,* not given.

Coney, *cuinínidhe, coiní,* rabbits.

Coneygar, *coinicéar,* not given.

Coneygar, *coinicér,* a rabbit warren.

Coneykeare, *cuinicéra,* a rabbit warren.

Confey, *coinfe,* not given.

Cong, *cunga, cong, conga,* a narrow strip of land, a narrow stretch of water between two larger ones, an isthmus, a strait, a narrow strait or a neck.

Conga, *conga,* not given.

Conge, *conga,* a narrow part of a river.

Conglas, *Conghlais,* not given.

Conglass, Cuglas, a male name.

Congo, *cunga,* a narrow strip of land, a strait, a neck.

Congor, *congar,* meeting place.

Congor, *cóngar,* not given.

Conicar, *cuinicéra, coinicér,* a rabbit warren.

Conicker, *coinicéar,* not given.

Conicker, *cuinicéra,* a rabbit warren.

Conickny, *Conmhaicne,* not given.

Conigane, *Uí-Chonnagain,* Cunningham, a family name.

Conigar, *coinigéar,* not given.

Conigar, *cuinicéra, coinicéar, coinicér,* a rabbit warren.

Coniker, *coinicéar,* not given.

Coniker, *coinicér,* rabbit warrens.

Conin, *choinín,* the rabbit.

Conkeine, *Concadhain,* not given.

Conlan, *Chonalláin,* Connallan, a personal or family name.

Conlan, *coinnleain,* stubbles.

Conlaun, *Uí-Chonaláin,* O'Connellan, a family name.

Conlawn, *Conlán-cinn-sein-tSléibhe,* not given.

Conleen, *coinnlín,* stubbles.

Conlester, *con-Liostair,* Liostar, Lister or Lester's (a male name) hound.

Conlig, *chonleic, choinleac,* flagstone of the hounds.

Conlig, *choinleic,* not given.

Conlish, *chin-lios, chin-lis, ceann-lios,* the head of the fort.

Conlish, *chinn-lis,* at the head of the ford(sic).

Conlore, *coinleoir,* the candlestick.

Conly, *Chonla,* a personal or family name and the founder of a Church in Galway.

Conly, *Connla,* not given.

Conmacht, Conn's (a personal name) place.

Conn, *ceann,* a head.

Conn, *con,* a hound.

Conn, *con,* pure.

Conna, *conachail,* hound wood.

Conna, *conadh-choill,* wood of firewood.

Conna, *Conaithe, Conchaidh,* not given.

Connabury, *coinicéar,* not given.

Connacht, *cúige-Chonnacht,* Connacht, 'Conn's' land.

Connacht, *Chonnacht*

Connacht, *Connachta,* the name of an ancient tribe, a personal or family name or a man from Connaught.

Connagh, *canach,* bog cotton.

Connagh, *conach,* abundance.

Connagh, *conadhach,* abounding in firewood.

Connagh, *seanchonach,* not given.

Connaghkinnagoe, *conadhachcinn-a'-ghabha,* the firewood-place of the head or hill of the smith.

Connaghty, *Chonnachtaigh,* the Connaughtman.

Connahy, *conachadh, con-achaidh,* hound field.

Connaught, *Chonnacht,* the name of an ancient tribe, a personal or family name or a man from Connaught.

Connaught, *connadh,* wood.

Connaught, *Chonnachtaigh,* not given.

Conneely, *Conaola,* Conaola or Conaol, a personal name.

Conneely, *Uí-Chonghaile,* Ua-Conáile, O'Connolly or O'Conneely, a family name.

Conneen, a little corner.

Connel, *Conall, Chonaill, Chonail,* St Conall.

Connell, *Chonaill,* Connal, a personal or family name.

Connell, *Conaill, Conall, Chonaill,* Conal, Conall, Connell, a male name.

Connell, *Cónaill,* O'Connell, a family name.

Connell, *congbhail,* a habitation.

Connell, *Uí-Chonaill,* descendants of Conaing(sic).

Connell, *Chonnell,* Connell, a personal or family name.

Connellan, *Chonalláin,* Conalláin or Connellan, a personal or family name.

Connello, *Conallaigh,* not given.

Connello, *Uí/Hy-Conaill-Gabra,* O'Connell Gabhra, the name of an ancient tribe.

Connelly, *Chonaíle, Chonaile,* not given.

Connelly, *O-Conghaile,* Connolly, not given.

Connelly, *Congallaigh,* St Connelly.

Connelly, *Chonglaigh,* St Congalach.

Connemara, *Conamara,* the Conmacne people of the sea or the sea coast territory of Conmac, Conmacc or Conmhac.

Connemara, *Conmacne-mara,* the seaside (mara) of Conmacne descendants of Conmnac.

Connemara, *conmaicne-mara, conmaicne,* the seaside.

Connemara, *corca Modhruadh, corcomruad,* the race (of people) of Modhruadh.

Connemara, *cuain-na-mara,* harbours of the sea.

Conner, *conaire,* a road or beaten path.

Connery, *chonaire,* a path-or defile.

Connery, *conaire,* not given.

Connery, *conaraidhe,* road or pass.

Connick, *Chonmhaic,* not given.

Connick, Conmhac, Conmac, a personal or family name.

Connick, *Cunmhaic,* Conmhac, a personal or family name.

Connigar, *coinicér,* rabbit warrens.

Connigare, *coinicér,* rabbit warrens.

Connoe, *chnudh,* nuts.

Connolly, *cluain-bhuaile, fiadhach-ruadh, fioch-rua, fiodh-ruadh,* not given.

Connonagh, *ceannannach,* a place of white heads.

Connor, *Chonchobhair,* O'Connor, a family name.

Connor, *Chonchubhair,* Conogher, a personal or family name.

Connor, *Chonchúir,* not given.

Connor, *Coinnire,* a personal or family name.

Connor, *chonaire,* the way.

Connor, *conaire, chonair,* the road or pass.

Connor, *doire-na-con, con-deire, coinnire,* oak wood of the hounds/dogs.

Connor, *Mhic-Chonchobhair,* Mac Conchuír, a personal or family name.

Connor, *Uí-Choncobhair,* O'Connor, a family name.

Conny, *chonnaidh, Connaidh,* not given.

Conny, *conaidh, conna, conadh, chonaidh,* firewood.

Conoal, *Chonóail,* O'Conole, a family name.

Conoal, *Conóail,* O'Conole, a family name.

Conor, *Chonchubhair,* not given.

Conor, Conra or Conor, a personal or family name.

Conra, *Connraighe,* not given.

Conra, *Conrá, Conra,* a male name.

Conragh, *conrach,* the treaty.

Conrath, *conarta,* pack of hounds.

Conrath, *conarta,* the covenant.

Conrath, *connrach,* not given.

Conrath, *Conrach,* Conra, a personal name.

Conrath, *conrach,* the path.

Conrea, *cunnradh,* covenant or treaty.

Conready, Conready, a personal or family name.

Conreafy, Conreafy, Canreafy, a family name.

Conreafy, *Con-Riabhche*, not given.

Conree, *Con-Raoi, Conraoi, Cúrí, Curoi, Cúraoi,* Curaois or Curaoi, an ancient Irish chief.

Conree, *Mhic-Conrai*, not given.

Conroe, *con-rauidhe*, red hound.

Conry, *Conáire*, St Cónaire.

Conry, *Conraoi,* Conraoi, a personal or family name.

Conry, O'Conry or MacConry, a family name.

Conry, *Ua-Conroí*, O'Conry, a family name.

Conspod, *conspoid*, controversy.

Contuort, *contabhairte*, danger.

Conty, *cointe*, not given.

Conty, *cuanta*, bays.

Conva, *conbhaidh*, not given.

Convoy, *conmhá, conmhaigh, con-mhagh,* hound plain.

Conwal, *chonbháil*, the establishment.

Conwal, *congbháil, congbhail*, habitation.

Conwald, habitation.

Conwall, *chonhbháil*, the establishment.

Conway, *ceann-mhaighe*, head of the plain.

Conway, *Conmhaigh,* Conway, a personal or family name.

Conway, *Mhic-Connmhaighe,* MacConway, a family name.

Conway, *Uí-Chonnmhaigh*, Ó Connmhaigh, a family name.

Conwell, *Conmhaoil,* Conwell, a personal or family name.

Coo, a channel or narrow neck.

Coo, *Chú, Có*, not given.

Coo, *cúnga*, narrow.

Coo, *Chua*, St Cua.

Coo, *cú*, a narrow stretch of water between two larger ones.

Coo, *cú*, narrows.

Coo, *cuach*, cuckoos.

Coo, *cuaiche*, a hollow.

Coo, *cumha*, lamentation.

Coo, *cumhadh, cumhaidh,* not given.

Coo, the hound.

Cooan, *chuain*, not given.

Cooan, *cuan*, a narrow inlet.

Coob, *cúm*, a valley.

Cooey, *cuaigh*, a cup or hollow.

Coofulla, *Cóigeuladh*, a nickname for the Province of Ulster.

Coog, *Chuag*, not given.

Cooga, *ciúgeadh*(sic), a fifth of a baile-biatach (a land measure).

Cooga, *coigeadh*, a fifth.

Cooga, *cúige*, not given.

Coogaun, *comhang*, a narrow place.

Coogaun, *cuagan*, poll of the narrow head(sic).

Cooge, *chuag*, the cuckoo.

Cooge, *cuaig*, not given.

Coogh, *Chua*, not given.

Coogh, *chuach*, cuckoos.

Coogh, *cuach*, cuckoos.

Coogue, *coigeadh*, a fifth.

Coogulla, *coig-Ulládh*, the province of leinster.

Coogulla, *cuige-Uladh*, literally 'the King of leinster'.

Coogulla, *cúige-Uladh*, not given.

Cooguquid, *cuigeadh-cuid*, a fifth of a ploughland.

Coogy, *chúige*, the province.

Coogyulla, *cuige-Uladh*, literally 'the King of leinster'.

Cooha, *cuach, cuaiche,* cuckoo/s.

Cooheen, *cuaichín*, the little cuckoo.

Cooheen, *cuaichíne*, not given.

Coohey, *cuachaí*, not given.

Coohy, *cuach*, cuckoos.

Cookera, *chócaire*, a cook.

Cool, *caol*, narrow.

Cool, *chúil, cúl*, a secluded spot.

Cool, *coill, choill*, a wood.

Cool, *cuaille*, a bare tree or a pole.

Cool, *Cuala, cúile*, not given.

Cool, *cúil*, a hill.

Cool, *cuil, cúil*, a corner, an angle, a nook, a recess or a secluded place.

Cool, *cul*, a back, usually of a hill.

Cool, *cúl*, remote.

Cool, *Cumhaill,* Cumhal or Cowell a personal or family name.

Coola, *cuaille*, the pole, stake, stock or point.

Coola, *cuailleach-na…, chuailleach, cúla*, not given.

Coola, *cúil, cúile*, corner, angle, nook or recess.

Coola, *cúil/chuile/chúil-an…, gCúl,* not given.

Coola, *cúil-an/a'/na…,* corneror angle of the…

Coola, *cúile,* a hollow(sic).

Coola, *cúl, cúile, culach,* a back place, angle, corner or a recess.

Coola, *cula,* a hill.

Coolacork, *cúil-a'coirce,* angle or corner of the oats.

Coolaflags, *(bi-lingual) cuailleach-na-leac,* not given.

Coolagh, *chúlach,* a corner, an angle, a secluded place, a back place, behind a hill etc.

Coolagh, *cuaileach,* a marshy place, a copse or thicket.

Coolagh, *cúileacha,* an angle or corner.

Coolagh, *cúl, cúile, culach,* a back place or land at the back of a hill.

Coolagh, *cúlach,* back land.

Coolagh, *cúlach, chuailleach, cúil-each, na-cualacha,* not given.

Coolagh, *cúlach,* corners.

Coolagh, *cuailleach,* a thicket or copse.

Coolagh, *culach,* a remote place, a back place, an angle, corner or recess.

Coolagh, *cúlag*(sic), peat or turf.

Coolaghansglaster, *glasdair-Mhic-Uallacháin*(sic), not given.

Coolaght, the company or colony.

Coolagorane, *cúil-Ó-gCuaráin,* not given.

Coolaha, *cúil-chatha,* not given.

Coolaherty, *cúil-Uí-Fhatharthaigh,* not given.

Coolaholloga, *cúil-Chalgaigh,* not given.

Coolamber, *cluain-sionnach*(sic), not given.

Coolamber, *cúl-umair,* hill back of the narrow channel.

Coolan, *cúil-an…,* not given.

Coolanagh, *cuileannach,* a place of holly.

Coolanheen, *cúil-Fhlaithnín,* not given.

Coolanimod, *cúil-an-adhmaid,* not given.

Coolaoh(sic), *cúlach,* the corner.

Coolapoge, *cúil-Lapóg,* not given.

Coolapogue, *cúil-na-gCupóg,* angle of the dockweed.

Coolatty, *cúil-leatáite,* not given.

Coolaun, *Cill-Chúláin*(sic), not given.

Coolaun, *cúlan,* little hill back.

Coolavin, *cuil-O'bhFinn,* corner of the O'Finn's.

Coolaw, *cul-atha,* back of the ford.

Coolawn, *culán,* a little rock.

Cooldurrin, *cúl-dorn,* the back of the fist.

Coole, *Chomhghaill, Comhghaill,* St Comgall/Comhghall.

Coole, *chúil, chúl, cúil,* the angle or recess.

Coole, *Chumnhaill, Cumhall,* a personal or family name.

Coole, *cúil,* a hill.

Coole, *cúil-an-Chnapaire, cúl-Chollainge,* not given.

Coole, *cúile, cúil, cul,* a secluded place or a recess.

Coole, *cúile, cúl,* a hillback, ridge back, a recess or secluded place.

Coole, *Cumhal, Cumhall, Cumhal,* a male name.

Coolea, *cúil/cúl-Áodh/Aodha,* Aodh's or Hugh's (a mans name) nook or angle.

Cooleagh, *chuailleach, chúil/cúil-liach/liath, cúil-liach,* not given.

Cooleagh, *chuailleach,* the wooden place.

Cooleagh, *cuáileach,* full of poles or tall trees.

Cooleen, *cholthailín,* a small gathering or 'pattern'.

Cooleen, *cuilín,* little angle or corner.

Cooleen, *cúilín,* a little hill(sic).

Cooleen, *cúilín,* little angles/corners.

Cooleena, *cuilin-na…,* recess of the…

Cooleena, *cuilin-a'…,* little recess of the…

Cooleens, *cúilíní, cuilíní,* small nooks.

Cooleeny, *na-cúilíní,* not given.

Cooleeny, *cuilínide,* little angles or corners.

Coolehill, *chúlchoill,* not given.

Coolehill, *cúl-choill,* back wood.

Cooleigh, *cuaileach,* land of poles or long trees.

Cooley, *chúile, cúile, cúil,* a corner, nook, recess, secluded place or angle.

Cooley, *chúile, cúille, cuaille,* not given.

Cooley, *Cuailgne, Cuailnge,* the name of a district and an ancient chief (son of Brogan).

Cooley, *cuil,* a corner.

Coolhill, *chollchoille,* hazel wood.

Coolhill, *chúlchoill,* not given.

Coolhill, *cúl-choill,* the back wood.

Cooli, *cúl-le…,* nook of the…

Coolia, *chuaille, cuaille,* a stake or pole.

Coolick, *cúil-lice,* land corner of the flagstone.

Coolicka, *cúil-lice,* land corner of the flagstone.

Coolicka, *cuil-lice,* nook of the flagstones.

Coolies, *cúilí,* not given.

Coolig, *cabhlaigh,* house ruins.

Coolimrick, *cúil-imris,* corner of contention.

Coolin, *cualann,* not given.

Coolin, *cuilín,* a little hill back or corner.

Cooline, *chúllín,* little angle or corner.

Cooliney, *cúilínidhe,* little angles or corners.

Cooliska, *an-chúil-loiscthe,* not given.

Coolle, *cúl-le…,* back to the…

Coollegreane, *cúl-le-gréin,* back to the sun.

Coollyduv, *cúil-Uí-Dhubh,* O'Duffs corner, angle.

Coolmain, *cúil-mholt*(sic), not given.

Coolmuckbane, *cúil-mholt-bhán*(sic), not given.

Coolnacran, *cuain*(sic)*-chrannacháin,* meadow of the wooded place.

Coolnaherin, *cúil-leathfhearainn*(sic), not given.

Coolnahinch, *cuar*(sic)*-leithinse,* not given.

Coolnaneagh, *cúil-na-smután*(sic), corner of the bogdeal humps.

Coolock, *chúlóg,* little secluded place.

Coolock, *cúlóc,* not given.

Coolock, *cúlóg,* the little corner.

Coologe, *an-tSaileog*(sic), not given.

Coologe, *chúlóg,* a small corner.

Coologue, *cúlóg,* little (hill) back.

Cooloo, *baile-Colbha,* not given.

Cooloon, *cúile-Uain,* not given.

Coolooney, *cúil-mhuine,* not given.

Coolooney, the big secluded place.

Coolougher, back of the rushes.

Coolreagh, *an-caladh*(sic)*-riabhach,* not given.

Coolreagh, *an-chúil-riabhach,* not given.

Coolroe, *cúl-ruadh,* ridge back(sic).

Cools, hill backs.

Cools, *na-cúlacha/cúla,* not given.

Coolstuff, *cúil-lios-dubh, Cill-Aodhgán,* not given.

Coolteen, *cuiltin, cuiltín,* little corner.

Cooltrim, *cluain-troim*(sic), not given.

Coolty, *coillte,* not given.

Coolugher, *cúil-luachra,* not given.

Coolum, *cuan-'Liam,* William's (a male name) haven.

Coolum, *cúllom,* bare ridge back.

Coolvoy, *an-chúlbhá,* not given.

Cooly, *choill,* hazel.

Cooly, *cuaille,* poles or stakes.

Cooly, *cúil-an…,* corner of the…

Cooly, *cúile,* an angle, nook or corner.

Cooly, *cúlach, Chúile,* not given.

Coolly, *culach,* an angle of land.

Coolyrua, *cúil-an-rua,* not given.

Coom, *cúm, cum,* a mountain hollow.

Coom, *cúm, cum, com,* a hollow, dell or valley.

Cooma, *com-na…, cúm-an/a'…,* hollow of the…

Cooma, *cúmhach, cúm,* a hollow, dell or valley.

Coomastow, *com-dhá-Stogha,* not given.

Coomb, *cham,* not given.

Coomb, *com, cúm,* a hollow, dell or valley.

Coombe, *com, cúmhach, cúm,* a hollow, dell or valley.

Coombs, *na-cúim,* not given.

Coomna, *com-na…,* hollow of the…

Coon, *cuan,* a curve in a river.

Coon, *cuan,* a harbour, haven, curve or winding.

Coon, *cuan,* a harbour, haven curve or winding.

Coona, *chaonaigh,* moss.

Coona, *Cuana,* St Cuana.

Coona, *Cuanna,* not given.

Coonagane, *chunachain,* a mossy place.

Coonagh, *an-Chuanaigh,* the garden of 'an Cuanach', not given.

Coonagh, *chuanach, Uí-Chuanach,* not given.

Coonagh, *cuanach,* a place of curves, bays or windings.

Coonagh, *Uí-Cuanach,* the people of *Hy Cuanach.*

Coonane, *cuanan,* a little dell or hollow.

Coonane, from *cuan,* a little harbour, haven curve or winding.

Coondera, *chomghair,* a short cut.

Coone, *cuain,* harbours.

Cooneen, *cuainín,* little cove.

Cooneen, *cuínín, cuainín,* a little harbour, haven curve or winding.

Cooneen, *cúinnín,* a little corner.

Cooneen, from *cuan,* a little harbour, haven curve or winding.

Coonera, *cuanaire,* sea inlets.

Cooney, *Chuana,* Cuana, a personal or family name.

Cooney, *Chuana,* Cuana, St Cuana.

Cooney, *Chuanna,* Cuana, Cuanna, not given.

Coonlough, *Cónla,* Conla, a male name.

Coonoge, *cuanóg,* a little harbour, haven curve or winding.

Coontraght, *an-phuntracht*(sic), not given.

Coony, *Cuana,* St Cuana.

Cooperhill, *mucinis,* not given.

Coor, *cuar,* a bay, a round hollow, a dell, a winding, a winding hollow, a curved hollow, a ring, a hoop, a circle, curve or curved.

Coor, *cuar,* a round hill.

Coor, *cubhar,* an angle of land.

Coor, *cubhar,* foam or froth.

Coora, *Chumhra,* not given.

Coora, *cuar-an…, cuar-a'…,* curve or round hollow of the….

Coora, *cumhraidh,* sweet smelling.

Cooraclare, *cúr-an-chláir,* not given.

Cooraghy, a place of boats.

Coorannel, *cuar-Randal,* Randal's (a personal or a family name) round plot.

Cooraun, *cuarán,* little dell or hollow.

Cooravane, *cúrabháin,* not given.

Coorevin, *comhar-Éimhín,* not given.

Coorha, *Chonrach,* Conrí, not given.

Coorha, *Chúmhra,* not given.

Coorna, *cuar-na…,* (see coor) of the…

Coorolagh, *cuar-a'locha,* curved land of the lake.

Coort, *chuairt,* the journey.

Coos, *cuas,* cave/s.

Coosan, *chuasáin,* a little cave.

Coosan, *chuasáin, cuasán,* a little cave.

Coosan, *cuasán,* a little cave, can also mean a small sea inlet or cove.

Coosane, *chúasáin, cuasán, chuasain,* a cavern, cove or cavity.

Coosane, *cuasán, cuasan,* a little cave or hollow.

Coosane, from *cuas,* little cave, can also mean a small sea inlet or cove.

Coosaun, *chuasáin,* little cave, can also mean a small sea inlet or cove.

Coosaun, *chuasán,* a hollow.

Coosaun, *cuasán,* a little recess or cave.

Coosaun, *Uí-Chuasáin,* O'Cussane or Cussan, a family name.

Coose, *cuais,* a cave.

Coose, *cuas,* a hollow.

Coose, *cuas,* cave/s or hollows.

Coose, from *cuas,* caves, can also mean sea inlets or coves.

Coosh, *cúas, cuais,* a cave.

Coosheen, *cuaisín,* a small hollow or creek.

Coosheen, from *cuas,* little cave, can also mean a small sea inlet or cove.

Coosna, *cuas-na…,* cave of the…

Cootehill, *muinchille,* not given.

Cop, *Chopa,* Coppa, a personal or family name.

Copal, *chapaill,* horse/s.

Copany, *copánach,* a place producing dock leaves.

Copay, *cluain-searbhóg,* not given.

Copney, *copánach,* a place producing dock leaves.

Coppanagh, *copánach,* a place producing dock leaves.

Coppanagh, *copanach,* not given.

Coppe, *capall,* horses.

Coppeen, *an-caipín, chaipín,* the little cap.

Coppinger, *Choipinéar,* Coppinger, a personal or family name.

Coppogagh, *copóg,* dock leaves.

Coppoge, *gCopóg,* dock or dock leaves.

Coppough, *gCeapach,* plots.

Coppul, *a'chapaill,* (of the) horses.

Cor, *chorr,* hills.

Cor, *chorraigh, churraigh,* not given.

Cor, *chorráin, chorra, chor, chartha, coirre,* not given.

Cor, *coire,* a hollow.

Cor, *cor,* a round pit, a hollow or a turn in the road.

Cor, *cor, corr,* a bend, twist or odd.

Cor, *cor, corr,* a round hill.

Cor, *cor,* smooth.

Cor, *coirre,* a hill.

Cor, *coradh, corra, cora, choradh,* a weir.

Cor, *corca,* the race (of people).

Cor, *corr,* a snout or beak.

Cor, *corr,* cranes or herons.

Cor, *corr,* unusually shaped.

Cor, *corran,* not given.

Cor, *garbh,* rough.

Cora, *chomhartha,* the sign.

Cora, *coradh, corra, cuarr,* a weir.

Cora, *cor,* a round hill.

Cora, *corr-an…,* not given.

Cora, *cumhraidhe,* sweet smelling.

Corabul, *baile-an-charbaid,* town of boulder(sic).

Coracow, *comhrac,* meeting.

Coracow, *comhrac-dhá-abha,* meeting of two streams.

Coragh, *currach,* not given.

Coragh, *corrach,* a moor or bog.

Corah, *córthach,* a moor or a bog.

Coran, *charnain,* a cairn.

Coran, *Chuaráin,* not given.

Coran, *Cuarain, Cuarán, Cuaran, Chuaráin,* St Cuaran.

Coran, *Chobhráin,* St Cobhran.

Coran, *cuarthainn,* winding or bending.

Corbally, *chorr-bhaile,* a jutting out place.

Corban, Carban or Corban, a family name.

Corban, *cor-bán,* a white district(sic).

Corban, *Uí-Chorbain,* O'Corban, a family name now generally made 'Corbett'.

Corberry, *Chairbre,* Carbery, a personal or family name.

Corbes, *Orbsen,* Orbsen, a male name and another name for Manannan Mac Lir.

Corbet, *carboid, carbad, carbaid,* a chariot.

Corbet, *an-carbad,* a jaw or boulder.

Corbet, *charbaid, carpait,* not given.

Corbo, *corr-bhó,* the cows snout.

Corbo, round hill of the cows.

Corboe, round hill of the cows.

Corbollis, odd townland.

Corboys, *cuir buidhe,* yellow hill.

Corbry, *Chairbre,* Carbery, a personal or family name.

Corbry, *Chorbaí(sic), Corbraí,* not given.

Corby, *Chorbaigh,* Corby, a personal or family name.

Corca, *corcach,* a marsh.

Corcaghan, *corcachán,* the marshy place.

Corcan, St Corcan.

Corcashy, from *corcas,* a marsh.

Corcaskea, *coirce-sciath,* oats of thorn bushes.

Corcaskea, *corr-sceitheach,* not given.

Corcaun, *corcán,* wild geranium.

Corclaragh, *cor-clárach,* a dyke with a plank across it.

Corco, *corca,* a race of people.

Corcoge, *chorcóige,* not given.

Corcoge, *corcóg,* beehive/s.

Corcomhid, *Corca-Muichit,* not given.

Corcomohide, *Corca-Mhuichead,* not given.

Corcomohide, *Corca-Muichit,* descendants of Muichet (a personal male name).

Corcomroe, *Corcamrua, Corcamruadh, Corcomruad, Corca-Mrua,* race or descendants of Modhruadh.

Corcoran, *Chorcrain,* Corcoran, a family name.

Corcoran, *corcorán,* purple.

Corcragh, *corcrach,* not given.

Corcran, *corcán,* wild geranium.

Corcran, *corcrán,* the pot.

Corcullioncrew, *cor-chuilinn-craobha,* not given.

Corcullioncrew, *cor-cuilinn-creamha,* holly-hill of wild garlic.

Corcush, *Churchais,* not given.

Cordal, *chordail, cordal, córdal,* not given.

Cordalea, *cor-da-liath,* hill of the two grey persons.

Corderry, *cora/corr-an-doire,* not given.

Cordrinan, *coir-droigheanain,* the black-thorn hill.

Core, *Chomhair, Cuair,* not given.

Core, *chór,* a snout.

Core, *Chuair, Cuar,* a personal or family name.

Core, *cóir,* just.

Core, *coir,* correctly arranged, right or symmetrical.

Core, *cór,* hillocks, an enclosure, a hillside, a district or a neighbourhood.

Core, *cora,* not given.

Core, *córr,* enclosed.

Core, *corr,* round or projecting.

Core, *cuar,* crooked or circular.

Core, *fuar,* bare.

Core, *Guaire,* Guaire, a personal or family name.

Coreen, *coirín,* a (little?) round hill.

Corelish, *corrlios,* not given.

Corey, *coire,* a cauldron.

Corey, *Uí-Chomhraidhe,* O'Curry, a family name.

Corgagh, *corcach, corcaig,* a swamp.

Corgarry, *corgardha,* hill of the garden.

Corgary, *corgardha,* hill of the garden.

Corgerry, *cor-dhoire,* the odd oakwood.

Corgrig, *an-chorrghráig,* not given.

Corha, *chairthe,* not given.

Corha, *coirrthe, coirthe,* a standing stone or a pillar stone.

Corhelshina, *cor-Shoilseánach,* not given.

Coricar, *cor-a'car,* round hill of the side cars.

Corick, *chomhraic, comhrac,* the meeting or conflict.

Corick, *comhraic, comhrac, chomhraic,* a meeting or confluence.

Corig, *chomhrais,* the meeting.

Corig, *comhraig, comhrac,* the meeting, conflict.

Corig, *comhraic,* not given.

Corin, *cairn,* a monumental heap of stones.

Cork, *choirce,* oats.

Cork, *Chorcaí,* not given.

Cork, *corcaigh, corcach,* the swamp or marsh.

Corka, *corca,* the race or descendants of...

Corka, *corcach,* a marsh.

Corkagh, *corcach,* a marsh.

Corkagh, *corcach,* a marsh.

Corkaghan, a little marsh.

Corkan, *corcach,* a marsh.

Corkan, *corcan,* wild geranium.

Corkanree, *corcach-an-Rí,* not given.

Corkar, *corcur,* wild geranium.

Corkaree, *corca-Raeidhe,* territories of 'Raidhe Orree', a male name.

Corkashy, *churchaisigh,* not given.

Corkashy, *corcaisidh,* marshy or waste land.

Corkashy, *corcas,* a marsh.

Corke, *corca,* not given.

Corkea, *chorcaighe,* a morass.

Corkeenagh, *cor-caonach,* hill of moss.

Corker, *carcair,* prison.

Corker, *carcragh,* a narrow pass or valley.

Corkey, *corcaigh, corcach,* a marsh or swamp.

Corkish, *an-churchais,* not given.

Corkish, *corcas,* a marsh.

Corkoge, *carcog, gCorcóg,* beehives.

Corkragh, *corcrach,* a marshy place.

Corkry, *Corcra, Corcraighe,* not given.

Corlan, *cartlann,* mint.

Corlane, *corr-oileán,* not given.

Corlis, *corrlios,* hill of the fort.

Corlisbrattan, round hill of Brattan's (a personal or a family name) fort.

Corlough, *corlach,* not given.

Corluddy, *corrloda,* not given.

Corluddy, *cathair-Luideach,* Luideach's (a personal or family name) fort.

Corlygorm, *corr-Lí-Ghoim,* not given.

Cormac, *Chormaic,* St Cormac.

Cormack, *Chormaic, Cormac,* Cormac, O'Cormac or St Cormac.

Cormick, *Chormaic,* not given.

Cormick, *Cormac,* Cormac, O'Cormac or St Cormac.

Cormick, *Cormaic, Cormac, Chormaic,* Cormac, a male name.

Cormick, *Uí-Chormaic,* Ó Cormaic, a family name.

Cormorant, *cró-inis, cró-inis-locha-ainninn,* not given.

Cormuck, *Chormaic,* Cormac, a personal or family name.

Corn, *carn,* a monumental heap of stones or a grave pile.

Corn, *cor-an/a'...,* round hill or hill of the...

Corn, *corrán,* not given.

Corn, *corr-an...,* not given.

Corna, *ceathrú-na...,* not given.

Corna, *corna,* a pit.

Corna, *cor-na...,* the quarter of the..., slope of the...

Corna, *corr-na..., cor-na...,* hill or little hill of the...

Corna, *corr-na...,* round hill or pointed hill of the...

Cornacallow, *corna-coilleadh,* pit of the grove or wood.

Cornalaur, *corr-an-urlár,* not given.

Cornaleck, *ceathrú-na-leac*(sic), not given.

Cornamramurry, *cor-na-mna mairbhe,* round hill of the dead woman.

Cornamult, *ceathrú-na-mBocht*(sic), not given.

Cornan, *Caornan*, St Cornan (6th cent).

Cornan, *Chornáin*, Cornán, a personal name and the name of a Church founder in Limerick.

Cornan, *Churnáin*, Cornán, not given.

Cornan, *Churnáin*, Curnáin, the name of a founder of a Limerick Church.

Cornan, *cornán-caisil*, the penny leaf plant.

Cornan, *corrnán*, a little ridge that sticks out.

Cornasore, *corr-na-sratha*, not given.

Corne, *cor-na...*, hill of the...

Corneagh, *corthanagh*, rugged land.

Cornee, *cor-Neidhe*, Neidhe's (a personal or family name) round hill.

Corneen, *Mhic-Chuirnín*, Courtney, a family name.

Cornels, *Choirnéil*, Cornel, a personal or family name.

Cornery, *cor-an-aodhaire*, shepherds hill.

Cornery, *cornaire*, not given.

Cornery, *corr-an-aodhaire*, shepherds peak.

Cornery, *cuar-nDoire*, round or crooked oak wood.

Corness, *cor-Aonghasa*, not given.

Corney, *Choirne*, not given.

Corney, *Cóirne, Coirne*, Coirne, a personal or family name and the founder of a Church in Cork.

Corney, the name of the Church founder of Kilcorney in County Clare.

Cornhill, *carn-clan-Aodha*, cairn of Hugh's (a male name) children.

Cornode, *corr-an-fhóid*, not given.

Cornreany, *carn-raithnighe*, carn of the ferns.

Cornyeal, *an-coirnéal*, not given.

Cornyeal, *corr-Uí-Néill*, O'Neill's (a family name) hill.

Corofin, *cora/coradh-Finne*, Finne's or Finna's (a male name) weir.

Corofin, *cora-finne*, weir of the white water.

Coronea, *carn-Aodha*, Aodh's, Hugh's (male names) cairn.

Coronea, *cro-Aodha*, Aodh's, Hugh's (male names) enclosure.

Corp, the slaughtered.

Corr, *chorr, an-choire*, not given.

Corr, *coirre, cor*, a hill.

Corr, *cora*, a weir.

Corr, *cor-an..., cor-a'...*, round hill of the...

Corr, *corr*, a round hill.

Corr, *corr*, herons or cranes.

Corra, a russet round hollow.

Corra, *carrach*, rough, rugged.

Corra, *choraidh*, a fish-weir.

Corra, *cor, corr*, odd.

Corra, *cor*, odd.

Corra, *coradha, coradh, corra, cora, choradh*, a weir.

Corra, Corra, a very ancient personal name.

Corr, *an-chorr...*, not given.

Corra, *cur*(sic)-*a'...*, round hill of the...

Corra, *corran*, round or projecting.

Corra, *currach, chorr, corr-an...*, not given.

Corra, *gCoradh*, weirs.

Corrabaun, Corrabaun, a family name now generally made 'Corbett'.

Corrabull, *baile-an-charbaid*, not given.

Corrachoill, *cor-choill*, round hill of the hazel.

Corradoon, *corrdhún*, not given.

Corragaun, *carragán*, rocky land.

Corragaun, *corragán*, rock.

Corragaun, *currachán*, rough land.

Corragaunnacalliaghdoo, *corragán-na-gCalliagh-dubh*, rock of the cormorants.

Corrageen, rocky land.

Corragh, *carrach, corrach*, stony, rough, rugged or barren.

Corragh, *cora, chorrach*, not given.

Corragh, *corrach*, rugged or marshes.

Corragh, *cuirreach*, a marsh.

Corragh, *cumhra*, fragrant, fresh.

Corragh, *currach*, boggy, moory land or marshes.

Corragina, *carraig-Eidhneach*, not given.

Corragina, *carraig-éidhneach*, rock covered in ivy.

Corraig, *carraige*, a rock.

Corrakan, *carragán*, not given.

Corrakan, *coracan*, quarrelsome.

Corramegan, *corr-Uí-Mhiagáin*, not given.

Corran, *carn*, a monumental heap of stones.

Corran, *carn-na-bh-fiach*, cairn (a monumental heap of stones) of the ravens.

Corran, *carn-na-bh-fiadh*, cairn (a monumental heap of stones) of the deer.

Corran, *chorráin, corran-cam*, not given.

Corran, *cor-a'...*, round hill of the...

Corran, *cor-an...*, round hill of the...

Corran, *corr-an...*, hill of the...

Corran, *Corran*, a personal or family name.

Corran, *corran, corráin*, a reaping hook, reaping hook shape or rocky land.

Corran, *corran*, a small hill.

Corranagh, *carranach*, rocky.

Corrane, *Chriochrain, Ciochran*, the name of an ancient chief.

Corraneary, *corr-an-aodhaire*, not given.

Corraneary, *corr-an-aoire*, the shepherds hill.

Corranewy, *corr-an-aobha*, not given.

Corranna, *beinn-na...*(sic), peaked hill of the...

Corranna, *corrán-na...*, not given.

Corranroo, *corádh-an-ruadh*, weir by the alder tree.

Corranroo, *corra-an-rubha*, weir of the 'rue' plant.

Corrasra, *cor-sratha*, round hill of the river holm.

Corraun, *cnoc-an-chorráin, corrán-Acaille*, not given.

Corraun, *corráin*, a reaping hook.

Corraun, *corrán*, a crescent/sickle shaped place.

Corravooly, *corr-bhuaile*, a round or crooked booley (dairying place).

Corray, *cunnradh*, covenant or treaty.

Corre, *corra*, a round hill.

Correal, *cor-aoil*, hill of lime.

Correel, *cor-aoil*, hill of lime.

Correen, *chairn*, a cairn.

Correen, *coirín*, a little round hill.

Correen, *coirrín*, not given.

Correens, from *coirín*, (with the English plural letter 's'), little round hills.

Correvan, *cor-Riabhán*, Revan's, (a male name) round hill.

Corri, *corr-a*, the cranes.

Corrib, *an-Coirb/Choirb/Coirib*, corrupted from *Orbsen*, Oirbse, Oirbsen, and Oirbsean, other names for Manannan Mac Lir.

Corrib, *Oirbsean*, not given.

Corrick, *comhraigh*, contention.

Corrie, *coire*, not given.

Corries, *caradha*, dams or fish weirs.

Corries, *gCoraí, cathraighe*, not given.

Corrig, *carraige*, the rock.

Corrig, *chomhraic*, not given.

Corriga, *carraigigh*, not given.

Corriga, *carriage, carraigeach, carraighidh*, rocks, rocky land or rocky hills.

Corrigeen, *carraicín, carraigín*, little rock.

Corrigina, *carraig-Aidhne*, not given.

Corrikeen, *carraicín, carraigín*, little rock.

Corrin, *card*, a monumental heap of stones (Cork usage).

Corrin, *carn*, a monumental heap of stones.

Corrin, *carn-Gael*, not given.

Corrin, *corr-na...*, round hill of the...

Corrinare, *cor-an-fhéir*, round hill of the grass.

Corrinary, *cor-an-aodhaire*, hill of the herdsman.

Corrinary, *corr-an-aoire*, not given.

Corrinenty, *cor-an-aen-tighe*, round hill of the one house.

Corrinenty, *cor-an-fheannta*, not given.

Corrinshigagh, *an-chorr-uinseogach*, not given.

Corrinshigagh, *cor-fhuinseogach*, round hill of the ash trees.

Corrintra, *cor-an-tSratha*, not given.

Corro, *coradh, cora, corr*, a weir or dam.

Corro, *cor-an...*, round hill of the...

Corrog, *curróg*, a small round hill.

Corroge, *corróg*, uneven land.

Corroge, *curróg*, a small round hill.

Corronea, *corr-an-eich*, hill of the horse.

Corroo, *coradh*, the fishing weir.

Corroon, *Charrúnaigh*, not given.

Corrowle, *cor, corr*, a round hill.

Corrowle, *corr/cor-abhall*, round hill of the apple trees,

Corrowna, *cor/corr-aibhne*, round hill by or of the river.

Corroy, *corr-ráithe*, not given.

Corroy, red/russet round hill.

Corry, *an-choraidh, na-coradh*, not given.

Corry, *coire*, a cauldron.

Corry, *cora*, a weir.

Corry, *corr*, not given.

Corry, corrdhoire, not given.
Corry, curraidh, moors.
Corry, curraigh, not given.
Corrybrackan, corr-Bhreacáin(sic), not given.
Corryolus, coraidh-Eoluis, weir of Eolus, (a personal or a family name).
Corsheerach, cas-siarach, corn land allowed to go to grass.
Corthy, córtaidh, a standing stone.
Corthy, Córthaidh, coirte, not given.
Cortial, Coirteail, not given.
Cortolvin, cor-Thí-Talmhan, not given.
Cortulla, chorr-Chealgach(sic), not given.
Corus, Mhac-Fheorais, not given.
Corus, Mhic-Fheoris, Mac Orish, a family name.
Corvalley, cor-an-bhealaigh, bend of the road.
Corveen, an-chorrmhín, not given.
Corville, an-corrbhaile, not given.
Corvoderry, cor-bhoith-doire, odd-booth of the oak wood.
Corwick, corrbhaic, not given.
Cory, Ua-Córaidhe, O'Curry, a family name.

Cos, cos, a foot, the foot of something, footed or bottom land.
Cosduff, cos-dubh, the maidenhaired fern.
Cose, cuas cave/s.
Cose, cuas, a hollow.
Cosgrave, Choscráin, Coscrán, not given.
Cosgrey, Uí-Choscraigh, O'Cosgraigh, a family name and means the descendants of Coscraigh.
Cosgry, O'Cosgary, a family name.
Cosh, cois, along, by or beside.
Cosh, cos, the foot, bottom, lower end, beside or along.
Cosh, coise, shaped like a foot.
Cosha, coise, not given.
Cosha, cos, the foot, bottom or lower end.
Cosheen, Chaisín, not given.
Coshkeam, coiscéim, a step or pass.
Coshlea, cois-sléibhe, foot of the mountain.
Coshma, cois-máighe, a place beside the river Maigue.
Coshone, cois-abhann, along or beside the river.

Coshown, cois-abhann, not given.
Coska, Cásca, easter.
Coskem, coiscéim, a step or pass.
Cosker, coscair, victory.
Cosker, Coscraigh, Coscragh, a personal or family name.
Cosker, Coscair, Cusker, a personal or family name.
Coskery, Uí-Choscraigh, O'Coscry, a family name.
Coskoran, Choscráin, not given.
Coskran, Choscráin, Coscran, a personal or family name.
Cosney, Chosnamhaigh, Cosnavagh, a personal name.
Cosquin, Choscáin, Choscán, a personal or family name.
Coss, a recess.
Coss, cos, a foot, the foot of something or footed.
Cossagh, chosach, footed.
Cossaun, a little cave.
Cossaun, chasáin, casán, cosán, a path.
Cossauna, casán-an/a'..., path of...
Costelloe, chasla, casla, an inlet of the sea.
Costia, cóiste, the coach.
Cot, chait, wild cats.
Cot, coite, a boat.
Cota, chótaigh, not given.
Coteenty, coitchínntidhe, common land.
Coteenty, na-coitiantaí, not given.
Cotteen, coitchionn, common land.
Cotteenagh, a place frequented by 'cots' or boats.
Cottia, coiti, coite, a small boat or canoe.
Cottian, coitchen, coitchionn, a common or common land.
Cottin, coitchín, a common.
Cotton, Choitín, Coitín, Cottin or Catan, a persons name.
Cotton, a small house.
Cotton, coitchen, coitchionn, a common or common land.
Cotty, choite, the boat.
Cotty, Chota, Cota, a personal or family name and the founder of a Church in Wexford.
Cotty, coiti, choite, coite, a small boat, skiff or canoe.
Couch, cuais, a hollow.

Cough, *chua,* not given.

Cough, *chuadh,* a hollow.

Cough, *cuaiche,* the cuckoo.

Coughlane, *Cochlán,* not given.

Coul, *cóll, coll,* hazels.

Coula, *chuaille,* not given.

Coula, *cuailli,* small trees

Coulagh, *chuaille,* the stake or tall branchless tree.

Coulagh, *cuaille, cuailleach,* a place of bare/branchless trees or poles.

Coulagh, *cualleach,* not given.

Coulaghta, *cuallachta,* an assemblage or tribe.

Coulaghta, *cuallachta,* the colony.

Coum, *cam,* winding, crooked or curved.

Coum, *cóm,* a hollow.

Coum, *com,* a river hollow.

Coum, *cúm, com,* a hollow, glen or valley.

Couma, *cham-an…,* not given.

Couma, *champa,* the camp.

Couma, *na-coma,* the hollows.

Coumalocha, *an-comlach,* not given.

Coumeen, *coimín,* not given.

Coumeenoole, *com-Dhíneol,* not given.

Coumeenoole, *comíneol,* Díneal's, (a personal or family name) hollow.

Coumfea, *com-fia,* not given.

Coumgagh, *com-Ga,* not given.

Coumha, *campa,* camps.

Coumha, *chamtha,* bends.

Coun, *Conn, Con,* men named Conn or Conn.

Coun, *cuan,* a bend.

Coun, *ceann,* the head.

Couney, *Cuanaigh,* Cooney a family name.

Countenan, *cointeannan,* disputed land.

Country, *colltrach,* a place of hazels.

County, *Cheanntaigh,* not given.

Cour, *cobhar,* froth.

Coura, *cuar-a'…,* hollow of the…

Coura, *cumhraidh,* sweet smelling.

Couragh, *cuarach,* abounding in round hollows.

Courcey, *Chursaig, Chuarsaigh,* Courcey or De Courcy, a persons name.

Courcey, *Cumhscraigh,* Cooscragh, a male name.

Courcey, *cúrsaí,* a racecourse.

Courcey, *Cuscraidh, Cumhascraigh,* not given.

Courcy, *Chuarsaigh,* Courcey or De Courcy, a personal or family name.

Courdea, *Chordaraodh,* Cordray, a personal or family name.

Courdra, *Chordraeigh,* not given.

Courha, *cumhraidh,* sweet smelling.

Courneenig, *Chuirninigh, Cuirnínig,* Curneen or Courtney, a family name.

Course, *cúrsa,* not given.

Coursey, *Chuairsaí, Chuairsaí, Cuairsighe,* not given.

Court, *cúirt, cuirt,* a court, a grand house or a mansion.

Court, *cuirte,* a mansion.

Courty, *court, cúirte, cuirte,* a court or mansion.

Cousane, *cuasán,* a little recess or hollow.

Couse, *cabhais, cobhas, chobhais,* a causeway.

Couse, *cabhas,* a crossing place, stepping stones or causeway.

Couse, *chabhais,* stepping stones.

Couse, *cuas,* caves, sea inlets or coves.

Couse, *cuis,* hollows or caves.

Coush, *chuais,* a hollow or a creek.

Coush, *chuais, cuas,* a cave.

Coush, *cuais,* not given.

Cousha, (na) *cuise,* (the) cause.

Cousha, *chabhsa,* stepping stones.

Cove, (of Cork) *cóf-Chorcaighe, an-cóf,* not given.

Cove, *cóbh,* not given.

Cove, *cuas,* a sea inlet.

Covedy, *coimheada,* watching or guarding.

Covedy, *coimheada,* watching or guarding.

Covet, *coimheada,* an observation post, watching or guarding.

Covety, *coimheadta,* watching.

Covit, *coimheada, coimhead, coimhéadta,* watching.

Cowan, *Caomhán,* not given.

Cowan, *Cobhainn, Cobhann,* a personal or family name.

Cowan, *Cuan,* St Cuan.

Cowan, McCowan, a family name.

Cowan, *Mhic-Abhainn,* son of Abhann/Aibhne, a personal or family name.

Cowey, *Cumhaighe,* Cooey, a male name.

Cowlaght, *cuallaghta,* a colony or company.

Cowley, *cobhlaigh, cabhlaigh,* Shannon fleet boats.

Cowly, *cabhlaighe,* a house ruin.

Cowma, campa, an encampment.

Cown, cean, a head.

Cowran, Chuaráin, Cuarain, Cuaran, St Cuaran.

Cowre, cobhar, froth.

Coxtown, coilleac, a woody place.

Coy, cuach, cuckoos.

Coyle, (river) *an-chaol,* not given.

Coyle, Comhghaill, Coyle, a family name.

Coyle, cuill, coll, coill, hazel.

Coyle, coille, a wood.

Coyle, MacDhubhghaill, a family name.

Coyle, mhic-giolla-Chomhghaill, MacKilcowel, McGilcoel, McGylcowill, MavGillillecoyl, family names.

Cozies, from *cuas,* caves.

Cra, crá, grief.

Craan, charráin, craane, a stony place.

Craan, chorráin, a crescent.

Craane, craane, a stony place.

Crab, crab, not given.

Cracken, chraicinn, craicinn, not given.

Cracken, croiceann, croicinn, craiceann, hides, skins or a tannery.

Craddock, an-Chradógaigh, not given.

Craddock, chreadóig, clay.

Craddock, Chreadóig, Craddock, a personal or family name.

Craddock, Cradóig, Chradóig, Craddock, a family name.

Craff, Cabha, not given.

Craff, creamha, creamh, a place of wild garlic.

Craffield, creamhchoill, wood of the wild garlic.

Craffroe, chreamh-ruaidh, not given.

Crag, chraig, creag, another form of *carraig,* a rock.

Crag, craig, not given.

Cragagh, cregach, a rocky place.

Cragg, chraig, not given.

Cragga, craiga, a stony field.

Cragga, craige, creaga, the rock or stony.

Cragga, creag-a'..., rock of the...

Craggach, chreagach, not given.

Craggagh, chreagach, creagach, a rocky or craggy place.

Craggan, chreagáin, not given.

Craggan, creagáin, creagain, a rock or a rocky place.

Craggana, creagán/creagan-na..., the little rock of the...

Craggane, creagan, the little rock.

Craggard, an-chreag-ard, not given.

Craggaun, chreagán, stony ground.

Craggaun, creagan, the little rock.

Craggera, cnagaire, a hard little hill.

Craggs, an-chreag(sic), not given.

Craggs, na-creaga, not given.

Craggy, creige, rocks.

Craggykerrivan, craig-Uí-Chiardubhain, O'Kirwan's rock.

Cragher, crachair, not given.

Craghy, crathaidhe, creathaidhe, a shaking bog.

Craghy, crathaigh, not given.

Crags, na-creaga, not given.

Craha, chradha, pain or torment.

Craheen, chraithín, not given.

Craheen, Craithín, Craheen, a personal or family name.

Craheen, creathach, a place of brushwood.

Craheen, curraichín, little moor or marsh.

Crahera, a rocky or craggy place.

Craig, chraobhaigh, craobhach, not given.

Craig, creag, creig, creaga, creige, another form of *carraig,* a rock or rocks.

Craig, creag-an..., rock of the...

Craiga, creag-a'..., creag-an..., rock/crag of the...

Craigavon, named after Viscount Craigavon.

Craigs, creaga, crags.

Craigue, an-ghráig, not given.

Craigy, crathaigh, not given.

Craigy, creige, rock/s.

Crain, crainn, the tree.

Cramph, craeibhe, a place of branchy, spreading trees.

Cramph, creamha, creamh, wild garlic.

Cramphill, creamh-choille, wild garlic wood.

Cramsy, Uí-Cnaimhsighe, O'Crampsie, a family name now often changed to 'Bonner' (from *cnamh* meaning 'bone').

Cran, cranach, crann, abounding in trees.

Cran, crann, a tree.

Cran, cranncha, chrann, not given.

Cran, gCrann, (unusually large) trees.

Crana, Chrána, Crana, a personal or family name.

Crana, chránaigh, crann-an…, not given.

Crana, Cranncha, Crannach, a river name meaning abounding in trees.

Crana, greanach(sic), not given.

Cranagh, chrannóg, crannog, a wooden structure.

Cranagh, crannach, trees, a place of trees, tree plantation/s, woods or woodland.

Cranagh, cránach, the sow (female pig).

Cranaher, crannach, abounding in trees.

Cranahurt, crannthairt, not given.

Cranalagh, crannalach, a place of trees.

Cranally, crannalach, a place of trees.

Cranareen, crannairin, a place of small trees.

Cranareen, crannarín, little tree.

Cranary, cranalaigh, a place of trees.

Crancreagh, crann-critheach, the aspen tree.

Crandy, cranda, stunted trees.

Crandy, crannda, bent or sloping trees.

Crane, charran, rough land.

Crane, corran, a sheep pen(sic).

Crane, corrán, not given.

Crane, craan, rocky land.

Crane, craane, craan, a stony place.

Cranfield, creamchoill, wood of wild garlic.

Cranfield, magh/maigh-chreamhchoille, má-creamhchaille, plain of the wild garlic wood.

Cranford, creamhghort, garlic field.

Cranfy, cranncha, not given.

Cranfy, creamhthaidhe, a place of wild garlic.

Cranig, crannaig, crannach, a place of trees.

Cranig, Mhic-Bhranaigh, Cranny, a personal or family name.

Crank, chrann, chrainn, a tree.

Crankill, creamhchoill, wood of the wild garlic.

Cranley, cranlaigh, cranach, crann, abounding in trees.

Crann, cranach, crann, abounding in trees.

Crann, crann, a tree.

Cranna, cranach, crann, abounding in trees.

Cranna, cránach, the sow.

Cranna, cranncha, crunn, crannaighe, crannach, chrannóg, crannóige, not given.

Crannach, cranncha, crannach, lots of trees.

Crannade, crannaí, stakes or hurdles.

Crannagh, crannach, the wooden structure

Crannagh, cranncha, not given.

Crannagh, crannnach, cranach, crann, abounding in trees.

Crannaghy, cranachaigh, crannachaidh, trees.

Crannareen, crannairín, the little grove.

Crannceo, crannceo, not given.

Cranne, a stony place.

Crannoge, crannóg, an artificial island.

Crannoge, crannoige, crannóg, a structure or dwelling of wood usually on a lake.

Crannogue, crannóg, an artificial island.

Cranny, an-chrannaigh, not given.

Cranny, cranach, crannach, crannaighe, cran-naigh, crann, abounding in trees.

Cranny, droichead-na-crannaighe, not given.

Cranoge, crannóige, not given.

Crany, cranaigh, cranach, a sow (a besieging machine).

Crap, cnap, a lump, a small round hillock.

Crappagh, an-chnapach, not given.

Crappagh, cnappach, hilly land.

Crappin, cnappain, a little hillock.

Craproo, cnap-ruaidh, not given.

Crarey, criartha, a bog.

Cratagh, creatalach, a sallow wood.

Crataloe, chreatalach, creatalach, a sallow wood.

Cratlie, croit-shliabh, humpbacked mountain.

Cratloe, chreatalach, creatalach, a sallow/willow wood.

Cratloe, creatlach, a place of frames.

Cratloe, creat-shuileóg, creath-saileóg, rough place of the sallies.

Craugh, cradhach, torments.

Craugh, creamha, wild garlic.

Craugh, currach, a marsh.

Craughill, creamhchoill, wood of the wild garlic.

Craughwell, creach-mhaoil, chreachmhaoil, creachmhaoil, place of plunders or plunder hill.

Craughwell, creamhchaoil(sic), wild garlic wood.

Craughwell, creamhchoill, not given.

Crauv, cnamh, bones.

Crava, chrabhaigh, devotion.

Crave, creamha, creamh, a place of wild garlic.

Craw, creamh, wild garlic.

Craw, *currach,* a moor or marsh.

Crawford, *Chráfard,* Crawford, a personal or family name.

Crawhill, *creamhchoill,* wood of the wild garlic.

Crawn, *carrán,* rough rocky land.

Craywell, *creamhchoill, creamh-choill,* wood of wild garlic.

Cre, *chraobh,* not given.

Cre, *craobh,* an ogham inscription.

Cre, *craobh,* tree.

Cre, *Cre,* Cre, a personal or family name.

Cre, *créach,* rough pasture.

Cre, *chriadh,* clayey soil.

Cre, *crioch,* country or district.

Crea, *chraobhaigh, chairrfhiadh,* not given.

Crea, *chraoibh,* a sacred tree.

Crea, *chraoibhe,* a branch or branchy place.

Crea, *chria, gCré, Crae,* not given.

Crea, *chriadh,* clayey.

Crea, *Cre, Cré,* a male name.

Crea, *Créde, Chréidhe,* St Crea.

Creadan, *créadáin, criadáin,* not given.

Creagh, a hard place beside marshy or soft land.

Creagh, *Crae,* Creagh, a family name.

Creagh, *craoibheach, craobhach,* a branchy place.

Creagh, *cré,* earth.

Creagh, *creach,* cattle prey.

Creagh, *créach,* rough pasture.

Creagh, *creag,* rocky ground.

Creagh, *creiche,* cattle spoil.

Creagh, *creiche, creach,* plunder.

Creagh, *crí,* an end, confine or a boundary.

Creagh, *chiche,* a boundary or territory.

Creagh, *cria,* a market.

Creagh, *criadh,* clay.

Creagh, *criothach, críche, chraoi,* not given.

Creagh, *critheach,* a shaking bog.

Creagh, *croiche,* a cross.

Creagha, *créacha,* brakes or shrubberies.

Creaghan, *criachán,* a copse.

Creaghan, *crícheán, creathán,* not given.

Creaghan, *criochan,* a shrubbery or grove.

Creaghlaghta, *crith-leachta,* abounding in monuments.

Creaght, *creagh,* a place frequented by men who protected cattle.

Creaght, *gCorraidhecht,* not given.

Creaghtan, Creighton, a personal or family name.

Creaghy, *chríochach,* a boundary.

Crean, *an-crián,* clayey(sic).

Crean, *chrián, craon,* not given.

Crean, *críon,* parched land

Creary, *criathrach,* abounding in pits.

Crease, *chraois,* not given.

Creasig, *chraosaigh,* the glutton.

Creat, *chríoch, chrioch,* a territory or boundary.

Creavagh, *craobhach,* branchy.

Crecora, *craobh-chomhartha, craebh-cumhradh,* sweet scented branch, tree or branchy tree.

Crecora, *craobh-chomhartha,* tree of the sign.

Crecora, *craobh-chortha,* palace of the sign.

Crecora, *craobh-cumhraidhe,* not given.

Crecrin, *craobh-dhruim,* branch ridge.

Crecrin, *creacrainn,* rocky land.

Credan, *Chríodáin, Criadáin,* not given.

Credaun, *Criadán,* not given.

Credaun, the crrion crwo.

Creddin, *Chreidin,* St Credan.

Cree, *chraoi, craí, chraobhach, craobhaighe,* not given.

Cree, *chroidhe,* hut or hovel.

Cree, *chruidhe,* a hovel or cattle hut.

Cree, *craoibhe,* a branch or branchy place.

Cree, *craoibhe,* the tree.

Cree, *crí,* a boundary.

Cree, *cria,* clay.

Cree, *criadh,* oak.

Cree, *crioch,* a bushy spot.

Cree, *criothach, crithach, criothaigh,* shaking bog or a morass.

Cree, *críothaigh,* quaking.

Cree, *crith,* shake, shaking.

Cree, *croidhe,* cattle.

Cree, *cróite,* pens for animals.

Cree, *cruidh,* milking.

Cree, *croí,* heart shaped.

Cree, *cruidhe, crodh, cria, cruidh,* cattle.

Creeagh, a boundary.

Creeagh, *chraobhaigh,* not given.

Creebe, cattle.

Creedan, *criadáin,* not given.

Creegh, *an-críoch,* the boundary.

Creegh, *cria,* a market.

Creeghagh, *chríochach,* not given.

Creeghagh, *críochach, criochach,* boundaries.

Creeghan, *chriocháin,* not given.

Creeghan, *criochán,* a shrubbery.

Creeghy, *chríochach,* not given.

Creeghy, *críche,* the boundary.

Creehar, *criathar,* the sieve.

Creehar, *criathrach,* the shaking bog.

Creehaun, *crítheán,* aspen tree.

Creehy, *críce,* not given.

Creehy, *croiche,* In Irish *croiche* means a cross but in townlands it can mean, a gallows, a hangmans rope, noose or a place of execution. In this case it means a gallows.

Creel, *chriathar, criathair,* bog, swamp or boggy.

Creelagh, *crithlach,* a shaking bog.

Creelogh, *caolach,* not given.

Creelogh, *crithlach,* shaking bog.

Creely, *Uí-Cruaidhlaoigh,* O'Creely or Crilly, a family name.

Creen, *chrainn, crainn,* the tree.

Creen, *cráinn,* wooded.

Creen, *craon,* not given.

Creen, *crian, chríon, críon,* withered.

Creen, *criathraigh,* waste or marshy ground.

Creen, *crioch,* a district.

Creen, *cruinn, cruin,* round.

Creen, *craobh,* branches.

Creena, *chríonaigh,* the withered bush-brake.

Creena, *críne,* withered tree/s.

Creena, *críoch/cró-na…,* not given.

Creena, *críona,* withered sticks.

Creenagh, *chríonaigh,* not given.

Creenagh, *crionach,* a place of withered grass.

Creenagh, *críonach,* anything withered.

Creenagh, *críonach, crinach,* withered wood.

Creenagh, *críonach,* things that are dry and rotten with age.

Creenaght, *cruthneachta,* wheat.

Creenary, *críonaire,* anything withered.

Creenery, *críonradh,* a place of withered growth.

Creenkill, *críonchoill, crion-coill,* the old(sic) wood.

Creenveen, *críon-mhín,* a smooth withered spot.

Creeny, *chríonaigh, chríonaigh,* withered bushes.

Creeny, *chrionagh,* withered shrubs or grass.

Creeny, *crinach,* withered land.

Creeny, *críonach, creenagh, chríonaigh,* withered brambles, trees or grass.

Creeny, *crionaigh,* anything withered.

Creeny, *an-crionaí*(sic), the withered place.

Creerach, *criathrach,* the shaking bog.

Creeragh, *criathrach,* pitted broken land.

Creeragh, *criathrach,* the shaking bog.

Creeran, from *criathrach,* the little shaking bog.

Creeraun, from *criathrach,* the little shaking bog.

Creesil, *craosail,* not given.

Creeslough, *craoslach, crioslach, craosloch, craos-loch,* the lake that swallows everything, gullet lake or the lake of gluttony.

Creestane, *Chríostáin,* Christopher, a male name.

Creeva, *chraobhach,* not given.

Creeva, *craebhaire,* branchy bushy land.

Creeva, *craoibhe,* a tree.

Creevagh, *chraobhach,* not given.

Creevagh, *cráebhach, craobhach,* bushy land.

Creevagh, *craeibhe, craibhi,* a place of branchy/spreading trees.

Creevagh, *craobhach,* a place of large branchy trees or a branchy place.

Creevagh, *craobhach,* a place of sacred trees.

Creevagh, *craobhach, craebhaire,* branchy bushy land.

Creevaghan, *craobhacháin,* a little branch or branchy tree.

Creevaghy, *craobhachadh, craobh-achaidh,* the bushy field.

Creevan, *craobhan,* little bushy spot.

Creevan, *Criomhthann,* a personal name.

Creevanagh, *chraoibheanach,* branchy or bushy.

Creevanty, *Craebhnatt,* Creevnat, the name of a Church founder.

Creevary, *craebhaire,* branchy bushy land.

Creevaun, *craobhan,* little bushy spot.

Creeve, *chraobh, craoibhe, criadh,* not given.

Creeve, *craobh,* a sacred tree.

Creeve, *craobh, craebh,* a branch, a branchy tree, bushy underwood or bushes.

Creeve, *créach,* rough pasture.

Creeve, *cria,* clay.

Creeve, *cria,* densely branched trees.

Creeveen, a little branch or a little branchy tree.

Creeveen, *craobhín, chraoibhín,* bushes or small trees.

Creevela, the grey branch.

Creevery, *craebhaire,* branchy bushy land.

Creeves, *an-chraobh/craobh,* the tree.

Creeves, *craobha,* sacred trees.

Creevin, *craobhín,* the little branch or branchy tree.

Creevnagh, *craobhnach,* a branchy place.

Creevy, a narrow branchy place.

Creevy, *chraobaí,* not given.

Creevy, *chraobhaigh,* dense trees.

Creevy, *craebh,* a large tree.

Creevy, *craebhaire, craoibhe, craobhe,* a branch, branchy/bushy land or a branchy cluster.

Creevy, *craobhach, craobhaigh,* bushy land, a branchy spot, a branch or a branchy tree.

Creevy, *craobhaigh,* a place of branches.

Creevy, *craobhaigh, craeibhe,* a place of branchy, spreading trees.

Creevy, *creevagh*(sic), a hill(sic).

Creewood, *craebh-fhoda,* long branchy tree.

Creg, *chreig,* not given.

Creg, *creag,* a rock, crag or rocky ground.

Cregagh, *chreagaigh, cregach,* a place of rocks or crags.

Cregagh, *creagach,* not given.

Cregan, *cregán,* little rock, rocky ground.

Cregg, *chreag, creag,* the rock, crag or rocky ground.

Cregg, *chreig,* not given.

Cregga, *creaga,* rocks.

Cregga, *creag-a'...,* rock of the...

Creggagh, *creagach,* rocky land.

Creggan, *chreagain,* not given.

Creggan, *creagáin,* rocky land, the rock or rocky round hill.

Creggan, *creagán,* a stony place.

Creggan, *creagán,* the little crag or stony place.

Creggan, *creagan,* little rock.

Creggan, *creag-an...,* rock of the...

Creggane, *creagan,* a little cliff.

Creggane, *creagán, chreagáin,* little rock or rocky ground/place.

Cregganna, *creagan-na...,* little rock of the...

Creggaun, *creagán,* a little rocky height(sic).

Creggaun, *criogán,* rocky ground.

Creggaun, *creagán, chreagáin,* little rock, little crag or rocky ground.

Creggauna, *chreagáin-a'...,* little rock of the...

Creggaunna, *creagan-na...,* field of the(sic)...

Creggogh, *cregach,* rocky.

Creggs, *na-creaga,* rocks.

Cregh, *creig,* rock.

Creghy, *croiche,* gallows.

Creha, *creiche, creach,* plunder.

Creha, *croiche,* gallows.

Crehan, *Uí-Chriocháin,* O'Crehan, a family name.

Crehanagh, *an-chreathánach,* not given.

Crehanagh, *criothánach, crithánach,* a shaking morass/bog.

Crehaun, *creathán,* not given.

Crehaun, from *crith,* a shaking bog.

Crehelp, *craobh-Elpi,* the ogham inscription of Elpi (a personal name).

Crehenagh, *chreathánaigh, criothanach,* not given.

Crehig, *chrochaig, chrochaigh,* gallows.

Crehig, *creiche,* cattle spoil.

Crehir, *criathar,* the sieve or shaking bog.

Crehir, *criathrach,* the shaking bog.

Crehy, *chreiche,* not given.

Creigh, *craobh,* a bush.

Creigh, *creiche,* cattle spoil.

Creigh, *croiche,* gallows.

Creighans, *na-creatháin,* not given.

Creighard, *crichard,* the high boundary.

Creman, *Mhic-Remoinn,* son of Redmond.

Cremorne, *críoch-Mhúrn,* not given.

Cremorne, *críoch-Moghdhorn, críoch-Mughdhorn,* country of the people called Mughdhorna.

Crenane, *Uí-Crionain,* O'Crenane or Crinion, a family name.

Crenian, *croiche-Naoimh,* the holy cross.

Crennagh, *crathnach,* shaking.

Crenode, *Chrionóid,* Crinnot, a family name.

Crenode, *Mhic-Reanóid,* not given.

Crenville, wood of wild garlic.

Cresig, *Chraosaigh,* the name of a particular west Cork glutton and spendthrift.
Cressy, *croise,* the cross.
Cretty, *crochta,* a croft.
Cretty, *crotaidhe,* humps.
Cretty, hillocks.
Creunata, *Craebhnatt,* Creevnat, the name of a Church founder.
Crev, *chraoibhe,* branchy.
Creve, *craobh,* not given.
Creven, *Criomhthainn,* Crimthann or Criffan, a personal or family name.
Crevinish, branchy island.
Crew, *chraobh, cró, craoithe,* not given.
Crew, *chrú,* blood.
Crew, *craeibhe, craoibh,* a branchy tree.
Crew, *craobh,* a sacred tree.
Crew, *craoibhe,* a bush, branch, branchy trees, dense tree or a branchy place.
Crew, *créach,* rough pasture.
Crew, *creamha,* a place of wild garlic.
Crew, *creamha, creamh,* wild garlic.
Crew, *creamha,* ramsons(sic).
Crew, *crú,* horse shoe.
Crew, *cru,* horse-shoe shaped.
Crewbane, *Cnodhbha,* Knowth, the name of the burial mounds of *Brugh-na-Boinne,* **Bane,** *bán,* white.
Crick, *chnoic,* not given.
Crick, *cnuic,* a hill.
Crickaun, *cnocán,* little hill, hillock.
Crickeen, *cnocán,* little hill, hillock.
Crickeens, *cnoicín,* not given.
Cricket, *chroitheach,* not given.
Criddoge, *Cradóg,* not given.
Criddogue, *Cradog,* Craddock, a male name.
Cridory, *chriathadera, chriathadora, chréither,* sieve or sieve maker.
Crieve, *craoibh, craoibhe, craeibhe,* a branchy tree, bushy or branchy land.
Criffer, *cruimhther,* the Priest.
Crighan, *critheán,* aspen trees.
Crih, *crith,* not given.
Crihaun, from *crith,* a shaking bog.
Crilla, *crithlighe,* a swamp.
Crillan, *crithleáin, crithleán,* a shaking morass or bog.
Crillaun, *crithleán,* a shaking morass or bog.

Crilly, *crithlach,* a shaking morass or bog.
Crilly, *crithleach,* a shaky or trembling place.
Crilly, *crithligh,* a quagmire.
Crim, *crom,* a bent or stooped man.
Crimeen, *Uí-Chruimín,* Cremen, a family name.
Crimlin, *cruimm-ghlin, cruim-ghlinn,* crooked glen.
Crimlin, *cruimm-ghlin, cruim-ghlinn,* crooked glen.
Crin, *chrainn, crainn,* the tree.
Crin, *chrainn,* not given.
Crin, *chrainn,* the (remarkable) tree.
Crin, *cranach, crann,* abounding in trees.
Crin, *crann,* a very large tree.
Crin, *crinn, crin,* not given.
Crin, *croin, críon, crann,* a tree/s.
Crin, *cruinn,* round.
Crina, *críon,* withered.
Crine, *crín, croin, críon, chrainn, crann,* a tree/s.
Crine, *cruinn, cruin,* round.
Crinken, *críonchoill,* not given.
Crinkill, *críonchoill,* not given.
Crinkle, *críonchoill,* withered wood.
Crinnaghtane, *cruithneachta,* wheat bearing place.
Crinnaghtaun, *cruithneachta,* wheat bearing place.
Crinnaloo, *crionna-Allua,* not given.
Crinnaughtaun, *cruinneachtán,* not given.
Crinnaughtaun, *cruithneachtán,* a place of wheat growing.
Crinnig, *chrionaig, chrionaigh,* withered or withered branches.
Crinnig, *chrionaig,* withered branches.
Crinnigan, *Uí-Chronagain,* O'Cronigan, a family name.
Crinnish, *cruinnis,* not given.
Crinny, *crionna,* not given.
Crinny, *cruinnidh,* round land or a round hill.
Crinode, *Chraenóid,* Crynol, a family name.
Crion, *críona,* withered.
Crippa, *coirbthe,* violation.
Crippaun, *cnappain,* a little hillock.
Crippoge, *crapóg,* a little hump.
Cris, *crios,* a girdle or circle.
Crish, *crois,* cross roads.

Crisha, *croise,* In Irish *croiche* means a cross but in townlands it can mean, a gallows, a hangmans rope, noose or a place of execution. In this case it means a cross.

Crishoge, *croiseóg,* not given.

Crislagh, *crioslach,* a girdle or circle.

Criss, *crios,* a girdle or circle.

Criss, *crois,* a crossroads.

Crissadaun, *críosadán,* not given.

Crissadaun, from *crios,* a little girdle or circle.

Crissane, *crosán, crosáin,* the cross.

Crissogues, *crosóga,* little crosses.

Cristora, *Chriostóra,* Christopher, a male name.

Cristora, *Criostabhaira,* Christopher, a male name.

Crit, *cruit,* a hump backed hill, hump/s or eminences.

Crittan, from *cruit,* a little hump backed hill.

Crivey, *craobhaighe,* brushwood.

Cro, *cro,* a hollow or valley.

Cro, *cró,* a hut, fold or pen for cattle.

Cro, *cro,* an enclosure.

Cro, *cruach,* a hill.

Cro, *cruadh,* hard.

Cro, *cruadh,* stiff or soiled.

Cro, *cruidh,* a milking place.

Croach, *croach,* a hill.

Croach, *cruach,* not given.

Croagh, *chróich, an-chruach,* not given.

Croagh, *chruaiche,* a round hill.

Croagh, *cróch,* a round hill.

Croagh, *cruach,* a rick, a hill, a stacked up hill, rick-shaped hillocks, a mountain, a round hill, a round rockpile, a pile of stones or a mound.

Croagh, *cruach, croagh,* a rick.

Croaghan, *chruacháin,* not given.

Croaghan, *crauchain,* a small mound.

Croaghan, *cruacháin,* a rick.

Croaghan, *cruachán,* a little round shaped hill or a little rick.

Croaghan, *chruachan,* a round hill.

Croaghan, *cruagh,* a stacked hill.

Croaghane, *cruachán,* a little round shaped hill.

Croaghane, *cruachán,* the heap

Croaghat, *croagh,* a stack like hill.

Croaghaun, *cruachán,* a little round shaped hill.

Croaghaun, *cruachán,* a peak or a little pile of stones.

Croaghaun, *cruagh,* a stacked hill.

Croagheen, *an-cruaichín/chruaichín,* not given.

Croaghlin, *cruachlann,* not given.

Croaghna, *cruachna,* peaks.

Croaghna, *cruach-na...,* not given.

Croaghrim, *cruachroim,* not given.

Croahy, *cruaiche,* a rick a stack or a rick-shaped hill.

Croan, *crón,* brown.

Croan, *cruán, cruan, cruadhán, cruadhan,* hard ground/land.

Croane, *Cróine,* not given.

Croane, *cruadhán,* a hard place.

Croane, *cruán, cruadhan, cruan,* hard ground/land.

Croanrudda, *cro-an-rudda,* not given.

Croase, *cruadhas,* hard land.

Crobally, *crua-bhaile, cruabhaile,* a place of har or stiff soil.

Crobally, *cruadh-bhaile,* townland of hard ground.

Crobh, a hand.

Crochtenclogh, little croft of stones.

Crock, *chnuic, cnoic, cnoc, gCnoc,* a hill.

Crocka, *cnoc-a'...,* hill of the...

Crockada, *cnoc-edar-da-greuch,* hill between two marshy flats.

Crockan, *cnocán,* not given.

Crockana, *cnoc-na...,* hill of the...

Crockanagh, hill of horses.

Crockaun, *cnocán,* little hill or hillock.

Crockauna, *cnocán,* a hill.

Crockeen, *cnocan,* little hill or hillock.

Crockna, *cnoc-na...,* hill of the...

Croe, *Chró, cró,* not given.

Croe, *gCró,* cattle.

Croe, *crú,* a hut, a cattle hut or huts.

Croe, *cruaig,* stunted.

Croff, *creamha,* not given.

Croft, *choradh,* a weir.

Crogh, *cruagh,* a stacked hill.

Crogha, *cruacha,* heaps or clamps.

Croghan, *cruachain, cruachán,* a round hill or a little rick.

Croghan, *Cruachan,* Cruacha, the name of Queen Maive's mother.

Croghan, *cruachan, cruachán, cruacha,* a little hill or mound.

Croghan, *cruagh,* a stacked hill.

Croghera, *chrochaire,* the hangman.

Croghery, *chrochaire,* the hangman.

Croghery, *crochaire,* a hangman or a gallows.

Croghig, *crochadh, crochaig, chrochaig,* hanging or a place of execution.

Croghill *creamhchoill,* wood of the wild garlic.

Croghnut, *cruachnaite, cruachnait,* not given.

Croghta, *crochta,* a small enclosed house-farm or croft

Croghteen, *croichtín,* a small croft.

Croghtena, *crochta-na...,* not given.

Croghten, *croichtín,* a little croft.

Croghy, *croiche,* In Irish *croiche* means a cross but in townlands it can mean, a gallows, a hangmans rope, noose or a place of execution. In this case it means a gallows.

Crogue, *cruach,* a stacked or round hill.

Croha, *croiche,* a gallows.

Croha, *crothach,* rough uneven land.

Crohan, *cruachán,* not given.

Crohan, *cruán, cruan,* hard ground or land.

Crohane, *chrócháin, cruachán,* not given.

Crohane, *Chróchán, Crócháin, Croachain,* St Cróchán/Crochan/Crohan.

Crohane, *cruachan, cruachán,* a hillock, a little round hill or a mound.

Crohane, *cruagh,* a stacked hill.

Croher, *chrochair,* a funerary bier.

Crohig, *chrochaidh,* of the hanging.

Crohy, *an-chruach/croich/croiche,* not given.

Crohy, *creathaighe,* ague.

Crohy, *croch, croiche,* a gibbet or gallows.

Crohy, *Crua,* not given.

Crohy, *crúaiche,* a rock pile.

Crohy, *cruaiche,* not given.

Croim, *croime,* winding.

Crois, *croise,* a cross.

Croise, *croise,* a cross.

Croke, *Crocach,* Croke, a male name.

Crokig, *Chrocaigh,* Croke, a family name.

Crokingle, *cro-Ceangail,* Ceangal's (a personal or a family name) enclosure.

Crokingle, *cro-ceangail,* enclosure of the binding.

Crolack, *cruach-leac,* not given.

Crolack, *cruadh-leaca,* hard stones or stony land.

Crolly, *craithlighe,* a shaking bog.

Crolly, *crochlí,* the steep way.

Crolly, *croithlí,* a quagmire.

Crom, *chrom, crom,* a bend, crooked, bent, curved, stooped, inclining or sloping.

Crom, *croime,* not given.

Cromac, a river bend.

Cromac, *cromóige,* not given.

Cromaghy, *crom-achadh,* sloping field.

Cromaglan, *cruimm-ghlin, cruim-ghlinn,* crooked glen.

Cromagloun, *cruimm-ghlin, cruim-ghlinn,* crooked glen.

Croman, *chromáin,* a crow or rook.

Croman, *croman,* the kite (bird).

Croman, *croman,* the stooped man.

Cromane, a sloped place.

Cromane, *cromán,* the hip.

Cromaun, *croman,* the stooped man.

Cromer, *chruimhthir,* of the priest.

Cromer, from *crom,* bent.

Cromlech, *crom-leac,* literally means a sloping stone but it is also used to describe three stones standing up and one on top to form a grave.

Cromlin, *cruimm-ghlin, cruimghleann, cruimghlinn,* crooked glen.

Cromoge, a little sloped place.

Crompane, *chrampáin,* not given.

Crompane, *chrompáin, crompán,* an inlet or creek.

Crompane, *crompain, crompan,* a little sea-inlet.

Crompane, *cromthan,* a curved place.

Crompaun, *crompán,* a little creek.

Crompaunvealduark, *crompán-bél-duairc,* little creek of the surly mouth.

Cromwell, *cnoc-Cromail,* not given.

Cromwell, *crom-choill,* stooped or sloping wood.

Cron, *corra,* a stone enclosure.

Cron, *crana,* trees.

Cron, *crón,* brown.

Crona, *crodhanna,* pens or enclosures.

Crona, *croine,* the (brown) cow.

Crona, *crón...,* the dark brown...

Crona, *cro-na...,* hut of the...

Crona, *cró-na…,* sheep fold of the…

Crona, *cro-na…,* valley of the…

Crona, *corr-na*(sic)…, hill of the…

Crona, *cruaine,* reddish.

Crona, *crunn, cróna, cró-na…,* not given.

Crona, from *corran,* sickle shaped.

Cronaghan, *cruithnechta*(sic), *Crothnachán,* not given.

Cronan, *Chrónáin, Crónáin, Cronain,* St Crónán/Cronan.

Cronan, *chronáin,* humming.

Cronan, *Cronáin, Cronain,* Cronan, a personal or family name.

Cronat, *Crónait,* not given.

Cronat, *Cruachnat,* St Cronat (the virgin saint).

Cronaun, *chrónáin,* not given.

Cronaun, *cronán, cronáin,* musical humming.

Cronavone, *crunnmhóin,* not given.

Crone, *chrón, coróin,* not given.

Crone, *crabhann,* an esker or river ridge.

Crone, *crabhann,* gravel ridge of the river(sic).

Crone, *cróine,* the (brown) cow.

Crone, *crón,* a hollow, a round hollow or a valley.

Crone, *crón,* brown.

Crone, *Crón, Cróine,* St Crone.

Crone, *crón,* dark.

Crone, *Crona,* a female name.

Crone, *cruadhán,* hard ground.

Croneen, *cran-a'…,* trees of…

Croneen, *cróinin,* a little hollow.

Croneen, *crón,* a brown spot of land.

Croneen, *Uí-Chroinín,* Cronin, a family name.

Croneen, *Uí-Chronín,* O'Cronin, a family name.

Croney, *chróna,* brown.

Croney, *Croine, Chróine, Chróne,* St Crona, (the virgin saint).

Croney, from *crón,* a hollow.

Cronghill, *creamhchoill,* wood of garlic.

Cronigan, *Uí-Chronagáin,* O'Cronigan, a family name.

Cronin, *crónainn,* dark brown pieces of land.

Cronny, *crona,* not given.

Cronock, *cruinneóige,* a lake dwelling.

Cronog, *crannóige,* not given.

Cronoge, *chrannóg,* not given.

Cronoge, *chrannóige,* a wooden structure usually on water.

Cronoge, *crannóg,* a structure or dwelling of wood usually on a lake.

Cronoge, *crónóg,* a little hollow.

Cronroad, *cro-an-rudda,* not given.

Crony, *an-chróinigh,* not given.

Crony, *corran-na…,* hill of the…

Crony, *Cróine, Cróine* or *Crón,* a womans, name.

Crony, *na-gCróineach,* of the O'Croin's, a personal or family name.

Crony, *Chróine,* Crone, a female name.

Crony, *cróine, croine,* a brown cow.

Crony, *crón,* brown.

Croo, *chrú,* not given.

Croo, *croch,* gallows.

Croo, *cruaidh, cruadh, cruadha,* hard.

Croob, *crúb,* claw, foot, hoof or paw.

Croob, *crúibe,* a claw.

Croobig, *chrubaigh,* club footed or clumsy.

Croobog, *crubóg,* crabs.

Croobog, *crúbóige,* not given.

Crooboge, *crúboge,* crabs.

Crooby, *crúibe,* a claw.

Crooeel, *cnudhaoil,* nut clusters or nut gathering.

Crooghie, *cruaice,* a clamp.

Crooha, *cruacha,* pinnacles or ramparts.

Crooha, *cruaiche,* a stack or a turf stack.

Croohen, *cruithne,* ancient Picts who settled here.

Croohy, *cruaiche,* a cross or gallows.

Crook, *cnoc, cruach,* a hill.

Crook, *cruach,* a stacked, round hill.

Crook, *cruaiche,* a rock.

Crook, *cruaiche,* the reek(sic).

Crooka, *chrúca,* a handful or crook.

Crooka, *cruaice,* a clamp.

Crooke, *cruach,* hard land.

Crooke, *crúc, cruac,* not given.

Crooken, *cnuicér,* rabbit warren.

Crookhaven, *an-cruachán,* (the haven of) the hillock/little rick or little round hill.

Crookhaven, *cruacán,* not given.

Croom, *croime,* winding.

Croom, *cromadh, chromtha, crometh, cromadh,* a sloping place.

Croom, *cromadh,* the crooked ford.

Croon, a well.

Croon, *cruithean, cruithne,* ancient Picts who settled here.

Croone, *Cruithne, Cruithean, Cruithen,* 'the Cruithin' or ancients Picts who settled here.

Croppan, *cnappain,* a little hillock.

Crory, *cruaire, cruaidhre,* hard land.

Cros, *cros,* a crossroads.

Crosh, *croise,* cross.

Crosheen, *crosán,* a little cross.

Cross, *clais,* a trench.

Cross, *crocea,* Church land.

Cross, *cros,* a cross or crossroads.

Cross, *cros, chrois, croise,* a cross.

Crossa, *na-crosa,* the crosses.

Crossagh, *crosach,* streaked or seamed ground.

Crossan, *chrosáin,* not given.

Crossan, *Crosáin,* McCrossan, Crossan or Crosbie, Crosby, a family name.

Crossan, *crosán,* a little cross.

Crossanagh, *chásanach*(sic), not given.

Crossane, *crosán,* a little cross.

Crossaun, *crosáin,* a cross.

Crossaun, *crosán,* a little cross.

Crossaun, *Crossáin,* Crossan or MacCrossan, sometimes changed to Crosbie, a family name.

Crossawn, *Chasáin,* Casan, a male name.

Crossayle, *crosaill,* not given.

Crossea, *crois/cros-Aodha, cros-Aedha,* Hugh's (a male name) cross.

Crosser, *crois-air…, cros/crois/croise ar…,* cross on or by the…

Crossery, *crosaire,* a crossroads.

Crosses, *na-crosa,* not given.

Crosshaven, *bun-an-Tábhairne, cros-tSeáin,* not given.

Crossig, *Chrosaigh, Crosaig,* Cross, a personal or family name.

Crosslair, *clais-Láir*(sic) , not given.

Crosslair, *clais-láir,* not given.

Crossna, *cros-an-aith,* cross of the ford.

Crossna, *cros-na…,* cross of the…

Crossna, *crosnach,* not given.

Crossnacaldoo, *crois-Mhic-Giolla-Dhuibh,* not given.

Crossog, Crossoge, *crosóg, crosog,* a small cross. There are many townlands with this name, in at least one instance it was a place where infants were buried.

Crossoge, *chrosóg,* not given.

Crossoges, *na-crosóga/chrosóg,* not given.

Crossone, Owen's (a male name) cross.

Crossterry, a cross shaped or bow shaped wood.

Crosstery, a cross shaped or bow shaped wood.

Crossy, *crosa,* crosses.

Crotees, *crotaí,* humps.

Crotlie, *croit-shliabh,* humpbacked mountain.

Crott, *crut,* a hump.

Crott, *cruit,* a humped hill.

Crott, *cruitt,* a harp.

Crotta, *chrotach,* not given.

Crotta, *crochta,* a croft.

Crotta, *crota,* humps, tummocks.

Crotta, from *cruit,* hump backed hills.

Crottan, from *cruit,* a little hump backed hill.

Crottees, from *cruit,* hump backed hills.

Crough, *carragh,* barren.

Crough, *cruach, chrúach,* a heap.

Crough, *chruach,* not given.

Crough, *cruach,* a rick, a hill, a stacked up hill, a natural rockpile, a round rockpile or a mound.

Croughal, *cruachal,* a little round hill.

Croughan, *cruachán,* a round hill.

Croughaun, *cruachán,* not given.

Croughil, *cruachal,* a little round hill.

Croughil, *cruáchoill,* not given.

Crought, *chrochta,* a croft.

Crought, *crochta,* not given.

Croughta, *crochta,* not given.

Croughteha, *crochta,* an enclosed field.

Croum, *chrom,* the lone bent….

Crour, *gCreabhar, creabhar,* woodcocks.

Crov, *cruadh,* hard land.

Crovane, *churraigh-bháin,* the white marsh.

Crove, *cró-bheithe,* the birch fold/enclosure

Crove, round hill of birch or a birch enclosure.

Crove, *croibh,* not given.

Croveen, *cruach-mhín/mheen…,* smooth round hill of the…

Crovehy, cró-bheithe/bhéithe, cróbheithe, not given.

Crovehy, round hill of the birch.

Crover, cruabhar, not given.

Crover, cruadhbhar, hard land.

Crover, cruadhbhar, hard surface or top.

Crow cro, chro, cró, a hut, fold or pen for cattle.

Crow, chró, gore.

Crow, chró, cró, a hut, enclosure or hovel.

Crow, cro, a valley.

Crow, cró, gcró, huts.

Crow, cró, hazel nuts.

Crow, cno, nuts.

Crow, cro, sheep or cattle sheds/huts.

Crow, croiche, the cross.

Crow, crua, craobh, croib, chróibh, not given.

Crow, cruach, a rick.

Crow, cruadh, hard, hard surfaced or hard land.

Crowagh, cruach, not given.

Crowan, cró-na/an…, not given.

Crowcor, crodh-corr, odd shed.

Crowdoo, dúchró(sic), not given.

Crower, gCreabhar, chreabhair, creabhar, woodcocks.

Crowey, cruaidhe, cruaidh, hard surfaced land.

Crowey, cruail, not given.

Crowhill, creamh-choill, cramhchoill, wood of wild garlic.

Crowhill, cruachoill, not given.

Crowhill, cruadh-choille, hard wood.

Crowin, chrobhain, not given.

Crowly, Uí-Chruadhlaoich, O'Crowley, a family name.

Crowm(sic), cróm, sloping.

Crown, cran, tree/s.

Crowna, cro/cró-na…, not given.

Croy, gray(sic).

Croy, chruaich, a rick.

Croy, chruaich, the peak.

Croy, chruaigh, the summit.

Croy, croiche, a gallows.

Croy, cruaidhe, cruadh, cruadha, hard.

Croyney, chroin, the tree.

Cru, chraobh, chraobha, not given.

Cru, cru, blood.

Cru, cruabhair, not given.

Cruagh, crebhach, craobhach, not given.

Cruagh, cruagh, a stacked hill.

Cruaig, Chruaidh, not given.

Cruaig, chruóige, hardness.

Cruaig, cruach, a stacked, round hill.

Cruan, cruan, cruadhán, hard land/soil.

Cruan, cruán, not given.

Cruary, cruadh dhaire, strong oak wood.

Cruary, cruaidhre, hard land.

Cruba, craoibhe, the bush.

Crubagh, crubach, talons.

Crubeen, cruba-enn, birds foot trefoil (a type of herb).

Crubeen, crúibín, little hoof or claw.

Crubinagh, abounding in hoofs or birds foot trefoil (a type of herb).

Crubogue, crúbóg, a small hoof, claw or paw.

Cruck, chnoic, cnoc, cnuic, a hill.

Cruckaun, cnocán, a hillock.

Cruckawn, cnocán, a hillock.

Crue, creamha, chneamha, not given.

Crue, crú, chru, blood.

Crue, cruaidhe, hard.

Cruell, creamhchoill, not given.

Cruell, cruadhail, hard land.

Cruemeragh, Cruimhthir-Fhiachrach, not given.

Cruffer, cruimhther, the Priest.

Crufty, croghta, a croft.

Crughwill, from crochabh and aill, the cliff height.

Cruha, croiche, a gallows.

Cruickagh, cnoiceach, not given.

Cruik, cnoc, a hill.

Cruimthir, cruimhther, the Priest.

Cruin, round.

Cruit, an-chruit, not given.

Cruit, cruit, a hump.

Cruit, cruite, cruit, a humped hill.

Crum, chrom, crom, bent, inclined, sloping or curved.

Crum, cruim, a valley.

Crumlin, croimghlinn, cruimhghlinn, curved glen.

Crumlin, cromghlinn, croimlinn, the crooked/winding valley.

Crumlin, cromlainn, not given.

Crummagh, cromach, sloping land.

Crummey, cromaidh, inclining ground.

Crummoge, curved or crooked.

Crummy, *cromach,* sloping land.

Crummy, *Uí-Chromaigh,* O'Crommy, a family name.

Crump, (island) *oilean-dá-chruinne,* not given.

Crumpane, *chrampáin,* not given.

Crumpane, *chrompáin,* a river valley.

Crumpane, *crompán,* a little creek, inlet at the mouth of a streamlet or branching off from a lake, riverbed or the sea.

Crumpane, *gCrompán,* inlets.

Crumpaun, *an-crampán,* not given.

Crumper, *cruimhther,* the Priest.

Crumper, *cruimthir,* not given.

Crumpin, *crompane,* a little inlet.

Crumraghragh, *cruimthir-Fhiachrach,* the Priest named Fiachra.

Crumreaghragh, *cruimthir-Fhiachrach,* the Priest named Fiachra.

Crumreragh, *cruimthir-Fhiachrach,* the Priest named Fiachra.

Crun, *crón,* brown.

Crun, *cruithin, cruithne,* ancient Picts who settled here.

Crunagh, *cruithneachta,* wheat bearing place.

Crunaght, *cruithneachta,* wheat or wheat bearing place.

Crunat, *cruithneachta,* not given.

Crunat, *cruthneachta,* wheat.

Crunaun, *chronáin,* not given.

Crunnet, *cruithneachta,* wheat.

Crunnion, *Croinnín,* not given.

Crunnoge, *cruinneóg,* round stones.

Crup, *cnap,* a lump or a small round hillock.

Crush, *crois,* crossroads.

Crusha, *croise,* a cross.

Crusha, *croisí,* a cross.

Crushea, *crois-Aodha,* Aodh's (a male name) cross.

Crusheen, *croisín, crosán, croisin* a small cross.

Crusheeny, *na-croisíní,* not given.

Crushy, *croise,* a cross.

Crussanagh, *crosánach,* full of crosses or intersections.

Crussera, *crosaire,* a crossroads.

Crussogue, *crosóg, crosog,* the small cross. There are many townlands with this

name. In at least one instance it was a place where infants were buried.

Crut, *cruit,* a hump backed hill.

Crutcheen, *cruitín,* a hillock.

Crutcheena, *cruitín-a'…,* hillock of…

Crutt, *an-chruit,* not given.

Crutt, *croit,* a hill or hump.

Crutta, *chrotach,* not given.

Crutta, *cruite,* a hump.

Crutta, *crota,* humps.

Crutta, from *cruit,* hump backed hills.

Cruttan, *cruite,* a little hump backed hill.

Crutteen, *chruitín,* hunchback or cripple.

Cruttera, *chruitire, cruitire, crotaire,* a harper.

Cruttia, *cruite,* not given.

Cruttin, *Chruitín,* not given.

Cruzha, *croise,* the cross.

Cry, *criothaigh, criothach, crithach,* shaking bog or a morass.

Crylough, *crithlach,* a shaking bog.

Cua, *cua,* a hollow.

Cua, *cúa,* not given.

Cuagh, *cua,* not given.

Cuan, *cuan,* a curve or winding.

Cuan, *cuan,* blind.

Cuba, *Cúba,* not given.

Cubba, *Uí-Chobthaigh,* O'Cowhig or Coffey, a family name.

Cubbin, *Ghobáin, Ghobain,* St Goban.

Cubby, *cabaighe,* gapped.

Cuckoohill, *cnoc-na/n-caillighe,* the hill of the hag.

Cuckoo-hill, *cnoc-na-caillí,* not given.

Cud, *coda,* a share or portion.

Cuddagh, *codacha,* divisions or shares.

Cuddahy, *Uí-Chuidighthigh,* O'Cuddihy, a family name.

Cuddihy, *Uí-Chuidighthigh,* O'Cuddihy, a family name.

Cuddoge, *codóige, codóg,* a lapwing or plover.

Cuddoo, *codamha,* divisions or shares.

Cuddy, *cuidighthe,* lodging or entertainment.

Cuddy, *Uí-Chuidighthigh,* O'Cuddihy, a family name.

Cuff, *cuaiche,* the cuckoo.

Cuffe, *Chuffe,* not given.

Cuffe, *cuaiche,* not given.

Cuffe, *Uí-Chobhaigh,* O'Cuffe, a family name.

Cuggaran, *Cugarain,* a male name.

Cugger, *cogair,* conspiracy or whispering.

Cuguilla, *coigile,* not given.

Cuibb, *goib,* a beak.

Cuil, *choill,* *coill,* a wood.

Cuil, *cúil,* not given.

Cuilcagh, *cuilceach,* *cailceach,* chalky or chalky mountain.

Cuileena, *coillín-na* , not given.

Cuilfea, *coille-fiadhadh,* wood of the deer.

Cuill, *coil,* hazel.

Cuill, *cuill,* *choill,* a wood.

Cuilla, *coill-an/a'...,* wood of the...

Cuillagh, *coilleach,* woodland.

Cuillaghan, *coilleachán,* a place of hazels.

Cuillair, *coiléir,* a quarry.

Cuillaire, *coiléir,* a quarry.

Cuillare, *coiléir,* a quarry.

Cuillaun, *coilleán,* underwood.

Cuilleachan, *coillean,* underwood.

Cuilleen, *an-coillín,* not given.

Cuilleen, *Mic-Cuilinn,* MacCullen, a family name.

Cuillew, *coilleadh,* *coille,* a wood.

Cuilloge, *coilleóg,* the young wood.

Cuilly, *coilleach,* woodland.

Cuilna, *coil-na...,* wood of the...

Cuilnaheron, *Cuil-le-h-Eirin,* its back turned to Ireland.

Cuilta, *coillte,* woods.

Cuiltia, *coil, coillte,* woods.

Cuilty, *coil, coillte,* woods.

Cuilty, *coilltidh,* not given.

Cuinereen, *cuinichiréin,* a rabbit warren.

Cuing, *cuinn, cuinne,* an angle.

Cuingareen, *cuininarín,* little rabbit warren.

Cuircnagh, *Cuircne,* Cuircne, a personal or family name and part the name of a barony in Kilkenny west.

Cuirke, *Uí-Chuirc,* O'Quirk or Quirk, a family name.

Cuirp, *choirp,* not given.

Cuirree, *gCaedhrí,* submerged rock faces.

Cuit, *chait,* not given.

Cul, *choill, coill,* a wood.

Cul, *coll,* hazel, a place of hazel.

Cul, *cul, chúil, cúil,* a corner, nook, angle or recess.

Cul, *cúl, cul,* back.

Culbin, *Cuilbin,* not given.

Culbin, *Chuilbín,* Culbin, a personal or family name.

Culdaff, *cúil-Dabhcha, cúl-Dabhach,* not given.

Culdaff, *cul-daighche,* back of the flaxdam.

Culdaff, Dabhcha's (a personal or family name) secluded spot.

Culdaloo, *coill-fhidh-dubh,* not given.

Culear, *choiléir,* a quarry.

Culeen, *coillín,* little wood.

Culeen, *cuilín,* little corner.

Culeeny, *coillínidhe,* little woods.

Cules, *cúille,* corners or angles.

Culew, *choillead,* moorland.

Culhane, *Uí-Chathláin,* Ó Cathláin, a family name.

Culhane, *Uí-Chathláin,* O'Culhane, a family name.

Culineen, *cúl-an-fhiona,* back place of the wine.

Culisky, *cuilisce,* not given.

Culkeen, from *cuilc,* a place of reeds.

Culkey, abounding in weeds(sic).

Culkey, *cuilcigh, cuilceach,* abounding in reeds.

Culky, abounding in reeds.

Cull, *cuill, coll,* hazel or a place of hazel.

Culla, *chodla,* sleep.

Culla, *Cholla,* not given.

Culla, *coille,* a wood.

Cullaan, *coiléain,* a hound whelp.

Cullaboy, *coill-bhuidhe,* yellow wood.

Cullagh, *choilleach,* not given.

Cullagh, *coilleach,* a woody place or woodland.

Cullagh, *coilleach,* grouse cocks.

Cullaha, *cuillithídh,* hazel.

Cullahill, *chúlchoill,* the black wood.

Cullahill, *collchoill,* hazel wood.

Cullahill, *cúlchoill, cul-choille/choill,* the back wood or the back of the wood.

Cullamore, *collamair,* not given.

Cullamus, *Colamas,* not given.

Cullan, *coll, coill,* hazels.

Cullane, *Chathláin, calláin,* not given.

Cullane, *Coilean, Coileáin,* Collins, O'Collins or O'Cullane, a personal or family name.

Cullane, *coll, coill,* hazels.

Cullane, *collán, collan,* a hazel grove.

Cullane, the puppy(sic).

Cullane, *Uí-Choileán,* Ó Coileáin, a family name.

Cullane, *Ui-Choileain,* O'Collins, a personal or family name.

Cullanter, a colander or bowl shaped strainer.

Cullata, *codlata,* sleepy.

Cullatag, *codlatach,* a sleepy place.

Cullaun, *callán,* shouting.

Cullaun, *cúlán,* the back angle.

Cullaun, *coiléain,* a hound whelp.

Cullaun, *colán,* a young cow.

Cullaun, *coll, coill,* hazel/s.

Cullaun, *collán, an-collán,* not given.

Cullaun, *cuileánn,* small holly-wood.

Cullaun, *Uí-Choileain,* O'Collins, a family name.

Cullaville, *baile-Mhic-Cullach,* MacCullagh's (a family name) town, MacCullagh means the son of Cullach.

Cullawn, *coilleán,* underwood.

Cullea, *culgha,* a hind.

Culleare, *choiléara, coiléir,* a quarry.

Culleare, *choiléir,* not given.

Cullee, *caillí,* not given.

Culleen, *Chillín,* a little Church.

Culleen, *choillín,* holly or holly land.

Culleen, *Chuilchín, Cuilcheann,* a male name.

Culleen, *Chuilín, coillín, choillín,* not given.

Culleen, *coillín, choillín, choillin,* a little wood.

Culleen, *coillín,* little wood.

Culleen, *coillín-Aodha,* not given.

Culleen, *coillíní,* little woods.

Culleen, *cuillionn, cuileann,* holly or holly land.

Culleena, *coillín-na...,* little wood of the...

Culleenagh, a place of woods.

Culleenagh, *choillíneach,* not given.

Culleens, *coillíní,* little hazel woods.

Culleens, *coillíní,* a place of small woods.

Culleens, *coillíní,* little woods.

Culleeny, *coillínach,* little wood.

Cullen, *Choileán, Cuilinn, Chuilinn,* St Cuileann, Cuilleann.

Cullen, *chuillen,* a holly wood.

Cullen, *chuillinn,* the slope.

Cullen, *Cill-Fhlainn,* St Flann's Church.

Cullen, *coileain,* a whelp.

Cullen, *Coileáin,* Collins, a personal or family name.

Cullen, *coillín,* a little wood.

Cullen, *cuil-Fhlainn,* St Flan's retreat.

Cullen, *cuilinn-Uí-Chaoimh, Coilín, choilleáin, chuilinn, ceatharlach*(sic), not given.

Cullen, *cuilleann, chuillinn,* a steep slope.

Cullen, *cuillionn, cuillinn, chuillion, cuilinn, cuileann,* holly or holly land.

Cullen, *Cullen,* a personal or family name.

Cullenach, *cuileannach,* holly.

Cullenagh, *chuileannach,* not given.

Cullenagh, *cuileannach,* a place of holly.

Cullenagh, *cuileanntrach,* a place/field or grove of holly.

Cullenane, *Uí-Chuileanain,* Cullinane, a family name.

Cullenane, *Uí-Chuilionnain,* O'Cullenan or Cullenan, a family name.

Cullendragh, *cuileanntrach,* a place of holly, a field or grove of holly.

Cullenoge, little holly or a place of holly trees.

Cullentra, *cuileanntrach,* a place of holly, a field or grove of holly.

Cullentragh, *chuileanntrach, cuileantrach,* not given.

Cullentragh, *cuileanntrach,* a place of holly, a field or grove of holly.

Cullentragh, *cuileanntrach,* a long steep slope(sic).

Cullentragh, *cullentragh,* sea-holly.

Cullentrough, *cuileanntrach,* a place of holly, a field or grove of holly.

Cullentry, *cullentragh, cuileanntrach,* (a place of) sea holly.

Cullenwaine, *cúil-Ó-nDubháin/O-nDubhan,* corner or secluded place of the O'Dwanes, (a family name). O'Dwane means the descendants of Duane.

Culler, *coiléir,* a quarry.

Cullew, *coilleadh, coille,* a wood.

Culley, *cuille,* woody.

Cullia, *choille, coille,* the wood.

Cullia, *coille,* wooded.

Cullia, *coillighe,* not given.

Culliagh, *coileach,* a cock.

Culliagh, *coilleach,* woodland.

Culliagh, *cúl-liath,* not given.

Cullies, *coilleadh, coillidhe,* woodland/s.

Cullig, *choilig, coileach,* a cock, a woodcock or a pheasant

Cullig, *coille,* a wood.

Cullig, *coilleach,* grouse cocks.

Cullig, *cullaig, chollaig, chollaigh,* a boar.

Culliheen, *Choilchín, Choilcín, Cuilcín,* not given.

Culliheen, *Chailchín,* Calchin, a personal or family name.

Cullin, *chuilinn, cuilinn,* not given.

Cullin, *chuilleann, cuillean, cuillionn, cullen, cuileann,* holly or holly land.

Cullin, *culolin*(sic), holly.

Cullin, *chuillinn,* a steep slope.

Cullin, *cúilín,* little corner.

Cullina, *Colna,* not given.

Cullinagh, *cuileanach, cuillenach,* a place of holly or hollies.

Cullinagh, *cuileannach, cuileanach,* not given.

Cullinan, *Cuilleanáin,* O'Cullenan, a family name.

Cullinan, Cullinan, a personal or family name.

Cullinane, *Uí-Chuilionnain,* O'Cullenan or Cullenan, a family name.

Culling, *chuilinn,* holly.

Cullingtree, abounding in holly.

Cullingtree, *cuileanntrach, cuileanntraighe,* not given.

Cullintraw, *cuileanntrach,* (a place of) sea holly.

Cullion, *chuilinn, coillín,* not given.

Cullion, *cuilleann,* a steep slope.

Cullion, *cuillionn, cuillean, cuilleann, cuileann, cuilinn,* holly or holly land.

Cullitha, *codlata,* sluggish or sleepy.

Culloge, *culog,* one seated behind the rider on a horse.

Cullomane, *Cill-Colmain,* Church of St Colman.

Cullomane, Colman, a personal or family name.

Cullomaun, Colman, a personal or family name.

Culloo, *Cholbha,* not given.

Culloville, *baile-Mhic-Cullach,* Mac Cullach's homestead.

Culloville, *collchoill,* not given.

Cullun, O'Collan, a family name.

Cully Water, *abha-coillidh,* not given.

Cully, *chloidhe,* ditch.

Cully, *choilig, coileach,* a cock, a woodcock or a pheasant.

Cully, *chúile, choillidh,* not given.

Cully, *choilligh,* a cock.

Cully, *Chuile,* Cuille, a personal or family name.

Cully, *coill, coillidhe, coillighe, coilleach, coilleadh, coille,* a wood, woodland or a forest.

Cully, *coill-na...,* wood of the...

Cully, *cullach, chullaigh,* the boar.

Cullybackey, *cúil-an-Bhacaigh,* not given.

Cullyhanna, *coillidh-Uí-Annaidh, coilleach-eanach,* not given.

Cullyhanna, *coil-Uí-hAnnaidh,* O'Hanna's (a family name) wood.

Cullyleenan, *coill-Uí-Líonain,* O'Leeanan's (a family name) wood.

Culna, *cúil-na...,* corner of the...

Culoge, *cúlóg,* little back.

Culray, *coil-réidhe,* wood of the moorland.

Culrush, *chúil-ruis, cúlruis,* back of the wood.

Culrush, *chúlrois,* not given.

Cult, *colt,* not given.

Culter, *alltair,* not given.

Culter, *Uí-Choltair,* Ó Coltar, a family name.

Cultia, *coil, coillte,* woods.

Culties, *coillte,* woods.

Cultra, *cúl-trá, cul-tra, cultragha,* secluded strand or the back of the strand.

Cum, *com, cúmhach, chuim, cúm,* a hollow, dell or valley.

Cumar, a confluence.

Cumask, *cumasc,* not given.

Cumasky, *Chumascaigh, Cumascaigh,* not given.

Cumasky, *Cummuscaigh,* Cummuscagh, a personal name.

Cumber, *chomair, comair, comer,* a confluence of rivers, lakes or both.

Cumber, *comar, chumair,* not given.

Cumberland, *Comhrann,* not given.

Cummane, *comán,* a little hollow.

Cummar, *comar,* a valley in which streams meet.

Cummaun, from, *cúm,* little hollow.

Cummawn, *comán,* a common.

Cummeen, *coimín,* little sheltered place, little hollow of the badger or just commonage.

Cummeen, *cuimin, cúimín,* a river valley, a glen, a hollow, a little glen, a commonage or secluded spot.

Cummer, *chomair, comer, comair,* a confluence of rivers, lakes or both.

Cummer, *comar,* a steep sided inlet or ravine.

Cummer, *chumair,* a ravine.

Cummer, *cumar, cumair, chumaír,* a valley or ravine.

Cummeragh, *chomarach, comrach,* not given.

Cummeragh, from *comar,* a place of confluences.

Cummin, *Chomainn, Chiomín, Coimín, Cuimin, Cuimín,* not given.

Cummin, *Chuimín,* O'Cummin, Cummins or Commons, family names.

Cummin, *Chuimín,* St Coimin/Cuimín.

Cummins, *Chuimín,* not given.

Cummirk, *chomairce,* not given.

Cummirk, *comairce,* protection.

Cummisk, *chumaisc,* not given.

Cummisk, *comasc,* contention or battle.

Cummisk, *cum-uisge,* back water.

Cumny, *Cuimne,* not given.

Cumper, *chlampair,* controversy (disputed lands).

Cumper, *coimir,* a confluence.

Cumran, *cumar-aran,* valley of the riverbed.

Cumreragh, *chruimthir/cruimthir-Fhiachrach,* the Priest named Fiachra.

Cumry, from *cummer,* a confluence.

Cumry, *na-comraigh,* not given.

Cun, *cionn,* a head.

Cun, *con,* a dog or hound.

Cunagh, *coinidhe, hcoineach,* rabbits.

Cunapoge, *cnapóg,* a mound or hillock.

Cunard, *ceannmhar,* not given.

Cunard, *cionn-ard,* the high head.

Cune, *ciuin,* quiet or silent.

Cuneen, *choinín,* rabbit/s.

Cung, *Cuing,* not given.

Cung, *cung,* the neck.

Cunghill, *conachail,* hound wood.

Cunghill, *conadh-choill,* wood of firewood.

Cunikeen, *cumarachin,* hills and vallies.

Cunikeen, *Mhic-Sheoinicín*(sic), not given.

Cunlagh, *connlach,* stubble.

Cunlagh, *connlaigh,* not given.

Cunlin, *coinnlín,* stubbles.

Cunna, *chonnadh,* trees.

Cunna, *chonnaidh,* not given.

Cunna, *chunna, cona, conna, conadh, chonnaidh, chonaidh,* firewood or a place of firewood.

Cunna, *coinne, choinne,* a rendezvous or meeting.

Cunnagavale, *chongbháil,* not given.

Cunnagavale, *congbhail,* a habitation.

Cunnagher, *conadhchair,* land of firewood.

Cunnahin, *Choinchinn,* not given.

Cunnahurt, *conthairt, conatuirt,* not given.

Cunnaker, *coinicér,* rabbit warrens.

Cunnamore, *conamar,* a place of fragments.

Cunneen, *Cuinnín,* O'Cunneen, a family name.

Cunneen, *Uí-Chuinín,* O'Cunneen, a family name.

Cunnell, *gCoinnle, gCáinlidh,* candles.

Cunnian, *gCoinín,* rabbits.

Cunnicar, *coinicér,* rabbit warrens.

Cunnier, *Conaire,* not given.

Cunnig, *chunna, cona, connaidh, conadh, chonaidh,* firewood.

Cunnigar, *coinicéar, coinigéar,* not given.

Cunnigar, *coinicér,* rabbit warrens.

Cunnihee, *Cuinchí,* not given.

Cunnihy, *Coinche, Coinchinne,* not given.

Cunning, *cGoinín,* rabbits.

Cunningham, *Uí-Chonnagain,* Cunningham, a family name.

Cunnion, *coinín,* rabbits or a rabbit warren.

Cunnion, *cuncheann,* the dogs head.

Cunnow, *gCnó.* Nuts.

Cunny, *chunna, cona, conna, conadh,* firewood.

Cuppage, from *copóg,* dock leaves.

Cuppanagh, *copánach,* land of dockleaves.

Cuppanagh, *cupánach,* abounding in rockweed(sic).

Cuppoge, *gCopóg,* dock leaves.

Cur, *cathair, an-chorr,* not given.

Cur, *churraigh,* a marsh or moor.

Cur, *cor,* odd.

Cur, *coradh, corra, cuarr,* a weir.

Cur, *gCorr, corr,* cranes or herons.

Cura, *coradh, corra, cuarr,* a weir.

Cura, *cor*(sic), round hill of the…

Curby, *Fhoirbe*(sic), not given.

Curby, *Chorrbhuí,* Corby, a personal or family name.

Curca, *corcadh,* a marsy or moory place.

Cure, *cru,* a bloody battle.

Curie, *corra,* an enclosure.

Curka, *coirce,* oats.

Curka, *corcach,* not given.

Curkeen, a little marsh.

Curkeen, *Uí-Cuircín,* O'Curkeen or Curkin, a family name.

Curkia, *coirce,* oats.

Curkin, a little marsh.

Curkin, *an-cuircín,* not given.

Curkish, *corcas,* a marsh.

Curkney, *Cuircne,* Cuircne, a personal name.

Curkoga, *curcóige,* not given.

Curkree, *Churcaí,* not given.

Curkree, *cnuic-Aodha, cnoc-Aoidh,* Aodh's/ Hugh's (male names) hill.

Curky, *coirce,* oats.

Curl, *Choirill, Caireall,* St Caireall.

Curl, *Chairill,* St Cairill.

Curlew, *(Mts) coirrshliabh,* not given.

Curlew, *(Mts) coirr-shliabh,* rugged or rough mountain.

Curlew, *(Mts) corrsliabh,* pointed (mountains).

Curley, *Choirill*(sic), not given.

Curluddy, *cathair-Luighdeach,* not given.

Curly, *Choireallaigh,* Coireallach, the name of a Church founder in Limerick.

Curly, *Choirle,* not given.

Curn, *chuirn,* a cup or goblet.

Curneen, a small round hill.

Curr, a pit or a round hill.

Curr, *corr,* a pointed hill.

Curr, *gCorr,* cranes or herons.

Curra, *charraigh, chorraigh, chora, gCorr, coirthe, corr, an-chorr,* not given.

Curra, *curra,* a homestead or enclosure.

Curra, *churraigh, cuirreach, currach, curraidh,* a marsh, a moor or a racecourse.

Curra, *coire,* a caldron,

Curra, *cora, corra, coradh,* a weir.

Curra, *coradh, cora, corra, cuarr,* a weir.

Curra, *corra,* a homestead or dwelling.

Curra, *corra,* a round or tapering hill.

Curra, *corra,* an enclosure, a pen or a round hill.

Curra, *corrach,* a marsh.

Curra, *corra…,* round hill of the…

Curra, *cubhar,* foam.

Curra, *cur a,* odd.

Currach, *currach,* a marsh.

Currachiane, *carraigín,* abounding in small rocks.

Curragawn, *carragín,* rocky spot of land.

Curragh, *chorr, cuirreach-life, cuirreach-Chill-Dara,* not given.

Curragh, *churraigh, cuirreach, currach, curraidh,* a marsh or a racecourse.

Curragh, *carrach,* rugged.

Curragh, *currach,* marshy land.

Curragh, *churraigh,* wet land.

Curragh, *cora,* a weir.

Curragh, *corra,* an enclosure.

Curragh, *gCurrach,* swamps.

Curragha, *currach,* not given.

Curragha, *curracha,* a marshy place.

Curracha, *curracha,* moors.

Curragha, *currach-an/a'…,* wet meadow/ marsh or marshy meadow of the …

Curraghakimikeen, *currach-Mhic-Thoimicín,* not given.

Curraghakimikeen, *currach-a'Chimicin,* moor of the Cimicin(sic).

Curraghan, *currach-an…,* moor/marsh of the…

Curraghatouk, *currach-a'-tseabhaic,* marshy meadow of the hawk.

Curraghavarbarna, *currach-an-Bhréanra*(sic), not given.

Curraghbola, *corrbhuaile,* not given.

Curraghbridge, *droichead-an-corann*(sic), not given.

Curraghchase, *an-chora*(sic), not given.

Curraghcloe, *currach, Ló, Ló's* or Lo's (a personal or family name) marsh.

Curragheen, *curraithín, curraichín, currachín,* little marsh/moor.

Curraghgraigie, *an-chorrghráig*(sic), not given.

Curraghna, *currach-na…,* moor/marsh of the…

Curraghy, *curragh,* a moor.
Curraginny, *Chorgine,* not given.
Curraha, *gCurraithe,* not given.
Curraha, moors or marshes.
Curraheen, *churraoin, curraichín,* a little marsh swamp, plot of wet land or moor.
Curraheen, *curraichín,* little wet place.
Curraheen, *currichín,* little swamp.
Currahill, *coirrchill,* not given.
Currahill, *cuiriothal,* marshy land.
Currahy, marshes, bogs or moors.
Currahy, *na-curraithe,* not given.
Curraineenbrien, *curra-Inghean-Brian,* the homestead/enclosure of Brian (Boru's) daughter
Curralanty, *currach-an-Leantaigh,* not given.
Curram, *chluain,* a meadow.
Curran, *chorrain,* a sickle or sickle shape.
Curran, *cor-an…,* round hill of the…
Curran, *corrán,* the curved headland or a crescent shaped place.
Curran, *currán,* the crescent.
Currane, *chorráin, Churtháin,* not given.
Currane, *corrán,* a reaping hook, a pointed hill, a crescent shaped place or rocky land.
Currane, sharp rocks.
Currane, *Uí-Charrain,* O'Carroll, a family name.
Currane, *Uí-Chiaráin,* O'Kearan, a family name.
Currane, *Uí-Chorain,* O'Currane, O'Corrane or Curran, a family name.
Currans, *corráin,* crescent shaped places.
Currany, *cor-raithne,* ferny hill.
Currauly, *cráilí, corr-Áille,* not given.
Curraun, *corrán,* a peaked hill or (shaped like) a reaping hook.
Curraun, *corrán,* rough marshy land.
Curraun, *corrán-lin,* corn-spurrey, a plant name.
Curravaha, *an-corrmhacha,* not given.
Curraveel, *gCoirrmhíol,* not given.
Curraveil, *corraimhiol,* midges.
Curraveil, *gairbhéil,* gravel.
Currawn, *corran,* rough land.
Curreal, *cor-aoil,* round hill of lime.
Curreen, *chuirrín,* the little peak.
Curreen, *churraoin, corraichín,* little moor.
Curreen, *corín,* a little corner.

Curreen, *cuirrín,* a little marsh.
Curreen, *Uí-Chorraidhín,* Curran or Crean, a family name.
Curreen, *Uí-Churraoin,* not given.
Curreen, *Uí-Curraidhin,* O'Curreen or Curren, a family name.
Curreen, *Uí-Curraoin,* O'Currin, a personal or family name.
Curreeney, *coirríní, cuirínidhe,* little moors.
Curreeny, *coiríní,* pointed hillocks.
Curreeny, *cuirínidh,* little weirs.
Curreeny, *na-gCoirríní / coirríní / coiríní,* not given.
Curren, *chuirrín, cuirrín,* a little marsh.
Curren, *churraigh,* the marsh.
Curri, a moor.
Curri, *coradh,* not given.
Curridan, *Uí-Curradán,* O'Curridan, a family name.
Curries, *curraigh,* moors or wet meadows.
Currig, *churraigh, curraidh, currach,* a marsh or racecourse.
Curriheen, *churraichín,* a small swamp or marsh.
Currihy, *Ciarraighe-Cuirche,* the name of an ancient tribe.
Currin, *Coirrín, curraoin,* not given.
Currin, *cuirrín, chuirrín, churraoin,* a little marsh or moor.
Currin, *cor-an-fhia,* round hill of the feer.
Currine, *Uí-Churraoin,* O'Currin, a personal or family name.
Curris, *na-currai,* not given.
Currish, *crois,* the cross.
Currow, *corra,* a weir.
Curry, *cairthe,* a standing stone.
Curry, *choile*(sic), a cauldron or whirlpool.
Curry, *choire,* a whirlpool.
Curry, *Chonaire, Conaire,* Conaire or Conary, a male name.
Curry, *corra, choraidh, Conaire,* not given.
Curry, *churaidh,* a hero or a knight.
Curry, *coire, choire,* a cauldron, a cauldron like pit or a hollow.
Curry, *cora,* a weir.
Curry, *currach, curraigh, cuirreach, churraigh, corrach,* a racecourse, a moor, swamp, morass or marsh.
Curry, *curraidh,* low land.
Curry, *curraigh, churraigh,* a morass or marsh.

Curry, O'Curry, a family name.

Currygurry, *corrdhoire,* not given.

Currynanerriagh, *an-curraoin*(sic), not given.

Curta, *cúirte,* a court or mansion house.

Curtaun, from *cor,* a little round hill.

Curtoga, *cortóga,* a little round hill.

Cus, *cois,* the foot or beside.

Cus, *cos,* bottom land.

Cus, *cuas,* a cave or cove.

Cusak, not given.

Cusduff, *cos-dubh,* black foot or black bottom land.

Cush, *bun*(sic), the mouth of the river named…

Cush, *chois, coise,* the foot.

Cush, *cois,* side.

Cush, *cois,* the foot, lower end, bottom, beside, along or adjoining a hill, farm, river etc.

Cush, *cois,* tree trunk.

Cusha, *cois-a'…,* along the…

Cusha, *coise,* the foot of something or bottom land.

Cushacorra, *cois-an-coradh,* hard by the weir(sic).

Cushaling, *cois-Loinge,* not given.

Cushan, *Cuisín,* Cushion, Cusheen or Cusheen, a family name.

Cushcam, *cois-céim,* a foot step, narrow road or pass.

Cushcam, *cois-chaim,* not given.

Cusheen, *chabhaisín, cabhaisín,* a small causeway or stepping stones.

Cusheen, *Cuisín,* Cushion, Cusheen or Cusheen, a family name.

Cusheen, *Oisín,* a personal name.

Cushen, *cois-abhann…,* the mouth or foot of the river….

Cushen, *cois-an…,* foot of the…

Cushen, *Cuisín,* Cushion, Cusheen, a family name.

Cushendall, *bun-abhann-Dalla, cois-abhann-Dalla/Dhalla,* mouth of the river Dall.

Cushendun, *bun-abhann-Duinne, cois-abhann-Duine,* mouth or foot of the river Dun.

Cushenny, *cos-seanaigh,* the foxes foot.

Cusher, *choisir,* not given.

Cushil, *chaisil,* a round stone fort.

Cushil, *chaisiúir*(sic), not given.

Cushin, *coisín,* the little foot.

Cushina, *cois-Aidhne,* not given.

Cushina, *cois-eidhní,* beside the ivy river.

Cushinyen, *cois-an-eidhin,* foot of the ivy.

Cushlawn, *chaisléan,* a castle.

Cushmaig, *coisméig,* a step, pass or pace.

Cushog, *cuiseoige,* straws or reeds.

Cuskeam, *gCoiscéim,* stepping stones.

Cusker, *casgair,* slaughter.

Cusker, *choimheascair,* strife.

Cusker, *choscair,* slaughters.

Cuskinny, *cois-Coinge/Cainnigh,* not given.

Cuskry, *coisgrigh,* a place of reeds.

Cuskry, *cuiscreach, cuiscrigh,* not given.

Cuskury, *cuiscreach,* not given.

Cuslea, *cois-sleibhe,* foot of the mountain.

Cuso, *cos-a'…,* foot of the…

Cuss, *cois,* the foot, bottom or lower end.

Cuss, *cos,* a land measurment equal to a quarter of a gníomh.

Cussa, *cosa,* feet.

Cussagh, footed.

Cussan, *casan, casán, chosán, cosán,* footpath.

Cussana, *chásanach,* not given.

Cussana, *gCosán,* path.

Cussana, *cosánach,* abounding in sloe bushes, blackthorn or pathways.

Cussane, *casán, chosán,* footpath.

Cussane, *chuasáin,* not given.

Cussane, *chuasan,* little caves.

Cussaun, *casán, chosán,* the footpath or pathway.

Cussay, *chosaigh,* not given.

Cussee, *cois-Sí,* not given.

Cutra, *Cútra,* Cútra, Cutra, a personal or family name.

Cuttean, *choitín, coiteáin,* a small boat or a little cot (a flat bottomed boat).

Cutteanta, from *coitchen, coitchionn,* a commons or common lands.

Cutteen, *coitchen, coitín, coitchiann, choitín, coitcheann, coitchionn,* a common, commonage or common land.

Cuttia, *choite,* the cot.

Cuttia, *coite,* a small flat bottomed boat.

Cuttin, *coitín, choithinn,* commonage, common land.

Cuttragh, *cotrach,* not given.

D

D'Loughtane, *Dlochtán,* not given.
Da, *da, dá, dha, dhá,* two.
Da, *Dháith,* not given.
Daar, *abhainn-na-darach,* river of the oak.
Daars, *dairghe,* oaks.
Dabrian, *dae-Bhriáin,* O'Brien's(a family name) house.
Dace, *déas, déise,* the ear of corn.
Dacker, *deacair,* difficult.
Dacklin, *dubh-chluain,* black meadow.
Dacon, *dá-chon,* two hounds.
Dadanan, a male name.
Dadreen, *dhá-draighean,* not given.
Daduff, *da-dubh,* two black visaged persons.
Daeagh, *da-fhiach,* two ravens.
Daeane, *dá-én,* two birds.
Daeigh, *dá-fhiach,* two ravens.
Daff, *dabhach,* a pool.
Daff, *daibhche,* a pit, hollow or a cauldron.
Daff, *daibhche, dabhcha,* sandhills.
Daff, *damh,* an ox or oxen.
Daff, *deafa,* not given.
Dagad, two sticks or rods.
Dagarve, *da-garbh,* two rough men.
Daggan, *daingin, daingean,* strong, stronghold or a fortress.
Daggin, *daingin,* not given.
Dagh, *dubh,* black.
Daghly, *da-chlaidhe,* two ramparts.
Daghtan, *dachtan, dachtáin,* not given.
Daghtan, *deachtain,* instruction.
Dagny, *daigne,* a stronghold.
Dagny, *daingean, daingne,* strong, stronghold or a fortress.
Dague, *Dhabhag,* not given.
Dague, *daigéad,* rocky.
Dague, *dTadhg,* Teige or Timothy, male names.

Dah, *damh,* poets or bards.
Dah, *Dhaith,* David, a male name.
Daha, *Daithí,* not given.
Daha, *Deaghaidh, Deaghadh,* the name of a mytical clan.
Dahadore, *dathadóir,* a dyer.
Dahadore, *dathadora,* dyers or painters.
Dahadore, *dathadóra,* not given.
Dahaen, *Dháithín, Dáithín,* little Dáithi (Dáthín) or David, a male name.
Daheen, *Dháitín, Dáithín,* little Dáith, a male name.
Daheen, *doibhchín,* little cauldron.
Daheen, from *Dau,* little David.
Daheen, little Davy, a male name.
Dahessiagh, *da-sheiseadh,* two-sixths.
Dahill, *dubhchoillidh,* black wood.
Dahin, *Daíthín,* little Davy, a male name.
Dahirr, *duithir,* gloom or blackness.
Dahy, *Dáithí,* not given.
Daiagh, *da-fhiach,* two ravens.
Daigh, *da-fhiach,* two ravens.
Daingean, *an-daingean,* the fortress.
Dairies, *daire,* places of oaks.
Daisy, *déise,* two (persons).
Dal, *dal,* a share.
Dalahasey, *dál-Uí-Chathasaigh,* not given.
Dalan, *Dallain,* a male name.
Dalane, *dalláin,* not given.
Dalaun, *dalán,* a standing stone.
Dalaun, *dá-lon,* two blackbirds.
Dalaun, *dTulán,* not given.
Dales, *dalas,* not given.
Dalgan, *dealgain,* not given.
Dalgan, *dealgan,* a place producing briars or thorns.
Dalgin, *dealgan,* a place producing thorns.
Dalin, *da-linn,* two pools.
Dalk, *Dealgan,* Dealga or Dealgan, a male name.
Dalkey, (island) *deilginis, delg-inis, dalk-ei,* thorn island.
Dalkey, (island) *deilginis-nó-inis-Bheigneata, Cill-Beagnait,* not given.
Dalkey, *Dealga,* Delga, the name of a firbolg chief and builder of a Church in Co Meath.
Dalkey, *dealga,* the thorn.
Dalkey, *Delca,* Delga's, a male name.

Dalkin, *Dolcan, Dolcáin, Dolcain,* Dolcán or Dolcan, a male name.

Dall, *daill,* a blind man.

Dall, *daill,* dark.

Dall, *dála,* the meeting.

Dall, *dalla,* blind.

Dalla, *da-ela,* two swans.

Dalla, *deala,* not given.

Dallan, Dallan, a personal or family name.

Dallane, *dalláin, dallan, dallain,* a standing stone or a pillar stone.

Dalleen, *Daitlin,* a male name.

Dalleen, *Duilín,* not given.

Dallig, *dealg,* thorns or thorn bushes.

Dalligan, *Dealgain,* Dealgain, a personal name.

Dalligan, *dealgan,* a place producing thorns.

Dallow, *Dala,* not given.

Dallow, *nDealbh,* phantoms.

Daloo, *Dalua,* Dalua, a personal or family name.

Dalouge, *Dealúigh,* not given.

Dalough, *dá-locha, dá-lachan,* not given.

Dalough, *dá-lough,* two lakes.

Dalraghan, *an-dearachán,* not given.

Dalraghan, *deallrachán,* little shining/shiny land.

Dalteen, *baile-dailtin,* town of the impudent young fellow.

Dalteen, *dailtín,* the horseboy.

Dalton, *an-Daltúnaigh,* not given.

Dalton, *Dátúnaigh,* not given.

Dalton, *Datúin,* Daton, Dalton, the name of the founder of a Church in Fiddown parish.

Dalty, from *dalta,* not given.

Dalua, *abhainn-dá-lua,* river of the two waters.

Dalulagh, *da-loilgheach,* not given.

Daly, *Dhálaigh,* Daly, a family name.

Daly, *Uí-Dalaighe, Uí-Dhálaigh/Dhalaigh,* O'Daly or Daly, a family name and means the descendants of Daly.

Dama, *Dámaí,* not given.

Dama, *dá-mhágh,* two plains.

Damh, *damh,* an ox.

Damlaght, *dTaimhleachta,* a plague cemetery.

Damma, *dámach,* not given.

Damma, *dá-mhágh, da-mhagh/mhaghe,* two plains.

Dampaun, *dTeampán,* round boulders.

Dampaun, *dTiompán,* not given.

Damph, *nDamh, damh,* an ox or oxen.

Dan, (lough), *Donn,* not given.

Danagh, *da-neach,* two horses.

Danesfort, *dún-feart, dunfert,* fort of graves.

Danesfort, *dún-na-bhFeart, dún-fearta,* not given.

Dangan, *daingean, daingin, dangan,* strong, a stronghold or a fortress.

Dangan, *daingean, dhaingean,* solid, firm or fortified.

Dangan, *daingean-Uí-Dhonabháin,* not given.

Dangean, *daingean,* strong, stronghold or a fortress.

Dangen, *daingean,* strong, stronghold, fort or fortress.

Daniel, *Dhomhnail, Dhomhnaill, Dhónaill, Daniel, Dónall,* Dónall, a male name.

Daniel, *Dónaill, Domhnaill, Domhnall, Dónall* or Donall, a personal or family name.

Danion, *daingean,* a fortress or fortified.

Danoge, *Domhnóige, Domhnóig,* Domnoc, a personal or family name.

Danoge, St Domhnog.

Danville, *Dainbhil,* not given.

Danville, *páirc-na-bhFuinsean,* field of the ash trees.

Dao, *dá-eó,* two yew trees.

Dao, *dubh,* black.

Daossan, *dá-dossan,* two bushes.

Daowen, *da-amhainn,* two rivers.

Dara, *darach,* not given.

Dara, *dó-róth*(sic), *dá-ráth, da-rath,* two forts.

Darag, *daraighe,* oakwood.

Darag, *dearg,* red.

Daragee, *daraighe,* oakwood.

Daragee, *dearg,* red.

Daragh, *darach,* oak.

Daralk, *doire-fhalc,* the oakwood of floods.

Darby, *Diarmada,* Dermot, a male name.

Dardan, *dair-doimhin,* deep oaks.

Dardis, *an-Dairdisigh,* not given.

Dare, *dara,* oak/s or an oak grove.

Daree, *dá-Rí/Riogh,* two kings.

Dareirke, *dá-radharc,* two views.

Dareirke, *deagh-adharc,* beautiful view.

Darg, *dhearg, dearg,* not given.

Dargan, *Deargain,* Dargain, a personal or family name.

Dargan, *Deargáin,* not given.

Dargan, *deargan,* sunburnt or red spot.

Dargan, *Uí-Deargain,* O'Dargan, a family name.

Dargle, *dargail, deargail,* little red spot.

Dargle, *dargail,* red rock.

Dargle, *dubhargail,* not given.

Darhanagh, *darthanach, darthánach,* oak bearing place.

Darhanagh, *darthanach,* oak bearing place.

Dariel, *idir-dhá-fhaill,* between two cliffs or slopes.

Darierke, *dá-radharc,* two prospects.

Darinis, *darinis,* oak island.

Dark, *dearc,* a cave.

Darkan, *dearcan,* acorns.

Darkin, *dearcan,* acorns.

Darkley, *dearclaigh,* a place of hollows, caves.

Daroge, *daróg,* a place of young oaks.

Daroge, from *dair,* an ancient oak tree.

Darra, *dara,* oak.

Darra, *daraigh, darach,* not given.

Darra, *doireach, doire, dairbhreach, dair,* an oak wood, a place of oaks.

Darragh, *an-dairtheach,* the oaken house.

Darragh, bulls.

Darragh, *daraigh, doire, dara, darach, dairbhreach, dharach, dair,* oak, an oak wood or a place of oaks.

Darraghlan, *doire-achaidh-Loinn,* not given.

Darrara, *dairbhre,* abounding in oaks.

Darraragh, *doire, dairbhre, dairbhreach, dair,* an oak wood or a place of oaks.

Darrary, *dairbhreach,* place of oaks.

Darree, *doiraidhe,* woods(sic).

Darren, *dairin, dairín,* a little oak wood.

Darrery, *dairire, dairbhre,* oaks, an oak forest or plantation.

Darrery, *doire, dairbhre, dairbhreach, dair,* an oak wood or a place of Oaks.

Darrif, *dearg,* red.

Darriff, *dTarbh,* bulls.

Darriff, *darach,* oaks or oakwood.

Darrig, *daraigh,* abounding in oaks.

Darrig, *derg, dearg,* red.

Darrigal, *deargail,* little red spot.

Darrigan, *deargain,* red land.

Darrigan, *Uí-Dhearcain,* O'Dearcain, a family name.

Darrigil, *deargail,* little red spot.

Darrigle, *deargail,* not given.

Darrigone, *dearg-mhóin,* red bog.

Darriv, *dTarbh,* bulls.

Darry, *daire,* an oak grove.

Darry, *daraigh,* oaks.

Dart, *dairt, dairte,* a heifer.

Dart, *dairt,* yearling heifers.

Dart, *dart,* heifers.

Darta, *dairt,* yearling heifers.

Darta, *dairte,* the heifer.

Dartan, *dartain, dartan,* the young bull or heifer.

Dartaun, *dartaun,* a heifer.

Dartree, *dartraí, dartraighe,* not given.

Dartrey, *dhartraí, dartraí,* not given.

Dartry, *dartraí,* not given.

Darum, *da-dhruim,* two ridges.

Darun, *da-dhruim,* two ridges.

Darush, *da-rubha,* two promontories.

Darver, *dairbhre, dhairbhreach, dairbhreach,* not given.

Darver, *darbhar,* a place pruducing oak.

Dary, *dáirigh,* not given.

Dary, *dairighe,* a place of oaks.

Daryark, *dea-radhairc,* (of the) pleasing prospect.

Daryrke, *dá-rhadharc,* two prospects.

Das, *deas,* beautiful.

Dasan, corrupted from *samhaidh, samadh,* sorrel.

Dasoon, *an-Dheasúnaigh,* not given.

Dass, *deas,* beautiful.

Dassoon, *Deasúnaigh,* Dawson, a family name.

Datha, *deatha, deata,* smoke.

Dau, *dá, dhá,* two.

Dau, *Daithí,* David, a male name.

Daugh, *damh,* oxen.

Daughtan, *deachtain,* instruction.

Daula, *dála,* the meetings.

Daulan, *da-lon,* two blackbirds.

Daulon, *dá-lon,* not given.

Dauroe, *dá-ghruadh, da-ruadha,* two red cows.

Dauroe, *dhá-Rú,* not given.

Dauwee, *Dáith-bhuí,* not given.

Dauy, *Dáith,* David, a male name.

Dav, *daimh,* an ox or a stag.

Dav, *damh,* an ox or oxen.

Dav, *dau,* two.

Davaddog, *Dabhaedog,* St Davaddog.

Davaddog, *Dabhaodóg,* not given.

Davagh, *dabhach,* the vat-like hollow.

Davagh, *dabhcha,* not given.

Davagh, *daimhche,* a caldron or flax pond.

Davan, *da-bheann,* two peaks or gables.

Daveagh, *da-bheithe,* two birch trees.

Daveog, St Dabeog, Daveog.

Davery, *damhghaire,* oxen.

Davick, *Damhaic,* not given.

David, *Dháith, Dáithí,* not given.

David, *Dháibhí, Dóibhí,* a personal or family name.

Davillaun, *damhoileán,* not given.

Davin, *Daithín,* little David, a personal or family name.

Davin, *Damháin,* St Davin/Damhán.

Davin, *deábhaidh,* a skirmish.

Davin, *Dháibhín, Daimhne,* not given.

Davis, *Dathi, Daithi,* David.

Davnet, *Damhnaita,* Dymphna or Damhnait, a 7th Cent Queen.

Davnet, *Damhnata,* not given.

Davnet, *Damhnata,* St Davnet, the martyr virgin saint.

Davock, *dá-bhoc,* not given.

Davog, *Dabhóg,* St Davog.

Davoher, *dá-bhothar,* two roads.

Davore, *da-bhothar,* two roads.

Davoun, *dá-bheann,* two gables.

Davuck, *Dhabhaic,* not given.

Davy, *Dathi, Daithi,* David.

Daw, *Dáith, Daith,* Davy, a personal or family name.

Daw, *Dháith, Dáith,* David, a male name.

Daw, *damh,* an ox.

Daw, *Dathi, Daithi,* David or Davy, a male name.

Daw, *Uí-Dheaghaigh,* Daw, a family name.

Dawan, *dá-éan,* not given.

Dawan, *damhain,* the doe.

Dawannagh, *dá-mhanach,* not given.

Dawley, *Uí-Dhalaigh,* O'Daly, a family name.

Dawn, *abhainn-dealgan,* not given.

Dawn, *dabhan, dá-abhainn,* two rivers.

Dawros, *damh-ros, damhros,* ox wood/ headland or peninsula.

Dawson, *dosáin,* the bush.

Dawson, *dosán, dosan,* a small bush.

Day, *Diagh,* not given.

Dayallig, *da-bhealaigh,* two mountain passes.

Dcheen(sic), *daibhchín,* a little cauldron.

De, *de,* two.

Dea, *Dheá, Deadha,* the name of a Church founder in Kildare.

Dea, *dia,* plenty.

Dea, *Uí-Aodha,* not given.

Dead, *dead,* a tooth.

Deady, *Deide,* Deady, a personal or family name.

Deady, *Déide,* not given.

Deag, *ghéag,* not given.

Dealidy, *diallaite,* the saddle.

Dealy, *Uí-Duibhghiolla,* O'Deely, a family name.

Deaon, *Dhubhain,* Devane or Downe, a personal or family name.

Deash, *déas, déise,* the ear of corn.

Deasig, *Deisigh, Deásaig, Déiseach,* Deasy, a family name.

Deaughreave, *dá-chríobh,* two bushes.

Deboye, *Aodha-bui/buí, Aedha-buidhe,* Yellow Aodh or Hugh (O'Neill).

Decies, *Déise-deiscirt,* not given.

Decies, *na-Déise/Desi,* an ancient tribe (*Fiacha-Suighdhe*) decended from 'southern' people.

Decies, *na-nDéise,* not given.

Decomet, *deagh-choimhead,* a good reconnoitering station.

Decoy, *clais-Chiaráin*(sic), not given.

Dee (river), *an-Níth,* not given.

Dee, *Daoi, abha-fhir-Dhaidh,* not given.

Dee, *daibhche,* a well.

Dee, *daibhche,* the caldron or hollow.

Dee, *duibhe,* black.

Dee, *Uí-Dheaghaidh,* O'Dea, a personal or family name.

Deebert, *an-Díbeart,* not given.

Deece, *déire-bhreagh,* not given.

Deece, *desi,* an ancient tribe (*Fiacha-Suighdhe*) decended from 'southern' people.

Deechomade, *deagh-choimhead*, a good reconnoitering station.

Deega, *díge*, a dyke.

Deegeen, *dígín*, little ditch.

Deegerty, *na-Dígirtí*, not given.

Deegvio, *díg-béo*, the living ditch.

Deegy, *diog, dige*, a trench or dyke.

Deehommed, *deagh-choimead*, a good reconnoitering station or observation post.

Deel, *daoile, daoil*, the chaffer.

Deel, *daol*, not given.

Deel, *Díl, Dil*, a personal or family name.

Deel, *doile*, the black river.

Deelada, *diallaite, diallada*, the saddle.

Deelagh, *daolach*, not given.

Deele, *daol*, not given.

Deele, *doile*, the black river.

Deeleen, *Daoilín*, a stream called the little Deel, (little chaffer).

Deelin, *dileann, díle, díleann*, flood.

Deelin, *dilíonn*, a place liable to flooding.

Deelion, *díleann*, flood.

Deelis, *dubh-lis, duibhlois, duibh-lios*, black fort.

Deelish, *dubh-lis, duibhlios, duibh-lios*, black fort.

Deelish, *duílis*, black enclosure.

Deely, *Dhaoile*, not given.

Deely, *daoil*, the river Deel. See **Deel**.

Deely, *Díle*, prone to flood.

Deema, *Díoma*, St Dimma, Dioma, daughter of an ancient galway chief.

Deema, *Díomadh*, St Díomadh.

Deema, St Dioma.

Deen, *dubhín*, black.

Deen, *Duibhín, Dinn*, not given.

Deen, *duinn*, of the chief.

Deenagh, *dianach*, not given.

Deenagh, from *deinín*, strong or vehement.

Deenish, *diadh-inis*, island of sorrow.

Deenish, *duibhinis, duibh-inis*, black island.

Deenisk, *Donnghusaigh*, Dennis, a male name.

Deenlea, *Uí-Duinnshleibhe*, O'Deenlea or Dunlea, a family name.

Deereeny, a small oak grove.

Deery, *doighre*, not given.

Deery, *doire*, an oak wood.

Deese, *déise*, the ear of corn.

Deese, *d'Taoisigh*, a chief.

Deeshart, *diseart*, a secluded retreat.

Deesirt, *diseart*, a hermitage.

Deevan, *daoimhín, díomhaoin, diomhaoin*, idle.

Deeveen, *dhiomhaoin*, idle, unpopulated or untilled.

Deeveen, *díomhaoin, diomhaoin*, idle.

Deevin, *díomhaoin, diomhaoin*, idle or lazy.

Deevna, *déabhaidh*, disputes or skirmishes.

Deeween, *diomhaoin*, idle.

Deffa, *daibhche*, a caldron.

Deffier, *dubh-fhér*, black grass.

Degil, *Déigil*, not given.

Degnan, *daingin*, a stronghold.

Deha, *duibhche*, a vat or round hollow.

Deheen, *daibhchín*, the little vat or pool.

Dehob, *de/dá-chab*, two gaps, mouths or openings.

Dehomad, *deagh-choimhead*, a good reconnoitering station.

Dehommed, *deac-cóimhead, deagh-choimhead*, a good reconnoitering station.

Deige, *d'Tadh*, Teiges or men name Timothy or Teige.

Deige, *d'Tadhg*, not given.

Deirdimus, *doire-diomas*, the proud oak grove.

Deish, *deimhis*, scissors or shears.

Delara, *dá-lara*, not given.

Delgany, *deilgne*, the thorny place.

Delgany, *deilgne-Mochoróg*, not given.

Delgany, *dergne*, little red spot.

Deligeen, *deilgín*, a little thorny brake.

Deligo, *deilge*, the thorn bush or bushes.

Dell, *daill*, a blind person or of the blind.

Dellig, *dealg*, thorns or thorn bushes.

Dellig, *deilge*, not given.

Delliga, *dealg*, thorns or thorn bushes.

Delligeen, *dealgín*, little thorn or thornbush brake.

Delligo, *dheilge, deilge*, the thorn.

Dellihy, *deilithe, deillithe*, separated, moving or moved.

Dellihy, *Doilithe*, not given.

Dellin, *deilinn*, not given.

Dellin, *duibh-linn, duibhlinn*, black pool.

Delour, *duilleabhar*, foliage.

Delphi, *fionnloch*, the white lake.

Delvin, (river) *an-Ailbhin*, not given.

Delvin, *Dealbhna,* the name of 7 ancient tribes and the territory of the descendants of Dealbaeth or Dealbhaeth.

Demesne, *Diméin,* not given.

Demock, *Dhíomóg, Deamóg,* St Deamog/Déamóg/Deamóg.

Demock, *Modhíomóg,* not given.

Demon, *deamhain,* demon/s.

Demon, *Demmáin,* a male name.

Demone, *diomóin, diomoin,* the river of two bogs.

Demone, *dúmóin,* not given.

Dempsey, *Dúinsí,* not given.

Dempsey, *Uí-Dhiomusaigh,* O'Dempsey, a personal or family name.

Den, *dionn,* a fortress.

Denaght, *dinigh,* medicine.

Denn, *dionn, denn, dinn,* fortress.

Dennet, *dianaid,* strong, vehement or swift.

Der, *doire,* oak wood.

Dera, *eadar, dir, eder,* between.

Deralaw, *idir-dhá-lágha,* not given.

Deramfield, *doire-amchoil,* oakwood(sic).

Derana, *doire-na…,* oakwood of the…

Deraowen, *dhá/dá-abhainn,* two rivers.

Deraowen, *idir-dha-abhainn, 'dir-dhá-abhainn,* between two rivers.

Derdaoil, *idir-da-fhaill,* between two cliffs.

Derdimus, *doire-díomais,* oak grove of pride.

Dereen, *doirín,* a small oak grove.

Derg (lough) *deirgdheirc, Geirg,* not given.

Derg, *dearg,* lake of the red hole.

Derg, *deirgeirt, deirgheirc,* the red eye (lake).

Derg, *dergdherc,* red eye.

Derg, *dhearg, dearg,* red.

Derg, *dheirg, deirg,* not given.

Derg, the red haired man.

Dergan, *Dargan, Dergan* or *Darragan,* a personal or family name.

Dergan, *Deargán,* not given.

Derganagh, *derganach,* a red place.

Derganags, *derganach,* a red place.

Dergany, *derganach,* a red place.

Derglin, *dearg-ghlin,* red glen.

Dergraw, *dearg-rath,* red fort.

Dergroagh, *an-deargchruach,* not given.

Derhig, *deirthig, deirtheach,* an oratory.

Deriel, *idir-da-fhaill,* between two cliffs.

Derigg, *derg, dearg,* red.

Derinch, *der-inis,* oak island.

Derine, *doirín,* a little oak grove/wood.

Derinis, *toir-inis,* not given.

Derk, *deirc, derc, deirce, dearc,* a cave.

Derlaw, *idir-dhá-lágha,* not given.

Dermeen, *Dírmín,* little Dermot, a male name.

Dermody, *Dhiarmada, Diarmada,* Diarmaid or St Diarmaid.

Dermody, *Diarmada,* Dermod, a personal or family name.

Dermody, *Diarmait,* a male name.

Dermot, *Diarmad, Diarmada,* Diarmad or Dermot, a male name.

Dermot, *Diarmuda,* not given.

Derna, *doireanach,* a woody place.

Derna, *doire-na…,* oak wood of the…

Dernan, *Ua-dTighearnáin,* Uí Tighearnáin, a family name.

Dernaweel, *doire-an-mhaoil,* the bald oakwood(sic).

Dernena, *doirín-an…,* not given.

Dernish, *toir-inis*(sic), *der-inis,* oak island.

Dernon, *Ó-dTighearnáin,* not given.

Dernory, *d-tórnóiridhe,* turners.

Dernved, *doire-na-bhFead,* not given.

Derny, *doireanna,* oak.

Derowen, *'dir-dha-amhainn,* between two rivers.

Derown, *dá-abhainn,* two rivers.

Derr, oak, oaks or an oak wood. See Darra.

Derra, *doire,* an oak wood.

Derra, *doire-an…,* not given.

Derrad, *doire-fhada,* long oak grove.

Derrada, *doire-fhada,* long oak wood.

Derradd, *doire-fhada,* long oak wood.

Derragh, *doire, daireach, darach, dairbhreach, daireach, dair,* an oak wood or a place of oaks.

Derragh, *doireach,* not given.

Derragh, *doire-each,* wood of the horses.

Derraghan, underwood.

Derrainy, *doirean-oidhche,* little oak grove of night.

Derrana, *doire-na…,* not given.

Derrane, *doireán,* little oak wood.

Derrard, *dorie-áird,* the tall oaks.

Derraree, *dairbhre,* oaks.

Derrary, *dairbhre,* oaks.

Derraulin, *doire-álainn,* not given.

Derraun, little oak wood.

Derravaragh, *dairbhreach,* place of oaks.

Derravarra, *dairbhreach,* abundance of oaks.

Derravarragh, *dairbhreach,* oak plantation.

Derravonniff, *doire-bhanbh,* not given.

Derravonniff, *doire-dha-bhanbh,* oakwood of the two suckling pigs.

Derre, *doire,* an oakwood.

Derree, *na-doirí,* the oak woods.

Derreen, *doireín*(sic), a little wood.

Derreen, *doirín, doireán,* little oak wood or thicket.

Derreen, *doirin,* little oak grove/s.

Derreen, *drinn, dreann, drinne,* conflict.

Derreen, *doirinidhe,* small oak woods.

Derreena, *dairin/doirín-na/a'...,* little oak wood of the...

Derreenna, *doirín-na...,* little wood of the...

Derreens, *doirin,* little oak groves.

Derreens, *na-doiriní,* not given.

Derreeny, *doirínidhe, nDoiríní, doiríni,* little oak groves or woods.

Derrew, *darmhagh,* not given.

Derrew, *doireadh,* a oak wood.

Derriana, *doire-iana,* oak wood of the drinking vesels.

Derriana, *doire-Ianna/Fhianna,* not given.

Derrica, *doire-Íce,* not given.

Derricknew, *doire-an-chneamha,* oakwood of garlic.

Derrie, *doirin,* little oak groves.

Derries, *na-doirí,* not given.

Derrig, *Deirg, Dearg,* the red haired man.

Derrig, *derg, dearg,* red.

Derrigra, *dearg-rath,* red fort.

Derrigrath, *deargráth, derg-rath, dearg-rath,* red fort.

Derriheen, *Doirchín,* not given.

Derriheen, *Doirithin, Dorahin,* a personal or family name.

Derrilla, *doire-Lach,* not given.

Derrin, *derrin, doirín,* an oak wood or a little oak wood.

Derrin, *doire-an...,* oak wood or grove of the....

Derrinea, *doire-an-fhiadh,* oakwood of the deer.

Derrins, *doirin,* little oak groves.

Derrins, *na-doiríní,* not given.

Derrintin, *doire-an-tuinn,* oakwood of the wave.

Derroge, *daireoige,* oak.

Derroo, *doiriú,* not given.

Derroogh, *darmhachaidhe,* oak fields.

Derroogh, *na-doiriu,* not given.

Derrow, *darmhaighe,* not given.

Derrow, *darú,* the oak plain(sic).

Derrow, *dermaigi, dair-mhuige,* the oak plain.

Derrow, *der-maigi,* the oak plain.

Derry, *doire-Cholmcille, doire-Calgaigh,* not given.

Derry, *doirí, daraidh, daire, doire,* an oak grove/wood.

Derry, *doirí,* not given.

Derry, *doire-an...,* oak wood of the...

Derry, *doire,* wood(sic).

Derry, *Uí-Doiridh,* O'Derry, a family name.

Derrya, *doire-atha,* oak grove of the ford.

Derryadd, *doire-fhada,* long oak grove.

Derryan, *doire-an...,* oak wood or oak grove of the...

Derryco, *doire-cuach,* wood of cuckoos.

Derrydruel, *doire-eadarúil,* not given.

Derryg, *dearg,* red.

Derrygrath, *deargráth,* not given.

Derrygrath, *dearg-rath,* red fort.

Derryhan, *doireachan,* underwood.

Derryholmes, *dairtheach-Sháráin, thigh-Moling,* not given.

Derryn, *doire-an/na...,* oak grove-wood of the...

Derryna, (full name) *doire-an-atha,* oak grove of the ford.

Derryna, *doire-an..., doire-na...,* oak grove, wood of the...

Derryna, *doire-na...,* not given.

Derrynea, *doire-an-fhéich,* not given.

Derryneece, *doirel-Aenghuis,* Aengus's (a male name) oak wood.

Derryowen, *doire-ghabhann/gabhann,* oak grove of the smith.

Derryreel, *doire-Uí-Fhrighil,* O'Freel, a family name.

Derryrellan, *doire-Oirealláin,* not given.

Derryroosk, *tír-Bhrochaisc*(sic), not given.

Derryvally, *doire-Mheitheán*(sic), not given.

Derryvullan, *Aireach-Mhaolán*(sic), not given.

Derva, *darmhagh,* not given.

Derver, *dirbhrighe,* an oak wood.

Dervin, *dairbhín,* a small oak grove.

Dervock, *dairbhóg, dearbhóg, dearbhog,* little oak grove.

Dervor, *dairbhreach,* not given.

Dervy, *darmhaighe,* not given.

Dery, *doire,* oak wood.

Descart, *deisceart,* not given.

Desco, *Deisce,* not given.

Desert, *desert, díseart, dísirt, diseart, disirt, disert,* a hermitage, wilderness, an abode of an anchorite or a desert.

Desertcreat, *díseart-dá-Chríoch,* hermitage of the two boundaries/territories.

Desertserges, *an-díseart,* not given.

Deshal, *dheiseal, deisiol,* southern.

Deshil, *deisil, deisiol, southern,* southwards or right hand.

Deshill, *dheiseal, deisiol,* southern.

Deshul, *deisiol,* southwards or right hand.

Deshure, *deiseabhar,* the sunny side.

Deskert, *deisceart,* south.

Deskert, *deisceart,* southern part or direction.

Desmond, *Deasumhan, Deasmhumhna,* Desmond, a male name.

Desmond, *des-mumna, deasmhumhna, deasmhumhain,* south Munster.

Deune, *deamhain,* demon.

Dev, *damh,* oxen.

Dev, *dubh,* black or dark coloured.

Devarrid, *da-barred,* two caps.

Deveen, *díomhaoin,* idle.

Devenish, *daimhinis, daimh-inis,* ox island.

Devesky, *dubhuisce,* black water.

Devet, *Daibhéid,* not given.

Devils bit, *bearnán-Éile/Eile, sliabh-Aildiúin, sliabh-an-bhearnán,* not given.

Devils glen, *bun-an-nEar,* not given.

Devils mother, *machaire-an-deamhain,* not given.

Devinish, *daimhinis,* ox island.

Devitt, *Mhic-Dáibhid,* MacDavid, MacDevitt or Devitt, a family name.

Devleash, *duibh-lios,* black fort.

Devlin, *dhuibhlinne, duibhleann, duibhlin,* not given.

Devlin, *duibh-linn, duibhlinn,* black pool.

Devlis, *dhuibhlis,* not given.

Devlis, *duibh-lios,* black fort.

Dha, *da,* two.

Dhu, *dubh,* black.

Dhuv, *dubh,* black.

Dhyng, *doimin,* deep.

Diag, *dhiaig,* hindermost.

Diamor, *diamar, diamhar,* a solitude or solitary.

Dian, *daingin, daingean, dian, dionn,* strong, stronghold or a fortress.

Dife, *duibhche,* a vat or round hollow.

Diff, *daimh, dhaimh,* the ox.

Diffager, *duibheachair,* the blackwater or the black river.

Differ, *duibhthir,* black district.

Diffin, *duibhchín,* black land.

Diffin, *duibhthin,* a small plot of black land.

Difflin, *duibhlinn,* black pool.

Diffreen, *dubh-thrian, trian,* black third.

Dig, *daoige,* not given.

Dig, *díge,* a trench.

Digeen, *digín,* a small dyke.

Digeen, *Duígín,* not given.

Digny, *daigne,* a stronghold.

Dingy, *deagánaigh,* not given.

Digny, *Dignigh,* Digny, a male name.

Digus, *dígus,* a ditch.

Diha, *daibhche, duibhche,* a vat, tub or round hollow.

Diha, *dige,* trenches.

Diheen, *doibchin, daibhchín,* the little vat, tub, round hollow or pool.

Dihy, *daibhche, doíbhche,* a vat or round/kneeve like hollow.

Dilisk, *duilisc, dulse,* an edible sea plant.

Dill, *daille,* blindness.

Dill, *daille, daill, doill,* a blindman or blindness.

Dillagh, *duilleach,* leafy.

Dillanig, *Diolanaig,* Dillon, a family name.

Dillar, *duille,* foliage.

Dillaver, *duilleabhar,* foliage.

Dillesk, *duileasg,* a sea plant.

Dilliga, *deilge,* the thorn bush or bushes.

Dillin, *duibhlinn,* black pool.

Dillisk, *duilisc, dulse,* an edible sea plant.

Dillon, *Díolúin,* Dillon, a personal or family name.

Dillon, *Díolúnaigh,* not given.

Dillon, *Iolladhan,* a personal or family name.

Dillur, *duille,* foliage.

Dillure, *duilleabhar, duilleabhair* foliage.

Dillure, *duilliúir,* not given.

Dilly, *duille,* foliage.

Dimo, *Díoma,* St Dima/Díoma.

Dimpan, *dTiompan,* standing stones.

Dimpaun, *dTeampán,* not given.

Dimpaun, *dTiompán,* a small hill.

Dimpaun, *tiompan,* a small abrupt hill, a hillock or a standing stone.

Dimus, *díomais,* pride.

Dinan, *Daighnín, Deighnín,* not given.

Dinan, *Deighnin,* Dinin, a river name, not given.

Dinch, *da-inse,* two river islands.

Dinch, *duínse,* not given.

Dine, a small stream.

Dine, *Dhiana,* O'Diana, a family name.

Dine, *dionn, daingin, daingean,* a fortress or stronghold.

Dine, *doimin, doimhin,* deep.

Dine, *Doinn, Dhoinn, daighin, doimhinn,* not given.

Dine, *domhain,* deep.

Dineen, *Duinnín,* Dinneen, a personal or family name.

Dineen, *Uí-Duinnín,* O'Dineen, a family name.

Ding, *dinn,* fortress.

Dingell, *daingean, dingin,* strong, stronghold or a fortress.

Dingin, *dingin,* strong, stronghold or a fortress.

Dingins, from *daingean,* fortresses.

Dingle, *daingean-Uí-Chuise/Chúire,* not given.

Dingle, *dingin, an-daingean,* fortress.

Dingy, *deagánaigh,* not given.

Dinin, *deighnín, deighnin,* not given.

Dinin, *deinín,* strong or vehement.

Dinin, Dinin, a personal or family name.

Dinis, *duibhinis, duibh-inis,* black island.

Dinish, *Daighinis,* not given.

Dinish, *duibh-inis,* black island.

Dinn, *denn, dinn,* a fortress.

Dinna, *deanna,* an aspect, a view.

Dinna, *dionn-a'...,* fortified hill of the...

Dinna, *doimhne,* a deep place.

Dinna, *duine,* a man.

Dinna, *duine,* people.

Dinneens, *dinnínidhe,* little fortified mounts.

Dinnery, *Dineara,* not given.

Dinnin, *Doininne,* not given.

Dinoregan, *doimhinn-Ó-Riagáin,* not given.

Dinta, *dTeine,* fire.

Dinta, *dTeinte,* not given.

Diongna, *denn, dinn,* a fortress.

Dionn, *denn, dinn,* a fortress.

Dir, *doire,* oaks.

Dir, *eadar, dir, eder,* between.

Diraowen, '*dir-dá/dhá-abhainn,* between two rivers.

Dirk, *dearc,* a cave.

Dirk, *deirc,* not given.

Dirra, *doire,* an oak grove.

Dirragh, *doireach,* oaky.

Dirraw, *darmhagh,* not given.

Disert, *díseart, disert,* a hermitage, wilderness or desert.

Dish, *déise,* the two persons.

Diskert, *disert,* a hermitage or a desert.

Diskirt, *deisceart,* southern part or direction.

Dissour, *an-deaseabhar,* not given.

Divanagh, *duibh-eanaigh,* black marsh.

Divane, *dubháin,* a fishing hook.

Divane, *Dubhain,* Divane or Dwan a family name.

Divann, *dubhén,* cormorant/s.

Dive, *daimh,* an ox.

Dive, *duibh,* black.

Diveane, *dubhén,* cormorant/s.

Diveen, *Daimhín,* Davin, a personal or family name.

Diveen, *diomhaoin, daoimhín,* idle or worthless.

Diveen, *domhain,* deep.

Diver, *dubh-thír,* black earth.

Divine, *Daimhin,* Devine, a personal or family name.

Diviny, *duibh-eanaigh,* black marsh.

Divis, *duibh-ais,* black hill.

Divish, *duibh-ais,* black hill.

Divish, *duibhis,* not given.

Divlin, *dileann,* flood, tide.

Divlin, *duibhlinn,* black pool.

Divva, *duibhe,* the black cow.

Do, *dú, dubh,* black.

Doagh, *dúa,* a high plane(sic).

Doagh, *dumhach,* a sand hill or sandbank.

Doagh, *dumhaigh, dumha, dabhcha, dabhach,* not given.

Doagheys, *dubhachaidh*(sic), not given.

Doalty, *Dubhaltaigh,* Dualtagh or Dudley, a male name.

Doan, *domhain,* deep.

Doan, *Duáin,* not given.

Doan, *dubhain,* the fishing hook.

Doart, *dubhghort,* not given.

Dobber, *tobair, dobair,* a well or spring.

Dobbin, *Dobain,* Dobbyn, a personal or family name.

Dobbin, *Doibín,* not given.

Dober, *dobair,* a well or spring.

Dober, *dTobair, dTobar,* not given.

Dock, *dugaí,* not given.

Dockera, *docrach,* difficult.

Dod, *dodaigh,* not given.

Dodder, *dothra,* not given.

Doe, *dá-eó,* two yew trees.

Doe, *na-d'Tuath, na-dtuath, na-doc,* of the districts, bondaries or territories.

Doe, *tua, dóithe,* not given.

Doemore, *tuadh-mór,* the big axe.

Doetha, *dóidhte,* burnt.

Doey, *Dubhthaigh,* Dubhthach, a personal or family name.

Dogherty, *Uí-Dochartaigh,* O'Dogherty, a family name.

Doghill, *Duachaill, Doghil,* the name of a ferocious monster.

Doghtura, *doctura,* a doctor.

Dogue, *Dhéig,* a personal or family name.

Doher, *doithir,* blackness or gloom.

Doher, *dothair,* there are several rivers of this name, *dothair* means river.

Doherdagh, *doicheartach,* not given.

Doherdagh, *doithirdeach, doitheardach,* gloomy.

Doherdough, *doithireach,* gloomy.

Dohilla, *dubh-choille,* black wood.

Dohir, *doithir,* gloom.

Dohir, *duithir,* not given.

Dohir, *tóchair,* a causeway.

Dohora, *dumhach-chorrach,* uneven mound.

Doill, *doill,* a blindman.

Doit, *doighte,* burnt.

Dolla, (two options here,) *Doladh, Dolaidh,* Mother-mountain and *dhá-Liath,* the two halves.

Dolla, *dala,* not given.

Dolla, *dolla,* loops.

Dollagh, *dá-loch,* two lakes.

Dollagh, *dólach,* not given.

Dollaghan, *dullaghan,* a hobgoblin who removes his head at will.

Dollas, *an-Doladh,* not given.

Dollig, *dealg,* thorns or thorn bushes.

Dolling, *Dalaing,* Dolling, a personal or family name.

Dollog, *dealg,* thorns or thorn bushes.

Dolly, *d-tulach,* little hills.

Dollymount, *baile-na-gCorr,* town of the herons.

Dolney, *Dalnaigh,* not given.

Dolphin's Barn, *an-carnán,* not given.

Doluskey, *dubh-luscaí,* not given.

Domeeny, *dTuaimíní,* not given.

Domeeny, *d-tuaim-ínidh,* little mounds.

Dommone, *diomoin,* the river of two bogs.

Domny, *Domhnaigh,* Sunday.

Domore, *dumhach-mhór,* great sandbank.

Don, *dún,* a fortress.

Dona, *Domhnach…,* Church of…

Dona, *dTona,* not given.

Dona, *dun-a'…, dún-an…, dun-na…,* fortress of the…

Donabate, *Domhnach-bát/baite/bat,* Church of the boat.

Donabate, *dún-dá-bhad,* not given.

Donabate, *dún-na-Bháid,* fort of the boat

Donacarney, *Domhnach-Cairne,* Cearnach or Carney's Church.

Donadea, *Domhnach-Dheá/Dá,* not given.

Donagah, *Donncadha,* Donough, a personal or family name.

Donagan, *Uí-Dhonnagain,* Donegan, a family name.

Donagh, *Damhnach, Domhnach,* the Church.

Donagh, *Domhnaigh, Domhnagh, Domhnach,* the (Catholic) Church or Sunday.

Donagh, *Donchadha,* Donagh, a personal or family name.

Donagh, *dTamhnach, Dhonnchaidh, Dhonncha, Donncha, Donnchadha,* not given.

Donagh, *Uí-Dhonnchadha,* O'Donohue, a family name.

Donagh, *Uí-Donchadha,* O'Donoghue or MacDonagh, a family name.

Donaghadee, *Domhnach-Daoi,* Church of St Diach.

Donaghadee, *Domhnach-Dí,* not given.

Donaghanie, *Domhnach-an-eich,* Church of the horse.

Donaghedy, *Domhnach-Caoide,* Caoide's Church.

Donaghedy, *Domhnach-Cheide,* St Caeide's, Cridoc's Church.

Donaghenry, *Domhnach-fhainre,* Church of the slope.

Donaghy, *Dhonnchadha,* Donough, a personal or family name.

Donaghy, Donaghy, a personal or family name.

Donaghy, *Uí-Donchadha,* O'Donaghy, a family name.

Donald, *Domhnaill,* not given.

Donald, *Dónaill,* Dónaill or Donall, a male name.

Donan, *Dhúnáin,* not given.

Donan, Donan or Downing, a personal or family name.

Donard, Domhangairt, St Domhanghart.

Donard, *Domhanghairt, Domhanghart,* St Donard, St Donart, (the son of King of Ulidia).

Donard, *Domhnach-árd,* not given.

Donard, *dún-ard,* the high fort.

Donarea, *Donchadha-riabh,* Donagh Riagh, (this means 'grey Donogh') a personal or family name.

Donaskea, *dún–na-scéithe,* fort of the Shields.

Donaskeagh, *dún-na-sciach,* not given.

Donaskeagh, *dún–na-sciath/scéithe,* fort of the shields.

Done, *doimhin,* deep.

Done, *domhain,* the world(sic).

Done, *dún-na...,* fort of the...

Donee, *dún/dun-Aodha,* Aodh's or Hugh's (a male name) fortress.

Donee, *Dunadhaigh,* O'Downey, a family name.

Donegal, *dún-na-nGall,* fort of the foreigners.

Donegan, *Uí-Dhonnagain, Dhonagain, Ó Donnagáin* or Donegan, a family name.

Donegare, *dún-na-nGabhar,* not given.

Donegore, *dun-O gCurra,* fortress of the O'Curra's (a family name).

Doneraile, *dún-ar-aill,* fort on the cliff. Previous names for Doneraile were Donoghraile, Downerahill, Donnerayle, Donnoughraile, Downerahyle, Bilboxtowne and Richardstown.

Doneraile, *dún-ar-dhá-aill,* not given, also see above for older names.

Doney, a male name.

Doney, a person or individual.

Doney, *domhnach, domhnaigh,* Sunday or of the Church.

Doney, *dona,* a stockade.

Doney, *dona, tSonnach,* a rampart, mound or fort.

Doney, *Donadhaigh,* Donadhach, a family name.

Doney, *Donaigh, duibheanaigh,* not given.

Doney, *duine,* a fortress.

Dongan, *dangain,* a fortress.

Dongan, *Dhonagáin,* Donnagan, a personal or family name.

Donna, *dona, tSonnach,* a rampart, mound or fort.

Donna, *Donaigh,* not given.

Donna, *tonnaigh,* enclosure.

Donnelan, *Uí-Domhnollain,* O'Donnellan, a family name.

Donnell, *Dhónaill,* Dónall, Dónal, Donal or Donall, a personal or family name.

Donnell, *Dhomhnaill,* Donal, a male name.

Donnell, *Domhnaill,* Donnell, a personal or family name.

Donnell, *Dónaill, Mhac-Dónaill,* not given.

Donnelly, *Dhonnaíle,* not given.

Donny, *Domhnach,* the Church.

Donny, *Domhnaigh,* not given.

Donnybrook, *Domhnach-Bhroc,* not given.

Donoghan, *Ua-Donachan,* O'Donaghan, a family name.

Donoghrevy, *Donncha-Riabhaigh,* not given.

Donohill, *dún-eochaille,* not given.

Donohill, *dún-eóchaille/eochaille,* fort of the yew wood.

Donohoe, *Ua-Donchadha,* Donough, a personal or family name.

Donohoe, *Uí-Dhonnchadha, Dhunchadha, Uí-Donchadha, Dhonnchú,* Ó Donnchú, O'Donoghue or O'Donohoe, a family name.

Donohue, *Uí-Dhonnchú,* Ó Donnchú, a family name.

Donore, *dhún/dún-Uabhair, dun-odhar,* not given.

Donore, *dúin-odhar,* a dun coloured fort.

Donough, *Dhonnchadha,* Church.

Donough, *Domhnach,* Denis, a male name.

Donoughrevy, *Dhonnchaidh-riabhaigh,* not given.

Donowley, *Dongoile,* Donelly, a family name.

Donowley, *dun-abhla,* fort of the apple trees.

Donowley, *dúnamhla*(sic), not given.

Dony, *Domhnach,* not given.

Dony, *duine,* a person.

Doo, *dTuath,* not given.

Doo, *dú, dubh, duibh,* black.

Doo, *dú, dumha,* a mound.

Doo, *du,* salty.

Doo, *dubh,* dark brown(sic).

Doo, *dubha, dubhach,* not given.

Doo, *dumha,* a sepulchral mound, leacht or tumulus.

Doo, *dumhach,* a sandbank.

Doo, *dub*(sic) , not given.

Dooa, *dumha,* a sepulchral mound or tumulus.

Dooagh, *dú-ach,* the black field.

Dooagh, *dú-acha, dumha-acha,* mound of the field.

Dooagh, *dubhach,* black surfaced.

Dooagh, *dumhach,* a sandbank.

Dooally, *dumha-aille,* mound of the cliff.

Dooan, *Damháin, Dubháin,* not given.

Dooan, *Dubhain,* Dwan, a family name.

Dooan, *Dubhan,* Duban, a personal or family name.

Dooan, *dubhán,* something black.

Dooan, Dwane, a personal or family name.

Dooary, *dubh-dhoire,* black wood.

Doobin, *dubhinn,* little black place.

Doobin, *dúbinn,* not given.

Doobrusna, *dumha-brusna,* burial mound of the faggot.

Doocatteen, *dumhach-Chaitín,* Caitín's mound.

Doocatteens, *dubhchoitchínídhe,* black commonages.

Doocharry, *dúchoraidh,* black weir.

Doochary, *dúchoraidh,* black weir.

Doocrow, *dúchruach,* not given.

Doody, *Ui-Dhubhda,* O'Dowd or O'Doody, a family name.

Doody, *Uí-Dubhda,* O'Dowd or Doody, a family name.

Dooega, *dumha/dú-Éige, dumhaigh-Ghéige,* not given.

Dooey, *dubhaidh,* black colouring dye.

Dooey, *dubhcha,* the cauldron.

Dooey, *dubhthaigh,* a sandhill.

Dooey, *Dubhthaigh,* Duffy, a family name.

Dooey, *dúiche, dúigh,* not given.

Dooey, *dumhach,* the sandbank.

Dooey, *dumhaigh,* sandbanks.

Dooey, *dumhaidh, dumha,* a sepulchral mound or tumulus.

Doogan, *Dhúgáin,* not given.

Doogan, *Uí-Dubhagain,* O'Duggan or O'Dugan, a family name.

Dooganig, *Dubhaganaig,* Duggan or O'Duggan, a family name.

Doogarry, *dubh-dhoire,* black oak grove.

Doogarry, *dubh-garrdha,* black garden.

Doogary, *dubh-dhoire,* black oak grove.

Doogary, *dubhgarrai,* tillage plot of black earth.

Doogary, *dúdhoire,* not given.

Doogary, *dúgharraí,* black garden.

Doogh, *daibhche, dabhach,* a caldron.

Doogh, *damh,* the ox, oxen.

Doogh, *dumhach,* a sandbank.

Dooghan, *dubhachan,* black.

Dooghta, *dubhachta,* black land.

Dooglasha, *an-dúglaise,* not given.

Dooglasha, *dubhghlaise,* black stream.

Doohat, *cnoc-riabhach,* not given.

Doohat, *dútháite,* not given.

Doohat, *dúthaite,* the black site.

Doohatty, *dútháite,* not given.

Doohooma, *dumha-thuama,* not given.

Doohy, *dumhach, dumhaigh,* a sandbank.

Doohyle, *dúchoill,* black wood.

Dooish, *cnoc-Damhais, Damhais,* not given.

Dooish, *dubhais, duibh-ais,* black hill or ridge.

Dookinelly, *dumhach-chinn-aille,* not given.

Dookinelly, *Dumha-cinn-aille-Uí-Thuathaláin,* O'Toolahans tomb at the head of the cliff.

Dooks, *dumhacha,* dunes or sandhills.

Dool, *Dubhghoill,* Dowell, a male name.

Doolagh, *dubhlocha,* black lake.

Doolagh, *duilleach,* leafy.

Doolaghs, *Dúilech,* St Dúilech.

Doolaghty, *Doolaghta,* a male name.

Doolaghty, *Dúbhlachtach,* O'Doolaghty, a family name.

Doolan, *dubhlán,* a challenge to fight.

Doolarty, *Dullartaigh, Dulartaigh,* Dullartach, Doolarty, a personal or family name.

Doole, *Uí-Dhúill,* Ó Dúill, a family name.

Dooleeg, *dumha-liag, duibhlíog,* not given.

Dooletter, *dúleitir,* not given.

Dooley, *Dubhlaoch, Dubhlaoigh,* the dark complexioned or dark visaged chief.

Dooley, *Uí-Dhúbhlaoich,* descendants of Dooley, a personal or family name.

Dooley, *Uí-Dhúlaoich, Dubh-laoigh, Uí-Dubhlaoigh,* Ó Dulach, O'Dooley or Dooley, a family name.

Doolieve, *duibhshliabh,* not given.

Doolig, *dubhlaidh,* dark or gloomy.

Doolin, *dubh-linn,* dark pool.

Doolin, *duibhlinn, duibh-linn,* black Pool.

Doolin, *dúlainn,* not given.

Dooling, *Dúnlaing,* not given.

Doolis, *dubh-lios/lis,* black fort.

Doolis, *dúlios, dúlas, dubhghlais,* not given.

Doolough, *dubhloch, dúloch, dubh-locha,* black lake.

Doolough, *dúlocha, dhúlocha,* not given.

Doolusk, *dúloiscthe,* not given.

Dooly, *dúbhlaidh,* dark ground.

Dooly, *Dúlaigh,* not given.

Dooly, *Dúlaoich,* Dooly, a personal or family name.

Dooly, the dark warrior.

Dooma, *dumha,* a mound.

Doon, *dúin,* a natural fort like hill.

Doon, *dúin, dun, dún,* a fort, fortress.

Doon, *dúin,* strong.

Doon, *dún,* 'a natural earth mound of rounded outline'.

Doon, *dún,* a natural rath like mound, an enclosure, a fortified residence or an enclosed homestead.

Doon, *dúnáin,* a little fort.

Doona, *duna,* a fortress.

Doona, *dúna,* forts.

Doona, *dun-a'...,* *dun-na...,* fort of the...

Doonagh, *dunach,* a fort.

Doonakeena, *dún-Mhic –Cionaoith,* Mac Cionaoith's fort.

Doonamo, *dún-na-mBó,* fort of the cows.

Doonan, *dúnáin,* not given.

Doonan, *dúnan, dúnán, dunín,* little fort.

Doonane, *dúnan, dunín,* little fort.

Doonane, *dúnán,* not given.

Doonans, from *dunín,* little forts.

Doonass, *Danainne,* Danann, a personal or family name.

Dooneen, *an-dúinín,* not given.

Dooneen, *Dunadhaigh,* O'Downey, a family name.

Dooneen, *dúnan, dunín,* little fort.

Dooneens, *duinni,* little forts.

Doonin, *dúnín,* little fort.

Doonis, *duibhinis,* not given.

Doonis, *duna,* forts.

Doonna, *dún/dun-na...,* fort of the...

Doonoor, *dun-uabhair,* not given.

Doonour, *dun-tighe-mhoir,* fort of Tighe's (a male name) house.

Doonour, *dún-Uabhair,* not given.

Doonties, *na-dúnta,* the forts.

Doonty, *dúnta,* forts.

Doony, *dún,* a fort.

Doony, *dúna,* a fortalice(sic).

Doony, *dúnaidhe,* forts.

Doora, *dúdhoire,* a dark oak grove.

Doora, *dúire,* an oak wood.

Doora, *dúire,* watery land.

Doora, *tuar-an...,* animal enclosure of ...

Dooraa, *dúrath,* not given.

Dooragh, black.

Dooragh, *dorcha,* dark.

Dooragh, *dubhdhaire,* not given.

Dooragh, *dúire,* watery land.

Doorah, the black fort.

Doorat, *dubh-rath,* black fort.

Dooravaun, *dubh-ruadháin,* not given.

Dooree, *dúraí,* not given.

Dooree, *dúraidh, dúrmhaighe,* oak plain.

Dooreel, *dumha-Fhrighil,* Freel's (a personal or a family name), grave or mound.

Dooregan, *dútha-Uí-Riagáin,* not given.

Doorian, *dúrian,* not given.
Doorish, *dubhrais, dubh-ruis, dúbhrais,* the black wood.
Doorish, *dúrois,* not given.
Doorless, *durlas, duirlios,* the strong fort.
Doorlis, *durlios,* the strong fort.
Doorlus, *durlas, duirlios,* the strong fort.
Doorlus, *durlas,* the oaken fort(sic).
Doornane, *dún-Fhionnain,* not given.
Doornane, *dún-Fhionáin,* Fionan's (a personal or family name), fort.
Doornane, *dúrnaun,* place of churlish, boorish plebeian people.
Doorock, *dubhrac,* black rock.
Doorog, *dubhróg,* little black land or stream.
Dooros, *dúros,* not given.
Doorosheath, *dúros,* not given.
Doorty, *Dubharda,* not given.
Doorty, *Uí-Dhúrtaigh, Dubhartaigh,* Ó Dúrtaigh or O'Doorty, a family name.
Doorus, *dubh-ros,* black meadow(sic).
Doorus, *dubhros, dubh-ros,* black copse.
Doorus, *dúrois,* not given.
Doory, *dubhdhoire,* not given.
Doory, *dubhraighe,* black land.
Doory, *dúr, dúire,* water.
Doos, *dubha,* black.
Doosis, *dubhrais,* the black wood.
Doosky, *duibhsce, dubh-sceith,* the black bush.
Doosky, *dúsceithigh,* not given.
Doovoge, *dubhóg,* the black spot.
Doowaun, *Dubhan,* Duane, a family name.
Dooy, *dumhaigh,* a sandbank.
Dooyeher, *dumhaigh-ithir,* not given.
Dooyork, *dumha-Dhearc,* not given.
Dora, *deóra,* tear, teardrop.
Doran, *dobharan, dobhráin, dobhran,* little water.
Doran, *Uí-Deorain,* O'Doran, a family name.
Dorane, *dobharain,* the otter.
Doras, *dorus,* a door or gate.
Dordan, *Dardain,* Dardan, a male name.
Dore, *dobhair, dobhar,* water.
Dore, *dor,* doors.
Dore, *Dor, Dore,* Dor, a personal or family name.
Dore, *dTor,* bushes.
Dorfe, *dorcha,* dark.

Dorgan, *deargain,* red land.
Dorgan, *Dorgáin,* not given.
Dorgan, *Uí-Dorgain,* O'Dorgan, a family name.
Doris, *dorus,* a door.
Dork, *dorc,* not given.
Dork, *dTorc,* boars.
Dork, *dTorc,* not given.
Dorn, *doirn,* a tidal pass.
Dorn, *doirn, duirn,* the fist or fist shaped.
Dorn, *Dornan,* Dorna, not given.
Dorn, from *doire,* oaks.
Dornan, *Dornáin,* not given.
Dornaun, *nDornán,* not given.
Dorneen, *Dhoirnin,* Durnin, a personal or family name.
Dorney, *díomoiridhe,* turners.
Dorney, *Uí-Torna/Thorna,* Ó-dTorna, Ó-dTorna, descendants of Torna, a personal or family name.
Dornogagh, *dornógach,* a place of handstones or round stones.
Dornory, *dTornóirí,* not given.
Dornory, *dTornóiridhe,* turners.
Dorough, *dorcha,* dark.
Dorragh, *dorcha,* dark oak wood.
Dorragh, *dorcha,* gloomy, dark or shaded.
Dorragha, *dorcha,* dark, darkness.
Dorraghy, *dhorcha,* not given.
Dorraghy, *dorcha,* dark.
Dorrery, *dairbhre, dairbhreach,* place of oaks or oak woods.
Dorrery, *dairbhre,* oaks.
Dorrha, *dura,* not given.
Dorris, *doruis,* not given.
Dorrish, *doruis,* a door or entrance.
Dorrus, *dorus,* a door or gate.
Dorry, a black oak grove.
Dorsey, *doirse,* the entrance or doors.
Dorsey, *dorsa,* gates.
Dorseys, *doirse-Eamhna,* not given.
Dort, *dairt,* a heifer or young girl.
Dort, *dart,* not given.
Dosan, *dosáin,* not given.
Dosan, *dosan,* a little bush.
Dosh, *dois,* not given.
Dossan, *dosáin, dosain,* a bush or a little bush.
Dossaun, bushes.
Dossaun, *dosán,* not given.

Dota, *dhóighte, doighte,* burnt.
Dotia, *dóite, dóite,* not given.
Dotia, *doithte, doighte,* burnt.
Doty, *dóite, dhóite,* not given.
Doty, *doitaidh, doighte, doithte,* burnt.
Douce, (Mt) *beann-Damhair,* not given.
Douce, *cnoc-Damhas,* not given.
Douce, *Digais,* a female name.
Doucharron, *dubh-charn,* black carn.
Dough, *dabhac,* sand hills.
Dough, *daibhche,* a caldron, vat or tub.
Dough, *damh,* the ox, oxen.
Dough, *dough, dubh,* black.
Dough, *dubhach,* dark or gloomy.
Dough, *dumach, dumhach, dumhcha,* a sand bank, sand hills.
Dougher, *dothair,* there are several rivers of this name, *dothair* means river.
Dougher, *dubh-charn,* black carn.
Doughil, *dúchoill, dubhchoill,* not given.
Doughill, *duchoill, dubh-choill,* the black wood.
Douglas, *Dúghlas,* not given.
Douglas, *dúglas, dúghlaise, dubh-ghlaise, dub-hghlaise,* black stream/let.
Douglasburn, *droichead-dubhghlaise,* not given.
Douglasha, *dubhghlaise,* black stream.
Doul, *diabhail,* the devil.
Dour, *dobhair,* water or watery.
Doura, *damhaire, damhshrath,* not given.
Doura, *damhghaire,* herd of deer(sic).
Dourn, *dorn,* a fist.
Dournadarrig, *dorn-a'-deirg,* fist of the red giant.
Dousky, *dubhuisce,* not given.
Dov, *dubh,* black.
Dove, *dubh,* black.
Dovea, *dhubhtha,* black clay for colouring.
Dovea, *dubhféith,* not given.
Dovea, *dubh-fhéith, duibhfhéith, dubh-fheith, dubh-feit,* black boggy stream, bog or marsh.
Dovegrove, *cluanachán,* not given.
Dovehill, *dúchoill,* not given.
Dovey, *dubhach,* black surfaced.
Dow, *damh,* an ox or oxen.
Dow, *Diughbha*(sic), not given.
Dow, *dumha,* a burial mound.

Dow, *dumha,* a mound, a sepulchral mound or a tumulus.
Dowa, *Dhubha,* O'Dowd, a family name.
Dowah, *davach,* a caldron.
Dowal, *Dubghoill,* Dugald, a male name.
Dowan, *dine, domhain, doimhin,* deep.
Dowan, *domhain,* not given.
Dowaun, *Duain,* a dark coloured man.
Dowd, *Uí-Dubhdha,* O'Dowd, a family name.
Dowel, *Uí-Dubhghoill,* O'Doyle or Doyle, a family name.
Dower, *dobhar,* water.
Dowery, *dubhthair,* uncleared forest.
Dowery, *duibh-aire,* black mountain of watching.
Dowery, *duibhthir,* abounding in heather and bushes.
Dowery, *duire,* watery.
Dowey, *Dubhthaigh,* Dubhthai, Dubhthach or Duffy, a family name.
Dowling, *dobhlainn,* not given.
Dowling, *dubh/ duibh-linn,* dark/black pool.
Dowling, *Dúnlaing,* Dunlang, a personal name.
Dowling, *Uí-Dunlaing,* O'Dowling, a family name.
Down, *domhain, dúnaidh, dTamhan, dhúin,* not given.
Down, *dhonn, donn,* brown.
Down, *dTonn,* waves.
Down, *dún, dúin, duna,* a fortress.
Down, *dun, dún, dúin,* a fort, fortress.
Down, *dúnáin,* a little fort.
Downan, *dunain,* a little fort.
Downea, *dun-Aodha,* Aodh's or Hugh's (a male name) fortress.
Downee, *Domhnaigh,* Donagh, Downey, a male name.
Downeen, *duinín,* a little fort.
Downeen, from *dunín,* little forts.
Downet, *Damhnait,* St Damhnait.
Downey, *Domhnaigh,* Donagh, Downey, a male name.
Downey, *Domhnaigh,* Sunday.
Downey, *duinín,* a little fortress.
Downey, *Dúnadhaigh,* Dúnadhach or Dúnadach, a personal or family name.

Downey, *Dunadhaigh,* O'Downey, a family name.

Downey, *tamhnaigh,* a green field.

Downfine, the fair fort.

Downies, *na-dúnaibh,* not given.

Downig, *Domhnaigh,* not given.

Downing, *dúnan, dunín,* little fort.

Downings, *dúiníní,* a fort or fortification(sic).

Downings, *dúnaibh,* forts.

Downings, *dúnaibh,* little forts.

Downis, *Dhonnghusa,* Dennis, a male name.

Downs, *an-dún*(sic), not given.

Downs, *na-dúna, na-dúnta*(sic), forts.

Downy, *Dhunadhaigh, Uí-Dunadhaigh,* O'Downey, a family name.

Downy, *Domhnaigh,* Sunday.

Dowra, *damhshraith, damh-shrath,* ox holm.

Dowrea, *damh-réidh,* mountain flat of the oxen.

Dowth, *dubhadh, dubad,* darkness or the dark place.

Dowth, *duthaidh, duthad, dothad,* not given.

Doyle, *Daill,* the blind person.

Doyle, *Dubghoill, Uí-Dubhghoill,* O'Doyle or Doyle, a family name.

Doyle, *Dúill, Dubhgall, Dubhghoill,* the blackor dark stranger, foreigner or Dane.

Dra, *dá-ráth,* two forts.

Draan, *doireáin,* a little oak wood.

Dragaun, *dragain, dragáin,* a warrior.

Dragon, *deamhain,* dragon.

Drain, *doire-eidhinn,* not given.

Drain, *drain,* a large round hill.

Drain, *draeighean,* sloe bushes, blackthorn.

Drains, *draeighean,* sloe bushes, blackthorn.

Drait, *droichid,* a bridge.

Dramagh, *dreamach,* tribes or multitudes.

Dran, *drean,* wrens.

Drane, *draoighinn,* blackthorn.

Drangan, *Drongán, Drongáin,* not given.

Drangan, *dun-drongáin,* not given.

Drangaty, from *dreancaid,* fleas.

Drankady, from *dreancaid,* fleas.

Dranna, *dreanna,* a quarrel or battle.

Drannan, *draighneáin,* not given.

Drannan, *Dreannan,* Drennan, a personal or family name.

Drantan, *dranntain,* growling or snarling.

Drasdil, *dreas-choill,* bramble thicket/wood.

Drastil, *dreascoill,* a briar thicket.

Draughteen, *druchtín,* a dewdrop or the herb 'dructin'.

Dreadeen, *droichidín,* little bridge.

Drean, *draoighean,* blackthorn.

Dredolt, *droichead-alt,* bridge of the steep glenside.

Dree, *droinge,* a portion.

Dree, *daireach,* wooded(sic).

Dree, *draoithe, drui, druadh,* druid/s.

Dree, *dríth,* not given.

Dree, *dTrí,* three.

Dreegeel, *dTrí-gCaol,* not given.

Dreela, *draoile,* a mire.

Dreelig, *Rialaigh,* not given.

Dreen, *doirín,* a little wood.

Dreen, *draeighean, draighean, draoighín, droighin, nDraoigheann,* sloe bushes or blackthorn.

Dreen, *draeighneach, draeighneachán, draeighean, draighín, draoighin,* abounding in sloe bushes or blackthorn.

Dreena, *draeighneach,* abounding in sloe bushes or backthorn.

Dreenaan, *draighneán, draighnéan,* little blackthorn.

Dreenaan, *droighnán,* blackthorn.

Dreenagh, *draoighneach, draeighneach, draighneach, draighnach, draighnech,* abounding in sloe bushes or blackthorn.

Dreenagh, *droighnach,* not given.

Dreenan, *draeighneach, drinan, draeighneachán,* abounding in sloe bushes.

Dreenan, *draighneach,* not given.

Dreenan, *draoigheanain,* a blackthorn or a sloe bush.

Dreeny, *dhraighnigh,* not given.

Dreeny, *draoighneach,* blackthorn.

Dreeny, *dreimhne,* fighting or fury.

Dreeny, *Drithne,* Drihne, a female name.

Dreerheene, *doirthín,* little oak grove.

Dreet, *droichid,* a bridge.

Drehid, *droichead, droichid,* a bridge.

Drehideen, *droichidín,* not given.

Dremeen, *dromin,* a ridge.

Drenagh, *dronnach,* not given.

Drennin, *Droigheanáin,* O'Drynan, a family name.

Drentagh, *dTreinteach,* not given.

Dresnagh, *dreasnach,* a little brambly place.

Dresrough, *dreisrigh, drishragh, drisreach,* a place of brambles.

Dress, *dreasa, dreas, dris,* a brambly place.

Dressagh, *driseach,* brambles.

Dressan, *dreasan, dressan,* brambles.

Dressigo, *dhriseogach, driseogach,* brambles or bushes.

Dressogagh, *driseogach, dressogagh, dreasógagh,* a place of briars, blackthorns.

Dressoge, *dressogagh, dreasógach,* a place of briars, blackthorns.

Dressy, *dreasach,* brambles or brambly.

Drestan, *dreastain,* brambles, briars.

Dresternagh, *dressogagh, dreasógach,* a place of briars, blackthorns.

Dresternan, *dreastarnán,* a place of briars, blackthorns.

Drian, *draoighinn,* blackthorn.

Drid, *druid,* a starling.

Drid, *druide,* starving(sic).

Drideen, *dTraighdín,* not given.

Dried, *droichead, droichid,* a bridge.

Drihara, *dTri-hEaghra,* the three O'Hara's (a family name).

Drihid, *droichíd,* the bridge.

Drillen, *dreólain, dreoilín,* the wren.

Drillen, *drislinn,* not given.

Drim, *drim,* the back, a hillside(sic).

Drim, *droimne, droim, druim,* a ridge of hills.

Drimagh, *dromach,* a place of ridges.

Drimeen, *droimín,* small hill ridge.

Drimeen, *dromin, druimín,* little ridge.

Drimina, *druimne,* a little hill ridge.

Drimma, *droim-an…, druim-a'…, hill-ridge of the…*

Drimmeen, *druimín,* a little ridge.

Drimmeenna, *druimín-na…, little hill ridge of the…*

Drimna, *droimne,* a ridge of hills or hill ridges.

Drimna, *dromina,* little hills(sic).

Drimna, *druimfhinne,* not given.

Drimna, *druim-na…,* hill ridge of the…

Drimna, *druimne,* the little hill ridge.

Drimnagh, *droimeanach, droimneach,* ridges or ridged land.

Drimnagh, *druimeanach, druim-eanaigh,* not given.

Drimneen, *droimnín, druimnín,* a little ridge.

Drin, *drinn, dreann, drinne,* conflict.

Drin, *droighin, dreithin,* not given.

Drin, *draighin,* blackthorns.

Drin, *droinne,* 'humpy'.

Drina, *draighnigh,* not given.

Drina, *draoigheannach, draeighean,* sloe bushes, blackthorn.

Drinagh, *draeighean, draeighneach, draighineach, draighneach, dráighneac(sic), draeighneachán, droighneach,* abounding in sloe bushes or blackthorn.

Drinagh, *dhraighneach,* not given.

Drinagh, *draighin, draoighneach, draeighean, droighnach,* abounding in sloe bushes or blackthorn.

Drinagh, thorny.

Drinaghan, *draeighneach, draeighean, draeighneachán,* abounding in sloe bushes or blackthorn.

Drinan, *draighean, draeighean, draeighneach, drinan, draghnain, draighnen, draeighneachán, droigheanáin,* abounding in sloe bushes or blackthorn.

Drinan, *draighneáin,* not given.

Drinan, *Uí-Dhroigheanáin,* O'Drenan, a personal or family name.

Drinan, *Uí-Droigheeanain, Uí-Droigheanain,* O'Drennan, O'Drynan or Drynan, a family name.

Drinane, *Draighneain,* Draighnean, a male name.

Drinane, *draighnean, drinan,* place of sloe bushes.

Drinaun, *draeighean, drinan, draighnen,* sloe bushes or blackthorn.

Drinaun, *draoighneach, draeighean,* sloe bushes, blackthorn.

Drine, *draighin, draoighin,* blackthorn or sloe bush.

Drine, *dreamhainn,* not given.

Drinee, *drine,* contest.

Driney, *droigheanaigh,* blackthorn.

Dring, *droing,* not given.

Dring, *druing,* a tribe or faction.

Dringa, *druinne,* a ridge or hump.

Dringeen, *druingín,* not given.

Drinin, *draighneáin,* brambly.

Drinine, *draighneáin,* brambly.

Drinn, *droinne,* stooped or hump-backed.

Drinna, a ridge.

Drinna, *drine,* contest.

Drinnan, *daingin*(sic), not given.

Drinny, *droinne,* stooped or hump-backed.

Driny, *draighní, draeighneach, draeighneachán, droigheanaighe,* abounding in sloe bushes or blackthorn.

Drippal, *dTripioppal*(sic), rushes.

Dripsey, *druipseach, dribsighe, dríbseach, dribseach,* the muddy river or abounding in mud.

Drish, *doras,* a door.

Drish, *dreas,* a place of briars or blackthorns.

Drish, *dries, an-drís/dris,* not given.

Drisha, *drise,* a thorn bush or a place of brambles.

Drishagh, brambles.

Drishaghaun, *driseachán,* a place of briars/blackthorns or a little brambly place.

Drishane, *drisean,* briars or brambles.

Drishane, *driseán, dreasaun, drisean,* a place of briars or blackthorns.

Drisheen, *drisín,* a place of briars or blackthorns.

Drishoge, *driseog,* not given.

Drishoge, *driséoige, driseoige,* brambles.

Drishogue, *dressogagh, dreasógach,* a place of briars, blackthorns.

Drishogue, *dressogagh, driséoige, driseog, dreasógach,* a place of briars, blackthorns or brambles.

Drisla, *drisle,* not given.

Drisla, *drisligh, dreasógach,* a place of briars, blackthorns.

Drislach, *drisleach,* brambles.

Drislagh, *drisleach,* brambles or brambly.

Drislane, *Drisleáin,* Drislane, a Munster family name.

Drislig, *drisleach, drislig,* brambles.

Drisly, *drisligh,* brushwood or brambles.

Drisoge, *dreasóg,* a place of briars or blackthorns.

Drissagh, *driseach,* brambles.

Drissoge, *driseog,* not given.

Drissoge, from *dreas,* a place of briars or blackthorns.

Dristernan, from *dreas,* a brambly place.

Dristernin, *dreasógach,* a place of briars or blackthorns.

Drod, *droichid,* the bridge.

Drod, *dTrod,* fights.

Drod, *dTroid,* not given.

Droe, *dobhar,* a well.

Droghed, *droichead, droichid,* a bridge.

Drogheda, *droichead-átha, droiched-átha/atha,* the ford bridge.

Droghill, *droch-choill,* bad wood.

Drohid, *droichead, droichid,* a bridge or bridges.

Droi, *druadh,* druids.

Droichit, *droichead, droichid,* a bridge.

Droim, *droim,* a ridge.

Droit, *droichead, droichid,* a bridge.

Drola, *drolaí,* not given.

Drolan, *dreólain, dreoilín,* the wren.

Drolane, *dreólain, dreoilín,* the wren.

Droleen, *dreoilín,* the wren.

Droles, *drolach,* a place of windings.

Drollach, *drolach,* a place of windings.

Drollagh, *drolach,* not given.

Drom, *droimne, druim,* a ridge of hills.

Droma, *droma, drom,* a hill ridge.

Droma, *drom-an...,* not given.

Droma, *druim-an/a'...,* hill ridge of the...

Droma, *druim-atha...,* ridge of the ford of...

Dromada, *drom-fhada,* the long ridge.

Dromagh, *n-dromach, dromach,* ridged, humps, ridges, backs or a place of ridges.

Dromalive, *droma leimhe,* ridge of elms or marshmallows.

Dromalta, *drom-Ealta,* not given.

Droman, *dromáin,* back-band (of cart)(sic).

Droman, *druim-an...,* ridge of the...

Dromana, *drom-Anna,* not given.

Dromana, *drom-eanaigh,* ridge of the marsh.

Dromaneen, *dromainín,* the little hill ridge.

Dromara, *droim-bearach,* heifer ridge.

Dromara, *droim-bhearach/bearach,* the pointed ridge.

Dromard, *dromárd, an-drom-ard,* not given.

Dromda, *drom-dhá...,* not given.

Dromeen, *dromín,* little hillside(sic).

Dromeen, *drom-Iníne,* not given.

Dromeen, *druimín,* little ridge.

Dromerillagh, *droma-eirleach,* ridge of the slaughters.

Dromerillagh, *drom-Oirbhealach,* not given.

Dromerk, *drom-riabhach, speckled/striped ridge.*

Dromin, *droim-Ing,* Ing's (a personal or family name) ridge.

Dromin, *droim-Ing,* little ridge(sic).

Dromin, *dromain, dromainn, druimín, little ridge.*

Dromin, *dromainn, ridges.*

Dromin, *drom-an…, ridge of the…*

Dromin, *dromann, a ridge.*

Dromin, *droman-Uí-Chleireacháin, dromainne,* not given.

Dromin, *druim-fhinn, white ridge.*

Dromin, *Uí-Droigheeanain,* O'Drennan/ Drynan, a family name.

Dromina, *droimneach, ridged land.*

Dromina, *drom-Aidhne,* not given.

Dromina, *dromainn-an…, ridge of the…*

Dromina, *drom-eidhneach,* not given.

Drominagh, *drom-Aidhne/Aidhneach,* not given.

Dromineer, *drom/druim-inbhir,* ridge of the river mouth.

Drominy, *dromainn-an,* ridge of the…

Drommahane, *drom-Átháin,* not given.

Dromna, *druim-na…,* hill-ridge of the…

Dromod, *dromad,* the ridge.

Dromod, *dromaid,* not given.

Dromond, the long ridge.

Dromore, *drom/droim-mór,* big or great ridge.

Dromore, *droma-mhóir,* not given.

Dromoyle, *an-droim-maol,* not given.

Dromoyle, *droim/druim-maol, bare ridge.*

Dromree, *drom-a'fhraoich, ridge of heather.*

Dromree, *drom-riabhach, grey ridge.*

Dromud, the long ridge.

Dromultan, *drom-ultáin,* ridge of the wethers.

Dronagh, *dTruaghanach, ascetics or hermits.*

Droo, *dithreabhach, a hermit.*

Drooa, *nDruadh, druadh, druids.*

Droohaun, *drútháin, dtruagháin,* not given.

Drool, *eadar-ghabhal, between two forks.*

Droose, *druadh,* the druid, *nDruadh,* druids.

Droose, *drúise, lust or adultery.*

Droose, *dTriubhas,* not given.

Drough, *droch, bad.*

Drought, *droichid, a bridge.*

Drought, *druinne, a ridge or hump.*

Droughtan, *Drúchtáin,* Droughtan, a personal or family name.

Droughtaun, *Drúchtáinn,* not given.

Droum, *dromand, backs.*

Droum, *drum, drom,* a ridge.

Drowse, *drobhaois, muddy or sluggish.*

Druckilla, *d-trucailidhe, cars.*

Druckilly, *dTrucaillidhe, 'truckles' or cars.*

Druckilly, *trocalaigh,* not given.

Druel, *druadh, druids.*

Drui, *druadh, druids.*

Druig, *druinne, a ridge or hump.*

Druim, *droimne, druim, a ridge of hills.*

Druimna, *druim-na…, ridge of the…*

Druish, *dhá-rúisc, two marshes.*

Drum, *dhroim, droma, dromainne, dhroma, dromann,* not given.

Drum, *droim, droimne, druim,* a ridge, a ridge of hills, a long hill or a long low hill.

Druma, *droim/druim-an/na/a'…,* ridge of the…

Drumaa, *druim-atha,* ridge of the ford.

Drumacon, *droim-dhá-chon,* not given.

Drumaconvern, *droim-achaidh-Chonbheirn,* not given.

Drumacoo, *droim-an-chú,* ridge of the hounds.

Drumacoo, *drom-Mochua,* ridge of St Mochua.

Drumacoon, *droim-Mhic-Comhainn,* not given.

Drumacrib, *droim-Mhic-Roib,* Mac Rob's (a personal or family name) ridge.

Drumacruttan, *droim-achaidh-Chruitín,* not given.

Drumadda, *druim-fhada,* the long ridge.

Drumaddagory, *droim-Mhic-Gofraidh,* not given.

Drumaddarainy, *dromad-raithnigh,* not given.

Drumagelvin, *droim-achaidh-Ghealbháin, droim-Ghealbháin,* not given.

Drumagh, *droim-achaidh,* not given.

Drumagh, *dromach, a place of ridges.*

Drumagh, *droim-an/a'…, ridge of the…*

Drumakeenan, *droim-Cianáin,* not given.

Drumalea, *droma-léith, grey ridge.*

Drumaliss, *droim-eachlaisce,* not given.

Druman, *droim/drom-an…, ridge of the…*

Druman, *dromainn, a ridge.*

Drumana, *dromana, drumana,* ridges.

Drumana, *droman-na…,* little ridge of the…

Drumanaghan, *dromainn-casin,* dangerous hill(sic).

Drumanan, *druim-meannán,* not given.

Drumanan, *druim-mionán,* ridge of the kid goats.

Drumane, *dromán,* not given.

Drumane, *druim-éan,* ridge of the birds.

Drumannon, *droim-meannáin,* ridge of the pinnacle.

Drumany, *drum-eanaigh,* marsh ridge.

Drumany, *droich-eanaigh,* hill of the swamp.

Drumar, *droim-áir,* not given.

Drumaroad, *droim-ar-rod,* stags hill(sic).

Drumary, *droim-Airí,* not given.

Drumass, *droim-Meas,* not given.

Drumate, *droim-Eite,* not given.

Drumaty, *druim-a'-tighe…,* ridge of the house of….

Drumaty, *drumadaigh,* a ridge.

Drumavan, *droim-an-mheáin,* not given.

Drumbad, *druim-baid,* a ridge of long hills(sic).

Drumbadmeen, *druim-bád,* ridge of the boat.

Drumbadmeen, *druim-bád-mhín,* smooth ridge of the boat.

Drumcliff, (river) *an-chodhnach,* not given.

Drumcliffe, *drom-cliabh,* not given.

Drumcru, *dhroim-chruabhair,* not given.

Drumeason, *droim-Miasan,* not given.

Drumee, *droim/druim-Aodha,* Aodh or Hugh's (a male name) ridge.

Drumeel, *druim-maol,* bald ridge.

Drumeela, *druim-míl ,* hill ridge of the soldiers.

Drumenagh, *druim-meadhonach,* middle ridge.

Drumer, *droim-ar…,* hill ridge on the…

Drummer, *druim-ar/air…,* ridge of the(sic)…

Drumer, *drumar,* ridges.

Drumerkillew, *druim-ard-coilleach,* high ridge of the wood.

Drumever, *droim-ramhar,* not given.

Drumganus, *droim-dhamh*(sic), not given.

Drumhart, *droim-U-Airt,* Art's (a personal or family name) ridge.

Drumilly, *druim-Milidh,* Myle's (a family or a personal or a family name) hill.

Drumin, *dromainn,* not given.

Drumin, *druim-an…,* ridge of the…

Drumin, *druimin,* the little ridge.

Druminda, *dromainn-Dáith,* not given.

Druming, *druim-Ing,* Ing's, (a personal or a family name) ridge.

Drumit, *dhroma-Eite,* not given.

Drumit, *drumod,* a long ridge.

Drumlaghdrid, *druimleach-druid,* the ridged hill of the starling.

Drumm, *druim, droim,* a hill ridge.

Drumma, *droma, druim,* a hill ridge.

Drummaan, *druim-meadhoin,* middle ridge.

Drummacool, *druim-Mhic-an-choill,* not given.

Drummagh, *dromach,* a little hill(sic).

Drummagh, *dromach,* ridged land or ridges.

Drumman, *dromainne,* not given.

Drumman, *dromán, droman,* little hill ridge.

Drumman, *dromann, droimne, druim, dromain,* a ridge of hills.

Drumman, *dromann,* a long hill or a ridge.

Drumman, *druim-an…,* hill-ridge of the…

Drumman, the little hills.

Drummana, *droman-na…,* little hillridge of the…

Drummaneen, *dromanín,* a little hill(sic).

Drummanna, *droman-na…,* little hill ridge of the…

Drummans, *an-dromainn*(sic), *na-dhromainne,* not given.

Drummans, *dromainn,* (with the English plural letter 's') ridges.

Drummany, *droim-eanaigh, ridge of the marsh.*

Drummaun, *druimín,* little ridge.

Drummaveg, *little ridge.*

Drummaw, *druim-atha,* hill-ridge of the ford.

Drummay, *druim-meith, fat or rich ridge.*

Drummed, *drom-art,* 'art' in this case means a house.

Drummeen, *droimín,* not given.

Drummeen, *druimín,* little ridge.

Drummeen, *Uí-Droigheeanain,* O'Drennan, a family name.

Drummeena, *druimín-na…, little ridge of the…*

Drummeenagh, *droimíneach,* not given.

Drummeenna, *druimín-na…, little ridge of the…*

Drummeer, *drom-shiár, western hill.*

Drummig, *dromaig, dromaigh, ridged land.*

Drummillion, *drummillion(sic), ridge of the angle.*

Drummin, *droimne, druim,* a ridge of hills.

Drummin, *dromain, dromainne, an-drom-mín,* not given.

Drummin, *dromainn, ridge/s.*

Drummin, *dromain-Uí-Chléirichín,* not given.

Drummin, *dromin,* the little hill(sic).

Drummin, *drummin,* a low hill.

Drummin, *drummín, dromainn,* a small ridge.

Drummina, *dromainn-na…,* not given.

Drummina, *droman-an…, druimin-na…,* ridge of the…

Drummina, *druim-eidhne,* ridge of ivy.

Drumminna, *dromainn-na…,* not given.

Drumminna, *druimin-na…,* ridge of the…

Drumminnion, *druimin-na-meannán,* ridge of the kids (goats).

Drummod, *druim-fhad,* long ridge.

Drummoher, *drom-Airchir,* not given.

Drummon, *droimne, druim,* a ridge of hills.

Drummon, *drumainn,* an extended ridge.

Drummona, *dromainn-an/na…,* not given.

Drummond, *droimne, dromain, dromainn, druim,* a ridge of hills.

Drummond, *drumainn,* a ridge, a little hill or little ridge.

Drummory, *druim-iubhraighe,* ridge of the yew.

Drummuck, *droma-muice,* pigs hill ridge.

Drummully, *droim-ailí,* ridge of the summit.

Drummy, *droma,* a hill back(sic).

Drummy, *druiminne,* the white backed cow(sic).

Drumna, *dhromainn/dromainn-na…,* not given.

Drumna, *droim/druim-na…,* ridge of the…

Drumna, *dromnach, druimne,* ridges.

Drumnaboy, *druim-na-buidhe,* ridge of the yellow cow.

Drumnacole, *druim-na-solais(sic),* hill of light.

Drumnaconagher, *dromainn-Connor,* Connor's(a personal or family name) ridge. Originally called '**Dromonticonnor'**, the ridge of/with Connors house.

Drumnagress, *druim-air-dreas,* hill-ridge over or on the bramble-brake.

Drumneen, *druimín,* little ridge.

Drumny, *droimne,* a ridge.

Drumny, *druimne,* ridges.

Drumny, *na-droimne,* not given.

Drumo, *droím-eo,* yew ridge.

Drumo, *drom-na…,* ridge of the…

Drumod, *droim-Fhuaid, dromad,* not given.

Drumod, *druim-fhad,* long ridge.

Drumone, *droim-Eamhna,* not given.

Drumourne, *druim-fhuáráin,* ridge of the spring well.

Drumsmith, *dhrom-Mhic-Gabhann,* not given.

Drumsna, *droim-ar-snámh,* swimming place ridge.

Drumwood, (bi-lingual) *coil-an-droma,* wood of the ridge.

Drumwood, *dromad,* not given.

Drung, *drong,* folk.

Drung, *drong,* the multitude, crowd or the place of meeting.

Drung, *drung, drong, druinge,* a party, sept, tribe or troop.

Drungan, from *drong,* the little place of the troop, tribe or faction.

Drunganagh, from *drong,* a place of septs or troops.

Drutan, *dhrúchtáin,* not given.

Dry, *druadh,* the druid.

Dryan, *draeighean,* abounding in sloe bushes, backthorn.

Dryd, *druide,* starving(sic).

Dryland, *Uí-Dhraoileáin,* O'Dreeling, a family name.

Drynin, *draighneáin,* brambly.

Drynine, *draighneáin,* brambly.

Du, *Daimh,* can be a Church or a house.

Du, *dú, dubh,* black or dark coloured.

Du, *dútha, duthaigh,* district.

Duag, (river) *dubhóg,* not given.

Duag, *dobhaig,* a cauldron.

Duag, *dubhog,* from *dubh,* black.

Duag, *dubhóige,* not given.

Duag, *Uí-Duach,* Duach, O'Duagh, a family name.

Duaga, *duaige,* black bog stuff(sic).

Duagh, *dubháth, dubh-ath,* black ford.

Duagh, *Uí-Dhuach, Uí-Duagh,* O'Duagh, a family and clan name.

Duagh, *Uí-Duach,* Duach or O'Duagh, a family name.

Duala, *duala,* not given.

Duald, *dubhalthach,* a dark complexioned lofty person.

Dualla, *dubh-aille, dúaille,* black cliff or slope.

Dualla, *dubh-bhaile,* black town or Blacks town.

Dualla, *dumha-aille,* not given.

Dually, *dubh-aille, dúaille,* black cliff or slope.

Dually, *dumha-aille,* not given.

Duane, *dha-deamhan,* two demons.

Duane, *Dubháin,* Dubhán, a personal or family name.

Duane, *Uí-Dhubháin, Dhubháin, Dubhain,* Ó Dubháin, O'Doane or Duane, a family name.

Duark, *duairc,* surly.

Duarrigle, *dubh-aireagal,* black habitation or oratory.

Dubban, *dTubán,* tubs.

Dubbaun, *dTobán,* tubs.

Dubber, *dothair,* name of a river.

Dubber, *d-tobar,* wells.

Dubber, *tobar,* a well.

Dublin, (Mts) *sliabh-ruadh,* not given.

Dublin, *dubh-linn, duibh-linn,* black pool, also known as *áth-cliath, Baile-átha-cliath,* town of the hurdle ford.

Ducalla, *duichealla, dubhchealla,* not given.

Duchile, *duchoill,* not given.

Dud, *Dodaigh,* Dodd, a personal or family name.

Dudley, *Dubhalthach,* a dark complexioned lofty person.

Duf, *dubh,* black.

Duff, (from Legnaduff) *duibhe,* the black cow.

Duff, *daimh,* an ox.

Duff, *dhubh,* not given.

Duff, *du, dubh,* black or dark coloured.

Duff, *dhuibh,* dark soil(sic).

Duff, *duibh,* the dark-complexioned man.

Duff, *Uí-Dhuibh, Dhuibh,* Ó Duibh or O Duff, *a family name.*

Duffe, *duibhe,* not given.

Duffer, *dubh-trian, black third.*

Dufferin, *dubhthrian, a black third part.*

Duffey, *Dhúbhthaigh, O'Duffy, a family name.*

Duffry, *dubhthar,* not given.

Duffry, *duibhthir, duibhthire, black territory.*

Duffy, *Duffy, a personal or family name.*

Duffyr, *duibhthir, duibhthire, black territory.*

Dufless, *duibh-lios, black fort.*

Dugan, *Uí-Dhugáin, Dubhagán,* Ó Dugán or O Dugan, *a family name.*

Dugennan, *Uí-Duibhgeannain, O'Duignan or O'Duignan, a family name.*

Duggan, *Dhubhgáin,* Dugan, a personal or family name.

Duggan, *Dubhgáin, Dúgáin,* not given.

Duggan, *Uí-Dhúgáin,* descendants of Duggan, a personal or family name.

Duggan, *Uí-Dubhagain,* O'Dugan, a family name.

Duggerna, *docairne, dogairne, a hindrance or an obstruction.*

Duggerna, *dogarna,* not given.

Dughile, *dubhchoill, dubh-choill, black* **wood.**

Dughlone, *dubh-clauin, black meadow.*

Dugort, *dubhghort,* not given.

Duhallow, *dútha/duthaigh-Ealla. district of the river Allo/Ealla.*

Duher, *Dothra,* not given.

Duhig, *Uí-Dhubhthaigh, Uí-Dubhthaigh, O'Duhig or O'Duffy, a family name.*

Duhig, *Uí-Dhúthaigh,* Ó Dúthaigh, a family name.

Duhir, *doithir, blackness or gloom.*

Duhir, *duithir,* not given.

Duige, *dubhaidh, black bog dye.*

Duige, *dumhaidh, a cairn or mound.*

Duigh, *dubh, black.*

Duinne, *brown river.*

Duiske, *dubhuisce, dubh-uisge, black water.*

Duivcloy, *dubh-chloidhe, black ditch.*

Dulane, *Dalláin,* Dallán, a personal or family name.

Dulane, *tuileán, tulán, tuilen, the little hill.*

Dulany, *Uí-Dubhshláine,* O'Delany, a family name.

Dulea, Dunlea, a family name.

Duleek, damhliag, daimhlaig, the stone house or Church.

Duleek, damhliag, the stone Church.

Duleek, duibhliag, not given.

Duleek, the stone Church or house.

Dulick, dubh-leac, black flagstone.

Dulin, Dunlaing, Dowling, a personal or family name.

Dulla, dola, the loop.

Dullagh, dTulach, d-tulach, hills or hillocks.

Dullaghaun, dTulchan, dTulán, hillocks.

Dullaun, dalláin, a pillar stone.

Dullaun, Doláin, not given.

Dullaun, dTulchan, dTulán, hillocks.

Dullerick, Doluaraic, Dolraic, not given.

Dullia, duille, a leaf of a tree.

Dullisk, duileasg, a sea plant.

Dullisk, duilisc, dillesk or dulsk, a broad leaved pond weed.

Dullisk, dulse, an edible sea-plant.

Dullow, dealbh, phantom.

Dulsk, duileasg, a sea plant.

Dulta, Dubhaltaigh, Duald, a personal or family name.

Dum, dTom, bushes.

Dumagh, dTomach, d-tomach, bushes.

Dumagh, dumha, a carn or a tumulus.

Dun, domhain, not given.

Dun, donn, brown or brown soil.

Dun, duinne, the dun cow, (a legendary cow).

Dun, dún, a fortress or fortified.

Dun, dún, a habitation(sic).

Dun, dun, fortified, strong or firm.

Dun, Uí-Dhuinn, O'Dunne, a family name.

Duna, dhún-na..., dún-a'..., fort or fortress of the....

Dunadry, dún/dun-eadradh, middle fort.

Dunadry, dún-eadaraigh, not given.

Dunaff, dún-dhamh, not given.

Dunamase, dún-Másc, the fort of Másc, a personal name.

Dunamon, dún-Iomadhain, Iomgan's (a personal or family name) fort.

Dunamon, dún-Iomáin, not given.

Dunanore, dún-na-nOthar, not given.

Dunany, dún-Áine, not given.

Dunbell, dún-bile, dort of the tree.

Dunbin, dún-binne, not given.

Dunboy, dun-Baoi, Baoi's (a personal or a family name) fortress.

Dundalk, dun-Dealgan, Delca, Delga's (a male name) fort.

Dundareirke, dún-dá-radharc, dún-Dea-rad-hairc, not given.

Dundareirke, dún-Dea-radhairc, not given.

Dundee, Donaid, Doney, a male name.

Duneane, dún-dá-éan, dun-dá-én, fortress of the two birds.

Duneen, Uí-Duinnín, O'Dineen, a family name.

Dunegan, dún-Géagáin, not given.

Dungan, Dhonnagáin, Donegan, Donnegan, a personal or family name.

Dungan, Uí-Dhonnagáin, Donnagán, a family name.

Dunganville, dún-gConmhaoile-Íochtarach, Cú Maoile's (not given) fort.

Dungar, dún-Gair, not given.

Dungloe, an-clochán-liath, not given.

Dungloe, dún-gleo, fort of contention or strife, also known by an-chochán-liath, the grey stepping stones.

Dungloe, dún-gloir, fort of the noise.

Dunglow, an-clochán-liath(sic), not given.

Dunglow, dún-cloiche, fort of the stone(sic).

Dunhill, Dhomhnaill, Donal, a male name.

Dunhill, dun-fhaill, dún-aill, fort on the cliff.

Dunican, Dhonnchon, Dunican, a male name.

Dunican, Dunican, Donegan or Duncan, a personal or family name.

Duniry, dún-Daighre, not given.

Duniry, dun-Doighre, Doighre's (a male name) fortress.

Dunlea, Uí-Duinnshleibhe, O'Deenlea or Dunlea, a family name.

Dunlo, dún-Lóich, not given.

Dunloe, (hill) dún-Laódha, not given.

Dunloe, dhún-Lóich, dun-Loich, fortress of Loch, a personal name.

Dunloe, dún-lóich, fort of the river Loe.

Dunn, dun, dún, a fort.

Dunna, Domhnach, a Church.

Dunna, dún, dun-na..., fort of the...

Dunnaluck, tír-Liúc(sic), not given.

Dunnamagan, *dún-Iomagáin/Iomagán,* not given.

Dunnamaggan, *dún-Iomagáin,* not given.

Dunnamaggin, *dún-Imagáin,* Imgan's (a personal or family name) fort.

Dunnaman, *dún/dun-na-mbeann,* fortress of the gables or pinnacles.

Dunnanew, *dún-na-cnú,* the nut hill(sic).

Dunnee, *Donaí,* not given.

Dunnee, *Donaidh,* Doney, a male name.

Dunneen, *dunín,* little fort.

Dunneill, (river) *abha-dhúin-Néil,* not given.

Dunny, *Uí-Dhunadhaigh,* O'Downey, a family name.

Dunnycove, *dún/dun-Uí-Chobhthaigh,* fortress of O'Cowhig, a family name.

Dunnyboe, *dun-na-mBo,* fort of the cattle

Dunoge, *dúnóg,* not given.

Dunrea, *dún-riabhach,* not given.

Dunsfort, *lios-an-dúna,* not given.

Dunshaughlin, *domhnach-Sechnaill,* Church of St Sechnall.

Dunsinare, *tamhsain-Aichir*(sic), not given.

Dunsy, *Duinseach,* St Duinseach or St Dunsy.

Dunville, *baile-Uí-Dhuinn,* not given.

Dunworly, *dún-Urlaing,* not given.

Duog, black streamlet.

Dur, *dair,* oaks.

Dur, *dTor, d-tor,* bushes.

Dur, *d-tor,* pointed hills.

Dur, *dur,* strong.

Dura, *dobhara,* marshy or beside water.

Durah, *dair-mhagh,* plain of oaks.

Durah, *dubh-rath,* black fortress.

Durcan, *Duarcáin,* Durkan, a personal or family name.

Durha, *durtheach,* a cabin or Church.

Durk, *torc,* a boar or swine.

Durless, *durlas,* strong fort.

Durly, *dTurlaighe,* half dried lake/s.

Durn, *Uí-Dornain,* O'Dornan, a family name.

Durneen, Durneen or Dornin, a personal or family name.

Durnian, boors.

Durnish, *dairinis,* oak island.

Durra, *daire, doire,* an oak grove/plantation.

Durraclogh, *dorchlach,* not given.

Durragh, *dorcha,* dark.

Durragha, *dorcha,* dark.

Durris, *dóras,* door.

Durrow, *darmhagh/darmagh-Coluim-Cille,* not given.

Durrow, *darwah, dar-mhagh, dairmhá, dair-magh, daurmhagh, darú, dermhagh, dearmagh, dermaigi, dearmhaighe, durúdh,* the oak plain or the field of oaks.

Durrow, *Daurmhagh, Dermhagh-Ua-nDuach,* the oak plain of Ui Duach.

Durrow, *doire,* not given.

Durrus, *dorus,* a door.

Durrus, *dúras,* not given.

Durrus, *dúros, dú/dubh-ros, dubhros,* black wood, grove or point.

Dursey, *dóirse,* gates.

Dursey, *na-dorsaí,* not given.

Dursey, *oileán-Baoi,* not given.

Durtaun, *dartáin,* the heifer.

Durtaun, *dortain,* a downpour or a gushing stream.

Durtaun, *dTortán,* not given.

Dury, *an-diúraidh,* not given.

Dush, *duis,* the bush.

Dussaun, *dosáin,* a little bush.

Dustara, *dostaire,* the swaggerer.

Duv, *damh,* an ox or oxen.

Duvana, *Uí-Dubhain,* Devane, a family name.

Duvane, *damháin, Dubháin,* not given.

Duvane, *Dhubhain,* Devane or Downe, a personal or family name.

Duvane, *Dubhaigh,* Dubhagh, an ancient chief.

Duvane, *Uí-Dubhain,* O'Doane or Duane, a family name.

Duvasig, *duibh-easaig,* the black cataract.

Duve, *dubh,* black.

Duveel, *dubh-Mhaoil,* not given.

Duvernagh, *duibh-fhearnach,* black alder land.

Duvillaun, *dubhoileán, dubh-oileáin,* not given.

Duvog, black streamlet or little black river.

Duvowen, (river) *dubh-abhainn,* not given.

Duvroga, *Dobhróige,* Dobhróg, not given.

Dwag, (river) *dubhaig,* not given.

Dwan, *Dhubháin,* Duane, a personal or family name.

Dwan, *Dubhain,* St Dubhan.

Dwyer, *Uí-Dubhuidhir,* O'Dwyer, a family name.

Dwyre, *Uí-Dubhuidhir,* O'Dwyer, a family name.

Dyan, *daingean,* strong, stronghold or a fortress.

Dye, *da-aghaidh,* two faces.

Dyre, *Deighir,* not given.

Dyrick, *Deighric,* not given.

Dysaghy, *duibhsacha,* not given.

Dysart, *díseart, disert,* a hermitage, wilderness or a desert.

Dysert, *dísert,* a wild country destitute of inhabitants(sic).

Dysert, *dísert, disert, díseart, dísirt, desert,* a deserted place, a hermitage, wilderness or a desert.

Dysert, *dísirt-Maoltuile,* not given.

E

Ea, *Aodha,* Hugh, a male name.

Ea, O'Hea or O'Hayes, a personal or family name.

Eachlann, *eachlann,* horse land.

Eacle, *fhiacail,* the tooth.

Eadan, *eadain,* a hill brow.

Eadan, *eadan,* the front or forehead.

Eadig, *Eadaigh, Eadig,* Eady, a personal or family name.

Eadin, *eadain,* a hill brow.

Eady, (island) *oilean-Éidigh,* not given.

Eady, *Eadaigh,* Eady, a personal or family name.

Eady, *Éide,* not given.

Eady, *eudaighe,* clothes.

Eag, *fhiaigh,* deer.

Eagh, *an-fheiche,* the raven.

Eagh, *Aodha,* Aodh or Hugh, a male name.

Eagh, *each,* horses.

Eagh, *Eachdhach,* Eochy, a male name.

Eaghra, *eachrach,* a place of horses.

Eague, *Éag/Éaga,* not given.

Ealane, *Fhialáin,* not given.

Ealga, *ealagach,* noble.

Ealty, *ealta,* flocks.

Ealy, *Éalaigh, Fhaidle, Fhaidhle,* not given.

Eamon, *Éamoinn,* Edmond, a male personal name.

Eamonn, *Eamoinn,* Samonn(sic), a personal or family name.

Eamush, *Sheamais,* James, a male name.

Ean, *éan,* birds.

Eana, *eanach,* marshy.

Eanach, *eanach,* a marsh.

Eanaghty, *Uí-Fhionnachtaigh,* O'Finnaghty, a family name now often made Finnerty or Fenton.

Eanaig, *aonaig,* the fair.

Eane, *éan,* birds.

Eanig, *aentaigh,* fairs.

Eanig, *aonaigh,* a meeting or fair.

Eanly, *éanlaigh,* not given.

Eanly, *éanlaith,* birds.

Eanna, *eanach, eanaigh,* a marsh.

Eanty, *aenaigh,* a fair.

Eany, *aenaigh, aonach, aonaigh,* a fair.

Eany, *Éanaigh,* Heny, a personal or family name.

Eany, *Eandha,* St Endeu.

Eany, *Éanna,* St. Eany.

Eany, *Éannaidh,* Enny, a personal or family name.

Eany, *eidhneach,* ivy producing or abounding in ivy.

Eany, *Éinne, Éinne,* a personal or family name and a founder of a Church in Galway.

Eany, *Fhéinne,* Enna, a personal or family name.

Ear, *fhéir,* grass.

Earagh, *iarthach,* west or western.

Earl, *Iarla,* an Earl.

Earl, *Iriail,* Irial, a personal name.

Earl, *Oirill,* not given.

Earla, *Iarla,* an Earl.

Early, *Iarla,* an Earl.

Earny, *Ereann,* Eire, a female name.

Eary, *aoire, aodhaire, aedhaire,* the shepherd.

Easan, *easan,* weasels.

Eascar, *eascair,* not given.

Eask, *iasc,* fish.

Eask, *iascach,* fishy.

Eask, *iascaidh,* not given.

Easkey, iasc, abounding in fish.

Easky, *iascach, iaseach,* fishy or abounding in fish.

Easky, *iascaigh,* not given.

Easter, *Esther,* a female name.

Eastlone, *lón-thoir,* not given.

Easton, *Uistín,* Austin or Augustine, a personal name.

Easton, *Uistin,* Austin, a male name.

Eatin, *Éitín, Éitin,* not given.

Eatly, flocks.

Eaton, *Éitín,* Eitin, a personal or family name.

Eaverie, *aimhreidh,* rough or complicated.

Eavy, *shléibhe, sleibhe,* mountain.

Ech, *eich,* a horse.

Eclary, *A-Chlaraigh,* De Clare, a male name.

Edagh, *éda,* cattle.

Edan, *eadan,* a hill brow.

Edan, *fheadáin,* a pit, a well or a brook.

Eddan, *fheadáin,* a streamlet or brook.

Eddrim, *eadar-dhruim,* middle ridge.

Eden, *an-tÉadan,* the face(sic).

Eden, *éadain,* not given.

Eden, *eadan,* the forehead(sic).

Eden, *eudan, eadan, éadan, edan, eudon,* a brow or hill brow.

Eden, *éadan,* a slope.

Edena, *éadan,* a hill brow.

Edena, *éadan-an…, eudan-na…,* hill brow of the…

Edenaferkina, *éadan-tí-Feirgean*(sic), not given.

Edenamo, *éadan-an-mBeatach,* not given.

Edenan, *eudan-an…,* hill brow of the…

Edenan, little hill brow.

Edenfinfree, *an-tÉadan-Anfach*(sic), not given.

Edenfinfree, white hill-brow of heath.

Edennagully, *eudan-dubh-gCaille,* hill brow of the wood.

Eder, *eder, dir, eadar,* between.

Edera, *eadortha,* a central place.

Edergole, *cor-treasna,* not given.

Edergole, *eadargóil,* not given.

Edermine, *eadardhruim,* not given.

Edernagh, *eadarnach,* the central place.

Ederney, *eadarnaigh,* the ambush.

Ederny, *eadarnach,* the central place or middle area.

Ederown, *eder-dá-abhainn,* between two rivers.

Edine, *éudain,* the front.

Edmond, *Éamainn,* Éamaninn, a personal or family name and a founder of a Church in Carlow.

Edmond, *Eamoinn,* Edmond, a male name.

Edna, *eudan,* a hill brow.

Edne, *eudan,* a hill brow.

Edoc, a personal name.

Edock, *Éadoc,* Edock,

Edra, *eadortha,* central.

Edy, *Chaeide,* St Caidoc.

Eedora, *fhigheadóra,* weavers.

Eedora, *fhígheadóra,* the weaver.

Eedy, *Íde,* St Ide.

Eel, *aeil, aol, aoil,* lime.

Eela, *Daoile,* of the river **Deel.**

Eel, *Uilre,* soldiers or warriors.

Eelan, *fhaoileann, bhFaeileán, faeileán,* seagulls.

Eelig, *aoilig,* manure.

Eelim, *Eibhlinne,* Evlin, a male name.

Eelinan, *Uí-Ileannain,* O'Heelinan, a personal or family name.

Eely, *aelaigh,* lime.

Eely, *aoiligh,* lime.

Eely, *daoile,* beetles, also the name of the river **Deol.**

Eely, *Daoile,* Daol, a personal or family name.

Eely, *Fhaeilenn,* St Faelenn, the virgin Saint.

Eely, *Fhaile,* not given.

Een, *án, ín, aun,* little.

Een, *Fhínín,* Fínín, a male name.

Eena, *aenach,* a fair.

Eena, *Eithne,* St Ethnea, the virgin Saint.

Eena, *fhíona, fhiona,* wine.

Eenagh, *áidhneach,* ivy.

Eenan, *Fhiónáin, Fhíonain,* Finan or St Finan.

Eenan, *Fhíonáin,* not given.

Eenaun, *Fhíonain,* Finan, a male name.

Eenaun, *Fhíonáin,* not given.

Eeneen, *Fhínín,* not given.

Eenloun, *Uí-Anluain,* not given.

Eeny, *án, ín, aun,* little.

Eeny, *aonaigh, aenach,* a fair.

Eeny, *Éunna,* Eany, a personal or family name.

Eer, *oirthir,* eastern.

Eeragh, *Fhiachrach,* Fiaghra, a personal name.

Eeragh, *iarthach, iarach,* west or western.

Eeran, *iarainn,* iron.

Eerin, *airtin,* little stones.

Eeroy, *Aodha-ruaidh,* red Hugh, a male name.

Eery, *Aodha-ruaidh,* red Hugh, a male name.

Eeshal, *iseal, íseal,* low, lower or low lying.

Eeshert, *díseart,* not given.

Eeshil, *íseal,* low.

Eeshill, *íseal, ísil,* not given.

Eeskeen, *Uí-Dhíscín*, O'Diskin or Diskin, a family name.

Eesteenig, *Esteenagh, Uístínig*, Hastings, a personal or family name.

Eesteenig, *Ístínigh*, not given.

Eetig, *Fhaoitigh, Fhaoitig*, White, a family name.

Eety, *Fhaoitigh*, White, a family name.

Eevan, *aeibhinn*, beautiful, joyous, delightful.

Eevan, *Laobháin*, St Laobhán, Laobhan.

Eever, *Iomhair*, Emer, a personal or family name.

Eevil, *Aeibhell*, the name of a particular banshee.

Eevin, *Aoibhinn*, not given.

Eevin, *aoimhinn, áoebhin*(sic), *aoibhinn, aoibhin, aeibhinn*, beautiful, joyous, pleasant, delightful.

Eevin, *Eimhin*, St Evin.

Effernagh, *Aifrionnach*, a place of (Catholic) masses.

Effernagh, *Oifreanach*, not given.

Effernan, *ithearnán*, corn producing land.

Effin, *Eifinn*, not given.

Effin, *Eimhín*, St Effin.

Effinchy, *bh-fuinnsean*, ash trees.

Effrin, *aiffrinn*, (Catholic) mass.

Effrinagh, *Aifrionnach*, a place of (Catholic) masses.

Effy, Eva, a female name.

Egan, *Aodhgáin*, not given.

Egan, *Mhic-Aodhagan*, MacEgan, a family name.

Egan, *Uí-Aodhagain*, O'Hagan, a family name.

Egar, *Adhgar, Adhgair*, a personal or family name.

Eggerton, *Éigeartáin*, not given.

Egish, *éigis, eigeas*, a learned man or poet.

Eglan, *Dhéagláin*, St Deaglán.

Egland, *Deaglán*, St Deaglán.

Eglen, the half glen.

Eglington, *an-mhá*, the plain.

Eglinton, *Domhnach-Bruachair*, not given.

Eglish, *eaglish, eaglais*, a Church.

Egny, *Eigne*, Egnagh, a personal or family name.

Egny, *Éignigh, Éighneach*, Egnagh or Egny, a male name.

Ehea, *Uí-Sheagha*, O'Shea, a family name.

Ehenny, *Eithne*, not given.

Eigh, *achaidh*, a field.

Eigh, *an-fheiche*, the raven.

Eigh, *ech, eich, each*, a horse.

Eigh, *fhia, fhiaidh, fhiadh*, deer.

Eight, *Eachdhach*, Eochy, a male name.

Eight, *Echach*, Eochaid, a personal or family name.

Eighter, *iochtar, íochtair, íochdar, iochtair*, lower or low lying.

Eighter, *íochtarach, íochtar*, not given.

Eighteragh, *íochtarach*, not given.

Eighterrush, *iachtair-ruis*, lower wood.

Eightragh, *íochtarach*, not given.

Eightragh, *iochtrach*, lower or low lying.

Eilean, (river) *an-Eibhleann*, not given.

Eilly, *Dhaoile*, the river **Dael**.

Eilte, *eillte, aillte*, precipices.

Eilty, *elite*, a doe.

Einagh, *aighneach, idhneach*, abounding in ivy.

Einaun, (island) *inis-eidhneáin*, not given.

Einean, *eidhneain*, ivy.

Eiragh, *iartharach*, western.

Eirin, *iarainn*, iron.

Eirk, *adharc*, a horn.

Eirk, *adharc*, a peak(sic).

Eirk, *h-adharc*, hunting horns.

Eirka, *adhairce*, the horn.

Eirky, *adhairce*, a horn.

Eiry, *eidhre*, an heir.

Eisc, *eisc*, not given.

Eisk, *éisc, eisc*, fish.

Eisk, *uisce*, water.

El, *aill*, a rock

Elagh, *aileach*, a stone house or fort.

Elagh, *Elaigh*, a male name.

Elan, *Fhaelain*, St Faelan.

Élan, *Fhaoláin*, not given.

Elan, *Uidhilín*, not given.

Eland, *Fhoilin*, Felan, a personal or family name.

Elane, *Áláin*, Alan, a male name.

Elane, *Eidhlean*, a personal or family name.

Elane, *eidhneain*, ivy.

Elane, *Eilean*, Helena.

Elane, *Fhaelain*, St Faelan.

Elane, *Oileain*, the island.

Elane, *Uí-Fhaolain*, Phelan, a family name.

Elarty, *Fhagharta,* not given.

Elder, *iolair,* an eagle.

Eldron, *eanaigh-Ealdrain,* not given.

Eleesh, *Eilíse,* Ellish or Eliza, a female name.

Elfinn, *aill-finn,* rock of the clear spring.

Elia, *Éille,* not given.

Eliagh, *Éileach,* not given.

Eline, *Eithleann,* Eithle, the name of a Church founder in Limerick.

Eliogarty, *Éile-Uí-Fhógartaigh / Fhogartaigh / Fhógarta,* Eile (Ely) O'Fogarty, the tribe of the descendants of Fogarty.

Elisa, *Eilíse,* Eliza, a female name.

Elisha, *aillise,* gangrene or abscess.

Ellagh, *aileach,* a stone house or fort.

Ellaha, *oilche,* rocks.

Ellan, *oileáin,* an island.

Ellana, *oileann-na...,* island of the...

Ellane, *oileáin,* the island.

Ellaun, *oileáin,* the island.

Ellen, *Eibhlín,* Eileen, a female name.

Ellery, *ailithre,* the pilgrim.

Ellery, *eilair,* a footpath.

Ellery, *Oilithre,* not given.

Ellida, *Oilealla,* not given.

Ellihy, *eilithe,* not given.

Ellin, *Eileann,* not given.

Ellinan, *Uí-Oileannáin,* Ó hOileannáin, not given.

Ellinure, *an-léana-úr,* not given.

Ellis, *Eilís, Eillis,* not given.

Ellis, *Eilghis,* Ellis, a personal or family name.

Ellis, *Eilíse,* Eliza, a female name.

Ellistragh, *felestar,* flaggers.

Ellistrin, *eileastran,* not given.

Ellistrin, *felestrom,* flaggers.

Ellistrom, *felestrom,* flaggers.

Ellistron, *felestrom,* flaggers.

Elly, *aileach,* a stone house or fort.

Elly, *ailí,* a boulder.

Elly, *aille,* a point of rock, a pointed rock, a 'spink', a pinnacle or an overhanging cliff.

Elly, *eallaigh, eallach,* cattle.

Elly, *Eile,* the district of Ely.

Elly, *eillighe, eilligh,* not given.

Elly, *Oiligh,* not given.

Elo, *éaloidh,* escaping.

Elogher, *Fhealachair,* Felchar, the name of an ancient chief.

Elphin, *ail / aill-finn, ailfinn, oilfinn,* rock of the clear spring.

Elphin, *ail-finn,* Fionn's (a male name) stone.

Elt, *eilit, eilte,* a doe.

Eltan, *aillteán, ailteain,* a little cliff.

Elteen, *ailtín,* little cliff or little glenside.

Eltia, *aillte,* not given.

Elton, *Eiltín,* Eiltín, a personal or family name.

Elton, *Eiltin,* Eltin, a personal or family name.

Elton, *Eiltín,* St Eiltin/Eltin/Elton.

Elton, *eiltín,* the little doe.

Elton, *Eiltiún*(sic), *cluain-Eiltín,* not given.

Elty, *eilite, eilit, elite, eilte,* a doe.

Elva, *Oilbhe,* not given.

Elvey, *Oilbhe,* not given.

Ely, (island) *inis-coiméadtha,* not given.

Ely, *aileach,* a stone house or fort.

Ely, *Éilí, Éile,* not given.

Emain, Emania, *eamhain,* the translation offered is 'neck brooch' but the true meaning is uncertain.

Ematris, *Ioma-Fhastraí,* not given.

Emin, *ime-an...,* dam of the...

Eminiska, *ime-an-uisce,* the water dam.

Emlagh, *imileá, an-tImleach,* not given.

Emlagh, *emlagh,* a marsh.

Emlagh, *imleach,* borderland.

Emlagh, *Imlig, Imleach,* (low) land beside a lake, marshy place or a marshy lake.

Emlagh, *imlioch,* a marsh or land bordering a lake.

Emleagh, *Imlig, Imleach,* (low) land beside a lake or marshy place.

Emly, *eimligh, imilligh,* a lough bank.

Emly, *imleach,* borderland.

Emly, *Imleach-iobhair/iubhair,* shortened version of the full name meaning the Lake marsh of the Yew tree.

Emly, *imlig, imlighe, imleach,* (low) land beside a lake, a lake border or a marshy place.

Emlygrennan, *bile-Ghroidhnín,* Grynan's (a male name) ancient tree.

Emlygrennan, *imleach-dhraighnín,* marginal land of the little blackthorn.

Emlygrennan, *imleach-draighnigh,* lakeland abounding with blackthorns.

Emmel, *imeall,* the border or margin.

Emmo, *iomaidh,* not given.

Emny, *Éime,* not given.

Emo, *Ioma,* the image.

Emo, *iomagh,* not given.

Emon, *Éamainn, Éamann,* a personal name.

Emon, *Emóin,* Eamonn or Edmond, a male name.

Emper, *béal-áth-Impir,* not given.

Emy, *Éime, iomadh,* not given.

Emy, *ioma,* not given.

Emy, *iomdhaigh, iomaidh,* a bed or couch.

Emyvale, *scairbh-na-gCaorach,* the shallow of the sheep.

Emyvale, *Uí-Méith-Tíre,* descendants of the rich land and then the word 'Vale' added.

Emyvale, vale of the bed.

Enagh, (Co Clare) *óenagh-Ua-Floínn,* the fair held in O'Flyn's territory.

Enagh, *an-fhéich, an-fheiche,* the raven.

Enagh, *aonaigh, aenach, tAonach,* a fair or assembly place.

Enagh, *aonaigh,* the assembly.

Enagh, *éanach,* birds.

Enagh, *eanaigh, eanaig, eanach,* a marsh.

Enagh, *eidhneach, eidhnech,* a place of ivy.

Enagh, *tEanach, aonach,* not given.

Enaghan, *eanachán, eanachan,* little marsh or marshy land.

Enaghan, *Uí-hEanachain,* O'Henaghan, a family name.

Enaghare, *an-tEanach-ghearr,* not given.

Enaghroe, *an-tAonach-rua,* not given.

Enare, *an-áir,* the slaughter.

Enas, *an-easa,* waterfall.

Enaule, St Naile.

Ench, *inse,* an island.

Endall, *abhann-Dalla,* the river 'Dall'.

Endrim, *aondruim,* not given.

Endun, *abhann-Duinne,* the river 'Dun'.

Eneen, *aneinín, éinin,* the little bird.

Eneen, *Fininghín,* Fineen, a personal or family name.

Enekare, *a'chnoicéir,* a rabbit warren.

Enerty, *Shinhartaigh,* Henerty, a personal or family name.

Eney, *eidhnigh,* ivy.

Enfield, *an-bóthar-buí,* the yellow road. Originaly it was called **Innfield** or the **Inn by the field** and changed by the railway company to **Enfield.**

England, *Aingleontaigh, an-Ingleontaigh, Aingleontach, an-tIngleontach,* not given.

Enilt, *an-eilit,* the doe.

Enish, *inis,* the island.

Enna, *Eithne,* not given.

Enna, *Ethne,* Ethne, a female name.

Ennel, *Ainnínne, Annin,* Ainneann, the name of an ancient firbolg chief.

Ennel, *ainninne,* great fairness.

Ennell, *Innill,* not given.

Enner, *inbher, inbhear, inbir,* the river mouth.

Ennereilly, *inbher-nDaoile,* not given.

Ennis, *inis,* an island, a meadow along a river, a holm or a ford.

Ennis, *inis-cluana-Rámfhada,* not given.

Enniskerry, *áth/ath-na-sceire/scairbhe,* ford of the rough river crossing place, rocky place, the rugged shallow ford or ford of the reef.

Enniskerry, *áth-na-scairbhe,* rough or rocky ford.

Enniskerry, *áth-na-sgeire,* ford of the rock.

Ennisnag, *inis-snag,* not given.

Ennisnag, *inis-snaig,* riverside land/holm of the woodpecker.

Enny, *eanach, eanagh,* a marsh or cut out bog.

Enny, *eanaigh,* marsh/es.

Enny, *Eithne,* Eithne, a female name.

Enny, *Eithne,* St Ethnea, the virgin Saint.

Enny, *Enna,* Enna, a personal or family name.

Enos, *Aengusa, Aenghusa,* St. Aengus/ Aongus.

Enos, *Aonghusa,* not given.

Envy, *aibhne,* a river.

Eny, *aonaigh,* the fair.

Eny, *eantaidhe,* little marshes.

Eny, *Eithne,* Enna, a female name.

Eny, *Enna,* a male name.

Eoca, *Eocha, Acha,* Eochy, a male name.

Eocht, *eochta,* the breast.

Eola, *bhláth,* flowers.

Eolan, *Fhaoláin,* not given.

Eonish, *eo-inis,* yew island.

Era, *iarach, iarthach,* western.
Erable, *eirball,* end or tail.
Eragh, *aerach,* airy or weird.
Eragh, *Fhiachrach,* Fiachra, the name of an ancient prince.
Eragh, *iarach, iarthach,* western.
Eragh, *iartharach,* western.
Eraghtish, *aireachtais,* assembly or assembly place.
Eraile, *ar-aill,* on the cliff.
Erard, *irarda,* not given.
Erdalliv, *ardtalaimh,* high land.
Ereen, trails.
Erg, *dhearg,* red.
Ergoole, *...air-gabhal,* ...on the river fork.
Erheeve, *air-thaoibh,* on the side.
Erher, *airthear,* east/eastern.
Erhin, *fhiorthainn, fiorin,* long grass.
Erhin, Oirthin, not given.
Erig, *dheirge,* red ground.
Erig, *Eirc,* St Earc.
Erigeen, *Meirigín,* Mergin, a family name.
Erilly, *oirbhealaigh,* not given.
Erin, *Éireann,* Éire or Ireland.
Erin, *Erin,* Ireland.
Erin, *Ernai,* an ancient tribe.
Erin, *iarainn,* iron.
Erin, *thrian,* a third part.
Erina, *airedhnadh,* salmon wiers
Erinagh, *Eireanach,* Irish.
Erinagh, *eireaneach,* proud.
Erinagh, *eiritheach,* rising.
Erinagh, *Oireanach,* not given.
Erk, *Eirc,* Erc, Erk, a male name. Nine Irish Saints had this name.
Erk, *erc,* cattle.
Erk, *hadhairce,* the horn.
Erkaun, Erkaun, a personal or family name.
Erke, *Adhairc,* not given.
Erke, *Eirc,* Erck, a male name.
Erkin, *Oircín, fheircín,* not given.
Erkina, (river) *an-eircne,* not given.
Erkinagh, *eircneach, oircneach,* salmon (river).
Erky, *aidhirceach,* horned or horny.
Erky, *Eirce,* not given.
Erla, *iarla,* a earl.
Erlough, *air-loch,* on the lake.
Ermogh, *Dermaighe,* not given.

Ernan, *airne,* sloes or blackthorn.
Ernan, *Earnain,* St Ernan.
Ernan, *fhearnán,* not given.
Ernane, *Earnáin,* a male name.
Erne, *Éirne, Ernaí,* the Erni, the name of an ancient tribe of Firbolgs.
Erneen, *Eirnín,* Erneen or Ernin, a persons name, a Saints name or a family name.
Eroe, *ruadh,* red.
Errarooey, *Oirear-dhumhaí,* not given.
Errew, *oireamh, aireamh, airech, airedh, oiredh,* good arable land.
Errew, *oiribh,* the ploughman.
Errey, *oireamh, aireamh, airech, airedh, oiredh,* good arable land.
Erriblagh, *earballagh,* tails or stripes of land.
Erribul, *earbuill, earball,* a tail.
Errick, *eiric,* a compensation fine.
Erriff, (river) *an-oireamh,* not given.
Erriff, *glean-na-hOirimhe,* not given.
Erriff, *oireamh, aireamh, airech, airedh, oiredh,* good arable land.
Errig, *dheirg, dhearg,* red.
Errig, *Eirig, Eirg, dheirge,* not given.
Errigal Keerogue, *aireagal-do-Chiaróg,* not given.
Errigal Keerogue, *Aireagal-Chiarán,* St Ciaran's oratory,
Errigal, *aireagal,* a small Church.
Errigal, *airecal,* a habitation.
Errigal, *earagail,* an oratory.
Errigal, *erghabál,* taking or seizing.
Errigal, *tAireagal, aireagal, aireagail,* a hermitage.
Erril, *Oirill, Oiliolla,* a male name.
Errill, *Airéill, Ailealla,* Olioll, not given.
Errill, *Eiréil,* not given.
Errily, *Iriala,* Irial, a personal or family name.
Errily, *oirbhealaigh,* eastern pass.
Errinagh, *erranac,* the end or tail.
Erris Head, *oileán-Dhamhaic,* not given.
Erris, *Iorras, Iorrais,* Iorrais, not given.
Erris, *iorrus,* a peninsula or promontory.
Erroon, *Eiriún,* not given.
Erroon, *Ereamhóin,* Eremon, Irvine or Harmon, a personal or family name.
Errul, *iar-iul,* western direction.
Erry, *aire,* a weir.
Erry, *eirre,* the end or limit.

Erry, *oireamh, aireamh, airech, airedh, oiredh,* good arable land.

Erry, *tOireadh, Oireadh, Oiridh,* not given.

Ersnaw, *air-snámh,* on or at the swimming place.

Ervallagh, *oirbhealach,* eastern pass.

Erveny, *airbheanna,* land divisions.

Ervey, *airbhe, airbheadh,* a land division.

Ervy, *Airbhe,* not given.

Erwinter, *ar-mhuinter,* on/of or belonging to the tribe.

Esh, *ais,* a marsh, wet meadow, low ground, a hill-back or the base of a hill.

Esha, *ais-an/a'...,* hill-base of the...

Eshagh, *Éiseach,* not given.

Eshan, *ais-an...,* marsh of the...

Eshcleagh, *eisc-liath,* not given.

Esher, *Laisreach, Laisr,* St Lassair, Lasair the virgin Saint.

Eshera, *eas-Eirí,* Ery's or Eriu's (a personal name) cataract.

Eshil, *iseal, íseal,* low.

Eshin, *Eision,* not given.

Eshin, *Uiseán, Oisín,* St Oisín.

Eshin, *Uiseán, Uissin,* Ossin, Ossian, the bard, son of Fin-Mac-Cumhail.

Eshna, *ais-na...,* marsh or hill-back of the...

Eshna, *ais-na...,* ridge of the...

Eshul, *íseal,* low.

Esk, *eascach,* fish.

Esk, *eisc,* a quagmire or marsh.

Esk, *eisce,* not given.

Esk, *esc,* a stream track.

Eska, *Eascann,* not given.

Eskaheen, *uisce-chaein,* beautiful water.

Eskan, *esc-an..., esc-na...,* river track of the...

Eske, *iasc,* fish or abounding in fish.

Eske, *iascach,* not given.

Esken, *esc-an..., esc-na...,* river track of the...

Esker, *eiscreach,* not given.

Esker, *escer, eiscir,* a sandhill, a sandy/gravel or glacial ridge, a ridge of high land or a line of sand hills.

Eskeragh, *eiscrach, eiscreach,* full of sand hills or eskers.

Eskine, *eisc-dhoimnin,* a deep fissure(sic).

Eskra, *eascrach,* not given.

Eskra, *eiscreach,* abounding in gravel ridges.

Eskragh, *eiscreach,* full of sand hills or eskers.

Esky, *eisceach,* not given.

Eslin, (river) *eas-Uí-Fhloinn, Aislinne,* not given.

Eslin, a male name.

Eslin, *na-hEislinne,* not given.

Esling, *na-hEislinne,* not given.

Esna, *ais-na...,* ridge of the..., place of the..., hill of the..., fort of the... or recess of the...

Esna, *eas-na...,* not given.

Espic, *Easpuig,* not given.

Espick, *Easpaig,* not given.

Espig, *Easpaig,* the bishop.

Ess, *easa,* a waterfall or a caratact.

Ess, *ess, easa,* a weasel(sic).

Essan, *easa, easan,* a little waterfall on a river, a little fall in a river, a little rapid or a little cataract.

Essaun, *easa, easan,* a little waterfall on a river, a little fall in a river, a little rapid or a little cataract.

Esset, Hasset, a personal or family name.

Essy, *easa,* a waterfall.

Ester, *Easra,* St Easra.

Estersnow, *díseart-Nuadhain/Nuadhan, disert-Nuadhan, issetnowne, issertnowne, tirs-Nuadhan,* St Nuadha's hermitage.

Estry, *estra,* a pond.

Eter, *iachtair, íochtair,* low, lower or low lying.

Etney, *Eithne, Eitinne,* St Eithtne.

Etra, *íochtarach, iochtrach, íochdar,* lower.

Etragh, *iochtrach,* lower.

Etre, *eatar,* central.

Etre, *íochdar,* lower.

Ettagh, *eiteach,* not given.

Ettra, *eitre,* furrowed land.

Eustace, Eustace or Fitz Eustace, an Anglo-Norman family name (14th-16th century).

Eustace, *nIústasach, Iústasach,* not given.

Eustace, *Ustáis,* Eustace, a family name.

Evagallahoo, *Uibh-Gallacha, Uíbh-Gallachú,* Hy Gallahoo, the name of a tribe and means the descendants of Gallchúr.

Evagh, *Eva,* a female name.

Evagh, *Mhéabha,* Maeve, a female name.

Evan, *Eibhin,* not given.

Evara, *Uí-Mheádhra, Mheara,* O'Mara, a family name.

Evegallahoo, *Úibh-Gallchú,* not given.

Even, *Íbheann,* not given.

Even, *Aobhin,* Evan, a personal or family name.

Evenew, *Mhic-Abhainn,* son of Abhann or Aibhne, a personal or family name.

Ever, *Eimhir,* Emer or Ever, a personal or family name.

Ever, *Íomhair,* not given.

Evin, *aoibhínn, aoibhinn, aoimhinn, aeibhinn,* beautiful.

Evin, *Éimhín,* not given.

Evin, *Eimhín,* St. Eimhin/Evin.

Evish, *eibhis,* a mountain meadow.

Evish, *eibhis,* coarse grass or coarse mountain pasture.

Evish, *éibhis,* not given.

Evit, *Ebhit,* Evit, a personal or family name.

Evlagh, *aibhleach,* a place of fires.

Evlin, *Dhoibhilin,* not given.

Evly, *Echmhilidh,* Evilly, a personal or family name.

Evneen, *an-tAibhnín,* not given.

Evy, *sleibhe,* mountain.

Ewry, *iubhraigh,* yew trees.

Ey, *…aigh,* as an ending to a word can sometimes mean, a place of…. or abounding in…

Eyeries, *na- hAoraí//hAedharaí,* not given.

Eyeries, *na- haraí, iar-righthe,* westering slopes.

Eynaun, *eidhneáin,* ivy.

Eyon, *eidhean,* not given.

Eyon, *eidhin,* ivy.

Eyrecourt, *dún-an-Uchta,* fort of the bank.

Eyries, *na-hAorí, eirighe,* rising or rising ground.

Eyster, *adhastair,* the halter.

F

Fa, *faiche,* a green.
Fachill, *fáchoill,* underwood.
Fachna, *Fachtna,* St Fachtna.
Fad, *fada, fhada,* long.
Fad, *feadh,* a wood.
Fadd, *fada,* long.
Fadda, *fada, fhada,* long.
Faddan, *feadán,* not given.
Faddaun, *feadan,* a small brook.
Fadden, *feadan,* a small brook.
Fadden, *Pháidín,* not given.
Faddock, *bFeadóg, bhFeadóg,* plover/s.
Faddock, *feadóg,* plovers.
Faddoge, *feadóige,* the plover.
Fadduaga, *feadh-dubhóige/dúbhoige,* not
given.
Fadduaga, *feadh-duaige,* the wood of the
black bog-stuff.
Faddy, *fada, fhada,* long.
Fadeen, *Phaidín, Paudeen,* Paddeen, little
Pat or Paddy, a male name.
Faes, *feá,* the wood.
Faes, *feadha,* woods.
Fafdeen, *Phadín,* little Patrick, a male
name.
Fagh, *faithche,* an exercise green, a green
plot.
Fagher, *Fiachrach,* Fiachra, a personal
name.
Faghla, *fochla,* a cave.
Faghy, *faithche,* a green or a play green.
Faghy, *faithche,* a play green.
Fah, *faithche,* a lawn.
Fah, *fatha,* not given.
Faha, *faiche, faithche, fhaiche,* an exercise
field, a sporting or hurling/field, green
or lawn.
Faha, *fatha,* fields.

Fahalea, *faithche,* a green lawn.
Fahan, *fán,* a slope.
Fahan, *fathain,* a burial place.
Fahan, *fathain,* little green plot.
Fahan, *fathain-Mhura,* not given.
Fahana, *faiche-na...,* green of the...
Fahane, *faithchean,* a little green plot, field
or exercise green.
Fahavan, *fathamhain,* not given.
Fahee, *fatha,* a field.
Faheen, *fhaichín,* not given.
Faheens, from *faithche,* little green plots.
Faheeran, *faiche-Chairáin, faithche-Chiarain,*
Ciaran's green or green plot.
Faher, *fachair,* a shelf or shelving land.
Faherlaghroe, *fatha-an-loch-rúadh,* red field
by the lake(sic).
Fahnia, *bhFaithnidhe,* warts.
Fahouragh, *faithche-ordha,* golden lawn.
Fahy, *fhaiche, faithche, faiche,* a green or an
exercise/sporting green.
Faia, *faithche, faiche,* an exercise green or a
green plot.
Failmore, *failmir*(sic), not given.
Fair, *for,* outlying.
Fairlane, *bóthar-an-aonaigh,* not given.
Fairtahy, *an-feartacha,* not given.
Faithlegg, *fáithling, féathlóg, feidlinn, féidh-
linn, féithlinn, féibhlinn, faithlig,* not given.
Fal, *fál,* a field, hedge, a fence, a close, a
hedged in or enclosed field, an enclo-
sure or wall.
Fal, *fál,* a boundary.
Fal, *fháil, fhál,* not given.
Faladin, *feleádain,* woodbine.
Falcon, *Faolcon,* not given.
Falcon, *phocáin,* a buck goat.
Faldra, *fallach,* not given.
Falee, *failghe,* a pig sty.
Fall, *fál, fall,* an enclosed field, a close, a
hedge or an enclosure.
Falla, *bhaile,* not given.
Falla, *faille, aill, faille,* slope/s.
Falla, *fal-an/a'...,* hedge or enclosure of
the...
Falla, *folach,* not given.
Fallagh, *Falach, fhallach,* not given.
Fallagh, *falach,* hidden.
Fallagh, *fálach,* hedged or a place of
hedges.

Fallaghearn, *fál-an-chaorthainn,* hedge of rowan.

Fallaghloon, *falach-glún-Phadraig,* not given.

Fallan, *abha-na-fallainge,* not given.

Fallan, *fallaine,* the cloak.

Fallaneas, *fál-Aonaosa,* not given.

Falleen, *faillin, faillín,* little cliff.

Falleen, *falluin,* hedges, enclosures.

Falleena, *faillín-an…,* little cliff of the…

Falleens, *falluínidhe,* little enclosures.

Falleeny, *na-faillíní,* not given.

Falleeny, *faluínidh, falluínidhe, faluinidhe,* (little) hedges, enclosures.

Fallen, *Faithleann,* not given.

Fallen, *Faithlenn,* Faithlenn, Faithle, Fathlenn or Faithleann, the name of an ancient pagan chief.

Fallia, *faille,* a precipice.

Fallin, *fall-an….,* hedge or enclosure of the…

Fallinerlea, *fall-an-fhir-liath,* hedge or enclosure of the grey haired man.

Fallougher, *fál-luachra,* rushy enclosure.

Fallow, a hedge or enclosure.

Fallow, *fál,* a boundary or hedge.

Fallow, *fala,* a field.

Falls (the, in Belfast), *tuath-na-bhFál,* district, land of the hedges or enclosures.

Falmore, *falmair,* not given.

Falna, *fál-na…,* field of the…

Falone, Faloon or Fallon, a personal or family name.

Falone, *Mhaoileoin,* not given.

Falsk, *failsce,* not given.

Falsk, *fal-sce, fal-sceach,* hedge of thorn bushes.

Faltagh, *fáltach,* not given.

Faltagh, from *fál,* a place of hedges.

Faltia, from *fál,* places of hedges.

Falty, from *fál,* places of hedges.

Faltybanes, from *fál,* place of white hedges or white enclosed fields.

Fama, *Fama,* not given.

Famma, *fásach, fasach,* not given.

Fan, *fán,* a slope, sloping land or a declivity.

Fan, *fionn,* white.

Fana, *fánaid, fánadh, fanach, fána, fanad,* sloping ground, slope or declivity.

Fana, *fán-an…,* hill slope of the…

Fana, *fán-an…,* not given.

Fana, *féanna,* not given.

Fanad, *fanad,* sloping ground.

Fanad, *fánaid,* not given.

Fanaghan, *fánaghan,* a little slope.

Fanaghans, from *fánagh,* little slopes.

Fanaghs, *fionn-achaidh,* white or whitish fields.

Fanaghy, *fionnachaidh, fionnchaidh*(sic), not given.

Fanaghy, *Fionna-chon, Fionnchon,* Finchu or Finn-chu, the name of an ancient chief. The names means 'fair hound'.

Fanahy, *fan-achadh,* sloping fields.

Fanahy, *fionnachaidh, fionn-achadh,* white field.

Fanahy, *fionn-fhaithche,* white excercise lawn or ground.

Fanan, *fán-an…,* slope of the…

Fancroft, *fionnchora, finn-choradh,* white weir.

Fancy, *fuinnse,* ash trees.

Fane, *abhainn-átha-féan, abha-bhán,* not given.

Fane, *abha-na-Féinne,* not given.

Fane, *mheadhon,* middle.

Fane, *Feinne,* the Fianna.

Fane, *feinne,* wild.

Fane, *Pháan*(sic), *Pháin,* St Pán.

Fane, *Phaoin,* St Paan.

Fanit, *fánaid, fánadh, fanad,* sloping ground, slope or declivity.

Fanit, *feánait,* not given.

Fannad, *fánaid,* the slope.

Fannan, a personal or family name.

Fannan, *Feanann,* not given.

Fanned, *Feannaid,* not given.

Fannog, *bhFeannóg,* scaldcrows.

Fannoge, *bhFeannóg,* scaldcrows.

Fanny, *feadhna,* not given.

Fanog, *bhFeannóg,* the crow.

Fanoky, *fionnoice,* a royston crow.

Fanta, *fánta,* slopes or hill sides.

Fantane, *fantán,* not given.

Fantane, from *fán,* (a slope), *fantáin, fántan, fánta,* sloping land, shelved hillside, little slope or slopes.

Fanure, *finnabhair,* a place of yews.

Fanygalvan, *fán-Ua-Galamhán,* O'Galvan's (a family name) declivity.

Far, *bhFear,* not given.

Far, *far,* outer.

Far, *fear,* grass, grassy.

Far, *bhFear, feara,* men.

Far, *fiar,* winding.

Far, *for, far,* top.

Far, *for,* outlying.

Farabogue, from *fearb,* a strip of land.

Faragh, *Farcha,* not given.

Faraghan, *farachain,* not given.

Faraghaun, *farrachain,* not given.

Faraghy, *farachadh,* not given.

Faragy, *fairche,* not given.

Faraha, *fairche,* territory.

Farahy, *fairche,* the parish.

Farbil, *fear-bile,* not given.

Farbill, *feara-bile,* men of the ancient tree.

Farboy, *bhFear-mbuidhe,* yellow men.

Farbreague, *fear-bréighe,* the false man.

Farbregagh, *fear-breige,* a tall rock in the sea or a standing stone called 'the false man'.

Farcan, *bhFarcan,* knotty oaks.

Farcan, *farcain,* not given.

Fardrum, *fardroim, fordrum,* not given.

Fardrum, *fordhroim, fardhroim,* top of the ridge.w

Fargarve, *bhFear-nGarbh,* rough men.

Fargy, *Fearga,* not given.

Faria, *pónaire,* beans.

Faris, *Feargus, Fergus,* a male name.

Farkshina, *faircsiona,* the prospect.

Farlough, *for-loch,* outlying lake.

Farlow, *for-loch,* outlying lake.

Farmley, *sceachanach,* not given.

Farmley, *fearann-lia,* territory or land of grey aspect.

Farn, *fearann,* land/s.

Farn, *fearna,* alder trees.

Farna, an alder plantation.

Farna, *fearnach,* a place of alders.

Farna, *fearran-an…,* land of the…

Farnagh, *fearnaidh, fearnach, fearna,* alder, alders or alder land.

Farnagh, *fornocht, farnocht,* an exposed or bare hill.

Farnaghan, *fearnacháin, fearnachán,* alders, an alder plantation.

Farnaghan, *fearnach-an…,* alder place of the…

Farnaght, *farnocht, fornocht,* a bare, naked or exposed hill.

Farnamurry, *fearann-Mhaolmhuire,* not given.

Farnan, *fearnáin, ferna,* alder or alder wood.

Farnan, *fearnán,* alder plantation.

Farnane, *fearnaidh, feárnán, fearnán, fearna, fearnain,* alders, alder land.

Farnanes, *na-fearnáin/fearnain/fearnáin,* a place of alders.

Farnans, *na-fearnáin,* not given.

Farnard, *fearann-ard,* high enclosures(sic).

Farnaught, *farnocht,* a bare hill.

Farne, *fearna,* alders.

Farnees, *fearnach,* a place of alders.

Farneigh, *fearnaigh,* not given.

Farney, *fearnaidh, fearna,* alders or alder land.

Farney, *fearnmhagh, fearn-mhagh,* the alder plain.

Farney, *fearnmhuighe,* place of alders(sic).

Farnham, *fearnáin,* alder.

Farnham, *Fearnáin, Farannáin, Farannain, Farannan,* a male name.

Farnham, Fearnan, a personal or family name.

Farnoge, *fearnaidh, fearna,* alders or alder land.

Farnoge, *fhearnóg, fearnóg,* not given.

Farnogh, *fearnaidh, fearna,* alders or alder land.

Farnoght, *fornocht,* an exposed hill.

Farnon, *fearnáin, fearnach,* not given.

Faroese (Islands), *na-Scigirí,* not given.

Farra, *bheara,* the spike.

Farra, *farrach,* the meeting place..

Farrach, *forrgea* (Latin) a place where meetings are held.

Farragans, *na-fargáin,* not given.

Farragh, *farrach* (Irish), *forrgea* (Latin) a place where meetings are held.

Farragh, *farrach,* an old measure of land.

Farrahy, *fairge,* the sea.

Farran, *fearann,* Church or glebe land.

Farran, *fearann,* land or territory.

Farran, *fearann-Bharra,* not given.

Farran, *fearann,* a ploughland (a land measure equal to 120 acres).

Farran, *fearn,* alders.

Farrana, *fearann,* not given.

Farrana, *fearran-na…, fearann-an/a'…,* land of the…

Farranaleen, *fearann-Mháibín*(sic), not given.

Farranaraheen, *fearann-Craithín*(sic), not given.

Farranasa, *fearann-Ásaigh,* not given.

Farrane, *fearann-na…,* land of the…

Farraneen, *fearainnín,* small townland.

Farraneesteenig, *fearann-an-Ístíngh,* not given.

Farraneshagh, *fearann-Eiseach,* not given.

Farranna, *fearran-na…, fearann-na/a'…,* land of the…

Farrassy, *Fheargasa,* not given.

Farrassy, *Fhearghusa,* Fergus a personal name.

Farrell, *Fearaíl,* not given.

Farren, *fearan, féaran,* land.

Farren, *fearan-na-seisíghe,* the land of the ploughland.

Farrihy, *fairche,* not given.

Farrihy, *fhairche,* territory.

Farrin, *fearan, féaran,* land.

Farris, *Fhearghuis, Feargus,* Fergus, a male name.

Farris, *fhoraoise, foraoiseach,* forest country.

Farrnagh, *fearnaidh, fearna,* alders or alder land.

Farrow, *forrgea* (Latin) a place where meetings are held.

Farry, *Fearadhaigh,* Farry, a personal or family name.

Farry, *forrgea* (Latin) a place where meetings are held.

Farsad, *feirste,* not given.

Farsan, *fearsan,* the spindle or sandbank ford.

Farset, *farset, fearsad, fast,* a river sandbank or sandbank ford.

Farset, *fearsad,* sandbank.

Farsid, *farset, fearsad, fast,* a river sandbank.

Farsid, *fearsad,* a sandbank at the mouth of a river.

Farsid, *fearsad,* a sandbank.

Farson, a parson or parish priest.

Farsoon, *pearsan,* the parson.

Farta, *fearta,* graves.

Farta, *feartach,* not given.

Fartagh, *ferta, feartach, fertach,* a grave, graves or a place of graves.

Fartha, *fearta,* graves.

Farthawn, *feartan,* little grave.

Farty, *fertach,* a place of graves.

Fas, *fás,* a wilderness.

Fasagh, *fásach,* uncultivated or a wilderness.

Fasey, *fhásaigh,* waste land.

Fasky, *Foscaidh,* not given.

Fasoge, *feasoige,* bearded.

Fassa, *fasach, fasach,* wasteland.

Fassagh, *fásach,* a wilderness.

Fassaugh, *fásach,* a wilderness.

Fassidinan, *fásach-an-dianin,* swift river pasture-lands.

Fassy, *fásaigh, fasaigh,* a wilderness.

Fast, *farset, feirste, fearsad, fast,* river sandbank/s.

Fastnet, *carraig-Aonair,* not given.

Fastry, *fástrach,* a wilderness.

Fastry, *fastraigh, fásdoire,* not given.

Fasy, *fásaigh,* wilderness.

Fatheen, *faiche,* a green.

Fathom, (hill), *feadan,* streamlet.

Fatten, *Phaidín, Paudeen,* little Pat, Paddy, a man or boys name.

Fatten, *Phaitean,* not given.

Fatten, *pheatan,* pets.

Fatthen, *faiteann, faithche-aiteann,* field of furze.

Faudeen, *Phaidín,* little Patrick.

Faugh, *fada,* long.

Faugh, *foathaigh,* giants.

Faughan, (river) *fachan,* not given.

Faughanvale, *nua-congbhail,* new habitation.

Faughanvale, *nuadhchonghbháil,* not given.

Faughara, *fachaire,* the shelving side.

Faughart, *fochaird, fachard-Mhuintheimhne,* not given.

Faughart, *fochart,* a cast or throw.

Faugheen, *faichín,* not given.

Faugher, *an-fhothair, foithreach, fachar,* not given.

Faugher, *fachair,* a shelf, a cliff shelf or shelving land.

Faughil, *fachlach,* a crack in moorland after drought.

Faughil, *fáchoill, fo-choill,* underwood.

Faughill, *fáchoill,* underwood.

Faughna, *Fachtna, Fhachtna, Fachtna,* St Fachtna/Faghtna/Fachtnan.

Faughny, *Fachtna,* Fachtna, a persons name.

Faugill, *fachlach,* a split in moorish ground from drought.

Fauhill, *fo-choill,* underwood.

Faul, *fál,* the hedge.

Faulagh, *fálach,* not given.

Faulagh, from *fál,* a place of hedges.

Fauleens, *failíni,* little hedges.

Fauleens, *na-fáilíní,* not given.

Faulish, a fairy fort.

Faulish, *phailíse,* not given.

Faulish, *phálais,* a mansion or palace.

Faulties, from *fál,* places of hedges.

Faun, *fáin, fán, fan,* a slope

Faun, *fan,* sloping,

Fauna, *fana, fáine,* a slope.

Fauna, *fánadh,* not given.

Fauna, *fán-na...,* declivity of the...

Faus, *fás,* waste or wilderness.

Fauskeen, *Pháiscín,* not given.

Faussagh, *fásach,* uncultivated, a wilderness.

Fawans, *fána,* slopes.

Fawans, *na-fánaibh,* not given.

Fawn, *fáin, fán,* a slope or declivity.

Fawna, *fána,* slope/s.

Fawna, *fán-na...,* not given.

Fawney, *fanaidh,* the slope.

Fawnia, *fáine,* the slope.

Fay, *bheithe,* birch.

Faythe, *faithche,* a sporting green.

Fea, a field.

Fea, *feá, fiadhaigh,* not given.

Fea, *feadh,* bulrushes.

Fea, *feadha,* strong or great.

Fea, feithe, a swamp.

Fea, *féich,* the raven.

Fea, *feigh,* ravens.

Fea, *feith,* a marshy stream.

Fea, *féith,* a shaking bog.

Fea, *féith,* a stream.

Fea, *feith,* a wet trench.

Fea, *fhéith,* not given.

Fea, *fia, fiadh,* deer.

Fea, *fia,* uncultivated land

Fea, *fiodh, fidh,* a wood.

Feacle, *fiacail, fiacla,* a tooth.

Feacle, *Fiachna,* Fiachna, a personal or family name.

Feadalea, from *fead/fid,* a whistle or whistling.

Feagarrid, *fhéith/féith-ghairid,* the short shaking bog.

Feagarroge, *fiadha-garabhróg,* a place of wild mustard.

Feagh, *féabh, fidh,* a wood.

Feagh, *feádh,* deer or a wood.

Feagh, *fiach, fhiaigha,* ravens.

Feagh, *fiaidh,* deer.

Feagh, *Fíoch,* not given.

Feagh, *fiodhach, fiodheach,* a woody place.

Feaghan, *Fhéicín,* Féichín, a personal or family name and the founder of a Church in Donegal.

Feaghna, *Fiachna,* not given.

Feaghna, *Fhachtna(sic),* Fachtna, a personal or family name.

Feaghna, *Fiachra*(sic), St Fiachra.

Feaghra, Fiachra, a personal or family name.

Feaghra, *fiadha,* bushes or underwood.

Feaha, *féithe,* the boggy stream.

Feahoe, *fiodh-átha-hO,* not given.

Feakle, *fhiacail, fiacla, fiacal, fiacall, fhiacal,* a tooth or teeth.

Feakle, (Kilfeakle) *Cill-Fhiacal,* not given

Feakle, *fhiadhchoill,* not given.

Feakle, *Fiacle,* a male name.

Feale, *abha-Fhéil/Fhéil/Feile,* a river in Limerick, not given.

Feale, from *Fiail,* river named after a woman who drowned in it.

Feale, *Feil, Fial,* Fial, a female name, wife of Lewy.

Feale, *Féile,* not given.

Fean, *feadhan,* overgrown with weeds.

Fean, *Feinne, Féinne, b-Fiann,* the Fianna.

Fean, *Liadhain,* Liadhan, a female name, (mother of St Kieran).

Feana, *bhFiann,* the Fianna, an ancient heroic militia.

Fear, *fiair, fear, fér, féur,* grass, a grassy place or a meadow.

Fear, *fiar,* not given.

Fearagh, *bFiarach,* lea fields.

Fearagh, *bhFiarach, fearagh, fearagha,* grassy fields.

Fearagh, *bhFiarach,* meadows.

Fearagh, *féarach, fiarach,* a grassy field or spot.

Fearagh, *Fiachrach,* not given.

Fearagh, *Fiarach,* St Fiarach.

Fearaghalee, *fiarachadh-liath,* not given.

Feard, *fiodha-Áird, feá/fiodh/feadha-aird,* the high wood.

Feargah, *Fhiachrach,* Fiachra, a personal or family name and a founder of a Church in Clare.

Fearn, *fearn, fearna,* alders trees.

Fearna, *fearann-na…,* land of the…

Fearnahan, *fearnacháin,* a place of alders.

Fearnog, *bhFearnóg,* alders.

Fearoe, *fia-rua,* not given.

Feathallagh, *fiataíolach,* not given.

Feathallagh, *fiataileach,* a place of coarse grass clumps.

Feaugh, *fiodhach,* woody.

Feckin, *Feichín, Féichín,* St. Fechin.

Feckin, *Féichín,* not given.

Fedamore, *feadamair,* abounding in streams.

Fedamore, *feadamair,* wood of Damar, not given.

Fedamore, *fedomair,* not given.

Fedany, *feadanach,* a place of streams.

Feddaly, *feadaíle,* not given.

Feddaly, from *fead, fid,* a whistle or whistling.

Feddan, *feadan,* a small brook.

Feddans, *an-feadán, na-feadáin,* not given.

Feddaun, *feadán,* a small brook.

Feddock, *feadog, feadóg,* plover/s.

Feddock, *Pheadoc,* not given.

Feddy, *feada,* not given.

Fedia, *fede,* a streamlet.

Fedoo, *fiodh-dubh,* not given.

Fedora, *fhíodóra,* not given.

Fee, *fiadha,* rough land.

Fee, *fidh, fioda, fiodh, feadha, fid,* a wood.

Feeagh, *fiadhach, fiobhach, fiobhach, fiodheach,* a woody place.

Feebagh, a woody place.

Feebagh, *fadhbach,* not given.

Feebeg, *fidh-beg,* little wood.

Feebeg, *fiodh-bheag,* not given.

Feed, *Fíd,* not given.

Feedarragh, *fiodh-darrach*(sic), wood of oak.

Feede, *Fíd,* not given.

Feedora, *fhigheadóra,* weavers.

Feedora, *fhíodóra,* not given.

Feedy, from *fead, fid,* a whistle or whistling.

Feeganny, *fiodh-gainimh,* not given.

Feegat, *fidh-gCat,* wood of the cats.

Feegh, *fiodh,* a wood.

Feeghs, from *fiodh,* woods.

Feeghs, *na-feá,* not given.

Feela, *feighile,* watching.

Feelagh, *fuighleach,* the 'other' portion.

Feelagh, *fuíollach,* not given.

Feelagh, *Fuíollach,* not given.

Feelough, *piodhlach,* shrubbery.

Feemore, *fidh-mór,* big wood.

Feemore, *fia-mór,* not given.

Feen, *fiadhian,* rough land.

Feen, *fionn,* clear, pleasant.

Feenagh, *fhiadhanach, fineach, fineadha, fiodhnach, fíonach,* a woody/wooded place.

Feenaghty, *Finachta,* Feenaghty or Finaghty, a personal or family name.

Feenan, *fiodhnán,* a woody place.

Feenan, *Fíonáin,* not given.

Feenaun, *Faonáin, Faonán,* not given.

Feenick, *fionnach,* old.

Feenish, *fiadh/fiodh/fidh-inis,* woody island.

Feenla, *faoilinne,* seagulls.

Feenune, *fineamhain,* an osier growth.

Feeny, *Fhíne, fíodhnach,* not given.

Feeny, *Fine,* Fine, a personal or family name.

Feeny, *fineadha, fiodhnach,* a woody place.

Feeny, *fineadhna,* woods.

Feeny, *Finne,* Fenny, a personal or family name.

Feeny, *Finna,* a female name.

Feeny, *Uí-Féinneadha,* O'Feeny, a family name.

Feepera, *piobaire, the* piper/s.

Feer, *feir,* grass.

Feer, *feir,* long.

Feer, *fior,* a stream.

Feeradda, *feir-fhada,* long grass.

Feeradda, *fiorfhada,* not given.

Feerina, *Fírinne,* not given.

Feerisca, *fior-uisce,* pure water.

Feerode, *Phéaróid,* Perrot, a family name.

Feerode, *Phiaróidigh,* Piaróideach, not given.

Feerulagh, *fíor-ullach,* proud stream.

Feeva, *fiodhbha,* the wood.

Feevagh, *fíodhbhach,* a woody place.

Fehadee, *bhFeithidí,* not given.

Fehadee, *feithe-duibhe,* black swamp/boggy stream.

Fehadee, *bFeithidí,* serpents or insects.

Fehanagh, *fiodhanach,* a woody place.

Fehil, *Uí-Fhithchill,* Fehil or Field, a family name.

Fehoonree, *Féichiúin-an-Rí,* not given.

Feigh, *faiche, faithche,* an exercise green, a green, a green plot or a playing/sports field.

Feigh, *fia, Mheidhbh,* not given.

Feigh, *fiach,* a raven.

Feigh, *fidh, fiodh, fidh, fid,* a wood.

Feigh, *fiodh,* a wood.

Feigh, *fíodhach,* woody.

Feighny, *Feichne,* not given.

Feightrin, *eachtrann,* strangers.

Feilim, *Feilim,* Feilim, a personal or family name.

Fela, *féile,* hospitality.

Felane, *faolán, faolan,* a wild place or a steep slope.

Felane, *Mhaolain,* Maolan, a male name.

Feley, *féile,* hospitality.

Felim, *Eibhlinne,* Eibhlinn, a personal or family name.

Felim, *Feidhlimidh, Feidhlim,* St Felim.

Felim, *Fhéidhlim,* not given.

Felimy, *Feilimidh,* not given.

Felin, *Feidhlim,* not given.

Felliv, *feillimh,* treachery.

Felly, *feille,* not given.

Feloree, *feileoirí,* not given.

Felt, *Fíolta, Fiolta,* Fiolta or Fíolta, a personal or family name.

Felt, rushy(sic).

Feltrim, *faeldruim,* wolf hill/ridge.

Feltrim, *faoldruim,* not given.

Fenagh, (lough) *loch-salach,* not given.

Fenagh, *fineadha, fiodhnach, fíonacha,* a woody place.

Fenagh, *fíodhnach, fiodhnacha, fíonacha,* a woody place.

Fenane, *fionán,* white coloured land.

Fenane, *fionnán, an-fionnán-mór,* not given.

Fenit, *fhianait, fianait,* the wild place.

Fenit, *fhiannait,* not given.

Fennagh, *fionnmhach,* the white plain.

Fennagh, *fionnmhagh,* not given.

Fennel, *Fionaíle,* not given.

Fennel, *Fionghaile,* murder or Fionghaile, a personal or family name.

Fennell, *Finéil,* Finéal, not given.

Fennor, *finnabhair,* a whitish place.

Fennor, *fionnabhair,* white field.

Fennor, *fionnúir,* not given.

Fennor, *fionnúr,* white water.

Fennor, *fionúbhair,* a fair hill.

Fenoagh, *fionnmhagh, fionnúch,* not given.

Fenor, *fionnabhair,* not given.

Fenor, *fionnúir,* white field.

Fenor, *fionnúr,* white water.

Fenor, the white spot.

Fenor, *fionnaghar,* whitish plain.

Fenora, *abhraoidh,* shaped like an eyebrow.

Fenora, *Fhionnúrach,* Fionnúir not given.

Fenora, *finnabhair,* a whitish place.

Fenora, *Fionnabhrach, Fhionnúrach,* St Fionnuir/Fionnúir.

Fenough, *fiodhnach,* woody.

Fenough, *Fhionnúdhach,* not given.

Fenrath, *fionnabhrach,* not given.

Fentony, *Fhionntain,* Fintan, a personal or family name.

Feohanagh, *fheothanach, feothanach,* a place of thistles.

Feola, *feóla,* the flesh.

Feorish, *fodras,* pale greyness.

Fer, *fear, feara,* men.

Fer, *féar,* grass or grassy.

Feragh, a grassy spot.

Feragh, *Fiachrach, Fíora,* not given.

Feragh, *Fiachra,* St-Fiachra.

Feraghs, *na-féaracha,* not given.

Ferbane, *féar-bán,* white grass.

Ferbane, *fhéir-bhain,* not given.

Fereen, *Phéirín,* not given.

Fereen, *Phirín,* Pierce, a personal or family name.

Fergus, (river) *an-Fhorgas,* not given.

Fergus, *Fhearghasa, Fhearghusa, Fheargusa, Feargus,* Fearghas or Fergus, a male name.

Fergus, *Fhearghasa,* St Fergus.

Ferguson, *Uí-Fherguis,* O'Fergus, a family name.

Ferigeen, *Aimhirgín,* Aimhirgín, a personal or family name.

Ferine, *feirín,* a small flange.

Feris, *Feargus,* Fergus, a male name.

Feris, *Phiarais,* not given.

Ferm, *feirm,* a farm.

Fermanagh, *fear-Manach, fir-Monach,* men of Monach, an ancient chief.

Fermanagh, *fearmonach,* not given.

Fermot, *Diarmuid,* Dermot, a male name.

Fermot, *Thormaid,* Thormund, a Norman personal or family name.

Fermoy, *feara-muighe-feine, fearamuighe,* men of the plain of the 'Fians' (a militia once led by Finn mac Coole.)

Fermoy, *fhear-maige, feara-muighe,* the men of the Plain.

Fermoy, *mainistir-fhear-muighe/maí/maige,* monastery of the men of the plain.

Fermoyle, *formaeil, formael,* a round hill.

Fermoyle, *formaoil,* not given.

Fern, *bhFearn, fearna,* alders,

Fern, *fearann,* land or territory.

Fern, *fearna,* alders trees.

Fernagh, *fearna,* alders.

Fernagh, *fearnach,* alders.

Fernagh, *fearnaidh, fearna,* alders or alder land.

Fernaghan, *fearnachán,* alders or an alder plantation.

Fernaghan, *fearnach an...,* alder place of the...

Fernanes, *fearnain,* a place of alders.

Fernasky, *fearnaisce,* not given.

Fernasky, *féarnascaigh,* long grass.

Ferney, *fearna,* alders.

Ferns, *bhFearn, fearna,* a place of alders.

Ferns, *fearna-Maodhóg, Fernigenan,* not given.

Ferr, *fear, feara,* men.

Ferrall, *Fearghaill,* Fearghal, a personal or family name.

Ferran, *fearan,* land.

Ferrard, *fir-arda/árda, feara-arda,* men of the height.

Ferridy, *Feardaigh,* Ferdy, a personal or family name.

Ferris, *Fearghusa,* Ferris, a personal or family name.

Ferriter, *Feirtéaraigh, Fheirtéaraigh, Fheirtéirigh,* Feirtéar or Ferriter, a family name.

Ferry, *peireadh,* not given.

Ferry, *pheire,* the ferry.

Ferrycarrig, *glas-charraig,* not given.

Fersey, *fearsad,* a sandbank at the mouth of a river.

Fersha, *feirste,* a sandbank ford.

Ferskel, *bhFeirscill,* a grassy field.

Ferst, *farset,* a sandbank ford or a spindle.

Ferst, *farset, feirste,* a ford or a sandbank ford.

Fert, *feirt, fhearta, ferta, fert,* a grave.

Ferta, *ferta,* a place of graves.

Fertagh, *fearta,* a place of graves.

Fertagh, *ferta, feartach, fertach,* a grave or a place of graves.

Fertaun, *an-féartán,* not given.

Ferti, *ferta,* a place of graves.

Fertiana, *feart-Éanna,* not given.

Fertiana, *feart-Uí-Eanna,* the grave of O'Henry.

Fest, *feirste,* the ferry.

Feston, *Phiastúin, Feistean,* not given.

Feth, *fidh, fiodh, fídh, fid,* a wood.

Fethard, *fiodh-ard/árd,* the high wood.

Fethereen, from *fead,* little streamlet.

Fethernagh, from *fead,* a place abounding in brooks.

Feugh, *fiodhach,* woody land.

Fevata, *féith-bháite,* land subject to flooding.

Fews, *fiodha, feadha, feadhna, feá,* woods.

Fews, *fiodh-Conaille, Parróiste-na-bhFíodh,* not given.

Fews, *Paráiste-na-bhFíodh,* Parish of the woods.

Fey, *faiche, faithche,* an exercise green or a green plot.

Ffolus, *follus,* bright.

Fha, giants.

Fhraoch, *fraoch,* heath.

Fi, *fidh,* a wood.

Fian, *bh-Fian,* Fians(sic).

Fian, *Fian,* not given.

Fiba, *fadhbach,* not given.

Fiba, *fiodhbhach, fiabach,* woody.

Ficka, *phice,* not given.

Fickil, *fiada-choille,* the wild wood.

Ficulla, *fiacla,* tooth shaped rocks.

Fid, *bhFead,* streamlets.

Fid, *feide,* a streamlet or runnel.

Fid, *feide, fead,* a whistle or streamlet.

Fid, *feide,* the end.

Fid, *fidh, fidh, fid,* a wood.

Fid, *fidh, fiodh, fidh, fid,* a wood.

Fidachta, *fhiodachta,* not given.

Fiddan, *feadan, feadán,* a small brook, runnel, hill or streamlet.

Fiddane, *feadán, feadan,* a small brook.

Fiddaun, *feadan,* a small brook.

Fiddaun, *feadan, feadán,* a small brook, runnel, hill or streamlet.

Fiddaunna, *feadán-na…,* not given.

Fiddown, *fiodh-dúin/dhúin,* wood of the fort.

Fide, *fid, fide,* a brook or brooklet.

Fidhane, *feadan, feadán,* a small brook, runnel, hill or streamlet.

Fie, *faithche, faiche,* a green, an exercise green or a green plot.

Field, *Ó-bhFicheallaigh,* Uí Fhicheallach, a family name.

Fienragh, *fionnabhrach,* the fair hill.

Fieries, *foidhrí, foithre,* woods, underwood or copse.

Fieries, *foidhrí,* slopes.

Fierna, a fairy.

Fierna, *firinne,* truth, truthful prediction.

Fiert, *Fírchirt,* not given.

Fiffy, *faithche,* an exercise green.

Figanny, *fiodh-gainimh,* sandy wood.

Figart, *fiadhghort,* not given.

Figart, *fiodh-ghart,* woody enclosure.

Figh, *fidh,* a wood.

Figile, *fhiodh-gaibhle,* wood of the fork, this is also the name of a river.

Figile, *fiodh-gaibhle,* not given.

Figlash, *fiodh-glaise,* not given.

Figullar, *fiodh-dhuilleabair,* wood of the foliage.

Figullar, *fiodh-Dhuilliúir/iolar,* not given.

Fiherta, *mítheirteach, fidh-fheartach,* woody land.

Fihertagh, *fiodhartach,* woody land.

Fihidy, *na-fichidí,* the twenties.

Fihoges, *na-faitheógaidhe,* little green lawns.

Fihoragh, *faithchorach,* grey plain.

Fika, *fic,* a spear.

Filan, *Bhaoighealláin,* Boylan, a personal or family name.

File, *faill,* slope of declivity.

File, *phoill,* an inlet.

Filea, *faill-a'…,* slope or declivity of….

Fillon, *bhFaoileann,* seagulls.

Fin, *fine,* territory or tribe.

Fin, Finn or O'Finn, a family name.

Fin, Finn, Finn McCoole.

Fin, *Finn,* Fionn, a personal name.

Fin, *Finna,* a female name.

Fin, *finne,* the white cow.

Fin, *fionn, finn,* clear, bright, fair, white or whitish.

Fin, *Fionn,* not given.

Fina, *faighne, phaghanaigh,* not given.

Fina, *fine,* white cow.

Fina, *fiodhíne,* a green field.

Fina, *na-Fianna,* na Fianna.

Finaghoo, *fionn-achadh,* whitish or fair field.

Finaghy, *fionnachadh,* the white field.

Finagle, *fionngaile, fiongaile,* not given.

Finagle, *fionghal,* fratricide (murder of a near relative).

Finahy, *fionnachadh,* white field.

Finan, *fionnán,* land of long whiteish grass.

Finanagh, *fidh-an-eanach,* forest land beside the marsh.

Finanagh, *fionnánach,* whitish land.

Finane, Fhionán, Fhionáin, Fhionain, St Fíonán/Finan.

Finane, *Fionnáin,* not given.

Finaway, *finn-mhagh,* white plain.

Finboy, *finnmhuigh,* the fair plain.

Finboy, *fionnmhaí,* not given.

Finch, *finch,* bubbling.

Finch, *fuinse,* a ford(sic).

Finch, *fúinse, fuinse, fuinnse,* ash.

Finchin, *fuinnsean, fuinseann, fuinsinn, fuinnsin,* ash trees.

Fine, *fhiadhain, fiadhain,* wild or wild land.

Fine, *fine,* a tribe or territory.

Fine, *Fionn,* not given.

Fine, *Phaghain, Paghan,* not given.

Finea, *fiodh-an-átha,* wood of the ford.

Fineela, *fionghal,* fratricide (murder of a near relative).

Fineen, *Fhingín,* Fhingin, a male name.

Fineen, *Fhínín,* not given.

Fineen, *Finghín, Finghin,* Fingin or Fineen, a male name.

Fineen, *Fingín,* Fingín or Finneen, a personal or family name or Florence, a female name.

Finegan, O'Finnegan, a family name.

Finelly, *fionaíle,* not given.

Finelly, *fionghal,* fratricide (murder of a near relative).

Fineshoge, *fuinseoige,* not given.

Finesker, *fineiscir,* white sand-ridge.

Fingal, *fine-Gall,* not given.

Fingall, land of the foreigners.

Finglas, *finn-glais, fionghlaise, fionghlas, fionghlais, fionnghlaise, fionnghlas,* clear or bright stream.

Finglash, *fiodh-glaise, finn-glais,* wood of the stream.

Finglasha, *finn-glais,* bright chrystal rivulet.

Finglass, *fionghlaise, fionghlais,* bright stream.

Finglass, *fionnghlaise,* not given.

Finglush, *finn-glais,* bright chrystal rivulet.

Fingrean, *finnghreann,* not given.

Finisclin, *fineasclainn, fineas-clainn,* rapid or strong stream.

Finish, *fidhinis, finise,* not given.

Finish, *fínis, Mhaínse,* not given.

Finish, *finn-inse,* white island.

Finish, *fionnuisce,* white or clear water.

Finisk, *an-fhinisc,* not given.

Finisk, *fionn-uisce, fionnuisce,* white water.

Finiskill, *fionn-ascaill,* white corner.

Finisklin, *fineas-clainn,* rapid or strong stream.

Finisklin, *fionasclainn,* not given.

Finlagan, St Finnluga or St Finnloga.

Finlay, *Finnlaoch,* Finlay, a personal or family name.

Finlehid, *finnleithid,* not given.

Finlough, *finnlocha, fionlocha,* clear lake.

Finlough, *finnoch,* not given.

Finn, *fhinn,* not given.

Finn, *Finne,* Finn, Finna, the name of Fergoman's sister.

Finn, *finne,* white or clear.

Finn, *fionn,* fair or whitish.

Finna, *fidh-na…,* wood of the…

Finna, *finn, finne,* white.

Finna, *finne,* the white cow.

Finna, *finn-na…,* whitish land of the…

Finna, *fionnan,* whitish land.

Finnagle, *fionghal,* fratricide (murder of a near relative).

Finnahy, *finnithe,* not given.

Finnahy, *fionn-fhaithche,* white flat, exercise field.

Finnan, *Fhíonáin, Fionain,* St Finan, Fhíonáin.

Finnan, *Fhíonáin, Fíonán,* a personal or family name.

Finnan, Finan, a personal or family name.

Finnan, *Fionnain,* Finnan, a personal or family name.

Finnan, *fionnain,* long coarse grass.

Finnan, *Fionnán,* not given.

Finnane, *Fhíonáin, Fináin, Fionain,* St Fionan/Finan/Fhíonáin.

Finnane, *fionnain,* coarse moor grass.

Finnaun, *fionnán,* not given.

Finne, *finne,* a beautiful woman.

Finnea, *fiodh/fidh-an-atha/átha,* the wood of the ford.

Finned, (river) *an-fhinnghid,* not given.

Finneen, *Finnén,* a personal or family name.

Finneen, *Uí-Fingín,* O'Fineen, a family name.

Finnell, *fionghal,* fratricide (murder of a near relative).

Finner, *finnabhair,* a whitish place.

Finner, *fionnabhair,* white field.

Finney, (river) *an-Ghairge,* not given.

Finnia, *finne,* the white cow.

Finnick, *feannog, fionóige,* a royston or scald crow.

Finnihy, deer stream.

Finnihy, *fhinnithe,* the clear stream.

Finnihy, *finnithe,* sparkling little river.

Finnila, *fionghaile,* not given.

Finnila, *fionghal,* fratricide (murder of a near relative).

Finnis, *fidh-innis*(sic)*, fiodh-Inis,* wooded island.

Finnis, *fionnais,* white ridge.

Finnisglin, *fineas clainn,* rapid or strong stream.

Finnish, *fidh-inis,* wood island.

Finnish, *fionnuisce,* bright water.

Finnisk, *finnisce,* not given.

Finnisk, *finn-uisce,* clear spring.

Finnoe, *fionnú, fionnmhagh,* not given.

Finnoe, *fionúd,* fair river.

Finnog, *feannog, finnoige, fionóige,* a royston or scald crow.

Finnog, *fheannóg,* not given.

Finnoge, *feannóige,* the hooded crow.

Finnoge, *fionnóige, a* scald crow.

Finnoge, *fionnóige, fionoige,* scald crow/s or a royston crow.

Finnoo, *fionnú,* bright hill.

Finnor, *finnabhair,* a whitish place.

Finnor, *fionn-ór,* white coast.

Finnow, *fionúd,* white or transparent river.

Finns, *na-fionna,* white lands.

Finnure, *finnabhair,* a whitish place.

Finny, *Fhinín,* not given.

Finny, *Finghín, Finghin,* Fineen, a personal or family name.

Finny, *Finín,* Finín, Finin, a 7th cent King.

Finny, *Finne,* Finna, a female name.

Finny, *finne,* white.

Finny, *finnfhidh,* fine woods.

Finny, *fiodhnaí,* a wooded place.

Finny, *fionaí,* wood/s.

Finny, *fionnaithe,* not given.

Finny, *fionnáithe,* the white kiln.

Finny, *fionnmhuigh,* not given.

Finny, *na-Fhicne,* not given.

Finoga, *fionoga,* the scaldcrow.

Finoge, *fionóige, fionnog,* scald crows or ravens.

Finogue, *fionóige,* scald crows.

Finora, *finnabhair,* a whitish place.

Finragh, *fionn-ratha,* white fort.

Finshin, *fuinnsinn,* an ash tree.

Finshina, *finsineach, fuinnse,* a place of ash trees.

Finshinagh, *finsineach,* a place of ash trees.

Finshinagh, *fuinseannach,* not given.

Finshoge, *bhfuinnseóg, fuinnseóg,* ash trees.

Fintan, Fintan, a male name.

Fintan, *Fintan,* St Fintan.

Fintan, *Fionntan,* not given.

Finter, *finntír,* not given.

Fintona, *fionntamhnach,* bright clearing(sic).

Fintona, *fionntamhnach,* fair arable field.

Fintona, *fionntamhnach,* white or fair coloured field.

Fintown, *fionntún, baile-na-finne,* not given.

Fintra, *fionn-traigh,* white strand.

Fintragh, *fionntrá, fionntraigh, fionn-traigh,* white strand.

Finuge, *fionnúig,* not given.

Finure, *fionnabhair-na-Ríog,* not given.

Finver, *finnabhair,* a whitish place.

Finvey, *finnmhagh,* bright plain.

Finvoy, *fhionnbhoith,* white cottage(sic).

Finvoy, *fhionnbhoth,* the white hut.

Finvoy, *finn-mhagh,* white plain.

Finvoy, *finnmhuigh,* the fair plain.

Finvoy, *fionnmhaigh, fionnmhagh,* not given.

Fir, (a corruption of) *tír,* land, territory or district.

Fir, *fear, feara,* men.

Fir, *fhír,* a man.

Fir, *fir,* not given.

Fir, *foithir,* a ravine.

Fira, *foithre,* underwood or copse.

Firbregagh, *fear-bréighe,* the false man.

Fircal, *feara-Ceall,* tribe or men of the Churches.

Fireen, *Uí-Mhuirisín,* Morrin, a family name.

Firies, *na-foidhrí,* not given.

Firkeel, *foithir-chaol,* narrow ravine.

Firoda, *fír-Ó-nDuach,* not given.

Firoda, *fioghar-Ó-nDuach,* border lands of Ó Duach (a personal or family name).

Firreen, *Phirín,* Pirín, not given.

Firrib, *feirbe,* cows.

Firrib, *feirbe, firb,* the cow.

Firrib, the stripe or groove.

Firry, *fuire,* not given.

Fish, *fhia, fia,* not given.

Fish, *fidh,* a wood.

Fishmone, *fhia-Múin,* not given.

Fishmoyne, *fia-Múin,* not given.

Fishoge, *fissoige, fuiseóg, fuiseóige,* a lark or larks.

Fishoge, *fuiseoige,* not given.

Fith, *fiodh,* a wood.

Fithmone, *fhia-Múin,* not given.

Fithmone, *fiodh-Mughaine,* wood of Mughain or Mughainia, a female name.

Fithmone, *fiodh-mughaine,* wood of the bog(sic).

Fivealley, *an-Chúirt,* not given.

Fivey, *fiodhbha, fiodhbhaighe,* the wood.

Flacony, *Flacana,* not given.

Flaherty, *Uí-Fhlaitheartaigh,* not given.

Flake, *phleidhce, pleidhce, bpleidhce,* stump or stake.

Flankerhouse, *gort-na-móinbhíolach,* not given.

Flannan, *Flannáin,* Flannan, a personal or faily name.

Flaskagh, *fleascach,* not given.

Flaskagh, from *fleasc,* land or rods.

Flatley, *Uí-Flaithile,* O'Flatley or Flahilly, a family name.

Flats, *magh-réidh,* not given.

Flean, *Flian, Fliain,* not given.

Flesk, (Rathflesk) Flesk, a personal name.

Flesk, (river) *an-Fhleisc,* not given.

Flesk, a bog or well.

Flesk, *fhleisc,* the rod.

Flesk, *fleisce,* a hoop.

Flesk, *fleisce, flesc,* wet.

Fleur, *bhFlúr, Fleur, bPiléar,* not given.

Fleur, *bPilear,* musket balls.

Flin, *Flainn,* Flann, a personal or family name.

Flinn, Flynn, a family name.

Fliuch, *fliuch,* wet.

Fliugh, *fhliuch,* not given.

Fliugh, *fliuch,* wet.

Flower, *lobhar,* the leper.

Fluddy, *ploide,* the puddle.

Fludig, *phlodaig,* a mire.

Fludig, *phludaigh,* not given.

Fludig, *ploda, plodach,* a puddle.

Flugh, *fhliuch, fliuch,* wet or marshy.

Flughan, *fluichain,* wet or spewy places.

Flughanagh, *fluichanach,* a wet or spewy place.

Flughany, *fluichanach,* a wet or spewy place.

Flugherine, *fliucharín,* little wet spot of land.

Flurry (river), *glais-ghalliagh,* not given.

Fly, *phlaigh,* plague.

Flyn, *Fhlainn,* not given.

Flyn, *Flainn,* Flann, a male name.

Flynn, *Flainn,* Flann, a male name.

Flynn, *Flainn,* Flann, a personal or family name and a founder of a Church in Kerry.

Foalies, *fualaí,* a wet place.

Foats, *leathbhaile-an-Iarla,* not given.

Foaty, *fód-Te,* not given.

Foble, *pioboil,* pebble.

Fobole, *phobóil,* not given.

Foda, *fhada, fada,* long.

Fodagh, from *fhóid,* place with a grassy surface or a soddy place.

Fodan, Fodan or Fodahan, a personal or family name.

Fodda, *fhada, fada,* long.

Fodeen, from *fhóid,* little sod or sod covered surface.

Fodeens, from *fhóid,* little sods or sod covered surfaces.

Fodrin, *Pheadraoin,* little Peter, a male name.

Fodry, *fóidre,* a place with a smooth green surface.

Fofanagh, *fofannán, fothannán,* a place of thistles.

Fofanny, *fochmhaine,* not given.

Fofanny, *fofannán, fofannaigh, fothannán,* thistle land or a place of thistles.

Foffanagh, *fofannán, fothannán,* a place of thistles.

Foghanagh, *fofannán, fothannán,* a place of thistles.

Fogher, *fachair,* a shelf or shelving land.

Foghill, *fo-choill,* underwood.

Fohanan, *fhothannáin,* not given.

Fohanan, *fofannán, fothannán,* a place of thistles.

Fohanaun, *fanach,* thistles.

Foher, *fothar,* a dell.

Foher, *fóthar, fóthair,* forest.

Fohera, *fhothrach,* not given.

Fohera, *foithre,* forests.

Foherish, *fothar,* a dell.

Foherish, *fothar-ois,* dell of the fawn.

Foherlagh, *fotharlach,* a place of swamps or woods.

Foherlagh, *fuarlach,* a sedgy place.

Fohill, *fo-thuile,* occasional flooding.

Fohona, *fofannán, fothannán,* a place of thistles.

Fohur, *foithir,* grassland sloping to the cliff edge.

Foil, *fail,* a sty or hut.

Foil, *f-aille, aille, faill,* a cliff.

Foil, *faillín,* a little slope.

Foil, *fhaill,* not given.

Foil, *phoill,* a hole or pool.

Foila, faill-an/a'..., cliff of the...
Foile, phoill, a hole or pit.
Foileen, faillín, a little cliff.
Foileye, faill-Fhiadh, not given.
Foiligh, faill leagha, an eroding cliff.
Foilrim, fhaill-drim, a steep valley(sic).
Foilyclera, O'Cleary's cliff.
Fola, fuil, fola, bloody.
Folan, fodhaladhn, litigation.
Folan, O'Fullan or O'Folan, a family name.
Folan, Uí-Fualain, a family name.
Foleen, Phóilín, Póilín or little Paul, a male name.
Foley, Fhoglúdha, O'Foley or Foley, a family name.
Foll, f-aille, aille, faill, a cliff.
Folla, fola, blood.
Folliard, Folliard, a family name.
Follistran, folastrann, flaggers.
Foly, Fallainge, not given.
Fomina, feamna, feamain, a type of seaweed.
Fona, phomhaire, beans.
Fona, póna, phóna, a pound.
Fone, mhóin, bog.
Fooey, fuaithe, the spectre or phantom.
Fooha, fothach, wildrness.
Fook(sic), *Fhuilc*, Fulk or Fulco, a personal or family name.
Fooka, phúca, púca, pooka, goblin or sprite.
Fookeen, Phúcúin, an-phúicín, not given.
Fookon, Phúcúin, Púcún, not given.
Fookoon, Phúcúin, Púcún, not given.
Foor, fhuair, fuar, cold.
Foora, fuaire, hard water or lime in the water.
Foora, fuaire, very cold.
Fooran, fuaráin, a cold spring.
Fooraun, fuarán, cold spring well.
Foore, fhuar, fuar, cold.
Fora, fóire, beans.
Fora, foithre, a woody swamp or hollow.
Foran, feorainne, a brink, river meadow or holm.
Foran, feoranna, beach or shore.
Foran, fuaráin, not given.
Foran, fuarán, cold spring.
Foraun, fuarán, cold spring.

Foravane, Furodhrain, St Furodhran.
Forawns, from *fobharán* or *fotharán*, not given.
Fore, feoir, a stream or rivulet.
Fore, feóir, not given.
Fore, fhuar, fuar, cold.
Fore, fobar, fobhair, fhobhair, fobhar, a spring or spring well.
Fore, fobhar-Féichín, fochaire, ford(sic), not given.
Fore, fómhair, harvest.
Fore, not given.
Forehill(sic), *fuarchoill*, bleak wood(sic).
Forekill, fuarchoill, not given.
Foremass, formhás, not given.
Forenaghts, from *fornocht*, exposed hills.
Forest, (Tipperary) *an-seisceann*(sic) , not given.
Forgney, forgnaí, fiorgnaidh, forgnaidh, an-edifice or building.
Forgney, forgnaidhe, not given.
Foria, phonaire, beans.
Forkeala, fóir-Chéile, not given.
Forkhill, fairceáil, not given.
Forkhill, foirceal-na-Cleire, the cold wood or sub-cell of the clergy.
Forkhill, fuar-choill, cold wood.
Forkill, fuar-choill, cold wood.
Forlagh, forlachta, the (exposed) shelving side.
Forlagh, forlachta, a deluge.
Forlorn, fearnóg, alders.
Formal, formaeil, formael, a round hill.
Formil, formaeil, formael, formaoil, a round hill.
Formoyle, formaeil, formaoil, formaoile, formael, a round hill.
Formweel, formael, a round hill.
Formwheel, formaeil, formael, a round hill.
Formwheel, formaoil, not given.
Fornaght, fórnachta, a very bare hill.
Fornaght, fornachta, not given.
Fornaght, fornocht, a bare, naked, cold or exposed hill.
Fornaght, fornocht, an exposed hill.
Fornaghts, from *fornocht*, bare, naked or exposed hills.
Fornocht, fornocht, not given.
Fornoght, fornachta, not given.
Fornoght, fornocht, an exposed hill.

Forra, *forrgea* (Latin) a place where meetings are held.

Forramoil, *na-foraí-maola,* not given.

Forriry, *foraire,* watching.

Forristeen, *foraoistín,* small forest.

Fortarla, *phuirtan-Íarla,* the Earls bank.

Fortel, *foirtil, fortola,* not given.

Fortetna, *cathair-na-Tanátha,* not given.

Forth, (Mt) *árd-leamhnachta,* not given.

Forth, *Fotharta,* inhabitants/descendants of the land of Ohy Finn Fothart, the leinster Prince.

Forth, *fotharta-Fea, fotharta-an-chairn,* not given.

Forthenry, *leargaidh,* not given.

Fortmoy, *fódmhaigh,* not given.

Fossa, *fosda,* a bank.

Fossy, *fosa,* not given.

Fostra, *faistre, faiscre,* cheese.

Fostra, *fastrach,* wilderness.

Fostrach, *fástrach,* a wilderness.

Fota, *fóite,* not given.

Fouder, *Bhruadair,* Bruadair, a personal or family name.

Foughart, *fochaird, fochairt,* not given.

Foughill, *fo-choill,* underwood.

Fouhnalium, *sruth-na-léim,* stream of the waterfalls.

Foughnane, *fothanan,* thistles.

Fouka, *puca,* a goblin.

Fouke, *puca,* a goblin.

Foul Sound, *bealach-na-fearbaighe, an-sonnda-salach,* not given.

Foulks, *phúcaigh,* not given.

Foulks, *Fúca,* a personal name.

Foulks, *Fhoilc,* (belonging to) Folco, a personal or family name.

Foulks, *Fhuilc,* (belonging to) Fulk, a personal or family name.

Foulkscourt, *cúirt-Fhuilc,* the court of Fulc or Fulco (a Christian name).

Foulksmills, *muileann-an-phuca, muileann-fúca,* not given.

Fouloo, *Uí-Fhoghludha,* Foley, a family name.

Foun, *fhionn, fionn,* white.

Fountain, *Fionntan, Fhiontain, Fhionntain, Fintan,* St Fintan.

Four knocks, *fuarchnoc,* the cold hill.

Four, *foithir,* a dell.

Four, *fuar,* bare.

Four, *fuar,* cold.

Fourcuil, *fuarchoill,* not given.

Fower, *fobhair,* a spring well.

Fowloo, *Fhoglúdha,* O'Foley or Foley, a family name.

Fown, *finn,* white.

Foxcover, *clais-an-rois,* hollow of the wood.

Foxfield, *cnocán-an-mhada-rua,* not given.

Foy, (river) *an-abha-bhuidhe,* not given.

Foy, *faithche,* an exercise/play or sporting green.

Foy, *fód,* sods.

Foyagh, from *faithche,* abounding in green plots.

Foyah, *faithche,* an exercise ground.

Foydragh, *fódragh,* a place of sods.

Foye, *Feá,* not given.

Foygh, *faithche,* an exercise green.

Foygh, from *faithche,* abounding in green plots.

Foyhin, from *faithche,* little green plot.

Foyl, *f-aill,* a cliff.

Foylan, *Fhialáin,* St Faelan.

Foylatalure, *faill-an-táilliúra,* not given.

Foyle, an estuary.

Foyle, *dá-pholl,* two pools.

Foyle, *f-aill,* a cliff.

Foyle, *fhaill, faill, feabhaill, feabhail,* not given.

Foyle, *faill,* a declivity.

Foyle, *fola,* blood.

Foyle, *phoill, poll,* a hole, pit.

Foyle, *phoill,* the pool.

Foyle, *phuill,* a hollow.

Foylea, *faill-an...,* declicity(sic) of the...

Foynes, *faing,* the raven.

Foynes, *faing,* the western boundary.

Foynes, *fainge,* not given.

Foynes, *fuinedh,* the end or limit.

Foyoges, from *faithche,* little green plots.

Foze, *feód,* not given.

Frack, *bhreac,* speckled.

Frack, *Fraic,* Fraic, Frac, a personal or family name.

Frahane, *phracháin,* not given.

Frahane, *pracain,* Prahane, not given.

Fraley, *Uí Fhreáile, Ó Freáile,* a family name.

Fraley, *Uí-Fearghaile,* O'Frawley or O'Fraley, a family name.

Fran, *Bhrain,* Bran, a personal or family name.

Fran, *Bhranduibh,* Brandubh, a personal or family name.

Fran, Black Bran, a personal or family name.

Franes, *thriain,* not given.

Franka, *Frangcach,* rats or Frenchmen.

Frankach, *Francach,* the Frenchman or the rat.

Frankagh, *Francach,* not given.

Frankee, *bhFranncach,* rats.

Frankfort, *baile-Chiaráin,* Ciaran's (a male name) homestead.

Franky, *Franncach,* French.

Frask, *phraisce,* kale.

Frask, *phraisce,* pottage or a place where wild cabbage grew.

Frask, *praisce,* not given.

Frask, *prasc, phraisce,* broken seaweed or cabbage.

Fraughan, *fraochán,* whortleberry or bilberry.

Fraul, *Fearáil,* Farrell, a personal or family name.

Frauns, from *ruadhán,* red lands.

Freach, *fraoch,* heath.

Freachane, *phreacháin,* a crow.

Freagh, *fraoch, fraech, fraeich,* heath.

Freagha, *fraoch-an...,* heath of the...

Freaghan, *fraechán,* place of whortleberries.

Freaghan, *phréacháin,* a crow.

Freaghana, *fraochanna, fraochnach,* not given.

Freaghanagh, a place of whortleberries.

Freaghane, *bhFraochán, phréacháin,* not given.

Freaghane, *fraechán,* place of whortleberries.

Freaghaun, *bh-fraochán, fraechán,* place of whortleberries.

Freaghaun, bilberries.

Freaghaun, *phréacháin,* the crow.

Freaghillaunluggagh, *fraoch-oileán-Logach,* not given.

Freaghoge, *fhraochóg,* not given.

Freaghoge, *freaghoge,* whortleberries.

Frecchaun(sic)**,** whortleberry.

Free, *fhraoigh, fraoich, fraoigh, fraoch,* heather.

Free, *fraech, fraoigh, fraeich,* heath.

Free, *fréadh,* plunder.

Freedy, *Bhroíle,* not given.

Freemount, *Cillín-an-Chrónáin,* not given.

Freeny, *Aifrinn,* Mass.

Freeny, *fhréinigh,* not given.

Freera, *Phrióra,* not given.

Freera, *Phrír,* Prior, a male name.

Frees, *fraoigh,* heather.

Freffans, *fraechán,* place of whortleberries.

Frehan, *bhFraochán,* not given.

Frehan, *fraechán,* place of whortleberries.

Frehane, *fraocháin,* little heath.

Frehane, *bFraochán,* whortle-berries.

Frehanes, *fraechán,* place of whortleberries.

Frehans, *fraecháin,* bilberries.

Frehans, *fraechán,* place of whortleberries.

Frehans, *na-fraocháin/fhraocháin,* not given.

Frehawn, *fraochán,* billberries.

Freigh, *fraech, fraoch, fhraoigh, heath,* heather.

Fremagh, *fraochmhaigh,* not given.

Freshford, *achaidh-úir, achadh-úr,* fresh green field.

Freugh, *fraech, fraeich,* heath.

Frevah, *freamhach,* abounding in roots.

Frevanagh, *freamhanach,* abounding in roots.

Frewin, *freamhainn,* not given.

Friar, *fraothrach,* heathery.

Friday, *bhraighde,* hostages.

Frilan, *Fraeileann, Fraoileann,* a male name.

Friland, *Bhraoilein,* not given.

Friland, *Fraoileann, Fraoile,* a personal or family name.

Froca, *phroca,* a crock or urn.

Froe, *fothar-ruadh,* red glen.

Frog, dwellings.

Froghan, *fraocháin, fraochan, fraochán,* a place of bilberries or whortleberries.

Frogmore, *glean-na-Réidhe-dóighte,* not given.

Frolic, *an-Fhrailic, na-frailice,* not given.

Frolic, *frochog, prochog,* a cave hollow or den.

Froot, *Phrútaigh,* not given.

Froot, *Phruit,* Prout, a personal or family name.

Froota, *an-Phrútaigh,* not given.

Froota, *Phrúite,* Prout, a family name.

Froska, praisge, the weed 'Brasica Rubra'.

Frossa, frasa, showers.

Frosses, na-frosa/frasa, the showers.

Frunk, Phroncaigh, not given.

Frunk, Frainc, (belonging to) the Frenchman or foreigner.

Frush, Frois, Fros, a personal name and the name of a Church founder in Limerick.

Fryland, Fraeileann, Fraoileann, a male name.

Fuad, Fuaid, Fuada, the name of an ancient hero and Milesian chieftain.

Fubble, phobail, congregation.

Fuddy, Fodaigh, not given.

Fuen, fion, white.

Fuerty, fiodharta, fiodharta, a wooded place.

Fuhery, na-foithre, the hollows, hills or swamps.

Fuhiry, na-foithre, not given.

Full, phoill, a pool.

Full, phuill, not given.

Fulla, (na-)fola, …of substance(sic).

Fulla, fola, blood or bloody.

Fullert, fulachta, a cooking place.

Fullert, Fulartaigh, not given.

Funcheon, fhoinnsean, ash trees.

Funcheon, fuinnsean, ash tree.

Funchin, bhFuinnsean, ash trees.

Funchinagh, fuinnseanach, finsineach, a place of ash trees.

Funchoge, fuinnseóg, a place of ash trees.

Fune, Fionn, Fhinn, Fionn, a personal or family name.

Fune, fhionn, white or pleasant.

Fune, finn, fionn, clear, bright or white.

Fune, fionn, fair or white.

Funga, fine, the white cow.

Funhin(sic), *fuinsín,* little ash trees.

Funnock, feannog, fionóige, a royston or scald crow.

Funsha, fuinse, fuinnseann, ash trees.

Funshadaun, fuinnseadáin, ash producing land.

Funshin, finsineach, fuinseann, fuinnse, a place of ash trees.

Funshinagh, finsineach, a place of ash trees.

Funshine, abounding in ash trees.

Funshion, an-fhoinnsean, not given.

Funshion, fuinsinn, fuinseann, fuinnseann, ash trees.

Funshog, finsineach, fuinnse, a place of ash trees.

Funshoge, fuinnseóg, a place of ash trees.

Fur, foithir, a wood or swamp.

Furara, foraire, a lookout rock.

Furbagh, forbach, not given.

Furbogh, furbach, land.

Furbogh, na-forbacha, not given.

Fure, feóir, grassy.

Furery, foraire, watching or guarding.

Furhane, fuarthán, a cold spring.

Furhee, foirtehí, dark.

Furish, easy.

Furnace, fornais, bléan-coilleadh, cnoc-an-iob-hair, not given.

Furnace, sorn, a smelting furnace.

Furness, fornocht, the bare hill.

Furness, frabacha, pasture lands.

Furnish, sorn, a smelting furnace.

Furnisha, Foirise, not given.

Furnisha, Furnaise, Furnish, a family name.

Furoor, fór-bhár, the hilltop.

Furoor, fo-úr, buried.

Furra, fhoradh, a wattle bridge.

Furra, foraidh, a mound.

Furra, forra, scaffold, bench or platform.

Furra, forraí, fhorradh, fhorrach, not given.

Furra, forrgea (Latin) a place where meetings are held.

Furra, furá, preparation.

Furraleigh, an-fhorrach-liath, not given.

Furrer, Forair, not given.

Furrish, foraoise, foraois, a forest.

Furroor, fobhair, not given.

Furroor, for-bhár, on the hilltop.

Furrow, forrgea (Latin) a place where meetings are held.

Furta, phorta, a bank (river).

Fush, fois, rest and tranquility.

Fushog, fuiseóga, the lark.

Fushogue, fuiseóg, skylark/s.

Fussough, fosach, the sheltered place.

Fy, faithche, an exercise green.

Fy, fiodh, a wood.

Fyagh, fidheach, not given.

Fyagh, from *faithche,* abounding in green plots.

Fybagh, an-fhadhbach, not given.

Fybagh, fiodhbach, fadhbach, a place of lumps.

Fye, *faithche,* a sporting green.

Fyfin, *faiche-fionn, faithche-fin,* whitish or fair (exercise) green.

Fyfin, *fiodh-Finn,* not given.

Fyla, *faille,* a cliff.

Fylane, *Fialáin,* Fialán, a personal or family name.

Fymore, *fiodh-mór,* not given.

Fyn, *finn,* white.

Fynchor, *finn-choradh,* white weir.

Fyncora, *finn-choradh,* white weir.

Fyne, *fiadhain,* wild.

G

Gabog, *gCabóg,* clowns.

Gabriel, *Giriam,* Giriam, a personal or family name.

Gad, *gad,* wythes, from a growth of osiers.

Gad, *nGad, ghad, ghadai,* not given.

Gadda, *gheadaigh,* not given.

Gadda, *ghuaduighe, ghaduighe, gadaighe,* a thief.

Gadden, *fheadáin,* a streamlet.

Gadden, *Gheadáin,* not given.

Gaddery, *gadaraigh,* the osier plantation for the wythes.

Gaddy, *gadai,* storyteller.

Gaddy, *ghadaí, gadáidhe,* the thief.

Gaddy, *ghadaí, ghuaduighe, ghadaighe, ghadaidhe, gadaighe,* a thief or thieves.

Gade, *gCéad,* hundreds.

Gadecran, *gCead-gCran,* a hundred trees.

Gadoe, *dá-dumha,* not given.

Gadragh, *nGadrach,* wythes.

Gaff, *gaimh,* winter streams.

Gaff, *gamh,* winter streams.

Gagagh, *gágach,* fissures or openings.

Gagan, from *gág,* a cleft or fissure.

Gagan, *ghéagain,* not given.

Gaggan, from *gág,* a cleft or clefts.

Gaggan, *géagánach,* not given.

Gaggin, *Choganaigh,* Gagan, Goggin or De Cogan, a family name.

Gaggin, Gagan or Goggin, a family name.

Gaggin, *géagán,* the arm.

Gaggin, *geaganach,* a place of branches.

Gaggin, *géagánach,* not given

Gagh, *Ga,* not given.

Gaghan, *Dhacháin*(sic), not given.

Gaghta, *geachta,* not given.

Gaghy, *'ic-Eachaidh,* MacGaghy, a family name.

Gagin, Gagan or Goggin, a family name.

Gah, *cath,* a battle.

Gah, *gá,* spears.

Gah, *gath,* a spear, lance or javelin.

Gaha, *gatha,* the spear.

Gahan, *gCathan,* Cahan, O'Cahan or O'Kane, a family name.

Gahan, *MacGathan,* MagGahan, a family name.

Gahaniff, *gaineamh,* sandy.

Gahaniff, *gathannaibh,* spears or gaffs.

Gaheen, Gahan or Gaheen, a personal or family name.

Gaheen, *gathín,* little javelin.

Gaheen, *Uí-Gaoithín,* O'Gahan, a family name.

Gahiny, *gCaithne,* arbutus trees.

Gahny, *ghainidhe,* sand.

Gaige, *géag, géug,* a branchy place.

Gaigue, *geug,* a branch or branchy place.

Gaile, *Gaedhail,* Irish.

Gaile, *Gael, Ghaeil, Gaola,* not given.

Gaine, (river) *an-Gháine,* not given.

Gainy, *Gháine,* Gaine, a personal or family name.

Gainy, *Gháithne,* not given.

Gairha, *gaorthadh,* a watered place or a wooded stream.

Gairha, *gearha, gairha,* bushy riverbank.

Gaithin, *gaithin,* a gaff or spear.

Gal, *cala,* a holm.

Gal, *ceala,* fair.

Gal, *gabhal,* the fork.

Gal, *geal,* bright or clear.

Gal, *geal, n-geal,* white.

Gal, *ghall,* not given.

Gal, *gheal, geal, geala,* bright or white.

Gal, *nGall, gall,* foreigner, sometimes an Englishman.

Galbally, *gallbhaile,* English town.

Galboy, *nGall-buidhe,* the yellow Englishman.

Galda, *ghaldia,* English.

Galda, *Gallda,* Gauls or foreigners.

Galdanagh, *Galldanagh,* belonging to an Englishman.

Galdanagh, *geal-eanach,* white marsh.

Gale, *gCailleach,* old women.

Gale, *giall, gháile,* not given.

Galey, *gáile,* a creek or inlet.

Galey, *gháile,* not given.

Galey, *Gháile,* a river named after an ancient tribe (Gaille).

Galid, *gallaid,* a standing, pillar stone.

Gall, bright.

Gall, *gall,* stone/s.

Gall, *gCál,* cabbage (lake).

Gall, *gCál,* Cál, a personal or family name.

Gall, *na-gCeall,* the Church(sic).

Gall, *nGall, gall,* a foreigner or foreigners.

Gall, *nGall,* stones or standing strones.

Galla, *geala,* white or bright.

Galla, of the foreigners.

Gallagh, *gaille,* a standing stone.

Gallagh, *gallagh,* rocks or standing stones.

Gallagh, *gCailleac,* hags.

Gallagh, *gCailleach,* nuns.

Gallagh, *gCoileach,* woodcock.

Gallagh, *g-coilleach,* woods.

Gallagh, *tamhlacht*(sic), *gallach,* not given.

Gallan, *gallán, gallan,* a standing stone.

Gallan, Gallan, a personal or family name.

Gallan, *Galline,* Gallen, the name of an ancient chief.

Gallan, *Uí-Chathaláin, Gathlán,* not given.

Gallanagh, *gallánach,* not given.

Gallanagh, *geal-eanach,* white marsh.

Gallane, *gallan, galláin, ghalláin, ghallain,* a standing stone or a pillar stone.

Gallane, *n-gallan,* standing stones.

Gallane, *Uí-Ghiolláin,* O'Gillan, a family name.

Gallanes, *gallán,* standing stones.

Gallarus, *gallaras,* not given.

Gallda, *galda,* English.

Galleen, *gCailín,* girls.

Galleen, *Ó gCoilín, Uí Choilín,* a family name.

Gallen, *choileáin, Gailine,* not given.

Gallen, *gaileang-an-Chorainn,* not given.

Gallen, *Gailenga,* a race of people decended from *Cormac Gaileng.*

Gallen, *Gailinne,* Gallen, a personal or family name.

Gallen, *ghailinne,* not given.

Gallen, the dishonoured spear.

Gallerus, *gallaras,* not given.

Galley, *Geithligh,* Geithleach, a personal or family name.

Galley, *Ó-gCeallaigh,* O'Kelly, a family name.

Galliagh, *cailleach, gCalliach, gCailliach, gCailleach,* nuns.

Galliagh, *garrdha-na-gCailleach,* not given.

Galliagh, *gCailleach,* old women.

Gallid, *gallid,* a standing stone.

Galligan, *Ghallagháin,* not given.

Gallin, *Uí-Galláin,* O'Gallen, a family name.

Gallion, *Callainn,* Callan, a personal or family name.

Gallion, *Gailenga,* a race of people decended from *Cormac Gaileng.*

Gallion, *gCalláinn,* noise.

Gallion, *gCallainn,* not given.

Gallion, *ghaillean,* standing stones.

Gallive, *nDealbh,* phantoms.

Gallive, *nEalbh,* not given.

Gallive, *n-geallabh,* images.

Gallogly, *gall-oglach, galloglach,* foreign soldiers.

Gallon, *Galláin,* not given.

Gallon, *gallan,* a standing stone.

Gallon, *gallanach, nGallán,* pillar stones.

Gallon, *galún, gallon,* a measurment of land.

Gallon, *Uí-Galláin,* O'Gallen, a family name.

Galloon, *gabhal-Liúin,* not given.

Galloon, *gealbháin, nGealbhún,* sparrows.

Galloon, *gealbhan,* not given.

Gallow, *gaille,* a standing stone.

Gallow, *galamh,* a place of standing stones.

Gallow, *gallagh,* rocks or standing stones.

Galluane, *gealún,* sparrows.

Gally, *Gallaigh, Ghallaigh,* not given.

Gally, *gCailleac,* hags.

Gally, *gCaladh,* not given.

Gally, *gCialliach, gCailleach,* nuns.

Gally, *Mhig-Amhalghadha,* Magally, a personal or family name.

Gally, *Geithligh, Geithlech,* Geithleach, a personal or family name.

Galmoy, *gabhalmhaigh, gabhalmaigh, galmaí,* not given.

Galough, *g-cailleach,* nuns.

Galroostown, *Galrastún,* not given.

Galros, *gallros,* not given.

Galshy, *Gaillseach, Gaillseach,* an Englishwoman.

Galt, *Gallta,* a foreigner. Usually an Englishman but can also be a Scotchman.

Galt, *nGealt,* the lunatic or the madmen.

Galtaun, *nGealt, ghealtain,* the madmen or madman.

Galtee Mountains, *gCoillteadh* woods.

Galtee Mountains, *na-gaibhlte,* of (the) woods.

Galtee Mountains, *sliabh-gCrot,* not given.

Galtee, *Gailte,* not given.

Galteemore, *beann-gCrot,* not given.

Galtrim, *ghalatroma, galatrom, calatruim,* not given.

Galty, (mountains), *gCoillteadh* woods.

Galty, (mountains) *nGaibhlte, Gaibhlte,* not given.

Galun, *gealún,* sparrows.

Galvally, *gallbhaile,* English town.

Galvan, *Gealbháin,* Galvin, Galvan, a family name who often call them selves 'Sparrow' (*Gealbhan,* sparrow).

Galvan, *Uí-Ghealbhain,* O'Galvin, a family name.

Galvin, *gaibhle,* the fork.

Galwally, *gallbhaile,* English town.

Galway, *Ghallaidhe,* Galway, a personal or family name.

Galway, *Gaillimhe, Gaillimh, nGaillimh,* unknown, various sources however speculate that it comes from;

(a) a *gallán* or large standing stone on the river corrib, now buried under the riverbank close to the bridge.

(b) *Gaillimh,* an ancient Princess who drowned there.

(c) *Gaillimh,* the place of foreign traders.

(d) A rocky place.

(e) *Gaillimh,* the stony/rocky river.

(f) *Gallmhaigh,* a place of standing stones.

Galwilly, *gallbhuaile,* the milking place of the foreigner/s.

Galwilly, *nGallbhaile,* not given.

Galwolie, *an-ghallbhuaile,* not given.

Gam, *gCam,* windings.

Gam, *gcéim,* tracks.

Gambon, *an-Ghambúnaigh,* not given.

Gambon, *Ghambúin,* Gambon, a personal or family name.

Gamboon, *gambún,* a nickname for crooked or ill made men.

Gammane, a family name.

Gammane, *gCamán, gCammán,* hurleys or hurling.

Gammane, *Ghamáin,* not given.

Gammon, *coman,* hurleys or hurling.

Gammon, *Ghámbúna,* Gambon, a family name.

Gamph, *damh, dhamh,* oxen.

Gamph, *gamh,* storms.

Gan, *can, cán, gan, gán,* little.

Gan, *gan,* without.

Gan, *gCeann,* heads.

Ganagh, from *gainíme,* little sandy place.

Ganagh, *gainíme,* sand/y.

Gananagh, *gainíme,* sand/y.

Gancan, *gan-cheann/ceann,* headless.

Gane, *gCeann,* heads.

Gane, *gCéin,* Cian or Kian, a personal name.

Gane, taxes.

Ganey, *gainíme,* sand/y.

Ganhue, *gainiú,* not given.

Ganhue, *gainthiú,* sandy.

Ganiffe, *ghainnimh,* sandy.

Gann, *gCeann,* heads.

Gannagh, *gainmhe, gainmheach,* sand or sandy.

Gannagh, *gCeannach,* not given.

Gannaughs, from *gainmhe,* sandy places.

Gannavagh, *gainmhe, gainmheach,* the sandy place.

Gannavane, from *gainíme,* little sandy place.

Gannavane, *gaineamhán,* not given.

Gannaveen, from *gainíme,* little sandy place.

Gannaway, *gainmhe, gainmheach,* sandy.

Gannee, *gCeannaigheadh,* peddlers or merchants.

Ganneen, *Gháinín,* not given.

Gannell, *gCoinnle, gCoinneall, gCáinlidh,* candles.

Gannew, *gainimh, gaineamh, sand,* sandy or a sand pit.

Ganniff, *ghainimh, gainimh,* sand or a sand pit.

Gannihy, *gCeannaidhte, gCeannaigheadh,* merchants.

Ganniv, *gainimh, gaineamh, sand,* sandy, a sand pit.

Ganniv, *gathannaibh,* spears or gaffs.

Gannive, *gainnive*(sic), *ghainimh, gaineamh,* sand or sandhill.

Gannon, Ceanann, a personal or family name.

Gannon, *gCanán,* not given.

Gannon, *gCanónach,* Canons.

Gannon, *Geanainn,* Gannon or Geanan, a male name.

Gannon, *Geanainn, Geanann,* a personal or family name.

Gannon, *Geannain,* Gannon or MacGannon, a family name.

Gannon, *Uí-Gheannain,* Gannon, a personal or family name.

Gannor, *dhanair,* the stranger.

Gannow, *gainimh, gaineamh, sand,* sandy or a sand pit.

Ganny, from *gainíme,* little sandy place.

Ganny, *gainimh, ghainimh,* sandy or a sand pit.

Ganny, *gainmhe, gaineamh, gainímhe, ghainimh,* sand.

Ganny, *gCeannaighthe, gCeannaigheadh,* peddlers or merchants.

Ganny, *geanaí, ghainimhe,* not given.

Ganny, *ghainmhe,* sandy.

Ganonagh, *gCanonach, gCananach,* canons.

Ganty, *ganntaidhe,* barren spots.

Ganvaghan, *gainmheachán, gaineamhachán,* a small sandy place.

Gany, a garden.

Gaorach, sheep.

Gap, *gCeap,* stakes, stumps or trunks.

Gap, *gCeap,* tree trunk/s.

Gappagh, *gCeapach,* tillage plots.

Gappary, *gCeapairí,* not given.

Gapple, *gCapul, gCapall,* horses.

Gappoge, *gCopog, gCopóg,* dock leaves.

Gappul, *gCapall,* horses.

Gar, *cearr,* crooked.

Gar, *gCearr, cearr,* wry.

Gar, *gár, gar,* near.

Gar, *garbh,* rough.

Gar, *garr, gearr,* short or wry.

Gar, *garraí, ghearr,* short.

Gar, *gCar, gCarr,* a car.

Gar, *gCarr,* carts.

Gar, *gCarr,* the waggon.

Gar, *gCearr,* not given.

Gar, *gearr, gearra,* short.

Gar, *gearra, ghártha,* not given.

Gar, *ghair,* a battle cry.

Gar, *ghairr,* offal.

Gar, *ghártha,* an enclosed garden.

Gar, *ghártha, garrdha,* a garden.

Gara, *Gadhra,* Gara, a personal or family name.

Gara, *Uí-Gadhra, Ghadhra,* O'Gara, a family name.

Garadice, (lough), *fionnmhuighe,* not given.

Garadice, *garbhros,* the rough peninsula.

Garadice, *garairis, gharairis, geirctheach, garadaghas,* not given.

Garagh, *dara,* oak.

Garagh, *gCurrach,* swamps.

Garagh, *ghearrtha,* of the cutting.

Garalt, *Ghearailt,* Gearalt, a personal name.

Garane, *garrain,* a shrubbery.

Garane, *garrán,* a shrubbery.

Garavaun, (river) *an-garbhán,* not given.

Garavaun, rough.

Garbally, *garbhaile,* not given.

Garbally, *garbh-dhoire,* rough oak wood.

Garbet, *carboid,* a chariot.

Garbragh, *gCairbreach, gCairbre,* the Carberrys, a family name.

Garbry, *gCairbreach, gCairbre,* the Carberrys, a family name.

Gard, *ceard,* an artificer.

Gard, *Gárda,* a guard.

Gard, *gCartha,* rocks.

Gard, *gCeard, ceard,* artificers.

Gard, *gCeard,* a craftsman.

Gard, tinsmiths.

Garde, *na-gCeárd/gCeard, ceard,* artificers or craftsmen.

Garde, *garha,* rocks.

Garden, *Garaidh,* not given.

Garden, *gharrdha,* the garden.

Gardice, *garbhros,* the rough copse.

Gardy, *gCeardcha,* forges.

Gare, *chearr,* crooked.

Gare, *gCaor, gCaor,* berries.

Gare, *gear,* sharp.

Gare, *gearr, gCarr, gCarr,* cars, carts or waggons.

Gare, *gearr, gear, gairrid, ghearr,* short.

Gare, *nGabhar,* not given.

Gareen, *gár,* near.

Gareen, *ghairín,* little garden.

Garey, *gCaorach, gCaerach,* sheep.

Garfinney, *an-ghairfeanaigh,* not given.

Garfinny, *an-ghairfeanaigh,* not given.

Garfinney, *garbhfhannaí,* the rough hilltop.

Gargan, Gargan or MacGargan, a family name.

Garha, *gaertha,* a river-thicket.

Garha, *ghearrtha,* the cutting or trench.

Garhagh, *gCairrthe,* rocks.

Garhoon, *gCeathramhan,* (land) quarters.

Garhoon, *geathramhna,* not given.

Garhy, *garrthaidh,* a garden.

Garif, *garbh,* rough.

Gariff, *garbh,* rough.

Gariffe, *gharbh,* rough.

Garig, *garg,* the fierce man.

Garinish, *garinis,* the near island.

Gark, *gCearc,* hens, heath hens or grouse.

Garkin, *dhearcan*(sic), not given.

Garlach, *nGárlach,* infants.

Garlagh, *Ghearla,* not given.

Garland, *baile-an-gárda/gharda,* the guards place.

Garland, *grealláin,* not given.

Garlegobban, *garraí-log-Bogan,* not given.

Garley, *garbhlaigh,* rough.

Garley, *garlach,* babies.

Garly, *garlaí,* not given.

Garly, *garlaigh,* children.

Garma, *garma,* headland.

Garn, *garran,* a shrubbery.

Garn, *gCarn,* a carn, cairn, a heap of stones usually an ancient monument or burial mound.

Garna, *carnadh,* (of the) slaying.

Garna, *cathair-na…,* not given.

Garna, *garrán,* a shrubbery.

Garna, *garrán-an…,* grove of the…

Garnagh, *gCarnach,* carns or monumental heaps of stones, usually a grave pile.

Garnaman, *gCearnamán, gCearnaman, cearnabhan,* wasps or hornets.

Garnaun, *carnán, garnán,* hillocks.

Garnaun, little cairns (monumental heaps of stones).

Garnish, *gar/gairbh-inis,* the rough island.

Garns, *gCarna,* carns or monumental heaps of stones, usually a grave pile.

Garode, *Gheaŕóid, Gearoid,* Gerrard, Garret, a male name.

Garogy, *gearróige,* little portion

Garr, *an-gearradh,* not given.

Garr, *gearradh,* a cut or trench.

Garr, *ghearr, gearr,* short.

Garra, *dhearach*(sic)*, ghártha, ghearra, ghearraidh, ghearrtha, gearra, garraí-an…,* not given.

Garra, Gara, Gara, a male name.

Garra, *garaidh,* cultivated land.

Garra, Garra, Garra, the name of a chief of the 'Morna'.

Garra, *garra,* short.

Garra, *gharrdha, garraí, garrai,* a garden.

Garra, *garrán,* a shrubbery.

Garra, *gearradh,* a cut or trench.

Garra, *gearradh,* a cutting.

Garra, *gearrfhaidh,* hares.

Garra, *garbha, gharbh, garbh,* rough.

Garra, *garra*(sic)*,* rough.

Garrafine, *garbh-fhiadhain,* wild rough land.

Garrafranes, *na-garfráin,* not given.

Garrafrauns, *na-garfráin,* not given.

Garragh, *garbhach,* rough.

Garragh, *gCairtheach, gCarrach,* rocks.

Garragh, *gCearrbhach,* gamesters or gamblers.

Garragh, *geirrfhiaghaigh,* the hare.

Garraghill, *garbh-choill,* rough wood.

Garrah, *garraithe,* not given.

Garraha, *garraithe, nGarraithe,* gardens.

Garrahan, *geartha,* cut away wood.

Garrahies, *garraithe,* gardens.

Garrahy, *nGarraighthe,* gardens.

Garrahylish, *garraithe-Eibhlíse,* not given.

Garralt, *Ghearailt,* not given.

Garran, *garrán, garran,* a shrubbery or copse.

Garran, *garrán, gharráin,* a grove, thin wood or plantation.

Garran, *gCarn, nGearán, na-nGrean,* not given.

Garran, *gCarran,* rocks.

Garran, *gearran, ghearráin,* the horse.

Garran, horses.

Garrana, *garrán-an…*, shrubbery or grove of the…

Garranacool, *garrán-Niocóil/Niochóil*, not given.

Garranagerra, *garbhdhoire*, not given.

Garranagle, *garrán-na-gCaol*, shrubbery of the narrow trees.

Garrandee, *carn-Daoi*, not given.

Garrandrew, *garraidhe-Aindriú*, Andrews garden.

Garrane, *garrán*, a shrubbery or grove.

Garrane, *garrán-an-ridire-finn, garrán-UíChearnaigh, nGearrán*, not given.

Garrane, *gharráin, gharrain*, a shrubbery or grove.

Garrane, *ghearráin, n-gearran*, of the nag, horse or gelding.

Garrane, *nGarrán*, shrubberies.

Garranena, *garrán-na…*, shrubbery or grove of the…

Garranes, *gearain*, cliff like inclines.

Garranes, *na-garrain, garráin*, groves.

Garranna, *garrán-na…*, not given.

Garranty, *garrantuidhe*, shrubberies or copses.

Garrarus, *garbhros*, not given.

Garraun, *Garrán*, abounding in bushes and brushwood.

Garraun, (in Coolaghmore parish) *Garrán-an-chonaidh*, shrubbery of the kindling.

Garraun, *gharráin, garrán, garran*, a shrubbery, grove or copse.

Garraun, *ghearráin, garran, garron*, a horse.

Garraun, *nGearrán*, old horses.

Garrauna, *garrán-na…*, abounding in bushes and underwood of the…

Garraunna, *garrán-na…*, shrubbery or grove of the…

Garravagh, *garbach*, rough land.

Garravagh, *garbhachadh*, not given.

Garravally, *garbhaile*, not given.

Garravaun, *ghearra-bháin*, white cutting or trench.

Garravin, *an-ghearrmhuine*, not given.

Garravlagh, *garbhlach*, rough land.

Garreen, *gairdín*, little garden.

Garreiny, *na-gearreidhní*, not given.

Garren, *ghearráin*, the horse.

Garret, *Gearóid*, Gerald, Gerard or Garrett, a male name.

Garret, *Ghairead*, not given.

Garret, *Ghearóid, Gearoid*, Gerrard, Garret, a male name.

Garrett, *Ghearóid, Gearóid or Geróid*, a male name.

Garrick, *carraige*, the rock.

Garrick, *gCarraig*, rocks.

Garrid, *ghairid, gharaid, ghearra*, short.

Garries, *nGarradha, nGarraithe*, not given.

Garriff, *gharbh, garbh*, rough or rugged.

Garriff, *Gairbh*, the name of a Church founder in Aghamore.

Garriffe, *garbh*, rough.

Garrifly, *garbhlaigh*, rough land.

Garrifly, *garbhthulaigh*, not given.

Garrig, *chairg*, the fierce man.

Garrig, *gCarraig*, rocks.

Garrigan, *gCarraigín*, not given.

Garrigan, *gearagain*, small rocks.

Garrigan, *Geargáin*, not given.

Garrigeen, *gairgan*, crowsfoot or a little cormorant.

Garrigeeny, *gCarraigínidhe*, little rocks.

Garrin, *garraí-an…*, not given.

Garrinch, *garinse*, not given.

Garriskil, *garascal*, the rough nook.

Garrison, *garastan*, not given.

Garrison, *gairisiúin, garastún*, a garrison.

Garriv, *garbh*, rough.

Garrive, *garbh*, rough.

Garrivhan, *Gairfine*, not given.

Garrivinnagh, *gairfean*, not given.

Garrogan, *gairgan*, crowsfoot or a little cormorant.

Garrolagh, *garbhlach*, rough land.

Garroman, *an-Gharmain*, not given.

Garron, *ceathramhan*, a quarter portion.

Garron, *gárán*, bushes.

Garron, *gCeathramhan*, quarter lands.

Garron, *gearrán*, not given.

Garron, *gharráin*, a grove.

Garron, *ghearáin*, a horse.

Garron, *ghearráin*, cut horse.

Garroose, *garbhas*, rough land.

Garrough, *garbhach*, rough land.

Garrow, *garbh*, rough.

Garrow, *gearradh*, a trench.

Garrowna, bream.

Garruragh, *garadh-ughra*, a moist flat(sic).

Garry, *gaorthadh*, a woody wet glen.

Garry, *garáidh,* cultivated land.

Garry, *garraí, garrdha, gharraidhe, garraidhe, gharraí, gárrdha, gharrdha,* a garden.

Garry, *garrdha,* a potato field or garden.

Garry, *gCurraigh,* marshes.

Garry, *gharbh, garbh,* rough.

Garry, *ghearra,* short.

Garry, *ghoraidhe,* smelting.

Garryan, *gaorthadh-an…,* woody wet glen of the…

Garryan, *gaorthadh-na…,* wooded glen of the…

Garryan, *garrdha-an…,* garden of the.

Garrycloyne, *garbh-chluain,* meadow garden(sic).

Garryhill, *garbh-choill,* rough wood.

Garryhundon, *coirthe-eó-Mughna,* not given.

Garryland, *garbhlán,* rough land.

Garryn, *garrán/garraí-na…,* not given.

Garryna, *garadha-an…, garraí-an/na…, garrdha-na/'n….,* garden of the…

Gart, *gairt, gart,* an older form of *gort,* an enclosed field, a tilled field or tillage plot.

Gart, *goirt,* a ploughed field.

Gart, *gCart,* carts.

Gart, *gCeart,* rights.

Garta, *Ghearta,* not given.

Garta, *gort-an/a'…,* field or enclosed field of the…

Gartan, *gartan, gartán,* a garden, a little garden or a little tilled field.

Gartan, *gCartán,* not given.

Gartan, *gCeardchan,* forges or workshops.

Garteen, a little enclosed field.

Garter, *an-Ghairtéil,* not given.

Gartford, *gort-forard,* high tilled field.

Gartin, *gart-na…,* enclosed field of the…

Gartina, *gart-an…,* enclosed garden of the…

Gartna, *gart-na…,* enclosed field of the…

Garty, *gort-an…,* field of the…

Garv, *garbh,* rough.

Garvagh, *garbhach,* a rough place.

Garvagh, *garbhachadh, garbh-achadh,* rough field or plain(sic).

Garvagh, *gCearrbhach,* not given.

Garvaghey, *garbhachadh,* rough field.

Garvaghy, *garbhachadh,* rough field.

Garvah, *gCearrbhach, cearrbhach,* gamesters or gamblers.

Garvahy, *garbhacadh, garbhachadh,* rough field.

Garvallagh, *garbhlach,* rough land.

Garvalt, *garbh-alt,* not given.

Garvan, *garbhádhn,* rough.

Garvan, *Garbhán, Garbháin,* Garbhán or Garvan, a male name.

Garvan, *garbhán,* rough land.

Garvan, *gearr-mhuine,* a short belt of shrubbery.

Garvan, *gearr-mhuine,* short shrubbery.

Garvan, *gharbháin, garbháin,* a rough stone.

Garvan, *Gharbháin,* not given.

Garvan, *Gharbháin,* St Garbhán.

Garvan, *Gharbhán,* St Grabhán.

Garvan, *gharráin*(sic), not given.

Garvan, *nGarbhán,* rough (mannered) people.

Garvan, *Uí-Gharbhain, Garbhain, Garbhán,* O'Garvan or Garvan, a family name.

Garvanagh, *garbhánach,* rough land.

Garvarry, *garbhaire,* rough land.

Garvary, *garbhaire,* rough land.

Garve, *garbh,* tough(sic).

Garve, *garb, garbh,* rough or rugged.

Garvery, *garbhaire,* the rough field.

Garvery, *garbhdhoire,* not given.

Garvetagh, *garbhtach,* rough land.

Garvey, *gairbh-fheithe,* rough bog vein.

Garvey, *garbhach,* rough land.

Garvey, *gCearrbhach, gCearbhach,* gamblers.

Garvey, *ghairbhíth,* not given.

Garvey, *Uí-Ghairbheith, Garbhaigh,* O'Garvey or Garvey, a family name.

Garvigan, Gargan or O'Garvigan, a family name.

Garvil, *gairbhéil,* gravel.

Garvillaun, *garbh-oileánn,* a stony riverside meadow(sic).

Garvlagh, *garbhlach,* rough grass.

Garvoge, a rough spot of land.

Garvoge, *garbhóige, gharbhóige,* mustard-plant.

Garvoge, *nGarbhóg,* not given.

Garvy, *cearrbhach,* gamesters or gamblers.

Gary, a garden.

Gary, *ghaire,* shouting or laughter.

Gary, *gharraí, gCoire,* not given.

Gary, *gharraidhe,* not given.

Gary, *ghaurthaidh,* old river bed.

Gascanane, *gascanán,* not given.

Gash, *cuas,* cave/s.

Gash, *gais, gaise,* the torrent, a swift water current, a rapid or a cascade.

Gasha, *gaise,* pine or fir trees.

Gashan, *gaise-an…,* the torrent of the….

Gasheen, *gCaisíneach,* not given.

Gasheen, *gCaisineach,* O'Cashen, a family name.

Gashel, *gCaiseal,* castles or circular stone forts.

Gashel, *gCaiseal, gCaisil, caiseal, cashel,* circular stone fort/s.

Gashleen, *gCaislínidhe,* stone-chatters (a type of bird).

Gashleeny, *na-gCaislíní,* not given.

Gashoge, *gCuiseóg,* a type of coarse grass.

Gask, *Gascin,* Gaskin, a male name.

Gask, *Ghaisce,* not given.

Gask, *gCasca,* Easter.

Gaskig, *gaiscighig, gaiscigheach, ghaiscígh, ghaiscigh,* a hero or champion.

Gaskin, *Sheascan,* not given.

Gassan, *gasan,* not given.

Gassan, *gasán,* sprigs, sprouts, shoots or branches.

Gassan, *gCasan, gCasán,* paths.

Gassane, *gCosán,* path.

Gassane, *gCrosán,* not given.

Gassen, *gCosán,* path/s.

Gassoon, *gossoons*(sic), young boys.

Gassy, *gasac,* bushy.

Gastell, *gheastal,* a deed or fact.

Gat, *gCat,* a cat.

Gate, *gCat,* not given.

Gate, *geata, gheata,* a gate or gap.

Gath, *ga, gath,* a spear, lance or javelin.

Gatha, *geata, geatha,* a gate.

Gatheran, *Gadráin,* not given.

Gaton, *gCeidin,* a flat topped eminence.

Gatt, *gCat,* (wild) cats.

Gatta, *gheata,* a gate.

Gattana, *geata-an…,* gate of the…

Gatters, *gCatach,* Catters, a family name.

Gaug, *Dhabhag,* not given.

Gaug, *Dháthóg, Dhathog,* little David.

Gaug, *gág,* a cleft, chink, split or chasm in rock.

Gaug, *n-gag,* jackdaws.

Gaugagh, *gágach,* clefts or splits.

Gaugane, from *gaug,* a long narrow sea inlet, a split or a cavern in a cliff.

Gauge, *gág,* a cleft, chink, split or chasm in rock.

Gaugh, *Gách,* not given.

Gaugin, from *gág,* a little cleft.

Gauhoge, *gCáthóg,* strawberry bushes.

Gaul, *gabhal,* a fork.

Gaul, *gall,* foreigner/s.

Gaul, *ghaill,* not given.

Gaul, *nGall,* stones or standing stones.

Gaula, *gallaigh,* a stranger.

Gauldrus, *gallros,* rocky land.

Gaulskill, *Cill-a-Ghaill,* Church of the foreigner.

Gaulstown, *cnoc-an-ghalliagh*(sic), not given.

Gaultiere, *an-Ghailltír,* not given.

Gaultiere, *gall-tír, tir, gaultiere,* district of the foreigners.

Gaum, *gCom,* hollows.

Gaune, *gabhann,* a smith.

Gaune, *gCeann,* heads.

Gaune, *gceann,* St Brigids headstone(sic).

Gaush, *gaise,* a torrent.

Gaushan, *gaise-a'…,* the torrent of…

Gaushee, *gaisidhe,* bog deals.

Gavelin, *gaibhlin,* a river fork.

Gavelin, a small river fork.

Gavenny, *gaimhne,* calves.

Gaver, *nGabhar, gobhair,* goat/s.

Gavla, *gaibhle,* the river fork.

Gavlen, *ghaibhle, gaibhle,* the fork.

Gavlin, *gaibhlín,* little fork.

Gavlin, *ghabhlín,* not given.

Gavna, *gabhnaighe,* stripper or milch cows.

Gavna, *ghabhna,* the calf.

Gavna, *ghamhna,* not given.

Gavna, *nGaibhne,* smiths.

Gavneen, *gaibhnín, gabhnin,* the little smith.

Gavny, *gaimhne,* calves.

Gavny, *gamhna,* not given.

Gaw, *Gá,* not given.

Gaw, *gabhar,* horse/s(sic).

Gaw, *gath,* a spear, lance or javelin.

Gawley, *Mhic-Amhalghadha,* MacAwley or Macaulay, a family name.

Gawley, *Uí-Dhálaigh,* Ó Dálaigh or O'Daly, a family name and means the descendants of Daly.

Gawlin, *gabhailin, gaibhlin,* little fork.

Gawna, *gamhain, gabhna, gamhana,* the calf.

Gawna, *gamhnach,* milch cows.

Gawna, *nGamhna,* calves.

Gawnagh, *gamhna,* not given.

Gawnagh, *gamhnach,* heifers, milking cows with a year old calf, a stripper cow, milch cows or a milking cow in the second year after calving.

Gawne, *gabhann,* a smith.

Gawne, *g-ceann,* heads.

Gawne, *nGhamhan,* calves.

Gawny, *gabhna,* a calf or calves.

Gawny, *gamhna,* not given.

Gawny, *gamhnach,* milch cows or stripper cows.

Gay, *gaeth, gaeithe, gaoth, gaoithe,* the wind.

Gay, *gCaoth,* quagmires.

Gay, *gedh, ghé, ghe, nGédh, ghedh, gédh,* a goose or geese.

Gay, *géidh,* geese.

Gaybrook, *baile-Réamainn,* not given.

Gayrour, *ghéill-ramhair,* the fat hostage.

Gaze, *géise,* not given.

Gea, *ghé,* not given.

Gea, *ghédh,* a goose, *n-gédh,* wild geese.

Geachta, *gCéachta,* ploughs.

Gead, *gCéad,* hundreds.

Geag, *géag,* a branch.

Geaga, *geige,* a branch.

Geagan, *Géagáin,* not given.

Geaghanach, *geaghanach,* a branchy place.

Geaglom, *géag-lom,* the bare branch.

Geagoge, *an-Iagógaigh,* not given.

Geal, *gile,* whiteness, brightness.

Geale, *an-Ghéill,* the hostage.

Geale, *Gaedhail,* Irish.

Geale, *Uí-Ghéill,* the hostage(sic).

Geana, *Uí-Geibheannaigh,* O'Geny, a family name.

Geanagh, *caoneach,* moss or mossy.

Geane, *Uí-Ghéibheannaigh,* Ó Géibheannaigh, not given.

Gear, *gCaor, gCaer,* berries.

Geara, *gairha,* bushy riverbank.

Geara, *gaorthadh,* a river glen.

Geara, *ghaorthaidh,* a woody glen.

Gearach, *gcaorach,* sheep.

Gearagh, *gCaorach,* sheep.

Gearagh, *gearha, gairha,* bushy riverbank.

Gearagh, *ghaorthaidh,* a woody glen.

Gearaun, *ghearain,* a steep slope.

Geardra, *Gheardra,* not given.

Geare, *gCaer,* berries.

Gearha, *gaertha, gearha, gairha,* a bushy riverbank or a stream-thicket.

Gearha, *gaortha,* a wooded valley or river grove.

Gearha, *gaorthadh,* woodland.

Gearhy, *gaorthadh,* a river valley.

Gearn, *gCeithearn,* not given.

Gearrea, *geire,* a sharp incline.

Geary, *gCaorach,* sheep.

Geary, *ghaoraigh,* not given.

Geary, *ghaorthaidh,* a wooded valley.

Geary, *ghearthaig,* river shrubbery.

Gease, *géise,* a swan.

Geashill, *géisill,* a place of swans.

Geata, *geata,* a gate.

Gee, *gaeth, gaeithe, gaoth, gaoithe,* the wind or windy.

Geeba, *gaeth, gaeithe, gaoth,* the wind.

Geegan, *Mhic-Eochagáin,* MacGeoghegan or Geagan, a family name.

Geeha, *gaeth, gaeithe, gáotha, gaoth, gáoithe, gaoithe,* the wind/windy.

Geeheen, *gaothín,* windy.

Geehin, *Uí-Ghaoithín,* O'Geehin or O'Gahin, a family name.

Geehy, *gaeth, gaeithe, gaoth, gaoithe,* the wind.

Geehy, *gaothach,* windy.

Geel, *an-gheimhil,* the fetter.

Geel, *gaill,* the foreigner.

Geel, *Gaodhael, Gaedheal,* the Gaels, Irish people or an Irishman.

Geel, *gCael,* narrow.

Geel, *gCaoil,* marshy streams.

Geel, *gCaol,* not given.

Geela, *geimhleach,* fetters.

Geela, *ghíle,* water.

Geela, *Ó gCaoilte,* not given.

Geelagh, *Gaodhlach,* Irish.

Geelagh, *geilleadh,* enclosure for sheep.

Geelagh, *geimhleach,* fetters or hostages.

Geelagh, *geimhleach,* the prisoner.

Geelagh, *gíleach,* not given.

Geelaun, *gCaolán,* narrow ridges.

Geeloge, *gCaológ,* little narrow ridges.

Geely, *gáile,* wind-beaten.

Geely, *Mhic-Caollaí, gaibhle,* not given.

Geemanig, *ghiománaig,* the steward or servant.

Geemanig, *Giomanaigh,* Steward, a personal or family name.

Geen, *Gaoine,* not given.

Geenan, *Gaoinean,* not given.

Geenly, *gCoinnle, gCáinlidh,* candles.

Geenly, *gCoinnlí,* not given.

Geenty, *nDingthe,* not given.

Geeny, *Gaoine, Géine,* not given.

Geeny, *gCaonaigh, caonach,* moss.

Geer, *caera, gCaorach,* sheep.

Geer, *fhiaghair,* lea land.

Geer, *gabhar,* horses(sic).

Geer, *gCaor, gCaer,* berries.

Geer, *gearr,* pointed or sharp.

Geer, *gearr,* short.

Geer, *ghír,* not given.

Geera, *gCaora,* sheep.

Geeragh, *an-ghaorthadh,* not given.

Geeragh, *caera, cáoradh, gCaorach,* sheep.

Geeragh, *gCiarraigheach,* (of the) Kerrymen.

Geeragh, *gCiarraíoch,* not given.

Geeraghan, *Mhic-Geachráin,* MacGaghran, a family name.

Geerah, *gCaorach,* sheep.

Geeraun, *gCaorán,* little clod or lump of turf.

Geerock, *gCaorán,* little clod or lump of turf.

Geeroge, *ciaróg,* chafers (beetles).

Geeroge, *gCiaróg,* not given.

Geery, *gCaoraigh, gCaorach,* sheep.

Geery, *i-Ghadra*(sic), O'Gara, a family name.

Geery, *Uí-Gadhra,* O'Geary or Guiry, a family name.

Geeth, *gaeth, gaeithe, gaoth, gaoithe,* the wind.

Geevagh, *gaothbhach, gaobach, ghobhach,* not given.

Geever, *an-Ghaobhair,* not given.

Geever, *Mhic-Iomhair,* MacKeever, a family name.

Geevoge, *gCiabhóg,* not given.

Geevraun, *Gaobhrán,* not given.

Gefin, *Géibhinn,* not given.

Gegan, *Mhic-Aogáin,* not given.

Gegaun, *geagan,* a branch.

Geggane, *geaganach, geganach,* a place of branches.

Geggane, *geaganach, geganach,* a place of branches.

Geha, *gaoithe,* wind.

Gehane, *ghaothain,* breeze, wind.

Geirr, *geire,* a sharp incline.

Gelagh, *Gaedhlach, Gaodhlach,* Irish, indicating that these were surrounded by non Irish people.

Gelagh, *Gaolach, Gaolach,* a family name.

Gelagh, *Ghaelach,* not given.

Gella, *gCoilleach,* heath-cocks.

Gellan, *cuillin,* holly.

Gellia, *greaillighe,* a swamp or mire.

Gelliff, *gaillimh, goilbh,* the storm.

Gelly, *Ghoile,* not given.

Gelly, O'Kelly, a family name.

Geloge, *gCaológ,* narrow ridges or ridges left from former tillage.

Gelshagh, *gaillseach,* an earwig or black insect.

Gelshagh, *geilseach,* not given.

Gelvin, *Ghaibhle, Gaibhleann,* not given.

Gelvin, *Mhic-Ghionnáin,* Mac Giollán, a personal or family name.

Gelvin, *n-gealbhan,* sparrows.

Genagh, *géanach,* not given.

Gennedy, O'Kennedy, a family name.

Geoghegan, *na-nGeochagán,* belonging to Mac Eochagáin, a personal or family name.

Geragh, *gaorthadh,* not given.

Geragh, *gCaorach, gCaeireach,* sheep.

Geragh, *ghaorthaidh,* a woody glen.

Gerahies, *gaorthaí,* woody vallies.

Gerald, *Gearóid,* Gerald or Garret a male name.

Gerald, *Ghearailt,* not given.

Gerd, *gCeard,* artificers or tradesmen.

Gereen, *ghaoraidhín,* a little river valley.

Gerig, *ghaorthaidh,* a wooded valley.

Gernal, *Gerlinn,* Gerlin, a personal or family name.

Gerril, *Ghoirill,* not given.

Gesh, *geis, géis,* a swan.

Gesh, *geis,* a spell or charm.

Gesh, *geis, geise,* taboo or prohibition.

Gesh, *gheis,* not given.

Gesh, swans.

Gevlagh, *nGeimhleach,* fetters.

Gevlin, *Gaibhle, Gaibhle,* a personal or family name.

Gevlin, *ghaibhle, geibhleann,* not given.

Ghal, *geal,* white.

Gharry, *gharraidh,* a garden.

Ghary, *chaire,* a wood.

Ghary, *charaidh,* a weir.

Ghaul, *geal,* white.

Ghevlagh, *nGeimhleach,* prisoners.

Ghill, *choill,* a wood.

Ghingergill, *Uí-Iongardail,* Harrington, a family name.

Ghlin, *ghlionn,* a glen.

Ghloon, *glún,* a glen.

Ghokera, *chóchaire,* the cook.

Ghoney, *chonaidh,* firewood.

Ghory, *choire,* a caldron.

Ghory, *chorraigh,* a marsh.

Ghrane, *gharrain,* a grove.

Ghug, *gClog,* bell/s.

Giants Causeway, *Clochan-an-aifir,* stepping stones of the giant, also known by the Anglicized name **'Clohanavowry'**, *clochán-na-bhFómorach, cloch-na-bhFo-mharaigh,* 'the stepping stones of the Femorians' who were giant legendary Sea rovers.

Giants Causeway, *bealach-an-Fhathaigh,* not given.

Gibbagh, *giobach,* rough, ragged, rugged or untidy.

Gibber, *gibber, tobar,* a well.

Gibbet, a gallows or a hanging tree.

Gibbogh, *giobach,* rough or ragged.

Gibbon, *Ghiobúin, Goibín,* not given.

Gibbon, *Giobhaín, Giobúin, Uí-Ghiobuin,* Gibbon or Gibbons, a family name.

Giblin, *Uí-Ghioballáin,* O'Gibellan or O'Giblin, a family name.

Gichagh, a wicker causeway.

Gid, *gaid,* a place of withes.

Gid, *ghaid,* wattle.

Gier, *gCaer,* berries.

Gigla, *gCioglach,* not given.

Gigla, *gCoigealach, gCuigealeach,* distaffs.

Giglach, *gCuigealeach,* distaffs.

Gil, *ghoill, gall,* foreigner.

Gilcagh, *giolcach,* a place of reeds or broom.

Gilcarry, *Mhic-Ghiolla/Giolla-Charraidh,* MacGilcarry, a family name.

Gilcash, *Mic-Gilla-Chuis,* MacGilcash, a family name.

Gilchrist, *Mic-Gilla-Chriost,* MacGilchreest or Gilchreest, a family name.

Gilduff, *Ghiolla-Dhuibh,* not given.

Gile, *coill,* shrubbery, underwood.

Gile, *gaill, ghoill, gall,* foreigner.

Gile, *gile,* white, whiteness or brightness.

Gilford, *áth-Mhic-Ghiolla,* ford of Giolla's sons.

Gilford, *gaillbheart,* not given.

Gilgan, *Uí-Ghiollagain,* O'Gilligan, a family name.

Gilhorn, *Ghiolla-chuirn,* Gilhurn or Glihorn, a family name and means servant of the cup or cup bearer.

Giliee, (sic) *nGiollaí,* youths.

Gilka, *ghiolcaigh,* not given.

Gilkagh, *giolcach, giolcaighe,* a place of broom.

Gilky, *giolcach, giolcaighe,* a place of broom.

Gill, *gaill, gall,* a foreigner or an Englishman.

Gill, *gCuil,* hazel.

Gill, *geal, gile,* white, whiteness or brightness.

Gill, *ghaill, ghoill, gall,* foreigner.

Gill, *Gill, caol,* not given.

Gilla, *gaibhle,* the fork.

Gilla, *geal, gile,* white, whiteness, brightness.

Gilla, *ghiolla,* a groom or servant.

Gilla, *gilla,* a fellow, a boy or a chap

Gillagancan, the headless man.

Gillaganleny, the shirtless fellow.

Gillagh, *gCailleach,* cormorants.

Gillagh, *gCoileach, gCoilleach,* cocks, grouse or woodcocks.

Gillaheen, *Ghiollachaoin,* Gillaheen, a family name.

Gillan, *Cuileannáin,* not given.

Gillane, *gallan,* standing stones.

Gillane, *Uí-Giolláin,* O'Gillan, a family name.

Gillaroe, *Giolla-ruaidh,* Gillaroe or Gilroy, a family name and means the red fellow.

Gillee, *nGiollaidhe,* attendant boys.

Gillee, *nGiollí,* not given.

Gilleen, *ghoilín,* little hollow.

Gilleeny, *gCillinidhe, gCillíní,* little Churches.

Gillen, *Ghiolláin,* not given.

Gillen, *Uí-Ghilín,* O'Gillen or Gilleen, a family name.

Gillew, *Gaileadh,* not given.

Gillew, *gCoilleadh,* woods.

Gilliagh, *gCoilleach,* grouse cocks.

Gillick, *'ic-Uillic,* MacGillic, a family name.

Gillick, *Giollaic,* not given.

Gillihy, *uillighthe,* angular.

Gillion, *gCuilleann,* holly trees.

Gillock, *Giolach,* Gillog, not given.

Gillock, *Giollóg,* not given.

Gilloge, *giolchóg,* a place of reeds.

Gilly, *gCoiligh, goilí,* not given.

Gilly, *giolla,* a servant.

Gilnahirk, *Cill-Ó-nDearca,* Church of Dearc's descendants.

Gilnahirk, *Cill-Ó-nDearca,* not given.

Gilnahirk, *eudan-giolla-na-hadhairce,* hill-brow or brae of the person called Gilnahirk. His name means the 'gillie or boy of the horn' (a horn blower).

Gilrevy, *Giolla-Riabhaigh,* not given.

Gilrevy, MacGilrevy, a family name.

Gilta, *gCoillte,* woods.

Gilta, *gioltach, cuilce,* reeds.

Giltagh, *gCoillteach,* woods.

Giltagh, *giolcach,* a place of broom.

Giltenan, *Mhic-Giolla-tSeanáin/tSeannain,* MacGiltenan.

Giltenane, *Mhic-Giolla-tSeanáin,* Mac Giolla tSeanáin, a personal or family name.

Gilty, *gCoillte, gCoillteach,* woods.

Gin, *gCeann,* heads.

Ginga, *na-ginge,* not given.

Ginity, *Shinhartaigh,* Henerty, a personal or family name.

Ginn, *gCeann,* heads.

Ginnane, O'Ginnane, a family name.

Ginnane, *Uí-Chuinneain,* Guinane, a family name.

Ginniff, *gainimh,* sandy.

Ginniff, *gainimhe,* not given.

Ginnive, *gainimh,* sand, a sand pit or a little sandy place.

Ginny, *gainimh,* not given.

Ginny, *gainimhe,* sand or sandy.

Ginny, MacGuiney, a family name.

Gippaun, *gCeapán,* stakes, stocks or tree trunks.

Gira, *gadhra,* dogs.

Gira, *ghaorthaidh,* a woody glen.

Gire, *ghadhair,* not given.

Gire, *nGadhar, gadhar,* a dog, dogs or foxes.

Girfin, *gairfean,* not given.

Girley, *greallach,* a marshy/miry place.

Girley, *greillighe,* a miry or trampled place.

Girmacan, *Uí-Ghormacain,* O'Gormagan, a family or clan name.

Girr, *nGiorra,* not given.

Girra, *n-girridhthe,* hares.

Girrawn, *gearráin,* the horse.

Girrea, *geirr,* the hare.

Girreen, *ghiodarín,* dung hills.

Girrha, *geirr-fiadgacha,* hares.

Girriha, *girrfhidhthe,* a place of hares.

Girrogue, *giorróg,* lots or cuts (of land).

Gisha, *ceiseach,* wickerwork causeways.

Gishagh, *cisach, gCiseach, gCiseach,* hurdle bridges, wicker causeways or improvised pathways.

Gittagh, *ciotach, gCiotach,* left handed men.

Gittagh, *gCiotach,* not given.

Givel, *gabhail,* a fork, forked.

Givel, *geimheal,* fetters.

Given, *geimhin,* a hide, hides or skins.

Givna, *goibhne,* smith/s.

Gla, stones.

Gla, *clach,* stone walls or stony.

Gla, *gCleath,* wattles or hurdles.

Glace, *glaise,* a stream.

Glace, *gléas,* tools or accoutrements.

Glack, *an-ghlaic,* not given

Glack, *glac, glaic,* a hollow or hollow place.

Glacka, *glaic-a'...,* hollow of the...

Glackaun, little hollow.

Gladree, *an-Ghleadraigh,* not given.

Glaggan, *gCloigeann,* skulls.

Glaggin, *gClaigean,* not given.

Glagh, *gCleath,* hurdles.

Glaghane, *clochán,* stony land.

Glah, *gCleath,* poles, wattles or hurdles.

Glan, *gleann, glean, gleanna, ghleanna,* a glen.

Glana, *ghleann-an…, gleann- na/a'…,* glen of the…

Glanahee, *Mhig-Fhlannchadha,* MacClancy, a family name.

Glanalin, *glean-annlainn,* valley of the pickles.

Glancy, *Mheg-Fhlannchadha,* MacClancy.

Gland, *gleann,* a glen.

Glandore, *cuan-dor*(sic), not given.

Glanna, *ghleanna, gleann,* a glen.

Glanna, *gleann,* a glen.

Glanna, *gleann-a'…,* glen of the…

Glannan, *gleannán,* the little glen.

Glannock, *gleannóg,* little glen.

Glannoge, *gleannóg,* little glen.

Glanntane, *gleantán,* a dell or small valley.

Glanntaun, *gleantán,* a dell or small valley.

Glant, *gleanna,* glens.

Glantane, *gleanntán,* the little glen.

Glantane, *ngleanntán,* little glens.

Glantauluskaha, parched glen(sic).

Glountane-Luskaha, parched glen(sic).

Glantaun, *gleanntán, gleantán,* a little glen.

Glanteen, *glenntín,* a little glen.

Glanthaun, a field.

Glanthaun, *gleanntán,* a small glen.

Glanthaune, *gleanntán,* not given.

Glantine, *ghleanntáin,* the valley or glen.

Glanworth, *gleannamhair, gleannamhnach,* glen of the waters/rivers, *(amhnach).*

Glanworth, *gleannúir,* glen of the yews.

Glanworth, *gleannúir,* watery glen(sic).

Glar, *gClar,* planks.

Glaragh, from *gClár,* planks.

Glare, *gClár, gCláir,* the board/s or planks.

Glare, *gClár,* boards, planks or flat fields.

Glary, *glaury,* muddy.

Glas, *ghlaise,* a stream.

Glas, *ghlas,* not given.

Glas, *glas,* a little stream.

Glas, *glas,* green or grey.

Glas, *glas,* locks or fetters.

Glascloon, *glaslochán,* not given.

Glascurram, *ghlaschluain,* green meadow.

Glasgorman, (River) *glaise-an-Airc/Earc,* not given.

Glash, *glas, glash, glaise,* a little stream.

Glasha, *ghlaise, glaise,* a stream.

Glasha, *glaise-an…,* not given.

Glasha, *glas,* green.

Glasha, *glasha,* a little stream.

Glasha, *nGlaise,* streams.

Glashagh, *an-ghlaiseach,* not given.

Glashagh, *glaiseach, glashagh,* streamy or watery.

Glashana, *glaise-na…,* stream of the…

Glashare, *glais-áir, glais-an-áir,* not given.

Glashare, *glaise-an-áir,* stream of the slaughter.

Glasheen, *ghlaisín,* a little stream or brook.

Glasheen, *ghlaisín,* a small vale(sic).

Glasheen, *glaisín-an…,* streamlet of the…

Glasheen, *Uí-Ghlaisín,* O'Glasheen, O'Glassin or Glassin, a family name.

Glasheena, a place of streams.

Glasheena, *glaisínídhe,* little lea spots.

Glasheens, *glaisíní,* little rills(sic).

Glashina, *glaisíneach,* abounding in streams/streamlets.

Glashling, *glaislinn,* not given.

Glashtin, *glais-tuinne,* a rapid rivulet.

Glashy, *gCalisighe,* trenches.

Glashy, *glaise,* a stream.

Glashy, *glaisigh,* not given.

Glaskan, *glascon,* a tribe named 'Glas cu' meaning grey leader.

Glaskenny, *clais-a-ghainmhe,* hollow of the sand.

Glasker, *glascar,* not given.

Glasker, *glas-sceir,* green rock.

Glaslaw, *ghlasláith,* not given.

Glaslin, *glas-lin,* green pools.

Glasn, *glas-an…,* stream of the…

Glasny, Glasney, a personal or family name.

Glasry, *glasraigh, ghlasraí,* not given.

Glass, *gClas,* furrows.

Glass, *gCleas,* feats.

Glass, *ghlais, glaise, glas,* a green place.

Glass, *ghlas,* green.

Glass, *ghlas,* green.

Glass, *glas, ghlais,* a grey place.

Glass, *glas,* grey or green.

Glassa, *glas-an…,* little stream of the…

Glassan, *ghlasáin,* the linnet.

Glassan, *glasáin,* not given.

Glassan, *glasán,* the streamlet.

Glassan, *glas-an…,* stream of the…

Glassaun, *ghlasáin,* not given.

Glasscloon, *glaschluain,* not given.

Glasserchoo, *glaise-Chú,* not given.

Glassers, *glasraidh,* herbage or verdure.

Glassick, *glasóg,* water wagtails.

Glassillaunvealnacurra, *glas-oileán-beal-na-cora,* little green island of or at the mouth of the weir.

Glassin, *Ghlaisín,* O'Glasheen, a family name.

Glassock, *glasóg,* water wagtails.

Glassog, *glasóg,* water wagtails.

Glassog, *nGlasóg,* wagtails.

Glasson, *Glasáin,* Glasson or Gleeson, a personal or family name.

Glasson, *glasán,* not given.

Glasson, *Glasson,* Glassan, a male name.

Glasson, *Uí-Glasáin,* O'Glassan, a family name.

Glassory, *gClas,* furrows.

Glaster, *glasdair,* not given.

Glaster, *glas-tir,* green land.

Glastrigan, *glas-deargáin,* not given.

Glastry, *glasdoire,* not given.

Glastry, *glasrach,* a grassy green place.

Glaughaun, *clochán,* stone walls.

Glaun, *gleann,* a glen.

Glauna, *gleann-an…,* glen of the…

Glaur, *gClár,* planks.

Glaush, *ghlas,* green.

Glave, *'ig-Lamha,* MacGlave, a family name.

Glavin, *Ghlaimhín,* Glavin, a family name.

Glavin, *Uí-Ghlaimhín,* O'Glavin, a family name.

Glea, *gCleath, gCliath,* hurdles.

Gleaan, *gCáelan,* narrow angles.

Gleagh, *gCliath,* not given.

Gleann, *gleann,* a glen.

Gleanna, *gleann/glean-an…,* glen of the…

Glear, *gCléir,* clergy.

Glear, *gléar,* not given.

Glear, *gleoir,* brightness, clearness.

Glearagh, *cléireach, cléirach,* priests or clergy.

Glearagh, *gCléireach,* not given.

Glearagh, *gCliathrach,* hurdle passages.

Gleath, *gCliath,* hurdles or harrows.

Gleav, *gCliabh,* baskets.

Glebe, *Cill-Ronan, an-bansha,* not given.

Glebe, *an-glaidhb/ghléib,* rented land owned by or attached to the parish Church.

Glebe, *seantoir,* rented land owned by or attached to the parish Church.

Gledane, *gliodán,* not given.

Glee, *gCladh,* mounds.

Gleensk, *glinsce,* not given.

Gleer, *gCliar,* clergymen.

Gleeragh, *Cléirach,* belonging to the priests.

Gleeraha, *gCléireac,* clergymen.

Glemig, *Ghlíomaigh,* not given.

Glen, *glinne, ghleann, ghlinne, gleann,* a glen.

Glena, *glean-na…, glean/glean-a'…, gleann-na/an…,* glen of the…

Glenaan, *glean-Áine,* Hanna's or Annie's (womens names) glen.

Glenaan, *gleannán,* the little glen.

Glenaboy, *glean-abha-buí,* not given.

Glenade, *glean/glen-Éada/Eada,* Eada's (a personal or family name) glen.

Glenade, *glean/glinne-Éada,* not given.

Glenagh, *glean/glean-each,* glen of horses.

Glenalla, *glean-Eala,* not given.

Glenane, *glean-Aidhein,* not given.

Glenane, *glean-Áine,* Hanna's or Annie's (womens names) glen.

Glenaree, *glean-Airí,* not given.

Glenary, *gleann-Áirí,* not given.

Glenastar, *glean-easa-aire, gleann-eas-Dáire,* glen of the cataract of the river 'Daar'.

Glenavy, *lann-Abhaigh/Abhaich,* Church of the dwarf.

Glenbevan, *an-gleann*(sic), not given.

Glenda, *gleann-dá,* glen/valley of the two…

Glendarragh, *glean-Fathroim,* not given.

Glendavagh, glen with deep pools along its course.

Glenealy, *gleann-Fhaidhle,* not given.

Gleneely, *glean/glean-Daoile,* not given.

Glenelly, *glean-Aichle,* not given.

Glengarra, *baile-an-tSean-chaisleáin,* not given.

Glenglassera, *gleann-Lasra*(sic), not given.

Glenish, *gleann/glen-ois,* meadow of the fawns.

Glenisland, *glean/gleann-Aoláin,* Aolan's glen.

Glenlee, *gCáinlidh,* candles.

Glenma, *gleann-Máighe,* valley of the Máigh(sic).

Glenmacnass, *glenn-luig-an-easa,* the district near the waterfall(sic).

Glenna, *glen-na…, gleann-na…, gleann-an…,* glen of the….

Glennagh, *glean-each,* glen of the horses.

Glennan, *gleanán,* little glen.

Glennanore, *glean-Fhionnúir,* not given.

Glennaun, *gleanán,* little glen.

Glennaun, *gleannán,* not given.

Glennyhorn, *cluain-na-hEorna*(sic), not given.

Gleno, *gleann-na…,* not given.

Gleno, glen of yews.

Gleno, *Glen-Ó,* not given.

Glenoe, *glean-eo,* glen of yews.

Glenoe, *gleann-Uamha,* not given.

Glenofaush, *gleann-Faisi,* Glen of '*Fas*' (wife of *Un* the Milesian).

Glen of the Downs, *gleann-dá-ghruadh,* not given.

Glen of the Downs, *gleann-dá-ghrua,* glen of the two brows.

Glenough, *glean/gleann-achaidh,* not given.

Glent, *gleann,* a glen.

Glentan, *ghleanntáin,* a little valley.

Glentane, *gleanntán, gleantán,* a dell or small valley.

Glentara, *gleann-dá-tharbh,* not given.

Glentaun, *gleanntán, gleantán,* a dell or small glen/valley.

Glentauna, *gleanntán-an/na…,* little glen of the…

Glentaunna, *gleanntán/gleanntan-na…,* little valley of the…

Glenties, *na-gleannta/gleanntaidhe,* glens.

Glenties, *na-gleanntaí,* not given.

Glentop, *árdach-mór, árdachadh,* not given.

Glenville, *gleann-an-phréacháin, ráth-Ronáin,* not given.

Glenwilliam, *glean-na-raithe,* not given.

Gleoir, *gleoir,* brightness or clearness.

Glera, *cleire,* clergy, clergyman.

Glera, *gCléireach, gCleireach, cléirach, clereach, clérech,* clergy or clerics.

Gleragh, *cléir, gCléireach,* clerics.

Glery, *gCleireach, gCléireach,* clerics or clergy.

Gleve, *gClaibh,* not given.

Glevragh, *cliabhrach, gCleavrach*(sic), baskets.

Glew, *gCliabh,* baskets.

Glew, *gColbha,* not given.

Gliddane, *gladán,* not given.

Glieve, *gCliabh,* baskets.

Gliggin, *cluigan, gCloigeann,* skulls.

Gliggizha, *gliogaire,* the babbling well.

Glima, *gluim-a'…,* not given.

Glin, *ghlinne, gleann,* a glen or valley.

Glin, *gleann-Chorbraighr, gleann-an-ridire, na-gleannta,* not given.

Glinch, *glinsce,* not given.

Glinn, *gleann, glinne,* not given.

Glinny, *ghleana, ghleanna,* a glen.

Glinny, *gloine,* not given.

Glinsk, *glinnsce,* not given.

Glinsk, *glinsce, glinsc', glin-sceach,* glen of the brambles.

Glish, *ghlaise,* not given.

Glish, *glais,* green.

Glisheen, *Uí-Ghlaisín,* O'Glasheen or Glashen, a family name.

Glissan, O'Gleeson, a family name.

Glissane, O'Glissane or Gleeson, a family name.

Glistenane, *glas-tSeanáin,* not given.

Glistinane, *Glisteaneáin, Glas-tSeanáin,* Senan's (a personal or family name) green place.

Gloc, *gCloch,* great stones.

Gloch, *gCloch,* great stones.

Gloe, *gleo,* contention or strife.

Glogh, *gCloch,* boulders.

Glogh, *gCloch,* stone/s or stony.

Gloghan, *gClochan,* stepping stones.

Gloghane, *gClochán,* not given.

Gloghaun, *gClochán,* ancient stone houses.

Gloghaun, *gClochan,* steping stones.

Glogher, *gClochair,* the stony place.

Glogher, *ghliogair,* a rattling or a whirling noise.

Gloishe, *glaise,* stream.

Glokee, *gClócaí,* cloaks.

Glokee, *gClócaidhe,* cloaks.

Glontach, *gCluainteach,* meadows.

Gloon, *glúine, ghluin, glún,* the knee.

Gloon, *glúing,* resembling a shoulder.

Gloon, *na-nGlún,* not given.

Gloor, *cealluire,* a Churchyard.

Gloor, *gColúr,* pigeons, doves.

Gloor, *gColúr,* pigeons.

Glooria, *gluaire,* purity, clearness or brightness.

Gloos, *cluas, gCluas,* ears.

Glor, *ghloir,* the noise.

Glora, *glóire,* glory.

Glora, *gluaire,* not given.

Glorach, *glórach,* not given.

Gloragh, *ghlórach, glórach,* noisy or voiceful.

Gloragh, *glórach,* purling, voiceful, babbling brook.

Glorane, *gClamhrán, gCluarán,* not given.

Glorane, *gClórán,* pignuts (*Bunium-Flexuosum*).

Glore, *an-ghleóir,* not given.

Glore, *gluaire, gleoir,* brightness or clearness.

Glore, *glór,* sound of the river.

Gloreen, from *glórach,* purling, voiceful or babbling brook.

Glory, *ghleórdha,* not given.

Glory, *glórach,* purling, voiceful or babbling brook.

Glory, *gluaire,* brightness.

Glos, *glas,* green.

Glosh, *glais, glaise,* a streamlet.

Gloshanaane, *glaise-an-gléan,* stream of the glen.

Gloss, *glas,* green.

Glosterboy, *clais-tSearbhóg,* not given.

Glough, *gCloch, cloiche,* stone/s.

Gloun, *gleann, glean,* a glen.

Glouna, *glean,* a glen.

Glounthane, *gleanntán,* not given.

Glounthaune, *an-gleanntán,* the little valley.

Glounthawns, *gleanntáin,* little glens or dells.

Glourane, *gCloithréan,* stones.

Glouria, *gluaire,* purity, clearness or brightness

Glown, *glean,* a glen.

Glowne, a glen.

Gloy, *gCloidhe,* ramparts or hedged fences.

Gluaire, *gluaire,* purity, clearness or brightness

Glug, *gClog,* bell/s.

Glugger, *ghlugair,* not given.

Gluggin, *gCloigeann,* skulls.

Glugh, *gCoilleach,* grouse cocks.

Glune, *glúine,* the knee.

Glunin, *glúinín,* a little bend.

Glunin, *Glúinín,* Glúnín, Glúinín or Gluinin, a personal or family name.

Glush, *glais,* green.

Glush, *glaise, glush,* a little stream.

Glushin, a little rivulet.

Glyde, (river) *an-casan,* not given.

Glyde, *Úlaid,* not given.

Glye, *glaoidhe,* shouting or calling.

Glyn, *gleann, glean,* a glen.

Glynn, *glean-Fhinneachta, glean-Moling,* not given.

Glynn, *gleann,* a glen.

Glynn, *Glinne,* not given.

Gnauv, *gCnamh,* bones.

Gnave, *gCnamh, gCámh,* bones.

Gneev, *gníomh,* not given.

Gneeve, *gniomh,* a measure of land, equalling 10 acres or a twelfth part of a ploughland.

Gneeve, *gníomh,* not given.

Gneeves, *gniomh, gniomha,* measures of land. One gneeve equals one twelfth of a ploughland or 10 acres.

Gneeves, *na-gnímh,* not given.

Gneevgulliagh, *gníomh-go/gniomh-ga-leith,* a gneeve and a half. A land measure equalling 15 acres.

Gno, (of the) nut.

Gnoe, nuts.

Go (island), *ghabha,* not given.

Go, *gobha,* a smith.

Goa, *gobha,* a smith.

Goa, *gotha,* the voice.

Goad, *gCóimhéad,* sentinels.

Goagh, *gCuach, cuach,* cuckoos.

Goagh, *Goach,* Goach, a personal name.

Goagh, *Góch,* not given.

Goan, *dhubháin*(sic), not given.

Goan, *nGabhann,* not given.

Goash, *gCuas,* caves.

Goash, *guaise,* not given.

Goask, *Guaise,* not given.

Gobadane, *gobadan,* a type of bird.

Gobbadagh, *gobadach,* pointed or beaked.

Gobban, *ghobain,* a small beak or gob.

Gobban, *Ghobáin,* Gobban a family name.

Gobban, *Gobán, Ghobain,* St Goban.

Gobban, *Uí-Gobáin,* O'Gobban, a family name.

Gobbane, Gobban, a personal or family name.

Gobbin, Ghobáin, Ghobain, St Gobán, Goban.

Gobbin, Gobbin, a personal or family name.

Gobbin, Mhac/Mhác-Gobáin, the sons of Goban, a personal or family name.

Gobbins, na-gobáin, points of rock or a rocky point.

Gobidane, nGobadán, n-gobadan, sandpipers or gobadanes.

Gobna, gob-na…, snout or land-point of the…

Gobnet, Gobnait, Gobnata, Ghobnait, Ghobnattan, St Gobnait/Gobnat/Gobinet/Gobnata, the virgin Saint.

Gobrooa, gob-ruadh, red point.

Goddaun, Goddaun or Goddan, a personal or family name.

Godee, ghadhaide, gadaidhe, thief.

Godoon, Ghodúnaigh, not given.

Godoon, Godún, Godwin or Godoon, a personal or family name.

Goe, góain, gobha, a smith.

Goe, Góain, not given.

Goe, Gobha, St Gobha, Gobanus.

Goe, Gon, a personal name.

Goff, dhamh, oxen

Goff, gaimh, the storm.

Goff, gomh, not given.

Goff, stone.

Goggan, Goggan, personal or family name

Goghlan, Ó gCochlán, Uí Chochláin, a family name.

Goghlin, Mhig-Cochláin, MacCochlan, a family name.

Gogona, O-gCuana, O'Cooney, a family name..

Goill, ghoill, ghaill, gall, foreigner.

Goill, giolla, manservant.

Goill, woods.

Goish, Gheois, Geoise, not given.

Goish, Uais, descendants of Colla Uais.

Gokane, geocan, a neck of land.

Gola, gaibhle, a river fork.

Gola, gComhla, gates.

Gola, ghabhla, not given.

Gola, gobhlach, forked, gabhla, a fork/s.

Gola, gualann, golan, gualainn, a shoulder.

Golagh, gCoileach, wood cocks.

Golagh, ghabhlach, gobhlach, forked, gabhla, gabhlach, a fork.

Golam, Gólam, not given.

Golan, gabhláin, the fork.

Golan, gabhlán, ghabhláin gualanna, not given.

Golan, ghabhláin, gabhailin, the small fork.

Golan, ghualann, gualainn, the shoulder.

Goland, gabhlán, little river fork.

Goland, gobhláin, gabhláin, a river fork.

Goland, gualann, not given.

Golat, gCullachta, not given.

Golban, Ghulbain, Gulban, the name of a Church founder in Limerick.

Gold, gúil, coal or charcoal.

Golden, ghabhailín, gabhailin, gabhailín, the small fork.

Golden, gualann, ghualainn, ghualann, a hill or shoulder.

Goldrum, an-ghabhail(sic), not given.

Gole, gabhaile, ghabhall, the fork.

Gole, gabhla, ghóbháil, not given.

Gole, gColl, hazels.

Gole, gCual, faggots (for firing).

Gole, góil, forks.

Gole, guail, charcoal.

Goleen, an-góbhailín, not given.

Goleen, gabhailin, the small fork.

Goleen, góilín, goilín, a small sea or river inlet.

Goley, gabhlaighe, river forks.

Goliagh, gCoileach, wood cocks.

Golier, guala, shoulder.

Gollagher, Ollaghan, Uallaghan, Ollaghan or Hoolahan, a family name.

Gollan, galláin, a standing stone.

Gollina, garaidhí, little garden.

Golloglagh, nGallóglach, not given.

Gollop, gColp, heifers.

Gollopy, gColpaí, grazing animals.

Gollum, gColmán, gColm, pigeons.

Gollyeen, coileán, a whelp.

Gollyeen, gCoilleán, little hazels.

Golman, gColmain, Colman, a personal or family name.

Golman, gColman, doves.

Golman, gColmán, gColm, pigeons.

Golman, Ua/O'-gColman, O'Colman, a family name.

Golmen, pigeons.

Gologue, *gabhlóg,* forks.

Golpagh, *gColpach,* not given.

Golree, *gabhalraigh*(sic), not given.

Golrick, *mhig-Ualghairg,* MacGolrock, a family name.

Golry, *gCalraidhe, g-Calruighe,* the people called 'Calry'.

Golum, *gColm,* pigeons or doves.

Golum, *gualainn,* not given.

Goly, *ghabhlaigh,* not given.

Goly, *ghualaidhe,* a charcoal burner.

Goman, *coman,* hurleys or hurling.

Gomartin, *gharraí-Mháirtín,* Martin's (a male name) enclosure or garden.

Gomaun, *gCamán,* not given.

Gomaun, *gComán, coman,* hurling.

Gomaun, *gComan,* hurleys.

Gommon, *gComan, gComán, coman,* hurleys or hurling.

Gomna, *gamhna,* calf.

Gomna, *gamhnach,* milch cows.

Gomon, *coman,* hurling.

Gon, *gCon,* hounds.

Gona, *Dhomhnaígh,* Sunday.

Gonachtagh, *Connachtach,* Connaught men.

Gonean, *gan-éan,* a birdless place.

Goneen, *gCoinínidhe, gCoinín,* rabbits.

Goneeny, *gCoiníní,* not given.

Goneeny, *gCoinínidhe,* rabbits.

Goney, *na-gConai,* rabbits.

Gong, *conga,* antlers of the buck.

Gonigan, *Uí-Dhonnagain,* O'Donegan, a family name.

Gonnaghtagh, *gConnachtach,* a Connaught man.

Gonnal, Conall, a family or personal name.

Gonnan, *gCanann,* not given.

Gonnell, *Conail, gConaill,* Conail, Conall, a personal or family name.

Gonnell, *gCoinnle, gCáinlidh,* candles.

Gonnell, *gConaill,* Connell, a family name.

Gonnell, *Ó gConaile, Uí-Chonaíle, O'gConnell,* O'Connell, a family name.

Gonnelly, Connolly, a family name.

Gonnelly, *Dhonnaíle,* not given.

Gonnelly, *Uí-Dhongaile,* O'Donnelly, a family name.

Gonnelly, *Uí-gConáile, Ghongaile,* Connolly or O'Connelly, a family name and means the decendant of Connoly.

Gonnilla, *congbhaila,* houses.

Gonny, *gConaidh,* firewood.

Gonoge, *gCuinneog,* not given.

Gonogue, *gCuinnneoig, g-cuinneóg, gCuin-neog, gCuineog,* churns.

Gony, *ghamhna,* not given.

Goodan, *Uí-Guadáin,* O'Goddan or Godwin, a personal or family name.

Googa, *gCoigéad,* provinces.

Googa, *gCúigí,* not given.

Googaun, *gagan,* a cliff-side split.

Googeen, *guaigín, gág, gáigín, goug, guag, guaigin, gobhaigin, gobhagán,* a narrow valley or little rock-cleft.

Googh, *gCuach,* cuckoos.

Googy, *Guaige,* not given.

Gooheen, *ghoithín,* a gurgling streamlet.

Goohy, *gCuaiche,* the cuckoo.

Gooig, *guaig,* not given.

Gooil, coal or charcoal.

Gool, *gCual, ghuail,* coal or fuel.

Gool, *gCúil,* corners.

Gool, *gabháil, ghabhall,* a fork.

Gool, *gúil,* not given.

Goola, *ghúlaigh,* not given.

Goola, *guala,* a shoulder.

Goola, *ghualaigh,* a charcoal burner.

Goolagh, *gCuailleach,* poles.

Goolan, *ghabhláin, gabhláin,* a river fork.

Goolan, *gualainn, gualann,* a hill or shoulder.

Gooland, *gabhláin,* a river fork.

Gooland, *cuillin,* holly.

Goold, *ghabhall,* a fork.

Goold, *Gúl,* not given.

Goolds Cross, *crosara-an-ghualaigh,* not given.

Goole, *gabhail, ghabhall,* the fork.

Goole, *ghóbail, ghabháil, gabhal,* forks.

Goole, *ghuail, guail, gual,* coal or charcoal.

Goole, *gualaigh,* not given.

Gooley, *Ghúilidhe,* (belonging to) Gooley, a personal or family name.

Goolny, *gualainne,* not given.

Goolny, *gualuinne,* (hill) shoulder.

Gooly, *gCuaille,* not given.

Gooly, *gCuailleadh,* stakes or poles.

Gooly, *ghualaidhe,* a charcoal burner.

Gooly, *guail, gual,* gualaigh, coal or charcoal.

Gooly, *guala,* a ridge, hill shoulder or shoulder of land.

Goon, *dhuim*(sic), a fort.

Goon, *ghabhainn,* not given.

Goon, *nGamhan, gamhan,* calves.

Goona, *gamhnach,* a stripper cow.

Goona, *ghamhna,* the calf.

Goona, *gúnach, n-gamhna, n-gamhnach,* strippers, milch cows or calves.

Goonagh, *gamhnach,* heifers, yearling calves or milch cows.

Goonan, *gCuanain,* Coonan or O'Coonan, a family name.

Goonan, *Guanain,* O'Goonan, a family name.

Goonan, *Ó gCuanáin, Uí Chuanáin,* a family name.

Goonaun, *Uí-Ghúnáin,* O'Goonan, a family name.

Gooneen, *gCoinín,* rabbits.

Goony, *dhamhna,* not given.

Goony, *gabhna,* a calf.

Goord, *gCuaird,* rounds, circuits or visitations.

Goord, *gCuard,* not given.

Goordagh, *guairdeach,* whirlwinds.

Gooreen, *guairín,* the little sandbank.

Goorland, *ghuairlcain*(sic), whirlwind.

Goosat, *guasachta,* danger.

Goose, *gCaas*(sic), *gCuas, gCuas, cuas,* cave/s, sea inlets or coves.

Goose, *gCabhas,* stepping stones.

Goose, *gCluas,* ears.

Goose, *Guaise, guas,* not given.

Gooter, *Gúitir,* not given.

Gopple, *gCapull, g-capal,* a horse/s.

Goppoge, *gCopóg,* docks or dock leaves.

Goppoge, *gCopóg,* Rumex Obtusifolius, (docks).

Goppul, *gCapull, gCapall, gCapal,* a horse/s.

Gor, *gCorr, corr,* herons, cranes or sandeels.

Gor, *Gor,* not given.

Gor, *gabhar,* goats.

Gor, *gortha,* scorched or burnt.

Gora, *gabhra, gabhrach,* goats.

Goragh, *gabhrach,* a place of goats.

Goran, *(na) nGabhrán,* not given.

Goran, *gabhran,* a place of goats.

Goran, *Uí-Ghabhráin,* O'Gowran, a family name.

Gorane, *gCorrán,* reaping hooks.

Gorane, *gharán,* shrubbery.

Gorave, *n-garbh,* rough (persons).

Gorbery, *gCairbre,* Carbery, a personal or family name.

Gorbet, *carboid,* a chariot.

Gorbet, *gCarbad,* not given.

Gordan, *Cordáin, Cordán,* a personal or family name.

Gorden, *gCuiridin,* parsnips.

Gordon, *gCuiridin,* parsnips.

Gordon, *gCuirridín,* equisetum or the weed 'horsetail' or 'horsetail grasses'.

Gore, *gabhair, gabhra,* horse(sic).

Gore, *gabhar, gabar, gabhra, nGabhar, nGobhar,* goat/s.

Gore, *gCaradh, gCuradh,* heroes.

Gore, *gCora,* weirs.

Gore, *gCorr, corr,* heron/s or crane/s.

Gore, *gCorr,* herons or cranes.

Gore, *gCorr,* round hills.

Gore, *ghabha, gahar*(sic)*, gabhar, gabhair, gobhair,* goat/s.

Gore, *ghabhair,* not given.

Gore, *na-cór,* round hills.

Gore, warriors.

Gorea, *gCairrfhiadh,* not given.

Goree, *gabhrach,* a place of goats.

Gorey, *gabhar,* goats.

Gorey, *gabhrach,* a place of goats.

Gorey, *Guaire,* Gorey, a male name and also a sandbank.

Gorey, *guaireach,* wooded or bristly.

Gorey, *Guara, Guaire, Guara,* a male name.

Gorgon, *Goirrgin,* not given.

Gorian, *Uí-Ghabhrain, Mac-Ghabhrain,* O'Gowran, MacGowran, MacGorian or Gorian, a family name.

Gorkagh, *gCnocach*(sic), not given.

Gorkagh, *gCorcaigheach, gCorcach,* Corkmen.

Gorm, *gorm,* blue or blueish.

Gorm, *ghorm,* dark green(sic).

Gormack, *Ó-gCormaic,* not given.

Gormack, *Chormaic,* Cormac, a male name.

Gormal, *Gormghal,* Gormal, a personal or family name.

Gorman, *garman,* a beam or a weavers beam.

Gorman, *garman,* gallows.

Gorman, *Goirmin,* Gormeen, a personal or family name.

Gorman, *Ghormáin, Garmán,* not given.

Gorman, *Uí-Ghormain, Ghormáin, Gormain,* Ó Gormán or O'Gorman, a family name.

Gormican, *O'Cormacain,* O'Cormacan, a family name.

Gormlee, *gormlaith,* blueish grey.

Gormley, *Ghormaile, Ghormlaithe,* Gormley, a family name.

Gormly, *Ghormaíle, Ghormla,* not given.

Gormly, *Gormly,* a family or personal name.

Gorms, *gorm,* blue.

Gormuck, Cormac, a personal or family name.

Gormuck, *Uí-Chormaic, Ó-gCormaic, a-gCormaic,* O'Cormac, a family name.

Gorna, *eorna,* barley.

Gorna, *gCoirneach,* not given.

Gornan, *gCarnan,* little carns or monumental piles of stones.

Gornmagh, *Gormach,* not given.

Gorp, *gCorp,* corpses or bodies.

Gorr, *gCorr,* cranes.

Gorra, *garraidhe,* garden.

Gorragh, *garbh,* rough.

Gorragh, *garbhach,* rough or rough land.

Gorran, *corráin,* not given.

Gorran, *garrán, garráin,* a shrubbery.

Gorrane, *garrán,* a shrubbery.

Gorraun, *garran, garran,* a shrubbery.

Gorraun, *gharrain,* not given.

Gorree, *gharraidh,* a garden.

Gorrif, *garb, garbh,* rough.

Gorriff, *garb, garbh,* rough.

Gorrive, *garb, garbh,* rough.

Gorro, *garbh,* rough.

Gorry, *garbhaí, Gofraidh, Ghofraidh, Gothraidh,* not given.

Gorry, *Godhfhraigh, Gothfraidh, Gothfraith,* Gorry or Godfrey, a male name.

Gorry, *Gofhraigh,* Godfrey or Geoffrey, a male name.

Gorry, *Uí-Ghuaire,* O'Guary, a family name.

Gort, *ghoirt, ghort, guirt,* not given.

Gort, *gort,* a field or a stone walled tilled field.

Gorta, *gorta,* hunger or famine.

Gorta, *gort-an/a'...,* field or enclosed field of the...

Gortagh, *gorta, gortach,* starved, hunger or famine.

Gortahill, *carraig-an-Bhuidheacháin,* not given.

Gortalia, *gort-tSaile, goirt-sháile,* not given.

Gortan, a little enclosed field.

Gortan, *gort-an...,* enclosed field of the...

Gortanoura, *gort-an-fhuaráin*(sic), not given.

Gortar, *gort-air...,* field of(sic) the...

Gortarevan, *gort-an-chraoibhín*(sic), not given.

Gorteanish, *gort-Aonghuis,* Angus's (a male name) field.

Gorteen, *ghoirtín, na-nGoirtíní,* not given.

Gorteen, *guirtín,* a little field or tillage plot.

Gorteen, *guirtínidhe, goirteen*(sic), *gortin,* (a place of) little fields.

Gorteena, *goirtín-na/a'..., goirtín-na/a'...,* little field of the...

Gorteena, *goirtin-a'...,* little field of...

Gorteenara, *goirtín-arbha,* small field of the corn.

Gorteenna, *goirtín-na...,* little field of the...

Gorteens, *na-gortáin,* not given.

Gorteeny, *nGuirtínidhe, nGoirtíní, goirtíní, goirtínidhe,* little enclosed gardens or little tilled fields.

Gorten, *guirtínidhe, gortin,* little fields.

Gorter, *gartan,* not given.

Gorter, *gort-air...,* field of the(sic)...

Gorter, *gort-ar...,* field on the...

Gortevy, *gort-an-bheithe,* not given.

Gorti, *gort-an/a'...,* field of the...

Gorticleave, *gort-a'chlaidhimh,* sword land, land conquered by the sword or field of the sword.

Gortin, *ghoirtín,* not given.

Gortin, *gort-an...,* field of the...

Gortin, *goirtín, gortin, gortín,* little field.

Gortinagin, *goirtín-na-gCeann,* tilled field of the heads.

Gortinea, *guirt-an-fhiaidh,* field of the deer.

Gortins, *gorteen,* enclosed fields.

Gortinty, *gort-teinte,* field of fires.

Gortiny, *goirtín,* a small field.

Gortiny, *na-ngortiní,* little fields.

Gortlandroe, *gort-oileáin-rua,* not given.

Gortlanna, *gort-glúna*(sic), not given.

Gortn, *gort-an…,* field of the…

Gortna, *gort-na/an…,* field of the…

Gortna, *gort-n-atha,* field of the ford.

Gortnada, *gort-an-Áraigh*(sic), not given.

Gortnafaha, *gort-an-atha,* field near the ford(sic).

Gortnatubbrid, *gort-na-Tiobratan,* not given.

Gortolee, *gort-Úlaí,* not given.

Gortrevy, *guirt-riabhaigh,* grey field.

Gortussa, *gort-tosaigh,* front field.

Gortussa, *gort-Osaidh/Usaidh,* not given.

Gorty, *gorta,* hunger or famine.

Gorty, *gort-tighe….,* the field of (a personal or a family name) house.

Gorty, *gort-Uí…,* the field of… (followed by a family or clan name).

Gorumna, (island) *garmna,* not given.

Gorv, *garb, garbh,* rough.

Gorvagh, *garbhach,* a rough place.

Gorvagh, *garbhachadh,* not given.

Gory, *Gabhra,* St Guara.

Gory, *gCoirigh,* malefactors.

Gory, *guaire,* rough.

Gory, *gCoirte,* a standing stone.

Gose, *cuas,* a cave.

Gose, from *cuas,* caves, sea inlets or coves.

Gose, *gabha*(sic), not given.

Goshaden, *goisidin,* not given.

Gosheden, *geósadán,* yellow ragweed or a stalk.

Goshel, *gCaiseal,* castles.

Goshel, *gCaiseal,* oratories or stone walls(sic).

Goshen, *gCoisín,* footmen.

Gospagh, *gCuspach,* uneven land.

Goss, *gas,* sprigs or white-ears.

Gotach, *gCiotach,* left handed.

Gotach, *gCotach,* small flat bottomed boats.

Gotoon, *Geotún,* not given.

Goug, *cubhog, gCubhóg,* jackdaws.

Gouga, *gCóigheadh,* provinces.

Gougane, *gabhagan,* a small crevice or cave.

Gougane, *gabhgán,* not given.

Gougane, *guagán,* a mountain recess.

Gougane, *guagán,* a rock cleft or rocky cave.

Gougeen, *gabhagán,* a small cleft.

Gough, *cuach, gCuach,* cuckoos.

Goul, *coll, gColl,* hazels or hazel bushes.

Goul, *gabhal,* a fork.

Goul, *gall,* strangers.

Goul, *ghabhla,* not given.

Goul, *gobhlach,* forked, *gabhla, gabhal,* a fork.

Goul, *guail,* coal.

Goul, *guaille, guala,* a shoulder.

Goul, *nGall,* foreigners.

Goula, *gabhal-a'…,* fork or opening of the…

Goula, *gabhalda,* a fork or forked.

Goula, *guaille, guala,* a shoulder.

Gouladane, *gabhaladáin,* little fork.

Goulane, *ghobhláin, ghalláin, ghallán,* not given.

Goulane, *gobhlán, gobhláin,* a little fork.

Goulaun, *gobhlán, gobhláin,* a little fork.

Goulda, *gabhal-an-dá…,* fork of the two…

Goule, *gabhal,* a fork.

Goule, *ghabhail,* not given.

Goulna, fork of the…

Gouloge, *gCúlóg,* not given.

Goum, *coom,* vallies.

Goum, from, *cum, cúm,* hollows.

Goum, *gCeann,* heads.

Goum, *gCom,* deep vallies.

Goun, *gabhann,* a smith.

Goun, *gCeann, g-ceann,* heads.

Goun, *n-gamhan,* calves.

Gour, *gabhair,* not given.

Gour, *gamhair,* winter streams.

Gour, *ghabhair,* goat/s.

Goura, *gabhra,* not given.

Gourdagh, *guair-deach,* whirlwinds.

Gourdeen, little field.

Gouree, *gaorthaí,* woody vallies.

Gouree, *guairí,* a rough covering or bristles.

Gourney, *Guairne, Guairne,* a personal or family name.

Gourney, *Uí-Dhoirinne,* Dorney, a family name.

Goush, *giumhas, giumhaise, ghiumhais,* fir.

Goushee, *giumhaise,* fir.

Goushee, *giumhaisí,* not given.

Gousta, *ghósta,* the ghost.

Gow, *gCabha,* caves.

Gow, *ghobha, ghaba, gabha, ghabha,* smith/s.

Gow, *gow, gabha, goba, gabhan, ghamnann, gobagobha,* a smith.

Gowan, *ghabhainn,* a stone cattle pen.

Gowan, *ghabhann, gabhan, goba, ghamnann, nGabhann, gobha,* a smith or smiths.

Gowan, *ghabhlach,* forked.

Gowan, *ghamhna,* not given.

Gowan, *gobhain,* a blacksmith.

Gowan, *Mhic-Ghabhann, Mhic-Gabhann,* MacGowan, Mac Gabhann, a family name.

Gowan, *nGabhann, nGamhan, gamhan, gamuin,* a calf or calves.

Goward, *guth-árd,* loud voice(sic).

Gowdan, *Uí-Ghabhadáin,* O'Gowdan, a family name.

Gowel, *gabhail,* not given.

Gowel, *gabhal,* a fork.

Gowel, *gobhlach,* forked, *gabhla,* a fork.

Gower, *fhobair, fhobhair, fobhair,* a spring, well.

Gower, *gabhra, ghabhar, ghabhair, ghobhair,* not given.

Gower, *ghabha, gabhar, gabhair, gobhair, nGabhar,* goat/s.

Gowes, *Gamhnach, Uí-Ghamhna,* not given.

Gowes, *gow, gabha, gabhan, gabhann, ghamnann, gobha,* a smith.

Gowk, *gCuach,* the cuckoo.

Gowla, *gabhlach,* a place of forks.

Gowla, *gaibhle, gaibhle, gabhla,* the fork.

Gowlagh, *gabhlach,* a place of forks.

Gowlan, *an-gabhlán,* not given.

Gowlan, *gabhailin, gabhláin, ghabhláin,* the small fork.

Gowlan, *gamhnaigh,* a calf.

Gowlan, *ghabhláin,* the fork.

Gowland, *gamhnaigh,* a calf.

Gowlane, *gabhlan, gabhlán,* a little fork.

Gowlane, *gabhlan,* branching off.

Gowlane, *gabhlán, ghabhláin, ghabhlain,* a fork.

Gowlane, *ghallain,* a standing stone.

Gowlane, *n-gabhlan,* small forks.

Gowlaun, *an-gabhlán,* not given.

Gowlaun, *gabhailin,* the small fork.

Gowlaun, *gamhnaigh,* a calf.

Gowle, *gabhal,* a river fork.

Gowley, *gabhlach, gaibhle,* forked.

Gowlin, *gualainn,* not given.

Gowloge, *gabhlóige,* not given.

Gowloge, *nGabhlóg,* river forks.

Gowloge, *Uí-Ghabhlóig,* O'Gowloge, O'Gowlog, a family name.

Gowly, *gabhla,* the fork.

Gowly, *gaibhle,* forks.

Gowlyawns, from *gabhalán,* forks.

Gown, corruption of *ghabhall,* the fork.

Gown, *gabhann, ghabhann, nGabhann,* not given.

Gown, *gCean, gCeann,* heads.

Gown, *gobha, gabhan,* a smith.

Gown, *nGabhan, ghamhann,* smiths.

Gown, *nGamhuin,* calves.

Gowna, *gamhnach,* heifers, yearling calves or milch cows.

Gowna, *gamhnach,* the barren cow(sic).

Gowna, *ghabhna, gamhna, gabhna,* the calf.

Gowna, *gobha, nGabhann,* a smith or smiths.

Gowna, *nGamhna,* not given.

Gownagh, *gamhna,* calves.

Gownagh, *gamhnach,* heifers, milch cows, milking cows with a year old calf, a stripper cow or a milking cow in the second year after calving.

Gownah, *gamhnach,* heifers, milking cows with a year old calf, a stripper cow or a milking cow in the second year after calving.

Gowne, *ghabhainn,* a stone cattle pen.

Gowney, *gamhnaigh, gamhna, ghamhna,* a calf.

Gowney, *nGaibhne,* not given.

Gowney, *Uí-Ghamhna,* O'Gowna or Gaffney, a family name.

Gowny, *gabhna,* a calf.

Gowny, *gamhna,* calves.

Gowr, *nGabhar,* goats.

Gowra, *ghabhra,* the goat.

Gowragh, *gamhrach,* abounding in winter streams.

Gowran, *bealach-Gabhran,* Gobhrán's (a personal or family name) pass or road.

Gowran, *bealach-Ghabhráin,* Gabhran's (a personal or family name) pathway.

Gowran, *baile-Ghabhráin,* Gabhran's (a personal or family name) homestead.

Gowran, *gabhrán, gabhran,* goats or horses.

Gowre, *gCorr,* round hills.

Goy, *gaoithe,* wind, windy.

Goyne, *gCadhan, cadhan,* a barcacle goose.

Goyne, *gCadhan,* ducks.

Goynig, *gamhnaighe,* a stripper cow.

Goynig, *n-gaibhne,* smiths.

Graan, *grán,* a corn field.

Grace, *ghrásaigh,* not given.

Grace, *gréis, gréise,* battle.

Gracedieu, *grás-Dé,* grace of God.

Grackan, *gCroiceann,* hides or skins.

Gracken, *gCraiceann,* not given.

Graddoge, *greadóg,* scorched or burnt land.

Graddum, *gradam,* not given.

Graddy, *Greadhaithe,* not given.

Gradoge, *graigeog,* a village or hamlet.

Gradoge, *greadóg,* scorched or burnt land.

Grady, *Ui-Ghreada,* O'Grady, a family name.

Graffa, from *grafaun/graifan,* a grubbing tool, meaning grubbed land, cultivated using a grubber or pickaxe.

Graffa, *grafach,* not given.

Graffa, *grafán,* land worked with a grubbing axe, grubbed land.

Graffan, *ghrafáin, grafán,* land worked with a grubbing axe, grubbed land.

Graffan, *grafainn,* not given.

Graffan, *Rafon,* Raffon, a family name.

Graffee, *na-grafaí,* not given.

Graffer, *ghrafaire,* a grubber, meaning grubbed land, cultivated using a grubber or pickaxe.

Graffin, from *grafaun/graifan,* a grubbing tool, meaning grubbed land, cultivated using a grubber or pickaxe.

Graffin, *ghrafainn,* not given.

Graffin, *ghrafuin,* grubbing axe or pickaxe.

Graffin, *grafán,* land worked with a grubbing axe, grubbed land.

Graffog, from *grafaun/graifan,* a grubbing tool, meaning grubbed land, cultivated using a grubber or pickaxe.

Graffoge, *grafán,* land worked with a grubbing axe, grubbed land.

Graffon, from *grafaun, graifan,* a grubbing tool, meaning grubbed land, cultivated using a grubber or pickaxe.

Graffon, *Rafon,* not given.

Graffy, *an-ghrafaidh/ghrafaigh/grafaidh,* not given.

Graffy, from *grafaun, graifan,* a grubbing tool, meaning grubbed land, cultivated using a grubber or pickaxe.

Graffy, *ghrafaig, grafán,* land worked with a grubbing axe, grubbed land.

Graffy, *grafann,* neighing horses(sic).

Grag, *grág,* cackling of birds.

Grag, *graig,* a village.

Graga, *gráig-an..., gráige,* not given.

Gragan, from *graig,* little villages.

Gragane, from *graig,* little villages.

Gragane, *grágán,* not given.

Gragara, *ghrágaire,* not given.

Gragara, *gragara,* cackling of birds.

Gragara, *gráig-an/na-rátha, graig-a'-raith,* hamlet of the rath.

Gragarnagh, *ghrágarnach,* not given.

Gragauga, *grágách* (Welsh language), a village.

Gragaugh, from *graig,* a hamlet.

Gragaugh, *gráig-átha,* not given.

Grageen, from *graig,* little villages.

Grageen, *graigín,* a little hamlet.

Gragh, *gCreach,* cattle spoils.

Gragh, *gréach,* a boggy plain or a mountian flat.

Graghil, *greamhchoill,* not given.

Gragra, *ghrágaire,* the croaker.

Gragra, *gr'igre*(sic), nose(sic) of cackling birds.

Gragullagh, *grágalach,* bird cackling.

Gragy, from *grág,* bird cackling.

Gragy, *ghráige,* not given.

Grahormack, *garrdha-Chormaic,* Cormac's (a personal or a family name) garden.

Grahormick, *garrdha-Chormaic,* Cormac's (a personal or a family name) garden.

Graig, *ghráig, graig, gráig,* a village or hamlet.

Graiga, *gráig/graig-an/a'...,* village or hamlet of the...

Graiga, *gráige,* a hamlet.

Graigaman, *gráig-Ghíomáin,* not given.

Graiganster, *gráig-Anstair,* not given.

Graigavine, *gráig-Ó-bhFinn,* not given.

Graigeen, from *graig*, little village.

Graigeen, *gráigín*, not given.

Graigna, *gráig/graig-na…*, village or hamlet of the…

Graigoor, *gráig-Iúir*, not given.

Graigue, *graife*(sic), *ghráig, na-grága*, not given.

Graigue, *ghraig, gráig, graig, graigue*, a village or hamlet.

Graigue, *gráige*, a herd of hroses.

Graiguea, *gráig/graig-a'…*, village or hamlet of the…

Graiguean, *graig-an…*, village or hamlet of the…

Graiguena, *gráig/graig-na…*, village or hamlet of the…

Graigues, *na-grága*, not given

Graigueswood, *coill-Ghreig*, Gregg's (a personal or family name) wood.

Grain, *ghréin*, the sun.

Grainey, *gréine*, of the sun.

Grallagh, *ghreallach, greallaighe, greallach*, a marsh, soft ground or a miry place.

Grallan, *ghrealláin, ghreallain*, a mire.

Grally, *greallaigh, greallaighe*, a marshy or miry place.

Gramph, *gCreamha, gCreamh*, wild garlic.

Gran, *gCrann, gCrann*, trees.

Gran, *gran, grean*, gravel.

Grana, *gCránach, gránach*, sows.

Grana, *gCranna*, trees.

Grana, *gráinne*, grain.

Grana, *gránna, grana*, ugly.

Grana, *greanach*, a gravelly place.

Grana, *na-gCanánach*(sic), not given.

Granagh, *gCanánach*(sic), not given.

Granagh, *gCoirneach*, clerics.

Granagh, *gCránach*, sows.

Granagh, *granach*, gravelly.

Granagh, *granagh*, grain, a place producing grain.

Granagh, *greanach*, sandy.

Granagh, *greanthach, greanach*, gravely or gravel pits.

Granaghan, from *greanach*, little gravely place.

Granaghan, *granagh*, grain, a place producing grain.

Granaghan, *greanach*, a place of gravel.

Granaghe, *garranaighe*, groves.

Granard, *gránárd, gránard*, the ugly height.

Granard, *gran-árd*, the grain hill.

Granard, *greancha, an-garrán-ard*, not given.

Granard, *gréine-árd*, hill of the sun.

Grane, *gCrann*, trees.

Grane, *gharráin, gharrain*, shrubbery.

Graney, *Ghráinne*, Grania or Grace, a personal or family name.

Graney, *greanach*, gravelly.

Graney, *Gréine, Gráinne*, daughter of Cormac mac Airt. She was buried at Tomgraney (Grainne's tomb/burial mound).

Graney, *Gréine, Greine,* …of the Grian, see **Greenane.**

Graney, *Greine*, Grian, a female name.

Grange, *ghráinseach*, a monastic farm.

Grange, *ghráinseach, gráinsí*, not given.

Grange, *gráinseach*, a farm and buildings, a monastic out-farm.

Grange, *gráinsighe, gráinseach, grainnseach, grainseach*, a place where grain is stored after harvest, generally monastic.

Grange, *graig*(sic)-*an…*, hamet of the…

Grangebellew, *gráinseach-an-dísirt-Muing-Gratan*, not given.

Grangecon, *gráinseach-an-chon*, not given.

Grangefertagh, *feartach-na-gCaorach*(sic), not given.

Grangesilvia, *gráinseach-na-coille*(sic), not given.

Grangi, *gráinseach*, a monastic farm or grange.

Grania, *Gráine, Gráinne, Ghráinne*, Grania, a female name.

Graniera, *garrán-iarthach*, not given.

Granig, *greanaigh, greanach*, gravelly.

Grann, *gCrann*, trees.

Grann, *gránna*, ugly.

Granna, *gCrann, g-cranna*, trees.

Granna, *gCranna*, trees.

Granna, *greancha*, not given.

Granny, *ghreanach*, not given.

Granny, *greannaighe, greanach*, gravelly land.

Granny, *Greine*, Grian, a female name.

Granoge, *gráineóg*, hedgehog/s.

Granoge, *Grainne-óg*, Granoge, the name of a Munster Queen.

Granogy, *gráineóg*, hedgehog/s.

Gransha, *ghráinseach*, not given.

Gransha, *gráinsigh, gráinseach, grainseach, grainseach,* a place where grain is stored after harvest, usually monastic.

Granshagh, *grainseach,* a place for storing grain after harvest, usually monastic.

Granshy, *grainseach, grainsighe,* a grange, monastic granary or farm.

Granshy, *gráinsí,* not given.

Grant, *Chrónata, Ghróntaigh,* not given.

Grant, *Ghranntaigh,* (belonging to) Grant, a personal or family name.

Granville, *darmhagh-mín,* not given.

Grassan, *gCrossan,* small crosses.

Grat, *gCreacht,* cattle preys, a place where rustlers kept the stolen cattle.

Grat, *gCreat,* not given.

Grattan, *gCreatán,* not given.

Graug, *nGráig,* hamlets.

Graugh, *gCruach,* ricks, stacks.

Graun, *gaineamh,* sandy soil.

Graun, *garran, garrán,* a shrubbery.

Graun, *gCorrán,* not given.

Graun, *gCran,* trees.

Graun, *gCrann, gCranna,* trees.

Graun, *grain,* corn.

Grauv, *gCnamh,* bones.

Gravale, *droibhéal,* barren land or wild country.

Gravale, *gairbhéal,* a gravely place.

Gravaun, *Garbháin,* Garvan, a personal or family name.

Grave, *gCnámh, gCnamh,* bones.

Grave, *gCraobh,* branches, bushes or branchy trees.

Gravery, *gCraobhdhoire,* not given.

Grawn, *garran, garrán,* a shrubbery.

Grea, *Cré,* not given.

Greach, *gréach,* not given.

Greagah, *gréagach,* sparkling (river).

Greagh, *gCreach,* cattle spoils.

Greagh, *gCruitheach,* not given.

Greagh, *ghréach, ghréagh, gréach,* not given.

Greagh, *greach, ghréich,* moorland or bog.

Greagh, *greach, gréagh,* a level moory place or a coarse mountain flat.

Greagh, *greagh, greach,* level spot between hills, a coarse mountain flat or just a mountain flat.

Greagh, sloping land that produces carse grass.

Greagh, *nGreadh,* steeds.

Greagha, *gréacha,* mountain flats.

Greagha, *gréach-a'…,* coarse mountain flat of the…

Greaghan, *Griochan,* Grehan a personal or family name.

Greaghans, little mountain flats.

Greaghna, *gréach-na…,* mountain flat of the…

Grean, *ghréine,* a sunny spot.

Greana, *Ghréine, Ghreine,* not given.

Greana, *greanach,* gravelly.

Greana, *greíne,* sun or sunny.

Greanagh, *greanach,* gravelly.

Greanagh, *nGrianach,* not given.

Greane, *Gréine,* not given.

Greany, *Ghráine,* Graine or Grace, a personal or family name.

Greany, *Ghráinne,* not given.

Greany, *ghréine, gréine,* the sun or a sunny rock.

Greany, *Ghréine,* Grian a personal name.

Greany, *Gréine, Gréine,* not given.

Greany, *grianan, grianán, grianáin,* a royal palace, a summer residence, a solarium, an eminent place, a sunny rock, a sunny place, a sunny nook or a fairy queen.

Greasy, *ghréasaí,* not given.

Greave, *gníomh,* a measurment of 10 acres.

Gree, *gCrioch,* boundaries.

Gree, *gCroidh,* cattle herds.

Gree, *gCroidhe, n'gCroidh,* cattle.

Gree, *gCroithe,* cattle pens.

Gree, *geroighe, geroithe,* cattle pens, folds or sheds.

Gree, *graí, gCroide,* horses.

Gree, *graí, groighe,* the stud.

Gree, *graighe,* not given.

Gree, *groighe,* a collection of stones.

Gree, *groighe,* cattle, horses or a horse-stud.

Gree, *gCruidh,* cattle or horses.

Greedan, *Críodáin,* not given.

Greehy, *gaoithe,* the wind.

Greek, *Ó-gCríc,* not given.

Green, *críom,* withered.

Green, *dhraighneach,* not given.

Green, Greenan, Greenane, Greenaun, *grianan, ghrianáin, grianán, grianáin,* a royal palace, fairy palace, bower, summer residence, solarium, balcony, gallery, eminent place, the sun, sunny place, important place, a sunny hill or a fairy queen.

Green, Grianna, not given.

Greena, gréine, the sun.

Greenagh, dhraighneach, not given.

Greenagh, draoineach, blackthorns.

Greenagh, grianach, sunny.

Greenaghan, greanachan, a small gravelly place.

Greenan, (island) oileán-an-tighe, not given.

Greenan, ghrianáin, grianán, not given.

Greenan, grianáin, a fairy palace, a summer house or summer hill.

Greenan, Uí-Ghríanáin, Ó Gríanáin, a family name.

Greenane, grianán, a summer dwelling place.

Greenane, grianán, ghríanáin, a sunny house, place, an important place or a palace.

Greenans, grianáin, important or sunny places.

Greenaun, grianán, an important or sunny place.

Greenoge, dhraighneog, blackthorns.

Greenoge, from grianan, a sunny little hill.

Greenoge, gráineóg, hedgehog/s.

Greenoge, grianóg, a sunny little spot.

Greenore, an-ghrianfoirt/grianfort(sic), not given.

Greenore, grianphort, the sunny landing place or port.

Greeny, dhraighnigh(sic), not given.

Greeny, grianach, sunny.

Greer, gCruidhe, cattle.

Greeragh, gCaorach, sheep.

Greese, (river) an-Ghrís, not given.

Greeve, gCraobh, branches or branchy trees.

Greeve, gríomh, a measure of land.

Greeve, na-craoibhe, not given.

Gregane, ghragáin, a little village.

Gregane, graigín, a little village.

Gregane, Mhic-Riagáin, not given.

Greggan, gCreagán, gCreagan, rocks or rocky.

Greggane, ghragáin, a little village.

Greggaun, gCreaggán, rocks.

Greggaun, gCriogán, nets.

Gregorlough, grágarlach, a place of tree stumps.

Gregory, Ghriaire, Gregory, a personal name.

Greigh, Creagh, a family name.

Greigh, gCraebach, branches.

Greigh, gCroighe, cattle.

Greish, gCrois, crosses.

Grella, gCléireach(sic), not given.

Grellagh, an-ghreallach, not given.

Grellagh, greallach, flat or clearing.

Grellan, griddle, a cromlech, (see **Cromlech**).

Grelly, Greallaigh, greallaigh, greallach, a marsh or slough.

Grelly, greille, a griddle.

Grena, gréine, sun, sunny or a sunny place.

Grena, O'Griana, Greny (a nickname of the O'Donovans).

Grenagh, an-ghreanach, not given.

Grenagh, greanach, gravelly.

Grenaghan, Gréineacháin, Gréineacháin, Gréinachán or Greinachan, a personal or family name.

Grenan, ghrianain, a palace.

Grenan, grianan, grianán, grianáin, a royal palace, a summer residence, an important place, a solarium, an eminent place, a sunny place or a fairy queen.

Grenane, ghríanáin, a sunny house or a palace.

Grenane, ghrianáin, the summer chamber or summer house.

Grenane, Uí-Ghrianáin, O'Greenan, a family name.

Grenaun, grianan, grianán, grianáin, a royal palace, a summer residence, a solarium, an eminent place, a sunny place and can sometimes mean a fairy queen.

Grenia, gréine, of the sun or a sunny place.

Grennan, from grianan, a sunny little hill.

Grennan, Ghroidhnín, Grynan, a male name.

Grennan, grianan, grianán, grianáin, a royal palace, a summer residence, a sun bower, a solarium, an eminent place, a sunny place/bower or a fairy queen.

Grennan, Uí-Dhroighneáin, Ó Droighneáin or Ó Donnchú, a family name.

Gresh, *gCros,* crossroads.

Gresha, *greise,* conflict, battle.

Gress, *dreas,* a bramble-brake.

Grevine, *gairbhín,* the rough place or gravely land.

Grevine, *grobhainn,* not given.

Grevisk, *greibhisc,* not given.

Grew, *gCnu,* nuts.

Grew, *gCraobh,* branchy trees.

Grew, *gníomha,* not given.

Grey, *groighe,* not given.

Grial, *gCrioll,* leather bags.

Grial, *nGrial,* not given.

Grian, see Greenane.

Grianan, *grianán,* a summer residence.

Grianane, *grianán,* not given.

Grib, *gribe,* a mire.

Gribban, *criadh/craidh-baine,* marl clay.

Griddle, *griddle,* a cromlech.

Griffey, *Ua-Gríobhtha,* O'Griffy, a family name.

Griffin, *gCriomhthann, Ghrífin, Ghrífin, Grifin,* not given,

Griffin, *Ghrifin,* Griffin, a personal or family name.

Griffin, *Mhic-Grifin,* not given.

Griffin, *Uí-Chriomhthain, Chriomhthain,* Griffin, a personal or family name.

Griffin, *Uí-Ghriobhtha,* O'Greefa or Griffin, a family name.

Griffin, *Uí-Gríofa,* Ó'Griofa, a family name.

Griffin, *Uí-Ghrifin,* Griffin, a personal or family name.

Grig, *ghráig,* a hamlet.

Grig, *grig,* not given.

Griggins, *na-grigíneacha,* not given.

Griggy, *griogaigh,* not given.

Grilla, *greille,* a griddle.

Grillagh, *ghreallach,* a place of mire, loam or clay.

Grillagh, *greallaighe, greallach,* a bare or moist place, beaten ground, a place of loam, clay or a marshy/miry place.

Grillagh, *nGriollach, griollach,* a mire or marshy land.

Grillane, *Greallán,* not given.

Grillaun, *greilleán,* an old rusty sword.

Grillighan, *greallachain,* a mire.

Grilly, *greallach,* not given.

Grilly, *greille, greideal,* the griddle.

Grilly, *griollach,* a mire or marshy land.

Grilough, *griollach,* a mire or marshy land.

Grim, *dhroim, dhruim,* a hill ridge.

Grim, *dhroim,* a hill or ridge.

Grine, *gCruinn,* not given.

Gris, *gCros,* crosses.

Grish, *nGris, gris, gríos,* embers.

Grisna, *nDrisneagh,* not given.

Grissane, *Uí-Chrosain,* Crossan, a family name.

Gristeen, ashes.

Gristin, *Dhristin*(sic), not given.

Griston, *baile-na-gCríostúnach,* not given.

Gro, *gCnó,* nuts.

Gro, *gCró,* flocks of sheep.

Groagh, *cró,* sheep flocks.

Groagh, *gCró,* huts.

Groagh, *gCruach,* a ridge.

Groagh, *gCruach,* ricks, stacks, pointed hills, round hills or rick shaped hills.

Groe, *gCruach,* ricks or stacks.

Grogagh, from *gruaig,* a place producing sedgy grass.

Grogan, from *gruaig,* a place producing sedgy grass.

Grogan, *Ghruagáin,* Gruagán, the name of a Church founder in Limerick.

Grogan, *grógán, grógáin,* the small heap.

Grogan, *gruagan,* a place of hard soil.

Grogan, *grogán, Gruagán,* not given.

Grogan, *Uí-Ghrógáin,* descendants of Grogan, a family name.

Grogan, *Uí-Ghrógáin,* Grogan, a family name.

Grogan, *Uí-Ghruagain, Uí-Ghruagáin,* O'Grogan, a family name.

Grogeen, from *gruaig,* a place producing sedgy grass.

Grogerny, from *grág,* cackling of birds.

Grogey, from *gruaig,* a place producing sedgy grass.

Grogey, *gruagach,* not given.

Groggan, from *gruaig,* a place producing sedgy grass.

Grogh, *gCruach,* ricks or heaped up stones.

Groghera, *gCrochaire,* not given.

Groghery, *gCrochaire, crochaire,* a hangman or a gallows.

Grogy, *Ghruaige,* not given.

Grogy, *gruaige, gruagach, gruagaigh,* hair or hairy, the long haired or hirsute fellow.

Grogy, *Gruaige,* Gruaige, a personal or family name.

Grohane, *gharrain,* a grove.

Grohery, *gCrochairí,* hangmen.

Grohoge, *gCrothóg,* the Pollock, a type of shellfish.

Groigy, an old man.

Groin, *groidhin,* a horse feeding place.

Grole, *Dhrol(sic),* not given.

Groman, *dhromann,* ridges.

Gromoolia, *nGormshuileach,* not given.

Grone, *Dhraighin*(sic), not given.

Grone, *gróin,* groundsel.

Gronna, *ghronna,* not given.

Groob, *gCrúb,* feet or hoofs(sic).

Groody, *an-Ghrúda,* not given.

Groogan, *Uí-Ghruagain,* O'Grogan, a family name.

Groom, *an-grúm,* not given.

Groom, *dhá/dha-dhrom,* two ridges.

Groom, *gruama,* gloom or gloomy.

Grooms, *an-ghiolla-ghruama,* the gloomy servant or doleful fellow.

Grosheen, *gCroisin,* little crosses.

Gross, *gCros, g-cros,* crosses.

Gross, *grasta,* grace.

Grot, *gCrot,* hillocks or tummocks.

Grot, *gort,* a field.

Grotty, *gCrochtaí,* not given.

Grotty, the hangman.

Grotty, *grotta,* hummocks.

Grough, *gCruach,* ricks, stacks or stacked up hills.

Groun, *gCrann,* trees.

Grouna, *gCrobhanna,* handfuls or clusters.

Grour, *gCreabhar, creabhar,* woodcocks.

Grour, *gCruach,* pinnacles.

Grovan, *Ghruabhain,* not given.

Grovan, *Ghrubháin,* Grovan, a personal or family name.

Grove, *garbh,* rough.

Grove, *garrán,* not given.

Groves, *Gnó*(sic), not given.

Grow, *gCnó, gCno,* nuts.

Grow, *gCro, gCró,* cattle huts.

Grow, *gCró,* huts or sheds.

Grow, *gCródh,* huts or cattle folds.

Grower, *gCreabhar,* not given.

Grower, *greabhar, greabhar,* woodcock/s.

Grown, *gcrann,* trees.

Gruag, *goruig,* abounding in long sedgy grass.

Grubby, *ghriobaigh,* not given.

Grubby, *griobach,* miry.

Grud, *crot, gCrot,* harps.

Gruig, *goruig,* abounding in long sedgy grass.

Grumoolia, *Uí-Ghormhaile,* Gormley, a family name.

Gruogy, *an-gruagach,* the hairy man.

Grus, *gCros,* crosses.

Gry, *gCoire,* not given.

Gry, *gCroidhe, groide, n'gCroidh,* ...of the cattle.

Gry, *graí,* horses or a horse breeding place.

Gry, *graigh,* a horse pasture.

Gry, *gróigh, groigh,* horses.

Gry, *groighe,* of the stud.

Guarallgh, *gCaeireach,* sheep.

Guardhill, *gardaill,* not given.

Gub, *giob,* ragged.

Gub, *gob,* a point or snout.

Guba, *gob-an...,* mouth of the...

Guba, *gub-a'...,* snout, peak or point of the...

Guban, *gob-an...,* point of the...

Gubb, *gob,* a point or snout.

Gubba, from *gob,* the peak.

Gubba, *Ghioba,* not given.

Gubba, *goba,* snouts.

Gubbacrock, *gob-dha/dhá-chnoc,* mouth, beak or point of the two hills.

Gubbaun, *gobán,* not given.

Gubbeen, from *gob,* little beak.

Gubbeen, Gubbin, not given.

Gubbeen, *guibín,* a small projection of sea into land.

Gubbyoosh, *gob-fhiodh-ghúise,* point of the spruce/pine wood.

Gubi, *goib,* the point.

Gubna, *gob-na...,* not given.

Gubs, from *gob,* beaks.

Gudden, *Uí-Ghodáin,* O'Goddan, a family name.

Guddin, *Uí-Ghodáin,* O'Goddan, a family name.

Guernal, *Grinneal,* not given.

Guff, *dhaimh,* not given.

Guff, *dhubh*, black.

Guhard, *guth-árd*, loud voice(sic).

Guib, *goib*, not given.

Guibb, *guib*, *goib*, a beak.

Guiggy, *gCúigeadh*, *gCuigeadh*, fives.

Guiggy, *gCuigidh*, fifths.

Guil, *Goill*, a personal or family name.

Guila, *coidhle*, *gCoidhle*, goats.

Guila, *gaibhle*, a fork.

Guilcagh, *ghiolcach*, not given.

Guilcagh, *goilcach*, *giolcach*, a place of broom.

Guilco, *giolcach*, a place of spartium Scoparium or broom

Guile, *caol*, narrows.

Guile, *gCaol*, narrows.

Guile, *gCoill*, a wood.

Guile, *ghoill*, *ghaill*, *ghall*, an Englishman, a stranger or a foreigner.

Guileataggle, *gaill-an-tSeagail*, foreigner of the rye.

Guileen, *gaibhlín*, the small fork.

Guiletaggle, *Ghoill-tseagail*, Englishmans rye.

Guilkagh, *ghiolcach*, not given.

Guilkagh, *giolcach*, a place of broom.

Guilkee, *giolcaí*, reeds.

Guilkee, *giolcaighe*, broom.

Guill, *gCuill*, hazel.

Guill, *Ghoill*, Goll, a personal or family name.

Guill, *Goill*, Guill, not given.

Guilla, *gáille*, *gaille*, *gallaun*, a standing stone.

Guilla, *giolla*, a man servant.

Guilla, *coille*, a wood.

Guilla, *go-leith*, not given.

Guillagh, *gCailleach*, ruins.

Guillagh, *gCoileach*, woodcocks.

Guillagh, *gCoilleach*, grouse cocks.

Guillamore, *ghiolla-mhóir*, the big youth

Guillamore, *Mic-Giolla-Mhuire*, MacGuillamore or Gilmore, a family name.

Guillew, *gCoilleadh*, woods.

Guillew, *gColbha*, not given.

Guilly, *gCoille*, *nGoillaí*, not given.

Guilly, *gCoilleadh*, woods

Guilly, *ghiolla*, an apprentice or attendant.

Guilly, *Ghiolla*, Gill, a personal or family name.

Guilly, *nGiollaí*, man-servants.

Guilsha, *Gaillsighe*, the Engligh woman.

Guilsha, *Gailsí*, not given.

Guin, *O'gCuinn*, O'Guin, a family name.

Guiness, *Mac-Aongusa*, named after Mac-Guinness, a personal or family name.

Guiney, *Dhuibhne*, name of a grandson of ancient King ConaryII.

Guinnell, *gCoinneall*, candles.

Guiny, *Dhuibhne*, Duibhne, name of a grandson of ancient King Conary II and son of the legendary Carbery Musc.

Guire, *ghadhair*, *gadhair*, dog/s.

Guiry, *Uí-Ghadhra*, O'Guiry or O'Gara, a family name.

Guise, *ghiúis*, pines.

Guitane, *coiteán*, not given.

Guitane, *goiteán*, *coiteáin*, a small boat.

Guiveragh, *gCuibhreach*, fetters.

Guivna, *goibhne*, smiths.

Guivnia, *goibhne*, smiths.

Gula, *gobhlach*, forks.

Gulane, *golan*, a gulley.

Gull, *gColl*, hazels.

Gull, *ghuill*, not given.

Gulla, *chodla*, sleep.

Gulla, *gaibhle*, a fork or forks.

Gulla, *gCailleach*, hags.

Gulla, *ghiolla*, a servant or guide.

Gulla, *ghoile*, a great appetite.

Gulla, *ghola*, a gulley.

Gulla, *guala*, *ghuala*, hill shoulder/shoulders.

Gulla, *nGiollaidh*, servant boys.

Gullagh, *gCollach*, *gCullagh*, boars.

Gullan, *gCuileann*, not given.

Gullan, *ghállain*, a pillar stone.

Gullanagh, *gCuilleannach*, not given.

Gullane, *gallan*, *galláin*, a pillar stone.

Gullane, *gallan*, standing stones.

Gullane, *ghalláin*, *gallán*, *ghallain*, a standing stone or a pillar stone.

Gullane, *O'gCoilean*, Collins, a family name.

Gullaun, *gallán*, a standing or pillar-stone.

Gullaun, *gallán*, *nGallán*, standing stones.

Gullaun, *gCoileán*, Collins, a family name.

Gullee, *gCoillighe*, grouse.

Gullee, *gCuilí*, not given.

Gulleen, *coileán*, a whelp.

Gulleen, *gCoilleán,* little hazels.

Gulleen, *ghoilín,* not given.

Gullen, *chuilinn,* the holly tree.

Gullen, *O'g-Cuilinn,* O'Cullen or Cullen, a family name.

Gullen, *Uí-Ghoillín,* Ó Goillín, a family name.

Gullia, *gaille,* a standing stone.

Gullia, *Guille,* Gullia, a female name.

Gulliagh, *gCoileach, gCoilleach,* cocks, grouse-cocks or wood-cocks.

Gullin, *gCuillinn,* holly.

Gullion, *cuileann, gCuillion, gCuilleann, gCuilinn, cuillion,* holly or the holly tree/s.

Gullion, *gCuilinn, cuilinn,* not given.

Gullion, *gCuillinn,* a steep slope or a steep unbroken slope.

Gullion, *gCulainn,* Culann, a personal or family name.

Gullion, the name of a particular Armagh artificer.

Gully, (river) *slogaire,* not given.

Gully, *guala,* shoulders.

Gully, *gCoillidhe,* woods.

Gulshy, *Gaillseach, Gaillsighe,* the Englishwoman.

Gummer, *gComar,* confluences.

Gummin, *gCuimin,* Cuimin, a personal or family name.

Gumna, *gamhna,* the calf.

Gun, *con, gCon,* hounds.

Gunahan, *O'gConachain,* O'Conaghan, a family name.

Guneen, *coinín, gCoinín,* rabbits.

Guneen, *Guinín,* a family name.

Gung, *gCuing,* cattle yokes.

Gunihy, *gCoincinne,* O'Conkin, a family name.

Gunleog, *gCoinnleog,* stubbles.

Gunnane, *O-gCoinnen,* O'Cunnane, a family name.

Gunned, *gConaid,* hounds.

Gunneen, *Guinín,* not given.

Gunneen, *O gCuinín,* O'Cuneen, a family name.

Gunnell, *gCoinneal,* not given.

Gunnell, *gCoinnle, gCáinlidh,* candles.

Gunnell, *O-gCoinnell,* O'Connel a family name.

Gunner, *Gunnair,* not given.

Gunner, *mhic-Gonair,* son of Gonar, a personal or family name.

Gunner, *Mheg-gConair,* Mac Conary, a personal or family name.

Gunnery, *gConairí,* paths.

Gunnery, *gConallach,* dogs or wolves.

Gunnet, *Gungaid,* not given.

Gunnigan, *OgCuinneagán,* O'Cunnagan, a family name.

Gunnion, *coinín, gCoinín,* rabbits.

Gunnion, *gCoincheann,* not given.

Gunny, *gainimhe, gainne,* sandy.

Gunny, *gConaidh,* firewood.

Gunny, *goine,* of the wounding.

Gunoge, *gCuinneog, gCuinneóg,* churns.

Gunogue, *gCanóg,* not given.

Gunogue, *gCuinneog, gCuinneóg,* churns.

Gunt, *dhunta,* closed, shut.

Guppaun, *gCopán,* not given.

Guppaun, *gCupán,* cups.

Guppoge, *capóg, copóg,* dockleaves.

Guppoge, *gCopóg,* dock leaves.

Guppoge, *gCupóg,* dockweed.

Gur, *gCorr,* cranes, herons or sandeels.

Gur, *gCorr,* sandeels.

Gur, *Goir, Gair,* not given.

Gura, *garbh,* rough.

Gurk, *Mhic-Oirc,* MacUrc or MacGurk, a family name.

Gurland,

Gurm, *gorm,* blue.

Gurney, *Ghuairne,* not given.

Gurnyawn, tuft of wool over a sheeps tail, a hillock or cairn.

Gurra, *garrdha,* a garden.

Gurra, *gCuradh,* champions.

Gurra, *Goireadh, Giorra,* not given.

Gurragh, *gCurrach,* moors or marshes.

Gurraha, *garrdhtha,* gardens or enclosures.

Gurrahy, *gCurraithe,* moors.

Gurraig, *na-nGheabhóg,* not given.

Gurran, a grove.

Gurrana, grove of the…

Gurrane, *garrán,* a shrubbery.

Gurrane, *garrán-na…,* grove of the…

Gurrane, *nGearrán,* old horses.

Gurranes, *garrain,* groves or small woods.

Gurraun, *garrán, gurraun,* a shrubbery or copse.

Gurraun, *gharráin,* not given.

Gurraun, *gurrán,* a copse.

Gurrawirra, *garbhdhoire,* not given.

Gurrawn, *garrán,* a shrubbery.

Gurrawne, *garrán,* a shrubbery.

Gurreen, *góire,* a cave.

Gurrihy, *gCurraighthe,* marshes.

Gurrihy, *geirr-fiadgacha,* hares.

Gurrihy, *gCuirche,* not given.

Gurrim, *mhaolghoirm*(sic), not given.

Gurroge, *curróg,* parsnips.

Gurroge, *geabhrog, gurrog, nGeabhróg,* seagulls or sea-swallows.

Gurssa, *gCros,* the cross.

Gurt, *gort,* a garden, a field or a stone walled tilled field.

Gurteen, *ghoirtín, goirtín,* a small field or garden.

Gurteen, *na-goirtín,* the gardens.

Gurteen, *goirtín, ghoirtín,* a small field, a small arable field or a small tilled field.

Gurteen, *na-ngortiní,* little fields.

Gurteena, *goirtín-a'…,* small field or garden or the….

Gurteenina, *goirtín-Aidhne,* not given.

Gurteenna, *goirtín-na…,* small field or garden or the….

Gurteeny, *goirtíní, goirtiní,* little tilled fields.

Gurtha, *gort-a',* field of the….

Gurtna, *gort-na…,* field or garden of the…

Gurty, *ghorta,* not given.

Gurtyogawn, *gort-Uí-Ógáin,* O'Hogans garden.

Gury, *gCorraí,* irrigular(sic).

Gus, *gCos, cos,* a foot or feet.

Guse, *ghiúis,* not given.

Guse, *giumhas, ghiumhais,* fir.

Gusetaul, *giustála,* athletic excercises.

Gussane, *gCasán,* paths.

Gusserane, *gosarán,* not given.

Gusserane, *na-gCosarán,* …of the trampling.

Gustaun, *gCasán,* paths.

Guth, *gCat,* cats.

Guy, *gadhair,* a hound.

Guy, *Ghuí,* not given.

Guyneen, *gCoinín,* rabbits.

Guyroe, *gadhair-ruaidh,* the red hound.

Gwee, *gaeth, gaeithe, gaoth,* the wind.

Gwee, *gaoth, gaot, gaeth,* a tidal inlet.

Gweedore, *gaeth-Dóir,* Doir's (the name of an ancient prince) tidal inlet.

Gweedore, *gaoth-dobhair,* inlet of the water.

Gweer, *gadhar,* dogs.

Gweesalia, *gaeth-sáile,* saltwater tide inlet.

Gweesalia, *gaoth-sáile,* not given.

Gweesidagh, (river) *an-ghaoisideach,* not given.

Gweestin, (river) *gaoistin,* not given.

Gwoly, *Ó-gCeallaigh,* O'Kelly, a family name.

Gyleen, *gaibhlín, ghaibhlín,* the small inlet.

Gyleen, *ghaibhlín, gabhailin,* the small fork.

Gyreeny, *nGadhairínidhe,* beagles.

Hack, *chac,* excrement or dung.

Hack, *hac, sheac, shac,* not given.

Hack, *Sheaic,* Jackman, a personal or family name.

Hackamore, *áthchomair,* not given.

Hackamore, *hacamar,* a dung stand.

Hackballs Cross, *crois-an-mhaoir, cnoc-an-maoir,* not given.

Hacket, *Haicéad,* not given.

Hacklim, *eichléim,* not given.

Hackmys, *eachinis,* not given.

Had, *hUada,* Wade, a family name.

Haddy, *fhada,* long.

Haden, *Aidín,* not given.

Haden, *O'hEideáin,* O'Haden, O'Hayden or Hayden, a family name.

Haffrey, *Sheafraidh, Sheaffraidh,* Geoffrey.

Haffrin, *an-Aiffrinn,* of the mass.

Hagan, *Uí-hAodhgáin,* O'Hagan, a family name.

Haggard, *an-tAigard,* not given.

Haggard, *an-iothla,* the haggard.

Haggart, *shagairt,* the priest.

Hagh, *Fhicha,* Fiach, a personal or family name.

Hagh, *h-aith,* fresh.

Hagh, *h-aithe, haithe,* a kiln.

Haghilly, *h-aith-choille,* fresh wood.

Haghny, *hAthchuinghe,* not given.

Haghny, *hEachaidhe,* the horseman.

Haght, *chéachta,* a plough.

Haght, *chiochtaigh, ciochtach,* not given.

Haghy, *heachaidhe,* the horseman.

Haglish, *eaglais, eaglaish, hEaglaise,* a Church.

Hague, *Uí-Thadhg,* O'Teige, a family name.

Haha, *h-aithe, haithche, hÁithe, haithe,* a kiln.

Haha, *hÁtha, aite,* a corn kiln.

Haha, *hátha, h-atha,* the ford.

Hahill, *dhá-thuile,* two floods.

Hahill, *Uí-Sháithil,* Ó Sáithil, a family name.

Hahilly, *haith choille,* young wood.

Hahilly, *haith-thuile,* sometimes floods.

Haia, *h-aithe, hÁithe, hAithche, hAithe,* a kiln.

Haire, *ethiar,* an air demon.

Haise, *éis, h-éis,* the track.

Haise, *Uí-hAodha,* O'Hea or Hayes, a family name.

Hala, *gheala,* white.

Halbert, *Halbart,* not given.

Halbert, *Thalbóid,* Talbot, a personal or family name.

Haldry, *Chalraighe,* Calry, a personal or family name.

Haldry, *Chaleridhe,* the sept 'Caldry' who were decendants of Lewy. Lewy was the grand uncle of Maccan, a third cent King of Ireland.

Hale, *chaoil,* not given.

Hale, *Héil, Haol,* Howel, a personal or family name.

Hale, *Héil, hÉil,* Haol, Howel or Hale, a family name.

Halia, *haile,* briny inlet/s.

Hall, *aill,* a cliff.

Hall, *hÁL,* Hall, a family name.

Hall, *Hálaigh,* not given.

Hall, *thall,* a mansion.

Halla, *chalaidh,* a ferry or riverside meadow.

Halla, *h-aileach,* a fort.

Halla, *haille,* a slope, declivity or cliff.

Halla, *halla,* a hall.

Halla, *hAlla,* not given.

Halla, *h-alla,* the ball(sic).

Halla, *hUla,* the monument.

Halla, *salach, shalach,* dirty.

Halla, *shaileach,* a place of sallies or willows.

Hallagh, *eallach,* cattle.

Hallagh, *shaileach,* sally trees or willows.

Hallagh, *shalach,* dirty.

Hallagh, *shalach, shailleach,* sally trees or willows.

Hallaghan, *Uí-hAllachain,* O'Hallaghan, a family name.

Hallan, *sallainn,* salt.

Hallan, *Thaláin,* not given.

Hallat, *taimhleacht, tamlagth,* a plague grave, monument.

Hallee, *na-hAilí,* the rocky place.

Hallia, *hAille,* a cliff or declivity.

Halloo, *chalbhaigh,* not given.

Halloo, *Shealbhaigh,* Shallow, a personal or family name.

Halls, *na-hOlladha,* tombs or penitential stations.

Hally, *sháile,* sea water.

Haloon, *thalamh-bháin,* lea ground or pasture land.

Halry, *Calraidhe,* the people called 'Calry'.

Halston, *baile-na-cúirte,* not given.

Haltar, *hAltórach,* not given.

Haltora, *altóir,* altar.

Haltora, *hAltóra,* not given.

Haltore, *haltóra,* the altar.

Halwan, *Cholmáin,* Colman, a personal or family name.

Halwick, *Shealbhaigh,* Sealbach or Sealbhach, a personal or family name.

Halwy, *Shealbhaigh,* Sealbhach, Shelly or Shalwy, a personal or family name.

Haly, *sháile,* sea water.

Haman, *shamhuin,* a pagan festival on Nov 1st for the end of summer and is usually held on hills.

Haman, *Thamhain,* not given.

Hame, *hame,* (Scottish) home.

Hamilton, *Uí-Thomultaigh,* O'Tumilty, a family name.

Hamlaght, *taimhleacht, tamlagth,* a plague grave/monument.

Hamlat, *taimhleacht, tamlagth,* a plague grave/monument.

Hamlat, *thamhlacht,* not given.

Hamlet, *Chaidhmlírt,* Hamlet, not given.

Hamlet, *Chaimléasaigh*(sic), not given.

Hamlet, *thamhlacht, tamlaght,* plague grave/monument.

Hamlet, *thamlacht,* a graveyard.

Hammer, *an-umair,* the narrow channel or trough.

Hammon, *Uí-hAmóin,* O'Hammon or Hammond, a family name.

Hamon, *Ámainn,* Hamon, a personal or family name.

Hamper, *an-umair,* the narrow channel or trough.

Hamper, *umar, amar, amuir,* a trough shape or hollow.

Hamsha, *hAimse,* archery.

Hamsherry, *Haimseire,* not given.

Hana, *h-aoine,* Friday.

Hanagan, *hOnchon,* not given.

Hanagh, *hAithne,* not given.

Hanagh, *thamhnach,* (of the) green fields.

Hander, *Shandair,* Sander or Saunder, a personal or family name.

Handle, *Shandair,* Saunder, a personal or family name.

Hane, *átháin,* not given.

Hane, *Sheáin,* John.

Hane, *tháin,* flock.

Hanee, *seanádh,* councel.

Hanik, *Uí-Hailmhic,* Hanick, a personal or family name.

Hank, *Uí-Hailmhic,* Hanick, a personal or family name.

Hank, *Sheanaic,* not given.

Hankard, *Thancáird,* not given.

Hankard, *Thankard*(sic), Tankard, a family name.

Hanna, *eananch,* a swamp.

Hanna, *Uí-hAnnaidh,* O'Hanna, a family name.

Hannan, *Ainnean, Uí-hAnáin,* O'Hannan, a family name.

Hannan, *Ua-Aithneadhan,* O'Hannan, a family name.

Hannon, *Eonáin,* Eonán, a personal name.

Hanny, *hEanaigh,* Tany, a male name.

Hanry, *Mhic-hAnroi,* MacHanry, a family name.

Happy, *ceapaighe,* not given.

Har, *car,* a rock.

Har, *hearr,* not given.

Har, *Ui-Achir,* Ó hAichir, a family name.

Har, *Uí-hÁir,* O'Hare, a family name.

Hara, *h-earradh,* wares.

Hara, *Uí-hEaghra,* O'Hara, a family name.

Haran, *fhearann,* land.

Harda, *h-Áirde,* the height.

Harda, *hArda,* not given.

Hardia, *hAirde,* not given.

Hare, (island) *inis-Aingín, inis-Uí-Eidirsceóil,* not given.

Haree, *hAithrighe,* not given.

Harigan, *Uí-hAragáin,* O'Harrigan, a family name.

Harkin, *Uí-Arcain,* Harkin, a family and tribal name.

Harlick, *hard-lice,* height of the flag (stone, s).

Harlow, *thurlaigh,* a half-dried lake.

Harmon, *thearmainn,* sanctuary or Church land.

Harnet, *Tharnocht,* not given.

Harney, *Athairne,* Aharny, a male name.

Harney, *Charna,* O'Kearney, a family name and means the descendants of Kearney.

Harney, *Charna,* Kearney, a personal or family name.

Harney, *charnaidh,* a pile a heap.

Harney, *Chearráin*(sic), not given.

Harney, *fhearna,* alder.

Harney, *fhearna,* alders.

Harney, *hÁirne,* Arney or Harney, a personal or family name.

Harney, *háirne, hAirne,* sloes or sloe tree/s(sic).

Harney, *Uí-Chearnaigh,* Ó Cearnaigh, a family name.

Harny, *airne,* not given.

Haron, *Sharain,* Saran, a personal name.

Harp, *Thórpa, Uí-Tharpa,* O'Torpy, O' Tarpey or Tarpey, a family name.

Harraghan, *Ua-Ádhrachán,* O'Harraghan, a family name.

Harraghan, *Uí-hArachain,* O'Harrahan, a family name.

Harragill, *haireagail,* a habitation or an oratory.

Harrahan, *Uí-hArachain, hArracháin,* O'Harrahan, a family name.

Harrahan, *Uí-hArracháin,* O'Harrahan, a personal or family name.

Harran, *Uí-h Eaghrain,* O'Harran or Harran, a family name.

Harriff, *thairbh, tarbh, tairbh,* a bull.

Harris, *Fhearghusa,* not given.

Harris, Harry, a male name.

Harriv, *tarbh,* a bull.

Harroon, *Sheathrúin, Seathrún,* Geoffrey, a male name.

Harrow, *bhráca,* a harrow or a hovel of boughs and sods.

Harrow, *tharbh,* bull/s.

Harry, *Araidh,* Harry, a male name.

Harry, *araidh,* the charioteer.

Harry, *Éinrí,* Henry, a male name(sic).

Harry, *haithrighe,* penance.

Harry, *na-carraige, na-choirthe,* the stone or the standing stone.

Harry, *na-carraige,* the stone.

Hart, *Airt,* Art, Hart or Arthur, a male name.

Harty, *Uí-hArtaigh,* O'Harty or Harty, a family name.

Harvey, *hairbhe,* the division (of land).

Harvey, *Uí-hAirmheadhaigh,* O'harvey, a family name.

Hary, *Araidh,* Harry, a male name.

Hary, *araidh,* the charioteer.

Hary, *shaire,* a sea inlet.

Hask, *heasca,* a quagmire.

Hask, *sheasc,* barren.

Haska, *theasgha,* lopping/felling trees.

Haskany, *heascaine,* the curse.

Hasket, *Uascaid,* not given.

Haskin, from *seascach,* a marsh.

Hasky, *h-eascon,* eels.

Hasky, *sheascaigh,* a marsh.

Hasley, *Aisle,* not given.

Hasna, *tharsna,* not given.

Hasragh, *hEasrach,* not given.

Hass, *deas,* south.

Hass, *eas, easa,* a waterfall.

Hassig, *casaig, casadh,* turning, twisting or returning.

Hassig, *chasaidh,* not given.

Hassig, *cheasaigh,* a wicker causeway.

Hassig, *cheasaigh,* boggy.

Hassig, *easaigh,* a cataract.

Hasty, *Hoiste,* not given.

Hasty, *Moiste,* Moysty, a family name.

Hat, *thaite,* the site.

Hatinna, *hAitinn,* gorse.

Hatta, *tháite, thaite,* quarter.

Hattan, Hattan, a personal or family name.

Hatten, *aitinn, hAitinne, hAitinn,* gorse or furze.

Hattin, *an-aitinn, aiteann,* furze.

Hattin, *hAitinne,* not given.

Hattina, *an-aitinn, aiteann,* furze.

Hattina, *hAitinne,* not given.

Hatty, *na-hÁite-Tí,* the site of the house.

Hau, *hÁithe,* not given.

Haugh, *an-fhaithche,* a sporting green.

Haugh, *Ua-hEachach,* not given.

Haugh, *Uí-hEachdhach,* O'Haughey, Hough or Hawe, a family name.

Haughly, *heachlaigh,* the horse stable.

Haughly, *Sheachlainn,* Seachlann or Mael-Seachlainn, a personal or family name.

Haught, *ocht,* eight.

Haughtha, *haite,* the place.

Haukish, *Sheácais,* not given.

Haulbowline, *inis-sionnach,* not given.

Haun, *athain,* the little ford.

Haune, *Sheagáin,* John.

Haunis, *hAmhnas, hAmhnais,* combat, battle or plundering.

Haurin, *charthainn, chaorthainn,* quicken tree.

Havanagh, *tamhnaigh,* a green field.

Havane, *iath-bhain,* white meadow.

Havane, *Uí-Chiabháin,* not given.

Havel, *Haibhil,* Haville, a personal or family name.

Havil, *abhaill, abhall,* apples, apple trees or an orchard.

Havil, *abhaill,* apples, apple trees or an orchard.

Haville, *haibhle,* the orchard.

Haw, *an-fhaithche,* a sporting green.

Haw, *cath,* a battle.

Haw, *chaithe,* chaff.

Haw, *chátha, chatha,* a battle.

Haw, *Echach,* Eochy, a family name.

Haw, *háith,* the ford.

Haw, *haithche,* a (lime) kiln.

Haw, *hÁithe,* not given.

Haw, *Ua, Uí,* grandson or decendant of…

Hawan, *shamhuin,* a pagan festival on Nov 1st for the end of summer and usually held on hills.

Hawan, *Thamhain,* not given.

Hawla, *hAbhaille,* the orchard.

Hawlagh, *taimhleacht, tamlagth,* a plague grave/monument.

Hawlaght, *taimhleacht, tamlagth,* a plague grave/monument.

Hawlan, *hAbhla,* not given.

Hawling, *atha-lin,* the ford of the flax.

Hawna, *shamhuin,* a pagan festival on Nov 1st for the end of summer and is usually held on hills.

Hawna, *thamhnaigh,* a cultivated field.

Hawnagh, *shamhnagh,* a grass-field.

Hawnagh, *thamnach,* a field.

Hawny, *thamhnaigh, tamhnaigh,* a field, a green field or a cultivated field.

Hawoer, *a-tuair,* a bleach green.

Hawragh, *Samhradh, Samhraidh,* summer.

Hay, *Chaoth,* not given.

Hay, *hAodha,* Aodh or Hugh, a male name.

Hay, *O'Hea,* a family name.

Hayden, *Uí-Éadáin,* O'Hayden, a family name.

Haye, *haithe,* a lime kiln.

Hayes, *carn-uamha,* not given.

Hays, *O'Hea,* a family name.

Hea, *eadhadh,* aspen trees.

Heabought, *Uí-Shé,* not given.

Headon, *Uí-hEidín,* O'Headon, a personal or family name.

Heafy, *Uí-Éafa,* O'Heafy, a family name.

Heagles, *eaglais,* a Church.

Heagny, *Egnach,* Eagny, a personal or family name.

Heakin, *Héicín,* Heakin, a family name.

Healy, *Shíle,* not given.

Healy, *Uí-hEilighe,* O'Healy, a family name.

Hean, *hÉin, héin,* the bird.

Hean, *Ian,* not given.

Hean, *Sheáin,* John, a male name.

Heanlish, the single fort.

Heark, *hAdhairce,* the horn.

Hearka, *hadhairce,* the horn.

Hearny, *Uí-Thighearnaigh,* O'Tierney, a family name.

Heary, *aedhaire,* shepherd.

Heary, *Uí-hAodhaire,* O'Heary, a family name.

Heashal, *íseal,* low.

Heashill, *Éisill,* not given.

Heashill, *Uí-hEisill,* O'Heashill, a family name.

Heckil, *seagal,* rye.

Heckna, *heicneach,* plunders.

Hederna, *eadarnaidh,* the ambuscade.

Hederny, *hEadarnaighe,* not given.

Hee, *chaoch,* not given.

Hee, *chaoich,* the blind man.

Hee, *h-oidhche,* the night.

Hee, *túibhe,* straw or thatch.

Hee, *Uí-Shidhe,* O'Hee, a family name.

Heean, *thíghean,* rich or fat.

Heean, *Uí-Shíadhain,* Sheean, a family name.

Heeda, *Shíoda, Sioda,* Sheedy, a family name.

Heedy, *Uí-Shioda,* O'Sheedy or Sheedy, a family name.

Heefy, *Ua-Iafa, Uí-Thíthfe,* O'Heefy, a family name.

Heeha, *h-oidhche,* the night.

Heel, *Siadhal,* Sheil, a personal or family name.

Heel, *Shiail,* Shiel, a personal or family name.

Heela, *h-aileach,* a fort.

Heela, *hÍle,* not given.

Heelan, *Chaoláin,* Keelan, a personal or family name.

Heelan, O'Heelan or Hyland, a family name.

Heen, *Hín,* not given.

Heen, *áithín,* little ford.

Heen, *chaoin,* pleasant.

Heena, *h-aoine,* Friday.

Heenan, Heenan, a personal or family name.

Heenan, *Uí-hEanáin,* O'Heenan, a family name.

Heeny, *hAoine,* not given.

Heeny, *h-aoine,* the name of a Co Cork stream meaning Friday.

Heeny, *Uí-hInidh,* O'Heeny, a family name.

Heer, *shiar, híar,* west or western.

Heer, *thír,* country.

Heeragh, *haoibhe,* delight.

Heeragh, *haoire,* delight.

Heeragh, *iartach,* west.

Heeran, *chaorthainn,* quicken trees.

Heerein, *Uí-Shírín,* Ó Sírín, a family name.

Heerin, *Uí-hUidhrin,* O'Heerin, a family name.

Heernabin, *thír-na-binne,* country of the peak.

Heeve, *thaoibh,* the side.

Hefernan, *Ifearnáin,* Ifearnán, a personal or family name and the name of a Church founder in Tipperary.

Heffernan, *Eithirneach,* not given.

Heffernan, *Uí-Iffearnáin,* O'Heffernan, a personal or family name.

Hegadon, Hegadon, a family name.

Hegan, MacEgan or Egan, a family name.

Heglis, *eaglais,* a Church.

Heglish, *heaglise, eaglais,* a Church.

Hegny, *Éignigh,* not given.

Hegny, *héigne,* compulsion.

Hehan, *Ua-Shéadhachain,* O'Sheahan, a family name.

Hehan, *Uí-hEacháin,* O'Heaghan, a family name.

Heifer, *Iomhair,* Ivor, a personal or family name.

Heige, *Thadg,* O'Tadhg, O'Teidg, Teige or Timothy, a personal or family name.

Heige, *Thaidhg,* Taidhg, a male name.

Heige, *Uí-Thaidg, Thaidhg,* Ó Taidhg or O'Taidhg, a family name.

Heige, *Uí-Thaidhg,* descendants of Taidgh(sic).

Heigue, *Thaidhg,* not given.

Heila, *hAidhle,* not given.

Heilla, *áille,* a steep hillside.

Heilla, *haille,* a cliff.

Hein, *hÉin,* not given.

Heive, *hÉimhe,* not given.

Hekeen, *Shéicín,* not given.

Hellan, *shaileáin,* not given.

Helly, *hOilí,* not given.

Helta, *h-eilte,* a doe.

Heltia, *heilte,* the doe.

Helty, *h-ailte, h-eilte, heilte,* the doe.

Helurabra, *heillúna, hoileamhnha,* nourishment.

Helvick, a Scandinavian word meaning rock shelf bay.

Helvick, *Heilbhic,* not given.

Hely, *chaolaigh,* saplings.

Hely, *hEidhle, hAidhle,* not given.

Hely, *hÉille,* latchet.

Hemery, *h-eimeirídh,* emigration.

Hemery, *hImitche,* removal or trekking.

Hemery, *hImrí,* not given.

Hemikin, a family name.

Hemikin, *Sheimicín,* Seimicin or Shemikin, a male name and means little James.

Hemikin, *Shimcín,* Simcin, a personal or family name.

Hemikin, *Shimicín,* not given.

Hemly, *Thiomalthaigh,* Timothy.

Hemush, Seamus, a male name.

Henar, *h-aenar,* lone, solitary.

Hench, *h-inse,* island.

Hendrican, *Ui-Annrachain,* O'Hanrahan, a family name.

Hendricken, *Heinricín,* not given.

Henebery, *Henebre,* Henebery, a personal or family name.

Henebery, *Hinibeire,* not given.

Henebry, *de-Hindeberg,* Henebry, a personal or family name.

Henesy, *Aonghasa,* Aonghas, a personal name.

Henna, *Eanna,* not given.

Henna, *sinneach,* foxes.

Hennessy, *Ue-Áenghusa*(sic), O'Hennessy, a family name.

Hennessy, *Uí-Aonghusa,* Hennessy, a family name.

Hennet, *Sheineid,* Jennet, a personal or family name.

Hennigan, *Ui-Choinneagain,* O'Coinneagain, a family name.

Hennigan, *Uí-hEanagain,* O'Hennigan or O'Hannigan, a family name.

Henny, *eanaigh, Theineadh, Thuinne,* not given.

Henoge, *Mhic-Shionoig,* MacShannock, a family name.

Henry, *…na-Riogh, …*of the kings.

Henry, *Hanraigh, Enrí, Anraí,* not given.

Her, *oir, east,* eastern.

Heran, *chaorthainn,* rowan trees.

Herberry, *Hiribeire,* not given.

Hergna, *airgne,* plunder.

Hergna, *hAirgne,* not given.

Hergny, *airgne,* plunder.

Heridan, *Uí-Shioradáin,* O'Sheridan or Sheridan, a family name.

Herin, *chaorthain,* blackthorn(sic).

Herin, *iarainn,* iron.

Herin, *thirim, thirn,* dry.

Herk, *coirce,* oats.

Herk, Erc or Erk, a male name.

Herk, *Thoirc,* boars.

Herkin, *Uí-Sheircín,* O'Sherkin, a family name.

Herkin, *Uí-Sheircin,* Sherkin, a family name.

Hern, *thirim,* dry.

Herna, *Uí-hAthairne,* O'Haherny or Harney, a family name.

Hernaun, *Thighearnáin,* Tiernan, a family name.

Herney, *áirne,* blackthorns and sloes.

Heron, *h-Eire, h-Eirin, h-Eireann,* Ireland.

Herragh, *sheirg,* clover.

Herriff, *thairbh, tarbh, tairbh,* a bull.

Herrish, *thairis,* cross or crosswise.

Herrive, *thairbh,* the bull.

Herty, *Rabhartaigh,* Rafferty, a personal or family name.

Hervin, from *thairbh,* the little bull.

Hervy, *hairbhe, airbhe, airbheadh,* the division.

Hesco, *hEisce, hEasca,* a bog-stream or a boggy/streamy quagmire.

Hesh, *sheis,* broom (the shrub).

Hesheragh, *seisreach,* ploughland.

Hesker, *heascra,* a sand ridge.

Heskeragh, *hEiscreach,* a sandhill or a sand ridge.

Hesseragh, *seisreach,* ploughland.

Hessery, *seisreach,* ploughland.

Hessiagh, *sheiseadh,* sixth/s.

Hest, *hEist,* Hosty, a personal or family name.

Hest, *Hoiste, Oistigh,* not given.

Hest, *sheis,* broom (the shrub).

Hesty, *iosta,* a store or an Inn.

Hesty, *theiste,* fame.

Hevelly, *haibhle,* an orchard.

Hevern, *Uí-Bhriain,* O'Brien, a family name.

Hevla, *hAibhle, abhal,* the orchard.

Hevnia, *haibhne,* the river.

Heyland, *Helan,* St Faolan or St Fillan.

Hibbin, *Thibín, Tibín,* not given.

Hickey, *Ua-Íocáidhe,* O'Hickey, a family name.

Hickey, *Uí-hIcidhe,* O'Hickey, a family name.

Hickey, *Ui-Ící,* not given.

Hierky, *h-adhairce,* a horn.

Hiernan, *Thiarnáin,* not given.

Hiernan, *Uí-Thiernain,* O'Tiernan, a family name.

Hiernaun, *Thiernáin,* St Tighernan, 5th cent.

Hierny, *Thighearnaigh,* Tierny a family name.

Hiery, *hUidhre,* dun cow.

Higeen, *Thaidhgín,* little Teige, Timothy or Tadhg, a male name.

Higgin, *Huigín,* not given.

Highhays, *an-garraí-uachtarach,* not given.

Highland, O'Heelan or Hyland, a family name.

Higue, *Thaidhg,* Tadg, male name.

Hihilan, *hiothlann,* a barn or a granary.

Hila, *aile,* a declivity.

Hila, *hadhla, aidhle,* a coopers or ship carpenters axe or adze.

Hila, *hAidhle,* not given.

Hila, *haille,* a cliff.

Hilan, *h-aibhleann,* a sparkling river.

Hilan, *haidhleann,* a shoulder top.

Hilan, *haidhlenn,* a coopers or ship carpenters adze.

Hile, *choill,* a wood.

Hill, *aill, aille,* a cliff.

Hill, *choil, choill,* a wood.

Hilla, *choilig,* a heath cock.

Hilla, *choiligh,* not given.

Hilla, *choill,* a wood.

Hilla, *eilidh,* deer.

Hilla, *hAidhle,* a staff.

Hilla, *hAille,* not given.

Hilla, *shillach,* sallows.

Hilla, *thuile,* buttercups.

Hillagh, *shaileach,* sallows or willows.

Hillan, *oileán,* an island.

Hillane, *hadhlán,* little place of the coopers or ship carpenters axe or adze.

Hillane, *hAidleann,* a shoulder top.

Hillaun, *oileán,* an island.

Hillion, *hUilleann,* not given.

Hilloge, *shaileóg,* sally trees, willows.

Hilly, *choiligh,* the cock.

Hilly, *choille,* a wood.

Hilly, *choilligh,* a heath cock.

Hilly, willows.

Hilt, *hEilte, eilte,* a female deer.

Hilty, *hEilte, eilte, eilil,* a female deer.

Hily, *hAille, háille,* a cliff.

Himikin, *Shimicín, Shimicin,* Simikin, Henikin or Jenkins, a family name.

Himman, *Thoimín,* Tomin, a personal or family name.

Himmin, *Thoimín,* Tommin or Timmins, a family name.

Himmin, *Thóimín,* Tomin or little Tom.

Himmirc, *himirce,* flitting, moving or departing.

Himock, *Sheamoig,* Young Seamus or James, a male name.

Himrissan, *himreasaine,* contention or controversy.

Hina, *haibhne,* a river.

Hinch, *hInse,* a holm.

Hinch, *h-inse, hInse, na-hInch,* an island, water meadow or river meadow.

Hincha, *hInse,* the island.

Hinchoge, *fuinnseóg,* a place of ash trees.

Hinds, *sraid-Uí-Eidhin, na-baic,* not given.

Hine, *Uí-hEidhin,* O'Hyne, a family name.

Hineena, *na-hInghíne,* not given.

Hineeny, *inghín, na-hInghine,* daughter/s.

Hineeny, *na-hInghíne,* not given.

Hinera, *hInneóna,* not given.

Hinnaught, *shneachta,* not given.

Hinneora, from *inneoin,* the anvil.

Hinnera, from *inneoin,* the anvil.

Hinnera, *hInneora,* not given.

Hinnery, from *inneoin,* the anvil.

Hinnion, *hingine,* the daughter.

Hinnis, *hInse,* the island or river meadow.

Hinode, *Shionóid,* Synott, a family name.

Hirk, *thoirc, thorc,* a boar.

Hirka, *circe,* a water hen.

Hirka, *hadhairce,* the horn.

Hirke, *choirce,* oats.

Hirm, *thirim,* not given.

Hirm, *thirm,* dry.

Hiry, *hUidhre,* not given.

Hiskey, *uisce, uisge,* water.

Hisky, *uisce,* water.

Hist, *Hist,* Hesty, a personal or family name.

Hist, *hist,* host.

Hist, *Hoiste,* not given.

Hist, Host or Hosty, a Welsh family name.

Hit, *chait,* the cat.

Hivenny, *hAibhne,* a river.

Hiveny, *haibhne,* the river.

Hivnia, *aibhne,* a river.

Hoagh, *uagh,* a cave or grave.

Hoaghry, *uacaire,* blanket thickener.

Hoarstone, *an-chloch-liath,* not given.

Hoash, from *cuas,* caves, can also mean sea inlets or coves.

Hob, *chab,* a mouth.

Hoban, *hObainn,* Hoban, a personal or family name.

Hober, *thobair, tober,* a well.

Hobert, Hobart, a family name.

Hobin, *Hóibín,* not given.

Hobin, *Thoibín,* Tobin, a family name.

Hobuck, *Hobac,* not given.

Hobuck, *Hoibín,* Hobb, a personal or family name.

Hockas, *hocais,* the mallow.

Hockya, *hocais,* the mallow.

Hoe, *cheoigh,* fog or mist.

Hoe, *chuadh,* a hollow.

Hoe, *hÓa, Thuaidhe, cheo,* not given.

Hoe, *hUamha, uaimh,* a cave or caves.

Hog, *óg,* young, young person.

Hoghter, *uachter,* upper.

Hogue, *óg,* young, young person/s.

Hogue, *Sheóg,* not given.

Hohan, *Uí-Thuathchain,* O'Hohan, a family name.

Hoimna, *hOmna,* oak/s.

Hoirke, *choirce,* oats.

Hola, *Chomhla,* Comla, Comhla, a personal name.

Hola, *hAbhla,* not given.

Hola, *thola,* flood.

Hola, *Thola,* St Thola.

Hola, *Thola,* Tola, a male name.

Hola, *Ula,* the name of an ancient chief.

Holahan, *Uí-hUallachain,* O'Holahan or O'Hoolahan, a family name.

Hole, *choill,* hazel.

Holet, *Fhachlait,* not given.

Holey, *Amhlaibh,* Auliff or Awley, a family name.

Holey, *buaile,* same as booley, a dairying place.

Holl, *chúil,* corner or angle.

Holla, *hUla,* a stone vault.

Hollahan, *Uí-hUallachain,* O'Holahan or O'Hoolahan, a family name.

Hollan, *Chollán,* not given.

Holland, *Mhaol-Challainn,* Maol-Callan or Mulholland, a family name.

Holland, *Thaláin,* Thaláin, Talan, a personal or family name.

Holland, *Thalan,* not given.

Hollis, *sholus, sholais,* light.

Hollish, the fleece.

Holloga, *choillóig,* hazel.

Holly, *chalaidh,* a landing place.

Holly, *h-ulaidhe,* an altar or monument stone.

Hollymount, *Maolla,* not given.

Holm, *Choilm,* Colm, a male name.

Holme, *hóm,* a creek.

Holmog, *Cholmóg,* St Holmog.

Holp, *cholpa,* a bullock, steer or heifer.

Holt, *chabhlagh, chabhalaigh, chobhlaigh, chabhaltaigh,* the fleet.

Holta, *h-alta,* projection or point.

Holty, *Abhalta,* not given.

Holty, *h-ealtai,* flocks.

Holty, *Ollta,* Ulstermen.

Holyhill, *cnoc-an-chuilinn,* hill of holly.

Homa, *thuama,* a mound.

Home, *Eoghain,* Owen, a male name.

Home, *Thuama, a female name.*

Homey, *Thóime,* Tomie, a male name.

Homin, *Thoimín,* Toimín, not given.

Homin, *thuaimin,* a little burial mound.

Homman, a hollow.

Homman, *choimín,* a little valley.

Homman, Timmons, a family name.

Hommon, *an-choimín,* not given.

Hommon, *Uí-Thiomáin,* O'Tiomain, a family name.

Homna, *omna,* oaks.

Homock, *Thómaic,* Tómac, a personal or family name.

Homuck, Homock, a family name.

Homuck, *Húmoc,* Homoc, a personal or family name.

Homuck, *Thómac, Thomac,* not given.

Homulta, *Thumaltach,* Toomaltagh, a personal or family name.

Homulta, *Uí-Thomulty,* O'Tomulty, a family name.

Honan, *Othanain,* Othanan's (a male name) *stone.*

Hone, *abhann, h-abhainn,* a river.

Hone, *Eoghain,* Eoghan, a male name.

Hone, *hEóin,* John.

Hone, *hAbhann,* not given.

Hone, *hÓn,* hole.

Hone, *h-Uamhain, hUamhan, hUamhann, uamha, uaimh,* a cave.

Hone, *Uí-Chuain,* not given.

Hone, *Uí-hEoghain,* O'Hone or Hone, a family name.

Honeen, Honeen, a family name.

Honey, *conadh, conna, chonaigh, chonaidh,* firewood.

Honock, *Sheánoig,* Shannock, a family name.

Honock, *Sheónac,* not given.

Honor, *uair,* cold.

Hony, *chomhnidhe,* residence or place of rest.

Hony, *chonaidh,* firewood.

Hoo, *chuaich,* a water basin.

Hoo, *shó, shú,* berries.

Hoo, *Hú, hUamha,* not given.

Hoo, *h-uagh, h-uaimhe, h-uamhain, uaimh,* a cave.

Hoo, *h-uaimhe,* a cave or a kiln.

Hoo, *h-uamhain,* the cave.

Hoo, *Hugh,* Hugh, a personal name.

Hooan, *úagheanna, uamhan, h-uamhain, na-uaimh/huamhan,* the cave/s

Hoogan, *Uí-Aodhagáin,* a family name.

Hoogh, *hUamha,* a cave.

Hooig, *thuaig,* north.

Hook, Hook, Hoke, a personal or family name.

Hoola, *abhall, ubhall,* apple or apple trees.

Hoola, *chuaile,* a pole.

Hoola, *chuaille,* not given.

Hoola, *cuailli,* stakes.

Hoola, *hUaille,* howling.

Hoolahan, *Uí-Uallacháin, hUallachain,* O'Holahan or O'Hoolahan, a family name.

Hoolahan, *Uí-Uallacháin,* Ó hUallacháin, a family name.

Hoole, *chúil,* not given.

Hoole, from *umhall,* owls.

Hooleen, *Chuilín,* the back of a hillock.

Hooleen, *Uí-Chuilín,* Cullen, a family name.

Hoolihane, *Uí-Uallachain,* Holland, a family name.

Hoolivan, *Uí-Shuileabhain/Shúileabháin/Shúilleabhain,* O'Sullivan, a family name.

Hooly, *chabhlaigh,* the fleet.

Hooly, *h-Ubhla, hÚlla, hUlla, abhall, ubhla, ubhall,* apple, apples or apple trees.

Hooma, *thuama,* a tomb.

Hoon, *h-uamhain, h-uamhan, hUamhan,* the cave.

Hoora, *hUidhre,* the dun cow.

Hoory, *hUidhre,* the brown cow.

Hoory, *hÚire,* not given.

Hoos, *chuais,* a cave.

Hoosh, *chiumhais,* a border.

Hoosh, *chuais,* not given.

Hoosy, *chuasaigh,* the cave.

Hoosy, *cusaigh,* caves.

Hoova, *na-huamha,* the cave.

Hora, *thorthach,* fertile.

Horahan, *Uí-hUarachain/hOdharachain,* O'Horahan, a family name.

Horan, *eorna, eórna,* barley.

Horc, *thuirc,* a boar.

Horey, *húraí, úireacht,* greenness or freshness.

Horgan, *Uí-hAimhragain,* O'Horagan or O'Houragan, a family name.

Horgan, *charragáin,* not given.

Horig, *chomhraic,* conflict.

Horig, *chomhraic/* Meeting.

Hork, *coirce, choirce,* oats.

Hork, *thorc,* a boar.

Horky, *choirce,* oats.

Horky, *chorcach,* not given.

Horn, *eorna, hEorna, hEórna, eórna,* barley.

Horna, *chóirnigh, chorine,* the carrion crow.

Horna, *choirnigh,* not given.

Horna, *eórna,* oats.

Horna, *h-airne,* sloes.

Horna, *hOrna, hEorna, hEórna,* barley.

Hornan, *Uí-Chornáin,* a family name and means the descendants of Fearnan.

Hornan, *Uí-Fhearnáin,* Ó Fearnáin, O Fearnan, a family name.

Horne, *eorna, eórna, heorna,* barley.

Horney, *Thorna,* Torna, a personal name.

Horra, *choraidh,* a weir.

Horragh, *Uí-Shearraigh,* O'Sherry, a family name.

Horrea, *chairfhiaidh,* not given.

Horrigan, *Uí-Arragáin,* a personal or family name.

Horsa, Horsa, a Danish personal name.

Horse and Jockey, *an-marcach,* the horseman or knight.

Horseleap, *baile-átha-an-urchair*(sic), not given.

Hose, *cuas*, a cave.

Hough, *achadh*, the field.

Hough, *Eacdach, Uí-Eachdach,* Hough, O'Hough, a family name.

Hough, *hUamha*, not given.

Hough, *uagh*, a cave or grave.

Houghtee, *hUchtaighe, h-uchtaighe,* fir tree or a house post.

Houl, *thall*, yon or far.

Houlahan, *Uí-hUallachain,* O'Holahan or O'Hoolahan, a family name.

Houlort, *hUbhallghuirt,* an orchard.

Houlourt, *haballúirte,* orchards.

Houn, *habhann*, the river.

Houne, *h-abhann*, a river.

Houra, *Abhradh, Fheabhrach, Feabhra,* not given.

Houra, *Fhearabhrat,* Feabhrat, Feamhrat or Abhra, the name of a half mythical ancient chief.

Hource, *hAbha-ruaidhe,* grey river.

Hourigan, *Uí-hAmhragain,* O'Hourigan, a family name.

Houry, *hAbhrai,* hill brows.

Houry, *hAmhraí,* not given.

House, *chuais*, not given.

Hove, *na-huamha,* the cave.

Hovel, *hovel*, a hovel.

How, *abhainn, habha, h-abha, h-abhainn,* a river.

How, *hAbha, abha, abhainn,* a river.

How, *hUaighe*, not given.

Howe, *h-abha, h-abhainn,* a river.

Howen, *hAbhna, hAbhann,* the river.

Howla, *cuil-Aodha,* Aodh's/Hugh's (a male name) corner.

Howla, *habhaille,* an apple tree or an orchard.

Howla, *h-abha-leithe,* grey stream.

Howlaght, *thaimleacht, taimhleacht, tamlaght,* a plague grave/monument.

Howlett, *taimhleacht, tamlaght,* a plague grave/monument.

Howlett, *taimhleacht, tamlagth,* a plague grave, monument.

Howly, *abhla*, apples.

Howly, *chobhlaigh,* the fleet.

Hown, *abhann, hAbhann, h-abhainn, hAbha,* a river.

Hown, *úaimhain,* caves.

Howna, *abhanna, h-abhainn, hAbhna, h-aibhne,* a river.

Hownagh, *thamhnach,* not given.

Howney, *h-aibhne,* a river.

Howth Summit, *mullach-na-binne,* not given.

Howth, *binn-Éadair,* not given.

Howth, from *Hoved*, a Danish word for head. The Irish name is *binn/beann-Éadair,* Eadar's peak.

Howth, *hofuth* (Norse), headland.

Hoy, *hÁithe, haithe,* a kiln.

Hoy, *thuaigh*, north.

Hoyle, *Chomhghaill,* St Comgall.

Hoyle, *Thuathaill,* Tohill, O'Toole or Toole, a family name.

Hubber, *thobair,* a spring.

Hubbert, *tubbrid,* a well.

Hubble, *pobul*, people, congregation or Parish.

Hubbock, *Hobag,* a diminutive form of 'Hub' (another version of the male name Robert).

Hubbock, *Hoboc,* not given.

Hubbrid, *tubbrid, tiobraid,* a well.

Hubert, Hubert or Hobart, a personal or family name.

Huby, *Ubaugh,* not given.

Hudda, *an-Hudaigh,* not given.

Hudda, Hudda, Huddy, a family name.

Huddart, *Eiderne, Eadread,* a personal or family name.

Hue, *uagh, uaimh,* the cave.

Hugh, *hAodha, Aodha, Aedha,* Aodh, Aedh or Hugh, a male name.

Hull, *choill,* a wood.

Hull, *chuill,* hazel.

Hulla, *coilleadh,* a wood.

Hulla, *hOlna,* not given.

Hulla, *hUla,* a monument or tomb.

Hulla, *hUla,* an altar.

Hulla, *hUladh, uladh,* an altar, monument or prayer station.

Hulla, *hUlaidh,* an altar-tomb or a penitential station.

Hulla, *hUlaidhe, uladh, olla,* altar or altar tomb.

Hulla, *hUlaidhe,* a penitential station.

Hulla, *thulaigh,* a hill.

Hullen, *Huilin,* Howlin, a personal or family name.

Hulliar, *choiléara, coiléar, hoiléir,* a quarry.

Hullin, *chuillean, chuilinn,* holly.

Hullion, *choillidhe,* not given.

Hullion, *chuillinn,* holly.

Hully, *hUille,* not given.

Hully, *hIulaidhe,* a monument.

Hulty, *heilte,* the doe.

Hulty, *hUltaighe,* the Ulster woman.

Hulty, *h-Ultaigh,* the Ulster person.

Hum, *thom,* bushes.

Human, *Chomáin,* not given.

Humana, *hiomána,* hurling.

Humana, *thumanach,* bushy.

Humblety, *Uí-Thomultaigh,* O'Tumilty, a family name.

Humma, *chuma,* invention, form, shape, fabrication or formation.

Humma, *choma,* not given.

Humma, *hUaimhe,* caves.

Humphry, *Iomchra,* not given.

Hunche, *hUinsinne, Uinseogach,* ash trees.

Hunco, *Dhunchadha,* Dunchadh, a family name.

Hune, *h-uamhan,* a cave.

Hunna, *chonna, cona,* firewood.

Hunna, *chonnaidh,* not given.

Hunshigo, *hUinsinne, Uinseogach,* ash trees.

Hunshin, *hUinseann,* not given.

Hunshin, *hUinsinn, uinseann,* the ash tree.

Hur, *oir, east,* eastern.

Hurk, *choirce,* oats.

Hurk, *thorc,* a boar or boars.

Hurk, *thurk,*(sic) boars.

Hurk, *torc,* hogs.

Hurka, *choirce,* oats.

Hurler, *hUrlair,* not given.

Hurley, *órdlach,* the hero.

Hurley, *Urthaille,* not given.

Hurlstone, *baile-na-cloiche,* not given.

Hurly, *Ua-Uarláidhe,* O'Hurley, a family name.

Hurly, *Uí-hUrthuile,* O'Hurly, a family name.

Hurney, *hUrnaí,* not given.

Hurney, *h-úrnaidhe,* an oratory.

Hurrin, a furnace.

Hurrow, *Uí-Rudha,* O'Roy, a personal or family name.

Hurry, *churraigh,* a curragh.

Hurst, *Hoiste,* not given.

Hurt, *thuirt, ghuirt,* fields.

Hurtim, *Fhordham, Hoirtim,* de Fordham, a family name.

Hurtim, *hoirtim,* not given.

Hushoge, *hUiseoige, fuiseóg,* skylark/s.

Huskard, *thuaisceart, thuaiscirt,* north.

Huskert, *thuaisceart,* northern.

Hussa, *Hosa,* not given.

Hussa, *Uí-hEoghasa, Uí-Hosaigh,* O'Hussey, a family name.

Hussey, Hussey, O'Hussey or O'Cush, family names.

Hust, *Hurst,* a personal or family name.

Husty, *Hoiste,* Hoiste, Husty or Hosty, a male name.

Husty, Host or Hosty, a Welsh family name.

Hutch, *chuais,* a cave or hollow.

Huv, *dhubh,* black.

Hy Kinsella, *Uí-Chinnsealaigh,* not given.

Hybla, *baile-an-fhiadh,* not given.

Hye, *h-oidhche,* the night.

Hyla, *haidhle, hAidhle,* the adze.

Hyle, *choill,* a wood.

Hylish, *hEilís,* Alice, a womans name.

Hylon, *hadhlann,* military equipment.

Hymen, *Thoimín,* Tomin, a family name.

Hyne, (lake) *Aidhne, Eidhnigh,* not given.

Hyne, (lake) *Oighin,* lake of the cauldron or whirlpool.

Hyra, *laidhre,* fork.

I

Iara, *Earrach,* Springtime.

Iaragh, *Iarthach,* not given.

Ibane, *Uí-Badhamhna,* not given.

Ibane, *Uí-Bhadhamha,* O'Fehilly, a family name.

Ibricken, *Uí-Breacáin,* not given.

Icarrane, *Uí-Chorrain,* Curran or Creane, a personal or family name.

Ickaweeny, *Mhic-a'Mhuimhnigh,* son of the Munster man.

Ickeen, *Ícín,* not given.

Ickilroe, *'ic-Giollaruaidh,* Gillaroe, MacGilroy or Gilroy, a family name.

Icknew, *'ic-Nuada,* Mac Noud, a family name.

Icknew, *'ic-Nuadha,* MacNoone, a family name.

Icmeelra, *'ic-Maoilre,* not given.

Icmeelra, *'ic-Meelra,* Mac Meelra, a family name.

Icmore, *'ic-Mhoire,* son of a woman named Mór or Mora.

Icmoyler, *Mhic-Mhaoilir,* Mac Maolir/ Moyland, a family name and means the servant of Mary (a womans name).

Icmurrin, *Mhac/Mhic-Muirinn,* not given.

Iconnor, *Uí-Chonchubhair,* not given.

Iconor, *Uí-Chonchobhair,* O'Conor, a family name.

Icronan, *Ui-Crónain,* St Cronan.

Ida, *Íde,* not given.

Ida, *Uí-Deaghaigh/Deaghdha,* descendants of Deaghadh or Dagaeus (a male name).

Ida, *Ui-Dheaghaidh,* O'Dea, the name of an ancient sept.

Ida, *Uí-Dheá,* not given.

Iddan, *fheadain,* not given.

Iddane, *fheadáin,* a streamlet.

Iddy, *Aidí,* not given.

Iddy, *Hyde,* a personal or family name.

Ider, *eadar, dir, eder,* between.

Ideraille, *idir-da/dha-fhaill,* between two peaks/cliffs.

Iderowen, *idir-dhá-abhainn,* not given.

Iderown, *eadar-dha-abhann,* between two rivers.

Idiclogh, *...a'-tighe-cloch,* ...of the stone house.

Idrone, *Uí-Drona,* named after the tribe of Hy Drona.

Idrone, *Uí-Dróna,* not given.

Iera, *iara,* west.

Iera, *iarthach,* not given.

Ieragh, *iarthach, iarthrach,* western.

Ieragh, *iarthach,* western or backward.

Ieran, *iarainn, iarain,* iron.

Ieraragh, *iartharach,* estern.

Ierher, *iarthach,* not given.

Ierher, *iarthair,* western.

Ierin, *iarainn, iarain, iárann,* iron.

Ierin, *Urrainn,* not given.

Ierna, *iarna,* the hank.

Iff, *dhaimh, damh,* the ox/oxen.

Iff, *duibh,* black.

Iff, St Affeen or St Effinus

Iffa and Offa, *Uibh-Eoghain-agus-Uibh-Fhathaigh, Uí-Eatach-Fothadh-Tíne,* not given.

Iffa, *Uí-Fátha,* the name of an ancient tribe.

Iffeen, *Ifín,* not given.

Iffeen, St Affeen or St Effinus.

Igally, *O'g-Ceallaigh, g-Ceallaigh,* O'Kelly, a family name.

Igarvan, *Uí-Gharbhain,* a family name.

Ighter, *iochtair,* lower or lower end.

Ighter, *íochtar,* not given.

Igrady, *Ui-Ghreada,* O'Grady, a family name.

Ihane, *an-fhiacháin,* the little raven.

Iheen, *Fheichín,* St Fechín.

Iher, *aith fheir,* new grass.

Iher, *iture,* tillage.

Ihery, *ithire,* arable land.

Ikane, *Uí-Chéin,* not given.

Ikeathy, *Uí-Ceatach,* the 'Hy' race or descendants of the tribe of Ceatach.

Ikeathy, *Uí-Ceathaigh,* not given.

Ikeeve, *Uí-Chaoimh,* O'Keeffe.

Ikerrin, *Uí-Caithrinn/Cairin/Chairín,* not given.

Ikilligan, *Uí-Ghiolgain,* O'Gilligan, a family name.

Ila, *oileáin,* not given.

Ilagh, *Aidhleach,* St Aidhleach.

Ilan, *Eibhlin,* Eveleen or Ellen, a female name.

Ilaneoynagh, *oileain-aibhneach,* island formed by the river.

Ilaun, *oileán,* island.

Ile, *choill,* wood,

Ilen, (river) *an-Aidhleann,* not given.

Ilen, *eibhlinn,* sparkling.

Ilkin, *Uilcín,* not given.

Ilkin, *Uilcín,* Wilkin, a personal or family name.

Illan, *Ilin,* not given.

Illan, *oileán,* not given.

Illan, *oilean, oilen, oileán,* an island.

Illan, *oilean-an...,* not given.

Illana, *oileán-a'...,* island of the...

Illane, *aillean,* a small cliff.

Illane, *oileain,* an island.

Illane, *oileán, oileáin,* an island.

Illanna, *oileán-na...,* island of the...

Illar, *iolair,* not given.

Illar, *iolar, fhiolair,* an eagle.

Illard, *iolaird,* not given.

Illard, *iolar,* an eagle.

Illaun, *oilean, oilen, oileán, oileáin,* an island.

Illauna, *oileán-an/na...,* oileán, Island of the....

Illaunagawna, *ré-ghamhna,* not given.

Illaunard, *an-tOileán-garbh*(sic), not given.

Illauninagh, *oileain-aibhneach,* island formed by the river.

Illaunna, *oileán/oilean-na...,* Island of the...

Illeagh, *dútha-Uí-Luigheach,* not given.

Illeny, *na-hUilliní,* not given.

Illeny, *uillinidhe,* elbows.

Iller, *iolair,* an eagle.

Illies, *na-hUillí,* not given.

Illies, *uillidhe,* elbows.

Illihy, *uillighthe,* angular.

Illin, *oileán,* an island.

Illintry, *oileántraigh,* not given.

Illion, *uilleann,* an angle or corner.

Illion, *uillinn,* an elbow.

Ilra, *iola, ilragh, iolar, iolra,* an eagle.

Ilt, *eilit, eilte,* a doe.

Ilterra, *Iltéaraigh,* Elliter, a family name.

Ilty, *eilit, eilte,* a doe.

Ima, *ime,* butter.

Imaal, *Ui-Máil,* another name for the parish of Donaghmore.

Imaal, *Uí-Máil,* descendants of Mal, a personal or family name.

Imaal, *Uí-Mhail,* Ui Mail, the name of an ancient tribe.

Imail, *Ó-Maoil,* Uí Maoil, a family, tribe name.

Imale, *Uí-Mail,* from *Hy Mail,* an ancient people, descendants of Mal, a male name.

Imana, *diamain,* sustenance.

Imana, *iomána,* hurling.

Imark, *O'Marcaigh,* O'Markey.

Ime, *ime,* a fence.

Imer, *Íomaí, Iomaí, Íomar,* St Íomaí/Iomar.

Imerish, *imreas,* controversy.

Imerisk, *imerish,* controversy.

Imeroo, *ime-rubha,* fence of the herb 'rue'.

Imeroo, *iomdha-ruadh,* not given.

Imill, *imeall, imill,* the boundary.

Imirish, *imreas,* contention.

Imlach, *imlagh, imligh,* a swamp or marsh.

Imlagh, *emlagh,* marsh.

Imlagh, *imleach,* not given.

Imlick, *imlic,* a navel or a central point.

Imma, *im, ime,* butter.

Immy, *ime,* butter.

Imogane, *imegan, imecan,* a small weir or dam.

Imokilly, *iomdha-caille,* not given.

Imokishy, dam or weir of the wickerwork causeway.

Imor, *Adhmaighe,* not given.

Imor, *Íomhar,* St Iomar/Imor.

Impaha, *iompoighthe,* the turning.

Imphrick, *iomarach,* not given.

Imrish, *imreas, imris,* contention, conflict, competition or strife.

Ina, *eidhnigh,* ivy.

Ina, *in-ath,* of the ford.

Ina, *inghine...,* the daughter of...

Inaboy, *inghine-Baoith,* daughter of Baoth or Boethius.

Inaddan, *an-fheadáin/fheadain,* the streamlet.

Inagh, *aidhneach,* not given.

Inagh, *aighneán, eidhnead, eidhneach, eidhnach, eidhneán,* a place of ivy.

Inagh, *an-atha,* the ford.

Inagh, *an-fhia/fhiadh,* the deer.

Inagh, *eanach,* marsh.

Inaght, *eidhnead, eidhneán,* a place of ivy.

Inah, *an-eich,* the horse.

Inah, *eidhneach,* ivy.

Inair, *an-air,* the slaughter.

Inalt, the hillside or cliff.

Inan, *eidhnead, eidhneán,* a place of ivy.

Inan, *Fhionáin, Fhionain,* Fionán or Finan, a personal or family name.

Inan, *Fhíonáin,* not given.

Inane, *an-nÉan/éin,* the bird.

Inane, *eidhnean, eidneáin, eidhneán,* a place of ivy.

Inane, *Fhíonáin, Fhionain,* St Finan.

Inane, *oighnean,* a little hollow.

Inar, *an-áir,* the slaughter.

Inarable, *an-earbail,* the tail or strip of land.

Inare, *an-fhéir,* of the grass.

Inargal, *an-airheann,* the plunder.

Inassa, *an-fhásaigh,* the wilderness.

Inaun, *fhionnáin,* long coarse grass.

Inaw, *an-ath,* the ford.

Inch St Lawrence, *Inse-Shan-Labhráis,* not given.

Inch, *inse,* a flat meadow(sic).

Inch, *inse, inis,* an island, land like an island in a bog etc, a river meadow, water meadow or wet meadow.

Inch, various places with this word as their only name;

Incha, *an-inse,* the island.

Incha, *inis-an…,* island of the…

Incha, *inse,* a wet meadow.

Incha, *inse,* an island or river meadow.

Incha, *inse, inis,* an island.

Inchaghaun, *inis-ghainmh,* not given.

Inchaguile, *inis-an-ghaille-chráibhthigh,* not given.

Inchan, *inse-an…,* not given.

Inchana, *inse-na…,* not given.

Inchee, *insí, insidhe,* islands or rivers/water meadows.

Inchenagh, *Inis-en-daimh,* island of the one ox.

Inchera, *inis-iarthach,* not given.

Inches, *inseacha,* river islands.

Inchi, *inci, inse,* an island, a river island or holm, also see **Inch.**

Inchi, *inse,* not given.

Inchi, *insi,* islands.

Inchicore, *inse-chór,* Guaire's (a personal or family name) island.

Inchicore, *inse-chór,* island of the snout.

Inchicore, *inse-Giúra,* not given.

Inchideraile, *inse-idir-dhá-aille,* not given.

Inchin, *uinsean, fhuinnseann,* ash tree/s.

Inchin, *inse-an…, inse-'n…,* river island or water/wet meadow of the…

Inchina, *inis-na,* island or river/water meadow of the…

Inchina, *insin-a…,* little islet of …

Inchinan, *inse-Fhionán,* not given.

Inchinan, *uinseanain,* a little ash plantation.

Inchna, *inse-na…,* island or river meadow of the…

Inchy, *inse,* a river meadow or an island.

Inchy, *inse-an…,* holm of the…

Inchy, *insidhe,* a river holm.

Indra, *Éandra,* not given.

Indra, *Aindriú,* Andrew, a male name and the name of a Church founder in Dunnamaggin parish.

Ine, *adhain,* the caldron.

Ine, *eidhinn,* ivy.

Ineely, *Chinnfhaelaidh, Kineely,* a personal or family name.

Ineen, *an-fhiona,* the wine.

Ineen, *inghine,* the daughter.

Ineer, *ahiar,* west.

Ineer, *inbhir,* river mouth or estuary.

Ineigh, *an-each,* the horse.

Inena, *an-Aonaigh,* the assembly.

Ineny, *aonaigh,* the assembly.

Inerlea, *an-fhir-leith,* the grey haired man.

Iness, *an-easa,* hill of the cataract.

Iney, full title '*inghen-Leinín*', daughters of Leinín.

Iney, *laighnigh,* a leinsterman.

Iney, St. Eany.

Ing, *íng,* a neck of land.

Ing, *eing,* not given.

Ing, *ionga,* nail, talon or hoof.

Inga, *einge,* a point (of land).

Inga, *einge,* (of) the territory.

Inga, *Innigh,* not given.
Inga, *ionga,* nail, talon or hoof.
Ingan, *iongan,* the nail.
Ingard, from *ionga,* high nail.
Ingaun, *Iongáin,* not given.
Ingergill, *Uí-Iongardail,* not given.
Ingin, *inghean,* daughter.
Ingle, *aingil,* the angel.
Ingley, *Ailgle,* an angel.
Ingna, from *ionga,* talons.
Inick, *Fhinneog,* St Finneog.
Inick, *Fhionnóg,* not given.
Inida, *an-fheide,* the streamlet.
Inidy, *an-fheide, the* noisy stream.
Inidy, *Inide,* shrove or Shrovetide.
Inierin, *an-Iarainn,* not given.
Inihy, *eidnach,* ivy.
Inihy, *Inthe, Inithe,* not given.
Inine, *an-einín,* the little bird.
Inine, *Fininghín,* Fineen, a personal or
    family name.
Inis, *inis,* an island, holm or river meadow.
Iniscal, *fhionn-ascail,* the white hollow or
    armpit.
Inisclan, *ineas-clainn,* rapid or strong
    stream.
Inish, *inis,* an island.
Inisha, *inis-a'...,* island of the...
Inishal, *inis-saille,* not given.
Inishammon, *inis-Samháin*(sic), not given.
Inishannon, *inis-Eoghanáin,* not given.
Inishannon, *inis-Eonáin/Eonain,* Eonán's
    (a personal or family name) island.
Inishargy, *inis-Cairge,* not given.
Inishark, *inis-Earc/Airc,* not given.
Inishbobunnan, cow island of the bitterns.
Inishee, *inis-Aedha,* Hugh's or Aodh's
    (mens names) island.
Inisheer, *inis-oírr/oirr,* eastern island.
Inisheer, *inis-soir/oirthir,* western island.
    (See Irish names of Places, P.W.Joyce,
    vol 2 page 451).
Inisheer, *inis-thiar,* west island.
Inisherkin, *Inis-oircin,* island of the piglet
    or whale.
Inishinny, *inis-sionnaigh,* not given.
Inishmore, *Árainn*(sic), not given.
Inishna, *inis-na...,* island or river meadow
    of the...
Inishnag, *inis-snaig,* not given.

Inishraher, *inis-raithin,* not given.
Inishshark, *inis-airc,* hardship island.
Inishsirrer, *inis-oirthir,* eastern island.
Inishtroghenmore, *inis-srathair*(sic), not
    given.
Inisk, *an-uisce,* of the water.
Iniska, *an-uisce,* of the water.
Iniskeen, *inis-caoin-Deagha,* not given.
Inisklin, *ineas-clainn,* rapid or strong
    stream.
Inisky, *an-uisce,* not given.
Inna, *Fhinne,* Finn, a female name.
Innane, *Fhionain, Fhionáin,* St Finan.
Innane, *Fhionnáin,* not given.
Inane, *Fhionáin,* Finan, a personal or fam-
    ily name.
Innfield, *an-bóthar-buí/buidhe,* not given.
Innha, *inithe,* not given.
Innick, *finnog, fhionnoige,* the scaldcrow.
Innishannon, *Inis-Eoghanain,* island of little
    Owen, a male name.
Inniskil, *Ionascail,* not given.
Innone, *inneoin,* the anvil.
Inny, (river) *an-Eithne, Eithne, glais-bear-*
    ramhain, an-Aoine, not given.
Inny, *Eithne,* Ethnea, the name of the
    founder of Killinny Church in Clare.
Inny, *Fhinnche,* not given.
Inny, *fhionnaidh,* long grass.
Inny, *h-eithne,* named after the wife of
    Conchobar McNessa.
Inny, *ningen,* daughters.
Innygraga, *Eing-na-gráighe,* not given.
Inode, *an-fhóid,* the sod.
Inrachty, *Iannrachtaigh,* Inraghta, Hanratty
    or Enright, a personal or family name.
Inse, *inis,* an island or river meadow.
Inse/inse-an-Phaoraigh, inis-an-ringce,
    inse-Mocholmóg, inis-cumhceraigh, inis-cuil-
    eantraighe, móta-an-loire, not given.
Insha, *inse,* not given.
Inshagh, *hInse, inse, inis,* an island.
Insheen, *insín,* little island or river holm.
Insheen, *insín,* little island or river holm.
Inshigagh, *fluinseogach,* ash trees.
Inshigo, *fluinnseoige,* ash trees.
Inshigo, *uinseogach,* not given.
Inshin, *fhuinnsinn, uinsinn,* ash trees.
Inshin, *inhsín*(sic), *a stream.*
Inshin, *insín,* a little holme(sic).

Inshinagh, *uiseannach, uinseannach,* a place of ash trees.

Inshugh, *inse, inis,* an island.

Insihore, *inis-mhór,* great island.

Insky, *uisce,* water.

Intack, the English word *'intake'* meaning a portion of land taken from uncultivated ground or an inclosure(sic).

Intee, *an-tighe,* the house.

Intenant, *an-teannail,* not given.

Intenant, *an-tSaighneain,* of the beacon.

Intendry, *an-sean-druadh,* the old druids.

Intennant, *an-tennail,* the bonfire.

Intin, *Fhionntain,* Finatan, a male name.

Intin, *Fhiontain,* not given.

Intin, *intinne,* the intention.

Inuan, *eidhneán,* abounding in ivy.

Inure, *an-iúir/iubhar/iobhair,* the yew.

Inure, *inniúir, Fhionnabhra,* not given.

Inver, *an-bhiorra,* a morass or watery fields.

Inver, *an-tInbhear,* not given.

Inver, *inbhear-Náile,* Naile's estuary.

Inver, *inbher, inbhear, inbhir,* the river mouth or estuary.

Inveran, *indreabhán,* a small estuary.

Inverin, *indreabhán,* not given.

Invy, *inbhear,* a river mouth.

Inward, *an-bhaird,* the bard or poet.

Iny, *eidhneach,* ivied.

Iquin, *Uí-Chúinn/Chuinn,* O'Quinn, a family name.

Ira, *adhar,* frost or snow.

Ira, *oighir,* ice.

Ira, *oighre, oidhre,* the heir.

Iragh, *adhras,* a residence.

Iraght, *oireacht,* inheritance.

Irahilly, *Uí-Raithille,* not given.

Irby, *Irby*(sic), not given.

Ire, brown.

Ireland, the following are various names used to denote Ireland;

Éire, Eire land.

Inis-na-bfiodhbhadh, island of the woods.

Críoch-na-bhfuineadhhach, end of the three divisons of the world. *Inis-Ealga,* noble island.

Eire, named after a Queen of the Tuatha-De Dannan.

Fódhla, named after a Queen of the Tuatha-De Dannan.

Banbha, named after a Queen of the Tuatha-De Dannan.

Inis-Fail, island of destiny.

Muicinis, Pig island.

Scotia, from Scota, a female name.

Hibernia, from the Latin *Hiberoc* and *Nyaon,* western island.

Iuernia, Iuerna, Ierna, Vernia, western island.

Irlanda, Land of 'Ir' son of Míleadh of the Clanna Míleadh.

Ogygia, most ancient island.

Others were, *Ériu, Érinn, Erenn, Hiberio, Ioueria, Iberio, Ywerddon, Iwerdon,* and *Iverdon.*

Irelands Eye, *Eria's-ey,* Eria's (a male name) island.

Irelands Eye, *inis-Mac-Neasain,* not given.

Irelands Eye, *inis-Mhic-Neasáin,* island of the son of Neasán, a personal name.

Irey, *oidhre,* not given.

Irin, *iarainn,* iron.

Iriston, *Ireastain,* Irestan, a personal or family name.

Irk, *Eirc,* Erc, a personal or family name.

Iron, (lake) *Orbhaidhe, iarin, Eirbhidh,* not given.

Iron, *iárann,* iron.

Irourke, *Uí-Ruairc,* not given.

Irragh, (na)-*nIorach,* not given.

Irrelagh, *mainistir-Oirbhealaigh,* not given.

Irrelagh, *oirbhealach,* eastern pass.

Irrer, *oirthir,* eastern.

Irril, *Iriail,* Irial, a personal or family name.

Irril, *Oirill,* not given.

Irrin, *fiorin,* coarse grass.

Irrus, *irrus,* a peninsula.

Iry, *daoighre,* the blast.

Iry, *oidhre,* not given.

Iry, *oighre,* the heir.

Isaac, *Isaac,* Isaac, a male name.

Isclin, *ineas-clainn,* rapid or strong stream.

Isert, *díseart, disert, desert, a* hermitage.

Ish, *ois,* a fawn, fawns.

Ishahane, *inse-Uí-Chathain,* Uí-Cathain's (a family name) island.

Ishal, *íseal,* low or low lying.

Ishal, *iseal,* lower.

Ishal, *isil,* low land.

Ishart, *disert, desert,* a hermitage, wilderness or desert.

Isheen, *oisín,* fawns.

Isheen, *Oisín,* Oisin, a personal name.

Ishert, *disert, desert,* a hermitage, wilderness or a desert.

Isk, *eisc,* fish.

Isk, *uisce, uisge,* water.

Iska, *uisce,* a pond or river.

Iska, *uisce, uisge,* water.

Iskan, *uisge-an…,* water of the…

Iskana, *eisc-na…,* marsh of the…

Iske, *uisce, uisge,* water.

Iskea, *uisce, uisge,* water.

Isker, *eiscir,* a sandhill, a sandy or glacial ridge, a ridge of high land or a line of sand hills.

Iskera, *eiscira,* not given.

Iskera, *eiscreach,* full of sand hills.

Iskera, *isceara,* a ridge.

Iskey, *uisce, uisge,* water.

Iskill, *ascal,* an angle of land.

Iskin, *Ineasclainn,* Ineasclann, a personal or family name.

Iskin, *ineasclainn,* the torrent.

Isky, *eisce,* a marsh or quagmire.

Isky, *uisce, uisge,* water, watery.

Isla, *oilleán,* an island.

Islandea, *oiléan-Uí-hAodha,* Ó Dubháin's (a family name) island.

Islandeady, *oileán-Éadaí,* not given.

Isle, *aille,* a cliff.

Isle, *choill,* a wood.

Isnagh, *Uisneach,* Uisneagh, a personal or family name.

Issane, *easán,* small waterfall.

Issert, *díseart,* wilderness.

Istalea, *lios-da-liath,* fort of the two grey persons.

Isteena, *Istiagh,* (St?) Istia, a founder of a Church.

Ister, *disert,* a hermitage.

Itereery, *íochtar/iochtar-thíre,* lower land.

Itra, *íochtarach,* not given.

Itra, *itra,* lower.

Itty, *Eitigh,* Etech, the name of an ancient princess.

Ity, *Eitigh,* Ita, a female name.

Ivaghan, *Uí-Mhochain,* Ó Mochán or O'Mohan, a family name.

Ivara, *Uí-Mheára/Mheara,* O'Mara, a family name.

Iveagh, *Uibh-Eachach,* Eochaidh Cobha's (a third century Ulster chieftain) descendants.

Iveagh, *Uibh-Eachach,* descendants of Echu.

Iveleary, *Uí-Laeghaire,* descendants of Laeghaire or O'leary, a family name.

Iver, *Íomhair, Ibhir,* not given.

Iveragh, *Uíbh-Ráthach,* not given.

Iverk, *Uibh/Uí-Eirc,* the name of a sept/ tribe and descendants of Erc.

Iveruss, *Uibh-Rosa,* the name of a tribe and means the descendants of Rosa.

Ivira, *Uí-Mheidheara, Uí-Mheadhraigh,* O'Meiry, a family name.

Ivor, *Íomhair, Íomhar, Iomhar,* Ivor, a male name.

Izod, *Iosóid, Iosóilde,* Izod, Yseult or Iseult, the name of an ancient princess.

Izod, *Ísirt,* not given.

J

Jamesduff, *Shéamuis, Shéamais-Dhuibh,*
James Duff, the name of an English
Officer in the 1798 rebellion.

Jamesduff, *Sheumais-dhuibh,* black James.

Jarney, *Cearnaigh,* Kearney, a personal or
family name.

Jeripont, *Seiripuin,* Jerry's or Jerimia's
(mens names) bridge.

Jerpoint, *Seripoint, Sheireapúin,* Jerimiah's,
Jerry's bridge.

Jerpoint, *Sheireapúin,* Jerpoint hill.

Jerpoint, *Seripúin,* not given.

Jerpont, *Seiripuin,* Jerry's or Jerimia's (mens
names) bridge.

Jiggins, *Shigín,* Jiggins, a personal or family name.

Johnboy, *Sheáin-bhuidhe,* yellow John, a
male name.

Jordan, *Shiurdáin,* Jordan, a personal or
family name.

Kally, *Caillí,* not given.

Kan, *ceann,* a head or a hill.

Kanaugh, *ceann-abha,* head water.

Kane, *Céin,* Kian, a personal or family name.

Kane, *Chatháin,* Cathán, a personal or family name.

Kane, *Ui-Chatháin,* not given.

Karaun, *chaorthainn,* the quicken tree.

Karaun, *Charráin,* not given.

Katierin, *Chaitighearn,* St Caithighearn, a 6th century Bishop.

Kay, *chéachta,* the plough.

Kayle, *caol,* not given.

Kea, *Aodha,* Cae(sic), a male name.

Kea, *Cae, Chaoch,* not given.

Kea, *cáidhe, caidhe,* muddy.

Kea, *caodh, caedh,* a quaw a quagmire or a marsh.

Kea, *cáoí,* a road.

Kea, *Cathaigh, Chathaig, Chathaigh,* St Cathach and Cathach, a male name.

Kea, *Cé,* Ce, a male name.

Kea, *Gé, Géidhe,* not given.

Keabrick, *Céibric,* not given.

Kead, *céad, cead,* one hundred and a measure of land.

Keadagh, *ceideach, ceide,* a smooth topped hillock.

Keadeen, *céidín,* a little smooth topped hillock, a little plateau or a flat hill.

Keadew, *céide, céideadh, ceide,* a green, an assembly place, a high level place with a smooth flat top or a hill.

Keadew, *céideadh-tíne-Tuathail,* not given.

Keadgran, *céad-cran,* one hundred trees.

Keadue, *céideadh,* a flat topped hill.

Keady, *cae-duibhe,* black quagmire

Keady, *caodaí, céideadh,* not given.

Keady, *chéide, céide, ceide,* a high level place with a smooth flat top, a plateau or a hill.

Keady, *chéide,* not given.

Keady, pass of the deer.

Keagh, *caech,* a disused mill.

Keagh, *caech, caoch, gCaoch,* blind.

Keagh, *sceach,* white thorn.

Keaghra, *Mhic-Fhiachrach,* MacFiachrach or Fiaghra, a family name.

Keaghta, *céachta, ceacht,* the plough.

Keal, *cael,* a narrow stream through a marsh.

Keal, *caoil, caol,* a marshy stretch or a marshy stream.

Keal, *caol,* a narrow marshy stream.

Keal, *chaol, caol, cael,* narrow or slender.

Keala, *caol-an/a'...,* narrow stream of the...

Keala, *caol-an...,* marshy stream of the...

Keale, *an-caol,* the narrow feature or place.

Keale, *caol, cael,* narrow, slender.

Keale, *Caola,* Caola, a male name.

Keale, *Gaela,* a male name.

Keale, *chaol, Gaola,* not given.

Kealfoun, *an-caol-fionn,* not given.

Kealid, from *cael,* the narrow place.

Kealig, *caolaig, chaolaigh,* slender rods or saplings.

Kealoge, *caológ,* a small marshy stream.

Kealties, *caolta,* marshy or marshy streams.

Kealty, *coillte,* woods.

Kealvaugh, *caolbhach,* a light plantation.

Kealvaugh, *caolmhagh, caol-mhagh,* a narrow plain.

Kealwee, *caolbhuí, caol-bhuidhe,* a yellow marsh stream.

Kealy, *Uí-Chadhla,* Ó Cadhla, a family name.

Keam, *ceim, céim, céime,* a step, a narrow mountain pass or a roadway between rocks or hills.

Keamna, *céim-na...,* pass of the....

Keamore, *caodh-mhór,* great quaw, quagmire or marsh.

Keamore, *ceim-mór,* a big pass.

Kean, *Céin,* a personal or family name..

Kean, *Uí-Chéin,* Ó Céin or O'Kean, a family name.

Keane, *caoin,* kind or fertile.

Keane, *Céin, Cein,* Cian, a male name and the name of Brian Boru's son-in-law.

Keany, *chaonaigh,* moss.

Keany, *Chiana,* not given.

Keany, *Cíana,* Cian, a personal or family name.

Kearagh, *caorach,* sheep.

Kearagh, *ghaorthaidh,* a woody glen.

Kearan, *Chiaráin,* St Ciarán.

Keare, *caor, caer,* berries.

Kearine, *ceirín,* plaster or a wound dressing.

Kearn, *cethern,* lightly armed foot soldiers.

Kearney, *carn-Eochaidh,* not given.

Kearny, *cethern,* lightly armed foot soldiers.

Keary, *Caora,* not given.

Keary, *Céire, Chéire, Céire,* St Ciar or Kiara.

Keary, *Ceiri,* St Ciara.

Keash, *chéis, céis,* a wickerwork/wattled causeway.

Keash, *ceis-Corainn,* not given.

Keasy, *Chóise, Céise, Chéise,* Céis, Caise, a personal or family name and a founder of a Church in Kildare.

Keating, *Chéitinn, Chéitinnigh,* not given.

Keating, Keating, a family name.

Keaton, *Gephtine,* Gephtine a personal or family name.

Keava, *ciabhach, céibh, céibhe, ciabhaigh,* long grass that grows in morasses.

Keave, *céibh,* long grass that grows in morasses.

Keavy, *ciabhaigh,* hazy.

Kebble, a cemetery.

Ked, *céad,* one hundred and a measure of land.

Kedagh, Kedagh, a persons name.

Kedna, *céad-na ,* land-measure of the…

Kedna, *céide-na ,* not given.

Kedra, *céad-racha, cead-ratha,* first forts(sic).

Kedragh, *céadrach, céadracha,* not given.

Kedragh, *céad-shrotha,* a hundred streams.

Kee, *Caidhe,* St Caidhe.

Kee, *caoich,* the one eyed man.

Kee, *Caoidhe, Chaoidhe, Chaoi,* St Caoi/ Caoidhe.

Kee, *chaeich,* a purblind fellow.

Kee, *Chaoich, Caoch,* Caech, the one eyed man or the half blind man named Hugh O'Neill.

Keeagh, *an-chaothach,* not given.

Keeagh, *caodhach,* marshy.

Keeba, *cíoba, cíbe,* a type of long coarse sedge grass.

Keedy, *Caoide,* St Caoide.

Keedy, *Chaoide,* not given.

Keefe, *chaoith,* a swamp.

Keefe, *Uí-Cháiomh,* O'Keeffe, a family name.

Keegane, *'ac-Aodhagain,* Mac Egan, a family name.

Keeghan, *caochan,* a morass.

Keeghan, *Caochan,* Keeghan, a personal name.

Keeghan, *chaocháin, chaochain,* the purblind man.

Keeghane, *Caochan, Caocháin,* Keeghan, a personal name.

Keeghaun, Keeghan, a personal or family name.

Keehan, *Caocháin,* not given.

Keehane, *Caochan,* Keeghan, a personal name.

Keel, (on its own) *caol,* a narrow ridge or marsh.

Keel, (on its own) *caol,* an isthmus.

Keel, *caoil, caol, caoile,* a marshy or narrow stream.

Keel, *caol, caola, cael,* narrow, slender.

Keel, *chaoil,* a narrow place.

Keel, *chaoille, chaol,* not given.

Keela, *caoile, caola,* narrow.

Keela, *chaola,* not given.

Keelagh, *caelach,* narrow.

Keelaghs, *caológa,* small ridges.

Keelan, *Caoláin, Chaolán, Caoláin,* not given.

Keelan, *Caolán,* Keelan, a personal or family name.

Keelan, *Uí-Chaoláin,* O'Keelan, a family name.

Keelaun, *caoladán, caolán,* narrow.

Keelaun, *Uí-Chaolain, Chaoláin,* O'Keelan, a family name.

Keelaraheen, *caol-raithin,* little fort of the marsh(sic).

Keeldra, *caidrach*(sic), a burial lace for unbaptised infants.

Keeldra, *caoldoire,* not given.

Keeldra, *cealdrach,* an old burying ground.

Keeldra, *cealdrach,* an unconsecrated burial ground.

Keeldragh, *caoldoire,* not given.

Keele, *cáol,* narrow.

Keelog, Keeloge, *caológ, caolog, caelóg, caolóige,* a narrow stripe, strait or ridge.

Keeloge, *chaológ,* not given.

Keeloges, *caolága,* strips or narrow places.

Keeloges, *na-chaológa,* not given.

Keeltane, *coilltán,* little wood.

Keelties, *coil, coillte,* woods.

Keelty, *Caoilte,* Keelty or Quilty, a personal or family name.

Keelty, *coil, coillte,* woods.

Keelwick, *Caolmhaic,* Kelwick, a personal or family name.

Keelwy, *caol-mhaighe,* narrow plain.

Keely, *caolaigh,* not given.

Keely, *chaolaigh,* slender sticks or rods.

Keem, *an-choim,* the pass.

Keem, *caoim, cuím,* beautiful valley.

Keen, *caein,* beautiful.

Keen, *caoin, chaoin,* level, smooth, pleasant or beautiful.

Keen, *chaim,* Cam, a persons name.

Keen, *chinn,* the head or end.

Keen, *Choinn,* Conn, a male name.

Keen, *cian,* a male name.

Keen, *cian,* outlying.

Keena, *caonach,* a place of moss.

Keena, *críona,* withered bushes.

Keenagh, *caenach, caonach,* moss or a place of moss.

Keenaghan, *caenach,* a place of moss.

Keenaghan, *caonachan, caonachán,* not given.

Keenaghan, from *caonach,* a place of moss.

Keenaghan, *caoanachan*(sic) a mossy place.

Keenaght, *Ciannachta, Cianachta,* the place of the race or descendants of Cian.

Keenaght, *coanach,* a place of moss.

Keenan, *Chianáin,* not given.

Keenan, *Chonáin, Conáin,* Conan, a male name.

Keenan, *Uí-Cianáin, Chianáin,* O'Keanan, O'Keenan or Keenan, a family name.

Keenane, *Chanáin,* not given.

Keenane, *Chonáin, Conáin,* Conan, a male name.

Keenera, *caonaire,* mossy land.

Keenheen, *caeinthín,* beautiful surfaced little spot of land.

Keenleen, *coinlín,* not given.

Keenleen, *coinnlín,* stubble.

Keenleon, *coinnle Eoghain,* Owen's or Eoghain's (a male name) stubble.

Keenly, *coille*(sic), not given.

Keenly, *coinnle,* a candle.

Keenog, *caonóg,* a place of moss.

Keenoge, *caonóg,* a place of moss.

Keenoge, *Cianóige,* not given.

Keent, *caointe,* keening or lamentatin.

Keenty, *caointe,* keening or lamentatin.

Keeny, *caoine,* not given.

Keeny, *caonach, caonaigh, chaonaigh,* moss or a place of moss.

Keer, *ciar,* dark coloured.

Keera, *caera, caoireach, caerach, gCaorach,* sheep.

Keera, *Céire,* St Kiara.

Keera, *chaora,* not given.

Keera, *cire,* a crest or top.

Keeragan, *Ciaragáin,* not given.

Keeragh, *caera, caora, chaorach, caorach, gCaorach,* sheep.

Keeragh, *caerach,* not given.

Keeraghan, *caorachan, caoracháin,* not given.

Keeran, *caorthainn,* rowan berry or rowan tree/s.

Keeran, *chaorthainn, caerthtainn, caorthann, caorthainn,* quicken trees, mountain ash or rowan trees.

Keeran, *chaorthainn, caorthainn,* blackthorns or sloe bushes.

Keeran, *Cheirín, Chaoráin,* not given.

Keeran, *Chiaráin, Ciarán,* St Ciarán.

Keeran, *Mac/ Mic-Cairthinn,* sons of Ciarán, Kieran, a male name.

Keeran, *Uí-Chiaráin,* O'Kieran, a family name.

Keerane, *gaoithe,* wind.

Keerane, *Uí-Chiarain,* Kearn, a family name.

Keeraun, *cairna,* not given.

Keeraun, *caorán,* a moor.

Keeraun, *chaoráin,* not given.

Keeraun, *cíorán,* a crest.

Keeraunna, *caorán-na* , moor of the...

Keereen, *caoirín,* not given.

Keereen, *ciaráin,* small place of black soil.

Keereen, *Cill-Riain*(sic), not given.

Keerhan, *caerthtainn*, quicken trees, mountain ash or rowan trees.

Keerhan, *caorán*, not given.

Keerhan, *caorthán*, a quicken trees grove.

Keerin, *caorthainn*, not given.

Keerin, *Mic-Cairthinn*, not given.

Keeroge, *ciaróg*, beetles.

Keeroge, *Ciaróg, Ciarán*, Kieran, a male name.

Keeroge, *Dachiaróg, Diachiarog*, St Dachiarog/Dachiaróg.

Keeroge, *Do-Chiaróg*, Do Chiaróg, a personal or family name.

Keery, *gCaoraigh*, sheep.

Keery, *caerthainn*, rowan tree.

Keevagh, *céabhach*, a place of long marshy grass.

Keevagh, *ciabhach, ciabhaigh*, long grass that grows in morasses.

Keevan, *Caomháin*, not given.

Keevan, *Chaomháin*, Caomhán, a personal or family name.

Keevan, *Uí-Chaomháin*, O'Keevan or O'Kevan, a family name.

Keevan, *Uí-Chiabháin*, Ó Ciabháin, a family name.

Keevican, *Uí-Chaomhaóin*, O'Keevican, a family name.

Keevin, *Chaoimhín*, Caoimhín or Kevin, a male name.

Keevin, *Ciabháin, Ciabhain, Caoimhghein*, not given.

Keevin, *Uí-Chaoimhghin*, O'Keevin, a family name.

Keevy, *caoimhe*, beautiful.

Keevy, *ciabhaigh*, not given.

Keherny, *ceitherne*, soldiers or kerns(sic).

Kehoe, *Mhic-Eochú*, Kehoe, a personal or family name.

Keify, *caoimhe*, beautiful.

Keighan, *Caocháin*, not given.

Keighan, *Céigeán, Caochán or* Keegan a personal or family name.

Keighan, *Céigeán, Chaechain*, Caechan, Keegan or Keeghan, a personal or family name.

Keilagh, *caelach*, narrow.

Keiloge, *caol-fhódh*, narrow land.

Keiloge, *caológ*, small narrow place.

Keiloge, *chaológ*, not given.

Keilty, *Chaoilte*, Caoilte, Keilty, a personal name.

Keim, *ceim*, a pass or gap

Keiman, *céim-an…*, pass or gap of the…

Keimin, *ceimín*, a small track or pass.

Kel, *coill*, wood.

Kele, *cael*, narrow.

Kelle, *Cille*, Church.

Kelliga, *ceilge*, treachery.

Kellin, *Caillin*, Caillin, a personal or family name.

Kellin, *Coillín, Coillin*, not given.

Kells, *Ceanannas, Ceanannas/Ceanannus-Osrai*, the chief fort of Ossary.

Kells, *Ceannanas*(sic)*-Osraidhe*, location or headship of authority in Ossory.

Kells, *Kenlis, Ceann-lios, Ceanannas*, not given.

Kells, *Ceanannas-Osraighe*, not given.

Kells, *Ceanannus, Ceanannas-mór*, (great) chief fort or great resisdence. The Anglo-Norman version of the name is 'Kenlis'.

Kells, *na-cealla*, the (monastic) cells.

Kells, *na-cealla*, the Churches.

Kellure, *cealluire*, a cemetery.

Kellure, *ceileabhair*, warbling of birds.

Kelly, *cailleach, caillighe*, the hag.

Kelly, *caillí, Cheallaigh, choiligh*, not given.

Kelly, *Ceallaigh, Cheallaigh*, St Ceallach.

Kelly, *Chealladh*, O'Kelly, a family name.

Kelly, *Cheallaig, Uí-Cheallaigh*, Ó Ceallaigh or Kelly, a family name.

Kelly, *choilligh*, (grouse) cock.

Kelly, *coille, choilligh*, a wood.

Kelly, *Uí-Cheallaigh/Ceallaigh*, O'Kelly, a family name and means the descendants of Kelly.

Kelsha, *coillseach*, brushwood or underwood.

Keltan, *coillteán*, not given.

Keltar, *Celtchair*, 'Keltar of the battles', a warrior of the red branch knights.

Kelter, *Chealtchair*, Keltchar, a personal name.

Kelure, *ceileabhair*, warbling birds.

Ken, *ceann*, a head.

Ken, *cionn, cinn*, a head or headland.

Kenagh, *caonach*, moss.

Kenagh, *cinn-eich,* not given.

Kenefick, *Kenefick,* a family name of English origin.

Kenmare, *ceann-mara,* head of the sea.

Kenmare, *neidín,* the little nest.

Kenna, *Cionaith,* Kenny, a personal or family name.

Kenna, *Geanach,* not given.

Kenna, *Uí-Chionaoith,* Ó Cionaoith, O'Cionaoth, a family name and means the descendants of Cionaoth.

Kennan, *Cianáin,* not given.

Kennan, *Kennan,* a male name.

Kennedy, *Ceannfhada,* not given.

Kennedy, *Ua-Cinneaida,* O'Kennedy, a family name.

Kennedy, *Uí-Chinnéide,* Ó Cinnéide, a family name.

Kennett, *Coinéad,* Coinéad, a personal or family name.

Kenno, *Uí-Chionaoith,* Ó Cionath, a family or clan name.

Kenny, *Cainnech,* Cainnech, a personal or family name.

Kenny, *Cannanan,* Cannon and O'Cannanan, family names.

Kenny, *Ceanainn,* O'Cannon, family name.

Kenny, *Ceannainn,* Ceanainn, Cannanan, a personal or family name.

Kenny, *Chainnigh, Cainneach,* St Canice/ Cainneach.

Kenny, *Cheannaigh,* Ceannaigh or Ceanach, a male name.

Kenny, *Cheinnigh,* Ceannach, a personal or family name.

Kenny, *cinn-eich, Coinnigh, Cannan, Chianaigh, Cionaigh,* not given.

Kenny, *Mac-Cionaoith,* Mac Kenny, a family name.

Kenny, O'Ceannann, a family name.

Kenny, *Uí-Chionaoith,* Ó Cionaoith or O'Kenny, a family name.

Kenry, *Caonrach, Choinne, Chaonraígh, Caonraíoch,* not given.

Kenry, *Caonraí,* not given.

Kenry, *Caonraighe,* the old territory of Kenry.

Kenry, *Chaonraí,* Caonraí, a personal or family name.

Kensale, *cionn-tSáile,* the sea head.

Kent, (lough) *ceann,* not given.

Kenty, *Cheantaigh,* not given.

Keo, *cheo,* not given.

Keo, *cheóig, ceo,* fog, foggy

Keoge, *ceoig,* fog or foggy.

Keoge, *cheoigh,* not given.

Keogh, *cheo,* mist or fog.

Keoghan, *Uí-Cheóchain,* O'Keohane, a family name.

Keole, *cheóil, ceól,* music.

Ker, *Ceir,* Ker, a personal or family name.

Kera, *Chéire,* not given.

Keragh, *caorach,* sheep.

Keraine, Kieran, a male name.

Keran, *Ciarain,* Kieran, a male name.

Kerane, *caérán,* a bog.

Kerane, *caerthtainn,* quicken trees, mountain ash or rowan trees.

Kerane, *caorán,* not given.

Kerane, *Chiarain,* Kieran, a male name.

Keraun, *caorán,* not given.

Keraun, *caorthainn,* quicken trees, mountain ash or rowan trees.

Kerdin, *Ceirdín,* Kerdin, a personal or family name.

Kerdin, *Cheirdín,* not given.

Kere, *céir,* wax candles.

Kere, *chéir,* not given.

Kereen, *ceirín,* plaster or a wound dressing.

Kereen, *Chéirín, Céirín,* not given.

Kereen, Kerin, a personal or family name.

Kereen, Kevin, a male name.

Kereen, *Ua-Céirín,* O'Kerin, a family name.

Kereight, *caeraigheacht,* a mountain booley (dairying place) or a shepherds temporary settlement.

Kergan, *Uí-Chiaragáin/Chíaragain,* O'Kerrigan, a family name and means the descendants of Ciaragáin.

Keribly, *Mic-Geirble,* MacKerbly or MacGerbly, a family name.

Kerin, *Cheirín,* Céirín, a personal name and a founder of a Church in Clare.

Kerin, *Ua/Uí-Céirín,* O'Kerin, a family name.

Kerk, *dearc,* a cave.

Kerka, *circe,* grouse.

Kerlevan, *Mhic-Oirleamháin,* not given.

Kerlevan, *Chiarleamháin,* Kierlevan, a personal or family name.

Kern, *cethern,* lightly armed foot soldiers.

Kern, *Uí-Chirín,* O'Kirrine, a family name.

Kernan, from *carn,* little carns.

Kerne, *cheithearnaigh,* a foot soldier.

Kerny, *Ceithirne,* not given.

Kerny, *cethern,* lightly armed foot soldiers.

Keroge, *Uí-Cearóg,* O'Keroge, a personal or family name.

Kerogue, *Ciaróg,* Keerock, a personal or family name.

Kerra, *choire,* a cauldron.

Kerragh, *chaorach,* not given.

Kerran, *caerthann,* not given.

Kerran, *caorthainn,* rowan or mountain trees.

Kerran, *Ciarán, Ciarain,* Kieran, a male name.

Kerreen, *chuirrín,* a round topped hillock.

Kerri, *ceithre,* four.

Kerrib, *cairbe,* abounding in large stones.

Kerricurrihy, *Ciarraighe-Cuirche,* the name of an ancient tribe.

Kerrig, *caorthach,* lumpy ground.

Kerrigan, *Uí-Chíaragain,* O'Kerrigan, a family name.

Kerrikyle, *ceithre-choill,* not given.

Kerril, St Caireall.

Kerrill, *cairéil,* a quarry.

Kerrin, *Caireann,* not given.

Kerrin, *Cairin,* Caire, a personal or family name.

Kerrin, *Chiaráin, Chiarín, Ciaran, Ciarán,* St Kieran.

Kerrin, *Choirín,* not given.

Kerrin, *choirín,* the little turn.

Kerrivan, *Uí-Chiardubhain,* O'Kirwin, a family name.

Kerron, *Ciaráin, Ciarán, Ciarán,* a male name.

Kerry, *ceathrú, cheathrú,* a quarter.

Kerry, *ceithre,* four.

Kerry, *chéarthaigh,* not given.

Kerry, *cheathramha,* not given.

Kerry, *Chiarraí, Ciarraidhe, Ciarraí, Ciarrai, Ciar-raidhe,* race or decendents of Ciar.

Kerry, *chiarraí, gCaorach,* sheep.

Kerry, *choire, coire,* a cauldron.

Kerry, *Ciarraighe-Cuirche,* the name of an ancient tribe.

Kerry, *scairbhe,* rough river crossing.

Kerwick, *Uí-Chiarmhaic,* O'Kerwick or Kerwick, a family name and now often call themselves Kirby.

Kesh, *ceiseach, cheis, ceis,* a causeway made from brambles and clay or wicker, usually over a bog, lake, small river or stream.

Keskeame, *choiscéim,* not given.

Keskeame, *choiscéime,* a footstep or pass.

Kessagh, *ceiseach,* a little wickerwork causeway.

Kétra, (river) *an-cheatra, ceatra-an-bhiolair,* not given.

Kett, *Ceit,* Kett or Ceat, a personal name.

Kett, *Ua-Cheitt,* O'Kett, a family name.

Kettle, *Cathail,* Cahill, a personal or family name.

Kettle, *Cital,* little Kitt, a personal or a family name.

Kettle, *Ceitil,* not given.

Keva, *ciabh, ceibhe,* long coarse grass.

Kevan, *Uí-Chaomháin,* O'Keevan or O'Kevan, a family name.

Kevan, *Uí-Chiabháin,* Ó Ciabháin, a family name.

Keveen, *Caoimhín, Caoimhin,* Kevin.

Kevin, *Caoimhghein,* not given.

Kevuee, *cae-bhuidhe,* yellow quagmire.

Key, *cae, caedh,* a quagmire or marsh.

Key, *Cé,* the quay.

Key, *chaoich,* not given.

Keyanna, *caothanna,* quagmires.

Keylod, *caol-fhód,* narrow sod.

Keylogue, *caológ,* a narrow ridge.

Keylong, *caológ,* a narrow ridge or strip.

Keylong, *chaológ,* not given.

Kib, *cib,* Ribb, a river name, meaning not given.

Kibb, *cib,* Ribb, a river name, meaning not given.

Kibberidog, *cibe-rideog,* sedgy land of the herb, 'rideog', 'bog-awl' or '*manna-na-mona*'.

Kibberidog, *ciob-Roideoige,* not given.

Kibbock, MacHobbock, a family name.

Kibbock, *Mhic-Lobuic,* Machobock(sic), a personal or family name.

Kiel, caol, narrow.

Kiel, choill, a wood.

Kiel, Cill, a Church.

Kiell, Chill, a Church.

Kiely, chaolaigh, fairy-flax (*linium-silvestre*).

Kiely, Uí-Chadhla, O'Kiely, a personal or family name.

Kieran, Chiaráin, Ciaran, a male name.

Kieran, Ciarán, Chiaráin, St Ciaráin, Ciaran, Kieran.

Kieran, ciaran, grey(sic).

Kiggaul, choigeáil, not given.

Kil, caol, narrow.

Kil, coill-a'..., wood of the....

Kil, coillidh, not given.

Kil, gCeall, a Church.

Kil, usually means a Church (*Cill, Cil*) but can also mean a wood (*coill, choill, coille*).

Kilan, coil-an..., wood of the...

Kilaned, Cill-Fhathnaid, not given.

Kilay, a'-tsléibhe, the mountain.

Kilbran, Chill-Bhreathnach, not given.

Kilbrew, Cill-Morubha, not given.

Kilcavan, St Kevins Church.

Kilchrist, Mhic-Giolla-Chríost, Gilchrist, a personal or family name.

Kilcline, Mhic-Giollachlaoin, Macklecleen or McGillechleene, a family name.

Kilcock, Cill-Cocca, Church of St Cocca the virgin.

Kilcock, cúil-coilig, corner of the grouse cock.

Kilcoe, Cill-Coiche, St Coch's Church.

Kilcommon, Cill-Chuimin, Church of St Coman.

Kilcommon, coill-Chuimin, Commane's/Coman's (a personal or family name) wood.

Kilcommon, poll-an-tSómais, Cill-Chomáin/Comainn/Coman, not given.

Kilcredaun, Cill-Cordain, not given.

Kilcreman, coillín-Mhic-Réamainn(sic), not given.

Kilda, Cill-dá..., Church of the two...

Kildalkey, Cill-Delga, Delgas Church.

Kildare, Cill-dara, Church of the oaks.

Kildea, Giolla-de, O'Gildea, a family name.

Kildea, Mhic-Giolla-dé, Mackledea, Kildea or Gildea, a family name.

Kilderry, coille-eidir-..., the wood between...

Kilduff, Mhic-Giolladuibh, Mackleduff or Kilduff, a family name. It means the son of the dark complexioned or black servant.

Kilduffahoo, Cill-dubh-dhá-thuath, not given.

Kildurrihy, Cill-Ura, not given.

Kile, choill, coill, a wood.

Kileragh, choill-Iarta, Fiachra's (a male name) wood.

Kileroe, coill-chró, not given.

Kiletaun, choillteáin, not given.

Kiletaun, coillteáin, underwood.

Kilfahavon, fa-hamhann(sic), the river.

Kilfine, Cill-Eilfín/Ifín, not given.

Kilgabriel, Cill-Ghiriam, not given.

Kilgarron, Cill-tighe-Garrán, not given.

Kilgarrylander, Cill-Gharrdha-Lóndraigh, not given.

Kilgarvan, coill-an-gharráin, not given.

Kilgrant, Cill-Cronnachtán, not given.

Kiliera, Cill-Fhiacrach, St Fiacre's Church.

Kilina, coill-an-feadha, wood of the rushes.

Kilka, caoilce, not given.

Kilka, cuilc, cuilceach, a place of broom.

Kilka, cuilce, cuile, reeds or brooms.

Kilkee, Cill-Caeidhe, St Kee/s Church.

Kilkeedy, Cill-Caeidhe, St Kee's Church.

Kilkeel, Cill-an-caol, Church of the narrow.

Kilkenny, Cill-Chainnigh, Church of St Canice,

Kilkenny, Cill-Chanaigh-na-cloch-n-aoil, Kilkenny of the limestones.

Kilkinamurray, coil-chon-Murchaidh, wood of Murchadh's (a personal or family name) hound.

Kill, (on its own) *an-Chill,* not given.

Kill, caill, choill, chuill, hazel.

Kill, chille, not given.

Kill, choill, a wood.

Kill, usually means a Church (*Cill, Cille, Cil*) but can also mean a wood (*coill, coille*).

Killa, Cill, a Church.

Killa, Cill-a'..., Cill-an..., Church of the...

Killa, *Cill-achadh…,* Church of the field of…

Killa, *Cille,* a Church or graveyard.

Killa, *coill-an/a'…,* wood of the…

Killa, *coille, coill,* a wood.

Killa, *coille-dá…,* wood of the two…

Killa, usually means a Church (*Cill, Cil*) but can also mean a wood (*coill, coille*).

Killaan, *Cill-Loebhain,* Lavan's or Loebhan's Church.

Killaboy, Kilboy, a male name.

Killabuonia, *Cill-Buaine,* not given.

Killachonna, *Cill-Dachonna,* Church of Dachonna, a personal or family name and a founder of a Church in Westmeath.

Killaconenagh, *Cill-achadh-nAoineach,* not given.

Killaconnor, *Cill-Chonaire,* not given.

Killacrim, *Cill-atha-cruime,* Church of the crooked ford.

Killadeas, *Cill-chéile/cheile-dé,* Church of Céle Dé or the Culdees (meaning the companions of God). These were 8th century monastic reformers.

Killadeas, *drom-ban,* not given.

Killaderry, *Cill-rátha/ratha-dairthí*(sic), not given.

Killadriffe, *Cill-Airdrí,* not given.

Killadriffe, *Cill-Maoldithribh,* not given.

Killadrown, *coill-idir-dhá-abhainn,* not given.

Killag, *Cill-liag,* not given.

Killagally, *Cill-Eaglaigh,* not given.

Killageer, *coille-gCaor,* wood of the berries.

Killagh, *coilleach,* woodland.

Killagha, *Cill-achaidh,* Church of the field.

Killaghin, *Cill-achaidh-an…,* Church of the …field.

Killagholehane, *Cill-Deochain-Liatháin,* not given.

Killaghtee, the Church of Aodh's (Hughs) lecht or monument.

Killagoola, *Cill-Ogúla,* not given.

Killaha, *Cill-achaidh,* not given.

Killaha, *Cill-atha,* Church of the ford.

Killahala, *coil-áth-shaile,* not given.

Killahaly, *Cill-dá-sháile, coill-dhá-sháilé, coill-an-sháilé,* not given.

Killahaly, *coill-áth-a'chalaidh,* wood of the ferry ford.

Killahara, *choill-Eachra/Echra,* not given.

Killahara, *Cill-Eachra,* not given.

Killahy, *Cill-Achaidh/Achadh,* Church of Achadh(sic).

Killala, *Cill-Ala, Cill-Alaidh/Alaid,* St Ala's Church.

Killalee, *Cill-Fhéilim*(sic), not given.

Killally, *Cill-Ailaidh,* not given.

Killaloe, *Cill-Dalua, Cill-Dha-Lua,* Church of St Dalua, Lua, Molua or Malua.

Killaloo, *Cill-Dalua, Dha-Lua,* Church of St Dalua.

Killaloo, *coil-an-lao,* wood of the calf.

Killamoyne, *Cill-Uí-Mhuadhain,* O'Mooan's Church.

Killan, *Cill-Áine,* St Anne, Áine's a female name) Church.

Killan, *Cill-an…,* Church of the…

Killan, *Cill-Anna,* St Anne/Ann's Church.

Killanafinch, *Cill-na-fuinseann,* not given.

Killane, *choillain,* hazel.

Killane, *Cill-Anna,* Anna's (a female name) Church.

Killane, *Cill-Lainne,* not given.

Killanigan, *coill-Lonnagáin,* not given.

Killaniv, *Cill-Chonduibh,* not given.

Killann, *Cill-an…,* Church of the…

Killann, *Cill-Anna,* Anna's (a female name) Church.

Killans, *coillíní,* little round hills(sic).

Killaranny, *coill-raithní,* not given.

Killard, *Cill-áird,* Church of the height.

Killard, *Cúl-ard,* high back or back land.

Killardy, *cillináirde,* a Church eminence.

Killardy, *coille-airde,* not given.

Killare, *Cille-láir,* central Church.

Killaree, *Cill-Laithrigh,* Laithreach's Church.

Killary harbour, *caolsháire, caolsháile-ruadh,* not given.

Killary, *caoláire,* the narrow sea inlet.

Killary, *Cill-Áirí/Áthraigh, coill-Áirí, caolsháile,* not given.

Killathy, *Cill-Aitche,* not given.

Killatten, *Cill-Leachtáin,* not given.

Killaun, *coilleán,* underwood.

Killawinnia, *Cille-Mhaonaigh,* Meaneys or Mooneys Church.

Killawn, *coilleán,* underwood.

Killboy, (Ballykillaboy) *Mhic-Bhiolla-bhuí,* Mac Gilloway, a personal or family name.

Kille, *Cill,* a Church.

Kille, *Cill-a'...,* Church of the...

Kille, *coill-a'...,* wood of the...

Kille, usually means a Church (*cille,cill, cil*) but can also mean a wood (*coill, coille*).

Killea, *choill/coil-liath,* grey wood.

Killea, *Cill-Aodha,* Hugh's or Aodh's (a male name) Church.

Killea, *Cill-Fhiadh/Fhiaich/Fhéich,* St Fiach's Church.

Killea, *Cill-liath,* grey Church.

Killea, *Cill-Réidh/shléibhe,* not given.

Killea, *Cill-Uí-Ráedh/Rae,* O'Reagh's Church.

Killea, *Cill-La,* Church of La, a deciple of St Finbar.

Killea, Cill-Aédha, St Aidus.

Killead, *Cill-Éad,* Faod (a personal or family name) Church.

Killeagh, *Cill-Fhiacha,* St Fiach's Church.

Killeagh, *Cill-Ia,* Ia's (a personal name) Church.

Killeagh, *Cill-liath, Cill-Éice,* not given.

Killeagh, *Cill-La,* Church of La, a deciple of St Finbar.

Killeague, *Coill-Líag,* wood of the flag-stones.

Killeane, *Cill-Liadhain,* Liadhain's Church.

Killeanly, *Cill-éanlaithe,* not given.

Killeany, *Cill-Fhéinne,* not given.

Killeavy, *Cill-shléibhe,* Church of the mountain.

Killedan, *Cill-Liadán,* not given.

Killee, *Cill-Aodha,* Hugh's or Aodh's (a male name) Church.

Killeedy, *Cill-Íde/Ide,* Church of St Ité/Idé.

Killeef, *coillidh-Liaf,* not given.

Killeek, *Cill-Íce,* not given.

Killeely, *Cill-Liaile,* not given.

Killeen, (from Rinakilleen) of the Churchyard.

Killeen, *Chillín,* the monks cell.

Killeen, *choillín,* not given.

Killeen, *cillin, cillínidhe, cillinach,* a burying place for children.

Killeen, *Cillín,* little Church.

Killeen, *Cillin,* St Cilleen.

Killeen, *coillín,* little wood.

Killeen, (Grangesylvia parish) *Cillín-lia,* the little old Church.

Killeena, *Cillín-an/a* , little Church of the...

Killeena, *coillíneach,* underwood.

Killeenadeema, *Cillín-a-Díoma,* not given.

Killeenadeema, *Cill-Inghíne-Díoma,* not given.

Killeenagarriff, *Cill-Mhic-Con-Ghairbh,* not given.

Killeenagh, *Chíllíneach, Cillíní,* not given.

Killeenagh, *Cillíneach, Cillineach,* the location of a little Church or cell, little Churches or burial places.

Killeenagh, *coillíneach,* underwood.

Killeenan, *coil-Línnan,* wood of water.

Killeenna, *Cillín-na* , little Church of the...

Killeenoghty, *Cill-Fhíonnachta,* Fíonnachta's Church.

Killeens, *Cillín,* a little Church or Churchyard for infant burial.

Killeeny, *Cillínidhe,* little Churches.

Killeeny, *Coillínidhe,* little woods.

Killeeny, *gCillíní,* not given.

Killeenyarda, *na-coillíní-arda,* the high little woods.

Killegar, *coille/coil-an-ghairr,* wood of the offal.

Killegar, *coill-an-ghairr,* wood of the turf-mould.

Killegland, *Cill-leithghleanna,* Church of the half-glen.

Killeheen, *Cill-Eichín,* Eichín's Church.

Killeigh, *Cill-liath, Cill-achaidh-drom-fhada,* not given.

Killeigh, *Cill-aichidh*(sic)*/achaidh,* Church of the field.

Killeigh, *Cill-Fhíach,* Fiach's Church.

Killeigh, *Cill-líath,* grey Church.

Killelane, *Cill-Fhaoláin,* not given.

Killeline, *Cill-Eithleann,* not given.

Killen, a wood.

Killen, *Ceithleann, Cethlenn, Ceithlinn,* Cethle, Ceithle or Cethlenn, a female name.

Killen, *choillín,* a little wood.

Killen, *chuilinn, cuilinn,* not given.

Killen, *Cill-an...,* Church of the...

Killen, *Cillín,* the little Church.

Killen, *cuilan,* secluded place.

Killen, *cúil-an...,* not given.

Killena, *Cill-Fhíne,* not given.

Killenagh, *Cill-Fhíne,* not given.

Killenagh, *cillíneach,* little Church site.

Killenaule, *Cill-an-áil,* the Church of the rock.

Killenaule, *Cill-Náile,* St Naile/Náile's Church.

Killenaule, *coill-an-Áil, Cill-Donáile,* not given.

Killenny, *Cill-Einne,* not given.

Killenny, *coill-leana,* wood meadow.

Killennybeg, *cnoc-na-greallaighe,* not given.

Killennymore, *tobar-bó,* not given.

Killenough, *coillíneach,* a woody district.

Killenough, *cuileannach,* a place of holly.

Killenure, *cuilan-Iúir,* secluded place of yew.

Killer, *Cill-ar...,* Church on...

Killererin, *Cill-fhear-Éireann,* not given.

Killery, *Cael-shaile-ruadh,* Church of the red narrow sea inlet.

Killery, *caolaire,* narrow sea.

Killery, *Cill-Oiridh,* not given.

Killester, *Cill-Lasra/Éasra,* not given.

Killew, *choille, coille,* the wood.

Killew, *coilleadh,* not given.

Killi, *coille,* a wood.

Killi, *coillo*(sic)*-an...,* wood of the...

Killiaghan, *Ceallachán,* the little Church.

Killian, *Cill-Liadhain/Liadhna,* St Liedania.

Killian, *Cill-Liadhan,* Church of St Liadhan.

Killic, *Cill-mhic...,* the Church of the son of...

Killickaforavane, *Cill-leice-Fórabháin,* not given.

Killimy, *coil-ime,* wood of butter.

Killin, *chuilinn,* holly.

Killin, *Cill-an...,* Church of the...

Killin, *Cilleán, Cillín,* not given.

Killin, *coillin,* a wood.

Killin, *coillín,* little wood.

Killina, *Cill-an...,* Church of the...

Killina, *Cill-Uí-Leannáin,* not given.

Killina, *coillín-na...,* little wood of the...

Killina, *coill-na...,* wood of the...

Killinaboy, *Cill-iíne/iníne/inghín,* Church of the daughter/s of Baoth.

Killinane, *Cill-Fhíonáin/Fhionnáin,* not given.

Killinchy, *Cill-Dúinsí/Duinsí/Dhúinsí/Dhuinsi,* Church of St Duinseach, Dúinseach or Duiseach.

Killined, *coill-an-nid,* wood of the nest.

Killineen, *Cill-Loinín,* Loinin's (a persons name) Church.

Killineer, *Cill-Ó-nDaighre,* not given.

Killineer, *Cill-Ua-nDoighre,* O'Deery's Church.

Killiney, *Cill-iníon/inion-Léinín,* Church of the daughters of Léinín, Léinin.

Killiney, *Cill-Fhinnche,* St Finnche's Church.

Killinga, *coil-einge,* wood of the groove or border.

Killinick, *Cill-Fhionnóg,* Church of St Finneóg/Finneog.

Killiskea, *coill-uisce,* not given.

Killistafford, *coill-an-Stafardaigh,* not given.

Killistia, *Cill-Istiagh,* Istia's Church.

Killistown, *Cill-Osnad/Osnadha,* Church of St Osnadh.

Killistristane, *coil-ros-Dristean,* not given.

Killo, *Cill-na...,* Church of the...

Killock, *an-chaológ,* not given.

Killock, *Cill-Eocha,* Eochy's (a male name) Church.

Killoe, *Cill-eo/eó,* Church of the yew.

Killonan, *Cill-Lónáin,* not given.

Killone, *Cill-Eoghain,* not given.

Killone, *Cill-Eoin,* Church of St John (the Baptist).

Killonecaha, *Cill-Ón-Chatha,* not given.

Killora, *Cill-Eora,* Church of St Eora.

Killorath, *Cill-na-ráth,* not given.

Killoscully, *Cill-Ó-Scolaí,* not given.

Killough, *an-coilleach,* the forest or woodland.

Killough, *Cill-acha,* Church of the fastings.

Killough, *Cill-Eochaidh/Eachaidh,* not given.

Killough, *Cill-Eocha/Eachach,* Eochy's (a male name) Church.

Killour, *Cill-Odhar,* not given.

Killow, *cóill-éó,* wood of yew.

Killower, *Cill-leabhair,* Chuch of the book.

Killucan, *Cill-Liúcainne,* Church of Liúcain, a personal or family name.

Killune, *Cill-Eoghain,* Owen's (a male name) Church.

Killurin, *Cill-Liúráin,* Church of St Luaithrenn.

Killusty, *Cill-Osta,* not given.

Killy, *caillighe,* the old woman.

Killy, *chille, choillí, caille, coill, cúil-na…,* not given.

Killy, *Cill-na…, Cill-an/a'…,* the Church of the…

Killy, *coilidh,* a cock.

Killy, *coill-a/a'/an/na…,* the wood of the…

Killy, *coilidh, coille,* the wood.

Killy, *coilleach,* grouse cock.

Killy, *na-cealla,* Churches or monastic cells.

Killy, *na-cealla,* the monaltic cells.

Killy, usually means a Church (*Coillidh, Cille, Cill, Cil*) but can also mean a wood (*coill, coille*).

Killycard, *coillidh-cairn*(sic), not given.

Killycarnan, *coill/choillidh-Charnáin,* not given.

Killycomain, *coill-Mhic-Giolla-Mhaoil,* Mac Giolla Maol's (a personal or family name) wood.

Killyleagh, Church of the descendants of laoch.

Killyleagh, *Cill-Ó-Laoch,* Church of Uí Laoch, a family or personal name and means the descendants of (the) heroes.

Killymard, *Cill-Ó-mBaird,* not given.

Killyn, *coill-na…,* wood of the…

Killyna, *coill-an/na…,* the wood of the…

Killynagh, *Cill-Luineachair,* Luineachair's (a persons name) Church.

Killynahar, *coill-an-Athair,* wood of the father.

Killyneece, *coil-Aenghuis,* Aengus's (a male name) Church.

Killyon, *Cill-Adhuin,* Church of St Kieran.

Killyon, *Cill-Liadhan,* Church of St Leidhan, Liadhan.

Killyon, *Cill-Liain,* Líadaine s (a womans name) Church.

Killyon, *Cill-Liain,* Lian's (a personal name) Church.

Killyon, *Cill-Liaine,* not given.

Kilmartin, *Chill-Mhártain,* not given.

Kilmartin, *Mhic-Giollamhartain,* Kilmartin or Gilmartin, a family name.

Kilmeelchon, *Cill-Ó*(sic)*-Mhíolchon,* not given.

Kilmeelicken, *béal-átha-na-mBreac*(sic), not given.

Kilmoe, *Cill-Mogha,* Church of St Mogha.

Kilmoylin, *Cill-átha-Maoilín,* not given.

Kilmurry, *'ic/ Mhic-Giolla-Mhuire,* MacGillamoire, a family name. It means the son of the servant of Mary.

Kilmurry, *Mhic-Giolla-Mhuire, Uí-Giolla-Mhuire,* MacGillemory or O'Macgillemory(sic), a family name.

Kilna, *Cill-na…,* Church of the…

Kilna, *coill-na…,* wood of the…

Kilnaboy, *Cill-iníne-Baoith,* Church of the daughters of Baoth, a personal or family name.

Kilnacor, *coill-na-coinne*(sic), the hill wood.

Kilnaharvey, *Coill-Chearrbhaigh*(sic), not given.

Kilnamach, *Cill-na-Mac,* Church of 'Seacht-Mac-Righ' which means the Kings seven sons.

Kilnamack, *Cill-na-mac,* the sons Church.

Kilnap, *Cill-an-Aba/Abba,* Church of the Abbot.

Kilree, *Chill-Rí,* not given.

Kilree, *Cill-Ruidhche,* Church of St Ruidhche.

Kilregane, *coill-chreagáin,* not given.

Kilroe, *Mhic-Giolla-ruaidh,* Mackilroe or Gilroy, a family name.

Kilroughil, *cóill-urchail,* hill of the spancil.

Kilt, *coillte,* woods.

Kilta, *coillte,* woods.

Kiltaan, *cóilltán,* little wood.

Kiltaan, *coilltéan,* underwood.

Kiltagh, *coillteach, coilltech,* wooded, woody or woodland.

Kiltaghan, *coillteachan,* underwood.

Kiltale, *Cill-tSiadhail,* Church of St Sedulius.

Kiltallaghan, *Cill-tSalchain,* not given.

Kiltallaghan, *Cill-tSealbhacháin,* Church of St Sealbhachan.

Kiltamagh, *coillte-amach,* outer woods.

Kiltamagh, *coillte-mach,* woods of the plain.

Kiltan, *Chailteáin,* Cailtean, a personal or family name.

Kilteen, *coilltín,* a little wood.

Kiltena, *coillte-na...,* wood of the...

Kiltennanlea, *Cill-tSeanán-léith,* The Church of 'St Seanan the grey'.

Kiltimagh, *coillte-mach,* wood of the plain.

Kiltown, *baile-na-Cille,* town of the Church.

Kiltown, *Cill-Donncha-na-Cille*(sic), not given.

Kilty, *coillte,* woods.

Kilty, *O Caoilte, Uí-Chaoilte,* O'Quilty or O'Keelty, a family name.

Kilty, *Ua-Coiltedh,* O'Kilty, a family name.

Kiltyfea, *coillte-feadha,* strong or great woods.

Kiltyna, *coillte-na...,* woods of the...

Kilvey, *coill-Bheithigh,* not given.

Kilvoy, *Cill-Bheódh-Aodha,* Church of St Beodh–Aodha.

Kilworth, *Cill-uird,* Church of the order.

Kimalta, *coimeálta, comailt,* not given.

Kimalta, *Comailte,* Kimalta, keeper hill.

Kimeheer, *caimthír,* winding land.

Kimmage, *cam-muighe, carn-cam-mhuighe,* not given.

Kimmeen, *an-coimín,* not given.

Kin, *chin, chinn, cin, cionn, ceann,* head or hill.

Kin, *Cinel...,* descendants or people of....

Kin, *cinn, Cian,* not given.

Kin, usually means a Church (*Cill, Cil*) but can also mean a wood (*coill, coille*).

Kina, *Chadhnaigh,* not given.

Kina, *Cheirdheanaigh,* Kyne, a personal or family name.

Kina, *chon,* hound.

Kina, *cionn-an/a'...,* head of the...

Kinaff, *an-chneamha,* not given.

Kinal, *cineál, cinel,* descendants, people of....

Kinalea, *cineál, cinel-Aodha,* the race (of people) of Aedh or Hugh.

Kinallia, *cinn-aille,* cliff head.

Kinally, *cionn-ailí,* not given.

Kinalmeaky, *cineál-mBéice,* not given.

Kinameaky, *cean-neal-meacan,* head of the noble root.

Kinameaky, *cinel-mBece,* the decenants of Bece, a mans name.

Kinamurry, *cine-Muireadhaigh,* the sept of Murray.

Kinase, *cinn-fhais, cinn-fhásaigh,* head of the wilderness.

Kinash, *cinn-easa,* not given.

Kinawly, *Cill-Náile/Naile,* St Naile's Church.

Kindry, *chriathadera, chriathadora, chria-thadóra, chréither,* a sieve or sieve maker.

Kindry, *chriathradóra,* not given.

Kine, *cáin,* sunny.

Kine, *Chadhain,* Kyne, a personal or family name.

Kine, *Uí-Chadhain,* O'Kine a family name.

Kine, *ceann,* high ground.

Kineely, *Cionnaola,* Cionnaola or Kenneally, a personal or family name.

Kineely, *Cionnfhaolaidh,* Cionnfhaoladh, a personal name.

Kineely, *Conghaile,* not given.

Kineely, *Mhic–Chionnfhaelaidh,* McKinneely.

Kineigh, *ceann-eich,* not given.

Kineigh, *cionn-ech,* head of the horse.

Kingarrow, *an-cionn-garbh,* not given.

Kinkeen, *choinncín,* old snout or nose.

Kinlalee, *cinn-Loilí,* not given.

Kinlar, *cainnléora,* not given.

Kinlar, *coinnleora,* the candlestick.

Kinlea, *chinn-shléibhe,* at the head of the mountain.

Kinlea, *Chonléith,* Conliath, the name of a Church founder in Limerick.

Kinlea, *cineal-Aodha,* descendants of Aodh or Hugh, a male name.

Kinlee, *chinn-sléibhe,* ...at the head of the mountain.

Kinleen, *chaoinlín,* stubbles.

Kinler, *coinleoir, coinnleora, caindloir,* the candlestick.

Kinler, *coinnleora,* candlesticks.

Kinlough, *cionn/cinn-locha,* the head of the lake.

Kinn, *ceann,* the hill or head.

Kinn, *coinn,* a burial place.

Kinna, *cine,* not given.

Kinna, *cionn/ceann-na…,* head or hill of the…

Kinnafad, *cionn-átha/ceann-atha-fada,* head of the long ford.

Kinnagin, *cionn-Cuincil*(sic), not given.

Kinnailia, *cinn-shaile,* sea side(sic).

Kinne, *cionn/ceann-na…,* head, headland or hill of the…

Kinnea, *cionn-eich/ech,* head of the horse.

Kinneagh, *Airchinneach, Airchinnigh,* name of an ancient chief.

Kinnefeake, *Chinféic,* Kinnefeake, the name of a family originally from Glamorganshire.

Kinnegad, *ceann-atha-gad,* head of the ford of wythes.

Kinnegad, *cionn/ceann-átha-gad,* head of the ford of the points.

Kinnegar, *coinigéar, gCoinigéar,* not given.

Kinnegar, *cuinicéra,* a rabbit warren.

Kinnegoe, *cinn-Gobha,* not given.

Kinneigh, *cinn-eich, ceann-eich/ech,* the hill/head of the horse.

Kinnelly, *Cionlaí,* not given.

Kinnigh, *chinn/cinn-eich,* the head of the horse or the horse-head.

Kinnikin, *Choinchinn,* Cu Chinn, a personal or family name.

Kinnity, *cinn/cionn/ceann-Eithigh, cionn-Eitigh,* the head of Etach, Eitach or Eiteach (an ancient princess) was buried here.

Kinny, *Cainnigh,* not given.

Kinny, *cinn-an…,* head of the…

Kinocko, hillock of the…

Kinsale, *cionn-tSáile, ceann-sáile,* not given.

Kinsaley, *Cill/cinn-sáile,* not given.

Kinsella, *Chinsealaigh,* Ó Cinsealaigh, a family name.

Kinturk, *cinn-tuirc,* not given.

Kinure, *cinnabhair,* head of the yew.

Kinure, *creamh-dhaire,* wood of garlic.

Kinvarga, *cinn-mhargaidh,* the head of the market.

Kip, *ceap,* tree trunk/s.

Kip, *chip, ceap, cip,* a tree, wooden stake/s, a stock or stump.

Kippa, *ceapach,* a wood.

Kippache, *ceaphacha,* plots.

Kippagh, a place full of stocks or tree stumps.

Kippagh, *ceapach,* an area of cleared wood.

Kippane, *cheapán, cheapchain,* not given.

Kippane, *ciopán,* a tree trunk or a stake or tree trunks.

Kippaunagh, *ciopánach,* abounding in tree trunks or stakes.

Kippeen, *gCipín, cipín,* little stick/s or trunk.

Kippin, *cipín,* little stick, a stock or tree trunk.

Kippure, *cíop-mhór,* great place of mountainy grass.

Kippure, *cip-iubhair,* trunk/stumps of the yew.

Kippure, *cipiúr,* the big place of mountain grass.

Kiproe, *cip-ruaidh,* red stock or trunk.

Kir, *Cill,* Church.

Kirby, *Uí-Chiarmhaic,* Kerwick, a family name.

Kircock, *Coirceog,* not given.

Kircubbin, *carr-Cobain,* not given.

Kircubbin, *Cill-Ghobáin,* Church of St Gobán.

Kirgeen, *charraigín,* little rock.

Kirikee, *Tir-meicc, tí-mhic-Í,* land of the son of Í (see *Athy*).

Kirk, *cearc, cark, circe,* hen/s or grouse.

Kirk, *circe,* the hen, heath hens or partridges.

Kirka, *chircigh,* not given.

Kirka, *circe,* a single grouse, hen/s or grouse.

Kirke, *circe,* hen/s.

Kirkeen, *chircín,* not given.

Kirkeen, *circín,* the little hen.

Kirky, *circe, cearc,* hens or grouse.

Kirky, *coirce,* oats or corn.

Kirn, *caorthainn,* quicken trees, mountain ash or rowan trees.

Kirwan, *Chiarabháin,* not given.

Kish, *ceiseach, ceis,* a wickerwork causeway usually through a bog or lake.

Kisha, *ceis-a'…,* wicker bridge of the…

Kisha, *ceiseach, cise, ceis,* a wickerwork causeway usually through a bog or lake.

Kishen, *chisín,* wickerwork causeway.

Kishen, *ciséin,* a small box.

Kishen, *cisín, chisín,* a little wickerwork causeway.

Kishkeam, bottom of the pass.

Kishkeam, *coiscéim (na-caillí),* the footstep (of the hag).

Kishkeam, *cois-céim,* a foot step, narrow road or pass.

Kishog, *ciseóg,* a little bridge made of wicker.

Kishta, *císte,* the treasure.

Kishy, *ceiseach,* a wicker causeway.

Kiskeam, *coiscéim-na-caillighe/caillí,* footstep of the hag/s.

Kissane, Kissane or O'Kissane, a family name.

Kista, *chiste, chíste,* the hoard, treasure or chest.

Kisteen, *Mhic-Oistín, Mic-Aistín,* not given..

Kistin, *Cistean,* not given.

Kit, *Ceat,* Keth, a personal or family name.

Kit, *chait, cait, cuit, cat,* a cat.

Kit, *Cheit,* Keith, a male name.

Kitt, *Ceat,* Ceat, Keth, a personal or family name.

Kitt, *Ceit,* Cet, a male name.

Kitt, *Cet,* Kitt, a personal or family name.

Kitt, *Cit,* not given.

Kitt, *Cuit,* Ceat, a personal or family name.

Kittagh, *ciotaigh,* the left handed person.

Kivet, *coimheada, coimhead, coimhéadta,* watching.

Kivey, *ciabaigh,* bushy or hairy.

Kivvy, *ciabhach, ciabhaigh,* long grass that grows in morasses.

Klogh, *cloch,* a stone house.

Kloon, *cluain,* a meadow or a lawn.

Knader, *cnadair,* burdocks.

Knap, *cnap,* a hill.

Knapp, *cnap, cnoc,* a hill.

Knappagh, *chnapach,* not given.

Knappagh, *cnapach, cnappach,* tummocks, small round hills, a bumpy area or hilly land.

Knappoge, *chnapóg, cnapóg,* hummock or a small hill.

Knappogue, *chnapóg,* the small hill.

Knavagh, *cneamhach,* a place producing wild garlic.

Knaveen, *Uí-Chnáimhín,* Ó Cnáimhín, a family name.

Knavin, *cnámhín,* the little bone.

Knevin, *Mhic-Cnaimhain,* Mac-Nevin, a family name.

Knick, *chnuic,* a hill.

Knickeen, *cnoicín, cnocán,* little hill or hillock.

Knigh, *cnaoi,* place producing nuts.

Knigh, *cnaoídh,* nuts.

Knigh, *eich,* horse/s.

Knocane, *cnocán,* a hillock.

Knock, *cnucha, chnoic, chnoc, chnuic, cnocach, cnoc,* a hill.

Knock, *gCnoc,* hills.

Knocka, *cnoc, an-cnoc…,* not given.

Knocka, *cnoc-an/a'…,* hill of…, hill of the…

Knocka, *cnoc-na/an…,* hill of the….

Knocka, *croc,* a hill.

Knockacurrin, *cnocán-Uí-Churraoin,* O'Curran, a personal or family name.

Knockadav, *cnoc-dá-dhamh,* not given.

Knockadee, *cnoc-Uí-Dheá,* not given.

Knockadorraghy, *cnoc-Uí-Dhorachaidh,* O'Darcy's (a family name) hill.

Knockafaugh, *cnuck*(sic)*–a-fada,* the long hill.

Knockagh, *chnocach, cnoc-each,* not given.

Knockagh, *cnocagh, cnocach,* a place of hills.

Knockahaduve, *cnock-faithche-dubh*(sic), hill of the dark field.

Knockahavaun, *cnoc-Uí-Thaobháin,* not given.

Knockalla, *cnoc-Colbha,* not given.

Knockalough, *cnoc-an-loig,* not given.

Knockan, *cnocáin, chnocáin, cnocan, cnocán,* little hill or hillock.

Knockan, *cnoc-na*(sic)*…,* hill of the…

Knockan, *cnoc-an…,* hill of the…, hill of….

Knockan, *gCnocán,* little hills.

Knockana, *cnocan-na…, cnocán-an/na…,* little hill of the…

Knockanaddoge, *cnoc-an-Dóigigh,* not given.

Knockanadoge, *cnocán-Ó-nDuach,* Hill of the Ó-nDuach, (a tribal name).

Knockanagh, *cnocánach,* a place of hills.

Knockanare, *cnocán-an-Ré,* not given.

Knockanarra, *cnoc-an-earraigh,*(sic), hill of springtime.

Knockane, *cnocáin, chnocáin, cnocán,* little hill or hillock.

Knockane, *gCnocán, cnocán,* not given.

Knockanea, *cnoc-an-fhia,* not given.

Knockanearis(sic), *cnocan-an-Phiarais,* not given.

Knockanena, *cnocán-na* , hillock of the…

Knockanes, *na-cnocáin,* not given.

Knockanna, *cnocán/cnocan-na* , little hill of the…

Knockannagad, *cnocan-na-gCat*(sic), hillock of the wild cats.

Knockanroe, little red hill.

Knockans, *cnocáin,* hillocks.

Knockar, *cnoc-ar…,* hill on the…

Knockaravella, *cnoc-an-Raibhile,* not given.

Knockarigg, *cnoc-airg,* hill of the chest.

Knockarigg, *cnoc-comhraic,* hill of the meeting, battle, confluence or encounter.

Knockarigg, *cnoc-Eirc,* Eirc's (a mans name) hill.

Knockaspur, *cnoc-na-sop*(sic), not given.

Knockattigan, *cnoc-Chéadagáin,* not given.

Knockaudoff, *cnoc-áith-duibh,* hill of the black ford.

Knockaughna, *cnoc-caithne,* hill of trees.

Knockaun, *cnocáin, cnocáin, cnocán,* little hill or hillock.

Knockaun, *gCnocán,* hillocks.

Knockauna, *cnoc-bhan-an…,* hill of the lea-ground of the…

Knockauna, *cnoicín/cnocán-an/na/a…,* little hill of the…

Knockaunan, *cnocán-an…,* little hill of the…

Knockaunna, *cnocán-a/na…,* little hill of the…

Knockaunnacarragh, *an-cnocán-carrach*(sic), not given.

Knockaunaglokee, *cnocán-na-gClócaí,* hillock of the cloaks.

Knockavurrea, *cnoc-Uí-Mhuireadhaigh,* O'Murray, a family name.

Knockbaun, *gCnocbán,* white hillocks.

Knockcurlan, *cnoc-urlann,* not given.

Knockdoe, *cnoc-Tuagha,* not given.

Knockdoe, *cnoc-tuath,* hill of axes.

Knockdoocunna, black hill of the firewood.

Knocke, *cnoc,* a hill.

Knockea, *cnoc-Aodha,* Aedh's/Hugh's (male names) hill.

Knockean, *cnocán,* a hillock.

Knockeare, *choinicéir,* not given.

Knockeare, *coinicéir,* the rabbit warren.

Knockeen, *cnoc-Fhinn*(sic), not given.

Knockeen, *cnocín,* little hills.

Knockeen, *cnoicín, cnuicín, cnocán,* little hill or hillock.

Knockeena, *cnoicín-na* , *cnuicín-a* , little hill of the…

Knockeenna, *cnoicín/cnuicín-a* , little hill of the…

Knockeens, *cnuiciní,* little hills.

Knockeevan, *cnco-an-anama*(sic), *cnoc-an-anama,* not given.

Knocken, *cnocán,* a hillock.

Knocken, *cnoc-an…,* hill of the…

Knocker, *cnocair, cnocaire,* a hill man, forester or lumberjack.

Knocker, *cnocar,* a hill.

Knockera, *cnocar-a'…,* hill of the…

Knockereen, little hill.

Knockerry, *cnoc-doire/dhoire,* oak grove/wood hill.

Knockgraffon, *cnoc-Rafann,* Rafainn's (a personal or family name) hill.

Knockieran, *cnoc-caorthainn,* rowan tree hill.

Knockieran, *cnoc-iarann,* hill of iron.

Knockilterra, *cnoc-an-Iltéaraigh,* not given.

Knockin, *cnoc-an…,* hill of the…

Knockin, *cnoicín,* a hillock.

Knockinane, *cnocáin, cnocán,* little hill.

Knocking, *cnocáin, cnocán,* little hill.

Knockma, *sidh-Meadha,* a fairy palace presided over by *Finnbhar/Fin'var.*

Knockmaa, *cnoc-Liamhna-siúil,* not given.

Knockmaroe, *cnoc-an-arbha,* not given.

Knockmoy, *Cnoc-Muaidhe,* Muaidh's (a female name) hill.

Knockn, *cnoc-na…,* hill of the…

Knockna, *cnoc-na…, cnuic-na…,* hill of the…

Knocknaquill, (bi-lingual) *cnoc-na-chleite/chleite/cletta,* hill of the quill.

Knocknaraha, cnoc-na-ratha, hill of the (from *ruith*) running away or flight.

Knocknasheega, *cnoc-na-síge,* hill of the stack or streak.

Knocknew, *cnoc-Tnútha,* not given.

Knocknew, *cnoc-tnú,* hill of contention.

Knocknew, *cnoc-Dhonnchadha,* Donogh's (a personal or family name) hill.

Knoco, *cnoc-a'...,* hill of the...

Knockown, *cnoc-gabhainn,* not given.

Knockpoge, *cnapóg,* a hillock or knoll.

Knockree, *cnoc-críothaigh,* not given.

Knockronaghan, *cnoc-chruithneacháin,* not given.

Knocks, *an-cnoc, na-cnuic/cnoca,* hills.

Knockumber, *cnoc-chomar,* hill of the confluence (where rivers meet).

Knocky, *cnoc-an...,* hill of the...

Knoohill, *cnóchoill,* nut hazels.

Knopoge, *chnapóg, cnapóg,* a little lump or hillock.

Knopp, *cnap,* a lump, a small round hillock.

Knopp, *cnoc,* a hill.

Knoppoge, *chnapóg,* not given.

Knoppoge, *cnapóg,* a small hill or knob.

Knowth, *Cnodhbha,* the name of the burial mounds of *Brugh-na-Boinne.*

Knoxter, Knockter or Noctor a personal name.

Knuc, *cnoc,* a hill.

Knuck, *cnoc,* a hill.

Knuckeen, *cnoicín,* little hillock.

Kock, *cnoc,* a hill.

Kody, *coíde,* brushwood.

Komagh, *camtha,* crooked.

Komeryk, *comairce,* not given.

Koskir, *choimheascair,* strife.

Koskir, *choscair,* slaughters.

Kough, *chuadh,* a hollow.

Kourea, *curra,* a weir.

Kreen, *cruinn,* round.

Krion, *crion,* old or withered.

Kriver, *creamh-dhaire,* wood of garlic.

Krogh, *chócaire,* cook.

Kuile, *Cill,* little burial place.

Kuile, *coill,* a wood.

Kunikeen, *Ciúinicín,* Runikeen, a male name.

Kuragh, *ciárach,* yewy.

Kye, *caedh,* a quagmire or marsh.

Kyla, *choill/coil-an...,* wood of....

Kyla, *an-choill...,* not given.

Kylanoreashy, *coil-an-Fhoiréisigh,* Forrest's (a family name) wood.

Kylanoreashy, *coill-an-Noiréasaigh/ Fhoraoise,* not given.

Kyle, *caol,* narrow.

Kyle, *choill,* wood/s.

Kyle, *chuill,* hazel.

Kyle, *an-chill,* not given.

Kyle, *Cill,* a burial place.

Kyle, *Cill, Cil,* a Church.

Kyle, *coill, coile,* a wood.

Kyle, *coll, choill, cuill,* hazel.

Kylea, *choill,* wood/s.

Kylea, *coill-a...,* wood of...

Kylea, *coill-an...,* hill of the...

Kylea, *coill-an...,* wood of the...

Kylea, *coill-Aodh,* Aodh's (a male name) hill.

Kyleera, *Cill-Fhiacrach,* St Fiacre's Church.

Kyleera, *iartha,* west Church or wood.

Kylena, *Cill-na...,* Church of....

Kylena, *coill-na...,* wood of the...

Kyleonermody, *coil-O nDiarmada,* wood of the O'Dermody's (a family name).

Kylesa, Church of Jesus.

Kyleta, *coillte,* woods.

Kyletaun, *coilltean,* the little wood.

Kylete, *coillte,* woods.

Kyleva, *coill-an-bháthaigh,* not given.

Kyleva, *coill-an-Bhádaigh,* de Bath's or Bath's (a family name) wood.

Kylevehagh, *coill-bheitheach,* not given.

Kyraun, *Ciarán,* Ciaran, a male name.

L

La, *lá,* not given.
La, *lagh, lagha,* a hill.
La, *lann,* a house or a Church.
La, *leth, leath,* half.
Laan, *léana,* a meadow.
Laba, *leabaidh, leaba,* a bed ora grave.
Laban, *labain, labán,* a plebeian, labourer or common vulgar fellow.
Laban, *lábáin,* not given.
Laban, *lábán,* a mire or dirt.
Labaun, *labán,* a plebeian, labourer or common vulgar fellow.
Labaun, *láibán,* mud, mire or a miry place.
Labba, *leabaidh, leaba,* a bed or grave.
Labbana, *leaba-na…,* bed or grave of the…
Labbin, *leaba-an…,* bed or grave of the…
Labby, *leabaidh, leaba,* a bed or grave.
Labodia, *leaba-doibhthe,* bed of the cauldron.
Laboge, *léabóg,* a little stripe.
Lac, *lough,* a lake.
Lacagha, *leaca,* flagstones.
Lacca, *leachach, leacach,* stony or flaggy.
Lach, *lach,* as an ending to a word can sometimes mean, a place of…. or abounding in…
Lacht, *leacht,* a monument or grave.
Lachta, *leachta,* monuments.
Lachtain, *lachtain, flagstones or a slatey place.*
Lack, *leacan,* a hillside.
Lack, *lic, leac, liag,* a great stone, a flagstone, a large flat stone or flagstones.
Lack, *lice, leaca, leac,* a stone, a flagstone or a slatey place.
Lacka, *leaca,* a hillside, a hill brow or a slope.
Lacka, *leaca, leacain, leacan,* a hillside or a stepped hill.

Lacka, *leaca,* spotted.
Lacka, *leaca-an…,* hillside of the…
Lacka, *leacach,* flagged or a flat rocky surface.
Lacka, *leice,* the flagstone.
Lackafin, *leaca-Fionna,* not given.
Lackagh, *leaca, leacach,* a place of stones or flagstones.
Lackaghane, *leacachán, leachachan,* abounding in flagstones, a flagstone place.
Lackakera, *Leaca-Céire,* St Kiar's flat rocks.
Lackan, *leaca, leacain, leacán, leacan,* a hillside or a stepped hill.
Lackana, *leaca-na…,* hillsode of the…
Lackaneen, *leacainín,* a small hillside.
Lackaneen, *leac-Fhínín,* not given.
Lackanna, *leacach-na…,* hillside of the…
Lackaun, *leacan,* a hillside.
Lackeen, from *leac,* a little flat, flagstone.
Lackeen, *Leith-caoin,* beautiful half.
Lackelly, *leac-Eille,* not given.
Lacken, *leaca, leacain, leacan,* a hillside or a stepped hill.
Lacken, *leacan,* flat stones.
Lacken, *leacan,* hill sides.
Lacken, *leicean,* hill slope/s.
Lacken, *leac-an…,* flagstone of the…
Lackena, *leacan-a'…, leaca-na…, lacka-na*(sic)…, hillside of the …
Lackenacoombe, *leacan/leacain-Mochomóg,* not given.
Lackenaireig, *leacain-aimhreidh,* an uneven/rough hillside.
Lackenareague, *leacain-aimhreidh,* an uneven, rough hillside.
Lackenna, *leacan-na…,* hillside of the…
Lacknacoo, *leac-na-con,* flagstone of the hound.
Lacky, *leacaidhe, leacach,* flaggy.
Lacky, *leachach, leacaigh,* flagstones.
Laconnell, *leac-Chonaill,* not given.
Lacroagh, *leathchruach, leath-chruach,* half hill or rick.
Lactify, *leachta-Feighe,* not given.
Lactify, *leachta-feadha,* fallow land(sic).
Laddan, *leadan,* a place of burdocks.
Ladeen, *leithidín,* a small area.
Lady, *leadhaidhe,* a sluggard.
Lafalla, *leithbhaile, leith-bhaile,* half-town.
Lafally, *leath-bhaile,* half town.

Laffan, *locháin,* a little lake.
Laffan, *locháin,* a little pond.
Laffin, *Lafáin,* Laffan, Lenfaunt, a family name of south Kildare.
Laffin, *locháin*(sic), not given.
Laffina, *leathfuini,* grey hill.
Laffina, *leath-mhuine,* half shrubbery.
Laffina, *leathmhuine,* not given.
Lafone, *leath-mhóin, leathmhóin,* half bog.
Lag, *lag,* a hollow, hollows or a hill.
Lag, *laga,* not given.
Lag, *leath,* one sided, half.
Laga, *lag-a'…,* hollow of the…
Laga, *log-an…,* not given.
Lagagh, *lagach,* hollow/s.
Lagan, *lagáin, log-an…,* not given.
Lagan, *lagan, lagán, lacán,* small hollow or dell.
Lagan, *lag-an…,* hollow of the…
Lagg, *lagh,* a hollow.
Laggagh, hollows.
Laggan, *lagáin,* hollow.
Laggin, *logáin,* a hollow or dell.
Laggins, *logáin,* a hollow or dell.
Lagh, *lach,* as an ending to a word can sometimes mean, a place of…. or abounding in…
Lagh, *leith,* half.
Lagh, *loch,* a lake.
Laghan, *Lachan,* not given.
Laghan, *leathan,* broad.
Laghdrid, *loch-Druid,* not given.
Lagheen, *leathchaoin,* half-beautiful.
Lagher, *leathair,* leather.
Laghey, *laithí, laithigh,* mire or mud.
Laghey, *laithigh, lathach,* a little slough.
Laghie, *leamhchoil,* an elm wood.
Laghil, *leamhchoill,* elm wood.
Laghil, *leathchoill,* not given.
Laghile, *leamhchoill,* elm wood.
Laghile, *leathchoill,* not given.
Laghill, *leamh-cóill,* elm wood.
Laghloony, *leath-chlunaidhe,* half lawns.
Laghnan, *Ua-Lachnáin, O Loughnane,* a family name.
Laght, *laght, leacht, leachta,* a monument, grave or burial heap/s.
Laght, *leacht,* a cairn or monumental heap of stones.
Laght, *laicht,* not given.
Laghta, *lachta,* a shelf.

Laghta, *laght, leacht, leachta,* a monument or burial heap/s.
Laghta, *leachta,* flagstones.
Laghta, *leacht-an…,* leacht of the…
Laghta, *lochta,* shelving or lofted, usually to do with a hill.
Laghtada, *leacht-a'-da…,* hillside of the two…
Laghtan, *leacht-an…,* hillside of the…
Laghtane, *an-leacht,* not given.
Laghtane, *leachtán,* a small grave.
Laghtea, *leacht-Aodha,* Hugh's or Aodh's (a male name) hillside.
Laghteen, *Laichtín, Laichtín,* St Laghteen.
Laghy, *an-laithigh,* the mire.
Laghy, *lataige,* broad.
Laghy, *lathach,* a little slough.
Laghy, *lathaí,* not given.
Laghy, *leathan, lathaighe,* a quagmire.
Laghy, *leathan,* wide.
Laghy, *lohagh,* miry, muddy or marshy.
Lagile, *leath-gCoill,* the half wood.
Lagna, *lag-na…,* hollow of the…
Lagneeve, *leath-gniomh/gníomh,* half of a gneeve (5 acres).
Lagore, *loch-gabhair/gabhra,* lake of the horse.
Lagore, *loch-gabhra,* goat lake.
Lague, *Laeg,* not given.
Lah, *leath,* half.
Laha, *lathach,* a quagmire.
Laha, *lathach, lathagh,* soft soil, marshy or a quagmire.
Lahadane, from *leathad,* a wide piece of land.
Lahadane, *leath-eadan,* a small hill breast.
Lahag, *lathach,* a quagmire.
Lahagh, *lathach,* a little slough.
Lahagh, *lathach, lathaighe, lathagh,* soft soil, marshy, a little slough or a quagmire.
Lahan, *leathain, Laithín, Lacháin,* not given.
Lahan, *leathan,* broad, wide.
Lahanaght, *leaca-nocht,* bare hillside.
Lahane, *leathan,* broad.
Lahanna, *leathana,* wide or broad.
Lahara, *leathara,* leather.
Laharan, *leath-fhearann,* half land, plough-land or townland.
Lahard, *leathaird,* inequity.
Lahard, *leathard,* not given.

Lahard, *leath-árd/ard,* a half height, gentle slope or sloping.

Lahard, *leath-ard,* half high field(sic).

Lahardan, *leath-árd,* a half height.

Lahardan, *leathardán, leathárdán, leath-árdán,* a half height.

Lahardan, *leath-ardun,* a half height.

Lahardane, *leathárdan, leath-árdán,* a half height.

Lahardaun, *leath-ardáin,* side of a plateau(sic).

Laharn, *leath-fhearann,* a half (town) land, half ploughland, half farm or half domain.

Laharran, *leath-fhearann,* half land, ploughland, townland.

Lahasery, *leath-easaire,* half layer.

Lahassery, *leathsheisrí,* not given.

Lahassery, *Leith-sheishreach,* half ploughland.

Lahee, *lathach,* a little slough.

Laheen, from *lathach,* a little slough.

Laheen, *leaithín,* small half.

Laheen, *leathchaoin,* half-beautiful.

Laheen, *leat*(sic)*-chaoin,* beautiful half.

Laheen, *loichín,* a pond.

Laheen, *leath-chaoin,* one side (of hill)(sic).

Laher, *láthair,* not given.

Laher, *lathair,* the place, a house site, building or the location of a battlefield.

Laher, *lathair-a'...,* the site of ...

Laher, *leathair, leathar,* leather.

Lahern, *leath-fhearann,* half ploughland.

Laherna, *lathair-na...,* site of the...

Laherne, *leath-fhearann,* not given.

Lahesery, *leith-sheishreach, leathsheisrí,* half ploughland.

Laheshera, *leith-sheishreach,* half ploughland.

Laheshery, *leith-sheishreach,* half ploughland.

Lahesseragh, *leith-sheishreach/sheisreach, leath-sheisreach, leithsheisreach,* half ploughland.

Lahessery, *leathsheisrí,* not given.

Lahid, *leathad,* breadth or a broad piece of land.

Lahid, *leithead,* not given.

Lahiff, *Amhlaoibh,* Amhlaoibh, a personal or family name.

Lahiff, *Laithimh,* Lahiff, a family name.

Lahiff, *Uí-Fhlaithimh,* Ó Flaithimh, a family name.

Lahiff, *Uí-Laithimh,* O'Lahy or O'Lahiff, a family name.

Lahinch, *an-leacht,* the grave.

Lahinch, *leacht-Uí-Chonchur/Chonchubhair,* not given.

Lahinch, *leath-inis,* half island.

Lahinch, *leath-inis, leithinsi,* half island or half peninsula.

Lahinch, *leath-inse,* peninsula(sic).

Lahode, *leath-fhóid,* the half sod.

Lahrath, *laithreach,* the old habitation.

Lahy, *Lacha, lathaighe,* not given.

Lahy, *lahagh, lathaighe,* a mire, slough or marsh.

Lahy, *lochan,* ducks.

Lahy, *Uí-Laithimh,* O'Lahey, a family name.

Laid, *leithead,* breadth.

Lair, *lár, lair, lair,* middle, centre.

Laira, *láthair,* a site.

Lakany, *leicne,* a hill brow.

Lakeen, *leacain,* a sloping hillside.

Lakill, *leath-gCoill,* the half wood.

Lakyle, *leamhchoill, leamh-choill,* elm wood.

Lakyle, *leathchoill,* half wood.

Lamagh, *leamach,* a place of elms, an elmy place.

Laman, *Lomáin,* Loman, a personal or family name.

Laman, *Lomán,* not given.

Lambay, *lamb-ey*(Norse), lamb island.

Lambay, *reachta,* not given.

Lambeg, *cluain-Colmóg,* not given.

Lambeg, *lann-bheag,* little Church.

Lame, *Latharna,* land of Lathair an ancient prince.

Lame, *léim,* jump.

Lamery, *Lamrach, Lamraí, Lamhraí, Lamhrach,* a personal name and the name of a founder of a Church in Kilkenny.

Lamfield, *leamhchoille, leamhchoill,* elm wood.

Lammy, *lamaigh,* not given.

Lammy, *leamhaigh, leamhach, leamhaidh,* a place of elms.

Lammy, *léime,* a jump.

Lamoge, a place of elms.
Lamoge, lamóg, a small bare place.
Lamogue, lamóg, not given.
Lamont, na-molt, the wethers.
Lamph, leamh, leamhain, leamhan, elm/s.
Lamphry, leamhraí, leamhraidhe, elms.
Lan, lann, a house or a Church.
Lan, lon, blackbird/s.
Lana, lann, a house or a Church.
Lana, lann-na…, Church of the…
Lanan, Fhlannáin, not given.
Land, Eileain, Helena.
Land, lann, a house or a Church.
Land, tulcáin, a little hill.
Landagivey, the Church of Agivey.
Landers, Londraigh, Landers or de Londra, a family name.
Landers, Lóndraigh, Londraigh, Landers, a family name.
Landrick, Bhlonaige, not given.
Lane, Laighean, láin, not given.
Lane, lán, full.
Lane, Léan, Eileaín, Ellen, a personal or family name.
Lane, lean, sorrows.
Lane, leathan, broad, wide.
Lane, Uí-Laighin, O'Lane, a family name.
Laneen, Uí-Laithnín, Ó Laithnín, O'Lannen, a family name.
Laneen, Uí-Laithnín/Fhlaithnen, O'Lahneen, a family name.
Laney, láine, not given.
Laney, léana, a meadow.
Langadon, Ui-Langadain, O'Langadon, a personal or family name.
Langan, Langáin, longáin, not given.
Langan, Langan or Longan a personal or family name.
Langan, linn-an…, pool of the…
Langley, Langley, a family name.
Langouch, langach, slender townland.
Langy, luinge, the encampment.
Langy, Uí-Longaidh, Long, a family name.
Lanigan, Lonnagain, not given.
Lanigan, Uí-Fhlannagáin/Fhlannagain, Ó Flannagáin or O'Flanagan, a family name.
Lankill, leamhchoill, an elm wood.
Lanly, Fhangaile, Flanelly, a personal or family name.

Lanly, Fhlannaíle, not given.
Lann, lann, a house or a Church.
Lanna, leana, a meadow.
Lanna, leanna, ale.
Lannaght, leamhnacht, the plant 'septfoil'.
Lannan, Fhlannáin, Flannan, a personal or family name.
Lannan, Leannáin, not given.
Lannat, leathnocht, not given.
Lannaun, Fhlannán, not given.
Lannav, leanbh, children.
Lanniv, leanbh, children.
Lannow, leanbh, children.
Lanny, lann, a house or a Church.
Laoghaire, Laoire, Laoghaire, Laegháire, Laoire or Laeghaire, the name of 5th century King.
Laoighis, Laoighis, not given.
Laoise, Laeighis, Laoise, ancient tribal name of the Moores.
Laoise, Laois, Laoise, named after the chieften called 'Lughaidh–Laeighseach'.
Laoughra(sic), rushes.
Lap, lapa, not given.
Lap, leapa, leaphta, a bed or grave.
Lappa, lapach, swamps.
Lappa, leaptha, leabtha, a bed or grave.
Lappa, leapacha, beds.
Lappan, an-lapán, not given.
Lar, láir, a thrashing floor.
Lar, lair, central.
Lar, láir, not given.
Lar, lár, lar, floor, a flat or ground.
Lara, laegh, lárach, a mare or mares.
Lara, lárach, lára, lair, láir, a mare.
Lara, láradh, a threshing place.
Lara, láthrach, láithreach, the site of something.
Lara, leathrátha, leath-rath, the half fort.
Larach, láithreach, not given.
Laracha, lárach, a mare.
Laragh, ladharach, not given.
Laragh, láithreach, laithreach, a site of an old ruin or where a battle was fought.
Laragh, lárach, mares.
Laragh, lárach, old ruins.
Laragh, lathrach, a site of a habitation or ruin.
Laragh, lathtach, láithreach, láthrach, latrach, the site of…

Laragh, *leath-ráth,* half ring-fort.

Laragha, *laracha,* places.

Larah, *leathrach,* not given.

Lard, *leath-árd/aird,* a half height or gentle slope.

Lare, *lair, láir, lár,* middle.

Lareen, *láthairín,* little site.

Larg, *learg,* a hillside or hill slopes.

Larga, *learg-a'...,* hillside of the...

Largan, from *learg,* a little hillside.

Largan, *leargaidh,* a hillside.

Largan, *leargan, leargáin, leargain,* a hill slope.

Largana, *leargain/leargan-na...,* hillside of the...

Largna, *lorg-na...,* not given.

Largy, *learg, leargaidhe, leargaidh, leirge,* a hillside or hill-slope.

Largy, *leargaidh, leargan,* a hill slope.

Largy, *leargain, leargaí,* not given.

Larha, *laithreach,* the house site of...

Larha, *leathrath, leathráth, leath-*ráth, a half fort.

Larheen, *laithrín,* little site.

Larheen, *latharín,* a little meeting place.

Larhig, *lathraigh,* the ruin.

Larhig, *lathtach, latrach,* the site of...

Larin, *lairthean,* the site.

Lark, *learg,* not given.

Lark, *leirge,* a hill-slope.

Lark, *lárc,* forking vallies.

Larkan, *Lorcán,* not given.

Larkin, *Uí-Lorcáin,* Larkin, a family name.

Larne, from *Latharna, Laharna,* Lahar, Lathaír, a male name.

Larne, *Latharna, Latharne,* people of Latharna, Lathair, son of Hugony the great.

Larney, *larnach,* middle.

Larra, *lára,* a mare.

Larraga, *learga,* a hillside.

Larragan, *leargan,* a hillside.

Larry, *laithreach,* the house site of...

Larry, *lathraighe,* the house site.

Lary, *larach, láire,* the mare.

Lary, *Láithrigh,* not given.

Las, *leasa, lios,* a earthen fort.

Lascaw, *leathscátha,* not given.

Lask, *leasc, leascaigh,* lazy or sluggish.

Laskagh, *lascach,* lights.

Lass, *leasa, lios,* an earthen fort.

Lassa, *lassa, leasa, lios,* an earthen fort.

Lassa, *leasa,* an enclosure.

Lassabrien, *leasa-Uí-Bhriain,* not given.

Lassan, *leasáin,* little fort.

Lassan, *leasan, leasán,* little forts.

Lassana, *leasana, leasanna,* forts.

Lassanagh, *leasanach,* full of forts.

Lassany, *leasanaidhe,* forts.

Lasser, *Laisre, Lasrach,* Lasrach, a personal or family name and a founder of a Church in Mayo.

Lasseragh, *Lasrach,* not given.

Lassy, *leasa, lios,* a earthen fort.

Lastra, *lasrach,* conflagration.

Lat, *leath,* half.

Lat, *lecht, leacht, leachta,* a sepulchral monument, grave.

Lata, *leacht- na/a'...,* monument or grave of the...

Latacapple, *leacht-a'-chapaill,* monument of the horse.

Lateeve, *leataoibh, leathtaoibh,* not given.

Lateeve, *leath-taebh,* half side.

Lateragh, *leatarach,* a hillside.

Lates, *na-léataí,* not given.

Lates, *léataí,* a low lying place intersected with drains.

Latha, *leacht-a'...,* monument of the...

Latieve, *leathaoibh,* the half-side.

Latin, *leachta-an...,* monument of the...

Latna, *leacht-na...,* monument of the...

Latoon, *leath-tua-Mumhan,* half of Thomond.

Latsy, *leacht-suidhe-Bolgadáin,* the monument of Bolgadan's (a male name) seat.

Latt, *leacht,* a monument.

Latta, *laghta,* a monument.

Latta, *laght-a'...,* the monument of the ...

Latta, *leachta,* the mound.

Lattallan, *leacht-Taláin,* not given.

Lattan, *leachtán,* not given.

Latten, *leachtáin,* not given.

Latteragh, *latracha-Ódhráin,* not given.

Latteragh, *leathracha, leatracha,* hillsides or hill slopes.

Latteragh, *leatrach,* not given.

Latteragh, *leatracha,* a wet hillside.

Latteragh, *letrecha-Odhrain,* St Odhran's wet hillside.

Lattery, from *letter*, wet hillsides.

Latti, *leachta*, a monument.

Lattin, *laitean*, not given.

Lattin, *leathtón*, bottom of the valley.

Lattin, *slaitín*, a bridge made of sticks.

Latton, *leath-tón*, half hill or half bottom.

Latton, *leatón, laitean*, not given.

Lattone, *leathtón, leath-tón*, half hill or half bottom.

Lattoon, *leathtón*, bottom of the valley.

Lattoon, *leath-tón*, half hill or half bottom.

Latully, *leath-tulaigh*, half hill.

Lauder, *Láidir*, Lauder, a male name and means 'strong man'.

Laugh, *lathaigh*, slough or mire.

Laugh, *lohagh*, miry or marshy.

Laughag, *luchógh*, rats.

Laugher, *chlochair*, stony.

Laughil, *leamhcoill, leamhchoill*, an elm wood.

Laughil, *leathchoill*, not given.

Laughill, *leamhchoille, leamhchoill*, elm wood.

Laughlin, St Lachtin.

Laught, *lecht, leacht, leacth(sic), leachta*, a sepulchral monument, grave.

Laughta, *lochta*, not given.

Laughta, *leacht, leachta*, a mound or grave-pile.

Laghta, *leachta*, flagstones.

Laughta, *lachtadh*, lactation or milk bearing.

Laughtin, *Lachtin, Laichtene*, St Lachtin, a 7th cent Saint.

Laughtin, *Lachtín*, not given.

Lauhir, *lathair*, a site or a battlefield.

Laun, *láin, lán*, not given.

Laun, *laun, lean, léana*, a wet meadow.

Laun, *oilean*, island.

Laun, *leathan*, broad.

Launa, *lána*, full.

Launa, *leathana*, broad.

Launan, *Fhlannán*, not given.

Laune, *leamhain*, elm.

Laune, *leamháin, leamhan*, elm/s.

Laur, *lair, lair*, floor or level surface.

Laur, *lair, lár*, middle.

Laur, *láir*, not given.

Laur, *lárs*(sic), floors or level surfaces.

Laura, *lair, lára*, a mare.

Lauragh, *lathrach, láithrigh, láithreach*, the site or location of something.

Laurane, *Labhrais*, Laurance, a personal or family name.

Lauree, *láthraighe*, not given.

Laurencetown, *cnoc-na-nGabhar, síol-Anmchadha*, not given.

Lauvlyer, *lámh-ladhar*, the hand of the fork

Lav, *leamh*, elms.

Lava, *leamhaigh*, not given.

Lavagh, *leamhach*, a place of elms.

Lavagh, *leamhaigh*, not given.

Lavaghery, *leamh-mhachaire*, the elm plain.

Lavalla, *leath-baile*, half townland.

Lavally, *leathbhaile, leath-baile/bhaile*, half town or townland.

Lavan, *leamhain*, elm.

Lavan, *leamnán*, not given.

Lavaran, *leamhrán*, little elm wood.

Lavareen, *leamhairin*, the small elm tree grove.

Lavareen, *leath-bairighean*, a little plot of ground.

Lavareen, *leath-bhairghín*, land in the shape of a half circle.

Lavaun, *leamhain*, elm.

Lavaur, *leath-bharr*, half top.

Lave, *leamh*, elm.

Lave, *shléibhe*, a mountain.

Laverty, *Uí-Laifeartaigh*, O'Laverty, a family name.

Lavey, *leamhaigh, leamhach, leamhaidh*, elms.

Lavin, *leamhain*, a place of elms.

Lavin, *Liamhna*, Liamania, a personal or family name.

Lavin, *Luadhain*, not given.

Lavin, *Luáin*, Luán, a personal or family name.

Lavis, *leamh*, elms.

Lavy, *leamhaigh*, a place of elms or an elm wood.

Law, *lá*, not given.

Law, *lagh, lách, lagha*, a hill.

Lawareen, *leath-bhairghín*, land in the shape of a half circle.

Lawaun, *leamháin*, elm.

Lawaus, *leath-mhás*, half hill.

Lawcas, *leamhchas*, a place of marsh mallows.

Lawcus, *Lácas*, not given.

Lawderdale, *droim-raithin,* not given.
Laweesh, *láimhis,* not given.
Lawn, *leathan,* broad.
Lawn, *oileán,* an island.
Lawney, *leamhnaigh,* a place of elms.
Lawny, *leamhnaighe,* elms.
Laxweir, *lax weir,* Danish for salmon weir.
Lay, *léith,* not given.
Lay, *liath,* grey.
Layd, *laethid,* broad.
Layd, *leithid, leithead,* broad or breadth.
Laydan, *leadáin,* burdocks.
Layde, *leithead,* breadth or broad.
Layden, *leadáin,* burdocks.
Laytown, *an-inse,* not given.
Le, *leac,* a flagstone.
Le, *leth, leath,* half.
Le, *liath,* grey land.
Lea, (on its own) *Caisleán-Léighe / Tuath-Léighe,* not given.
Lea, from *liath,* grey spots.
Lea, *laegh, lao, laogh,* calves.
Lea, *Lé, léith, liatha,* not given.
Lea, *lia, léithe, liath,* grey or a grey place.
Lea, *liath, liatha,* grey spot of land.
Lea, *shliabh, sliabh,* mountain.
Leaan, *léana,* meadow land.
Leaan, *Uí-Leáin,* O'Leane, a family name.
Leab, *leadhb,* a stripe of land.
Leaba, *leadhba,* not given.
Leaba, *leadhbatha,* stripes or patches.
Leabrannagh, *leadhb-Reannach,* not given.
Leachta, *leachta,* monuments.
Lead, *léad, lead,* not given.
Lead, *leithead, leithid,* breadth, broad, wide or a wide piece of land.
Lead, *liath,* grey.
Lead, *loid,* a pond or pool.
Leadinton, *baile-an-Leidean,* not given.
Leadmore, *ceathramhadh-leid-mór-Mhic-Mhathghamhna,* Mac Mahons wide division.
Leaffony, (river) *an-Gleóir,* not given.
Leaffony, *liathmhuine,* grey shrubbery or thicket.
Leafin, *lia-Finn,* not given.
Leafin, *liathmhuine,* grey shrubbery or thicket.
Leafonny, *liathmhuine,* grey shrubbery or thicket.

Leafony, *liathmhuine,* grey shrubbery or thicket.
Leag, *Fhleadha,* not given.
Leag, *leag,* a flagstone.
Leag, *liag,* flagstones.
Leagan, *liagáin,* a standing stone or pillar stone.
Leagane, *liagán,* a standing stone or pillar stone.
Leagard, *liag-árd,* the high pillar stone.
Leagaun, *liagan, liagán,* a standing stone or pillar stone.
Leagh, from *liath,* grey spots.
Leagh, *laoch,* heroes.
Leagh, *leamhaigh, na-liathacha, léith,* not given.
Leagh, *leath,* half.
Leagh, *liagha,* physician.
Leagh, *lia, liath,* grey.
Leagh, *liathach,* the grey people.
Leaghan, from *liath,* grey spots.
Leaghany, *log-thamhnaigh,* hollow grassy uplands.
Leaghort, *leith-phort,* the little landing place.
Leaghort, *liath-ghort,* grey tillage field.
Leaghs, from *liatha,* grey spots of land.
Leaght, *lecht, leacht, leachta,* a sepulchral monument or grave.
Leaghtafin, white *leacht* or burial heap.
Leaghys, from *liatha,* grey spots of land.
League, *léige, liege,* a pillar stone or a standing stone.
League, *líag, liag,* a flagstone, flagstones or standing stones.
League, *liag,* piller stone/s, flagstones, stones or a stony place.
League, *liag,* the stone, stones or boulders.
League, *liaigh,* not given.
League, *liege,* a rock.
Leagy, *liaga,* flagstones.
Leaha, *latha,* a dog.
Leaha, *léithe,* the grey cow or the grey mare.
Leaha, *liath,* not given.
Leaha, *liatha,* grey spot of land.
Leaha, deer(sic).
Leahan, *leathan,* broad space.
Leaheen, from *liath,* little grey spots.
Leaheen, *leathín,* little half.

Leaheth, *leithead, leatad,* breadth.
Leahill, *leamh-choill,* elm wood.
Leahill, *Leith-choill,* grey wood.
Leahys, *na-liatha,* the grey spots of land.
Leak, *leac, líag,* flagstones.
Leak, *líag,* flagstones.
Leakin, *leacainn,* not given.
Leam, *léim,* jump.
Leam, *leim, léime,* the (remarkable) jump.
Leama, *léim-a'…,* the leap or pass of the…
Leama, *léime, leime, leama,* a jump or leap.
Leamacrossan, *léim-Mhic-Crosain,* MacCrossan's (a family name) leap.
Leamanch, *léim-an-eich,* leap of the horse.
Leamaneh, *léim-an-eich,* leap of the horse.
Leamanish, *léim-an-ois,* not given.
Leame, *léime,* a leap or pass.
Leamirlea, *léim-fhir-léith, leim-fhir-leith,* leap of the grey man.
Leimirlea, *léim-Irlé,* not given.
Leamna, *leim-na…,* leap or pass of the…
Leamy, *Uí-Léimigh,* O'Lamy, a family name.
Leamy, *Uí-Léimigh, Uí-Laimigh,* O'Leamy, a family name.
Lean, *leána,* a meadow.
Lean, *leathan,* broad, wide.
Leana, *léana, leana,* a wet or marshy meadow.
Leananeh, *léim-an-eich,* leap of the horse.
Leane, *léin,* not given.
Leane, *léine,* a shirt.
Leannaght, *leathan-ucht,* a wide hill breast.
Leannan, *(river) an-leannan,* not given.
Leansaghan, from *leana,* wet land.
Leany, *léana,* a meadow or a marshy meadow.
Leap, *léim,* a leap.
Leap, *léim-Uí-Donnabhan,* not given.
Lear, *ladhar,* a fork of glens or river/s.
Learden, *ladhardáin,* little fork.
Leary, *Laegháire, Laeghaire,* a male name.
Leary, *Laoghaire,* not given.
Leary, *Uí-Laoghaire,* O'Leary, a family name.
Leas, *lios,* a fort.
Lease, *léis, lias,* huts.
Lease, *léisigh, léiseach,* not given.
Leash, *lios,* a fort.

Leasty, *Léiste,* Leiste a male name.
Leasty, *Léistigh,* not given.
Leat, *leacht, laght,* a monument, a monumental heap of stones or a grave pile.
Leath, *leath,* half.
Leatilla, *Liatuile,* not given.
Leava, *léabha,* marsh mallows.
Leavalliagh, *Liafala,* not given.
Leavan, *Laobhain,* Laobhán, a personal or family name and a founder of a Church in Monaghan.
Lebagh, *leadhbac, leadhbach,* ragged, straggling, untidy or patchy.
Lebally, half townland.
Lebane, *leadhbain,* a stripe of land.
Lebane, *Liobáin,* Liban, a personal or family name.
Lebe, *leadhb,* rags.
Lec, *lag,* a hollow.
Lecade, *leth-chéad,* a half hundred.
Lecale, *leath-Cathail/Chathail, Leith-Cathail,* Cathal's (a male name) half.
Lecale, *leath-Cahail,* Cahail's portion.
Lecamy, *leac-mhuighe,* not given.
Lecanvy, *leic-Ainbhe,* not given.
Lecarrow, *leithcheathramha, leithcheathrú, leith/leath-ceatamhradh, leath-cheathru/ceathramhadh,* the half quarter.
Lecarrown, *leath-ceatamhradh-na…,* half quarter of the…
Leck, *leice,* flagstone/s.
Leck, (Annaleck), *Liac,* a personal or family name.
Leck, *lic, leac, leic, leice, liag,* a great stone, a flagstone or a large flat stone.
Lecka, *leice,* the flagstone or a flaggy place.
Leckagh, *lecach, leachach,* flagstones or flagstony.
Leckan, *leacan,* a hillside or a hill slope.
Leckanvy, *leac-Ainbhe,* Ainbhe's (a personal or family name) stone.
Leckanvy, *leacán-mhaigh,* hillside of the plain.
Leckaun, *an-leacán,* the hillside.
Leckaun, *leacan, leacán,* a hillside.
Leckna, *leic-na…,* not given.
Leckna, *leicne,* flagstones.
Leckna, *leicne,* sloping land.
Leckna, *leicneach,* flaggy.
Lecknagh, *leacnach,* a hillside.

Leckney, *leicne,* a place of flagstones.
Leckny, *leicne,* a place of flagstones.
Lecky, *leice,* not given.
Lecky, *leacach,* flaggy.
Leconnell, *leac-Chonaill,* not given.
Lectrum, *liath-druim* grey ridge.
Ledder, *leathair,* leather.
Lederg, *leth-derg,* the red half.
Lee, (river) *an-Lí,* not given.
Lee, (river) *laoi,* water, an older name for this river is *an-tSabhrain,* not given.
Lee, *laeich,* the hero.
Lee, *leagh, laoigh, lao, laoi, laogh,* a calf or calves.
Lee, *Lí,* Li or Lí, a personal name.
Lee, *lia,* a physician
Lee, *lia,* a pillerstone or physician.
Lee, *liagh,* a healer.
Lee, *liath,* not given.
Lee, *lighe,* the grave.
Lee, *Lughaidh,* Lughaidh, Laidhe, the name of an ancient tribe.
Leea, an ancient territory and the descendants/tribe of Leea.
Leean, *luighean,* centre (townland).
Leeaun, *liaghain,* the trowel.
Leedigan, *Laghadagáin,* not given.
Leeds, *lias,* the lambs hut.
Leedy, St. Mid or Ité.
Leeg, *an-líg,* not given.
Leeg, *liag,* flagstones.
Leeg, *liag, leac,* a stone, flagstone.
Leega, *léige,* stone.
Leega, *líge,* flagstones.
Leega, *líoga,* not given.
Leegane, *liagán,* a standing stone.
Leegawn, *liagán,* a pillar stone.
Leegawn, *liagan, liagáin,* a standing stone.
Leek, *leac, liag,* a flagstone.
Leek, *leice,* a rocky ford.
Leek, *liag,* made from stone.
Leek, *liagaigh,* not given.
Leeke, *liag, leac,* a flagstone.
Leeke, *liag, liag,* made from stone.
Leeks, *leice,* the flagstone.
Leel, *Laoighill,* Lyle, a personal or family name.
Leel, *laoi-fheoil,* not given.
Leel, *Laoill,* not given.
Leen, *Fhlainn, lighean,* not given.

Leen, *laoigheann,* calves.
Leen, *lín, lin,* flax.
Leen, *lion, lión,* linen or nets.
Leena, soft ground.
Leena, *line,* flax.
Leena, *luinge,* the encampment.
Leenagh, *Líonach,* not given.
Leenaghan, *líonachain,* flax.
Leenaghan, *líonáin, líneacháin,* not given.
Leenan, *línnan, línn,* water.
Leenane, *líonán, líonan, lionán-chindmara,* the tide filling spot at the head of the sea.
Leenane, *lionan,* where seaweed grows or a shallow sea bottom.
Leenane, *líonán, líonáin,* not given.
Leenaun, *leannáin,* not given.
Leenaun, *lionan, líonán,* shallow sea-bed.
Leenty, *lianta,* meadows.
Leenty, *Líontaigh,* not given.
Leeny, *Laighnigh,* Ó Leighin,(sic) not given.
Leer, *ladhar,* a river fork.
Leer, *léir,* clear.
Leer, *Léire,* Léire, a personal or family name.
Leer, *léri,* austerity.
Leere, *ladhair,* river-fork or a protruding piece of land.
Leeriska, *léir-uisce, fhíoruisce,* not given.
Leese, *lias,* huts.
Leesha, *Eilíse,* Eleesha or Eliza, a female name.
Leesha, *Laoisigh,* not given.
Leet, a corruption of *leice,* a flagstone or flaggy place.
Leevan, *Laobháin,* Laobhán, not given.
Leevan, *leamhain, leamháin, leamhan, liomhain,* elm/s.
Lefanta, *liathbhánta, liath-bhánta,* grey fields.
Leffin, *locháin,* a little lake.
Lefinn, *leithmhín,* not given.
Lefinn, *liathmhuine,* grey thicket.
Leg, *lag,* hollow/s.
Leg, *lec,* flaggy.
Leg, *liag,* a flat stone or flagstone.
Leg, *lig, lug,* a hollow.
Leg, *Loig,* not given.
Lega, *lag-an/a'…,* hollow of the….

Lega, *lag-an…,* hollow of the….

Legagh, *leagach,* stones or flagstones.

Legagh, *liagach,* the boulder.

Legan, *lag/lug-an…,* hollow of the…

Legan, *liagán, liagáin,* a pillar stone.

Legan, *liagáin,* a standing or pillar stone.

Legan, *liagan, lacán,* small hollow.

Legan, *liagan, liagáin,* a standing stone.

Legan, *liagan, liagán,* a standing stone or standing stones.

Legane, *liagán,* a standing stone.

Legar, *liagar,* not given.

Legat, *Eileagóid,* not given.

Legaun, *lacán,* small hollow.

Legaun, *liagán,* a standing stone.

Legaun, *liagan, liagáin,* a standing stone or pillar stone/s.

Legg, *lag,* a hollow.

Legga, *lag-an/a'…,* hollow of the….

Legga, *leacach,* abounding in flagstones.

Leggagh, *lagach,* a place of holes.

Leggan, *lagan,* a hollow.

Leggan, *liagan,* a little hollow.

Leggan, *logáin,* not given.

Legge, *lag,* a hollow.

Legge, *lag-a'…,* hollow of the….

Leggets, *…an-Leigéadaigh,* not given.

Legghimore, *lag-thighe-mhóir,* hollow of the great house.

Legghimore, *na-leachta-Móra,* not given.

Leggs, *na-laig,* hollows.

Legilly, *lug-gile,* bright hollow.

Legland, *leithghleann,* side of the valley or the half glen.

Leglands, *leithghleann,* not given.

Legna, *lag-na…,* hollow of the…

Legoniel, *lag-an-aoil,* hollow of the line(sic).

Legoniel, *lag-an-aoil/aoilh,* hollow of the lime.

Legoniel, O'Neill's (a family name) hollow.

Legvoy, *leag-mhagh,* flag surfaced plain.

Leha, *Leith-an…, leath-a'…,* half of the…

Lehan, *leathan,* broad.

Lehanagh, *leitheanach,* nor given.

Lehanagh, *líathánach, léithíneach, liathanach,* grey or grey land.

Lehane, Lehane, *Liatháin,* not given.

Lehane, *Uí-Liatháin,* O'Lehane, Lehane or Lyons, a family name.

Lehanes, *lohain,* little lakes ponds or pools.

Lehardan, *leath-ardán,* half little height.

Lehaun, *Uí-Liatháin,* O'Lehane, Lehane or Lyons, a family name.

Lehaunstown, *baile-lochán,* not given.

Leheen, *leithín,* little or near at hand.

Leheen, *léithín,* the small grey man.

Leheen, *lithín,* not given.

Lehenagh, *leitheanach,* the extension.

Lehenagh, *leitheanach,* the wide plain.

Lehenagh, *leithinach,* grey land.

Lehenagh, *leathanach, leithineach,* not given.

Lehenagh, *líathánach, léithíneach,* grey land.

Lehenagh, *liath-eannach(sic),* grey marsh.

Lehery, *leath-a'righ,* the Kings half.

Lehesery, *leath-sheisrighe,* not given.

Lehid, *leathfad,* a declivity.

Lehid, *leithead,* a wide piece of land.

Lehid, *leithid,* wide.

Lehillan, *leith-uilleann,* half angle or elbow.

Lehinch, *an-leacht,* not given.

Lehinch, *leath-inse,* peninsula(sic).

Lehinch, *leithinse,* not given.

Lehinch, *leithinsi,* half island or peninsula.

Lei, *leath,* half.

Lei, *liath,* grey.

Leidy, *Uí-Lideadha,* O'Leidy or Liddy, a family name.

Leig, *leig, leige,* a ridge.

Leigh, *laegh,* calves.

Leigh, *lao,* a calf.

Leigh, *liatha, laogh,* not given.

Leigh, *leith,* half.

Leigh, *liag,* flagstones.

Leigh, *liath,* grey, grey land or grey spots.

Leigh, *liath, litahach,* grey.

Leigh, *liath-mochoemhóg,* (ancient name), grey land.

Leigh, *Uí-Luighdheach,* Hy Leea, an ancient territory.

Leighan, from *liath,* little grey spots.

Leighin, from *liath,* grey spots.

Leighlin, *leightlannia,* white plain.

Leighlin, *leithghleann, leath-gleann, leith-ghlinn, leath-ghlionn,* half glen.

Leighlin, *leithghleann,* side of the valley.

Leighon, from *liath,* little grey spots.

Leighon, *laidhean,* not given.

Leigue, *liag,* flagstones.

Lein, (lake) *loch-Léibhinn,* not given.

Leinster, *Cúighe-Laighean,* land of broad spears.

Leinster, *Labhradh-linshagh, Labraid-long-seach,* (territory of) Lavra the mariner. The ancient name of **Leinster** was *cuige-laighean,* the province of spears.

Leinster, *Laighean,* not given.

Leinster, *Laighin,* the place of the Lagin people.

Leinster, the place of broad spears.

Leiny, *Laighnigh,* the leinsterman.

Leise, *leighis,* the cure.

Leiter, *leiter,* not given.

Leiterra, from *liath,* grey or grey land.

Leitir, from *liath,* grey or grey land.

Leitir, *leitir,* a wet hillside.

Leitra, from *liath,* grey or grey land.

Leitra, *leitrach,* a marshy place.

Leitra, *liataire,* not given.

Leitrim, (County Clare) *leith-tirim,* half-dry land.

Leitrim, *liath-druim/droim, liatroim, liath-droim, liathdroma,* grey hill or grey hill ridge.

Leitrim, *liatruim,* not given.

Leitry, grey or grey land.

Leitry, *leitrí,* wet hillsides.

Leitry, *liathdoire,* not given.

Leix, *Laeighais, Laoise, Laeighis,* an ancient tribe and territory.

Leixlip, *laxhlaup,* an ancient Danish name for the salmon leap. The Irish name is *léim-an-bhradáin,* leap of the salmon.

Lekaun, *an-leacán,* not given.

Lelagh, *laioleach,* not given.

Lelagh, *laoileac,* a Danish fort.

Lem, *léim,* leap, jump.

Lemanaghan, *liath-Manchain/Mancháin/ Manacháin/Manachain,* St Manchans grey place, land.

Lemane, *loman,* bare rocks.

Lemlara, *léim-lára,* not given.

Lemna, *léim-na…,* leap of the…

Lemnagh, *léim-an-eich,* leap of the horse.

Lemnaroy, *léim-na-eich-ruadh, leim-an-eich-ruaidh,* leap of the red horse.

Lemoge, young William.

Lemokevogue, *lia-Mochaomhóg,* not given.

Lemonfield, *léim-an-fhia,* leap of the deer.

Lemy, *léim,* leap, jump.

Lemy, *léime,* not given.

Len, *leathan,* broad, wide.

Lena, *léana,* a meadow.

Lena, *léana,* swampy land, meadow.

Lena, *léana,* wet meadows.

Lena, *lena, leana, léana,* a marshy or wet meadow.

Lenaderg, *lathreach-dair-Thighe,* site of the oratory.

Lenadoon, *léana-an-dúna,* not given.

Lenagh, *leana,* a marshy meadow or wet meadowy land.

Lenagh, *leanach,* not given.

Lenagh, *leathnach, leathan, leathanach,* broad.

Lenaghan, from *leana,* wet meadowy land.

Lenaghan, *Uí-Luineacháin,* O'lenaghan, a family name.

Lenahaun, *léanachain,* a holm.

Lenahauns, *léanaidhe,* wet meadows.

Lenana, *léana-na…,* not given.

Lenane, *Uí-Leanáin,* O'Lannane, a personal or family name.

Lene, *Léibhinn, Léibhinn,* a personal or family name.

Lenish, *leith-inis,* grey river holm.

Lennaght, *leathnocht,* not given.

Lennaght, *lemnacht,* new milk.

Lennan, *líonán,* not given.

Lennan, *Uí-Leanáin,* O'Lennan, a family name.

Lennane, *Uí-Leanáin,* O'Lennan, a family name.

Lennon, *Uí-Leanáin,* O'Lennan, a family name.

Lenny, *linne,* not given.

Lenty, *léantaidhe,* wet meadows.

Leny, *léana,* a meadow.

Leny, *léine,* a shirt.

Leny, *lena, leana, léana,* marshy or wet meadow/s.

Leny, *Luíne,* not given.

Leo, *leamh,* elm tree.

Leo, *leamhach,* land producing marsh mallows.

Leode, *léath-fhóid,* the half sod.

Leoh, *leamhach,* land producing marsh mallows.

Leonagh, *leamhnach,* an elmy place.

Leons, *leamhain,* not given.

Leopardstown, *baile-na/an-lobhar,* town of the lepers.

Lerane, *Ailearain,* St Aileran.

Leraw, *leath-rath,* half fort.

Lerga, *learg-a'...,* hillside of the...

Lerga, *leirg-an...,* not given.

Lergan, *leargán,* a small hillside.

Lergan, O'Ciaragan, a family name.

Lergina, *leirgín-an...,* not given.

Lergyna, *leargaidh-na...,* hillside of the...

Lergyna, *learga-na...,* not given.

Lerha, *leath-rátha,* half rath, fort.

Lerhin, from *lathair,* little site.

Lerr, *ladhair,* not given.

Lerrig, *leirg,* a slope.

Lerrig, *leirg, leargan,* a hillside.

Lesh, *leis,* sheltered.

Lesha, *Luiseach, Lucy,* a personal or family name.

Lesha, *Léise,* Lacey, a personal or family name.

Lesheen, *lisín,* a little fort.

Lesher, *Laisre,* not given.

Lesk, *leisc,* the lazy man.

Lesk, *Leisc,* Lesk, a personal or family name.

Lesk, *leisce,* not given.

Leskirt, *desceirt,* south.

Lesky, *leascaigh,* lazy or sluggish.

Less, *leasa, lios,* a circular earthen fort, sometimes associated with the fairies.

Lessan, *liosáin,* little fort.

Lessans, from *lios,* little forts.

Lessery, *leith-sheishreach,* half ploughland.

Lesson, *leasán,* the fort or little forts.

Lesson, *liosán,* little forts.

Lessy, *leasa,* a fort.

Lester, *leastair,* a beehive.

Lester, *leastair,* a small boat.

Lester, *leastar,* not given.

Lester, *lestar,* the vessel, cup or household vessel.

Lestrane, *Loiscreain,* not given.

Lestrane, *Loistreáin,* Loistreán, a personal or family name.

Lestraun, *loistreain,* corn burning.

Lestraun, *loistreáin,* not given.

Let, *leachta,* a sepulchral mound or tumulus.

Letra, *leatrach,* not given.

Letrim, *liath-dhruim,* the grey ridge.

Lett, *leacht,* tombs or grave stones.

Lettan, *leadan,* a place of burdocks.

Letter, *leitir,* a marsh(sic).

Letter, *leitreach,* not given.

Letter, *letter, leitir,* a wet hillside/hill slope.

Lettera, from *letter,* wet hillsides.

Letteragh, from *letter,* wet hillsides.

Letteragh, *leitir-riabhach,* not given.

Letteragh, *leitreach,* spewy or a wet hillside.

Letteran, *leitir-an...,* hillside of the...

Lettercus, *leitir-cos,* not given.

Lettereeneen, *leitir-Fhínghin,* not given.

Lettereeragh, *leitir-Iartharach,* not given.

Letterna, *leitir-na...,* hillside of the...

Lettery, from *letter,* wet hillsides.

Lettery, *litirí,* not given.

Lettiff, *leath-taoibh,* the half-side, one of a two sides.

Lettin, *leitean,* stirabout or porridge.

Lettra, a hillside.

Lettybrook, *an-cluainín,* not given.

Leuch, *leamhach,* a yew wood.

Leucra, *liúcra,* not given.

Leucra, *Liúceanna, Luiceanna,* belonging to the family known as the 'Luke's'.

Leugh, *leamhach,* land producing marsh mallows or elms.

Leva, *shliabh, tSléibhe,* a mountain.

Levagh, *leamhach,* elms.

Levaghery, *leath-mhachaire,* the half plain, farm.

Levaghy, *leamh-achaidh,* fields of elm.

Levallinree, *leath-bhaile-an-righ,* half of Ballinree (**Bhaile-an-righ,** townland of the king) townland.

Levally, *leathbhaile,* half townland.

Levallyclanone, *leathbhaile-chlann-Eoghain,* not given.

Levallyclanone, *leath-bhaile-clan-Eoghain,* half of the townland of **Ballyclanone.**

Levan, *lemhain, leamhain, leamhan,* elm/s.

Levanagh, *leamhanach,* elm.

Levane, *leamhain, leamháin, leamhan,* elm/s.

Levaun, *leamhain, leamhan,* elm/s.

Leveelick, *leth-mhílic,* half of the townland called Meelick. See **Meelick** or **Veelick.**

Levera, *Leibhre,* not given.

Levern, *liath-bhearn,* grey gap.

Levery, *Leibhre,* not given.

Levick, *Lamhaic,* not given.

Levin, *leamhain, leibheann,* not given.

Levin, *leamhán,* elms.

Levoy, *leathmahol,* not given.

Levoy, *leathmhaoil,* partially-derelict.

Levy, Lughach, a personal or family name.

Levy, *shliabh, shléibhe,* a mountain.

Lew, *leamha,* elm.

Lewagh, *leamhach,* a yew wood.

Lewagh, *leamhach,* land producing marsh mallows.

Lewis, *Lobhaois,* not given.

Lewy, *Lúiche, Lughaidh,* Lughaidh, *a* celebrated Dedannan Chief called 'Lewy of the long arm'.

Lewy, *Lúiche,* Lughdhach, a personal or family name.

Lewy, *Luigheach,* not given.

Leyney, *machaire-Luighne,* not given.

Leyny, *Luighne,* descendants, posterity of Lugaid/Luigh-Laigne.

Lhackinn, *leacain,* a hillside.

Liafin, *liathmhuine,* grey shrubbery or thicket.

Liam, *Liam,* Liam, a male name.

Liambue, *Liam-buidhe,* 'Tawny William', a male name.

Liamgow, *Liaim-gabha,* William the smith.

Libane, *leadhbain, leadhbáin, leadhbhain,* a small or rough patch.

Libane, *thighe-Líobáin,* not given.

Libbert, *liobar,* the flap or lip.

Libber, *liath-beirt,* two grey (horses?)

Libernagh, *liobarnach,* untidy or slovenly.

Libert, *Halberd,* Halberd, Halburd, a personal or family name.

Licaun, *leacán,* little glenside or slope.

Lick, *leac, lice,* flat rocky surface, a stone, flagstone or slate.

Lick, *leic, Loic,* not given.

Licka, *leac-an/a'...,* flagstone or flagstone surfaced land of the...

Licka, *lecach, leice,* flagstony or a flagstone

Licka, *lica,* a flagstone.

Lickacrue, *lice-cruaidhe,* hard slate.

Lickacrue, *lice-ruadh,* red slate.

Lickafinna, *lice-finne,* the white flagstone.

Lickana, *licana,* flagstones.

Lickane, *leacan,* a hillside.

Lickane, *leicne,* a hill brow.

Lickaun, *lecnán,* little flagstone or flag surfaced land.

Lickeen, *licín,* a little flat stone or a little flagstone.

Lickeen, *ligín*(sic), a small flagstone.

Licken, *leicin,* abounding in flagstones.

Lickey, *lice, leice,* the flagstone.

Licklash, *lic-ghlas,* not given.

Licknaun, *licenán,* little field of flagstones.

Lickny, *leicne,* a place of flagstones.

Lickoran, *leic-Dhobhráin,* not given.

Lickoran, *lic-Uarain,* the stone of St Deóran/Odranus/Furaran.

Licky, (river) *lice,* not given.

Licky, *leice,* flagstones.

Licky, *lice,* a flagstone, large flagstones, a slatey or flaggy spot or flag surfaced land.

Licky, *Luice,* Licky, not given.

Licky, *Luicean,* not given.

Liddan, *Liodáin,* Liddan, a family name.

Liddane, *Ua-Luidán,* O'Liddane, a family name.

Liede, *loid,* a pond or pool.

Lier, *ladhar,* a river fork.

Lier, *laidhre,* not given.

Lieragh, *ladhrach,* forks.

Lieve, *shliabh, tSleibhe,* a mountain.

Liff, *lubh, luihh,* herbs.

Liff, *luibh, luibhe,* herbage.

Liffane, *leathbhán,* half portion of lea land.

Liffe, *luibhe,* herbage.

Liffeany, *luihrnach,* weeds or herbs.

Liffen, *Liffín,* not given.

Lifferny, *luibhearnaigh,* weeds.

Liffey, *an-life,* not given.

Liffin, *Lia-Finn,* not given.

Liffin, *lifin,* a halfpenny.

Liffin, *Liffín, Lifín,* Liffin, a personal or family name.

Liffin, *luifinn,* weedy.

Liffin, *luibh,* herbs.

Liffock, *leitóg,* the small half.

Lifford, *leifear, leithbhearr,* side of the water.

Lifford, *lia-phort,* flagged landing place.

Lig, *leac, liag,* a stone or a standing stone.

Lig, *liag, lag, luig,* not given.

Lig, *lug, log,* a hollow.

Liga, *lig-a'...,* flagstone of...

Ligg, *lug, log, lag,* a hollow, hollows or a hill.

Liggins, from *liagán*, standing stones.

Ligh, *leagha*, eroding.

Ligna, *lag-na…*, hollow of the…

Lihen, *Liphthen*, Liffen or Lihen, a personal or family name.

Lihen, *Lithean*, not given.

Lileagh, *laoighille*, not given.

Lileagh, *loilgheach*, milch cows.

Lim, *leim*, jump.

Lima, *leim/léim-an*, jump or leap of the…

Limerick, *luimnigh, luimních, luimnech, luimneach, luimnaech*, bare spot/s of land.

Limerick, *luimneach, luimnigh*, bare land.

Limin, *léam-an…*, pass or leap of the…

Liminary, *léam-an-aodhaire*, pass or leap of the shepherd.

Limnagh, *luimneach*, bare spot/s of land.

Limp, *leamh*, elm.

Lin, *chluain*, a meadow.

Lin, *Fhlainn*, Flann or Flinn, a personal or family name.

Lin, *Fhlainn, Loinn*, Flann, a male name.

Lin, *ghlinn*, curved.

Lin, *lainne*, a Church.

Lin, *lín*, flax.

Lin, *Liní*, not given.

Lin, *linne, linn*, a pool or river.

Lin, *Uí-Fhloinn*, Ó Floinn or O'Flynn, a family name.

Lina, *Laighean*, leinstermen.

Lina, *Laighneach*, the Leinsterman.

Lina, *Luíne, Laighnigh, líne*, not given.

Linagh, *Laighneach*, Leinstermen.

Linan, *laidhghnean*, Linon, a personal or family name.

Linan, *Laoigheanáin*, Lynan, a personal or family name.

Linan, *Uí-Laigheanáin*, Ó Laigheanán, a family name and means the descendants of Linan.

Linane, *leanán*, boggy mountain meadow.

Linane, *lionáin*, filling.

Linane, *lionain*, flooding.

Linane, *Uí-Leannáin*, Ó Leannáin, a family name.

Linane, *Uí-Lionnain*, O'Linnane, a family name.

Linch, *Uí-Loingsigh*, Lynch a family name.

Linch, *Uí-Loinsigh*, O'Linchy or Lynch, a family name.

Linchy, *Loingsigh*, not given.

Linchy, *loingsighe*, sailors.

Linchy, *Uí-Loingsigh*, Lynch a family name.

Linchy, *Uí-Loinsigh*, O'Linchy or Lynch, a family name.

Line, (Carrigaline), *Uí-Leidhin/Leighin/Laighin*, O'Lyne, a family name.

Line, *Floinn*, Flynn, a family name.

Line, *láighean, laighean*, the spear/s.

Line, *Laighean*, Leinstermen.

Line, *Laighin, Fhlainn, Laighill*, not given.

Line, *lin, lín*, flax.

Line, *linna*, a deep pool.

Line, *Uí-Fhloinn/-Fhlainn*, O'Flynn, a family name.

Lineen, *Loinín*, Loinin, a personal or family name.

Liney, *Laidhghuín*, Lynam, a male name.

Liney, *Laighnigh*, leinstermen.

Ling, *linne*, the pool.

Ling, *Uí-Fhloinn*, O'Flynn, a family name.

Lingady, *laingide, loinnide*, not given.

Lingaun, from *ling*, to spring or leap forward.

Lingaun, *loinneán, linneán*, not given.

Lingo, *linne*, not given.

Lining, *Laighnigh*, Lyons, a family name.

Linn, *Fhlainn*, Flann, a personal name.

Linn, *linne, linn*, a pool.

Linnan, *Lonáin*, Lonnin, a personal or family name.

Linne, *linne*, a pond.

Linnen, *Uí-Lionnain*, O'Linnane, a family name.

Linns, *lann*, the Church.

Linns, *na-Linne*, not given.

Linny, *Line*, Line, a male name.

Linny, *linneen*, Linneen, a personal or family name.

Linny, *Loinne*, not given.

Linsfort, *lios-Linne*, not given.

Linsky, Linsky, a family name.

Lintan, *liontán*, not given.

Lintan, *líontán*, nets.

Lintaun, *líntán*, a place of flax.

Lintaun, *linnteán*, abounding in pools.

Lintaun, *liontan*, not given.

Liny, *Laighneach*, the Leinsterman.

Lion, *Laighean*, Leinstermen.

Lion, *laighin*, the spear.

Lion, *Laighneach,* Leynaghne, a family name.

Lion, *Uí-Laighin,* O'Lyon or Lyne, a family name.

Lios, *lios,* a circular earthen fort, sometimes associated with the fairies.

Liosaniska, *lois*(sic)*-an-uisge,* a water Lois(sic).

Lippa, *an-Lipe,* not given.

Lira, *ládhghar,* a fork or junction.

Lira, *ladhaire, laidhre,* a river fork.

Lire, *Laghra,* not given.

Lire, *laidhre,* a river fork.

Lis, *lios,* a circular earthen fort, sometimes associated with the fairies.

Lisa, *lios-an/a'...,* fort of the...

Lisabuck, *lios-Oboc,* not given.

Lisagh, *liosach,* a fort.

Lisahane, *liosachán,* the fairy mount.

Lisannagh, *leasána,* little forts.

Lisatoo, *lios-a'-tsamhaidh,* fort of the sorrel.

Lisburn, *lios-na-Bruidhne,* not given.

Lisburn, *lios-na-gCearrbhach,* ring fort of the gamblers.

Liscale, *lios-Cathail,* Cathal's (a male name) fort.

Liscall, *lios-Cathail,* Cathal's (a male name) fort.

Liscaw, *leath-scatha,* partial or half shadow.

Liscelan, *lios-Fhaoláin,* Faolan's (a personal or family name) lios.

Lisda, *lios-dá...,* fort of the two...

Lisdoolin, *lios-Trólin,* Trolin's (a personal or family name) fort.

Lisdowney, *lios-dúin-fhiach,* the lios of Fiach's (a personal or family name) fort.

Lisfarbegnagommaun, *Lios-fear-beg-na-gComán,* fort of the little hurlers.

Lisgall, *lios-Cathail,* Cathal's (a male name) fort.

Lisgenan, *Lios-Géibheannáin, an-Ghráinsigh,* not given.

Lish, *leasa, lios, lis,* a circular earthen fort or ring fort.

Lish, *loiscthe,* not given.

Lish, *luis,* not given.

Lisha, from *lios,* a circular earthen fort.

Lisheen, *liosín, lisín,* a little fort.

Lisheen, *lisín,* a small enclosure.

Lisheena, *lisín,* not given.

Lisheena, *lisín-a'...,* little fort of the...

Lisheena, *lisín-a'..., lisín-na...,* little fort of the...

Lisheenagh, *liosín-Aodh,* Aodh's (a male name) little home.

Lisheenan, *lisín-an...,* a little fort of the...

Lisheenleigh, *lios-Ainleithe,* Ainleiths (a personal or a family name) fort.

Lisheenna, *lisín-na...,* little fort of the...

Lisheenydeen, *liosín-a-domhain,* little lios of the hollow place.

Lishen, *lisín,* a little fort.

Lisin, *lios-an...,* fort of the...

Lisk, *leisc, laisc, luisc,* not given.

Lisk, *leisce, lisc,* the lazy man.

Lisk, *loiscthe,* burnt.

Liska, *leisgidh,* the lazy man.

Liska, *loiscthe,* burnt.

Liskea, *lios-sciath,* fort of the shield.

Liskeagh, *lios-sciath,* fort of the shield.

Lisket, *lios-cata,* a sheep fold(sic).

Liskey, *lios-caoch,* not given.

Liskey, *loiscithe, loiscthe,* parched, scorched or burnt.

Liskilly, *lios-chúil-na-beithe,* enclosure of the birch corner.

Liskinbwee, *lios-cinn-buidhe,* fort of the yellow top or head.

Liskincon, *lios-cinn-con,* fort of the hounds head.

Liskinfere, *lios-cinn-féir/Fhéir,* not given.

Liskinlahan, *lios-Scanláin,* not given.

Lisky, *lios-caoich,* fort of the blind man.

Lislynchahan, *lios-Uinseogáin,* not given.

Lisna, *lios-na...,* fort of the...

Lisnagowan, fort of the smith or fort of O'Gowan, a personal or family name.

Lisnahanathen, *liosach-an-eudain,* fort of the hill brow.

Lisnalinchy, *lios-Uí-Loinsigh,* Ó Loingseach's (a personal or family name) fort.

Lisnanagh, *lios-an-fheadhnaigh,* fort of the company or troop.

Lisnanroum, *lios-na-dhróm/nDrom,* not given.

Lisnaveane, *lios-Suibhne*(sic) , not given.

Lisquillibeen, *Lios-Scoilbín,* not given.

Liss, *lios,* a circular earthen fort, sometimes associated with the fairies.

Liss, *Lis,* not given.

Lissa, *liosa,* forts.

Lissa, *lios-a'...,* fort of ...

Lissa, *lios-an/a'...,* fort of the...

Lissadober, *lios-Ó-dTobair,* not given.

Lissagarvan, *Lios-a' Garbháin,* Garvan's fort.

Lissahane, *liosachán,* little fort.

Lissalway, *lios-Shealbhaigh/Sealbhaigh,* Sealbhach's (a personal or family name) fort.

Lissamona, *lios-Ó-Móine,* not given.

Lissan, *lios-Aine,* Aine's (a female name and the name of a fairy queen who was supposed to live here) fort.

Lissan, *liosán, leasán, lisín,* little (ring)fort.

Lissan, *lios-an...,* enclosure of the...

Lissan, *lios-an...,* fort of the...

Lissana, *liosanadh,* forts.

Lissane, *liosán,* little forts.

Lissard, *lios-aird...,* fort of the height of the...

Lissardowlin, *lios-árd-abhla,* not given.

Lissaroon, *lios-Urumhan,* not given.

Lissarulla, *lios-Arúla,* not given.

Lissarulla, *lios-a'Rúla,* ploughed fort.

Lissava, *lios-a-mheadha,* fort of the metheglin or mead.

Lissava, *lios-an-mheatha,* not given.

Lisse, *lios,* a circular earthen fort.

Lisseagh, *lios-each,* fort of the horses.

Lisseagh, *lios-fhéich,* not given.

Lisseen, *lisín,* little fort.

Lisseenna, *lisín-na...,* not given.

Lisselton, *lios-Eiltín,* not given.

Lisselton, *lios-Lachtín,* not given.

Lissen, *lisín,* little fort.

Lissenhall, *lisín-an-airgid,* not given.

Lisser, *liosar,* a fort.

Lisser, *lios-ar...,* not given.

Lisserdrea, *lios-aird-reidh,* fort of the smooth hill.

Lissernane, *lios-Earnáin,* not given.

Lisshane, *liosachán,* the fairy mount.

Lissian, *lios-fhiadhain,* the wild fort.

Lissin, *lios-an...,* fort of ...

Lissina, *lios-na...,* not given.

Lissina, *lisín-na...,* little fort of the...

Lissindonal, *lios-Uí-Dhomhnaill,* O'Donnels little fort.

Lissindragan, *lios-Iondragain,* Hendragan's (a personal or family name) fort.

Lissofin, *lios-Aodh-Fionn, lios-Aedha-Finn,* fort of Hugh (a male name) the fair.

Lissoy, *lios-eoigh/eo/eó,* fort of the yew.

Lissoy, ring fort of the cave.

Lissue, *lios-Aodha, Aedha,* Aedh's (a male name) fort.

Lissy, *lios-an,* fort of the...

Listerlin, *lios-Airglinn,* not given.

Listerlin, *lios-ar-glinn,* fort on the glen.

Listerlin, *lios-thar-ghlinn,* fort overlooking the glen.

Listoke, *lios-Dubhóige,* not given.

Listra, *listrach,* a fort.

Listrahee, *listrach-Aodh,* Aodh's or Hugh's (a male name) fort.

Listrahenny, *lios-rátha-Éignigh,* not given.

Listrane, *loistreáin, loiscrean, loiscreáin,* a place where corn is burnt in the ear.

Listrolin, *lios-Tróilín,* not given.

Litter, a retreat.

Litter, *leitir,* a hillside.

Littin, *Litean,* not given.

Livaun, *leamhain, leamhain, leamhan,* elm/s.

Liveraun, *libhearán,* a leveret.

Lixnaw, *leic-snámha, lic-snamha,* the flag-stone of the swimming.

Lixnaw, *leic-snámha,* the floating island(sic).

Lo, *Leodha, Leodh,* Leo, the name of a old chief.

Lo, *loch,* lake.

Load, *lóid,* a load.

Loaghan, *Luacháin,* not given.

Loan, *Luán, na-leamháin,* not given.

Loanends, *cairthe-muighe,* not given.

Lobawn, *lúbán,* not given.

Lobbus, *leaba-ois,* bed of the fawn.

Lobbus, *lobhuir,* the leper.

Loben, *Loibín,* not given.

Loch Carrick, *carraig-loch-an-tairbh,* not given.

Loch Hackett, *loch-Cime,* not given.

Loch Inisterry, *loch-doire,* not given.

Locha, *loch-an...,* not given.

Lochain, *lochán,* a little lake.

Lochan, *loch-an...,* not given.

Lochann, *loch-na...,* not given.

Lochash, *loch-Chais,* not given.

Lochaverra, *loch-burrann,* not given.
Loch-Katherine, *loch-Uí-Mhaoldubháin,* not given.
Lochna, *loch-na…,* not given.
Lock, *leac,* flat rocks or flagstones.
Lody, *lóide,* mud or puddle.
Lody, *lóidigh,* not given.
Loe, *ghleo,* strife or tumult.
Loe, *Lautha,* Luath, a male name and means 'swift'.
Loe, *Logha,* Lughaidh, a personal or family name.
Loe, *loich,* Loch, a personal name.
Loe, *Lua,* Lua, a personal name.
Loe, *luaigh,* pleasant.
Loe, *luatha,* ashes.
Loe, *Lugha,* Lugh or Lewy, a male name.
Lofty, *leachtai,* graves or monuments.
Lofty, *lochta,* the shelf, shelving or lofted, usually to do with a hill.
Log, *lag, log,* a hollow.
Loga, *log-an/a'…,* hollow of the…
Logan, *liagan,* a little hollow.
Logan, *lócháin,* not given.
Logan, *lochan,* a pond.
Logan, *Uí-Locháin,* O'Lochan, a family name.
Logane, *logáin,* not given.
Logane, *logan,* small lakes or hollows.
Logar, *ló-garr*(sic), rough bend.
Logg, *lag, log,* a hollow.
Loggagh, *logach,* not given.
Loggan, *lagáin,* the cavity.
Loggan, *logán,* a little hollow.
Loggy, *logaigh,* a hollow.
Logha, *locha,* a pond.
Loghan, *locháin,* the pond.
Loghan, *Lochan,* a personal name.
Loghan, *Lochan,* Lochan, a personal or family name.
Loghaun, *lochán,* a small pond.
Logher, *luachair,* not given.
Logher, *luachrach,* sedgy.
Loghera, *luachra,* reeds, rushy.
Loghig, *lochaigh,* not given.
Loghill, *leamhchoill,* elm wood.
Loglos, *log/lag-glas,* green-grey hollow.
Logna, *log-na…,* hollow of the…
Logue, *Laodhog,* Logue, a family name and a personal name.

Logue, *Leog,* Leog, not given.
Logurt, *lubhgoirt,* a herb-garden.
Loha, *luaithe,* ashes.
Lohan, *Lócháin,* a personal name.
Lohan, *locháin, lócháin,* chaff(sic).
Lohane, *lochán,* little lake.
Loheen, *lochín,* a pond.
Loher, *an-lóthar,* not given.
Loher, *lothar,* a hollow or trough.
Loher, *luachra, lúachra,* rushes.
Lohera, *luachrach,* rushes.
Lohert, *lubh-ghuirt,* the herb plot or garden.
Lohery, *luachra, lúchra,* rushes.
Lohorig, *lotharaigh,* rough land.
Lohort, a garden.
Lohort, *lothairt,* not given.
Lohort, *lubhghort, lúbhghuirt,* a herb garden or kitchen garden.
Loighag, *luchógh,* rats.
Loirc, *loirc,* murder.
Loist, *losaide, loiste,* a kneading trough or fertile spot.
Loman, *Lomáin, Lóman,* a male name.
Loman, *loman,* bare spots.
Loman, *Lomán,* not given.
Loman, *Loman,* St Loman.
Lomanagh, *luimnaech,* bare spot/s of land.
Lomane, *loman, lomain,* bare.
Lomane, *lomán,* not given.
Lomaunagh, *lománach,* not given.
Lomaunagh, *luimnaech,* bare spot/s of land.
Lomcloon, *lomchluain,* not given.
Lome, *lom,* bare.
Lomina, *luimnigh,* the bare spot.
Lon, *lón,* a marsh(sic).
Lon, *lon, londubh,* blackbirds.
Lona, *Lóna,* not given.
Lonagh, *leamhnach,* an elmy place or a place of elms.
Lonagh, *leamhnachta,* new milk.
Lonan, *Lonáin, Lonain,* Lonán, Lonan, a personal or family name and the name of a Church founder in Limerick.
Lonart, *longphort,* a fortress or encampment.
Lone, *leamhan,* elm.
Lone, *lón,* blackbirds.
Lone, *Lúain, Luain,* Luan, a male name.
Lone, *luain,* a hunch like hill.
Lone, *luán, lubhán, lubháin,* lambs.

Lonehort, *longphort,* a fortress or encampment.

Lonehurt, *longphort,* a fortress or encampment.

Loney, *Luinigh,* Luinigh, a personal or family name.

Loney, *O'Luinigh,* O'Looney, a family name.

Long, *loinge,* the house.

Long, *long,* houses.

Long, *loinge,* the ship(sic).

Long, *long,* ships.

Long, *longa, luinge,* the encampment.

Long, *Longaigh,* not given.

Longa, *longa, luinge,* the encampment.

Longa, *longaigh,* not given.

Longane, *Uí-Longáin,* O'Longan, a family name.

Longfield, *leamhchoille, leamh-choill, leamh-choille,* elm wood.

Longfield, *páirc-an-Longaigh,* not given.

Longford, *áth-fhada, an-tÁth-fada, an-Longfort,* not given.

Longford, *longphoirt, longfoirt, longphort,* a fortress or encampment.

Longford, *longphoirt, longphort,* the fortified house.

Longig, *Longaig,* Longagh or Long a personal or family name.

Longig, *Longaigh,* Longach, not given.

Longna, *long-na…,* house or ship of the…

Longueville, *glean-riabhach,* not given.

Longwood, *maighe-Dearmhaí,* not given.

Longy, the encampment.

Lonhurt, *longfoirt,* not given.

Lonhurt, *longphort,* a fortress.

Lonnan, Lonnan or O'Lonan, a family name.

Lonty, *leonta,* provisions, supplies.

Lonty, *Lonta,* Lundy, a male name.

Lonty, *lóntaigh,* not given.

Loo, *Lú,* an ancient God.

Loo, *luaidhe,* lead or a lead mine.

Loo, *lúb,* not given.

Loo, *lubh,* herbs.

Loo, *Lugh,* Louis, a male name.

Loo, *Lugha, Lua,* Legh, Lugh or Lewy, a male name, also used for St Molua.

Loo, *Lughaidh,* Lewy a personal or family name.

Looart, *lubhghort,* the herb garden.

Looart, *lúghort,* not given.

Looaun, *leamháin,* elm.

Loob, *loop,* an enclosure.

Loob, *lúb,* loop/s or winding/s.

Loobagh, *lúbach,* full of loops.

Loobanagh, *lúbanach,* loops or windings.

Loobaun, *lubán,* windings.

Loobinagh, *leamhánach*(sic), not given.

Loobinagh, *lúbanach,* loops or windings.

Loobna, *loop-na…,* enclosure of the…

Loobroe, *brúgha-Lúgh,* the otherworld resting place of the sun God named 'Lúgh'.

Looby, *lúba,* winding.

Looby, *lúbaigh,* a winding river or river loops.

Looby, *lúbaigh, lúba,* a winding fort.

Looby, *Lúbaigh,* Luby or O'Looby, a family name.

Looby, *lúbtha,* not given.

Lood, *Lút,* not given.

Loogh, *leamhach,* marsh-mallows.

Loogh, *Lua,* not given.

Looghan, *fhliuchain,* wet, spewy land.

Looghra, *luachra,* rushes.

Looha, *luaithe,* ashes.

Loon, *cluain,* a meadow or a lawn.

Loon, *leamhan,* a place of elms.

Loona, *Lughna, Lugna,* Lugna or Lugna, a male name.

Loonagh, *chluaineach,* a meadow.

Loonagh, *chluanach,* meadow lands.

Loonaghtan, from *lemnacht,* little land of the new milk.

Loonigan, *Lonagáin,* not given.

Loonogs, *lannóg,* a small building/Church.

Loop, from the Danish 'hlaup' and *léim/ léime* in Irish, a leap, jump.

Loop, *lúb,* a loop or winding.

Loop, *lúb,* leap.

Loopy, *lúb,* a loop or winding.

Loora, *Luraigh,* St Lurach.

Loorican, *chlúracháin,* a leprachaun.

Looricaun, *gClúracán,* not given.

Loortan, *lubhghortán,* the herb garden.

Looscane, *luascan,* swinging.

Looscaun, *luascán,* swinging or rocking.

Looscaunagh, *luascánach,* rocking or swinging.

Loose, *lus,* herbs.

Loose, *lús,* not given.

Looskaun, *luasgán,* a cradle.

Loran, *leamhran,* a place of elms.

Loran, *Lóthrán, Lúrain,* not given.

Lorcan, *Lorcáin, Lorcain,* Lorcan, a male name.

Lore, *Labhrain, Lór,* not given.

Lore, *lobhar, lobhair,* the leper.

Lorgan, *Lorcain,* a male name.

Lorrha, *lothra,* a place of oaks.

Lorrigan, *lorga-an...,* the track of the...

Lorrug, *lorg,* a track.

Lorton, *lugh-bhurdán, lubh-ghortán, lughb-hortán,* the herb plot or garden.

Lorum, *leamhdhrom, leamhdhru*ím, ridge of the elms.

Lorum, *leamh-dhruim,* the elm ridge.

Loscan, *loscáin, of the burning.*

Loscarane, *loiscreán,* scorched land.

Loscran, *loisgreáin, corn burned in the ear.*

Losh, *lois,* not given.

Loskaha, *loscaithe,* not given.

Loskan, *losgáin, loisceáin,* burning.

Loskeran, *loiscreán,* burnt/scorched ground.

Loskeran, *loisgreán,* place where corn was burned.

Loskeraun, *loisgreán,* place where corn was burned.

Loskeraun, *losca,* (of the) burning.

Loskin, *loscáin,* the burning.

Losky, *loscathaidhe, loiscthe, loisgthe,* burnt.

Loss, *glas,* green.

Lossary, *Lasrach,* Losar, Lasair, a personal or family name.

Losscragh, *Lasrach,* St Lasser.

Lossera, *Lasrach, Lasrach,* a personal or family name.

Losseragh, *Lasrach,* not given.

Losset, *loiste,* not given.

Losset, *an-losad,* the well laid out field.

Losset, *lusaid, losad, losaid, kneading trough/s, well tilled plots, fertile or rich productive land.*

Lossets, *na-loiste,* not given.

Lossot, *lusaid, a kneading trough.*

Lost, *loiscthe,* not given.

Lost, *loiste,* a kneading trough or fertile spot or good land.

Lost, *loiste,* burnt.

Losta, *loiste, a kneading trough or well culti-vated land.*

Lota, *luaith-teach, an-luaitigh,* not given.

Lotteragh, *latrach,* rough scrubby land.

Loucht, *leacht, a monument.*

Lough, *cnoc,* a hill.

Lough, *lach,* not given.

Lough, *lachan,* ducks.

Lough, *latach, lathaighe, quagmire/s.*

Lough, *leaca,* a hillside.

Lough, *leacht, a monument.*

Lough, *loch, locha,* lakes.

Lough, *log,* hollow.

Lough, *loiche,* not given.

Lough, *lough, locha, lougha,* a lake.

Lough, *Lua, Lua, a personal name.*

Lough, *luach,* reward.

Lough, *lucht,* people.

Lough, *mallows.*

Lougha, *loch, lough, lougha,* a lake.

Lougha, *locha,* a lake or pond.

Lougha, *locha,* lake/s.

Lougha, *loch-a'...,* lake of the...

Lougha, *loiche,* a pond.

Loughag, *luchógh,* rats.

Loughan, a small place.

Loughan, *lachain, lachan,* ducks or duck shaped.

Loughan, *leathan,* wide.

Loughan, *locháin/lochain/lochán/locán/loughaun,* little lake or a pond.

Loughan, *lochán,* a lake.

Loughan, *loch-an...,* lake of the...

Loughan, *na-lougháin,* the lakes.

Loughan, *fhliuchaine,* wet land.

Loughana, *lochán-na/an/a'...,* little lake of the...

Loughane, *locháin,* not given.

Loughane, *lochán,* a place of lakelets.

Loughane, *lochán, locán, loughaun,* a little lake, a pool or a pond.

Loughaneeg, *loch-an-eug,* lake of death-or decline.

Loughaninish, *lough/loughan Aonghuis,* Aongus's, (a male name) lake.

Loughanna, *lochan-na...,* little lake of the...

Loughannadown, *lochan-na-dtonn,* little lake of the waves.

Loughanstown, *baile-lochán,* not given.

Loughanunna, *loch-an-ghoinne,* not given.

Lougharnagh, *luacharnach,* a place of rushes or rushy land.

Lougharoe, red lake.

Loughaun, *loch-Óna, locháin,* not given.

Loughaun, *lochán, locán, loughaun,* a little lake, a pond.

Loughaunna, *lochán-na…,* little lake of the…

Loughavoy, *locha-bhaidhidh,* lake of drowning.

Loughavoy, *loch-an-bhealaigh,* not given.

Loughawn, *lochán, locán, loughaun,* a little lake or a pond.

Loughbarra, *cruaichín,* not given.

Loughcurrane, *loch-Luíoch*(sic), not given.

Loughduff, *an-lathaigh-dhubh,* not given.

Loughea, *loch-Éa,* not given.

Lougher, *Lochair, Lochar,* a persons name.

Lougher, *Lothair, Lothair,* a personal or family name.

Lougher, *luchra, luachair, luachrach,* a rushy place.

Lougher, *luachrach, luachra, lúchra, luacha,* rushes.

Lougheraherk, *loch-dhoire-thoirc,* not given.

Lougherny, *luacharnaí,* not given.

Lougherny, *luacharnaigh,* rushes.

Loughglinn, *loch-Glinne,* lake of Glinnia, a female name.

Loughil, *leamhchoill,* the elm wood.

Loughile, *leach-choill, leamh choill, leath-choill,* half wood.

Loughill, bright lake.

Loughill, *leamhchoill,* the elm wood.

Loughin, *loch-an…,* lake of the…

Loughin, *loughan,* a little lake.

Loughinsholin, *loch-innse-Uí-Fhlann,* lake of O'Flynn's (a family name) island.

Loughinsholin, *loch-inse-Uí-Fhloinn,* not given.

Loughkent, *loch-ceann*(sic), not given.

Loughlin, *lochán*(sic), not given.

Loughlin, *Lochlainn,* Lochlann or Loughlin, a personal or family name.

Loughlin, *Lochlannach,* a Dane.

Loughlin, Loughlin or Melaghlin, a personal or family name.

Loughlin, *Maoilsheachlainn,* Malachy, a male name.

Loughlin, *Uí-Lachtnain,* O'Lachtnan, O'Loughnane, a family name.

Loughlin, *Uí-Lochlainn,* O'Loughlin or O'Melaghlin, a family name and means the descendants of Loughlin.

Loughlinstown, *baile-lochán,* not given.

Loughmoe East, *na-Cealla-beaga,* not given.

Loughmoe, *luachma,* not given.

Loughmoe, *luaghmhagh, luach-mhagh,* prize plain or plain of reward.

Loughmore, (Tipperary) *lough-moe, luach-mhagh,* the plain of the reward or the prize field.

Loughmore, (Tipperary) *luachma,* not given.

Loughna, *leacan-a…,* glen-slope of the…

Loughna, *Lóchna,* not given.

Loughna, *loch-na/an*(sic)…, lake of the…

Loughnaan, *Uí-Lachnáin/Locháin,* Ó Lachnáin, a family name.

Loughnafin, *lough-na-finne,* bright lake(sic).

Loughnane, *O'Lachtnain,* Loughnane, a family name.

Loughnane, *Uí-Lachnáin/Lachnáin,* not given.

Loughnane, *Uí-Lachtnain,* O'Lachtnan, O'Loughnane, a family name.

Loughoge, *luchóg,* mice.

Loughooly, *loch-Chúile,* not given.

Loughra, *luchair, luachra,* rushes.

Loughrain, *Uí-Luachrain,* O'Loghran, a family name.

Loughran, *Uí-Luacharáin,* Loughran, a family name.

Loughrim, *clochdroma,* stonyridge.

Loughris, *luachrais,* rushy land.

Loughros, *luacharos, luachras,* a rushy place.

Loughros, *luacharos,* rushy headland.

Loughros, *luachros,* not given.

Loughry, *lúchra,* rushes.

Loughry, *luachraigh,* a rushy place.

Loughryman, *luprachaun, luchorpán,* leprechaun/s.

Loughshillin, *loc-innse-Uí-Fhlann,* lake of O'Flynn's (a family name) island.

Lought, *leacht,* a monument.

Loughta, *leacht, leachta,* a sepulchral monument, a grave or a grave pile.

Loughta, *lochta,* not given.

Loughtee, *lucht-teach,* people of the house.

Laughter, *luachra,* rushes.

Loughthea, *leacht-Aodha,* Hugh's monument.

Loughty, *lucht-tighe,* people of the house.

Loughure, *loch-odhar,* a weatherbeaten sea inlet.

Louhy, *luaithe,* ashes.

Loum, *lóm, lom,* bare.

Loumanagh, *luimnaech, lomanach,* bare spot/s of land, a bare place.

Lounaght, *leamhnachta,* new milk.

Lounaghta, *leamhnachta,* not given.

Loundash, *Londais,* not given.

Lounty, *lóinte,* stores.

Lounty, *Lóintigh,* not given.

Loup, *lúb,* a bend or loop.

Lour, *Iúir,* tower(sic).

Lour, *lair,* the middle.

Lour, *leabhar,* books.

Lour, *lobhar,* lepers.

Lour, *lobhar,* lepers.

Loura, *labhartha,* a stream or babbling brook.

Loura, *lobhar,* lepers.

Lourish, *labhrais,* speak, speaking.

Lousybush, *sceach-na-míol,* white-thorn of the lice.

Louth Hall, *baile-an-Tallúnaigh,* not given.

Louth, *Lú,* plain(sic).

Louth, *lúbhadh,* not given.

Louth, *Lugh,* the hollow.

Louth, *Lugh-mhaigh,* plain of Lugaid/Lugh.

Louth, *lughmaigh,* hollow of the plain.

Louth, *Lughbhadh,* named after the Celtic God 'Lugh'.

Low, *leamhach,* a place of marshmallows.

Low, *Lughdach,* not given.

Lowan, *leamhan,* elm trees.

Lowan, *luain,* the lamb.

Lowart, *lubh ghuirt,* the herb plot or garden

Lower, *lobhar,* leper/s.

Lowerton, *lugh-bhurdán, lubh-ghortán, lughb-hortán,* the herb plot or garden.

Lowertown, *lugh-bhurdán, lubh-ghortán, lughbhortán,* the herb plot or garden.

Lowertown, *lúghortán, lubhghortán,* not given.

Lowery, *leamhraidhe,* a place of elms.

Lowforge, *drom-Conra,* not given.

Lownagh, *leamhnachta, leamhnacht,* new milk.

Lownan, *leamhnán,* elm plantation.

Lowran, *leamhrán,* little elm wood.

Lowrish, *labhrais,* speak, speaking.

Loy, *lathaí,* a mire.

Loy, *Lughdhach,* not given.

Loyer, *ladhar,* a fork.

Loyst, *loiste,* a kneading trough or fertile spot.

Luagh, *luach,* the prize.

Luaghna, *luach-na…,* not given.

Luatha, *Luatha,* not given.

Lubitavish, *lub/lúb-a'tsamhais,* the winding of the sorrel.

Luby, *lubaidh,* a sloping place.

Lucan, *leamhcán,* a place of elms.

Lucan, *leamhcan,* not given.

Lucan, *livecan,* (latin) *leamhcán* (Irish), land producing marshmallows.

Lucas, *Lúcáis, Lucas,* Lucas, a pesons name.

Luce, *lios,* a circular earthen fort, some-times associated with the fairies or a palace.

Luchoge, *luchog,* mice.

Luchraman, *luchraman,* a leprachaun.

Luchraman, *luchraman,* small trouts.

Luck, *luic,* an animal shelter or pen.

Lucumpher, *lag-umair,* hollow of the cup.

Lucy, *Luasaigh,* Lucey, a personal or family name.

Lucy, *lus-mhuighe,* herb plain.

Ludden, *lodain,* not given.

Ludden, *lodan,* a place of puddles.

Luddy, *Lúidigh,* not given.

Ludigan, St Ludigan or St Ludadan.

Luffany, *fhliuchaine,* wet land.

Luffany, *fhliuchmhuine,* not given.

Luffertann, *lugh-bhurdán, lubh-ghortán, lugh-bhortán,* the herb plot or garden.

Luffertaun, *lubhghortán, magh-na-bheithe,* not given.

Luffertaun, *lugh-bhurdán, lubh-ghortán, lugh-bhortán,* the herb plot or garden.

Lug, a hole(sic).

Lug, *lig, loig, lug,* a hollow.

Luga, *log-an/a'…,* hollow of the…

Lugagh, the holes.

Lugan, *log-an…,* not given.
Lugga, *loga,* the hollow.
Lugga, *log-an/a'…,* hollow of the…
Lugga, *lug,* a hollow.
Luggagh, holes.
Luggagh, *logach,* not given.
Luggala, *log-an-lagha, log-a'lagha/lágh,* hollow of the hill.
Luggan, *log-an…,* hollow of the…
Luggaun, *lugaun, logáin,* little hollow.
Luggy, *logaigh,* hollows or hollow spots.
Lugh, *lig, lug,* a hollow.
Lughanagh, *fliuchaine, fliuchanne,* wet land.
Lughany, *liuchanach,* wet or spewy place.
Lugher, *an-fhliuchair,* the wet place.
Lughil, *leamh-coill/choill,* the elm wood.
Lughinny, *an-fhliuchmhuine,* not given.
Lughinny, *an-fhliuchaine/fliuchaine/ fliuchanne,* springy or wet land.
Lughoga, *luchóg,* mice.
Lughoge, *luchóg,* a mouse or mice.
Lughraman, *loughryman*(sic), can be a type of trout, a fairy or leprechaun/s.
Lughraman, *luchramán,* not given.
Lughros, *luacharos,* not given.
Lughros, *luachros,* peninsula of reward or hire.
Lughveen, *an-fhliuch-mhín,* the wet field.
Lughveen, *an-liuchmhín*(sic), not given.
Lugna, *log-na…,* hollow of the…
Lugnaquillia, *lug-na-gCoilleach,* hollow of the cocks/grouse.
Luideen, *luidín,* a small dint or mark.
Luig, *lig, lag, lug,* a hollow.
Luig, *Lughadhaigh,* Lowe, a persons, name.
Luin, *loin,* the bird or blackbird.
Luirc, *Luirc,* Lorc, a personal name.
Lulagh, *loilgheach,* milch cows.
Lulleagh, *loiligheach, loilgheach,* milch cows.
Lulleegh, *loilíoch,* milch cows.
Lully, *laoilgheach,* milch cows.
Lum, *lom,* bare.
Lumber, *Lumar,* not given.
Lumford, *longphoirt, longphort,* the fort.
Lumford, the long ford.
Lumin, *Lomon, Lománin,* Lomond, a family name.
Lumma, *loma,* bare.
Lumman, *Lomán,* not given.
Lumman, St Loman.

Lummery, *Lomra,* not given.
Lummery, *lomradh,* fleece.
Lummin, *Lomáin,* Loman, Lomand, a personal or family name.
Lumminy, *luimnigh,* a bare spot.
Lummon, *lomain,* not given.
Lummon, *lomann,* bare.
Lummon, *Lomon, Lománin,* Lomond, a family name.
Lummon, *luman,* a shield.
Lummon, St Loman.
Lumnagh, *lománach,* not given.
Lumnagh, *luimnaech, lomnach,* bare spot/s of land.
Lumney, *lomnaigh, luimnigh,* the bare place.
Lumny, *linmnagh, luimnigh, lumna,* a bare spot of land.
Lumpera, *Lompairne,* not given.
Lumpera, *Lompuirne, Lampora,* Lamprey, a family name.
Lun, *lon, londubh,* blackbirds.
Luna, *Lughna,* not given.
Luna, *Lúna,* not given.
Luna, St Luana.
Lunaghan, *luigheachán,* the ambush.
Lunaght, *leamhnachta,* new milk.
Lunaghta, *leamhnacda*(sic), *leamhnachta,* new milk.
Lune, *luíne, luaighne,* not given.
Luney, *leamhnaigh, leamhnach,* a place of elms.
Lung, (river) *an-luing,* not given.
Lung, *long,* a boat or a house.
Lung, *mágh-Lunga,* not given.
Lungs, *longa,* houses.
Lunkard, *longfoirt,* not given.
Lunkard, *longphuirt, longphort,* a fortress or encampment.
Lunkard, *longphuirt,* the boatstead
Lunkard, *lúngfort,* the stronghold.
Lunn, *lon,* blackbirds.
Lunniagh, *an-luinnigh,* not given.
Lunnig, *Longaigh,* Long, a family name.
Lunny, *linne,* a pond.
Luocar, Luochar, *Labraine,* not given.
Luoge, *Uí-Laoghog,* Luogue, a family name.
Luogh, *leamh, leamhach,* land producing marsh mallows.
Luppan, *lopán,* not given.
Luppercadane, *luprachaun, luchorpán,* leprechaun/s.

Lupraghaun, *luprachaun, luchorpán,* leprechaun/s.

Lura, *lobhar,* not given.

Lurcher, *lurchaire,* the foal.

Lurcher, *urchair,* not given.

Lurg, *loirge,* not given.

Lurg, *lorg,* a ridge.

Lurg, *lorg, lurg,* a track.

Lurga, *lorgain,* a shank, ridge or a strip of land.

Lurga, *lurga,* shins, stripes, long hills or ridges.

Lurgagh, from *lurga,* shins, stripes or ridges.

Lurgan, *leargain,* not given.

Lurgan, *lorgain,* a shin or ridge.

Lurgan, *lorgain, lorgan,* a strip of land.

Lurgan, *lorgan,* a long ridge.

Lurgan, *lurgain,* a ridge or a shank.

Lurgan, *lurgan,* a long low hill or hills.

Lurgan, *lurgan,* leg shaped.

Lurgan, *lurraga, lorgain, lurgain, lurga,* a long stripe of land, a long low ridge.

Lurgana, *lurgan-na...,* long hill of the...

Lurgans, *an-lorgain*(sic), not given.

Lurgoe, *an-lorga,* not given.

Lurgoe, *lurga,* shins.

Lurgy, from *lurgach,* a long hill.

Luricane, *luprachaun, luchorpán,* leprechaun/s.

Lurin, *Liobhráin,* Liobhrán, a personal or family name and the name of a founder of a Church in Wexford.

Lurkaun, *lurgán,* leg shaped.

Lurkin, *Lorcáin,* named after Archbishop Lorcán Ó Tuathail.

Lurkin, *Uí-Lorcain,* O'Lorcan or O'Larkin, a family name.

Lurraga, *lorga,* a shin.

Lurraga, *lorga, lurga,* a long stripe of land, a long low ridge.

Lurrig, from *lurg,* a long hill.

Lurriga, *lorga,* a long hill or a little ridge of hills.

Lurrigadane, *luprachaun, luchorpán,* leprechaun/s.

Lus, *lus,* a herb or herbs.

Lush, *luis,* not given.

Lush, *lus,* leeks.

Lusha, *luise,* a quicken tree.

Lushaha, *loisgithe,* burnt.

Lusheen, *luisín,* a little herb or plant.

Lushkinnagh, *loiscneach,* burnt land/place.

Lusk, *bhloisce,* the noise.

Lusk, *bhlosc,* not given.

Lusk, *loiscthe, loisgthe,* burnt.

Lusk, *luisc,* a cripple.

Lusk, *lusc,* not given.

Lusk, *lusca,* a cave.

Luska, *loisgthe,* burning or burnt.

Luska, *lusca,* not given.

Luska, *an-loiscthe,* not given.

Luskaha, burning or scorching.

Luskaha, *loiscighthe,* little burnt....

Luskan, burnt.

Luskan, *luascáin,* swinging.

Luskan, *lusc,/lusca-an...,* cave of the...

Luskane, *luascáin,* swinging.

Luskeran, *loisgreán,* place where corn was burned.

Luskinagh, *loiscneach,* burnt land.

Lusky, *Leasca,* Duibh-Leasc, the name of an ancient chief.

Lusky, *loisgthe, loiscthe,* burnt or burnt land.

Lusky, *lusca,* not given.

Lusmagh, *lusmhaigh, lusmágh,* plain of herbs.

Luss, *lus,* herbs or leeks.

Lusseraun, *lusore,* 'male speedwell' (a plant).

Lust, *loiscthe,* not given.

Lust, *loiste, losad, losaid,* a kneading trough, fertile spot, well tilled or good land.

Lustia, *loiste,* a kneading trough, well tilled land or fertile spot.

Lustran, *loisgreán,* place where corn was burned.

Lustraun, *loisgreán, loistreáin, lusgraun, lustrun,* place where corn was burned.

Lustrin, *loisgreán,* place where corn was burned.

Lusty, a kneading trough or a fertile spot of land.

Lusty, *loisgthe, loiscthe,* burnt.

Lusty, *losaide, loiste,* a kneading trough or fertile spot.

Lyan, *laighean,* a long strip of land or a lance.

Lyan, *leana,* a wet meadow.

Lyardane, *ladhardáin,* little fork.

Lybagh, *leadhbach,* an elongated strip of poor land.

Lybe, *leidhb,* a long strip of land.

Lybe, *leidhbach,* a long strip of land.

Lybes, from *leidhb,* long strips of land.

Lydacan, *lideachán, an-laighdeacán,* not given.

Lylo, *cailleoc*(sic), little wood(sic).

Lyn, *lann,* a house or a Church.

Lyn, O'Lynnn, a family name and a personal or family name.

Lyna, *Laighneach, Laighnigh,* the Leinsterman.

Lyna, *Laighneadh,* Leinstermen.

Lynagh, *Laighneach,* Lynagh, a family name.

Lynagh, *Laighneadh,* Leinstermen.

Lynally, *lainn-Eala,* not given.

Lynally, *lann-Ealla, lann-Eala, lann-Elo, lann-Ella,* Church of Eala/Ela.

Lynan, *Uí-laigheanáin, Laighneain,* Ó Laigheanán or O'Lynan, a family name.

Lynch, *Leithinnse,* not given.

Lynch, *Uí-Loingsigh,* Lynch a family name.

Lyneen, *Laighnín,* little Leinster.

Lynen, O'Lynan, family name.

Lynin, *Laighnín, Laighnin,* not given.

Lynn, *lann,* a house or a Church.

Lynn, *lann-Mhic-Luacháin/Luachain,* Mac Luacháin's Church.

Lynn, O'Lynnn, a family name and a personal or family name.

Lyon, *Laighean,* Leinstermen.

Lyon, *Liama,* not given.

Lyons, *Ó-Liatháin, Uí-Liatháin,* O'Lehane, a family name.

Lyr, *ladhair, ladhar,* a (river) branch or fork.

Lyra, *ladhair/ladhar-an/a'...,* fork of the...

Lyra, *ladhar-ruadh,* red fork.

Lyra, *ladhra,* river fork/s.

Lyra, *laidhre,* not given.

Lyradane, *ladhair-fheadán,* not given.

Lyradane, *ladhardáin,* little fork.

Lyradaun, *ladhardáin,* little fork.

Lyragh, *ladharach,* a river branch or a place of branching streams

Lyragh, *ladhrach,* forked.

Lyran, *ladhar-an...,* fork of the...

Lyrane, from *ladhar,* little (river) branch or fork.

Lyraneag, *ladhar-an-fhiadhaig,* river fork of the deer.

Lyranes, from *ladhar,* little (river) branches or forks.

Lyrath, *rath-an-Lígh,* not given.

Lyrath, *ráth-an-lighe,* rath of the grave.

Lyrath, *ráth-Léigh,* Leye's (a personal or family name) rath.

Lyrattin, *ladhar-aitinn,* river fork of the furze.

Lyre, *ladhair, ladhar,* a (river) branch or fork/forks or forked.

Lyre, *laidhre,* not given.

Lyre, *leadhb,* poor land.

Lyreen, from *ladhar,* little (river) branch or fork.

Lyren, *ladhar-an...,* fork of the...

Lyrena, *ladhair/ladhar-na/an...,* fork of the...

Lyroe, *ladhar-ruadh,* red fork.

Lyroge, *ladharóg,* little fork.

M

Ma, *má,* a plain or a field.

Ma, *magh, machaire, muigh,* a plain, a flat place.

Ma, *máighe,* not given.

Maam, *mhám, mám,* a mountain pass.

Maam (cross), *an-teach-dóite,* not given.

Maan, *meadhanach, meadhán, Meana,* not given.

Maan, *meadhon, meáin, meadhoin,* middle.

Maas, *más,* a hill or buttock.

Maas, *más,* a thigh.

Mabeen, *Maibin,* little Mab/Mabbina, a personal or family name.

Mabilla, *muighe-bile,* plain of the ancient tree.

Mabin, *Maibín,* not given.

Mabin, *Mhaibín,* Mabin, a personal or family name.

Mac, *magh, machaire, muigh,* a plain, a flat place.

Mac, *mic, mac, Mac, Mic, Mhic, Mhac,* son of….

Macabea, *Macabeach,* the Macabees.

Macabea, *Mochaoi-bheo,* Mochaboeus or Macabee, the name of the founder of Kilmacabea Church in Cork.

Macaberry, *Mhac-Cairbre,* son of Carbre (a personal or family name).

Macachapple, *MacCopple,* a family name.

Macacullen, *MacCullen,* a family name.

Macadam, *Mhic-Ádaim,* not given.

Macadam, *Mhic-Adam,* son of Adam, a male name.

Macaderrig, *Mac-an-deirg,* son of redness.

Macadoyle, *Mhic-an-Daill,* not given.

Macady, *Mhic-Éadaigh,* not given.

Macaffrey, *Mhic-Gafraidh,* not given.

Macaffry, *Mhic-Gofraidh,* Mac Gofraidh, a personal or family name.

Macahill, *Mac-Cathail,* O'Cahill(sic), a family name.

Macahill, *Mhic-Cathail,* not given.

Macahill, *Mhic-Chathail,* Mac Cahill, a personal or family name.

Macahilly, *Mhic-Eachmhildiagh,* MacCaughley, a personal or family name.

Macaladdery, MacGladdery, a family name.

Macaladdery, *Mhic-an-Leadra,* not given.

Macallion, *Mhac-Ailín, Mhacailín,* McAllion, a family name. It means the son of Allion.

Macan, *Mhic-Anfa,* not given.

Macan, *MacCanna,* MacCann, a personal or family name.

Macanab, *Mic-an-Abba,* MacNab, a family name.

Macandrick, *Mac-Onraic,* not given.

Macane, *Mhic-Céin,* not given.

Macanearla, *Mhic-an-Iarla,* son of the earl.

Macannon, *Mhic-Chanainn,* Mac Cannon a family name.

Macanoge, *Mocheanóg,* St. Mochonog, St. Mochonog.

Macanogue, *Mocheanóg,* St. Mochonóg.

Macantire, *Mic-an-tSaoir,* MacIntyre, a family name.

Macantrim, *magh-ceann-truimm,* plain of the head of the elder bush or boor-tree.

Macar, *Mic-Cheara,* MacCarr, a family name.

Macar, *Mocheara,* not given.

Macarbery, son of Cairbre.

Macarbry, *Mhic/ Mhac-Cairbre,* Mac Carbre, a family name and means the son of Cairbre.

Macarbry, *Mhic-Aodha,* MacHugh, a family name.

Macarn, *Mac-Carnaig,* McCarney. A personal or family name.

Macarret, *Mhic-Ghearáid, Mhic-Gearóid, Mic-Gearoid,* Mac Gearóid or MacGarret, a family name and means the son of Carrett or Carret.

Macart, *Mac/ Mhic/ Mhac/ Mic-Airt,* Mac Art, a family name and means Art's (a personal name) son.

Macarty, *Mhic-Cárthaigh, Mic-Carthaigh,* not given.

Macash, *Mic-Cais,* MacCash, a family name.

Macashel, *Uí-Mhaolchaisil,* Ó Maolchaisil, a family name.

Macashen, *Mhic-Chaisín,* not given.

Macask, *Mocháisc, Maol-Chaisc,* not given.

Macask, *Mhaolchaisc,* Mac Cask, a family name.

Macat, *Mhic-Ceit,* Mac Ceit, a personal or family name.

Macatall, *Mac-a -táil,* Macatall, a family name and means 'son of the adze'.

Macateer, *mhic-an-tSaoir,* not given.

Macatreer, *Mic-a -trír,* son of the three persons.

Macaula, *Mac-Aula,* Mac Auley, a family name.

Macauliffe, *Mac-Amhlaoibh,* not given.

Macaun, *Macáin,* not given.

Macave, *Mhic-Ádhaimh,* Mac Ádhaimh, a personal or family name.

Macavoy, *Mhic-Cúmhaí,* not given.

Macaw, *Mac-Ádhaimh,* not given.

Macaw, *mhic-Dháibhró,* MacDavid, a personal or family name.

Macaw, *Mhic-Dháith/Dhaith,* Mac Dáith, a family name.

Macaward, *Mhic/ Mic-an-Bhaird,* Macaward, MacWard, a family name and means 'son/s of the Bard'.

Macbreed, Mac Bride, a family name.

Macbrennan, *Mac-Breanáin, Mic-Bhrannain,* MacBrennan, a family name.

Macbride, *Mhic-Bhride,* Mac Bride, a personal or family name.

Macbride, *Mhic-Giolla-Bhríde,* not given.

Macbrien, *Mhic-Bhriain,* not given.

Macclanchy(sic)**,** *Mac-Fhlancaidhe,* MacClancy, a personal or family name.

Maccomb, *Mochuma,* not given.

Maccurragh, *mag-corrach,* uneven plain.

Maccurragh, *muc-churrach,* pig moor.

Macdoe, *madadh,* dogs.

Macdonagh, *Mhic-Dhonnchú,* Mac Donnchú, a personal or family name.

Macdonnell, *Mac-Domhnall,* Mac-Donnell, a family name.

Macduagh, *Mhic-Duach,* Mac Duach/ Duach, Duach's (a male name and 8th

in descent from Dathi, King of Ireland before the time of St Patrick) son. The name means 'son of Duach'.

Macduagh, *Mhic-Duach,* the son of Duach also know as St Colmán.

Macduan, *Mac-Duan,* the nmame of a County Clare saint.

Macduane, *mhec-Dubhain,* son of Dubhan.

Macduff, *muc-dubh,* black pigs.

Macduff, *muice-duibhe, Mac-Duibh,* not given.

Macdugh, *Mhic-Dhuach,* Mac Duach, a personal or family name.

Mace, *más,* a thick hill, a long low hill, a thigh or a buttock.

Mace, *mháis,* a hill.

Mace, *mhása,* not given.

Macecrump, *Mhása*(sic), *an-Más*(sic), not given.

Macedmond, *Mhic-Éamainn,* not given.

Macedmond, *Mac-Eamoinn,* Mac Edmond, a personal or family name.

Macedmund, *Mhic-Éamainn,* not given.

Macegan, *Mhic-Aogáin,* not given.

Macegan, *Mhic-Thadhgair,* MacKeegan, a family name.

Macegan, *Mic-Aodhagain, Mac-Aidhagain,* MacEgan or McEgan, a family name.

Macelligot, *Mac-Uileagáid,* not given.

Macelligott, *Mhic-Eileagóid,* Mac Eileagód, a family name.

Macfadden, *'ic-Phaidin,* not given.

Macfelim, *Mac-Féilim,* Mac-Felim, a personal or family name.

Macfinn, *magh-Mhac-Fhinn,* not given.

Macforban, *Mhic-Fhearbháin,* not given.

Macgillycuddy' Reeks, *na-gCruach-dubh/ crucha-dubha,* not given.

Macha, *Mhacha,* Macha, the name of a legendary Queen and Goddess, see **Armagh.**

Machenry, *Mhic-Anraic,* not given.

Machenry, *Mac-Enrí,* Mac Henry, a family name.

Macher, *machaire,* a plain or field.

Machin, *meacan,* root vegetables.

Machro, *machaire,* a plain.

Machro, *machaire,* a plain.

Machugh, MacHugh, Macay or Hewson, family names.

Machugh, *Mhic-Aodha,* MacAodha or MacHugh, a family name and means the son of Hugh.

Macilcurr, *Mic-Giollchuir,* Macgilcor, a family name.

Macilhoyle, *Mic-Giolla-Chomhghaill/ Chomhgk-*(sic)*aill,* Macklehoyle, a family name.

Macilroy, *Mic-Giollaruaidh,* Mackleroy or Gilleroy, a family name.

Maciniff, *meacain-dhuibh,* the plant 'comfrey'.

Maciniff, *Mhic-Chonduibh,* McNiff, a family name.

Macjames, *Mhic-Sheamais,* not given.

Mack, *Mac,* sons.

Macka, *meacan,* not given.

Mackagh, *mBacach,* beggars or cripples.

Mackalin, *Mhic-Giolla-Eoin,* not given.

Mackan, *meacanaidhe, meacan,* a place of or abounding in parsnips or other tap rooted plants.

Mackanagh, *meacanach,* a place of wild carrots, parsnips or other tap rooted plants.

Mackane, *Mhic-Céin,* not given.

Mackanee, *meacanaí,* not given.

Mackanee, *meacanaidhe,* a place of or abounding in parsnips or other tap rooted plants.

Mackaney, *meacanach,* a place of wild carrots, parsnips or other tap rooted plants.

Mackaquim, *Mhic-an-chaim,* son of the crooked fellow.

Mackatall, *Mac-an-Táil,* not given.

Mackateer, *Mac-Tíre,* the wolf.

Mackaun, *mBacán,* stakes.

Mackea, *Mac/ Mic-Aodha,* Mac Aodha or Mackay, a family name.

Mackea, *Mac-Áodh,* Mac Aodh/Hugh, a personal or family name.

Mackeamore, *Mhic-Aodha-Mór,* not given.

Mackean, *Mhac-Chéin,* not given.

Mackean, *Mhic-Chathain,* Mac Keane, a family name.

Macken, *mágh-Ceitne,* not given.

Macken, *Maicín,* not given.

Macken, *meacan,* parsnips.

Mackeogh, *Mhic-Ceoch,* not given.

Mackeown, Mac Keown, a family name.

Mackerrilla, *Mac-Irghiala,* son of Irial O'Connor, (Co Clare).

Mackerrin, *Mhic-Iarainn,* not given.

Mackesy, *Uí-Macasaigh,* O'Mackesy, a family name.

Mackesy, *Uí-Mhacasa,* Ó Macasa or Mackessy, a family name.

Mackey, *Mhic/ Mic-Aodha, Mhacaí,* Mackey, Mackay, a family name.

Mackey, *Uí-Mhacaí,* Ó Macaí, a family name.

Mackgillagill, *Mhic-Giolla-Ghil,* not given.

Mackilduff, *Mic-Giolladuibh,* Mackilduff or Kilduff, a family name.

Mackillagill, *Mic-Giollagil,* MacGillagil, a family name.

Mackilmartin, *Mhic-Giolla-Mhártain,* not given.

Mackilmurry, *Mic-Giolla-Mhuire,* Macklemurry, Gilmore or MacGilmore, a family name.

Mackilowney, Mackilowney or Mackledowney, a family name.

Mackilreiny, *Mic-Giolla-ráighne,* Macklereany, a family name.

Mackilroy, *Mac/ Mic-Giollaruaidh,* Mackleroy or Gilleroy, a family name.

Mackilroy, *Mhic-Giolla-Rua,* not given.

Mackin, *meacán,* wild parsnips.

Mackina, *meacanaigh, meacanaí,* not given.

Mackinroe, *Mic-Conruaidhe,* MacConrua or Mackinroe, a family name.

Mackirilla, *Mic-Iriala,* MacIrilly, a family name.

Mackmaine, *magh-Maein,* Maen's (a personal or family name) plain.

Mackmanus, *Mhic-Maghnusa,* not given.

Mackmine, *magh-Maein,* Maen's (a personal or family name) plain.

Macknagh, *meacanaidhe, meacan,* a place of or abounding in, parsnips.

Macknan, *meacnaon, meacan,* a place of or abounding in parsnips or other tap rooted plants.

Macknee, *Mac-Naoi,* the sons of Naoi, a family or personal name.

Mackney, *Macnaí, meacanaigh,* not given.

Mackney, *meacanaidhe, meacan,* a place of or abounding in parsnips.

Mackon, MacConn, a family name.

Mackowen, *Mhic-Eoghain,* Mac Owen, a family name.

Macky, *Mic-Aodha,* Mackay, a family name.

Maclancy, *Mic-Fhlancaidhe,* Mac Clancy, a family name.

Maclane, *Mac/ Mhic-Calláin,* Mac Callán, a personal or family name.

Maclane, *Mac-Leighin,* the scholar(sic).

Maclare, *Mhocléir,* Mockler, a family name.

Maclaughna, *Mic-Lachtna,* MacLachtna, a family name.

Maclaughny, *Mac-Lachtna,* not given.

Maclea, *mhaí-Cliara,* not given.

Macleague, *Mhic-Liaig,* MacLiag, a personal or family name.

Macleague, *Mac-Liag,* St Mac Liag.

Macleane, *Mac-Lean,* a personal or family name.

Maclenine, *Mhic-Leinín,* MacLenine, also known as St Colman of Cloyne.

Maclin, *Mhic-Fhloinn,* not given.

Maclinan, *Mac-Linán,* Mac Linnane, a personal or family name.

Maclode, *Mhic-Leód,* McLeod, a personal or family name.

Maclode, *Mhic-Leoid,* not given.

Maclone, MacClone or Maglone, a family name.

Macloneigh, *mag-cluaineich,* not given.

Macloon, *Mac-Clún,* Mac Clune, a personal or family name.

Macloonagh, *na-cluanach,* of the lawn or meadow.

Macmague, *Mhic-Maodhóig,* McMaigue, a personal or family name.

Macmague, *Mhic-Mhág,* not given.

Macmanus, Mac Manus, a family name.

Macmara, MacMara, a family name.

Macmine, *magh-Maein,* not given.

Macmoe, *Mic-Mogha,* Mac Mow, a family name.

Macmow, *Mhic-Mhó,* not given.

Macmurragh, *Mhic-Mhurchú,* not given.

Macnadile, the nickname 'son of the idol'.

Macnaghtan, *Mac-Neachtain,* not given.

Macnaghten, *Mhic-Nactain,* Mac Naghten, a personal or family name.

Macnahanny, *meacnach-eanigh,* not given.

Macnally, *Mhic-an-Fhailígh,* not given.

Macnamara, Macnamara, a personal of family name.

Macnamee, *Mic-Conmidhe,* MacConmee, MacConway or MacNamee, a family name.

Macnass, *Mac-Neasa,* the sons of Neasa, a personal or family name.

Macnean, *Mac-nÉan,* Mac Nean, a personal or family name.

Macnee, *mac-nAedha,* sons of Aedha.

Macneil, *Mhic-Néill,* not given.

Macnevin, *Mac-Neabhain,* son of O'Nevan, a family name.

Macnevin, *Mhic-Nemhín,* Mac Nevin, a personal or family name.

Macney, *machnaidhe,* not given.

Macnicholas, *'ic-Niocláis,* MacNicholas, a personal or family name.

Macnoise, *maccu–Nois,* the sons of Nos/ Noas.

Macnoise, *Mhic/Mac-Nóis,* not given.

Macnoise, *Mic-Nois,* descendants(sic) of Noas.

Macnoran, *macn-Odhrain,* sons of Oran, a male name.

Macnowen, *Mac/ Mic-nEoghain,* clan or descendants of the son of Eoghain O'Kelly, (Galway).

Macnowen, *macn-nEoghan,* sons of Eoghan, Owen, a male name.

Macoda, *Mhac-Óda,* Mac Códa or MacÓda, a family name and means the son of Óda or Oda.

Macoda, *Mhacóda,* not given.

Macoda, *Mic-Giolla-Mhochuda,* MacGillacuddy, a family name. It means the son of of the servant of St Mochuda or Carrthach of Lismore.

Macody, *Mhic-Óda,* not given.

Macoe, *Mochua,* St Mochua.

Macogue, *Macuag,* a male name.

Macogue, *Mochuóg, muchóige,* not given.

Macogue, *muc-óg,* young pigs.

Macoliver, *Mhic-Oiliféara,* not given.

Macoliver, *Mhic-Oiliféir,* Mac Oliver, a personal or family name and the name of a Church founder in Kilkenny.

Macoll, *Mic-Cholla,* MacColla or MacColl, a family name.

Macomb, *Mochumb, Mochoma,* St Mochuma.

Macombe, St Maconna/Machoma.

Macomma, *Mochuma, Mochoma,* St Mocomma.

Macomoge, *mo-Cholm-og,* Colman, the name of a 7th century Abbot.

Macomoge, *mo-Choman,* St Coman.

Maconaghy, *Mic-Dhonchadha,* MacDonaghy or MacDonogh, a family name.

Maconna, *Mac-Conadh,* O'Conna(sic), a family name.

Maconnell, *Mac/ Mhic-Conaill,* Mac Conaill, a personal or family name.

Maconnell, *Mac-Chonaill,* not given.

Maconnelly, *Mhic-Conaile,* Mac Conaile, a family name.

Maconnelly, *Mhic-Dhonghaile,* not given.

Maconor, *Mhic-Conchúir,* not given.

Maconvy, *meacan-bhui,* wild carrot(sic).

Maconway, *meacan-bhui,* wild carrot(sic).

Maconway, *Mhic-Chonmhaighe, Mac-Conway,* McConway, a family name.

Macoo, *Mac-Eochadha,* Mac Gough, a family name.

Macoo, *mic-con,*(sic) MacConn, a family name.

Macoo, *Mochua,* St Mochua.

Macooda, *Mac-Cúdagh,* O'Cooda(sic) a family name.

Macoog, *Mhic-Cúg,* MacHugo or MacHugh, a family name.

Macoog, *Mho-Cúga,* St Mho-Cúga.

Macool, *Mac-Cumhaill,* not given.

Macool, *magh-cuil,* recessed plain.

Macoolaghan, *Mic-Uallacháin/Uallachain,* MacCuolahan or Cuolahan, a family name.

Macooleen, *magh-cuilin,* plain of the little corner or field.

Macoom, *Mochoma,* St Mocomma.

Macormick, *Mhic-Chormaic,* Mac Cormack, a family name.

Macorra, Mac Corra, a family name.

Macosker, *Mac-Coscair,* not given.

Macosquin, *magh-Coscain/Cosgrain, maigh Choscáin, má-Choscain,* Coscán's (a personal or family name) plain.

Macotter, MacCotter, a family name.

Macough, *mhic-Dhuach,* a personal or family name.

Macow, *Mhic-Bhúith,* Mac Búith, a personal or family name and the founder of a Church in Kilkenny.

Macow, *Mochua, Mhachua,* Machua, a personal or a family name, and also the name of a Saint.

Macow, *Mochua,* St Mochua.

Macowen, *Mhic-Eoin,* Mac Keown, a family name.

Macowney, *Mhic-Uaithne,* Mac Uaithne, a personal or family name.

Macpatrick, *Mhic-Padraig,* son of Patrick.

Macphadin, *Mhic-Pháidín,* not given.

Macquiggan, *Mac-Cuigín,* Mac Quiggin, a family name.

Macquin, *Mhic-Chuinn,* MacConn, a family name.

Macrade, MacRade, a family name.

Macrah, *Mac-Craith,* Magrath or Magraiden, a family name.

Macraheen, *Mac-Criothain,* Mac Crahane or Mac Crohan, family names.

Macrandal, *Mhic-Raghnaill,* MacRandell, a personal or family name.

Macravan, *Mac-Rabháin,* Mac Ravan, a family name.

Macrea, *mácraidh,* cattle distemper/disease.

Macrea, *Mochridhe,* St Mochridhe.

Macreary, *magh-criathrach,* plain abounding in pits.

Macreary, *maigh-créithre, magh-creichin,* not given.

Macredmond, *Mhic-Reamoinn,* Mac Redmond, a family name.

Macredmond, *Mhic-Reamon,* Redmond, a personal or family name.

Macreehy, *Mhic-Creithe,* sons of Creithe, a personal name.

Macreelly, *Mic-Cruadhlaoich,* Mac Crilly, a family name.

Macreese, *Mhic-Rís,* not given.

Macreeve, *Mic-Riabhaigh,* MacCreevy, a family name.

Macrelly, *Mic-Cruadhlaoich,* Mac Crilly, a family name.

Macrenan, *Macn-Eain, Mac-nEnain, Mhic-Réanáin,* sons of Énáin, a family name and the founder of a Church in Donegal.

Macrenan, *mac-nEnain,* sons of Enan.

Macrenan, sons of Neanan.

Macrerk, *Mhic-Oirc,* not given.

Macrevan, *Mac-Creabhan,* MacCrevan, a personal or family name.

Macrih, *machraidh,* distemper.

Macrilly, *Mic-Cruadhlaoich,* Mac Crilly, a family name.

Macrin, *maighe-crainn,* not given.

Macroan, *mac-nEoghain,* sons of Eoghain, a male name.

Macrogan, *Mac-Rogain,* Mac-Rogan, a personal or family name.

Macrone, *mac-nEoghain,* sons of Eoghain, a male name.

Macroney, *móin-Muicrinne,* not given.

Macroom, *magh-cromhtha/chromtha/cromtha,* the sloping, inclining plain or plain of the crooked fork.

Macroom, *maigh-Chromtha,* the crooked plain.

Macrory, *Mhic-Ruaidhrí,* not given.

Macrory, *Mhic-Ruairí,* Mac Ruairí, a personal or family name.

Macross, *mhachaire/machaire-rois, machaire-ruis,* the plain of Ross or the plain of Magheross. Magheross are the districts called the 'Rosses' or woods.

Macross, *mhachaire-rois,* grove of the plain.

Macrossan, McCrossan, a family name.

Macrossan, *Mhic-Crosain,* not given.

Macrowley, *Mhic-Chruadh-Laoich,* MacCrowley, a family name.

Macrown, *Mhic-Eireamhon,* Irwin, a male name.

Macrusheen, *Mac-Roisin,* Mac Rusheen, a personal or family name.

Macsaint, *muighe-samh,* plain of sorrel.

Macscanlan, *Mhic-Scannláin,* son of Scanlon, a personal or family name.

Macshane, *Mhic-Sheáin,* Mac Shawn, a personal or family name.

Macshaneboy, *Mac-Seáin-Buidhe, Mhic-Sheáin-bhuí,* son of yellow John.

Macsheedy, *Mac-Sioda,* Mac-Sheedy, a personal or family name.

Macsherron, *Mhic-Shéathrúin,* not given.

Macsherron, son of Jeoffrey.

Macsherry, *an-Tseafraidh,* Mac Sherry, a family name.

Macsherry, *Mhic-Sheafraidh/Shéafraidh,* MacSherry, a family name and means the son of Jeoffrey.

Macshoneen, *Mac-Sheoinín,* Jennings, a family name.

Macshoneen, *mac-Shoneen,* Jennings, a personal or family name.

Macsimon, *Mhic-Shimeoin-Pleimeann,* Mac Simon Fleming, a family name (West Cork).

Macsradeen, *Mic-Shráidín/Sráidín,* Mac Sráidín, a personal or family name.

Macstay, MacStay, a family name.

Mactalway, *Mic-tSealbhaigh,* Mactalway, the name of the founder of Kilmactalway Church in Dublin.

Macteera, *mac-tire,* correct translation is son of the country but it is used to denote a wolf.

Macteige, *Mac-Tadhg, /Mhic-Thaidhg,* Mac Teige, a family name.

Macthomas, little Thomas(sic).

Macthomas, *Mhic-Thomáis,* Mac Thomáis, a personal or family name.

Macthomas, *Mhic-Thomáisín, ic-Thomaisín,* Mac Thomáisín, MacThomas, a family name and means the sons of little Thomas.

Mactigue, *Mac-Tigue,* son of Tighe or Tadhg (a mans name).

Mactranny, *Mhic-Treana,* Mac Trean/Treana, a personal or family name and the founder of a Church in Sligo.

Mactrasna, *Mhic-Thransa,* not given.

Macuagh, *Mhic-Dhuach,* St Colman MacDuagh.

Macuddy, *Mhic-Cuidithigh,* not given.

Macuddy, *Mochuda,* St Mochuda or Carrthach of Lismore.

Macue, *Mhic-Aodha, Mic-Aoda,* MacHugh a family name.

Macue, *Mhic-Aoidh/Aodha,* not given.

Maculick, *Mic-Uilic,* MacUlick, a family name, and Ulick is a personal name.

Macullen, Mac Cullen, a family name.

Macullig, *Mhic-Uilic,* Mac Uilick, a family name.

Macullig, *Mhic-Uileag,* not given.

Macully, *Mic-Cholla,* MacColla or MacColl, a family name.

Macun, *Mac-Con-Cu,* not given.

Macurkey, *muighe-coirce,* not given.

Macurly, *Mhic-Thoirdealbhaigh/ Thoirdhealaigh,* Mac Thoirdhealaigh, a family name.

Macurly, *Mhic-Thorlaigh,* not given.

Macurtain, *Mac-Curtáin,* O'Curtin(sic), a personal or family name.

Macus, *Macus,* Macus, a personal or family name.

Macushin, MacCushin, a family name.

Macward, *Mhic-an-Bháird, Mic/ Mhic-an-Bhaird,* Mac an-Bhard or son of the bard or poet.

Macward, *mic-an-bhaird,* son of the bard.

Macwilliam, *Mhic/Mac-Liam,* not given.

Macwilliam, *Mhic-Uilliam,* MacWilliam, a family name.

Mada, *maide,* wood.

Madadoo, *mada/madra-dubh,* the black dog.

Madame, *magh-damh,* plain of oxen.

Madane, *Uí-Mhadáin, Mhadáin,* Ó Madaín or Madden, a family name.

Madara, *magh-darach/dara,* oak plain.

Madavagh, *maigh-Dabhcha,* not given.

Madda, *madadh,* dogs.

Madda, *maide,* wood.

Maddadoo, *mullach-chu,* summit of the hound.

Maddagh, *mbodach,* churls.

Maddaroe, *mhadaigh-ruaidh,* the red dog or fox.

Madden, *Mhadáin, magh-Dreana,* not given.

Madden, *Uí-Mhadáin,* O'Madden or Madden, a family name.

Madder, *mether, meadar,* a drinking vessel.

Madderee, *madraidhe,* dogs.

Maddock, *Madóg, Madog,* Maddock, a personal or family name.

Maddoo, *madadh, madradh,* dogs.

Maddox, *Mhadóg,* not given.

Maddra, *madadh, madradh,* dogs.

Maddree, *madadh, madraí, madrai, madradh,* dogs.

Maddree, *mBodairi,* churls or landlords.

Maddree, *meidri,* churns.

Maddry, *madhraidhe,* dogs.

Maddy, *madadh,* curs.

Maddy, *madra, madadh, madradh,* dogs.

Maddy, *maide,* stick/s.

Maddyroe, *madadh-ruadh,* a fox or red dog.

Mademoge, *Modhíomóg,* St Modiomog.

Mademoge, *Mo-Dhíomóg,* Modíom(sic) the younger, the name of a Church founder in Kilmademoge parish.

Maderie, *madrai,* dogs.

Maderie, *mBodairi,* churls or landlords.

Maderie, *meidri,* churns.

Madigan, *Madagáin,* not given.

Mado, *madadh,* dogs.

Madog, *Madog,* Maddock, a personal or family name.

Madog, *Mhadóg,* Madóg, a personal or family name from a Welshman named Rhys Madoc.

Madore, Dore's (a personal or family name) plain.

Madown, *Mhic-Dhubháin,* not given.

Madra, *mhadra,* not given.

Madranna, *mag-Dreana,* not given.

Madree, *madraí,* dogs or foxes.

Madrum, *maí/muighe-droma,* plain of the hill-ridge.

Madum, *Modhoma,* not given.

Madum, *Mho-Dhíom,* Modhiom, the name of a Church founder in Kilmadum parish.

Madun, *Macdun, Mac-Dun,* Macdun, a personal or family name.

Mael, *maol,* bare.

Maelra, *maolráth,* not given.

Magaghran, MacGaughran, a family name.

Magaha, *maigh-Gheithe,* not given.

Magan, *Mhag-Cana,* not given.

Magan, *Mhic-Cionaoith,* Mac Cionaoith, a family name.

Maganey, *Maigh-Géine,* not given.

Maganlis, *Mic-Ainleis,* Maganless, a personal or family name.

Maganny, *Mogeanna,* not given.

Maganshin, *Magaintín,* a personal or family name.

Magar, *Mogharaidh,* not given.

Magaraghan, *Mhic-Garachain,* not given.

Magarry, *mo-gharraí,* my garden.

Magarry, the enclosed garden.

Magart, Mac Art, a family name.

Magauran, *Mic-Shamradháin/ Shamhradhain,* Macauran or MacGouran, a family name.

Magee, *Mag-Aoidh / Aodha, Mhic–Aodha, Mac–Aedhas,* Magee, a personal name and a family name and means the son of Hugh or Aodh.

Mageney, *magh-Aebhna,* not given.

Mageragh, *Mhic-Fhiachrach,* not given.

Maggan, *mBogán,* soft ground.

Maggan, *mBogán,* soft men(sic).

Magh, *magh, mach, machaire, muigh,* a plain, a flat place.

Magh, *mBeach,* not given.

Magha, *macha,* a lawn or milking field.

Maghan, *macha-ʹn...,* field of the...

Maghan, milking place of the...

Maghan, *Uí-Miodchain,* O'Meehan, a family name.

Maghana, *macha-na...,* lawn or milking field of the...

Maghar, *machaire,* a plain or field.

Magharee, *na-machairí,* not given.

Magharees, *machairidhe,* plains or flat islands.

Maghaura, *...a'-chairrthe, ...*of the pillarstone.

Magher, a family name.

Magher, *Ui-Mheachair / Mheacháir,* not given.

Maghera, *machaire,* a field.

Maghera, *machaire, machaira,* a plain.

Maghera, *machaire-an / a'...,* plain of the ...

Maghera, *machaire-rátha / ratha,* plain of the fort or plain of the ring forts.

Maghera, *Machaire-Riabhach,* streaked plain.

Magherafelt, *machaire-fiogaidh,* the rushy plain.

Magherafelt, *machaire-theach-Fíolta / Fíolta,* the plain of Fioghalta, Fíolta's (a personal name) house.

Magheralin, *machaire-lainne,* plain of the Church.

Magherally, *machaire-Uladh,* not given.

Magheramayo, *Machaire-muighe-eo,* plain of the small plain of yew.

Magheramorne, *machaire-Dhamoerna,* not given.

Magheran, *machaire-an...,* plain of the...

Magherana, *machaire-ʹn-atha,* plain of the ford.

Magherana, *machaire-an / na...,* plain of the....

Magherareagh, *an-machaire-riabhach,* streaked plain.

Magheree, *machairí,* plains.

Maghereen, *machairin,* a little plain.

Magherin, *machaire-ʹn...,* plain of the...

Magherin, *machairin,* a little plain.

Magherna, *machaire-na...,* plain of the...

Magheross, *machaire-rois,* plain of Magheross. Magheross are the districts called the 'Rosses' or woods.

Magherow, *machaire-Eabha,* not given.

Maghery, *an / na-machaire,* the plain or a level farm.

Maghery, *machaire,* plains or open fields.

Maghery, *machairidhe,* plains or level farms.

Maghery, *mhachaire,* a field, meadows or lawns.

Magho, *macha-eo,* milking field of the yew.

Maghon, *an-mheitheán,* not given.

Maghroe, *Murchadha-ruaidh,* not given.

Maghy, *macha,* not given.

Magibboge, *Moghobóg, Mogiobóig,* Mogibog, a personal or family name.

Magillagill, *Mhic-Ghiollagil,* Mac Giollagil, a family name.

Magilligan, *aird-Mhic-Giollagain, árd-Mhig / Mhic-Ghiollagáin,* MacGilligan's (a family name) height or point.

Magillycuddy's Reeks, *cnuacha-dubha-Mhic-Giolla-Mochuda,* not given.

Magin, *Mic-Fhinn,* Magin, a family name.

Maginaghy, *Mic-Fhionn-Chadha,* Maginaghy, a family name.

Maging, *Mic-Fhinn,* Magin, a family name.

Magirril, *Mic-Ireoil,* Mac Ireel or Magirril, a family name.

Maglaff, *Mágh-Laithbhe,* not given.

Maglaff, *Mic-Lamha,* Mac Glave, a family name.

Maglancy, *Mhic-Fhlannchaidh,* not given.

Maglancy, *Mic-Fhlannchadha,* MacClancy or Maglancy, a family name.

Maglane, *maingleann,* swampy.

Maglane, *Mhic-Ghiolla-Eáin, not* given.

Maglasderry, *Mhac-Laistre,* not given.

Maglava, *Mhic–Lamha,* MacGlave, a family name.

Maglave, *Mac-Glave*(sic), *Mic-Lamha,* Mac / Mc Glave, a family name.

Maglave, Maglave, a personal or family name.

Maglavy, *Mic-Lamha,* Mac Glave, a family name.

Maglen, *Mhic-Lionnáin,* Mac Lionnáin or Mac Lionnan, a family name and means the son of Lionnan or Lionnán.

Maglen, *Mhig/meg-Fhloinn,* Flanns (a male name) son.

Maglin, *meg-Fhlainn,* Maglin, a personal or family name.

Maglin, *maigh-ghlinne,* not given.

Magoney, *maigh-Gamhnaí,* not given.

Magonway, *Ó-gConnmhaigh*(sic), not given.

Magoo, *maí-ghubha,* not given.

Magoo, *magha-gabha,* valley of the smith.

Magorban, *magh-Gurbán/Gorbáin,* Corban's or Gorban's (a male name) plain.

Magorban, *maigh-gCorbáin,* Corbán's palin.

Magorman, *Magh-Orbán, Meg-Gormáin,* not given.

Magorry, *Mhic-Gofraidh,* Mac Gofraidh or MacGorry, a family name and means son of Gorry.

Magorry, *Mic-Gafraidh,* not given.

Magourney, *Mágh-Guairne,* not given.

Magourney, *magh-Uí-Dhoirinn,* O'Dorney, a family name.

Magowna, *magh-gamhnach,* field of the stripper cow.

Magowry, *magh-Góra,* Gora's (a male name) plain.

Magowry, *maigh-Gabhra,* not given.

Magran, *Mac-Granna,* not given.

Magrath, *Magraith,* Magrath, a personal or family name.

Magrath, *Mhic-Craith,* Magragh, a personal or family name.

Magreehan, *MacCriochain,* Magreehan, a family name.

Magrine, *Mic-Roidhin,* McGrine, Magrine or MacRoin, a family name.

Magroarty, *Mag-Robhartaigh,* not given.

Magrorty, *meg-Rabhartaich,* Magroarty, a family name.

Maguigan, *Mac-Guagáin,* not given.

Maguigan, *Mhic-Ghuigín, Mic-Guigín,* MacGuigan or MacQuiggan, a family name.

Maguiggan, *Mic-Guigin,* MacGuigan or MacQuiggan, a family name.

Maguire, *Mhic/ Mag-Uidhir,* Maguire, a family name. It means the son of the pale faced man.

Maguirk, *Mag-Uirc,* MacGuirk, a family name.

Magulleene, *maingleann,* swampy.

Magunihy, *Mag/magh-gCoinchinn,* O'Conkins plain.

Magunshin, *Mac-Uinseann,* not given.

Magy, *mágach,* the hare.

Mah, *Midhigh,* Meagh or Meade, a personal or family name.

Maha, *Macha,* not given.

Mahaan, *meathán,* oak slits (for sieves).

Mahan, *meathain, meathan,* oak slits for sieves or sieve slits.

Mahanagh, *Mág-Eanna/Sheanaigh,* not given.

Mahanagh, *meathanach,* a place of sieve slits.

Mahanagh, *meathanach,* abounding in twigs or saplings.

Mahane, *meathan, meathán,* oak slits (for sieves) or sieve slits.

Mahane, *meathan,* twigs or saplings.

Mahas, *máis,* a hollow.

Mahee, *inis-Mochaoi,* St. Mochaei/ Mochaoi.

Maher, *machaire,* a plain.

Maher, *Máthair,* Mother.

Maheraneig, *mathair-an-fhiag,* mother of the raven.

Mahoe, *Mochua,* St Machua.

Mahoge, *mhothóige,* not given.

Mahoge, *muchóige,* wild vetch.

Mahon, *(river) an-mhachain,* not given.

Mahon, *Machan,* Mahon, Machain, a river name, not given.

Mahon, *Mhathúna, Ó-mBádhamha, Mhachan, Machan, Mathghamhna,* not given.

Mahon, *Mathgamhna,* MacMahon, a family name.

Mahon, *meathan,* saplings.

Mahon, *Mhathghamhna, Mathghamhna,* Mahon, a family name.

Mahon, *Mochain,* Móchán, a personal or family name.

Mahon, *O'Mathghamhna,* O'Mahony, a family name.

Mahon, *Uí-Bhadhamha,* Mahon, the name of an ancient tribe also known by the name 'Ibane'.

Mahon, *Uí-Mhatháin/Matháin,* Ó Matháin, Ó'Matháin or O'Mahan, a family name and means the descendants of Mahon.

Mahonoge, *Mhathúna-óig,* not given.

Mahony, *Ua-Mathghamhna,* O'mahony, a family name.

Mahoonagh, *magh-tamhnaigh,* plain of the cultivated field.

Mahoonagh, *magh-thamhnach,* not given.

Mahoonagh, *maigh-thamhnach,* plain of clearings.

Maice, *Mhaelíora,* not given.

Maiden, *Maighdean, dá-mhailidhe,* not given.

Maiden, *Mhiadáin,* St Miadan.

Maigue, *an-mháigh,* not given.

Maigue, *mháig, maigh, magh,* a plain.

Main, *an-mhin,* the water.

Main, *maighin,* a plain.

Main, *meadhan, meadhon,* middle.

Main, *mein,* a cleft or opening.

Main, *Mheáin, mhaing, maein,* not given.

Main, *mín,* smooth.

Maina, *mainge,* a hillock or rounded peak.

Maine, *maighean-an-bradáin, mainge, meáin, mheáin, méin, mhaighne,* not given.

Maine, *Maighne,* Maon, a personal or family name.

Maine, *maighin,* a plain or the little plain.

Maine, *maoine,* riches or wealth.

Maine, *meadhoin, mheáin, meadhona, meadhun,* middle.

Maine, *mhaoidheachain,* boasting.

Maine, *Mhugháin,* Mughan, a personal or family name.

Mainham, *Mhaighneann, Maighnenn,* St Mainen, Maighne, a 17th century Bishop.

Maive, *Mheidhbhe,* Queen Maeve.

Major, *Mhéidsir,* not given.

Makaevoge, *Mhocaomhóg,* Mochaomhóg, the name of Kilmakaevoge Church.

Makane, MacKane, a family name.

Makaroge, *Maciaróg,* St Mociaróg.

Makate, *Mic-Ceit,* MacKeth, a family name.

Makay, *Mhic-Eathach,* not given.

Makeady, *Mhic/ Mac-Éide,* not given.

Makeady, *Mhic-Éadaigh,* Mac Éadaigh or Keady(sic), a family name and means the sons of Éadach.

Makeady, Son of Edach, a personal or family name.

Makee, *Mhic-Aoidh,* McHugh or Magee, a personal or family name.

Makee, *muicidhe,* a pig drover.

Makee, *Mhic-Shíthigh,* not given.

Makee, *Mic-Aodha,* Mackay, a family name.

Makee, St Mochaidhe.

Makeera, *Mhic-Íre,* Son of Íre, a personal or family name.

Makeeran, *Mochiarán,* not given.

Makeery, *Mac-Ciardha,* not given.

Makeery, *Mhic-Íre,* Mac Íre or Macíre, a personal or family name and means son of Ire.

Makeery, *Mhic-Thíre,* Mac Tire, a personal or family name.

Makeeve, *Mac-Ciomh,* Mc Keefe, a family name.

Makeeve, *Maí-Caoimh*(sic), not given.

Makeever, *mac-Iomhar,* Makeever, Mac Ivor, a family name.

Makeever, *Mhac-Íomhair,* not given.

Makelagher, MacCeileachair or MacKelleher, a family name.

Makellett, *Mhic-Eileoid,* not given.

Makellis, *Mhá' Ceillis,* MacEllis, a family name.

Makellis, *Mhic-Eilís,* not given.

Makeltar, Keltar's (persons name) son.

Makenna, *Mhic-Cionnaith,* not given.

Makenny, *Mhic-Cionnaith,* MacKenny, a family name.

Makenny, *Mhic-Éinigh/Cionaotha,* not given.

Makeon, *Mic-Eoghain,* Makeon, a family name.

Maker, *Mhic-Céir,* not given.

Makerrila, *Mic-Iriala,* MacIrilly, a family name.

Makevoge, *Mochaomhóg,* Mochaemhog, St Mochaemhog.

Makiff, *Mhic-Dhuibh,* not given.

Makill, *mhaí-coille,* not given.

Makilladuff, *Mhic-Giolla-Dhuibh,* not given.

Makilladuff, *Mic-Giolladuibh,* MacGilladoff, Kilduff or MacKilduff, a family name.

Makilloge, *Mochilleóg, Mochilleog,* St Mocheallog/Mochilleog/Mocheallóg.

Makilly, *'ic-Gilla,* Mac Hilduff a family name.

Makin, *Macáin,* not given.

Makin, *Mic-Finn,* Mackin, a family name.

Makina, *meachanach,* abounding in carrots.

Makinlan, *Mhic–Coindelbhain,* Mac Kinlan, a family name.

Makinna, *Mhic-Cionaith,* not given.

Mal, *Mal,* Mal a personal or family name.

Mal, *meall,* hillocks.

Malady, *Mhaoiléidigh,* not given.

Malady, *Uí-Maoiléidigh,* O'Meleady, Melody or Meleady, a family name.

Malahide, *Baile-atha-Thíd,* town of Teud, Theud's (a male name) ford.

Malahide, *mallach/mullach-Íde,* Íde, Ide's (a personal or family name) hilltop.

Malahide, *maol-a-hÍde, maol-aHíde, malahíde,* not given.

Malausa, *Molásaí,* not given.

Male, *maol,* derelict.

Male, *mhaol,* not given.

Malea, *Mailia,* not given.

Malea, *Mhailéith,* Malea, a personal or family name.

Malee, *maoilín,* not given.

Maleen, *Moilín,* Moling, a personal or family name.

Maleer, *Mhic-Laoighill,* not given.

Maleery, *Moleirc,* St Moleirc.

Maley, *Mháille, Mhaille,* Máille, a personal or family name and the founder of a Church in Clare (St Maille).

Maley, *Ua-Maillaidhe,* O'Malley, a family name.

Maliere, *Maelughra, Maolughra, Maoluidhir,* the male name (Maolughra) and the name of an ancient tribe.

Malin, *málainn, malainn,* small brow/brae or the hill brow.

Malin, *Mháilín,* Mailin, a male name.

Malin, *Moling, magh-déileann,* not given.

Maline, *Moiling,* St Moiling.

Maline, *Moling,* not given.

Maline, *Mo-Lua,* Mo-Lua, the name of a Church founder

Malis, *Málais, Máluis,* Malas, Malus, a personal or family name.

Malkedar, *Maoilchéadair, Maolchéadair, Maeilchetair,* St Maolchéadar/Mailkedar/ Maolcheadar.

Mall, *meall,* a knoll.

Mall, *meall,* hill/s.

Malla, *meala,* honey.

Malla, *mealla,* mounds.

Malla, *mhala, mala,* a hill brow.

Mallagh, *mallach,* not given.

Mallagh, *mallacht,* curses, cursing.

Mallaght, *mallacht,* curses, cursing.

Mallan, *Maoláin,* Mullan or Mallon, a personal or family name.

Mallard, *mallacht,* curses.

Mallard, *marclach,* horse loads.

Mallavoge, *mealbhóg,* a lump or hillock.

Mallen, *malainn,* a hill brow.

Mallin, *Mhálainn,* not given.

Mallina, *mullagh-na…,* hill of the…

Mallock, *Mocheallóg, Mocheallag,* St Mocheallog, Mocheallóg or Mohallog.

Malloe, *Maolmuadh,* Maolmuadh, the name of an ancient King of Munster.

Mallow, *mala,* a hill brow.

Mallow, *mala,* plain of the rock.

Mallow, *mala/mágh-Ealla, magh-Eala, magh-Ealla,* plain of the river Allo, Allow or Eallo.

Mallow, *mealadh, míl,* honey.

Mallusk, *Magh/má-bhloisce,* plain of the noise.

Mally, *malaidhe,* hill brows or braes.

Mallyna, *mullagh-na…,* hill of the…

Maloe, *Ó-Mhaolmhuaidh,* Molloy, a family name.

Maloge, *Malóig,* Mallock, a personal or family name.

Maloge, *Mológ,* not given.

Malogue, *Malóg,* St Malock.

Malogue, *Molaga,* not given.

Malone, *magh-leamha,* not given.

Malone, *magh-luan,* plain of the lambs.

Malone, *má-lón, ma-lon,* plain of elms.

Malone, *má-lón,* plain of meadows.

Malone, *Maollúin,* the mule or Malone, a family name.

Malonga, *Míolchon,* not given.

Maloo, *Molua,* a personal or family name.

Malooda, *Mo-Luada,* St Luada.

Maloon, *magh-luan,* plain of the lambs.

Malora, *Maoiluidhre,* Malire, a personal or family name.

Malora, *maighe-ladhar,* plain of the river confluences.

Malra, *malradh,* not given.

Malra, *mannragh,* stalls or mangers.

Malragh, *mallsrath,* not given.

Malragh, *malrach,* boys.

Malragh, *malrach,* horseloads.

Malug, *Molaga,* St Moluag or St Molaga.

Malug, *Moluga,* not given.

Malur, *Malar,* not given.

Malure, *Maolúra, Maoiliúra,* Maolúra, a personal or family name.

Malure, *Molura, Maoilughra,* a personal or family name.

Malure, the servant of Iura, a personal or family name.

Malvoge, *mealbhóg,* uneven land.

Mama, *madhma, maam,* a mountain pass.

Mama, *mama,* a pass, a mountain pass.

Mame, *madhma, maum,* a high pass.

Man, *mBan, m-ban,* a woman or women.

Man, *mBeann,* points.

Man, *Mochain,* not given.

Manach, *meana, manach,* monks, the same word is used for nuns.

Managh, *maghneach,* plain of horses.

Managh, *meadhonach, mheadhonach, mhead-ahn,* middle.

Managh, *meana, mhanach, manach, monach,* monks or friars.

Managh, *meánach, mheánach,* not given.

Managhan, *Mainchín, Manchain,* St. Mainchín/Manchan.

Managhan, *Mhainchín,* Munchin, a personal or family name.

Managhan, *Mhancháin,* not given.

Managher, *manachair,* monks.

Managher, *mBeannchoir, m-Beannchair,* a place of gables or pointed rocks.

Manaheen, *Mhainchín, Mainchín,* Manchin, Mainchin or Manaheen, founder of the Church of Kilmanaheen.

Manaheen, *Mhainchín, Mainchín,* St Mainchín, founder of the Church of Kilmanahan.

Manahin, *Mhainchín,* St Mainchin.

Manan, *meanáin,* kid goats.

Mananearla, *mac-an-Iarla,* son of the Earl.

Manaway, *mBeann-buidhe,* yellow pinnacles.

Manch, *ma/magh-inse,* plain of the river island/meadow.

Manch, *máinse, ma-inse,* river meadow plain.

Mandis, Manda, a personal or family name.

Mandra, *mannra,* mangers or stalls.

Mane, *meadhon,* bare.

Mane, *meadhon,* middle.

Maneen, Maneen or Manning, a family name.

Maneen, *Mhinín,* not given.

Maneen, *Mo-Fhinghin, Mainchín,* St Mainin.

Maneenaside, *moinín-na-soighead,* little bog of the arrows or darts.

Maneve, *mBannaomh,* saintesses or holy women.

Manfin, Finn's wives.

Mangan, *Mongán,* a personal or family name.

Mangan, *mongán,* an overgrown place of coarse grass, a thicket or place of coarse herbage.

Mangans, *mongan,* a marshy or sedgy place.

Mangeen, *muingín,* a swamp or a morass.

Manger, *mainnear,* an enclosure for cattle.

Manger, *mainnsér,* a manger.

Mangerton, *mangartach,* mountain of fawns.

Mangerton, *mhangarta, mangartach,* mountain covered with hair like grass.

Manicholas(sic)**,** *Mhic-Niocláis,* not given.

Maniheen, *Mainchin,* Mainchin, a personal or family name.

Manister, *mhainistir, mainister,* a monastery.

Mann, *mBeann,* angles or projections.

Mann, *meann,* not given.

Manna, *magh-Ana,* Anna's (a female name) plain.

Manna, *magh-neach,* plain of the horses.

Manna, *mana, meánach, mhanach,* not given.

Manna, *meana, manach,* monks.

Mannagh, *manach,* not given.

Mannagh, *monoch*(sic), monks.

Mannan, *Manannáin,* Mannan, a male name.

Mannan, *meanán,* kid goats.

Mannan, *Mhaine,* not given.

Mannave, *mBan-naoimh,* the female saints.

Manniff, *m-banbh, mBanbh, bainbh,* young pigs.

Mannin Bay, *cuan-Manainn,* not given.

Mannin, (loch) *loch-Manainn, loch-na-nAirneadh,* not given.

Mannin, (loch) *Manán,* a personal or family name.

Manning, *dún-Manainn,* not given.

Manning, *manaigh,* of the monk.

Mannock, *manach,* monks.

Mannoge, *mBánóg,* little green fields, lea fields.

Mannon, *meanán,* kid goats.

Mannon, *meannáin,* the pinnacle.

Mannon, *Mhananáin,* Mananán Mac Lir (a Tuatha de Danann magician).

Mannow, *mBanbh,* suckling pigs.

Manny, *Maine,* not given.

Manny, *manach, managh, manaigh,* monk/s.

Manoge, *mBánóg,* green fields or small green fields.

Manoge, *Munnóg,* not given.

Manor, *mainéar,* a manor.

Manragh, *mannrach,* mangers.

Manragh, *mBanrach,* enclosures.

Manragh, *mBanrach, manrach, mannrach,* mangers, enclosures or pounds.

Manroe, *mBan ruaidh, mBan-ruaidh,* the red (haired) woman.

Manry, *mannrach,* mangers.

Mansel, *Mainseal,* Maunsel, a male name.

Manserghshill, *cnoc-an-mahinséaraigh,* manger hill.

Manserghshill, *cnoc-an-mhainséaraigh,* not given.

Mansheefrog, *mBan-siadhbhrog,* the fairy women or the women of the fairy dwelling/mansions.

Mansher, *mainséar,* mangers.

Mantagh, *mhantach,* gapped.

Mantagh, *Mhantach, Mantaigh, Mantagh,* Mantagh, a male name and means toothless.

Mantan, *meantán,* snipes.

Mantua, *móinteach,* moorland.

Mantuar, *magh-an-tuair,* plain of the bleaching green.

Manucky, *magh-muice,* plain of pigs.

Manulla, *Magh-Nulla/Fhionnalbha/Fionndalbha,* Fionnalbha or Finalva's (a personal or family name) plain.

Manulla, *maigh-Nulla, magh-Fhiondalbha,* not given.

Manus, *mainis,* a spear.

Manus, *Manuis, Mánais, Maghnuis, Mánas, Manas, Manus* or Magnus, a male name.

Manus, *Mhánais, Mághnusa, Mághnuis,* not given.

Manus, *Mhánais, Mánas* or Manus, a male name.

Manus, *Mhánasa, Mánas,* a personal or family name.

Manway, *mbeann,* pinnacles.

Manway, *mbeann-mbui,* yellow turrets.

Manway, *ma-bui,* tallow plain(sic).

Manway, *abahainn-bui*(sic), yellow river.

Manway, *Mahon-bui,* yellow Mahon, a o personal or family name.

Manway, *Maonmhuighe, Mánmhaí, Mánmhai,* not given.

Manway, *meadhon-mhuighe,* middle plain.

Many, *Maine,* Maine or Mainy, a personal or family name.

Many, *mBáine,* Báine, a personal or family name.

Many, *manaigh, mhonaigh,* the monk.

Many, *manaigh,* monks,

Many, *meánach,* middle.

Maol, *maol,* bare, bald or the hornless cow/s.

Maon, *meadhon,* middle.

Maon, *Muain,* not given.

Maperath, *caisleán-na-Mábach,* not given.

Maquage, *Macuag,* Mac Cuag, a family name.

Maquage, *Mochuóg, mo-Chuaigh,* St Mocuac.

Maquin, *mac-Chuinn,* Conn's (a male name) sons.

Maquin, *Mhic-Coinn,* not given.

Mara, *mara,* the sea.

Mara, *marbh,* the dead.

Mara, *Meara, Mearagan, Mearagan,* the name of a Firbolg chief.

Mara, *Mhaire,* Mary, a womans name.

Marahill, *marbhchoill,* the dead wood.

Marbh, *marbh,* the dead.

Marcach, *marcach,* horsemen.

Marcahaun, *Marcacháin,* the horseman, rider or knight.

Mard, *mBárd, mBard,* bard/s or poets.

Mardyke, *mairdíog, an-mhairdíog,* not given.

Mare, *mara,* the sea.

Maree, *áth-cliath-meadhraighe,* not given.

Mareen, *maothairín,* a little grove or a woody swamp.

Mareen, *Moirín,* Moirín, not given.

Marega, *mharga,* a market.

Marg, *marga,* market.

Margy, *margadh,* a market.

Margy, *mBairche, mairge,* not given.

Marheen, *mothairín,* a little thicket or grove.

Marhin, *Márthain,* not given.

Maricat, *magheri-cath,* field of battle.

Marino, named after the Italian town of Marino. Irish names for this location is *dún-an-Óir,* fort of the gold and *rinn-an-dúna,* headland of the fort.

Mariscal, *mharascail,* a marshal.

Mark, *marc,* horses.

Mark, *mBarc,* barks, ships.

Markagh, *marcach,* horsemen.

Markahan, *Marcacháin,* the horseman rider or knight.

Markahan, *Ua-Marcachán,* O'Markahan, a family name.

Markey, *mairce,* a mark.

Markey, *marcaigh, mharcaigh,* the horseman.

Marklann, *marclann,* a stable.

Marklin, *marclann,* stables.

Marks, *Mharcais,* (belonging to) Mark, a personal or family name.

Marky, *marcaigh,* the horseman.

Marla, *márla,* marl clay.

Marla, *mharla,* not given.

Marlay, *baile-Bhearlaí,* not given.

Marley, *cnoc-dubh,* not given.

Marley, *márla,* rich clay.

Marll, *mhárla,* yellow clay.

Marlow, *poll-an-mharla/marla,* not given.

Marly, *mharla,* marl clay.

Marnagh, *mBáirneach,* limpets.

Marnell, *Mhairnéalaigh,* not given.

Marnock, *Mearnóg,* St Mernoc or St Eirnín, Earnan.

Maroon, *Mhaolruáin,* Maolruan, a personal or family name.

Marra, *marbhtha,* murder.

Marraff, *marbh,* the dead.

Marragh, shaped like a boat.

Marran, Marrin or Morrin, a personal or family name.

Marran, *Uí-Mhearáin, Murchain,* not given.

Marrane, *Mearain,* Maran, a personal or family name.

Marriff, *marbh,* dead bodies.

Marrig, *Meara,* Mearagan, Mearagan, the name of a Firbolg chief.

Marroge, Marroch, a family name.

Marroge, *mBarróg,* rods or alder trees.

Marroge, *mBarróg,* wickerwork.

Marshal, *Marshal,* a personal or family name.

Mart, *mart,* beeves, an ox, a bullock or a full grown cow.

Marta, *Mhártain, Mhartain, Mártain, Máirtín,* Martin, a male name.

Martara, *martra,* martyr/s.

Marteran, *martran,* relics.

Marteren, *martran,* relics.

Martery, *martra,* not given.

Martin, MacMartin or O'Martin, a family name.

Martin, *Mártan, Mártain, Máirtín, Mhártáin, Mháirtin, Mháirtín,* not given.

Martin, *martin, martán,* heifer/s.

Martin, *martran,* relics.

Martin, *Mháirtin, Mhairtín,* Martin, a male name.

Martin, *Mharitín*(sic), Máirtín, a personal or family name.

Martin, *Mhic-Giolla-Mhártain,* Mac Giolla Mhártain, a family name and means devotees of St Martin.

Martle, *Mhaineil,* Martel, a family name.

Martle, *Mhairtéal,* Mairteal, a family name.

Martle, *Moirtéalaigh,* not given.

Martola, *mairtfheola,* of the beef.

Martra, *martra,* martyr/s.

Martra, *martra,* relics.

Martray, *martra,* martyr/s.

Martry, *martra,* martyr/s.

Martry, *martrach,* not given.

Martry, *martraigh*, a place of killing or wounding.

Martyr, *martra*, relics, martyr/s or relics of martyrs.

Marv, *marbh*, the dead.

Marva, *marbh, mairbhe*, death, dead.

Marve, *marbh*, death, dead.

Marvila, *Mhúrmíle*, Murvil, a male name.

Mary, (loch) *loch-Laeghaire*, not given.

Mas, *más*, a long low hill.

Mas, *meas*, not given.

Mascanlan, *Mhic-Scanláin*, Mac Scanlán or MacScanlan, a family name meaning son of Scanlon or Scanlan.

Mase, *Masg*, Masc, the name of an ancient chief.

Mase, *Méise*, an altar slab.

Mase, *mías*, dishes.

Mashanaglass, *magh-seann-glaise*, not given.

Mashanaglass, *maigh/má-seanghlaise, magh-sen-eglaise*, plain of the old Church.

Mashoge, *Mosamhog*, St Mosamhog or St Mashoge.

Mask, *Mheasca, Measca*, not given.

Maskanlan, *Mhic-Scanláin*, son of Scanlán, a personal or family name.

Mason, *Máisean*, not given.

Mass, *más*, a hill.

Mass, *más*, a long low hill.

Mass, *measa*, fruit, nuts or nut-fruit.

Massa, hill of the…

Massareene, *Más-a'rioghna*, the Queens hill.

Massereene, *coill-Ultach*, Ulster wood.

Mast, *Maistean*, Maiste, a personal or family name.

Mast, *Maistean*, Maiste, not given.

Mast, *Maistean*, Maistiu, the name of a mythical maiden.

Master, *maistir*, churning.

Master, the master.

Mastra, *mostra*, the master of…

Mastulla, *Mhac-Stola*, not given.

Mastulla, *Mhá-Stollaé*, McStully, a family name.

Matehy, *magh-Mac-Teichthe*, plain of Teichthech's son.

Matehy, *magh-tuaith*, not given.

Matehy, *ma-teithe*, the smooth plain.

Mateige, *Mhic-Thaidhg*, not given.

Mather, *mether, meadar*, a drinking vessel.

Matigue, *Mac-Thaidhg*, Mac Teigue, the name of a founder of a Church in the parish of Knocktopher.

Matoskerty, *muige-tuaiscertaighe*, the north plain.

Matrix, *Bhun/Bun-Tráisce*, not given.

Matt, *Meata*, not given.

Mattle, (island) *oileán-an-Mhatail*, not given.

Mattock, (river) *an-Mhaiteóg/Mhaiteog*, not given.

Maudlin, *Maidilín*, not given.

Maugh, *macha*, a farm, a farmyard or a milking and feeding field for cattle.

Maugh, *magh*, a plain.

Maugha, *macha*, a field, a lawn, an enclosure, a farm, a farmyard or a milking and feeding field for cattle.

Maughan, farmyard of the…

Maughana, *macha-na…*, field of the…

Maul, *meall*, a lump, a mound, a knoll or a small round hill.

Maula, *meall*, a hillock.

Maula, *meall-a'…*, hillock of…

Maula, *meall-an/a'…*, knoll of the…

Maulan, *meall…*,(sic) hillock/hill of…

Maulane, *millín*, a little hill.

Maulee, *Málaí*, not given.

Maulee, *malaidhe*, bags.

Maulimile, *mealla-mille*, knolls of fuschia or honeysuckle.

Maulin, *málainn*, not given.

Maulin, *maoileann*, a bleak eminence.

Maulin, *maolghleann*, not given.

Maulna, *meall-na…*, knoll of the…

Maum, *madhm, maum*, an eruption, a chasm or a high mountain pass.

Maum, *maidhm*, erupted.

Maum, *mám*, a pass.

Mauma, *mám-an…*, not given.

Maumakeogh, *madhm-a'-ceo, mám-an-cheo*, pass of the mist.

Mauman, *mám-an…*, not given.

Maumeen, *maidhmín*, the little pass.

Maumeen, *máimín*, not given.

Maumeen, the little mountain pass.

Maumkeogh, *mám-an-cheóigh*, not given.

Maumna, *mám-na…*, pass of the…

Maun, *meadhoin*, middle.

Maun, *móin,* bog.

Maunagh, *mBánach,* green fields.

Maunagh, monks.

Maune, *meadhón, meadhon,* the middle or centre point.

Maunvough, *meadhon-mheacha,* middle of the hill.

Maurice, *Muirisc, Muiris,* not given.

Maurnach, *m-báirneach,* limpets.

Maurnagh, *m-bairneach, mBairneach,* limpets.

Maus, a bullock.

Maus, *más,* a long low hill or a thigh.

Mausna, *más-na* , thigh of the...

Mauteoge, *máiteog,* watery land.

Mautiagh, *máiteach,* watery land.

Mavy, *Méabha,* Maeve, a female name.

Maw, from *magh,* plains.

Maw, *magh, machaire, muigh,* a plain, a flat place.

Mawillin, *magh-mhuilinn,* plain of the mill.

May, *má, maighe, mágh, magh,* a plain.

May, *meith, fat or rich.*

Mayle, *Máil,* not given.

Mayle, *Máile,* Malley, a family name.

Mayle, *Maille,* Mailey or Malley, a personal or family name.

Mayne, *áth-Maighne,* not given.

Mayne, *maighín,* a field(sic).

Mayne, *maighin,* a little plain.

Mayne, *meadhun,* middle.

Mayne, *mhaighean, méin,* not given.

Maynooth, *maigh/má-Nuad, mágh/magh-Nuadhat, maigh-Nua,* Nua's, Nuadhat's or Nuadu Necht's, (a personal name) plain.

Mayo, *maigh-eo, magh-eó, maigh-eó* the plain of yews. The original full Irish name was *maigheó-na-Sacsan,* yew tree plain of the Saxons.

Mayo, *muigheó,* not given.

Mayogall, *magh-guail,* not given.

Mayogall, *má-ghuala,* plain of the shoulder.

Maze, *magh, má, an-má, an-ma,* the plain.

Mbraddan, *mBradán,* not given.

Mbraher, *mBrathar,* friars.

Mbrisklaun, *mBriosclán,* wild tansy weed.

Mbrock, *m-broc,* badgers.

Mead, *míde,* middle.

Meadagh, *Méadach,* not given.

Meadan, *Meidín,* 'my little Ita'.

Meadan, *Mhíodáin, Mhiadáin,* Miadán, founder of the Church of Kilmeadan.

Meade, *na-Míoch,* of Na Mígh, not given.

Meaden, *Meidín,* not given.

Meaden, *Mhiadáin, Mhíodáin,* St Miadan, Míodan, Mhíodáin.

Meadle, *maidhahm,* bursting streams or a pasture.

Meadle, *méadal,* not given.

Meadle, *miadull,* thongs.

Meagh, *Mheadhach,* Mede, a family name.

Meagh, *Míoch,* not given.

Meagher, *Mheachair,* Maher, a family name.

Meaghsland, *fearann-na-Míoch,* not given.

Meague, *Maodhóg,* Maodhóg, a personal or family name and the founder of a Church in Kildare.

Meaky, *mBece, mBeice,* Bece, a male name.

Meal, *mael, maol,* bald, bare.

Meal, *máol,* low.

Meal, *maothail,* soft.

Meal, *meall,* a hillock.

Meal, *Míl,* not given.

Meal, *moil,* the beast.

Mealagh, (river) *Maolach,* not given.

Mealaghans, *maelachán,* bare hillocks.

Mealcly, *maol-chladh,* the bare rampart.

Mealclye, *maolchlaí,* not given.

Mealdown, *Maoldomhnaigh,* not given.

Mealdown, *Mhaoldomhnaigh, Maeldomhnaigh, Mhaoldonn, Maoldomhnach,* Maeldowney, a male name.

Mealdown, *Mhaoldomhnaigh,* Muldoney, a personal or family name.

Mealdown, *Mhaoldomhnaigh,* Muldowney, a personal or family name.

Meale, *mael, maol,* bald.

Mealisheen, *maol-lisín,* bare little fort.

Meallagh, *meallach,* a hillock.

Meallagh, *mhéalach,* not given.

Meallaghmore, *meallach-mór,* abounding in hillocks(sic).

Meallis, *maol-lios,* the bare fort.

Mealough, *maelagha,* a round hill or abounding in hillocks.

Mealuane, *Maoldubhain,* Maoldubhan, a personal or family name.

Mean, *meán, meadhon,* middle.

Meana, *mianach,* mines.

Meana, mines.

Meanagh, *meanfhach,* a wide stream that cuts its way deeply.

Meanagh, *mianach,* the mine.

Meane, *meáin, meadhon,* middle.

Meaney, *Mhaonaigh,* Meaney or Mooney, a personal or family name.

Meanla, *mean-chaladh,* mouth passage.

Meanus, a mining place.

Meanus, *Méanas, Meanas,* not given.

Meanus, *mianus,* a mine.

Mearacaun, *méaracán, mearacán,* fairy thimbles an old name for foxgloves.

Mearacaun, *méaracán,* not given.

Mearn, *Méarán,* not given.

Mearoga, *mearoga,* fingerstones.

Mearogafin, *mearoga-Finn,* Fionn's (a male name) fingerstones.

Meath, *na-mí, an-mhí,* the middle.

Meath, *an-Mhidhe,* not given.

Meath, *meadhach,* stallions.

Meath, *na-Méad,* of the Meade's, a family name.

Mee, *Midhe,* Mee, a personal name and a family name.

Mee, *Ui-Mhídhe,* not given.

Meean, *mBian,* not given.

Meean, *mían,* desires.

Meece, *mias,* dishes.

Meedan, *míadan,* a meadow.

Meedy, *Míde,* St. Midé/Ité/Ide/Íde.

Meedy, *Mo-Ide,* St Ita.

Meegan, *Míogáin,* Meegan, a personal or family name.

Meehan, *mhidheacháin,* not given.

Meehan, *Miodhacain, Miocháin, Mhiadhacháin, Uí-Mhithidhin, Mhithidheain,* O'Meehan, a family name.

Meehan, *mitheán,* middle land.

Meehan, *Uí-Mhithigin, Mhithidhéin,* not given.

Meehaun, *mitheán,* middle land.

Meeing(sic)**,** smooth field.

Meekery, *Mhic–Thire,* Mac Teer, a Family name.

Meel, *maol,* a bald hill.

Meel, *maol, mael,* bald, bare, roofless, hornless.

Meel, *moil,* the beast.

Meela, *maoile, maoil,* a hornless cow.

Meela, *maothaile,* low marshy land.

Meela, *míl ,* hill ridge of the soldiers.

Meela, *mill-an…,* not given.

Meelaboe, *mhaoile-Mhuaidh,* not given.

Meelagh, from *moil,* midges.

Meelagh, *mBialach, mínleach,* not given.

Meelagh, *míolach,* cattle.

Meelagh, *míolach,* lousy, brutish or abounding in cattle.

Meelaghans, *an-maothlachán,* not given.

Meelaghans, *maelaghan,* little bare hills.

Meelan, *Maoláin,* not given.

Meelchon, *Ua-Mílchon,* O'Milchon, a family name.

Meeleboe, *Mhaoilmuaidh,* Maolmuadh, a personal or family name.

Meeleen, *maelán, maelín,* a little round backed island in the sea or round bare rocks.

Meeleen, *mhaoilín,* a bare eminence.

Meelia, *maoile,* bare.

Meelick, *míleac, mileac, mílic, mhílic, miliuc, imleac,* low marshy ground usually beside water.

Meelick, *míleac, Milecc,* an insulated piece of land.

Meelick, *míliuc,* a marsh.

Meelikon, *Maolacáin,* Meelickin, a personal or family name.

Meelin, *an-maolinn,* a small hill.

Meelin, *an-mhaoilinn,* not given.

Meelish, *Mílis,* Myles, a personal or family name.

Meelode, Meelod or Mylod, a family name.

Meelon, *maelán, maelín,* a little round backed island in the sea or round bare rocks.

Meelon, *maoileann,* a bleak eminence.

Meelshane, *maoil-sidheáin,* not given.

Meelta, *míolta,* midges.

Meeltan, from *moil,* midges.

Meeltanagh, *maoltanagh*(sic), the bare hill.

Meeltog, *míoltóg,* midges.

Meeltog, *maoltog,* a hillock or knoll.

Meeltoge, *míoltóg,* a place of midges.

Meeltogue, *míoltóg,* midges.

Meeltogues, *míoltóg,* a place of midges.

Meeltran, *maoltrán,* a bare little hill.

Meeltraun, *maoltrán,* a bare little hill.

Meely, *maoile,* the hornless cow.

Meen, *mhín, mín,* small.

Meen, *mhín, míne,* smooth or a smooth place.

Meen, *mhóin,* bog.

Meen, *mine, mín,* a mountain meadow, pasture or smooth field.

Meena, *Meena,* Meena, a personal or family name.

Meena, *mín,* a mountain meadow or a smooth field.

Meena, *míne,* smooth or smoothness.

Meena, *mín-na/a'...,* smooth field/place or mountain pasture of the...

Meena, *mín-na...,* smooth place of the..., or mountain meadow of the...

Meena, *Miodhna,* St Miodhna.

Meena, *Míona,* not given.

Meena, *moing-na...,* swamp of the...

Meenacahan, *mín-Mhac-Catháin,* mountain pasture of Cathán's sons.

Meenachan, *mí-Mhac-Catháin,* MacKanes (a family name) mountain meadow.

Meenagh, *meadhonach,* middle land.

Meenagh, *mithgheineach,* not given.

Meenagh, *Muimhneach,* Munstermen.

Meenaghan, *mineachan,* a little smooth green place.

Meenahony, *mín-an-chomhnuidhe,* not given.

Meenan, *mín-an...,* mountain meadow of the...

Meenan, *mionán,* kids.

Meenan, *mionnáin,* not given.

Meenanare, *mín-an-áir,* smooth green field of the slaughter.

Meendrane, *mín-doire-*eidhinn, not given.

Meengar, *mín-gearr,* short-smooth surfaced.

Meenirroy, *mín-an-fhir-ruaidh,* mountain meadow of the red haired man.

Meenlagh, *mín-loch,* small lake.

Meenna, *mín-na/a'...,* smooth field of the...

Meens, *muingí,* not given.

Meenta, *mínte,* smooth fields.

Meentagh, abounding in smooth patches.

Meentagh, *na-mínte, mínteach,* not given.

Meentoges, *míntóg,* small green spots.

Meentolla, *míntulach,* not given.

Meenty, *mínte,* a wet mountain pass.

Meenvane, *min-bhan,* white field.

Meenvane, *min-mheadhon,* middle tract of pasture.

Meeny, *Uí-Mianaigh,* O'Meeny, a family name.

Meenychannon, *mín-Uí-Chanann,* not given.

Meenyvougham, smooth field of the hut.

Meer, *maoir,* a steward.

Meer, *mín,* not given.

Meera, *míora,* land divions.

Meera, *mio-rath,* bad luck(sic).

Meere, *mír,* top.

Meere, *Meere,* a personal or family name.

Meeshal, *magh-iseal,* the low plain.

Meeshal, *midh-iseal,* a middle low lying district.

Meetagh, *mBiadhtach,* victuallers.

Megan, *Meagan,* Meagan, the name of a Church founder in Co Down.

Meggagh, *meagach,* earthy.

Meggagh, *miogac,* smiling or sunny.

Mehigan, *Uí-Mhaothagain,* O'Mehigan, a family name.

Mehill, *maethail,* soft spongy land.

Mehill, *maothail,* not given.

Mehill, *meitheal,* bands of workmen.

Mehill, *Mícil, Mhichíl,* Michael, a male name.

Mehonoge, St Mohenoge.

Meige, *Maodhóg,* not given.

Meigh, *maigh, magh,* a plain.

Meiltron, *maol-droim,* flat topped or bald ridge.

Mel, *meala,* honey.

Mel, *meall,* a lump.

Melagh, *mBialach,* not given.

Melagh, *méallach,* not given.

Melan, *Maelain,* St Maelan or St Maolan.

Melan, *Maolán,* Maolán, a personal or family name.

Melan, *Mhaoláin,* not given.

Melan, *Moylan,* a male name.

Melcom, *Maolchuinn,* Mulquin or Mulqueen, a family name.

Meldrom, *maol-drom,* bald ridge.

Meldrum, *maoldrom, maol-druim,* bare ridge or back.

Melican, *maoilcheann,* bare hilltop.

Melkernagh, *miolcearnaigh,* Carneys hill.

Mell, bare.

Mell, *Meille,* not given.

Mella, *méile,* not given.

Mellan, *Meallain,* Mellon, a personal or family name.

Mellaw, *mBéal-ath,* mouth of the ford.

Mellia, *Meille,* not given.

Mellick, *mileac, imleac/ Miliuc,* low marshy ground usually beside water.

Mellick, *mílic,* wet ground.

Mellifont, (latin), *fons-mellis,* fountain of honey. The Irish name is *an-mhainistir-mhór,* the great monastery.

Mellison, *magh-liosain,* plain of the little forts.

Mellisson, *an-maoileasain,* not given.

Mellisson, *muighe-liosáin,* plain of the little fort.

Mellon, *maelán, maelín,* a little round backed island in the sea or round bare rocks.

Mellon, *Mealláin,* not given.

Mellon, *Milain, Milain, Miolan, Miláin,* Milán or Milan, a male name.

Mellon, *mullán,* the hillock.

Melsh, *milis,* sweet.

Melton, *Mealtain, Melltain,* Mealtan, Mealltan, a personal or family name.

Melton, *Mealtain,* Meltan, a personal or family name.

Melville, *an-slogaire,* the swallow hole.

Melvin, *loch-Meilge,* not given.

Melvin, *Meilbhe,* Meilbhe, not given.

Melvin, *Meilghe,* a legendary ancient King.

Melvin, *Meilí,* not given.

Memory, *an-cuimhneachán,* not given.

Men, *mín,* little.

Mena, *meadhonach, mheánaigh, mheadahn, meanach, meánach,* middle.

Mena, *meadhónach,* not given.

Mena, *Mhaonaigh,* Maonach, not given.

Mena, *míne, a* smooth face.

Mena, *móna,* bog.

Menagh, *meadhónach, meadhonach, mheadahn, mednach, meánach,* middle.

Menagh, *meadhonach,* middle land.

Menagh, *muinngeanach,* shaggy.

Menan, *mináin, mhionnáin,* not given.

Menawn, *mionnáin,* not given.

Meneenagh, *mBiníneach,* not given.

Meneenagh, *miníneach,* coarse grass.

Menlagh, *mín-loch,* small lake.

Menlough, *meanloch-Ó-Mainnín,* not given.

Menlough, *mionlach,* a small place.

Menlough, *mionlagh,* not given.

Menlough, *mionloch,* small lake.

Menny, *meanaith,* the awl.

Menta, *mínte,* a wet mountain pass.

Meone, *meadhon,* middle.

Meoul, *maol,* a hillock.

Meoul, *meall, mhaoil,* not given.

Meragaun, *méaracan,* fairy-thimbles, fairy-fingers or foxgloves.

Merans, *Meadhráin,* Meran, a personal or family name.

Merin, *méaraghan,* foxglove.

Merlin, *Mheirlín,* not given.

Merlin, *Méirlín,* Merlin, a personal or family name.

Merret, *Mairghread,* Mairgread or Margaret, a female name.

Merrigan, *Uí-Muireagain,* O'Merrigan, a family name.

Merrion, *muirbhtheann,* not given.

Merrion, *muirfín, muirfean,* the sea-shore or land along the sea shore.

Mertinagh, *mairtineach,* deformed persons or cripples.

Mertinagh, *mBirtíneach,* small bundles.

Mertinagh, *mBritíneach,* not given.

Mescan, *mescan,* shaped like a butter pat.

Mesha, *meise,* a stone altar or table.

Mesha, *méise,* the dish.

Mesk, *meisc,* not given.

Mesker, *meascair,* the conflict.

Messan, *Mheasáin, Measáin,* St Measán/ Measan.

Met, *Méid,* not given.

Metagh, *mBiatach, mBiadhtach,* victuallers.

Metagh, *m-biadhteach,* hospitallers or hostel keepers.

Metagh, *mBiathach, m-biatach,* hospitallers or hostel keepers.

Methan, *Meathan,* not given.

Mether, *mether, meadar,* a drinking vessel.

Meva, *Meadhbha,* Queen Maeve.

Meva, *Mheidhbhe,* Maive, a female name.

Mevagh, *Midhbheach, Míobhaigh, Miobhach,* not given.

Mew, *Meadhbha,* not given.

Mhingy, *moing,* a morass.

Mhingy, *muing-a'...,* swamp of...

Mhinisteir, *Mhinisteir,* a Minister.

Mhoan, *móin,* a bog.

Mhuire, (Mt) *Fuire,* not given.

Michael, *Mhicheáil, Mhichil, Michil, Mhichíl,* Michael, a male name and the founder of a Church in Cork and Wexford.

Michan, *Uímhíadhacháin,* O'Meehan, a family name.

Michane, *nigheachain,* of the washing.

Mickatreer, *Mhic-an-Trír,* not given.

Micklon, *Ó/O'Míolchon,* O'Milchon, a family name.

Micmanus, *Mhic-Mághnuis,* MacManus, a family name.

Mictreer, *Mic-Trír,* not given.

Middleknock, *an-meanchnoc,* the middle height.

Middleton, *mainistir-na-corann,* not given.

Midisil, *muighe-isle,* low plains(sic).

Mien, *maighain,* a plain.

Mien, *mín,* not given.

Mihil, *Mhichíl,* Michael, a male name and the name of a founder of a Church in Clare.

Mihil, *Mhichíl, Michil,* St Michael (the Archangel).

Mihil, *Michíl, Michil,* Michael a male name.

Mihin, *mheithean, meithean,* saplings or splinters.

Mihin, *mheithean,* saplings.

Mihin, *mithean,* not given.

Mihoonagh, *mBitheamhnach,* thieves.

Milane, *maelán, maelín,* a little round backed island in the sea or round bare rocks.

Milane, *maoileann,* a small bare or bald hillock, hill, mound or eminence.

Milane, *meallan,* a bald mound or hill.

Milane, *meilleán,* not given.

Milcashel, *Uí-Mhaolcaisil,* O'Mulcashel or Cashel, a family name.

Milcon, *Maolchuinn,* Mulqueen, a family name.

Milcon, *mhaoilcon,* a mythical hound.

Milcon, *Mhílchon,* not given.

Mile, *maoil,* not given.

Mileen, *millin,* a hillock.

Miles, *Mhílis,* not given.

Miles, *na-maoil,* bare peaks or summits.

Mill, *meall,* a lump, a small round hill.

Milla, *mhaol,* peaks.

Milla, *mille,* honeysuckle or fuschia.

Milla, *mullach,* heights.

Millan, *mhuillinn, mhuilinn,* the mill.

Milland, *mhuilinn,* the mill.

Millar, *iolar,* eagle.

Millard, *iolar,* eagle.

Milleen, *millín,* a little hill/knoll.

Milleena, *meillín-na,* not given.

Milleena, *millín-an...,* little hill of the...

Milleena, *millín-na...,* smooth little plain of the..., or little hill of the...

Milleenan, *meillín-an...,* not given.

Milleens, *meilliní,* hillocks.

Milleeny, *millinidhe,* little hillocks.

Milleeny, *na-Millíní,* not given.

Miller, *mhuilleora,* the miller.

Millford, *bél-na-ngalloglach,* ford of the gallowglasses or foreign soldiers.

Milligan, *maelaghan,* little bare hills.

Milligan, *Milleogáin,* not given.

Milligans, *maelaghan,* little bare hills.

Millin, *millín,* a small mound.

Million, *Mhiolúin,* not given.

Millis, *milis,* pleasant.

Millis, *milís,* sweet.

Millish, *milis,* sweet.

Millon, *Mhiolúin,* Mellon, a personal or family name.

Mill Tenement, in the Parish of Ardclinis in Co Antrim. This is the supposedly smallest townland in Ireland, reported to be a quarter of an acre but is listed in the 1851 census as being one acre, 1 rood and one perch.

Milltown Malbay, *sráid-na-cathrach,* not given.

Milmorane, *mill-Mearáin,* not given.

Milshoge, *milseóg,* anything sweet, sweet grass etc.

Miltown Malbay, *sráid-na-cathrach,* not given.

Min, *mhean,* not given.

Min, *mionn,* a field.

Min, *muing,* marsh.

Mina, *mine,* a small sized plot.

Minalns (sic), (Kilkenny), *míneáin,* smooth tracts of land.

Minan, *mionnan, mionán,* kid goats.

Minane, *meannán, mhionnáin,* not given.

Minane, *mionáin,* a kid (goat).

Minane, *mionnan,* a small rocky place, a rocky point of land.

Minanes, *mineáin,* small smooth green places.

Minard, *mhin-aird, mine-airde, binn-árd,* not given.

Minaun, *meannán, mionnan,* kid goats.

Minch, *minse,* not given.

Minda, *Mionda,* not given.

Mine, *Míne,* not given.

Mine, *mionn,* the high crown.

Mine, *muing, mong,* morass.

Mines, *Maghna,* not given.

Mines, *Maoineas,* not given.

Mines, *Maoinis,* Maoinis, Maoineas, a personal name.

Mines, *Maonais,* de Moenes, a family name.

Mines, *mathna,* smooth.

Mines, *mín,* smooth.

Minfoyle, *Maolphoil,* Mulfoyle, a male name.

Minick, *Mionóg,* St Minog.

Minioge, *M Fionnóg,* personal or family name and means 'little Finn'.

Minna, *mine,* a meal.

Minna, *mine,* small.

Minna, *na-mine,* not given.

Minnan, *meannán,* not given.

Minnan, *mionan,* a kid goat.

Minnane, *meanán,* kid goats.

Minnane, *mionnán,* not given.

Minnaun, *mionnán, meanán,* kid goats.

Minnawn, kids.

Minnick, *Mhinic,* not given.

Minnin, *Mhinín, Bheinín,* not given.

Minnis, *magh-ínse,* river holm plain.

Minoge, *Bhionóg, Mo-Innog dha-fionóg, Dha-Mhionóg, Damhionog,* St Winnoc.

Minoge, *M Fionnóg,* little Finn, a personal name.

Minoge, *Mionóg,* not given.

Minoge, *Ua-Minóg,* O'Minogue, a family name.

Minoge, *Uí-Mineóg,* O'Minnoge, a family name.

Minsha, *mBeinnse, mBínse,* benches.

Minsha, *minseach,* not given.

Mintiaghs, *mínteach,* not given.

Mintiaghs, *mínteacha,* smooth green patches of mountainy pasture.

Minton, *meantán,* snipes.

Mintra, *mBaintreabhaig, mBaintreabhaigh, mBaintreabhach,* widows.

Mintra, *mBaintreach,* not given.

Mintry, *mBaintreabhach,* widows.

Mintry, *min-tire,* smooth green spot(sic).

Minus, (Island) *Maínis,* not given.

Mira, *maighre,* a level place.

Miran, *mireann,* divisions.

Mire, *maghair,* a plain.

Mire, *Maghair,* Maghar, a personal or family name.

Mire, *maor, maer,* a steward or keeper.

Mire, *Mír,* not given.

Mirigan, *meireagán,* foxgloves.

Miscaun, *mioscán, mhioscáin,* roll or shaped lumps of butter, a cairn shaped like a butter roll.

Miscaun, *miosgán,* butter.

Mish, *meissi,* phantoms.

Mishills, *muighe-isle,* low plains.

Misk, a mountain meadow or a smooth field.

Misk, *Meascáin,* a personal or family name.

Miskis, *mioscais,* not given.

Miskish, *mioscuis,* enmity, spite or hatred.

Mitchelstown, *baile-an-Mhistéalaigh,* Mitchel's town.

Mitchelstown, *baile-Mhistealaigh-na-dton,* town of Mitchell of the waves.

Mitchelstown, *baile-Mhistéala-na-dTamhan,* not given.

Mizen Head, *ceann-Moiscne,* not given.

Mizzen Head, *carn-Uí-Néid,* not given.

Mna, *mna,* a woman or women.

Mnamarva, *mna-mairbhe,* the dead woman.

Mo, *má, magh, maigh, machaire, muigh,* a plain,

Mo, *mBó,* cattle.

Mo, *mogh, maigh, magh,* a plain.

Moage, *Maedhog,* a personal name.

Moan, *Madháin,* Muadhán, a personal or family name.

Moan, *Modhain,* Modhan, Madain, a male name.

Moan, *moin,* a bog.

Moana, *móin-na* , bog of the…

Moananagh, *magh-n'Aonach,* the fair green(sic).

Moanarche, *móin-Airse,* Archy's (a personal or family name) moorland.

Moanna, *móin-na* , bog of the…

Moano, *móin-an* , bog of the…

Moanreel, *móin-réil,* rightful landed property(sic).

Moanroe, (river) *an-mhaighean-nó, an-mhóin-ruadh,* not given.

Moantaun, *mointán,* a place of bog.

Moanteen, *mhainntín,* a small gap.

Moanteen, *móintín, mointín, mointeán,* little bog.

Moanvaun, *an-mhóin-bhán, na-móna-baine, mín-bhuí*(sic), not given.

Moarhaun, *motharán,* a little stone structure for 'folding' lambs.

Moat, *mot, móta, mhóta, mhota,* a moat, high ground or a mound.

Moata, *mota,* a moat or fort.

Moate, Moategranoge, the great mound of *Grain óg.*

Moate, *móta,* the moat or mound.

Moati, *móta, a moat.*

Moaty, *mótaidhe,* forts or moats.

Mobarnon, *maigh/magh-bearnáin,* plain of the little gap.

Mocar, *Mochara,* St Mochara.

Mochonna, *Mochonna,* St Mochonna.

Mochuda, *Mochuda,* Mochuda, the name of the founder of Lismore.

Mochy, *Mothaigh,* not given.

Mockagh, *mBacach,* cripples or beggars.

Mockan, *meacan,* parsnips.

Mockler, *Mhóicléir,* Mockler, a family name.

Mockler, *Moiclearach, Moicleir,* and the French version '*Mauclerc*' meaning bad scholar/cleric, a family name.

Mockler, *Mocliar*(sic), not given.

Mocmoyne, *magh-'ic-Maoin,* plain of Maon's (a personal name) son.

Mocollop, *maigh-Cholpa, magh-Colpa,* not given.

Mocollop, *magh-colpa/cholpach,* the steer plain.

Mocolmock, *Mocholmoc,* St Mocholmoc.

Mocomoge, St Mochaemog.

Moculla, St Moculla.

Modaghe, *mBodach,* a churl.

Modan, *Mhudain,* Mudan, a personal or family name.

Modan, *Muadán,* not given.

Modderee, *maddraighe,* dogs.

Modderee, *maigh-doirí,* not given.

Moddy, *madadh,* dogs.

Modeese, *maigh-Dís,* not given.

Modeligo, *magh-Deilge/Dheilge,* the thorn plain.

Modelligo, *magh-deilge, maigh-dheilge,* plain of thorns.

Modeshil, *maigh-Dheisil, mag-Deisil,* not given.

Modreeny, *maigh-Drithne,* not given.

Moe, *mBó,* cattle.

Moe, *Mó, Mogha,* Mo, Mogh, a personal or family name.

Moe, *mBoth,* not given.

Moe, *Modha,* not given.

Moe, *móigh, magh,* a plain.

Moe, *moin,* a bog.

Mofey, *both,* tent, hut or booth.

Mog, *Magáid,* not given.

Mog, *mo-Aodhóg,* St Mogue/Megath.

Mog, *mogh,* a plain.

Mogagh, *mBogach,* bogs.

Moganny, *Mogeanna, Mogeanna,* a personal or family name and the founder of a Church in Kilkenny.

Moganny, *Mocheana,* St Mocheana.

Mogar, *Mochara,* St Mogara.

Moge, *Moig,* Moge, a personal or family name.

Mogeely, *magh-Éile/Il* , the plain of Ely.

Mogeely, *maigh-Dhíle,* Éile's (a personal or family name) plain.

Mogeesha, *magh-Oésigh,* not given.

Mogh, *maigh,* not given.

Moghalaun, *mBuachalán,* yellow regweeds.

Moghan, *Mocháin,* not given.

Moghan, *Uí-Móchain,* O'Mohan, a family name.

Moghaun, *muchán, múchán,* smothered or suffocated.

Moghil, *mBuachaill,* boys.

Moghill, *mBachall,* staffs or crosiers.

Moghill, *mBouchail, mBouchaillidhe,* boys.

Moghillie, *mothallaighe,* rough shaggy place.

Mogland, *maigleann,* not given.

Mogouhy, *magh-gaothach,* a windy place(sic).

Mogue, *Maodhog,* Mogue, a personal or family name.

Mogue, *Mhodóg,* Modóg, a personal or family name.

Mogue, *mo-Aodhóg/Aodh-óg,* 'my dear little Hugh' the name of St Mogue who was also known as Maidoc.

Mogue, *Mhóg, Maodhóg, Maodhóig,* St Maodhóg/Mogue.

Moguee, *Maedhog,* a personal or family name.

Mohalagh, *mBachlach,* shepherds.

Mohalagh, *mothallach,* place of rough bushes.

Mohalagh, *muclagh,* place of pigs/piggeries.

Mohan, *mBothán,* little huts.

Mohanagh, *muchánach,* abounding in quagmires.

Mohaun, *mBothán,* cabins (for animals).

Moheen, *Mhochaidhín,* O'Moheen, a family name.

Moheen, *Mhoithín,* not given.

Moher, *machaire,* a plain.

Moher, *mBóthar,* roads.

Moher, *mhothair, mothair, mothar,* an old ruin or a ruined fort.

Moher, *mothar,* a patch of shrubbery/trees or a thicket.

Moher, *mothar,* a sheep fold.

Moher, *mothar,* the ruin of a caher, rath, fort or building, a thicket or a wooded swamp.

Moher, *mother, móthar,* a shrubbery or a cluster of trees or bushes.

Mohera, *mothara,* ruins of a cahers, raths or buildings.

Mohera, *mother-an…,* fold of the…

Moheragh, *mothracha, mothrach,* not given.

Moheramoylan, *mothar-maoilínn,* sheep-fold with low stone walls(sic).

Mohereen, *moherín,* ruin of a little caher, rath-or building.

Mohernagh, *motharnach,* abounding in thickets.

Mohernagh, *mútharnach,* not given.

Moherough, *motarac,* ruin.

Mohide, *Mhuiche, Muichet,* the race (of people) of Muichet, an ancient druidic acolyte.

Mohil, *an-mhaothail,* not given.

Mohill, *maothail,* cheese(sic) or soft land.

Mohill, *maothail, maethail,* soft spongy land.

Mohill, *maothail-Mhancháin,* not given.

Mohill, *mBuachaill, mBouchaillidhe,* boys.

Mohilly, *mBouchaillidhe,* boys.

Mohilly, *mBuachaillí,* not given.

Mohily, *mothallaighe,* rough shaggy place.

Mohober, *maigh-Thobair,* not given.

Mohoge, *mBothóg,* not given.

Mohona, *magh-a'chonnaidh,* plain of the wood or kindling.

Mohona, *ma-tona,* plain of quagmires or bottom land.

Mohonok, St Mohenoge.

Mohorough, *motharach, motharacha,* ruin/s.

Moicyawn, *móinteán,* boggy land.

Moicyawn, *múchán,* souterrain(sic).

Moig, *magh, má, machaire, maigh, muigh,* a plain, a flat place.

Moigh, *maigh, magh,* a plain, a flat place.

Moigh, *mBoith,* a tent or hut.

Moin, *móin, moin,* a bog.

Moine, (river) *an-mhaighean-nó, an-mhóin-ruadh,* not given.

Moinen, *móinín,* little moor(sic).

Mointragh, *mBaintreabhach,* widows.

Moira, *machaire,* a plain.

Moira, *magh-rath,* the plain of the fort.

Moira, *maigh-rath, má-ráth,* plain of the ring fort/s.

Moira, *maoir,* not given.

Moira, *má-roth,*(sic) not given.

Moiry, *mhaighre,* salmon.

Moiry, *mhoighre,* not given.

Mokea, *Mac–Aodh,* Mac Aodh, Hugh or Mogue, a personal or family name.

Mokevoge, *Mochaemhog,* St Mochaemhog.

Molada, *Mo-Luada,* St Luada.

Molaga, *Molaga,* St Molaga.

Molagga, *Molaga,* not given.

Molana, *Mholana, Molanfhaidh, Molanfhaidh,* St Molanai or St Molana

Molash, *Molaise,* St Molaise/Molaisi/Molash.

Molassy, *baile-an-bhailéisigh,* not given.

Molassy, *mágh/magh-leasa,* plain of the fort.

Molassy, St. Molaise.

Molavasagh, *Mul-Mhasaig,* Mulmassy, an ancient Milesian name.

Moleague, *Molaga,* not given.

Moleague, *Molaige, Molaga,* St Molaga.

Moleran, *Moilearáin,* not given.

Moleran, *Moelodhráin,* St Moeloran.

Moley, *Mhóiligh,* a personal or family name.

Molgum, *m-bolgam,* mouthfuls.

Molin, *Moling, Mholing, Moling,* St Moling.

Molin, *muilinn,* the mill.

Molina, *Mhaelfhina,* Mullaney a male name.

Molina, *Mhaoillíona, Mhaolíona,* Maolfhina, Maolíona or Maoilfhoina, a male name.

Molina, *Uí-Mhaolfhíona,* not given.

Molire, *Maoiluidhre,* Malire, a personal or family name.

Molire, *maighe-ladhar,* plain of the river confluences.

Mollaneen, *molánín, mullainín,* the little hill.

Mollogha, *magh-locha,* the field beside the lake(sic).

Molly, *mala,* a hill brow.

Molly, *málaighe,* hillbrows or braes.

Molly, *molaidhe,* hill brows.

Molly, *mullach,* a summit.

Mollyna, *mullach-na...,* summit of the...

Moloney, *Moaldhomhnaigh,* O'Moloney, a family name.

Moloogh, *mBulbhach,* not given.

Molosky, magh-loscathaidhe, burnt plain.

Molough, *mhaigh-locha,* not given.

Molt, *molt,* wethers.

Moltaun, *moltán,* wethers.

Moltra, *mannragh,* stalls or mangers.

Molua, *Maolmuadh,* Maolmuadh, the name of an ancient King of Munster.

Molum, *mágh/magh-lom,* the bare plain.

Molum, *Mólam,* not given.

Molyn, *Moling,* not given.

Molyon, *Molaidhghein,* not given.

Molyon, *Moliain, Moladhain,* Moladhan, a personal name.

Momony, *maigh-Mónann,* not given.

Mon, *mBan,* women.

Mon, *móna,* a common(sic).

Mon, *magh-an...,* plain of ...

Mon, *mona, móin,* bog.

Mon, *mugh,* a plain.

Mon, *Munna,* St Munna.

Mona, *moin-na..., móin-na/an/a ...,* the bog of the....

Mona, *móna, mona, móin,* bog, turf or peat.

Mona, *móna,* rough land(sic).

Mona, *Mona,* St Mona.

Mona, *muin-a...,* shrubbery of the...

Mona, *muine,* a thicket.

Monachan, *Manacháin,* St Manachán, Monachan, Manchán.

Monadee, *móna-duibhe,* black bog.

Monafrica, *móin-an-phriocaigh,* not given.

Monagay, *móin-achaidh-Ghae,* not given.

Monage, *maigh-nÓis(sic),* not given.

Monagh, *manach,* monks.

Monagh, *Manaigh,* the name of a a people.

Monagh, *mónach,* rough ground.

Monaghan, *mhuineacháin, mhancháin,* not given.

Monaghan, *muineachain,* the place of little hills.

Monaghan, *muineacháin,* the bushy place.

Monaghan, *muineachan, muineachán,* a place of thickets or little thickets.

Monaghan, *muineachán,* the little shrubbery.

Monagor, *an-mhune-gearr,* not given.

Monaire, *mónfhéur,* bog grass or a mountain meadow.

Monalea, *Chonaill-Aodha,* not given.

Monalee, *mona-léithe,* grey bog.

Monalia, *maigh-Náille,* not given.

Monalia, *móináille,* beautiful bog.

Monalty, *munilte,* not given.

Monam, *moin-na...,* the plain of the....

Monan, *móinín,* little bog.

Monana, *muine-na...,* not given.

Monanaleen, *móin-an-lín,* flax producing place(sic).

Monane, *meanan,* kid goats.

Monang, *mhóin-Fhinn,* not given.

Monang, *móin-abhann,* river bog.

Monang, *móin-Fhinn,* Finn's (a personal or family name) bog.

Monanimy, *móin-Ainmne,* not given.

Monanny, *maigh-nEanaigh,* not given.

Monarchie, *móan-Áirse,* not given.

Monargan, *magh-an-airgeann,* bog of the plundering.

Monas, *móin-easa,* the cataract of the bog or bog of ....'s (a persons name) cataract.

Monassa, *móan-fhásaigh,* not given.

Monassa, *móin-an-fhásaigh,* bogland of the wilderness.

Monaster, *mainistreach, mainister,* Monastery.

Monasteraden, *Mainistir-Réadáin/Réidin,* not given.

Monasternalea, *Mainister-na-Liatha,* Monastery of the grey Friars.

Monasteroris, *Mainistir-Fheorais,* not given.

Monavea, *an-mhóin-bhui,* not given.

Monchree, *móin-chriadh,* clayey bog.

Monclassa, *móinín-a'leasa,* little bog of the fort.

Mondra, *mannrach, manrach,* sheep cotes or folds.

Mondra, *mBanrach,* not given.

Mone, *Móghan,* not given.

Mone, *móin- na/a'...,* bog of the...

Mone, *móin,* bog.

Monea, *magh-an-fhiaidh,* plain of the deer.

Monea, *má-nia, magh/má-niadh, maigh-niagh/nia,* the plain of the champion or heroes.

Monea, *móin-Aodha,* not given.

Monear, *móinéar,* not given.

Monear, *mónfhéur,* bog grass or a mountain meadow.

Moneash, *muinéas,* a brake or shrubbery.

Moneel, *muinéil, muineul,* the neck.

Moneen, *mhóinín,* not given.

Moneen, *móinín,* a little bog.

Moneena, *móinín..., móinín-na...,* little bog of the...

Moneenaun, *móin-Fhíonáin/Fhionáin,* Finan's (a personal or family name) bog.

Moneenaun, *móin-Fhionnáin,* Finan's (a personal or family name) bogland.

Moneenna, *móinín-na...,* little bog of the...

Moneens, *moininí,* small bogs.

Monellan, *magh-Nialláin,* Niallan's (a personal or family name) plain.

Monelty, *muinilte,* the sleeve.

Moneour, *an-mhóin-odhar, móinodhar,* the brown bog.

Monesteragh, *mainistreach,* Monastery.

Moneteen, *móintín, mointín, mointeán,* a little bog.

Money, *bonad, buanaigh,* not given.

Money, *Maonaigh, muine-na...,* not given.

Money, *mhonaidh,* the moor or moorland.

Money, *móin-a'...,* bog of the...

Money, *móin-na/a'...,* bog of the...

Money, *móna, monaidh,* a bog.

Money, *monaidh, móin,* a bog.

Money, *Mughaine,* St Mughain.

Money, *muine,* a shrubbery, thicket grove or brake.

Money, shrubs.

Moneygold, *muine-Dhúltaigh/Dhubhaltaigh,* Dualta's (a personal or family name) thicket.

Moneygold, *muine-Dubhachtaigh,* Duald's (a personal or a family name) shrubbery.

Moneyna, *muine-na...,* shrubbery or brake of the...

Moneysterling, O'Lynn's Monastery.

Mong, *móin-a'...,* bog of the...

Mong, *mong,* a quagmire, a swamp, long sedgy grass or quagmire grass.

Mongagh, *mhongach,* not given.

Mongagh, *mongach,* a morass that produces sedge grass.

Mongan, a morass that produces sedge grass.

Mongan, *mangan,* sacks.

Mongan, *mBuinneán,* not given.

Mongan, *Mongáin, Mongain,* Mongán, Mongan, a male name.

Mongan, *Ui'Mongáin,* O'Mongan, a personal or family name.

Mongaree, *mangaire,* peddlers or merchants.

Mongaun, a morass that produces sedge grass.

Mongaun, *Ua-Mongán,* O'Mangan, a family name.

Mongaun, *Uí-Mhongáin, Ui'Mongáin,* Ó Mongán or O'Mongan, a personal or family name.

Mongna(sic), *mongán,* a fen or swampy place.

Mongragh, *monghráireach,* howling or roaring.

Monie, *muine,* shrubbery.

Monilea, *muine-liath,* not given.

Monin, *móinín,* the little bog.

Monintin, *móin-intinne,* bog of the intention.

Monivea, *muine-mheá, muine-an-mheadha,* shrubbery/grove of the mead.

Monkeal, *an-mhóil-chaol,* not given.

Monnagh, *mongach,* a morass or a place of long coarse marsh grass.

Monneill, *an-mhuinchille,* not given.

Monnery, *muineire,* a brake or shrubbery.

Monog, *moinóg,* little bog.

Monog, *mónóg,* bogberries.

Monoge, St Mohenoge.

Monra, *moin-ruadh,* red bog.

Monroe, *an-mhóin-rua,* not given.

Monsea, *maigh-Saotha, muing-suidhe,* not given.

Monsea, *maigh-saotha,* not given.

Monsea, *mugh-sáeth,* plain of diseases.

Monslatt, *maigh-slat,* plain of twigs/rods.

Mont, a hill.

Montaigh, *móinteacha, mointeach,* a boggy place.

Montana, *móinthean-a'…,* boggy land of the …

Montanavoe, *móin-tSeanbhoithe,* not given.

Montane, *móintéan,* boggy lands.

Montanovoe, *mointeán-a'boith,* boggy land of the tent.

Monteenmore, *móintín-mór,* big moor(sic).

Montiagh, *móinteacha, móinteach, mointeach,* a boggy place.

Montore, *móin-an-tSeantuar/tSeantauir*(sic), not given.

Montore, *móin-tuair,* bog of the bleaching, bleach green or drying place.

Montry, *mBaintreabhach,* widows.

Monty, *mínte,* not given.

Mony, *maigh-na..,* not given.

Mony, *mona, móna, mónadh,* bog.

Mony, *Mónann,* not given.

Mony, *muine,* a thicket.

Monyglen, *bun-an-ghleanna,* not given.

Moo, *mBó,* cow, cattle.

Moodan, *Mhódain,* a personal or family name.

Moodane, *múdán, mBúdán,* not given.

Moodranagh, *mBódránach,* Bodran, a personal name.

Moodranagh, *mBúdránach,* Bowdren, a family name.

Moody, *madaidhe,* dogs.

Mooge, *Maedhog,* a persons name.

Mooghaun, *muchán,* a morass.

Mooghaun, *múchán, múchan,* an underground passage or tunnel.

Mooghaun, *múchán,* smothered or suffocated.

Mooghna, *móna,* rough tracts of land(sic).

Moohan, *mucháin,* a quagmire.

Moohane, *múchán,* smothered or suffocated.

Mooley, *bhuaile, buaile,* a dairying place.

Mooley, *Mhúiligh,* not given.

Mooly, *buaile,* a dairying place.

Moon, *Maodhán, Mún, an-mhaoin,* not given.

Moon, *Mhumhan, Mumha,* Munster, one of the four provinces of Ireland.

Moon, *Móghain,* Moghan, a personal or family name.

Moon, *mona, móin,* a bog.

Moon, *Móin, Muáin, Món*(sic) not given.

Moon, *mona, moin, muín,* a bog.

Moon, *Muaghaine,* Mughain, a female name.

Moon, *Mudhain,* Muadhan or Modan, a personal or family name.

Moon, *Mughaine,* St Mughain.

Moon, *Mughna, Mughain,* Mughan, a personal or family name.

Moon, *Mughna, Mughaine, Mughania,* a personal or family name.

Moon, *Mugna,* Mughan, Mooan, a personal or family name.

Moon, *Múna,* Múna or Muna, a personal or family name.

Moona, *móna,* not given.

Mooncoin, *móin-Choinn/Chaidhn,* Coyne's (a personal or family name) bogland.

Moone, *an-mhaoin,* the possession.

Moone, *maon, maoin,* gift.

Moone, *maon-Choluim-Cille,* not given.

Mooney, *Mhaonaigh,* not given.

Mooney, *Uí-Maonaigh,* O'Mooney, a family name.

Mooney, *Uí-Mhaonaigh,* a family name.

Moonhall, *móin-Ail,* Hall's (a personal or family name) bogland.

Moor, *Múir,* not given.

Moor, *múr,* a wall, house, rampart or fortress.

Moord, *an-mord,* not given.

Moord, *móird, magh-ard,* high plain.

Moore, *mór,* great or big.

Moore, *Uí-Mhórdha, Uí-Mhaolmhordha/
Mhórdha,* Moore or O'Moore, a family
name.

Moorna, *Mhuirne,* Murna, a female name.

Moorna, *Múirne,* Muirne, a personal or
family name.

Moorock, *Múrac,* not given.

Mor, *machaire,* a plain.

Mor, *mór,* big, great.

Mora, *baile-na-móna,* not given.

Mora, *maighe, magh,* a plain.

Mora, *Móradh,* not given.

Mora, *Mórdha,* Moore, a family or a persons name.

Moraghy, *maigh-rátha,* not given.

Moraghy, *mór-achadh,* great field.

Morahaun, *Moráin,* O'Moran, a family
name.

Moral, *Mhoireil,* not given.

Moral, *mór-áille, aille,* the big cliff.

Moral, *muighe-Luain,* not given.

Moran, *Mhóráin,* Moran, a family name.

Moran, *Morna*(sic), not given.

Moran, *Uí-Mhcráin*(sic), O'Moran, a personal or family name.

Morane, *moran,* mountain rushes or rock
plants.

Morath, *Moiréadach,* not given.

Moraun, *morán,* a meadow.

Moraun, Moran, a personal or family
name.

More, *mhagh,* a plain.

More, *mór, mhór, mhó*(sic), big or great.

Moreagh, *ma/magh-riabhach,* the grey, dot-
ted, speckled or striped plain.

Moreagh, *motarac,* ruin.

Moree, *mór,* big, great.

Moreen, *mBoithrín,* little roads or boreens.

Moreen, *Moirín,* Moreen, a female name.

Moreen, *mothairín,* a small grove or thicket.

Moreen, *Muirín,* not given.

Moreen, *Muirnín,* Muirne, a personal or
family name.

Morenane, *boirneán,* a rocky place.

Mores, *mor,* great.

Moress, *mór-easa,* the great cataract.

Morett, *magh-reicheat/réata,* not given.

Morett, *magh-riada,* the chariot driving
plain.

Morgal, *Murgail,* not given.

Morgallion, *machaire-Gaileang,* plain of the
tribe 'Mór-Gaileanga'.

Morgan, *Muireagháin,* Moregan, a personal
or family name.

Morgan, *Murchon,* St Muirchu.

Morgans, *Muireagán,* not given.

Morheeny, *mBóithrínidhe,* little roads or
borheens.

Moria, *Móire,* Mora's (a female name).

Moriarty, *Uí-Mhuircheartaigh,* Moriarty or
O'Moriarty, a family name.

Morilly, O'Murhilly, a family name.

Morin, *Mhóráin,* not given.

Morish, moorish(sic).

Morisheen, *Mhuirisín,* little Maurice, a
mans/boys name.

Morive, *marbh,* the dead.

Mork, *morc,* swine, hogs.

Mormeal, *mór-meall,* great little hill.

Mormeal, Mir-Muichil, St Michaels portion.

Morna, *Mhaonaigh,* not given.

Mornan, *Mórnán,* not given.

Mornane, *boirneán,* a small stony place.

Mornane, *Moirneán,* not given.

Morne, Moran, a family name.

Morne, Morn, not given.

Morne, Morna, the Morna, a tribal or family name.

Morne, *Múrn, Mughdhorna,* the Mournes (a
people), the Mugdorn tribe.

Morne, *Moirne,* Moirne, a personal or
family name.

Morney, *Murnaigh,* Morna, a personal or
family name.

Morningstar river, *an-chamhaoir,* not given.

Mornington, *baile-Uí-Mhornáin,* town of
Ó Mornán.

Moroe, *maigh/má-rua, magh-ruadh,* reddish
plain.

Moroghoe, *Uí-Mhurchadha,* Murphy, a family name.

Morony, *Maolrunaidh,* Maolrunaidh, a personal or family name and the founder of
a Church in laois.

Morris, *Mhairéasaigh, Mhairéisigh, Uí-
Mhuirgheasa,* not given.

Morris, *Mhuirgheasa, Mhuirghis, Mhuirris,
Mhuiris, Muiris,* Muiris, Morris or
Maurice, a male name.

Morris, *Muirgís,* O'Murgis, a family name.

Morris, *Murghis,* a male name.

Morrisey, Morrissey, a family name.

Morrish, *Mhuiris,* Maurice, a personal or family name.

Morrisheen, *Mhuirisín, Muirisín,* little Morris, a mans or boys name.

Morrishmeen, *Mhúiris-mhin,* smooth Maurice.

Morrive, *marbh,* not given.

Morrow, *marbh,* the dead.

Morsough, *m-brosach,* bruses or broases(sic).

Mortagh, *Muircheartaigh,* Moriarty, a family name.

Mortely, *mhairtealaigh,* martyrs or cripples.

Mortgage, *Morgáiste,* not given.

Mortyclogh, *mother-tighe-cloch,* the stone house ruin.

Morvila, *Mhúrmíle,* Murvil, a male name.

Mosney, *maigh-Muirí, má-Mhuireadha,* Muirid's (a personal or family name) plain.

Mosog, *Mosóg,* not given.

Mosside, *magh-saighde, má-sáide,* not given.

Mossley, *magh-soile,* not given.

Mostrim, *meathas-troim, meathustruim,* the fertile ridge.

Mot, *adhmuid,* timber.

Mot, *Mochta,* St Mochta, 10th cent.

Mota, *móta, mhóta, mhota,* a moat, high ground or mound.

Mote, *mhóta,* a castle mound.

Mote, *Mhóta, móta, mhota,* a mote, moat, high ground or a mound.

Mothel, *maothail, maethail,* soft spongy land.

Mothell, *maothail, maethail,* soft spongy land.

Mough, *magh,* a plain.

Mough, *mBoth,* huts.

Mought, *mBocht, m-bocht,* the poor.

Moughty, *Mochta,* St Mochta, 10th cent.

Moula, *meall-a'…,* hillock of…

Moun, *madhm,* an eruption.

Moun, *moin,* a bog.

Mount, a castle(sic).

Mount, *cnoc,* a hill.

Mount, *cnocán,* a hillock.

Mount, *mannt,* a chasm.

Mount, *moin, móin,* bog.

Mount, *móinteach,* a moor.

Mount, *montiagh,* bogs, boggy land.

Mountain, *meantán, mhóintín,* not given.

Mountain, *mointeain,* reclaimed bog, moor or coarse land.

Mountain, *móintín,* the little bog.

Mountain, *móinteán,* moory land or coarse herbage(sic).

Mountallon, *maidhm / madhm-talmhan,* a land slip or eruption of the earth.

Mountin, *mointeán, mointin,* boggy land, little bog.

Mountrath, *maighean-rátha,* bog of the ring fort.

Mountshannon, *baile-Uí-Bheoláin,* not given.

Mouragh, *mBanrach,* not given.

Mouragh, *mBuarach,* cow-spancels.

Mourne (Abbey), *móin, moin, mona,* the bog.

Mourne, *Mhuirne, Moghdhorn,* not given.

Mourne, *Morna,* Morna, a personal or family name.

Mourne, Morney, a personal or family name.

Mourne, *Mudhorn, Múirne,* not given.

Mourne, *Múrn, Mughdhorna,* (mountains) the Mournes (a people), the Mughdhorna/Mugdorn tribe. The Irish name for these mountains is *beanna-Boirche,* peaks of Boirche, ascribed to a 3rd cent shepherd named 'Boirche'.

Mourneen, *boirnín,* a little hill.

Movaun, *mBóbhán, mBo-bhán,* white wcows

Movee, *Mobhí, Moibhú, Mobhi,* St Mobhí/Mobhi/Movee.

Moveedy, *maigh-Mhíde,* not given.

Moveen, *má / magh-mhín,* the smooth district/plain.

Movenis, *magh-inis,* a level river holm or island.

Mover, *Módhmhar,* not given.

Moville, *bun-an-phobail,* the end of the parish.

Moville, *maigh / magh-bhile,* plain of the ancient tree.

Mow, *m-bó,* cows.

Mowhan, *má-bhán,* white plain.

Mowhan, *Múchán,* not given.

Mowney, *maigh-Abhna,* not given.

Moy, *má, magh, machaire, muigh, muigh, maigh, maighe, máo, muaide, muighe,* a plain, a flat place.

Moy, *maí, mhaí, Moighe,* not given.

Moy, *m-buidhe,* yellow.

Moy, *Mhidhigh,* Meade, a personal or family name.

Moy, *Muaidh, Muaidhe,* Muaidh, a female name.

Moy, *muaidh,* stately.

Moy, *muaidhe,* clouds.

Moya, *magh-na…,* plain of the…

Moyacomb, *magh-da/dá-chon,* plain of the two dogs.

Moyagh, *maigheach,* level land.

Moyagh, *mBoitheach,* cow houses.

Moyah, *mBoitheach, mBoitheach, bo-teach,* cow-sheds, cow house/s or byres.

Moyaliff, *magh-Ailbh,* plain of flocks.

Moyaliff, *maigh-Ailbhe,* not given.

Moyaliffe, *magh-Ailbh, Ailbhe's* (a personal or family name) plain.

Moyaliffe, *magh-ailbh,* plain of flocks.

Moyally, *maigh-Eille,* not given.

Moybrick, *ma-thoirc,* plain of the wild pig(sic).

Moyeda, *mágh-Éide,* not given.

Moyella, *magh-Éille,* not given.

Moyemoge, *Modhíomóg,* not given.

Moyemoge, *mo-Dhiomóig,* St Dimoc.

Moyeoge, *Modhiomóg,* St Dimog/Dima.

Moyer, *magh,* a plain.

Moygalla, *mágh-eallach,* cattle plain.

Moyge, *magh,* a plain.

Moygh, *magh,* a plain.

Moygoish, *mag-Uais,* not given.

Moygoish, *Uí-mic-Uais,* the name of an ancient tribe.

Moyhill, *maethil, maethail,* soft spongy or marshy land.

Moyhora, *maigh-Theamhrach,* not given.

Moyhora, *mágh-thorthach,* fertile plain.

Moykarkey, *muigh-na-coirce,* the plain of the oats.

Moylagh, *magh-locha/lacha,* not given.

Moylagh, *maolach,* a flat or bald hill.

Moylan, *maelán, maelín,* a little round backed island in the sea or round bare rocks.

Moylan, *Mhaoldubháin,* Maoldubhán, a personal or family name.

Moylan, *Maelan,* St Maelan.

Moylan, *Mhaoláin,* Maelan, a male name now used as the surname Moylan.

Moylan, *Maoláin, Maoilín, Maolán, Mhaoláin,* not given.

Moylan, *Mhaoilín,* Maoilín, a personal or family name.

Moylan, *Uí-Maoilin,* Moylan, a family name.

Moylaun, *maelán, maelín,* a little round backed island in the sea or round bare rocks.

Moyle, *mael,* a hill.

Moyle, *maethail,* soft spongy land.

Moyle, *maoil, maol, mael,* bald, roofless, dilapidated or hornless.

Moyle, *maoile, maoil, maol, mael,* bare or a hornless cow.

Moyle, *maol,* a bare hill.

Moyle, *maol,* flat.

Moyle, *maothail, maothal, mhaol,* not given.

Moyle, *mhile,* a mile.

Moyleen, *maelán, maelín,* a little round backed island in the sea or round bare rocks.

Moyleen, *mhaoilín,* a small eminence.

Moyleen, *mhaolín,* a small rise.

Moyler, a family name and means the son of the servant of Mary.

Moyler, *Mhaoileachair,* not given.

Moyler, *Mhaolmhuire,* Moyler, a family name.

Moylerane, *Maelodhrain,* St Mailodhran/ Mailoran.

Moyles, *an-mhaoil*(sic), *na-maola,* not given.

Moylet, *magh-leacht,* plain of the gravestones.

Moyley, *mhaoile,* the bald person.

Moylin, *Mhaolín, Mhaoilinn, Moling, Moilin,* not given.

Moylin, *Uí-Maoilin,* O'Moylin or O'Moylan, a family name.

Moylish, *maoilis,* not given.

Moyliskar, *maol-eiscir,* not given.

Moylough, *maolach,* a flat or bald hill.

Moyly, *Mhaoile,* not given.

Moym, *maidhm,* erupted.

Moynagh, *maghnach,* a plain.

Moynagh, *Muimhneach,* Munstermen.

Moynaghan, a small flat place.

Moynalty, *magh-nEalta,* plain of (bird) flocks.

Moynan, *Maighnéain,* not given.

Moynas, *magh-neasa,* plain of the.......... cataract.

Moyne, *mágh-ain,* land of rushes.

Moyne, *maighean, an-mhaighean,* the precinct.

Moyne, *maighean, maighin,* a little plain.

Moyne, *maighean, maighin, mhaighin,* a plain, a little plain.

Moyne, *maighean,* a message(sic).

Moyne, *maoin,* wealth.

Moyne, *Mhuadhain,* St Modan.

Moyne, *món,* a bog.

Moyne, *Múin, maighne,* not given.

Moyne, *muing,* a morass.

Moyne, plain of the abbey enclosure(sic).

Moyneard, *maighin-árd,* the high little plain.

Moynehall, *maighean-eóchaille,* not given.

Moyney, *magh-abhna,* not given.

Moyney, *maighne,* the precinct(sic).

Moyney, *maigne,* plains.

Moyng, *an-mhoing*(sic), not given.

Moyng, *muing, muinga,* a sedgy place, a morass.

Moynoe, *magh-eó* the plain of yews.

Moynsha, *mágh-inse,* not given.

Moyntagh, *móinteach,* boggy land.

Moyntiagh, *móinteach,* boggy land.

Moyntragh, *mBaintreach,* not given.

Moyny, *maighne,* not given.

Moyny, *maighnigh,* the small plain.

Moyock, *Maidhioc, Maidhioc* or Mayock Barrett, a male name.

Moyode, *magh-fhoid,* field of the grass surface or sod.

Moyode, *mágh-fhót,* not given.

Moyola, *magh-Dhula,* not given.

Moyra, *maigh-ráithe, magh-rátha,* not given.

Moyra, *Maighre,* Moyer, a personal or family name.

Moyra, *maighreach,* a place of salmon.

Moyre, *magh-Adhair,* not given.

Moyree, (river) *abha-Maghríogh,* not given.

Moyrisk, *maoroisc,* not given.

Moyrus, *maíros, muigh-iorras,* not given.

Moys, plains.

Moystown, *magh-Istean,* Istean's (a personal or family name) plain.

Moystown, *maigh-Eistean,* not given.

Moyteoge, *máiteóg-acadh-gabhair,* not given.

Mrack, *mBreac, breac,* trout (from 'breac' speckled skin).

Mrahar, *mBrathar,* friars.

Mraher, *mBráthar, mBrathar,* friars.

Mreel, *mBroighiall, bruigheal,* cormorants.

Mrock, *mBroc, m-broc,* badgers.

Mronty, *mBróinte,* mill stones.

Mrossagh, *mBrosach,* not given.

Mryall, *mBruigheal,* cormorants.

Mu, *magh,* a plain.

Muacailly, *m-buachaillí,* boys.

Muc, *muc, muic,* pig or pigs.

Much, *much,* great, big.

Much, *na-muc,* of the pigs.

Muck, *mongach,* not given.

Muck, *muc, muic,* a pig or a piggery.

Muck, *muigh,* a plain.

Mucka, *muca,* not given.

Mucka, *muice,* pig.

Muckalee, *maigh-Coillí, mucfhalaighe,* not given.

Muckalee, *magh-thulaighe,* the hill plain.

Muckaly, *muclaigh,* piggeries.

Muckamore, *ma/maigh-chomair, magh-comair,* the plain of the confluence, joinings (of rivers, lakes or both.)

Muckanagh, *muc-eanach,* pigs marsh.

Muckanagh, *muiceanach, muiceannach,* a place of pigs a pig feeding place or a piggery.

Muckanaghederdauhaulia, *muicenach-idir-dhá-shaile,* not given.

Muckanaghederdavhalia, *muiceannach-eder-dau-haile,* piggery between two briny inlets.

Muckanaght, a place of pigs.

Muckduff, *mongach-dubh,* the black marsh grass.

Muckee, *Mhic Aodha,* Mac Kee, a family name.

Muckee, *mucaidhe, mhuicidhe,* a swine herd.

Muckelty, a place of pigs.

Muckenagh, *muiceannach,* a place of pigs.

Mucker, *mucar,* a place of pigs.

Mucker, *mucair,* not given.

Muckera, a place of pigs.

Muckery, a place of pigs.

Muckinagh, *muiceannach, muiceanach,* a place of pigs, a piggery or a pig feeding place.

Muckineagh, *muicineach,* not given.

Muckinsh, *muc-ais,* piglike.

Muckish, back of the pig.

Muckish, *mucais,* ridge of the pig.

Muckla, *muclach,* piggeries.

Mucklagh, *muclach, muclagh,* piggeries, a place of pigs/swine herds or a place of piggeries.

Mucklagh, *muclach,* not given.

Mucklaghan, *muchlachán,* a piggery.

Muckleheany, *Mic-Giolla-Sheanaigh,* Mackilheany, Gilheany or Heany, a family name.

Mucklemurry, *Mac-Giollamhuire,* Mackilmurry or Gilmore, a family name.

Muckley, *muclach,* a piggery.

Muckley, *muclaí,* a drove of swine or a place of pigs.

Mucklin, *Mhídheacháin,* Meehan, a male name.

Mucklin, *Mhíolchon, mhuclainn, muclainn, Mhic-Luain,* not given.

Mucklin, *muc-chluain,* pig meadow.

Mucklin, *muicliom,* pig land.

Muckloon, *muc-chluain,* pig meadow.

Muckly, *mucfhalaighe,* not given.

Mucknagh, *muiceannach,* a place of pigs.

Muckno, *mhucnú, mucnú, mucshnámha,* not given.

Muckno, *muc-shnámh,* lake of the pigs(sic).

Muckno, *muc-snamh,* a pigs swimming place.

Mucknoe, *machaire-mucsnámha,* plain of the pig swimming pace.

Muckoge, *Mocóg,* not given.

Muckoge, *mucóg,* young pigs.

Muckoo, *mucadh,* pigs.

Muckoo, *Mucú,* not given.

Muckridge, *Mhucraise, Mocraise,* St Mochraise.

Muckrum, *muc-dhroma,* pig ridge.

Mucks, *muc,* pigs.

Mucksna, *muc-snamh,* pig swimming.

Mucky, *mhuicí,* not given.

Mucky, *mucuidhe, mucaidhe, muicidhe,* pigs, swineherd.

Mucky, *muice,* the pig.

Mucky, *muicí,* swineherds.

Muclagh, *muclach,* piggeries.

Muclone, *muc-chluain,* not given.

Mucrarey, *magh-criartha,* plain of the bog.

Mucrus, *muc-ros,* copse or headland of the pigs.

Muddagh, *mBodach,* low-bred persons.

Muddagh, *mBodach, m-bodach,* churls, clowns.

Muddough, *m-bodach,* clowns.

Muddy, *mBodach,* a churl.

Mude, *Mhochuada,* St Mochuda.

Muff, *magh, má, muigh,* a plain.

Mugga, *mBogaighe,* a boggy or soft place.

Muggal, *mogul,* a cluster.

Muggaunagh, *magh-gamhnach,* plain of the milch cows.

Muggy, *mBogaigh,* bogs.

Mugh, *macha,* not given.

Mughana, *macha-na...,* not given.

Muhagh, *mothach,* fertile.

Muigh, *muighe,* not given.

Muilra, *mael-reidh,* smooth mountain flat.

Muilrea, *maoilréidh,* not given.

Muinard, *muine-aird,* the high brake or shrubbery.

Muine, *muine,* shrubbery.

Muineagh, *muineach,* a brake or shrubbery.

Muineaghan, *muineachan,* a brake or shrubbery.

Muineal, *muinéal,* a neck.

Muing, *moing,* not given.

Muing, *muing, muinga,* a sedgy place, a morass.

Muinga, long marshy grass.

Muinga, *moing-an...,* not given.

Muinga, *muing, muínge, muinge, muinga,* a sedgy place, a morass.

Muinga, *muing-a'...,* boggy morass of...

Muinga, *múinge,* rough grass.

Muingan, *moing-an...,* not given.

Muingan, *muing-an...,* boggy stream of the..., boggy morass of the...

Muingatlaunlush, *Muing-an-tSlánluis,* not given.

Muingatlaunlusk, *muing-a'tSlanluis,* sedgy place of the rib grass.

Muingelly, *muing-Eili,* Elly's marshy streaf(sic).

Muingna, *moing-na…*, not given.

Muingna, *muing-na…*, sedgy place, bog of the…

Muings, *na-moingí*, the ferns.

Muings, *na-monga/muingí*, not given.

Muiniagh, *an-mhuineach*, not given.

Muiniagh, *muingach*, a boggy morass or a sedgy place.

Muintervary, *muinntir-Bháire*, not given.

Muker, *Mocair*, Mockar, a personal or family name.

Mul, *mael*, a bald hill.

Mul, *maoile, maol, maoil*, a hill.

Mul, *maol*, partly levelled.

Mul, *mhala*, a hill brow.

Mul, *mhaoil*, a current.

Mul, *mhaol*, not given.

Mul, *mul*, a hill.

Mul, *mullach*, a summit.

Mulalla, *Uí-Mhaolalaidh*, O'Mulally, a personal or family name.

Mulbreeda, *maól-Bríghde*, servant of St Bridget.

Mulcah, *maoilcatha*, not given.

Mulcah, *Mhulcatha*, Mulcah, not given.

Mulchan, *maelchan*, Maelchan, a male name.

Mulchen, *Maolchon*, Maelchon, a personal or family name.

Mulclohy, *maolchloiche*, not given.

Mulderg, *Maoildeirg*, O'Mulderg, a family name.

Muldonagh, *maol/mul-Domhnaigh*, hill of the Church or Sunday.

Muldonagh, *maoldomhnach*, not given.

Muldorry, *Uí-Maoldoraigh*, O'Muldory, a family name.

Muldowney, *Maoldomhnaigh*, Muldowney or Moloney, a family name.

Muldrogh, *maoil-dorcha*, dark round/bald hill.

Mulgee, *Uí-Mhaolgaoithe*, Wynne(sic).

Mulkaun, from *mullán*, a little summit.

Mulkear, (river) *an-mhaoilcearn*(sic)/*mhaol-céar*, not given.

Mull, *mael*, a bare headland.

Mull, *maol*, bald.

Mulla, *mullach*, a summit.

Mulla, *na-mBuillí*, the blows.

Mullach, *mullach*, a summit.

Mullagh, *mallach, mullaigh*, not given.

Mullagh, *mallacht*, the curse.

Mullagh, *mhullach, mullach*, a summit or summits.

Mullagh, *mullach*, a hilltop.

Mullagha, *mullacha*, summits.

Mullagha, *mullach-an/a'…*, summit of the…

Mullaghan, *mullachan, mullaghán*, little summits.

Mullaghan, *mullach-an…*, summit of the…

Mullagharlin, *mullaigh-Chairlinn*, not given.

Mullagharn, *mullach-chairn*, summit of the carn.

Mullagheruse, *mullach-an-ruadhais*, not given.

Mullaghna, *mullach-na…*, summit of the…

Mullaghroe, *mullach-na-nDruadh, mullagh-ruadh*, not given.

Mullaghruttery, *mullach-chrotaire/otraigh, mallacuttra*, not given.

Mullaghusker, *mullach-Coscair*, not given.

Mullakill, *Uí-Mhaolábhail*, Ó Maolábhail, a family name.

Mullalough, *maol-locha*, not given.

Mullamarakill, big/great hilltop of the wood.

Mullan, *Maoláin*, Maolán, a personal name.

Mullan, *maolán*, a bald hill.

Mullan, *mBulán*, young bulls.

Mullan, *Mealláin, Meallain, Maelain,* Meallán, Meallan or Maelan, a male name.

Mullan, *Meallin*, a personal name.

Mullan, *Mhaolain*, Moylan or Mullan (a personal or a family name) height.

Mullan, *muileann*, a mill.

Mullan, *mullachan, mullach*, a little summit/s.

Mullan, *mulláin, mullán*, a little summit/s.

Mullan, *mullán*, a hillock.

Mullan, *mullach-an…*, hill of the…

Mullan, *mullán*, a little mill(sic).

Mullana, *muileann-na…*, mill of the…

Mullana, *mullach-na…*, summit of the…

Mullanafinnog, *mullach-Mheitheánach*(sic), not given.

Mullanan, *mullach-an…,* summit of the…

Mullanary, *mullan-aidhaire,* little hill of the shepherd.

Mullanarycortannel, *mullach-an-fharaidh-thoir*(sic), not given.

Mullanatinna, *mullán-aitinne,* a furry(sic) hillock.

Mullanderg, *mullach-dearg*(sic), not given.

Mullane, *Mothláin,* Mollan or Mullan, a personal or family name.

Mullane, *mullain,* a green summit.

Mullane, *O'Maolain,* O'Mullane, a family name.

Mullanlary, *mullach-chloichrí,* not given.

Mullannagaun, *mullan-na-gCeann,* green field(sic) of the heads.

Mullans, *mulláin,* a green field(sic).

Mullans, *na-mulláin,* little summits or hillocks.

Mullantra, *múl-na-tsratha,* hilltop of the holm.

Mullany, *mullach-an…,* height of the…

Mullarts, a place of elders.

Mullary, *má-Lamhraí,* plain of Lamhrach, a personal or family name.

Mullary, *Mól-Áirí, magh-Lamhraighe,* not given.

Mullatee, *mullach-an-tSí,* not given.

Mullaun, *mBullán,* young bulls.

Mullaun, *meallán,* not given.

Mullaun, *maolán, mhullain,* a hillock.

Mullaun, *mulláin,* little green fields(sic).

Mullaun, *mulláin, mullán,* little summit/s.

Mullaunna, *mullán-na* , little hill of the…

Mullauns, *mulláin, mullán,* little summits.

Mullavil, *Uí-Maolfhabhaill,* O'Mulavill, a family name usually now know as Lavelle.

Mullavill, *O'Maolabhal,* a family name.

Mullawna, *mullán-na…,* not given.

Mullen, *Maelan,* a male name.

Mullen, *Maoláin, Mealláin,* not given.

Mullen, *Maolín, Maolín,* a personal or family name.

Mullen, *mhuilinn, muillean, muileann, muil-leann,* a mill or mills.

Mullen, *Moling,* St Moling.

Mullen, O'Mullen or O'Moylan, a family name.

Mullena, *muilean/muileann-an/a'…,* mill on, of or beside the…

Mullena, *muileann-a'…,* mill on, of or beside the…

Mullenan, *mileannáin,* the little mill.

Mullenna, *muileann-na…,* not given.

Mullennahone, *muine*(sic)*-na-hUamhan,* not given.

Mullet, *mhuirthead,* mullet (peninsula).

Mullia, *mBuillí, mBúille,* strokes or blows.

Mullia, *muille,* not given.

Mullies, *mullaigh,* hills or summits.

Mullig, *mBolg, mBuilg,* bags or bellows.

Mullig, *mBulóg,* knolls.

Mullin, *Meallain, Maelain,* Meallan, Maelan, a male name.

Mullin, *mhuilinn, muilín, muillean, muileann, muilleann,* a mill.

Mullin, *mullagh-na…,* hill of the…

Mullina, *muileann-na…,* mill of the…

Mullina, *mullagh-na…,* summit/hill of the…

Mullina, *mul/mull-na…,* summit of the…

Mullinabro, *muileann-Ó mBróithe,* O'Brophy's (a family name) hill.

Mullinacuff, *muileann-Mhic-Dhuibh,* Mac Duibh's or MacDuffs (a family name) mill.

Mullinahack, *muilenn-a'chaca,* mill of the bad smell.

Mullingahill, *craon-Moling,* not given.

Mullinoly, *muileann-Uala,* not given.

Mullion, *muilleann,* a Mill.

Mullivan, *Maoldubhain, Maoldubhan,* a personal or family name.

Mullog, *mBulóg,* bullocks.

Mulloge, *mBallóg,* not given.

Mulloge, *mBullog,* bullocks.

Mullogh, *magh-lacha,* plain of the lake.

Mullough, *muileach,* top or summit.

Mully, *muilinn*(sic)*, mhullaigh,* not given.

Mully, *mullach, mullaigh,* a summit or hilltop.

Mullyash, *mullach-Aise,* not given.

Mullyera, *mullach-Ara,* not given.

Mullyera, *mullan-aidhaire,* little hill of the shepherd.

Mullyna, *mullaigh-na…,* summit of the…

Mulmoney, *maol-muine,* flat topped hazel bushes.

Mulmosog, *mull -Mosóg,* not given.

Mulna, *mul-na…,* hill of the…

Mulona, *mullagh-na…*, hill of the…

Mulqueen, *Maolcúine*, Mulqueen, a personal or family name.

Mulqueeny, *Uí-Maolchaoine*, O'Mulqueeny, a family name.

Mulrennan, *Uí-Maoilbhreanain*, O'Mulrenan, a family name.

Mulroy, *mael-ruadh*, red bald hill.

Mulroy, *maoile-ruaidhe*, not given.

Mult, *muilt, moilt, molt*, wether/s.

Multeen, *muiltín*, a little mill.

Multeeny, *m-buailtínidh, m-buailtinidhe*, flails.

Multeeny, *moiltíní*, not given.

Multimber, *Uí-Mhaoltomair*, O'Multomar or Multimber, a family name.

Multina, *mBuiltíneach*, of the Beltons or Boltons, a personal or family name.

Multina, *Moiltineach*, not given.

Multrean, *Uí-Maoiltrea*, O'Multrea, a family name. This name means servant of St Trea (the virgin saint).

Multy, *muilte*, mills.

Multy, *mullach-tighe…*, summit of the house of…

Mun, *bun*, not given.

Mun, *mhong, Munna*, not given.

Mun, *móin*, bog.

Mun, *muin*, a neck or flat.

Muna, *muine*, not given.

Munady, *muinide*, not given.

Munam, *muine*, a shrubbery.

Munder, *Muinire*, not given.

Mundry, *Mhondraí*, not given.

Mung, *moing*, not given.

Mung, *mong*, a sedgy place.

Mung, *muing*, a quagmire.

Mung, *muinge*, sedge or sedge grass.

Munga, *mong, muinge*, a morass that produces sedge grass.

Munga, *mong-a'…*, quagmire of the…

Munga, *mongach*, grassy or sedgy.

Munga, *muinga*, sedge grass.

Munga, *muing-a'…*, quagmire or sedgy place of the…

Munga, *mongach*, not given.

Mungan, a morass that produces sedge grass.

Mungan, *mongán*, not given.

Mungaun, a morass that produces sedge grass.

Mungo, *mongach*, marsh grass.

Mungret, *Mhungairit, Mhungairt, Mungairit*, not given.

Munhin, (river) *muinchinn*, not given.

Munie, *muine*, a shrubbery.

Munna, *moinge*, not given.

Munna, *muine*, a morass.

Munna, *muine*, a shrubbery.

Munnadesha, *bun-na-deise*, bottom land of the ear of corn.

Munnagashel, *bun-na-gCaiseal*, hill base of the stone forts.

Munnane, *muinean*, a small thicket, shrubbery.

Munnauns, *na-mionnáin*, not given.

Munnia, *muine*, a shrubbery or bushes.

Munnie, *muine*, a shrubbery.

Munnig, *muinigh*, a brake, shrubbery or thicket.

Munnilly, *mhuinchille*, not given.

Munnilly, *muinillidh, muinchille, muinichille, muinthille, muinirtle, muinilte*, the sleeve.

Munnion, *mBuinneán*, torrent or flood.

Munsburrow, *móin-na-Láirge*, not given.

Munsha, *minnse, muinse*, goats.

Munsha, *minseach*, not given.

Munster, *an-Mhuma*, place of Mumu or land of the men of Mumha.

Munster, *cúige-Muman, an-Mhumhan*, land of Mumha's men.

Munster, *Mhuimhneach*, not given.

Munter, *muintir*, the clan, tribe, family or people of…

Murchan, *Murchán*, O'Morahan, a family name.

Mureen, *O'Mhuirtin*, O'Morris, a family name.

Murgasty, *morgáiste*, not given.

Murgasty, the mortgage.

Murhaugh, *múroch, murbhach*, moory or marshy.

Murhaun, *múrthán*, little wall.

Murhevne, *muirtheimhne*, not given.

Murhur, *muigh-airthir*, eastern plain.

Murilly, *muirchille*, the sleeve.

Murirrigane, *Murorgán*, not given.

Murkogh, *marcach*, the rider.

Murlane, *Smurláin*, Smurlan, a mans name.

Murle, *muirlighe*, a marsh.

Murleog, *muirleog*, a basket for catching eels.

Murlough, *murbholg, murbhuilg,* a sea inlet.
Murlough, *murbholg,* sea swell.
Murlough, *murbholg,* the sea belly.
Murlough, *murloch,* not given.
Murn, *Mhúráin, Bhoirne,* not given.
Murn, *Murn, Muirne,* a female name.
Murn, *Uí-Mhuráin,* Ó Muráin, a family name.
Murnagh, *muirneach,* not given.
Murneen, *muirnín,* a lovable thing, an agreeable pleasant place or a pretty spot.
Murnogh, *muirneach,* a small marsh or swamp.
Murphy, *Mhurchaidh,* not given.
Murphy, *Mhurchúdha, Murchadha,* Murrough, a family name.
Murphy, *Murchuda,* O'Murphy, a family name.
Murphy, *Ua-Murchadha,* O'Murphy, a family name.
Murphy, *Uí-Mhurchú,* O'Murchadha, Ó Murchú or Murphy, a family name and means the descendants of Murphy.
Murra, *Murchad,* Morgan, a family name.
Murragh, *Mhurchaigh, muiritheach, muirbheach,* not given.
Murragh, *mór-ath,* big or great ford.
Murragh, *muighe-ratha/rátha,* plain of the ring fort.
Murragh, *Muircheartaigh,* Murtogh or Murkertagh, a personal or family name.
Murragh, *murach,* a rampart.
Murragh, *murbhach,* a flat piece of land along the sea or a salt marsh.
Murragh, *Murcha, Mhurcha, Morogha,* not given.
Murragh, *Murchadh, Mhurchadha, Murchadha,* Murchadh, Murrogh or Murragh, a male name, and the name of the first Bishop of Killala.
Murragh, *Uí-Mhurchú,* Ó Murchú, a family name.
Murragh, *Mhurchaidh,* Murrough, a personal or family name.
Murragha, *Mhurchadha,* Murrough, a personal or family name.
Murragha, *Mhurchaidh,* not given.
Murragha, *Morchadh,* Morrogh, a personal or family name.
Murraghill, *urchaille,* the cold wood.

Murraghoe, *Murchoe,* Murphy, a family name.
Murraghue, *Uí-Mhurchadha,* Murphy, a family name.
Murraghue, *Uí-Mhurchú,* not given.
Murrahin, *muigh-raithin,* plain of ferns.
Murrahin, *muirithin,* swampy ground.
Murrahin, *muirithin,* swampy land.
Murraugh, *Uí-Mhurchú,* Ó Murchú, a family name.
Murray, *Muireadhaigh,* Muireadhach or Muirdach, a male name.
Murray, *Muireadhaigh,* Muiredach or Murray the name of the first Bishop of Killala.
Murray, *Muiri,* Muireadhach, a personal or family name.
Murray, *Muirígh,* Muiríoch, a personal or family name.
Murray, *Uí-Mhuirígh,* Murray, a family name and means the descendants of Murray.
Murray, *Uí-Murchadha,* O'Muireadhaigh, O'Murray, a family name.
Murray, *Uí-Murchadha,* O'Muireadhaigh, O'Murray, a family name.
Murreagh, *an-mhuiríoch,* not given.
Murreagh, *muirbheach,* low sea board or sandy soil.
Murreagh, *muiríoch,* a beach.
Murreagh, *murbhach,* a flat piece of land along the sea, a salt marsh or flat marshy land by the sea.
Murreda, *Mairgheada,* Margaret, a female name.
Murree, *muiridhe,* the marine lake.
Murren, *mhoirinn,* not given.
Murren, *muirin,* sea grass.
Murrida, *Muireadach,* Muireadach, a personal or family name.
Murriheen, *Muirghaidhín,* little Murrough, a personal or family name.
Murrihy, *Muirithe,* Murray, a family name.
Murrikin, *Mhuireagáin,* Morgan, a male name.
Murrin, *Mhuirín,* Moreen, Martha or Muirne, a womans name.
Murrin, *Mhuirnín,* Muirne, Muirni, Boirne, a personal or family name.
Murrish, *muirisc,* a seashore marsh.

Murrisk, *muraisc,* a sea marsh.

Murriskna, *muir-riasc-na...,* sea marsh of the...

Murroe, *maigh/magh/mhá-rua,* red plain.

Murroe, *muirbheach,* not given.

Murroo, *muirbheach, murbhach,* a sea marsh or sea plain.

Murroogh, *murmhagh,* the sea plain.

Murroogh, *murúch,* a beach.

Murrough, *murbhach,* a flat piece of land along the sea or a salt marsh.

Murrow, *murbgach,* a flat marshy piece of land by the sea, a salt marsh.

Murry, *Mhuirígh, Muireadhaigh,* not given.

Murry, *Muire, Mhuíre, Mhuire,* Mary or St Mary.

Murry, *Muireadach, Mhuireadhaigh,* Murry, a family name.

Murry, *muireadaigh,* big an smooth.

Murry, *Muirí,* Muireadhach, a personal or family name.

Murry, *Muirí,* Murry, a personal or family name.

Murry, *muirigh,* monks.

Murry, *Muirithe,* Murray, a family name.

Murry, *Uí-Muireadhaigh, Uí-Mhuireadhaigh,* O'Murry or O'Murray, a family name.

Murryely, *Mhuire-Éile,* not given.

Murtagh, *mortach,* stagnant.

Murtagh, *Ua-Muircheartach,* Murtagh, a family name.

Murtagh, *Uí-Muircheartaigh,* O'Moriarty or O'Murkertagh, a family name.

Murtela, *mhairtealaigh,* martyrs or cripples.

Murvaclogher, *muir-ba-clochair*(sic), stoney place under the sea.

Murvagh, *muirbeach,* not given.

Murvagh, *murbhach,* a flat piece of land along the sea or a salt marsh.

Murvey, *mhuirbhigh, murbhach,* a flat piece of land along the sea, the seashore or a salt marsh.

Murvey, *muirbheach, mhuirbhigh,* the shore or sandy shore.

Murvy, *mhuirbhigh,* the beach.

Murvy, *murbhach,* a flat piece of land along the sea or a salt marsh.

Muse, *mús,* pleasant.

Musgrave, *Muscraíghe,* Muskerry an ancient territory.

Mushera, *muisire,* rough land.

Muskeagh, *magh-sciathach/sceach,* plain of thornbushes.

Muskerry, *Muscraidhe,* descendants/race of Carbery Músc/Muse/Musc, son of Conary II.

Muskerry, *Muscraighe, Múscraí,* not given.

Muskin, *muscán,* loose clay.

Muskry, *Muscraighe-Chuire,* the name of a lake of an ancient territory.

Musly, *mussailidhe,* mussels.

Muttoge, *mútóg,* a stump.

Mwee, *magh,* a plain.

Mweel, a bare hilltop.

Mweel, *maoil, maol,* a hill.

Mweel, *maoil-an...,* not given.

Mweel, *maol, mael,* bald, bare, roofless, hornless, or hornless cows.

Mweel, *míl,* animals.

Mweela, *maoil-an/a'..., maol-na...,* hill of the...

Mweela, *maol-a'...,* bare or bald hill of the...

Mweelan, *maelán, maelín,* a little round backed island in the sea or round bare rocks.

Mweelaun, *maoláin,* a bare hill.

Mweelaun, *maolán,* not given.

Mweeleen, *maelán, maelín,* a little round backed island in the sea or round bare rocks.

Mweelin, *an-mhaoilinn,* not given.

Mweelin, *maigh-mhuilinn,* not given.

Mweelin, *maoilean,* a bleak (bald) hill.

Mweelin, *maoilín, maoilin,* a little round bare hill.

Mweeling, *maelán, maelín,* a little round backed island in the sea or round bare rocks.

Mweeling, *maoilinn,* a hill summit.

Mweeling, *mhaoilinn,* not given.

Mweeloon, a bare or bald hill.

Mweelrea, *maoil-réidh,* smooth hilltop.

Mweenagh, *Muimhneach,* Munstermen.

Mweenish, *máinis,* not given.

Mweenish, *muigh-inis,* flat island.

My, *magh, muigh,* a plain.

My, *miodh,* middle.

Mylane, *maoilean,* a bare place.

Mylone, *magh-luan,* plain of the lambs.

Mynagh, *maghnach,* a plain.

Myre, *maer,* a steward or keeper.

Myre, *mhaighe,* not given.

Myroe, *má-rua,* red plain.

Myroe, *muigh-ruadh,* not given.

Myros, *miodh-ros,* middle headland.

Myross, *midhros,* not given.

Myrtleville, *baile-an-chuainín,* not given.

Myshal, *magh-iseal,* the low plain.

Myshall, *magh-iseal,* the low plain.

Myshall, *midh-íseal,* not given.

Myshall, *míseal, mísil,* a low central place.

N

Na, *na,* …, of the…
Naan, *ain,* a ring.
Naas, *nás,* meeting place or the assembly.
Naas, *nás-na-Ríogh,* not given.
Nabania, *na-báine,* the white cow(sic).
Nabba, *'n-Abba,* the Abbot.
Nabiree, *na-mBioraí,* the reeds.
Nabla, *nablaithe,* a ravine or hollow.
Nabol, *na-bPoll,* not given.
Nabrackalan, *na-breac-elainn,* the beautiful trouts.
Nabrackbady, *na-mbreac beadaidhe,* the saucy or dainty trouts.
Nabrackbautia, *na-breac-báidhthe,* the drowned trouts.
Nabrackbeg, *na-breac-bheag,* the little trouts.
Nabrackdeelion, *na-breac-díleann,* the flood trouts.
Nabrackkeagh, *na-breac-caech,* the blind trouts.
Nabrackmore, *na-breac-mór,* the big trouts.
Nabrackrawer, *na-breac-remmhar,* the fat trouts.
Nabro, *na-bro,* the flood or gush.
Nabron, *na-brón,* the millstone.
Nacard, *na-cor-rátha,* the odd ford.
Nacnocky, *na-cnoca,* the hills.
Nacole, *Niocóil, Niocól,* a personal or family name.
Nacole, *Niocóil,* St Nicholas.
Nacrin, *an-ao'chrainn,* one tree.
Nacung, …*na-cuinge,* …of the yoke.
Nad, *nead,* nest/s.
Nadane, *an-fheadain,* of the streamlet.
Naddan, *an-fheadain,* a little stream.
Nadneagh, *an-fheadánach,* not given.
Nadrid, *nead-druid,* the enclosure.

Nadrid, *nead-druide,* nest of the starving(sic).
Nadryd, *nead-druid,* the enclosure(sic).
Nadryd, *nead-druide,* nest of the starving(sic).
Nady, *chnáidí,* of annoyance.
Nafarty, *na-fearta,* not given.
Naff, *nDamh,* oxen.
Nafflan, *na-bhFlann/bh-Flann,* (of the men called) 'Flann'.
Naffrin, *an-Aifrinn,* mass offering.
Nafin, *na-finne,* of the white cow.
Nafina, *na-fine,* of the white cow.
Naflan, *na-bhFlann/bh-Flann,* (of the men called) 'Flann'.
Nafooey, *na-feothaidh,* not given.
Nafooey, *na-fuaithe,* the phantom.
Nag, a woodpecker.
Nagalt, *na-ngealt,* the lunatics.
Nagar, *na-gCarr,* of the cars.
Nagard, *na-gCeard,* artificers.
Nagarde, *na-gCeard,* artificers.
Nagaug, *na-gCadhóg,* the jackdaws.
Naggin, *na-gCeann,* the heads.
Nagh, …*nach,* as an ending to a word can sometimes mean, a place of…. or abounding in…
Nagh, *neach,* troops,
Nagh, *n-eich, n-each, nEach, neach, eich,* horse/s.
Naghill, *'n-eochaill,* the yew wood.
Naghill, *cnámhchoill,* not given.
Naghtan, *Uí-Neachtain,* O'Naughtan, a family name.
Naghten, *Mic-Neachtain,* MacNaughten, a family name.
Nagin, *na-gCeann,* the heads.
Nagin, *na-gCionn,* not given.
Nagire, *n-gadhar,* dogs.
Naglantane, *na-ngleanntán,* little glens.
Nagle, *an-gCailleach,* of the old women.
Nagles, (Mt) *an-mhóin-mhór,* not given.
Nagnady, *Iognaide,* St Ignatious.
Nagora, *na-g-corr,* the cranes.
Nagown, *na-gCeann,* the heads.
Nagran, *na-gCrann,* of the trees.
Nagree, *na-ngroigheadh, na-graigh/groigh,* the horses.
Nagrus, *na-g-cros,* of the crosses.
Nagry, *na-gCruidh, gCruidhe,* the cattle.

Nagry, *na-graí/groighe,* not given.

Nagry, *na-ngroigheadh, ngroidheadh, na-graigh/groigh,* the horses.

Naha, *na-háith*(sic), the ford.

Naha, *na-haithe/haithche, n'Áithe,* the kiln.

Naha, *na-hÁtha,* not given.

Nahan, *na-heanaigh,* the marshes.

Nahan, *Natháin,* Nathan, a male name.

Nahana, *na-nEagaig,* not given.

Nahau, *na-háithe,* the kiln.

Nahaw, *na-haithe,* the kiln.

Nahay, *na-haithe, haithche,* the kiln.

Naheelis, *na-hIallais,* abounding in bind-weed.

Naheer, *na-huidhre,* of the dun cow.

Naheera, *na-hUidhre,* the brown stream.

Naheery, *na-huidhre,* of the dun cow.

Naher, *an-Athar,* the father.

Naher, *n-Eachair,* of the horses.

Nahera, *na-huidhre,* of the dun cow.

Nahevla, *na-abhal,* the orchard.

Nahiry, *na-hUidhre,* the brown stream.

Nahod, *'n-ath-fhoid,* the ford of the sod.

Nahoe, *na-hUaimhe, huamha,* the cave.

Nahoo, *na-huamha,* the cave.

Nahoora, *na-huidhre,* of the dun cow.

Nahulty, *na-Hultach,* the Ulsterwoman.

Nahur, *na-hIora,* not given.

Nahur, *Nathar,* not given.

Nahyla, *na-hAidhle,* not given.

Nail, *ionga,* not given.

Nakil, *tóin-na-hOlltaí,* not given.

Nalbanagh, *na-nAlbanach,* not given.

Naliv, *nDealbh,* phantoms.

Nallagane, *nDealgán,* thorn bushes.

Nallis, *fhionnghlaise,* the white stream.

Nallog, *nDealg, n-dealg,* thorn or thorn bushes.

Nally, *na-hAilighe,* not given.

Nally, *na-hailighi,* stone fort.

Naloo, *na-lugh,* the hollow.

Nalour, *na-lobhar,* the lepers.

Nalower, *na-lobhar,* the lepers.

Nalty, *nEalta, nealta,* (bird) flocks.

Nalyer, *na-ladhar,* the river forks.

Namagh, *na-mach,* not given.

Namagh, *na-mbeach,* the bees.

Naman, *na-mBan,* the women.

Naminnoo, *na-Minneamh,* not given.

Namna, *na-mna,* of the women.

Namoe, *na-mBó,* of the cattle

Namon, *na-mban,* the women.

Namph, *nDamh, n-damh,* oxen.

Nample, *leamhchoille,* not given.

Nana, *an-eanaigh,* the marsh.

Nana, *an-fheá,* not given.

Nana, *na-nÁith,* kiln.

Nana, *na-nÁth,* the fords.

Nana, *na-nEach,* not given.

Nanagh, *an-fhia,* not given.

Nanagh, *na-neach/nEach,* the horses.

Nanagh, *nEanach,* marshes.

Nanane, *na-néan,* the birds.

Nanar, *na-n-ár,* of the slaughters.

Nanav, *na-nDamh, n-damh,* oxen.

Nane, *Fhíonáin, Fhionáin,* Fíonán, Fionán or Fionnan, a personal or family name.

Nane, *Fhionain, Fhionáin,* St Finan.

Nane, *néan, n-éan,* the birds.

Naneen, *na-nÉan,* not given.

Naneill, descendants of Niall, a personal name.

Nanerriagh, *na-naodhaireach,* shepherds.

Nangle, *naingeal,* angels.

Nanima, *an-anama,* not given.

Nannig, *an-eanaigh, eanaig,* the marsh.

Nanny, (river) *an-Ainge,* not given.

Nanny, *na-eanaigh,* the marsh.

Nanoone, *na-n-uan,* of the lambs.

Nanooney, *nUaithne,* Owney, a personal or family name.

Nanoose, *nan-mhas,* the hired soldiers.

Nanoose, *na-n-ús,* the soldiers. (compare **Nhus**)

Nant, *neanta,* nettle/s.

Nant, *neantanán, neantach, neantaná, neanta,* a place of nettles.

Nanta, *neannta, neanta,* nettle/s.

Nantinan, *neanntanán, neantanán, neantaná,* a place of nettles.

Nantoge, *neanntog, neantóg,* little place of nettles.

Nantoge, *neantóige,* not given.

Nanty, *fhantaigh,* not given.

Nanty, *na-neanta/neannta,* nettle/s.

Nanty, *neantadh,* not given.

Nanty, *Uí-Neachtain,* Ó Neachtán, a family name.

Nanum, *an-anama,* not given.

Nanum, *an-anam,* the soul or spirit.

Nanus, *na-nOis, na-nos,* fawns.

Nanuss, *na-nOs,* the deer.

Naon, *én,* birds.

Nap, *an-appa,* the abbot.

Nap, *cnap,* a lump, a small round hillock.

Nappagh, *cnappach,* hilly land.

Nappan, *cnapán, cnappain,* a small hill.

Nappan, *cnapan,* a knob shaped hillock.

Nappy, *an-Apadh,* the Abbot.

Nar, *nár,* slaughters.

Naraha, *na-rátha,* the rath or fort.

Naran, *na-reanna,* not given.

Naranad, *na-nDeargnat,* not given.

Naraw, *na-ratha,* the fort.

Nard, *n-Ard,* the heights.

Nare, *an-fhéir,* not given.

Narea, *na-ria/riaghadh,* the executions.

Nareera, *na-reimhre,* the (sea) swell.

Narget, *an-airgid,* not given.

Narin, *fhearthainn,* place of rain.

Nariska, *an-uisce,* the water.

Narnane, *an-airnéain/airneain,* not given.

Narnane, *an-áirneáin,* the night work.

Narney, *nAirne, nÁirne,* not given.

Narney, *nAírní, nÁirneadh, nAirneadh,* sloes.

Narra, *an-fhorrach,* not given.

Narra, *an-fharrach,* the assembly place.

Narra, *naraidh,* the charioteer.

Narragh, *an-fhorrach,* the area of land.

Narragh, *an-fhorrach/fharrach,* not given.

Narragh, *nDarach,* oaks.

Narrew, *an-arbha,* not given.

Narriagh, *naireamhach,* ploughmen.

Narrick, *...na-dTorc,* not given.

Narrick, *...na-nDaróg,* ...of the oak or small oaks.

Narrid, *an-airid,* not given.

Narrigle, *n-aireagal,* a prayer house.

Narry, *an-aodhaire,* not given.

Narry, *Fhearaígh, Fearaíoch,* not given.

Narry, *n-aedhaire,* of the shepherd.

Nart, *an-fhearta,* not given.

Nart, *an-fhearta/fheart,* the grave.

Nart, *neirt,* strength.

Narullagh, *na-saileach,* the sally trees.

Naryagh, *na-naodhaireach,* shepherds.

Nasa, *an-easa,* the waterfall.

Nash, *an-Naisigh, an-Naiseach,* not given.

Nash, *nás,* meeting place.

Nasherry, *an-oisire,* the oyster.

Nashig, *Naisig,* Naiseach, not given.

Nask, *nEasc,* not given.

Nask, *neasg,* tethering ropes.

Nasker, *na-sceire,* the sharp rock. Sometimes an inland rock but mostly a sea rock.

Naskollia, *na-scoile,* the school.

Nasop, *na-sop,* straw wisps.

Naspol, *nAspal, nAspol,* not given.

Nass, *an-easa,* the cataract, waterfall.

Nassa, *an-easa,* the cascade, waterfall or cataract.

Nassan, *Neasáin,* Nessan, a male name.

Natooey, *na-Tuaithe,* not given.

Nattin, *an-aitinn,* furze.

Naugh, *n-each,* horses.

Naugh, *n-gall,* the English.

Naught, *nocht,* not given.

Naul, *an-áil,* litter(sic).

Naul, *an-áill, an-aill,* the cliff or the rock.

Naule, *an-áil,* the rock.

Naule, *an-shail,* salt water.

Naule, *Náile,* St Natalis.

Naunagh, wanderers.

Nav, *nDamh,* oxen.

Navaag, *na-feadh,* the bulrushes.

Navad, *na-bhfead,* the whistles.

Naval, *na-bhfál,* of the hedges.

Navall, *na-bhfál,* of the hedges.

Navan, *an-uaimh,* the cave.

Navan, *Nabhainn, an-eamhain,* not given.

Navan, new habitation.

Navar, *na-bh-fear, na-bhfear,* the men.

Navart, *na-bhfeart,* the graves or miracles.

Nave, *Naoimh,* Saint/s, holy.

Nave, *nDamh,* oxen.

Navea, *na-bfhiagh, na-bhfiadh,* the deer.

Navea, *na-fhéich,* the raven.

Naved, *na-bhfead,* (fairy) whistling.

Navee, *na-b-fhiagh,* the deer.

Naveen, *na-bhFiann,* the Fianna or Fena the ancient heroic militia.

Naveen, *na-bhFionn,* the white spots.

Naveigh, *na-bhFiach/bhFia,* not given.

Naveigh, *na-bhFiagh,* the deer.

Navglaun, *...na-bhFlann,* not given.

Navin, *Cnaimhín, 'ic-Cnaimhin,* McNevin, or Nevin, a family name.

Navode, *na-bhfód,* the green sods or patches.

Navune, *na-bhFionn,* the white spots.
Nawal, *na-bhfál,* of the hedges.
Nawengland(sic), *baile-na-nGall,* homestead of the English.
Nawly, *Naile,* Naile, a male name.
Ndiahab, *nDiabhal,* the devils.
Ndial, *nDiabhal,* devils.
Nea, *an-fhiaidh,* the deer.
Nea, *an-fhiaigh,* the raven.
Nea, *naí,* the infant.
Nea, *néidh,* windy.
Neadan, *an-Éadain,* the brow.
Neagh, *an-fheiche,* the raven.
Neagh, horse.
Neagh, *an-tAonaigh,* a meeting place, a fair.
Neagh, *nEachach, Neachach, nEathach, nEchach,* Eochadh, Eochaidh or Eochy, a 1st cent Munster chief, King who drowned in this lake.
Neagh, *nEathhach,* Eochaid, a male name.
Neague, *an-fhiaig,* the deer.
Neal, *neal,* noble.
Neal, *neall,* clouds.
Neal, *neal-uisge,* water-crow root.
Neal, *Uí-Néill,* Ó Néill, Néill or O'Neill, a family name.
Neale, *an-Éill,* the bird flock.
Neale, *nDaol,* beetles or chafers.
Neale, *Uí-Néill,* Ó Néill, a family name.
Nean, *nÉan, n-éan/én,* birds.
Neane, *nÉan/en/én,* birds.
Neaner, *an-aonfhír,* not given.
Neaney, *na-nIonadh,* of the wonders.
Neaney, *na-nIongnad,* not given.
Neanor, *an-aonfhir,* the lone man.
Neanor, *n-eaner, nEanor,* lonely.
Neany, *an-aonaigh,* the fair.
Neany, *na-nIonadh,* of the wonders.
Nearla, *an-iarla, n'arla,* (of the) Earl.
Nearla, *na-nEirleach,* not given.
Neary, *an-aoire, n-aedhaire,* of the shepherd.
Neary, *an-aoire,* the satirist.
Neary, *fhearaigh,* grassy fields.
Nease, *Aenghusa,* not given.
Nease, *Naois,* Naois, a personal or family name.
Neashagh, *n-Aeseach,* not given.
Neashagh, *nDéiseach,* (of the) Decies (a family name).
Neaska, *náosga, naosca,* snipes.

Neaskagh, *naosgaidh,* snipes.
Neaskeagh, *naosgaidh,* snipes.
Neaskin, *'n-easgainn, an-eascain,* the marsh.
Neaskin, *naosc,* a place of snipes.
Neasky, *naoscaighe,* the snipe bog.
Neasky, *naosgaidh,* snipes.
Neasy, *na-nDeisi, nDeise, nDeisí,* ford of Desii (an ancient territory).
Neav, *naomh,* saints.
Neave, *naobh,* river rafts.
Neave, *naomh,* saint/s or holy.
Neaveen, *Naoimhín,* not given.
Nebber, *an-abair,* the mire.
Neck, *cnoc,* a hill.
Ned, *nead,* a nest or a birds nest.
Ned, *nead,* haunt or lair.
Nedan, *an-eudan,* the hill brow.
Nedanone, *nead-an-eóin,* the birds nest.
Neddan, *an-fheadain,* the streamlet or brook.
Neddans, *feadáin, bh-feadáin,* brooks or streamlets.
Neddans, *fearann-an-neadáin, na-neadán/neadáin,* not given.
Neddaun, *neidán,* the skirmish.
Nedeen, *neadín,* the little nest.
Neden, *an-éadain,* not given.
Nedinagh, *nead-an-fhia,* deers nest.
Nee, *an-fhiadh,* the deer.
Nee, *Eidhnighe, Ní,* not given.
Nee, *Naoi,* a male name.
Nee, *naoimh,* holy.
Nee, *Neidhe,* a male name.
Nee, *nighthe,* washing.
Neechy, *Naoise,* Naoise, a personal or family name.
Needle, (island) *snáthadán,* not given.
Neelagh, *n-iallach,* flocks or herds.
Neen, Finin, a personal name.
Neena, *an-aonaigh,* the fair.
Neenagh, *fhíona,* wine.
Neenan, *Naoidheanain,* Naoidheanan or Neenan, a personal name.
Neenaun, *Naíonán,* not given.
Neening, *Fhaininigh,* Fanning, a family name.
Neeny, *an-aonaigh,* the fair.
Nees, *naosg,* snipes.
Neese, *Aenghuis,* Aengus, a male name.
Neese, *Aonghasa,* not given.

Neesk, *naosc,* snipes (birds).

Neesk, *naosca,* not given.

Neeskan, *naosgan,* snipes (birds).

Neestin, *Nístin,* not given.

Neeta, *an-Faoitig, Fhaoitigh, an-ite, an-Fhaeite,* White, belonging to White, a family name.

Neety, *an-Faoitig/Fhaoitigh, an-Ite, an-Fhaeite,* White, belonging to White, a family name.

Neety, *an-Fhaoitigh,* de Faoite, a family name.

Neeve, *naomh,* saints.

Neevin, *naoibhinn,* beautiful.

Neevin, *Naoimhín,* not given.

Neevoge, *Naomhóg, Naomhog, Naomhóig,* Neevoge, mans name and means 'little saint'.

Negal, *na-ngall,* foreigners.

Negish, *an-Éigis,* not given.

Negish, *n-eigeas,* of the learned man or poet.

Neigham, *Niachaim,* not given.

Neighan, *an-fhiachmagh,* the hunting plain(sic)

Neighvaun, *an-eich-bháin,* the white horse.

Neill, *Neill,* Neill, Niall or O'Neill, a family name.

Neill, *Neill,* Niall, a male name and the name of an ancient chief.

Neill, *Uí-Néill,* Ó Néill, a family name.

Neillan, *Niallain,* O'Neylan, a family name.

Neillean, *Ua-Nialáin,* O'Neylan, a family name.

Neiphinn, *néimh-bheann,* bright peak, summit.

Neirc, *nadharc,* horns.

Neirk, horn/s.

Neiry, *nDaighre,* not given.

Neiry, *Néire,* not given.

Neity, *an-Faoitig, Fhaoitigh, an-ite, an-fhaeite,* White, belonging to White, a family name.

Nelestrum, *an-fheiliostruim,* flaggers.

Nelligan, *Ui-Niallagáin,* O'Nelligan, a family name.

Nelly, *n'Aile,* standing stones.

Nemar, *na-marbh,* (of) the dead.

Nen, *naoin, naon, naen,* nine.

Nenagh, (river) *abainn-Ó-gCathbhadh,* not given.

Nenagh, *an-aonach,* the fair or assembly.

Nenagh, *an-t-aenach,* the fair, *Aonach-Urmhúmhan/Urúmhan/Urmhumhan,* fair town, assembly place of the Ormonds, an East Munster tribe.

Nenagh, *na-nAonach,* not given.

Nenagh, *neíneach,* morasses.

Nenagh, *nénach,* birds.

Nendrum, *naoi-nDruim,* not given.

Nennan, *an-fhionnáin,* not given.

Nennan, *Néanaín,* Nunan, a male name.

Nenor, *naonbhair,* nine persons.

Neor, *nDéor,* drops or tears.

Neor, *nDeoraí,* not given.

Nephin, *Neimhtheann, Néifin,* not given.

Neppy, *neipe,* turnip.

Nera, *an-Iarla,* the Earl.

Nera, *an-oidhre,* not given.

Neroon, *na-nEireamhóin/nÉiriún,* belonging to the Naroon's or Irwin's, a family name.

Nerree, *nDoirí,* not given.

Nerree, *nDoiridhe, n-dairghe,* oaks or oak woods.

Nerriagh, *na-naodhaireach,* shepherds.

Nerriff, *nAireamh,* not given.

Nerriff, *noireamh,* ploughmen.

Nerrig, *an-eirrig,* not given.

Nerrig, *na-deirg,* red colour.

Nerroon, *na-nAiriún,* not given.

Nerrowne, *na-nÉiriún,* belonging to the Naroon's or Irwin's, a family name.

Ness, *eas, ess, an-tEas/easa,* a waterfall on a river, a fall in a river, a rapid or a cataract.

Ness, *inis,* an island or river holm.

Neth, *nead,* nest/s.

Nether, *an-iochtair,* the lower.

Nevan, *Ua-Neabháin,* O'Nevan, a family name.

Nevan, *Uí-Chnaímhin,* O'Knavin, a family name.

Nevan, *nEimhin,* St Evin.

Nevin, *Naeidhen, Naeidhe,* name of a pagan chief.

Nevin, *naíon,* infants.

Nevin, *Naíon,* the child.

Nevin, *Naomhan,* Nevin, a family or a persons name.

Nevin, *Neimhin,* Nevin, a male name

Nevin, *Naoimhín, Noidhean,* not given.

Nevin, *Uí-Naomháin,* O'Nevin, a family name.

Nevoga, *Naomhóga,* Nevoge, a male name.

Nevoga, *Naomhóige, Naemhóige,* not given.

New, *cnúdh,* nut producing place.

New, *Naoi,* Naoi or Noé, a male name.

New, *nua,* new.

Newbliss, *cúil-darach,* not given.

Newgrange, *caiseal-Aonghusa, ros-na-Ríogh,* not given.

Newragh, *an-Iúrach,* not given.

Newrath, '*n-Iubhrach,* the yew land.

Newrath, *an-rátha-nua, an-Iúrach,* not given.

Newry, (river) *abhainn-gleann-Ríghe*(sic), *an-Rí,* not given.

Newry, *an-iúraigh, an-tIúr, an-tIúir,* a place of yew trees. The ancient name was *Iubhar-cinn-tragha, Iobhar-chind-tráchta/ trachta,* yew at the head of the strand.

Newry, *an-tIúr,* the yew tree.

Newry, *iúr-chinn-trá,* not given.

Newtownbalregan, *baile-nua- dealgan*(sic), not given.

Newtownfane, *baile-nua-áth-Féin*(sic), not given.

Newtownsandes, *maigh-Mheáin*(sic), not given.

Newtownstalaban, *tigh-Líobáin*(sic), not given.

Ney, …*nach,* as an ending to a word can sometimes mean, a place of…. or abounding in…

Nhus, *na-n-ús,* wild dogs, gallowglasses or mercenaries.

Nichol, Nichol or MacNichol, a family name.

Nick, *chnuic, chnoic, cnoc,* a hill.

Nickawn, *cnocán,* a hillock.

Nickeers, from *cnuicéir,* rabbit warrens or coney boroughs.

Nicker, *coinicéar,* not given.

Nicker, shortened version of *cuinicér,* a rabbit warren.

Nickeres, *na-coinicéir,* not given.

Nicole, Nichol or MacNichol, a family name.

Nid, *nead,* a birds nest.

Nid, *nid,* not given.

Niddan, *an-fhiodáin/feadan,* the small brook.

Niddane, *an-fheadain,* the streamlet.

Niddane, *nid-án(*sic), birds nests.

Niddaun, *an-fheadáin,* the streamlet.

Nidon, *Adain,* Adain or Aydon, a personal or family name.

Nidon, *fhiodh-duin,* wooden fortress.

Nier, (river) *an-uidhir,* not given.

Nier, *an-uidhir,* dun coloured (river).

Nier, *n'ier,* grey river.

Nierin, '*n iárann, an-iarainn, the* iron.

Niggan, *nUigin,* …of the Higgin's, a family name.

Nilard, *an-Aighleardaigh,* not given.

Niller, *an-iolair/iolar/fhiolair,* the eagle/s.

Nilly, *na-bhile,* the ancient tree.

Nilteen, *n-ailtín,* the little glenside, declivity or ravine.

Nim, *n'im,* of the butter.

Ninch, *an-inse,* the island.

Nine, *an-adhainn,* the caldron.

Ninny, *Ninnidh,* St. Ninnidh/Ninny.

Nira, *eidhre,* the heir.

Niree, *nDoirí,* oaks.

Nish, *inis,* an island.

Nisk, *an-uisce, na-uisge,* the water.

Niskan, *Neascán,* not given.

Niske, *n-eisce,* river, quagmire.

Nisky, *an-uisce, na-uisge,* the water.

No, *nua,* new.

Noan, *an-uamhain,* the cave.

Noan, *nuadhainn,* caves.

Noan, *n-uamhainn,* the cave.

Noard, *núrd, nua-ard,* new hill or height.

Nobber, *an-obair,* the work or construction.

Nobber, *obair,* work.

Nocht, *nocht,* naked.

Nock, *cnoc, cnoich, chnuic,* a hill.

Nockan, *chnocáin,* a hillock.

Nockans, *cnocáin,* hillocks.

Nocum, *Nócam,* Nocam, a personal or family name.

Nod, *namhad,* enemies.

Node, *an-fhóid,* the sod, soil or land.

Node, *noide,* a Church or hermitage.

Nody, *Noide,* the Church.

Noe, *an/n-eó,* yews.

Noe, *núadh, nua,* new.

Noe, *Nuadh, Nuad,* not given.

Noge, *nÓg,* not given.

Noggin, *chnocáin,* hillock/s.

Noggin, *Naigín,* Noggan, a personal or family name.

Noggins, *chnocáin,* not given.

Noggus, *Cnogús,* not given.

Noghan, *namhachan, n-uamhchan,* the little cave.

Noglagh, *na-nÓglach,* not given.

Nohoval, *nuachabháil,* new enclosure.

Nohoval, *nua-chongbhai, nuadh-chongbháil,* new habitation or settlement.

Nohovoldaly, *nuadhchonghbháil-Uí-Dhálaigh,* not given.

Noise, *Nois,* Nos, a male name.

Noise, *nós,* noble.

Nolah, *'n-ulaigh,* the prayer station or altar tomb.

Nolan, *Nualláin,* not given.

Nolan, *Ó Nialláin,* Uí Nialláin, a family name.

Nollag, *Nodlag,* Christmas.

Noly, *Nualla,* Nuala, a female name.

Nomasna, *Uí-Lom Masna,* O'Lomasney, a family name.

Nona, *inneoin,* the anvil.

None, *n-uan,* the lambs.

Noneen, *nóinín,* daisies.

Noney, *inneoin,* the anvil.

Noney, *inneona, inneóna,* not given.

Nonshagh, *nÓinseach,* female idiots.

Nonshie, *nÓinseach,* female idiots.

Nonty, *fhantaigh,* the spectre.

Nonty, *fhantaigh,* the nobleman.

Nony, *néona,* violence.

Noo, *nua,* new.

Noo, *n-ubh,* eggs.

Nooaff, *an-uamh, n'-uaimh,* the cave.

Nooag, *nDubhóg,* not given.

Nooan, *n'-uamhainn,* the cave.

Nooan, *na-úamhan,* the caves.

Nooan, *nDubhan,* of the Duanes, a family name.

Nooan, *Nuadhan,* St Nuadha.

Noodan, *Nuadain,* Nuadan, Nuodan, a personal or family name.

Nooey, the cave.

Nook, *ráth-Gualann,* not given.

Nooker, *an-úcaire,* the fuller (person who thickened cloth).

Nookery, *an-úcaire,* the fuller (person who thickened cloth).

Nool, *n-Ábhall, n-Abhall,* the orchard.

Nool, *nubhall, nubhull,* apples.

Noon, *dún,* a fort.

Noon, *na-bhann,* streams.

Noon, *na-bhann,* streams.

Noon, *núan, n-uan,* the lambs.

Noonan, *naoidhgeanain,* a young child.

Nooneen, *nóinín,* daisies.

Nooney, *inneoin,* the anvil.

Noony, *inneonaigh,* not given.

Noony, *Inneona,* Inneon, a personal or family name.

Nooran, *nuaran,* cold springs.

Noose, *Aenghuis,* Aengus, a male name.

Noose, *na-hAmhas,* mercenaries.

Noose, *núis,* new milk.

Noose, *núis,* biestings(sic).

Noose, *nÚs, nUs, núise,* not given.

Noosh, *nGiumhais,* a wood of fir.

Noosh, *núis,* the first milk after calving, also known as 'beastings'.

Nooth, *Nuadhat,* Nuadhat, an ancient King.

Nora, *an-fhabhra,* the hill brow.

Nora, *Nóra,* Nora, a female name.

Nora, Honora or Nora, a female name.

Nora, *Noraidh,* Norris, a personal or family name.

Noran, *an-uaráin, an-fhuairáin/fhuaráin,* the cold spring or well.

Nore, (the river) *fheóir, fheoir,* the feoir, not given.

Nore, a stream.

Nore, *an-óir,* the gold.

Nore, *nDeór,* tears.

Noreshy, *an-Urraéise,* Norris, a male name.

Norig, *an-Óraig,* not given.

Norig, Honora or Nora, a female name.

Norman, *Normáin,* not given.

Nornoge, *nDornóg,* round stones.

Norone, *na-ruan,* the rowan.

Norrus, *nDorus,* the doors.

Nort, *Ó nDúrtaigh,* Uí Dhúrtaigh, not given.

Nossig, *an-fhosaigh,* the encampment.

Nough, *neacht,* horses.

Noughaval, *nuachabháil,* new cloister.

Noughaval, *nuachongbháil, nua/nuadh-cong-bhail,* new habitation or establishment.

Noughaval, *nuadh-gabhail,* new settlement.

Noul, *nAbhall,* apples.

Noulagh, *nOllthach,* Ulstermen.

Novally, *nua-bhaile,* the new town.

Nove, *damh, dhamh,* oxen.

Now, *nua,* new.

Nowen, *Neóna,* not given.

Nowen, *n-uamhain, an-uamhainn,* the cave.

Nowl, *n-úll, nAbhall, n-abhal,* apples.

Nowl, *nDall,* blind men.

Nowl, *nÚll,* not given.

Nowlagh, *neamhlach, nabhlach, n-abhlach,* apples or apple trees.

Nowlagh, *Neamhlach,* not given.

Nowle, *na-nubhall,* the apples.

Nroum, *nDrom,* backs or ridges.

Nubber, *'n-abar, an-abair,* the mire.

Nuckle, *an-fhocail,* not given.

Nuddy, *an-Uaigh, an-Udaig,* O'Huid, Hoode, a family name.

Nuenna, *an-uaithne,* a green river.

Nuffy, *nDubhthaigh,* O'Duffy, a family name.

Nugent (Mount), *droichead-Uí-Dhálaigh,* not given.

Nuller, *an-iolair, fhiolair,* the eagles.

Nuller, *an-iolar,* the eagle.

Nultagh, *an-Ultaigh, nUltach, na-nUltaigh, nUltagh,* the Ulstermen.

Nultagh, *nUltach,* Ulstermen.

Nulty, *n-Ultach,* the Ultonians(sic).

Nulty, *nUltach,* Ulstermen.

Num, *anama,* not given.

Nunane, *Nunáin,* Nunane a family name.

Nunry, *an-ionra,* not given.

Nunry, *an-ionra,* (of the) hill tillage.

Nunty, *inbhair,* yew.

Nunty, *Nontaigh,* Nunt, a male name, also the Anglo Norman name 'Funt'. (P.W.Joyce, Irish names of places 172, Vol 2).

Nuran, *niubhrán,* little yew trees.

Nurcher, *an-urchair,* a cast or throw.

Nurchossy, *fhuar-chosach,* cold foot or cold bottom land.

Nure, *inbhair, an-iúraig, ni-úbhar, nIubhar, an-iubhar, an-Iuir, an-iubhair, an-nIur,* the yew or yew trees.

Nurlar, *n'urlar,* the floor.

Nurney, *an-iurnaidhe,* not given.

Nurney, *an-urnaidh / ernaidhe / urnaí,* the prayer house / oratory.

Nurra, *an-fhiora,* sharp edged rock.

Nurra, Orr, a family name.

Nurrus, *nDorus,* doors.

Nusly(sic), *murailí,* mussels.

Nuss, *nOs,* deer.

Nuv, *nUbh,* eggs.

Ny, …*nach,* as an ending to a word can sometimes mean, a place of…. or abounding in…

Nymph, cormorants.

O Dempsey, *Toghroinn-cheantair-Uí-Dhíomasaigh,* not given.

O, (Wood of O), *eó,* Yew.

Oaghtragh, *uachtrach,* upper.

Oakhill, *eochaill,* yew wood.

Oankeagh, *uamhin-cáidhe,* muddy cave.

Oar, *odhar,* light brown or pale grey.

Oark, *amhairc,* the view.

Oarty, *Robhartaigh,* not given.

Obarravane, O'Barravan, a family name.

Obegley, *Ó-Beigfhile,* not given.

Obihane, *Ó-mBaotháin/mBaothain,* not given.

Ocheasty, *Ó-Séasta,* not given.

Ochesty, *Uí-Séasta,* O'Cheasty, a personal or family name.

Ock, *óg,* small.

Ockan, *eocán,* yew land.

Od, *fhad,* long.

Odagh, *O-nDuach,* O'Duagh, a family name.

Odagh, *Teampull-bhabhún-Ó-nDuach, bábhún-Ó-nDuach,* not given.

Odder, *odhra,* a pale grey spot of land.

Ode, *fhoid,* sward, soil, strip, sod or land.

Ode, *fhóid,* the sod.

Odea, *Ua-Deadha/Déadha,* O'Dea, a family name.

Odfoy, *fhóid-bhuidhe,* yellow sod.

Odiernan, *Ó-dTiarnáin,* not given.

Odiernan, *O-dTioghearnan,* O'Tiernan, a family name.

Odonnell, *O-dTomhrair,* O'Tomrair, Toner, a family name.

Odonnell, *Ua-Dómnail,* O'Donnell, a family name.

Odorney, *O-dTorna,* O'Torna, Torney, a family name.

Odough, *críoch-Ó-nDuach,* not given.

Odras, *odras,* pale greyness.

Oe, *abha,* a river.

Oe, *eo, eó,* yews.

Offa, *O'Fátha,* the name of an ancient tribe.

Offa, *Uí-Fothaidh,* not given.

Offaly, descendants of Ros, (a personal name) of the rings. The name of an ancient King.

Offaly, *Ó-Failghe,* not given.

Offaly, *ros-Failghe,* the *ros* (peninsula or wood of) the descendants of the son of king Cahirmore.

Offaly, *Uíbh/Uí-Failghe,* place of the 'Hy' or descendants of the tribe of Failghe.

Offaly, *Uíbh-Fhailí,* not given.

Offelimy, *Hy-Felimy,* descendants or tribe of Felimy.

Offerlane, *Ó/Uí-Foircealláin,* place of the descendants of Foircealláin/ Foircheallán.

Ofin, *Ua-Finn,* a County Clare saints name.

Og, *óg,* small.

Ogaha, *O-gCathaigh,* O'Caha, O'Cahy, a family name.

Ogahane, *O-gCatháin,* O'Cahan or Kane, a family name.

Ogan, *ogán,* trees or branches.

Ogan, *Ua-Ógáin,* O'Hogan, a family name.

Ogarney, O'Carney, a family name.

Ogartha, *Ó-gCáirthinn, Uí-Cháirthinn,* a family name.

Oge, *nÓg,* not given.

Oge, *óg,* small.

Ogeary, *Uí-Gheidhre,* O'Geary, a family name.

Ogeena, O'Geibheannaigh, O'Geany, a family name.

Ogeena, *O-gCíona,* O'Keena, a family name.

Ogeenagh, *O-gCianacht,* O'Keenaght, a family name.

Ogeenaghan, *Ó-gCuinneagáin, O'gCianachain, Ui-Cuinneagáin* or O'Keenaghan, a family name.

Ogelly, *O'gCeallaigh,* O'Kelly, a family name.

Ogham, *eo-cham,* the crooked yew tree.
Oghanaun, *fhochannan,* thistles.
Ogher, *eochair,* a margin, edge or brim.
Ogher, *eochrach,* the border.
Oghery, *eochaire,* not given.
Oghery, *eochairidhe,* margins.
Oghil, *eóchaill,* eochaill, *eochaille,* yew wood.
Oghill, *Achaille*(sic), *Uí-Thuathghail,* not given.
Oghill, *eochaill, eóchaill, eóchaille, eochaille,* yew wood/s or yew grove.
Oghilly, *eochaille,* yew woods.
Oghly, *eochaille,* yew woods.
Oght, *ucht,* breast.
Ogilleen, *O gCillín,* O'Killeen, Killeen, a family name.
Oginna, *O'gCiona,* O'Kinna, a family name.
Oginna, *Ó-gCineadh,* O'Kinney, a personal or family name.
Oginna, *Ó-gCinneá,* not given.
Oglagh, *óglagh,* youth/young persons.
Ognaveen, *O'gCnaimhín,* O'Knavin or Nevin, a family name.
Ogohig, *O'gCobhthaig,* O'Coffey, a family name.
Ogonnell, *Ua-Chonnaill, O'gConaill,* O'Connell, a family name.
Ogonnelloe, *O-gCoingialla,* O'Conneely, a family name.
Ogonnelloe, *tuath-Ó-gCoinghialla,* not given.
Ogonnelloe, *tuath-Ó-gConáile, Uí-Chonaíle,* O'Conaile's or O'Connolly's (a family name) district.
Ogorra, *O'gCorra,* O'Corra, a personal or family name.
Ogra, *fhógra,* the proclamation.
Ogra, Ogra, a personal or family name.
Ograda, O'Grady, a family name.
Ograne, *O'gCorran,* Curran, a family name.
Ogreana, *O'gCríona,* O'Creena, a family name.
Ogue, *óg,* small.
Ogue, *óg,* youths.
Ogue, *oige,* youth.
Ogulla, *Oghdhealla,* not given.
Ogullane, *O-gCoileán,* of the Collinses, a family name.

Ogunnell, *Ó-gCoinneall, Uí-Choinneall,* a family name.
Ogunnell, *ó-gConaill,* O'Connell, a family name and means the son of Connell.
Ohea, *Aedha,* Hugh, a male name.
Ohen, *Uí-Thuatháin,* O'Tuathan, a family name.
Oher, *fhothair,* not given.
Ohill, *eochaille, eóchaill,* yew wood.
Ohine, *Baeithin,* St Baeithin.
Oid, *fhoid,* sod, soil or land.
Oilgate, *maolán-na-nGabhar,* not given.
Oiltiagh, *ailltach,* cliffy.
Oiltiagh, *aillteach,* not given.
Oine, *Eoghain,* Owen, a male name.
Oir, *óir,* gold.
Okane, *achadh-Caoin,* not given.
Okane, *Uí-Chéin,* Ó Céin or O'Keane, a family name and means the descendants of Cein.
Okelly, *Ó-gCeallaigh,* not given.
Okennedy, *Ua-Cinnaíde,* O'Kennedy, a family name.
Okyle, *Ógchoill,* not given.
Okyle, *óg-choill,* young wood.
Okyne, *Mhic-Aodáin,* not given.
Ola, *nÉola,* Éola, a personal or family name.
Ola, *oll,* great.
Olagher, *Olchobair,* Olchobar, a personal name.
Olam, *Ólaim,* not given.
Oland, *fodhaladh,* litigation.
Olderfleet, Ulflich's (a personal name) fjord.
Ole, *ubhall,* apple trees.
Oleague, *dhá-liag,* the two standing/pillar stones.
Olee, O'Lee, a family name.
Oleem, *Oluim, Olom, Olioll Olom,* the name of the 3rd century king of Munster.
Oleigh, *Uí-Luigheach,-Luighdheach, Ó-Luigheach,* the descendants of Luigheach.
Olin, *Eolaing,* Eolang, a personal name.
Olin, *Uí-Fhloinn,* not given.
Oline, *Ó-Laighin, Uí Laighin,* a family name.
Oliver, *Otfáigh,* not given.
Olla, *oll,* great.

Olla, *olla, ollan,* wool.
Ollaghan, *Ollacháin,* not given.
Ollatrim, (river) *ollatruim,* not given.
Ollatrim, *calatroim,* not given.
Olomer, *almair,* not given.
Oltore, *altóir,* altar.
Om, *om,* an oak.
Omadaun, *amadán,* fool/s or clown/s.
Omadaun, *Ó-mBuadáin,* not given.
Omagh, *an-ómaigh,* the plain.
Omagh, *Óghmagh,* not given.
Omagh, *omaigh, Ómaigh, oghmagh,* the sacred plain.
Omagh, *ómaigh,* the untilled, untouched or virgin plain.
Omalus, *O'Malghus,* O'Malus, a personal or family name.
Omard, *om-ard,* the high oak.
Omarka, *Ó-Marcaigh,* not given.
Omaun, *hiomána,* hurling.
Omeath, *Ó-Méith,* place of the descendants of Méith, a personal or family name.
Omeath, *Uí-Méith, Uí-Meith,* Hy Meath, the descendants of Muiredach Meith.
Omeath, *Uí-Méith-Mara,* not given.
Omedan, *amadán,* a fool.
Omeen, *omin,* green(sic).
Omer, *umar, umair, amar, amuir,* a trough shape, trough shaped depression or a hollow.
Omey, *iomaidh, iomhaidh-Feichin,* St Fechin's seat or bed.
Omongan, *O'Mongan,* a family name.
Omoy, *O-mBuidhe,* of the O'Boy's, (a family name).
Omoyne, *O'Múain,* O'Moane, a family name.
Omra, *ómra,* pleasant.
Ona, *Una,* a female name.
Onagh, *abhnach,* a place by a river, a marshy/watery place or a place of rivers.
Onagh, *dDomhnach,*(sic), a Church.
Onagh, *Dhonchadh,* Donach, Donogh or Denis, a male name.
Onagh, *eanach,* not given.
Onagh, *Eoghanach,* Owen, Eoghain, a male name.
Onaghan, Honohan, a family name.
Onaght, *Eoghanacht,* place of the descendants of Eoghan, a personal name.
Onahan, *Onchon,* not given.

Onan, *Adhamhnán,* Adam, Eunan, Adamnan, a male name.
Onan, *Eoghanáin,* Owenan, a personal or family name.
Onan, *Fhóthannáin,* not given.
Onan, *Othanáin,* Ohanan or Onan, a personal or family name.
Onan, *Ua-Onáin,* O'Honan, a family name.
Onane, *Eoghanáin,* Owenan, a personal or family name.
Onane, *uarnhain,* a cave.
Onaun, *Eoghanáin,* Eoghanan or Owenan, a personal or family name.
One, *Eamhna, Eóghain,* not given.
One, *Eóin, Eoghain, Eoin,* Eoghain, Owen or John, a male name.
One, *uamhaín,* the cave.
Onea, *O-n'Aodha,* O'Hea, a family name.
Onea, *O-nDeaghaidh,* O'Dea, a family name.
Onear, *an-iarthar,* of the west.
Oneary, *an-aodhaire,* the shepherd.
Oneary, *an-fhearaigh,* the grassy fields.
Oneen, *Eoghanín, Eoghainín,* Oweneen or little Eoghan, a personal or family name.
Oneer, *O-nDubhuidhir,* O'Dwyer, a family name.
Oneil, *an-Iarla,* the Earl.
Oneil, *Uí-Neill,* O'Neill, a family name.
Oneill, the Earl.
Oneill, *Uí-Neill,* O'Neill, a family name.
Oneilland, *Hy-Niallain,* ancient tribe or race of Niallan.
Oneilland, *Niallán,* a male name.
Oneilland, *Uí-Nialláin,* place of the ancient tribe or race of Niallán/Niallan.
Onellan, *O'Niallain,* O'Neilan, a family name.
Onellan, *ua-Nialláin,* O'Nealan, a family name.
Onermody, *O'Diarmada,* O'Dermody, a family name.
Onermody, *Ó-nDiarmada,* not given.
Onerry, *O'nDeirigh,* O'Derry, a family name.
Onerry, *Ó nDoighre, Uí-Doighre,* a personal or family name.
Onerry, *Ó-Neire,* not given.
Oney, *chonaidh,* firewood.

Oniel, *an-Iarla,* the earl.

Oniel, *Ua-Neill,* not given.

Oniell, *an-Iarla,* the Earl.

Onig, *Óinigh,* not given.

Onig, *uaine,* green.

Onna, *onna,* furze, gorse.

Onoane, *an-uamhain,* the small cave.

Onomy, *Omna,* not given.

Onora, *Onóra,* not given.

Onuffy, *Ó/O-nDubhthaigh,* O'Duffy, a family name and means the descendants of Dubthach.

Onum, *anam,* souls.

Onum, *anma,* the soul.

Ony, *Damhna,* Damhna, a personal or family name.

Ony, *uaine,* green.

Ony, *Uaithne,* Owney, a personal or family name.

Oo, *na-huamha,* the cave.

Oo, *uaighe,* a cave or grave.

Ooan, *uamhainn,* a cave.

Ooangloor, *uaimh-na-gColúr,* pigeons cave.

Oodonagha, *uaimh-Dhonnchadha,* Denis's (a male name) cave.

Oognagh, from *uaigneas,* solitude.

Ooha, *uathaidh,* one or single.

Oohig, *fhuathaig, fhuathaigh,* 'Foohagh', the name of a particular phantom or spirit that haunted various places.

Ooker, *úcaire, úcairí,* not given.

Ookery, *ucaire,* a cloth tucker or fuller.

Ool, *abhall, ubhall,* apple, or apple trees.

Oola, *hUlla, úlla, ubhla,* an orchard, apple trees or apples.

Oolagh, *shúlach,* sunny.

Oolagh, *uallach,* proud.

Oolagh, *ubhla,* an orchard or apples.

Oole, *ubhaill,* the orchard.

Oole, *umhall,* owls.

Ooley, (Lough) *Úiligh,* Ooley, a personal or family name.

Oolia, *uaille,* wailing.

Ooly, *Amhlaí, úllaigh, abhla,* not given.

Ooly, apple trees.

Ooly, *ubhlaighe,* apples.

Ooly, *Amhlaoidh,* Humphrey, a male name.

Oon, *uamhan, uamhaín,* the cave.

Oona Water, *an-fhúbhna,* not given.

Oona, *uaimh-na...,* cave of the...

Oona, *uamhanna,* caves.

Oona, *Uamhna, Uaine,* not given.

Oona, *Úna, Una,* Una, a female name.

Oonagh, *thamhnaigh,* a fertile spot.

Oonagh, *Uhgoine,* Ughoin, a personal or family name.

Oonarontia, *uaimh-na-rón,* seals cave.

Ooney, *mhuine,* a thicket.

Ooney, *uaithne,* not given.

Ooney, *Una,* a female name.

Oonia, *uaithne,* green, greenish.

Oony, *uaithne,* not given.

Oor, *bhuair,* pride.

Oor, *Iúir, iubhair,* yew.

Oora, *fhuaire,* cold.

Ooragh, *iúbhrach,* yews.

Ooragh, *tuartha,* paddocks, cattle fields.

Oordrane, *Urdráin,* not given.

Oorid, from *uar,* cold.

Oorid, *Úraid,* not given.

Oorin, *fhuarthainn, fhuarthain,* not given.

Oorin, *uairthinn,* cold spring.

Oorla, *urla,* long grass.

Oorta, *úrta,* wet or damp.

Oory, *iubhraighe, iubhrach,* yew or yew lands.

Oory, *Úraí,* not given.

Oose, *amhus, amhas,* a hired soldier.

Oosh, *ghuise,* spruce or pine.

Oosh, *uais,* the cave.

Ooskny, *fhuasnadh,* fighting.

Ooval, *ubhall,* apples.

Oquirk, *Ó-gCuirc,* not given.

Ora, apple trees.

Ora, *odhar,* light brown or pale grey.

Ora, *úartha, fhuardha,* cooling.

Orah, *úartha,* cooling.

Oram, *eo-dhruim,* yew ridge.

Oram, *eoroim,* not given.

Oran, *Eoghainín, Óráin, dhobhráin,* not given.

Oran, *Ódhráin, Odhráin, Odhran,* St Odran/Odhran/Oran.

Oran, *Ódhráin, Odhráin, Odrain,* Oran, a male name.

Oran, *Odhrain, Odhrán,* a personal name.

Oran, *Oran,* a personal or family name.

Oran, *óran, uarain, uaráin, uarán, uaran, úráin, fhuaráin, fhuarán, fhuairain,* a cold spring.

Oran, *uainín*, little verdant.
Oran, *Uí-hOdhrain*, O'Horan or Horan, a family name.
Oranian, *Odhrain*, Oran, a male name.
Oraun, *na-nÓrán*, the cold springs.
Orban, *orban*, a holding or glebe land.
Orbsen, *Orbsen*, Orbsen, a male name and another name for Manannan Mac Lir.
Orc, *orc*, pigs.
Ordan, *ordan*, glory or dignity.
Ordan, *ordán, órdán*, little sledge/sledges.
Ordan, *ordanin*, sledge hammer.
Ordinary, *Ordoire*, not given.
Ore, as a word ending, Danish for a ford.
Ore, *feoir*, grass.
Ore, *fhoghair*, harvest.
Ore, *nDeoraí, fheoir, fhoghmhair*, not given.
Ore, *odhar*, brown, light brown, pale, grey or pale grey.
Ore, *ór*, by the sea coast.
Ore, *ór, óir*, gold.
Ore, *óre*, iron.
Ore, Scandanavian for a sandy point.
Ore, *uabhar, uabhair*, pride.
Organ, *Aragáin*, Aragan, a personal or family name.
Organ, *Árgain*, not given.
Organ, *Uí-Árgáin, Argáin, Ó hÁrgáin, hArgáin*, a family name.
Organ, *Uí-Argáin*, Organ or Horgan, a family name.
Orglin, *Orglan*, Orgla, a male name.
Orglin, *Orglan*, St Orgla.
Oriel, *oir-ghialla*, golden hostages.
Oriel, *oirtheara*, the name of an ancient Kingdom and means easterns or eastern people.
Orig, *Óraigh*, not given.
Orior, *oirthear*, not given.
Orios, *oirthear, airtheara*, easterns or eastern people.
Oris, *Feorais, Fheóras, Feoras*, Pierce, a family name.
Oris, *Fheorais*, Feora/Feoras, the name of an ancient monk also called Birmingham. It is also a family name.
Oris, *órthaidhe*, easterns or eastern people.
Orish, *fheorais*, not given.
Oritor, *cora-Críche*, not given.
Ork, *orc*, pigs.

Orkneys, *átha-an-mhaí*, not given.
Orlagh, *orrla*, not given.
Orlaghan, *oirleachain*, slaughter.
Orlar, *urláir*, a level place.
Orlar, *úrlár, úrláir*, floor or valley floor.
Orley, *úrlaidh, órlaidh*, slaughter.
Ormond, *Uarmáin*, cold spring.
Ormond, *Urumhain, Urmhumhain*, not given.
Orna, *eorna*, barley.
Ornan, *eórnan*, not given.
Orney, *hEornan, eorna, eornan*, barley.
Oroher, *ruathair*, an attack.
Oroher, *urchair*, a missile, cast or throw.
Oroon, *Urumhan*, Irvine, a family name.
Orra, *Bharraigh*, Barry, a male name.
Orrery, *Orbhraighe, Orbraige*, a tribe and later a territory.
Orry, *airthir*, eastern.
Ortan, *Ortain*, Ortan, a personal or family name.
Ortla, *ordlach*, a hero.
Orum, *Fhothram*, Fothram, a personal or family name and a founder of a Church in Kilkenny.
Orum, *Ódhráin, Ódhrán*,
Odhran, the name of a Church founder in Fiddown parish.
Orum, Oran, a personal or family name.
Ory, *iubhraighe*, yew.
Ory, *Óraí*, not given.
Oscar, *Oscair*, Oscair, a personal or family name.
Oscobe, *O'Scoba*, O'Scoba, a family name.
Oscully, *Ó Scolaí, Ó Scolaí*, a personal or family name and a founder of a Church in Tipperary.
Oscully, *O'Scaille*, Asgal, a male name (Danish).
Osheen, *Oisin, Oisín*, a male name.
Oshulan, *Ó'Siúláin, Uí-Shiubhláin, Uí-Shiúláin, O'Siubhlain*, O'Shulan, a family name and the name of a founder of Killoshulan Church in Kilkenny.
Osist, *O'Siosta*, a family name.
Oskehan, *Ó-Sceacháin*, not given.
Oskil, *oscail*, a hollow or an angle.
Osseragh, *Lasrach*, Lasser, a persons name.
Ossery, *Lasrach*, Lasser, a persons name.
Ossian, *Oisín, Oisín*, a male name.

Ossig, *Osaidh,* not given.

Ossory, *Osraí, Osraí,* the name of an ancient territory.

Ossory, *Osraighe,* not given.

Ossy, *fosadh,* an enclosure.

Ote, *fhóid,* the sod.

Oteragh, *uachtar achadh,* upper fields.

Oteragh, *uachtar-ratha,* upper forts.

Oteran, *Odhráin,* not given.

Oteran, *Fhuathráin, Fhuaradhráin,* St Furaran.

Otra, *otra, uachtarach, uachtrach, uachdar,* upper.

Otray, *Otraigh,* not given.

Otre, *uachdar,* upper.

Otteran, *Ódhran,* Oran, a personal or family name.

Ou, *abh, abha,* a stream, a river.

Oua, *uagh, uaimh, uath,* a cave.

Ouganish, *uaigneas,* solitude.

Ough, *abha,* a river.

Ough, *Eachaidh,* O'Hough, a family name.

Ough, *Eocha, Acha,* Eochy, a male name.

Ough, *ocht, ucht,* a bank or hill breast.

Ough, *oucht,* breast.

Oughaval, *nua-congbhail,* new habitation.

Ought, *ucht,* breast.

Oughtagh, *ochtach, uchtach,* the breast.

Oughter, *úachdar,* high lying.

Oughter, *uachtair, uachtaraigh, uachdarach, uachtar, uachdar, úachdar, uachdar,* upper.

Oughter, *hUachtair,* not given

Oughtera, *uachtrach,* upper.

Oughteragh, *uachdarach, uachtrach,* upper or high lying.

Oughteragh, *uachtarach,* not given.

Oughterany, *uachtar-Fhine,* not given.

Oughtiv, *Ochtaibh,* not given.

Oughtminee, *ucht-mine,* mountain breast of the level plain.

Oughtra, *uachdarach,* upper.

Oughtragh, *uachdarach,* upper.

Oughtragh, *uachtrach,* not given.

Oughty, *Ochta,* not given.

Oughty, *ochtaighe,* breasts.

Oughty, *uchta, uachta, ucht,* breast.

Oughy, *achaidh,* not given.

Ouk, *abhaic,* not given.

Ouk, *abhaich,* a dwarf.

Oul, *abhall, abhaill,* apples trees or an orchard.

Oula, a circle.

Oula, *ubhall, abhla,* apples.

Oulagh, *abhallach,* apple trees.

Oulart, *abhall-ghort/gort, abhalghort,* the orchard field.

Oulart, *abhall-gort,* apple field.

Oulart, *abhallort, úllord,* the orchard.

Oulart, *an-tAbhallort,* the orchard.

Oulart, *an-tAbhallort, ubhallghort,* not given.

Ouler, *iolar,* the eagle.

Ouler, *urlár,* not given.

Ouley, *abhalaigh,* abounding in apple trees.

Oulort, *abhall-ghort, abhalghort,* the orchard field.

Oultagh, *Ultach, Oltach,* Ulstermen.

Oultha, *Ultach, Oltach,* Ulstermen.

Oultha, *Ultaigh,* not given.

Oultort, *abhaltort,* (sic) an orchard.

Oulty, *abhalta, abhla,* not given.

Oulty, *alltaigh,* a bleak wild place.

Oulty, *olltaigh, oltaigh, ultaigh,* Ulstermen, Ulsterman.

Oun, *abh,* a river.

Ouna, *abh-na...,* river of the...

Ounagh, *ounagh, abhnach,* marshy, a watery place or a place of rivers.

Ounce, *fhuinsigh,* not given.

Ounce, *uinsighe,* ash trees.

Oune, *Eoghain,* Owen, a male name.

Ountain, *Fhinntain,* St Finntan.

Ountain, *Fhionntain,* St Fintan.

Ountaine, *Fhionntain,* St Fintan.

Ountane, *Fhinntain,* St Finntan.

Our, *amhair,* singing.

Our, *odhar,* dun or fawn coloured.

Our, *ódhar, odhar,* light brown, dark grey or pale grey.

Our, *Odhar,* St Odhar.

Our, *uabhar, uabhair,* pride.

Oura, *abhra,* a hill brow.

Oura, *odhardha,* pale grey, yellow or light brown.

Oura, *Orrtha,* not given.

Ouragan, *Amhragan,* Ouragan or Houraghan, a personal or family name.

Ouragan, *Uí-Anragáin,* Ó hAnragáin, a family name.

Ouragan, *Uí-hOdhragain,* O'Houragan, a family name.

Ouragh, dun coloured land.
Ourane, abhráin, song.
Ourane, Odhrain, St Odhran.
Ourane, Uí-hOdhráin, O'Horan, a family name.
Oure, uabhair, pride.
Ourea, corra, a weir.
Ouris, cnoc-an-amhrais, not given.
Ourna, eorna, eórna, barley.
Ourna, O'Dharna, Ourney, a male name.
Ourna, odharna, dun coloured (lake).
Ourney, abhernaidh, marshy.
Ourney, urnaighe, a oratory.
Outeragh, uachtar-achadh, upper field/s.
Outeragh, uachtar-rátha/ratha, upper forts.
Outragh, uachtarachaid, not given.
Outrath, ráth-uachtar, uachtar-rath/rátha/ratha, the upper fort.
Ouvane, abh-bhán, white/whitish river.
Ouveg, an-abhainn-bheag, not given.
Ouvry, aimhréidh, aimhreidh, rough or complicated.
Ovane, a'mhein, of the opening or cliff.
Ovannan, an-bannach, the foxes.
Ovaun, abha-bhán, white river.
Oveenoge, oighe-Mhineóg, the virgin named 'Mineóg'.
Oveeny, O'bhFéinneadha, O'Feeny, a family name.
Ovens, na-hUamhanna, uamhanna, the caves.
Ovens, uaimh-Bharra, not given.
Over, uabhar, uabhair, pride.
Ovey, (baile)-Óbha/Odhbha/Odhbha, not given.
Ovin, Ó-bhFinn, not given.
Ovoca, tráigh-dá-abhainn, not given.
Ow, abh, abha, a stream, a river.
Ow, abhainn, a river.
Owan, Eóghain, not given.
Owang, abha, abhainn, a river.
Owel, Uair, Uair, the name of an ancient firbolg chief.
Owen, abhainn, a river.
Owen, Eaóghain, Eoghain, Eoghain or Owen, a male name and the name of about 12 Irish Saints.
Owen, uamhainn, the cave.
Owen, uamhanna, caves.
Owena, abha/abhainn-na..., river of the...

Owenagarney, abhainn-Ó-gCearnaigh, not given.
Owenan, abhainn-na..., not given.
Owenass, abha-an-easa, not given.
Owenavorragh, abhainn-an-bhorraid, river liable to flood.
Owenea, abha-an-fhiadh, not given.
Owenea, abhainn-an-fia, abha-an-fia/fhia, deer river.
Oweniny, abhainn-Aidhne, not given.
Owenna, abha/abhainn-na..., river of the...
Owenur, abhainn-fhuar, cold river.
Owenure, abhainn-fhuar, cold river.
Ower, odhar, dark grey.
Ower, odhar, dun coloured.
Ower, odhar, light brown, pale grey or dun coloured land.
Ower, uabhar, uabhair, pride.
Owey, uamhaigh, the cave or grave.
Owin, abhann, a river.
Owl, abhail, abhall, ubhall, apple, trees.
Owla, abhla, the apple tree.
Owlan, abhla, apple or orchard.
Owlart, abhalloirt(sic), not given.
Owle, abhall, abhla, ubhall, apple tree/s.
Owle, abhall, ubhall, an orchard.
Owley, abhlach, not given.
Own, abhainn, a river.
Own, Eoghain, Owen, a personal or family name.
Owna, abhainn-a'..., river of the...
Owna, aibhne, a river.
Owney, Uaithnín, not given.
Owney, Uaitne, Anthony, a male name.
Owney, Urnaí(sic), Uaithne, a personal or family name and a founder of a Church in Offaly.
Ownia, Áine, Ania or Hanna, a female name.
Ownia, uaithne, green.
Ownim, an-anama, not given.
Owning, Ónainn, Onang, not given.
Owny, Mhughaine, St Mughain.
Owny, Uaithne, Uaithne, a personal or family name and a founder of a Church in Offaly.
Owra, ábhar, abhra, shaped like an eyebrow.
Owra, an-odhra, reddish.

Owran, *Odhrain,* Odran, a personal or family name.

Owry, *Abhra,* Abhra, a personal or family name.

Owvane, *abh-bhán,* white/whitish river.

Ox, (mountains), *gamh,* not given.

Ox, (mountains), *ghamh,* storms.

Ox, (mountains), mountain of the stones.

Oxman, *ostmen,* 'eastmen', Scandinavians or Danes.

Oy, *uaimhe,* the cave.

Oyle, *aill,* rock.

Oyle, *aille,* a cliff, slope or declivity.

Oylegate, *muileann-na-nGabhar, bearna-na-hAille,* not given.

Oyne, Eoghan, a male name.

Oyster, (island) *Oilean-na-nOistre,* not given.

P

Padarine, *phaidrin,* beads.
Padden, *Pháidín,* little Patrick.
Padder, *Peadair,* St Peter.
Paddin, *Pháidín,* not given.
Paddock, *na-paidic, an-paideac/peadoc,* not given.
Paddock, *buaile,* a milking enclosure or paddock
Padeen, *Pháidín, Phaidín,* little Patrick.
Padin, *Phádin,* little Paddy.
Padin, *Pháidín,* not given.
Padinn, *Phádin,* little Paddy.
Pake, *péac,* a peak.
Palace, *pailís,* a stockade or palisade.
Palace, *pailis, palas,* a palace or royal residence.
Palatine, *na-bPalaitíneach,* not given.
Paleen, *bairghine,* cake.
Pallace, *pailís,* a fairy palace.
Pallas, *pailís,* a palisade.
Pallas, *pailís,* a stockade or palisade.
Pallas, *pailis, phailís, palas,* a palace, palisade or royal residence.
Pallas, *pailíse,* not given.
Pallas, *palas,* a fairy fort.
Pallas, *palas,* a fishing pallice, a hut for curing fish.
Pallis, *pailís,* a stockade, a fairy palace or a palisade.
Pallis, *pailis, palas,* a palace or royal residence.
Panace, *an-phailís,* not given.
Paps, *dá-chích,* the two breasts.
Parisee, *parasaidhe,* parish land.
Parishagh, *pairiseach,* parish land.
Park, *pairc,* a park or a field.
Park, *phairc, páirc, páirce,* a pasture field.
Parka, *pairc-agh...,* field by the...

Parka, *páirc-an/a'...* field of the...
Parka, *páirce,* not given.
Parkan, *páirc-an...,* field of the...
Parkana, *pairceanna,* parks or fields.
Parkeena, *Páircín*(sic), not given.
Parkeenna, *Páircín-na...,* not given.
Parklane, *Páirc-Eiléin,* not given.
Parson, *Pearsuin,* Parson, a personal name.
Parson, *phearsáin,* the parish priest.
Parson, *Phearsúin,* a parson.
Parsonagh, Parsons, a family name.
Parteen, *partín, poirtín, phoirtín,* a haven or little landing place.
Parteen, *Phairtín,* not given.
Particles, *na-páirteagail,* not given.
Partry, *Partraí,* not given.
Pass, *pasaiste,* a causeway.
Pasta, *peiste,* a reptile, monster.
Paste, *péiste,* a monstrous worm or reptile.
Pasteen, *páistín,* children.
Pastime, *na-Fastaím,* not given.
Patrick, *Phádraig, Pádraig, Padraigh* or Patrick a male name.
Paudeen, *Pháidín,* not given.
Paudeenour, *Phaidín-odhair,* not given.
Pawlart, *Páil-airt,* Art's (a personal or family name.) pailing.
Pawlerth, *an-Páileard,* not given.
Peacaun, *péacán,* cowslips.
Peacon, *Bécáin,* St Peacan.
Peacon, *peicin,* a small peak.
Peacon, *Pheacáin, Peacán,* the name of a Church founder in Limerick.
Peacon, *Phéacáin,* not given.
Peacon, *Picheain, Pichan,* a male name.
Peak, *an-phéic/péic,* not given.
Peak, *peac,* a stake or peak.
Peaka, *péice, peice,* the peak.
Peakaun, *peacán,* a sharp pointed hill.
Peake, *peac,* a peak.
Peake, *péac,* not given.
Peake, *péic,* red ferns.
Peaky, *péice,* long tailed.
Peast, *bPéist,* worms.
Peast, *péist,* not given.
Peast, *piast, péiste,* serpent.
Peasta, *péiste,* any kind of animal.
Peasta, *piast,* a monster.
Peastia, *péiste,* not given.
Peasty, *peiste,* a reptile or insect.

Peasty, *piast,* a beast or monster.

Pedder, *Pheadair,* St Peadar/Peter.

Pee, *peithe,* the dwarf elder.

Peebra, the piper.

Peiste, *peiste,* a dragon, serpent or monster.

Peiste, *péiste,* the serpent, worm or pest.

Pekane, *Phíocáin,* St Becan.

Pellick, *peilic,* not given.

Penane, *pionnán,* not given.

Penane, *poinán,* a little peak.

Pepperstown, *baile-an-Phiobaraigh,* not given.

Peragh, *Paorach,* Power, a family name.

Perish, *Phiarais,* Pierce, a male name.

Pet, *Peata,* not given.

Pettigo, *paiteago,* lump.

Pettigo, *paiteagó,* the blacksmiths patch.

Pettigo, *paiteagó,* the lump.

Pettigo, *paite-gobha,* not given.

Pettigoe, *paiteagó,* not given.

Pettigoe, *paiteago,* the lump.

Pettigoe, *paitíghe-gobha,* the place of the smiths house.

Phale, *bheil,* mouth.

Phaleesh, *pailis, palas,* a palace or royal residence.

Pharis, *faras,* foundation.

Pharson, the parish priest.

Pharsoon, *Phearsúin,* a Parson.

Phaudeen, *Pháidín, Phaidín,* little Pat or Paudeen, a male name.

Phausthee, *bPáistídhe,* children.

Pheak, *Phéic,* Peake or Bec, a male name.

Pheasteen, *phéistín,* not given.

Pheasty, *phéiste,* a great reptile.

Pheebera, *phíobaire,* not given.

Pheeby, *phíoba,* the (musical) pipe.

Pheepa, *phíopa,* a musical pipe.

Pheepera, *píopaire,* the piper.

Pheepra, *píopaire, piobaire,* the piper/s.

Phehane, *feitheain,* swampy.

Phehane, *féitheán, fhéitheán,* not given.

Phehane, *Uí-Fhiachain,* Feehan, a family name.

Pheirish, *Phiarais,* Pierce, a personal or family name.

Phelagh, *bhéal-átha,* not given.

Phelagh, *féileach,* woodbine.

Phelim, territory of the tribe of Hy Felimy.

Phellic, *pheilic,* the basket.

Phellic, *Phelic,* Fell, a personal or family name.

Phellic, *Philligh,* not given.

Phenane, *féitheán,* osiers.

Pheonix, (Pheonix Park), *fhionnuisce, fionn-uisg',* clear water.

Pherode, *Phéaróid,* Perrot, a family name.

Phierish, *Phiarais,* Piaras or Pierce, a personal or family name.

Phile, *phoill,* an inlet.

Philibeen, *Mic-Philibín,* MacPhilbin, a family name.

Philimy, *Feidhlimidh,* Feidhlimidh, a male name.

Philip, *Philib,* Philip, a personal name.

Philipeen, *Philibín,* not given.

Philipeen, *Phillibín,* little Philip (a male name) or a plover.

Phillabeen, *phillibín,* a plover.

Phillip, *Philib,* not given.

Philips, *Philib,* not given

Phin, *Fin,* Finn, a male name.

Phleasure, *phleisiuir,* enjoyment.

Phlick, *Phelic,* Fell, a personal or family name.

Phobble, *pobual, phobuail,* potash.

Phole, *Phóil, Phoil, Póil,* Paul, a male name.

Phoner, *phonaire,* beans.

Phonery, *phónaire, phonaire,* beans.

Phonta, *phónta,* a cattle pound.

Phooca, *phouca, phúca, phuca, púca,* a spright, a fairie/s or a pooka.

Phooka, *phúca,* not given.

Phooleen, *phuillín,* a little hollow.

Phoria, *bPónaire,* beans.

Phoria, *phopraigh,* propagation.

Phoria, *phóire,* not given.

Phort, *phoirt,* not given.

Phort, *phuirt,* a ferry, port, bank or a landing place.

Phouca, *phouca, phuca,* a sprite, a fairie/s or a pooka.

Phreaghane, *phreachain, bPríochán,* crows.

Phreaghaun, *phréacháin, phréachain,* not given.

Phreaghaun, *phreachain, preaghaun,* ravens or rooks.

Phreaghaun, *preaghaun, prehaun, bPreachan,* crow/s.

Phreechawn, fraughan, not given.

Phreeson, phriosúin, prison.

Phrumpa, phrompa, not given.

Phubble, phobail, the congregation.

Phubble, phubaill, not given.

Phuca, phouca, phuca, phúca, púca, a spright, a fairie/s, a pooka or hobgoblin.

Phuill, poll, a hole or pit, sometimes in a river.

Phukeen, phuicín, a small hut or shelter.

Phull, poll, phuill, a hole or pit, sometimes in a river.

Phunta, phónta, púnta, phúnta, a cattle pound.

Phuntaun, phúntáin, the little cattle-pound.

Phutteen, phoitín, poteen, moonshine or illicit whickey.

Phutteen, putín, a small hare.

Piast, peiste, a dragon, serpent or monster.

Pibrum, Padhbram, not given.

Piedmont, baile-Mhic-Dhónaill, not given.

Pierce, Phiarais, not given.

Pigeon, gColúr, Phidsean, not given.

Pike (the), paidhc, a turnpike, a place where road tolls were paid.

Pil, phoill, a hole.

Pile, poill, a creek.

Pile, puill, not given.

Pill, phoill, a hole.

Pill, pill, a small inlet branching off.

Pilltown, baile-an-phoill, homestead of the river inlet.

Piltown, baile-an-phoill, homestead of the creek.

Piltown, baile-an-phoill, town of the hole.

Pilltown, baile-an-Phoill, place of the Pill river.

Pingina, pingine, marsh pennyworth (a plant).

Pingina, pingíne, the penny.

Pingina, pingne, not given.

Pins (the twelve). In Connemara, collectively they are known as beanna-Beola. Individually they are… an-chailleach, binn-bhán, binn-Bhraoin, binn-breac, binn-breac. binn-chorr, binn-doire-chlár, binn-fraoigh, binn-gabhar, binn-glean-uisce, binn-leitrí, and meacanach. They are also knows as the twelve bens.

Pintown, (cattle) pen-top(sic).

Pintown, baile-an-Phionna, not given.

Pipe, phíopa, píopa, the pipe.

Pipe, Popa, a saints name.

Pisa, píse, pease or vetches.

Pise, píse, pease.

Pish, pise, peas.

Pisha, pise, peas.

Pishanagh, piseanach, a place producing peas.

Pishanagh, piseánach, vetches.

Pishy, pise, peas.

Pistol, piostail, not given.

Pistole, phiostoil, pistole, pistil, a pipe, channel or stream.

Pistole, phiostólaigh, not given.

Pistole, phistóla, the pistol.

Pistole, pistol, a rivulet or a narrow tube-like stream channel.

Pitmave, Maeve's (a female) pudenda(sic).

Plaia, plaigh, the plaque.

Plaia, pláighe, not given.

Plaster, plástar, not given.

Plau, phlaigh, plague.

Plaukarauka, Plácaráca, not given.

Plaw, plaighe, a plague.

Plawy, phlaighe, plague.

Pledulagh, pléideála, pleading or controversy.

Plezica, plaoscach, shelly.

Plicawn, Bolcáin, Bolcan, a male name.

Ploopluck, clogh-púca, stone fortress of the pooka, sprite, fairy or fairies.

Ploresk, brock-lusc(sic), badger cave.

Ploresk, prochlusc, plotharaisc, the cave.

Pluck, pluc, a lump, protuberance or swelling.

Pluckanes, plucáin, plucain, small knobs or stumps.

Pluckeen, plucín, little swelling.

Plud, plud, a puddle.

Plughoge, phlochóige, plochóg, not given.

Poagh, kissing.

Pobble, pobul, people, congregation or Parish.

Pogaree, fhraoich, heather.

Pogaree, riaghaidh, executions.

Poge, phouca, phuca, púca, a spright, a fairie/s or a pooka.

Pogue, a kiss.

Poilin, *Phóilín,* little Paul, a male name.

Pol, *poll,* a measurment of land.

Pol, *poll,* a pool.

Poland, *pollach,* a place of holes.

Poldoody, *poll-Dubhda,* Dooda's (a personal or a family name) pool.

Pole, *Póil,* Paul, a male name.

Pole, *póil,* the pool.

Poleen, *Phóilín,* not given.

Poles, *na-pollaí,* the pools.

Polin, Paulin or little Paul, a personal or family name.

Polin, *poll-an...,* hole of the...

Poll, *poll,* a hole, pit, cavern, excavation in the ground, river or bog.

Poll, *poll,* a measurment of land.

Polla, *polla, poll,* a measurment of land.

Polla, *poll-a'..., poll-an...,* hole of the...

Pollach, *phollach,* a place of pits.

Pollagh, *phollach,* abounding in pits.

Pollagh, *pollagh, pollach, phollach, phollaigh, pullagh,* a place of holes.

Pollagh, *pollach,* hollow/ed land.

Pollagh, *pollach,* a hallowed(sic) place.

Pollagha, *pollacha,* holes.

Pollagha, *pollagh, pullagh,* a place of holes, pits.

Pollaghan, *pollagh-an...,* hole of the...

Pollaghna, *pollagh-na...,* hole of the...

Pollan, *polláin,* not given.

Pollan, *poll-an...,* hole of the...

Pollanaroo, *poll-an-arbha,* hole of the corn.

Pollanea, *poll-an-fhiaidh,* hole of the deer.

Pollans, from *pollán,* little holes or caverns.

Polleens, from *pollán,* little holes or caverns.

Polleeny, from *pollán,* little holes or caverns.

Polleeny, *na-poillíní,* not given.

Polleha, *poille,* not given.

Pollet, *pollaid,* not given.

Pollna, *poll-na...,* hole of the...

Pollnagh, *poll-na-neach,* hole of the horses.

Pollough, *pollagh, pullagh,* a place of holes.

Pomeroy, *cabhán-an-chaorthainn/chaortain,* hill of the rowan tree.

Pomeroy, *priomrae,* main level place.

Ponra, *bPónaire,* beans.

Ponra, *ponaire,* beans.

Pontoon, *pont-abhann,* not given.

Pook, *phouca, phuca,* a spright, a fairy, fairies or a pooka.

Pook, *phúcaigh,* not given.

Pooke, *phouca, phuca,* a spright, a fairy, fairies or a pooka.

Pookeen, *poicín, puicín,* a little eminence.

Pookeen, *puicin,* a little fairy or a place of the small cattle hut.

Pookeen, *puicín,* a secluded spot.

Pookeen, *puicín, púicín,* a place of sparrow hawks or kites.

Pool, *poll,* a hole.

Poole, *Phoil,* St Paul.

Poor, *Phaoraigh,* Power, a family name.

Popple, *pobul,* congregation parish or people.

Porcha, *pairc-a...,* field or park of the...

Poreen, *poirín, póirín,* a little hole.

Poreen, *Póirin,* Poreen, a personal or family name.

Poreen, *póirín,* round stones.

Poria, *ponaire,* beans.

Porsoon, *Parsún,* a priest.

Porsoon, *poirsiún,* a portion.

Port, *phuirt, port,* a bank or a landing place.

Port, *portúdhach,* not given.

Port, *puirt, portach,* a bog.

Porta, *port-an/a'...,* port or landing place of...

Portacloy, *port-an-chlaí,* harbour of the wall or fence.

Portacloy, *port-an-chlóidh/chlaidhe,* not given.

Portagh, *portach,* a bog or turf banks.

Portally, *Port-Ailigh,* not given.

Portan, *portán,* a bank.

Portan, *portán,* crab.

Portan, *port-an...,* landing place of the...

Portane, *an-portán,* not given.

Portane, from *portán,* little landing places.

Portane, *portán,* the little landing place.

Portane, *port-an...,* landing place of the...

Portarlington, named after Sir Henry Bennet, AKA Lord Arlington. The Irish name is *cúil-an-tSúdaire,* secluded place of the tanner.

Portaugh, *portach,* bog.

Portauns, *na-portáin,* not given.

Porteen, *portín,* the little landing place.

Portglenone, *port-chloinne-Eoghain,* not given.

Portglenone, *port-chluain-Eoghain*, port of Eoghans (a male name) meadow.

Portilan, *Oileán-na-dTuath*, not given.

Portin, *port-an…*, landing place of the.

Portland, *port-an-tolchain*, the bank or landing place of the little hill.

Portland, *port-tulcháin*, not given.

Portlaw, *port-cladhach*, *port-lách*, not given.

Portlick, *magh-lice-Pádraig*, not given.

Portn, *an-portan*, not given.

Portolohane, *port-an-tolchain*, the bank or landing place of the little hill.

Portoonaka, *port-uaithne*, a green haven or small inlet.

Portora, *port-abhla-Faeláin*, not given.

Portora, *port-abhla-Faoláin*, the harbour of Faolán's (a personal or family name) apples or apple trees.

Portoughnaboe, *port-Úth-na-bó*, not given.

Portrane, *port-rahern/rachrann/reachrann*, the landing place of 'rachra' which was the custom of sending sheep to an island in the spring. *Reachrann* is the Irish name for Lambay island nearby.

Portroyal, *partraí*, *portraighe*, not given.

Porturlin, *port-Durlainne*, not given.

Posey, *posae*, *pósae*, not an Irish word, the Irish given spellings are phonetic.

Potaley, grey pots(sic).

Potteen, *phoitín*, poteen or illicit whiskey.

Pottiagh, *paiteach*, a place of holes.

Pottiaghan, *paiteachán*, a place of holes.

Pottiaghan, *poiteacháin*, bad ground.

Pottinger, *baile-abhann-lagan*, not given.

Pottle, *photaire*, belonging to the potter.

Pottle, *potteal*, *poitéal*, *poll*, a measurment of land.

Poul, *poul*, *poll*, a hole, pit, hollow, a cavern or excavation in the ground/river or bog.

Poula, *poll-a'…*, holl of or on the…

Poula, *poll-an…*, hole of the…

Poulacapple, *póll-an-capaill*, horses cave(sic).

Poulacapple, *poll-an-chapaill*, not given.

Pouladuff, *poll-an-daimh*, not given.

Pouladown, *poll-a'deamhain*, dragons hole.

Poulan, *poll-an…*, hole of the…

Poularick, *poll-Lairge*, hollow or pool of the river 'Lairge'.

Poulavone, *pollmhóin*, not given.

Pouldine, *poll-domhin*, a deep hole.

Poule, *poll*, the hole.

Pouleen, *pollín*, *puillín*, the little hole.

Pouleen, *puillín-a'…*, the little hole of the…

Pouleennacoona, *poillín-na-cuana*, the small fissure beside the fields.

Poulna, *poll-na…*, hole of the…

Poultar, *poll-a'Tara*, hole of the river Tara.

Pour, *Poeraigh*, Power, a family name.

Pousta, *Púiste*, not given.

Powel, *poll*, a hole or pit.

Power, *Phaoraigh*, Power, a personal or family name.

Powlas, *pálás*, a palace.

Powra, *bPónaire*, beans.

Poyntz, *Phointe*, named after English Lt Pointz.

Prap, *phrap*, cluster of houses.

Prap, *prap*, *phraip*, not given.

Prapoge, *prapóg*, not given.

Prask, *praisc*, wild cabbages.

Preaghane, *préachán*, the crow.

Preaghaun, *preachán*, rook/s.

Preaghaun, *prehaun*, *bPréachán*, *bPreachan*, crow/s.

Preavan, *phreamháin*, tree root.

Preban, *preabán*, a patch.

Prebaun, *preabán*, a patch.

Preghane, *preachan*, periwinkle.

Prehane, *phreachain*, ravens.

Prevan, *phréamháin*, not given.

Pribbaun, *preabán*, a patch.

Priest, *Príost*, not given.

Primult, *brí-muilt*, not given.

Prior, *an-Phríóreacht*, *Príor*, not given.

Prior, *phrióra*, the Prior.

Prior, *Phrír*, Prior, a family name.

Prisoon, *príosun*, prison.

Privaun, *preamhain*, roots.

Procklis, *broc-lusc*, the badger den.

Proclis, *prochlais*, a cave or den, possibly of badgers.

Prohas, *pruchas*, a cave.

Prohoness, *bruadhnas*, a place of rushes.

Prohus, *prothuis*, *pruchas*, a cave or vault.

Prohus, *pruis*, *pluais*(sic), a foxes lair.

Prohust, *pruchas*, a cave.

Proleek, *Phroilig*, *Proilíg*, *Prailic*, not given.

Prologue, *an-Phrológ,* not given.

Prologue, *prochlais,* a daw or cave.

Prolust, *prolusc,* a cave.

Proogep, a little post or prop.

Proonts, *Prointe,* not given.

Prop, a post or prop.

Propoge, *prapóg,* not given.

Propoge, *propóg,* a stack–like, round hill.

Prosperous, *an-Chorrchoill,* not given.

Prucklish, *broc-laige,* badgers warren.

Prucklish, *proclais,* a cave or a badgers warren, den

Prughlish, *prochlais,* a cave or den, possibly of badgers.

Pubble, *phobail, pobul,* people, congregation or Parish.

Pubble, *phobóil,* not given.

Pubble, *pobal,* descendants of…

Puck, *phocaide,* not given.

Puck, *phouca, phuca, púca,* a spright, fairie/s or a pooka.

Puckane, *pocan,* elevated ground.

Puckane, *pocán,* little bag.

Puckane, *pócan,* little mounds or hills.

Puckaun, *pocán,* little heap.

Puckaun, *pocán,* the bag or the little bag.

Puckawn, *phocáin, pocán,* a buck goat or male goats.

Pulla, *polla,* a pole or a pill.

Pulla, *polla,* holes.

Pullagh, *phollaigh,* not given.

Pullagh, *pollach,* a place of holes.

Pullagh, *pollagh, pollach, pullagh,* a place of holes.

Pullan, *pollagh, pullagh,* a place of holes.

Pullan, *pollán,* little hole or pit.

Pullans, from *pollán,* little holes or caverns.

Pullans, *na-polláin,* not given.

Pulleen, *poillín,* a small pool.

Pullen, *pollán,* little hole or pit.

Pullens, from *pollán,* little holes, caverns.

Pullis, a place of holes.

Pullis, *phailís,* not given.

Pupple, *pobul,* people, congregation or Parish.

Pursheen, *puirsín,* spearmint.

Purtagh, *portach,* a bog.

Purth, *port,* a river bank.

Pust, *post,* a prop or post.

Putiachan, *puiteachán,* abounding in holes, pits or pans.

Puttaghan, *an-Puiteachán,* not given.

Q

Quade, *comhfhad,* remarkable tomb.

Quage, *Chuag,* not given.

Quaid, *Mic-Uaid,* MacQuaid, a family name.

Quaig, *Chuaig,* Cuaig, a personal or family name.

Quain, *Chuain,* Cuan, St. Cuan.

Quale, *caol, cael,* narrow, slender.

Quane, *Cúan, Cuan, Chúain, Chuáin, Chuain,* St. Cúan/Cuan.

Quane, *Uí-Chuain,* O'Quane, a family name.

Quay, *caedh,* marshy.

Quay, *Mhic-Aodha,* MacHugh, a family name and means son of Hugh/Aodh.

Quelly, *coille,* a wood.

Querin, *caor,* a blaze of firelight(sic).

Querrin, *caorthann,* the quicken tree or trees.

Querrin, *cuibhreann,* tilled field.

Querrin, *cuibhreann-coille, cuibhreann,* not given.

Quig, *cuigeadh,* a fifth.

Quigga, *cuige,* a fifth.

Quiggan, *Chomhgáin,* Comhgán, a personal or family name and the founder of a Church in Wicklow. .

Quiggin, *Comhgáin,* not given.

Quiggin, from *caodh,* a quagmire or marsh.

Quiggy, fifths.

Quiglough, *Coigealach,* not given.

Quigna, a fifth part of the….

Quigny, *cuigne,* not given.

Quilabeen, *Cuilibín,* Culbin, a family name.

Quilcagh, *cailceach,* chalky.

Quileagh, chalky.

Quilina, *cuilleanach,* holly.

Quill, *caol,* not given.

Quill, *chleite,* a feather.

Quill, *chleite, cletta,* a quill.

Quill, *choill,* a wood.

Quill, *choil*(sic)*, collach, chuill, cuill, coill,* hazel.

Quilla, *coille,* the wood.

Quillia, *coille,* the wood.

Quillia, *coilleach,* not given.

Quillia, *gCoilleach,* grouse.

Quillin, *Mic-Uidhilín,* MacQuillin, a family name.

Quilly, *coille,* a wood.

Quilly, *coillidh,* woodland.

Quilly, *cuaille,* a pole or branchless tree.

Quiltinagh, *coillteanach,* woodland.

Quiltinan, *coillteanán,* woodland.

Quilty, *choilltigh,* not given.

Quilty, *coil, coillte,* woods.

Quin, *'ic-Chuinn,* MacQuinn, a family name.

Quin, beautiful.

Quin, *cainche, chainche, cuince, cuinche,* arbutus trees or arbutus land.

Quin, *caoin, caein,* beautiful.

Quin, *caoin, caein, caeine,* beautiful or pleasant.

Quin, *caoin,* smooth(sic).

Quin, *choim,* shelter(sic).

Quin, *chuin, chuim,* a hollow.

Quin, *Chuinn,* Conn, Con, a personal or family name.

Quin, *Choinn, Chuinn,* Conn, a male name.

Quin, *Coinn, Choin, Mhic-Mhaing,* not given.

Quin, *cúinne,* a nook.

Quin, *Ua-Cúinn, Uí-Chuinn,* O'Quin or Quin, a family name.

Quin, *Uí-Choinn,* Ó Coinn, a family name.

Quinchy, *cuinche,* arbutus trees or arbutus land.

Quinhie, *cuinche,* arbutus trees or arbutus land.

Quinlan, *Chaoinleáin,* not given.

Quinlevan, *Uí-Coindealbhain,* O'Quinlevan, a family name.

Quinny, *cuinche,* arbutus trees or arbutus land.

Quinsheen, from *cuinche*, little arbutus island.

Quintagh, *cuanta*, windings.

Quintin, *chointinn*, not given.

Quintin, *cóintin*, controversy or disputed lands.

Quintin, *Cumhaighe*, Cooey, a male name.

Quirk, *Chuirc*, Corc or Quirk, a personal or family name.

Quirk, *Uí Choirc*, Ó Coirc, a family name.

Quirk, *Uí-Chuirc*, Ó Cuirc or O'Quirk, a family name.

Quirke, *Cuirc*, Corc, a personal or family name.

Quirke, *Uí-Chuire*, a family name.

Quiveen, *Chaoimhín, Choimhín*, not given.

Quiveen, *Uí-Chaomhglir*, O'Keevan, a family name.

Quivvy, *cuibhidh*, proper or fit.

Quivvy, *ciabhaigh, ciabhach, ciobhach*, abounding in long coarse grass.

Quoile, *caol*, narrow or narrow water.

Quoile, *choill*, the wood.

Quoile, *cuaille*, a pole or stake.

Quoy, *caedh*, a quagmire or marsh.

R

Ra, Raa, *ráth, rátha, rath,* a fort or rath.

Rable, *earbail,* at the end or a tail.

Rabows, *an-ráth*(sic), not given.

Rabrachan, *raith-Bhreacain,* Brackan,s (a personal or a family name) rath or fort.

Raby, *Ráibe,* not given.

Racahill, *raith-Chathail,* Cahill's (a family or a a persons name) fort.

Race, *Rás,* not given.

Rack, *ráth, rath,* not given.

Racka, *raca,* the wreck.

Rackwallace, *rath-'ic-Mhaluis,* the fort of Malus's (a male name) son.

Rackwallis, *ráth-Mhic-Mhailis,* not given.

Racreeghan, *ráth-chríocháin,* not given.

Rad, *ráid,* not given.

Radeerpark, *páirc-na-bhFianna,* not given.

Rademan, *rath-Deman,* Deman's(a personal or family name) fort.

Rademon, *rath-Deamáin,* Deamán's (a personal or family name) fort.

Rademon, fort of the demons fort.

Radoon, *raith-dúin,* the strong rath or fort.

Raduffe, *rátha-duibhe,* not given.

Raferagh, *ráth/rath-Fiachrach,* not given.

Raffeen, *rath-Finn,* Fionn's (a male name) fortress.

Raffeen, *ráth-mhín,* the level fort.

Raffeen, smooth ring fort.

Rafferty, *Laifeartaigh,* not given.

Raffline, *ráth-Flainn,* Flan's (a personal or family name) habitation.

Raffrey, a place beside water.

Raffrey, *ráth-Mhuireadhaigh,* not given.

Rafian, *ráth-Fian,* Fian's (a personal or family name) fort.

Raford, *ráth-Fulrach,* not given.

Rafter, *Reachtaire,* the provost.

Rafter, *Uí-Reachtabhra,* O'Raghtora (Power), a family name.

Rafwee, *rath-Buidhbh,* Bove Derg's (an ancient chief and prince) fort.

Ragamus, from *ragam,* horseradish.

Ragamus, *rágamas,* not given.

Ragee, *re-gaeith,* of the wind.

Ragg, (The) *buaile-dhubh,* not given.

Ragget, *ragad,* a churl.

Ragget, *Ragad,* Ragget or Le Ragged, an Anglo-Norman family name.

Ragget, *Raghat,* a personal or family name.

Raggett, Raggett a family name.

Raggy, *ragaidh,* rough coarse land.

Ragh, *...rach,* as an ending to a word can sometimes mean, a place of.... or abounding in...

Ragh, *rath, ratha, ráth,* a rath or fort.

Ragh, *reach,* grey.

Raghan, *Bhrachain,* Braghan or Berchan, a male name.

Ragheen, *raithneach,* ferns.

Ragheenagh, *raithíneach,* a place of forts.

Raghery, a place beside water.

Raghie, *rátha,* a fort, rath.

Raghly, *reachla,* not given.

Raghool, *raith-Chumhail,* Cumhal's (a family or a persons name) fort.

Raghra, *Rachra,* not given.

Raghter, *Uí-Reachtabhra,* O'Raghtora, a family name.

Rah, *ráth,* a ring fort.

Rah, *rath, raith, rátha, ratha,* a fort.

Raha, *ráithe,* the ring fort.

Raha, *rátha*(sic), *reatha, reithe,* (of the) ram.

Raha, *rátha, ratha,* a fort.

Raha, *ratha,* forts.

Raha, *rath-an...,* fort of the...

Raha, *riabhacha,* grey.

Rahagan, *ráth-Eochain,* Eochain's (a personal or family name) fort.

Rahan, *rathain, raithain,* a little fort.

Rahan, *raithin,* ferns.

Rahan, *rátháin,* a small rath.

Rahan, *ráth/rath-an...,* fort of the...

Rahan, *rathain, raithean, raithean, raithnighe, raithin,* a place of ferns.

Rahan, *ráthan,* a ring fort.

Rahan, *Rohaun,* Rowan, a personal or family name.

Rahan, *ruacháin,* not given.

Rahanagh, *raithneach,* not given.

Rahanane, place of the fort.

Rahanna, *ráth-Eanchú,* not given.

Rahans, *raithnigh,* not given.

Rahara, *ráth-Era/Fhearaidh,* not given.

Rahard, *ráth-aird, an-ráth-ard,* not given.

Rahasane, *rath-orán,* not given.

Raheanbo, *rath-aen-bo,* fort of the one cow.

Raheelan, *ráth-Chaolain,* Keelan's (a personal or family name) fort.

Raheen, *an-ráithíneacha,* not given.

Raheen, *raithin,* bracken.

Raheen, *raithin, ráithín, raithín,* a small rath, ring-fort or circular earthen fort.

Raheen, *raithnigh,* not given.

Raheen, *rathain,* a place of ferns or fermy ground.

Raheen, *reithín,* the little ram.

Raheena, *ráithín/raithín-na* , little fort of the…

Raheenagh, *ráithíneach,* abounding in small raths.

Raheenarran, *ráithín-an-fhearainn,* small rath of the land holding.

Raheenna, *ráithín/raithín-na* , little fort of the…

Raheens, *ráithíní,* small forts or small ring forts.

Raheeny, *ráithíní,* not given.

Raheeny, *raithínidhe,* little forts.

Rahelty, *ráth-eilte/éilte,* not given.

Rahena, *rathína,* little dwellings.

Rahenes, *ráithínidhe,* little raths or little forts.

Rahenes, *na-ráithíní, not given.*

Raheny, *ráth-Eanaigh,* fort of the marsh/ marshes.

Raheny, *rath-Éanna/Enna,* Eanna's or Enna's (a male name) fort.

Raher, *arathair,* tillage.

Raher, *mBratar,* friars.

Raher, *rahen,* a place of ferns.

Raherd, *raith-aird,* the high fort.

Rahillakeen, *rath-Uillicín,* not given.

Rahillakeen, *ráth-Uilicín,* Ulic's (a personal or family name) fort.

Rahilly, *Raghallaigh,* Raghallach, a male name.

Rahilly, *Rathaile,* Rahilly, a male name.

Rahilly, *Uí-Rathaile,* O'Rahilly, a family name.

Rahin, *rahin,* a place of ferns.

Rahin, *raithín,* little fort.

Rahin, *rathain, raithnighe,* a place of ferns.

Rahina, *ráth-Aidhne,* Aidhne's (a personal or family name) rath.

Rahinagh, *raithineach, raithneach,* a place of ferns.

Rahinane, *ráth-Fhionnáin/Fhíonáin,* not given.

Rahine, *ráithín,* a little ring fort.

Rahine, *rath-chaoidhin,* fortress of the marsh.

Rahinnane, *ráthanáin,* not given.

Rahins, *rathain, raithnighe,* a place of ferns.

Rahnee, *raithní,* bracken.

Rahnee, *rathain, raithnighe,* a place of ferns.

Rahona, *ráthóna,* not given.

Rahona, *ráth-thonnach,* a fortified ráth.

Rahone, *ráth-Eoghain,* not given.

Rahoon, *raith-Iugaine,* Iugane's, Ooney's or Owney's (mens names) fort.

Rahoon, *rathún,* not given.

Rahoonagh, *an-rathúnach,* not given.

Rahora, *ráth-Hóraigh,* not given.

Rahylin, *raithleann,* not given.

Rahyvira, *rath-an-Mheidhrigh,* not given.

Raigh, *an-ráithe,* not given.

Raigh, *rath,* a fort.

Raighland, *Réidhleáin,* not given.

Raile, *Ráiligh,* Raile, a family name.

Raily, *Ráile,* Rawley, a male name.

Raily, *Ráiligh,* not given.

Rain, *raithin, rathain,* ferns.

Rain, *ruáin,* red ground.

Raine, *raithin, rathain, raithnighe,* ferns.

Raine, *raithní,* not given.

Raine, *Riáin,* Rían, a personal or family name and the founder of a Church in Donegal.

Raineach, *raithneach,* ferns.

Rainee, *raithne,* ferns.

Rainee, *raithní,* not given.

Rainey, *raithinighe,* not given.

Rainey, *raithneach, raithnighe, rathain,* ferns.

Rainy, *Ráine, raithinighe,* not given.

Rainy, *raithní, raithnighe, raithneach, rathain,* ferns.

Rainy, a queen.

Raischoha, *réidh-scotha,* plain of the flowers.

Rakenny, *rath-Cuinge,* not given.

Ralahiv, *rath-Amhlaoibh,* Humphrey's (a male name) fort.

Raleagh, *rath-leith,* grey round fort.

Raleagh, fort of the grey people.

Raleigh, *rath-Luighdheach,* Lughaidh's (a person name) fort.

Raliogh, *ráileach,* abounding in oaks.

Ralla, *rálach,* place of oaks.

Rallagh, *rálach,* place of oaks.

Rallaghan, *rálach,* place of oaks.

Ralloo, *ráth-Lugha,* not given.

Rally, *rálach,* place of oaks.

Rally, *Rothlaibh,* not given.

Ralph, *baile-an-ratha,* homestead of the earthen fort.

Ralph, *ceathrú-na-rátha/átha,* not given.

Raly, *rálach, ralach,* place of oaks.

Ram, *Ráma,* not given.

Ramelton, *rath-Mealltain,* not given.

Ramer, *ramhar,* thick or fat.

Rammer, *ramhar,* broad.

Ramor, *Reamhor,* not given.

Ramore, *rath-mór,* great fortress.

Rampark, *pairc-an-reithin,* not given.

Rampere, *rampier,* a rampart.

Ran, *Rán,* pleasant.

Ran, *rann,* divisions.

Ran, *ráthan,* a small ráth or fort.

Ran, *ranna, rinn,* the point or headland.

Ran, *rathain,* rushes(sic).

Ran, *reanna,* not given.

Rana, *ráth/raith-na,* the fort of the....

Ranagh, *raithneach,* ferns.

Ranaghan, *raithnigh, raithneachán,* a place of ferns.

Ranah, *reana,* the point.

Ranahan, *raithneachán,* a place of bracken.

Randle, *Randail,* Randal, a Danish personal name.

Randle, *Randalaigh,* not given.

Randoges, little divisions.

Randox, from *rand,* little divisions.

Rane, *raithin,* little rath.

Rane, *raithin, raithnaighe,* ferns.

Rane, *ruáin*(sic), ferns.

Raneese, *rath-Anghuis,* Angus's (a male name) fort.

Ranelagh, *Raghnaill, Raghnallach,* Raghnal's (a personal or family name) place.

Ranelagh, *Randalach,* Randal, a male name.

Ranelagh, *Rannaileach,* not given.

Ranelagh, *rannaireach,* the verses.

Ranelagh, *Rannairech,* Rannaire, a personal name and possibly a saints name.

Raney, *raithne,* ferns.

Ranga, *reanga,* a ridge or border.

Ranhy, *raithneach, raithnighe,* ferns or ferny.

Rankin, *Raincín,* Rankin, a personal or family name.

Rankin, *Uí-Annrachain,* O'Hourihane, a family name.

Ranky, *Fhraincigh,* not given.

Ranky, *rinceadh, rinnce, raince,* dancing.

Ranna, *raithneac*(sic), ferns.

Ranna, *rann-a'...,* division of the...

Ranna, *rann-na...,* point of the...

Rannagh, *an-Reannagh,* not given.

Rannagh, *raithneach, raithnigh,* a place of ferns.

Rannaghan, abounding in ferns.

Rannell, *Raghnaill, Raghnall,* Randal, Reginald or Reynolds, personal and family names.

Rannig, from *rathain,* a place of ferns.

Rannig, *reannaigh,* not given.

Rannock, *ráth-a'-chnuic,* fort of the hill.

Ranns, from *rann,* divisions.

Ranny, *raithnigh, raithní, raithneach,* a place of ferns.

Ranny, *raithnigh, raithnighe,* not given.

Ranny, *rannaidhe,* divisions or land portions.

Ranny, *reanna,* the point.

Rantoge, from *rann,* little divisions.

Rany, *raithní,* ferns.

Rap, *rap,* fragments.

Rapalagh, bad land.

Raphoe, *ráth/rath-bhoth,* ring fort of the huts/tents or fort of the hut.

Rapla, a male name.

Rapla, bad land.

Rapla, *raplach,* noisy.

Rapla, *ropalach,* not given.

Rappa, *ropuigh, ropaigh,* plundering.

Rappala, bad land.

Rapparee, *ropaire,* the robber.

Rapparree, *ropaire,* noisy.

Rappery, *ropaire,* robbers or noisy.

Rara, *reára,* blackbirds.

Rark, *radharc,* the prospect, view.

Ras, *ras,* a wood.

Rash, *rath,* a fort.

Rash, *reas,* the fight.

Rash, *ros,* a wood or grove.

Rashane, *ráth-Seáin,* John's fort.

Rashee, *ráth-sidhe/sí, rath-sidhe,* fairies fort.

Rasheen, underwood.

Rashina, *ros-eidhneach,* not given.

Rask, *Rasca,* not given.

Raska, *rásca,* a type of herb.

Raskeagh, *ráth-sciach,* not given.

Rasker, *ráisceir, rath-sceire,* fort of the rock.

Raskill, *ras-choill,* brushwood or underwood.

Raskin, *Rascain,* not given.

Raskin, *riascain,* little moor.

Rass, *ras,* shrubbery or underwood.

Rassa, *ras-a'…,* wood of the…

Rassa, *rassa,* a copse.

Rassan, *rasán,* the little wood.

Rassaun, *rasán,* the little wood.

Rast, *raist,* rest.

Rast, *reaist,* not given.

Rastill, *rastail,* a hand rake.

Rat, *Raithe,* not given.

Rat, *ráth, rátha,* a fort.

Ratahan, *Uí-Reachtagain,* O'Ratigan, a family name.

Ratallen, *ráth-tSailainn,* ring fort of the salt.

Ratarnet, *réidh-tarnocht,* a bare mountain flat.

Ratass, *ráth-teas,* south/southern ring fort.

Ratawragh, *rath-teamhrach,* fort of the conspicuous hill.

Rath, *rath, rátha, ratha,* a fort.

Rath, *rubha,* a brake or salient.

Rathaleek, *ráth-Áilíocáin,* not given.

Rathaleek, *ráth-Uilic,* Ulick's (a male name) rath.

Rathanny, *ráth-Eine/Chana,* not given.

Rathardeacher, *rath-ard-Fhiachrach,* Fiachra's (a personal or famly name) high fort.

Rathavin, *ráth-an-bhinnigh,* not given.

Rathbourn, *ráth-ard-mhór,* not given.

Rathconnell, *rubha-Chonaill,* Conaill's (a personal or family name) salient.

Rathcool, *ráth-Cuala,* not given.

Rathcool, *reidh-chul,* smooth hill back.

Rathdrumin, *rath-droma-Nao,* not given.

Rathe, *rath,* a fort.

Rathea, *ráth-Aodha,* not given.

Rathealy, *ráth-Aola,* not given.

Rathealy, *ráth-Aolmhaigh,* Aolmhach, a personal or family name.

Rathene, *ráithín,* a little rath.

Rathenee, *raithínidhe,* little forts.

Ratherrig, *rath-dhearg,* red fort.

Rathfalla, *rath-bhaile,* not given.

Rathin, *ráth-an…,* rath of the…

Rathlin, *reachlainn, reachra, rachrann,* the landing place of 'rachra' which was the custom of sending sheep to the island in the spring.

Rathlin, rough island.

Rathna, *ráth/rath-na…,* fort of the…

Rathnarrow, *rath-an-arbha,* fort of the corn.

Rathnaveoge, *ráth-Mobheóg*(sic), not given.

Rathoath, *rath-Tó,* fort of Tó, a male name.

Rathoe, *ráth-Tó,* not given.

Rathoma, *ráth-Coma,* not given.

Rathoonagh, *rath-thamhnagh,* the rath field.

Rathruane, *ráth-Dhreamháin,* not given.

Rathruane, *ráth-Ruadhain,* Rowan's (a personal or family name) fort.

Rathrush, *ráth-Faolascaigh,* not given.

Rathurles, *ráth-durlais,* not given.

Rathurlisk, *rath-thurluisc,* fort of the oak.

Rathwire, *ráth-Guaire,* not given.

Ratoath, *ráth-Tabhachta,* not given.

Rathora, *ráth-Hóra,* Hora's (a personal or family name) fort.

Ratoran, *rath-teórann,* fort on or of the boundary.

Ratrass, *rath-treasa,* fort of the battle.

Ratta, *rata,* a hare or rabbit.

Ratteen, *rath-teine,* fort of fire.

Ratten, *raitín,* a type of freise.

Rattin, *raitín,* ratteen, a type of homespun.

Rattin, *raitin, reitín,* not given.

Rattoo, *ráth-Tó,* Tó's (a personal or family name) fort.

Rattoo, *ráth-tuaidh,* northern fort.

Ratty, *Raite,* Raite, a river name, not given.

Ratyn, *rath-teine,* fort of fire.

Raubaun, *ráth-bán,* white fort.

Raugh, *rath,* a fort.

Raugh, *ráthach,* forts.

Raughts, *reachtais,* legislation.

Rausa, *rása,* copses.

Rausker, *Gamhscair*(sic) , not given.

Rava, *rubha,* a brake.

Ravan, *ramhan,* the spade.

Ravanny, *ráth-Mhaonaigh,* not given.

Ravarnet, *ráth-bhearnain,* not given.

Ravel, *Rábháil, Fhreaghbhail,* not given.

Raven, *riabháin,* not given.

Raven, *riabháin,* the swarthy person.

Raven, *riabhán,* greyish land.

Raven, the small bird.

Raverty, *Rabhartaigh,* Raverty, a personal or family name.

Raverty, *Uí-Raithbheartaigh,* O'Rafferty, a family name.

Raw, *rath, rátha,* a rath.

Rawanney, *rath-a'mhanaigh,* fort of the monk.

Rawer, *ramhar,* thick or fat.

Rawer, *reamhar,* the fat men.

Rawes, *raths,* a forts.

Rawley, *Raighléid,* Rawley, a family name.

Rawley, *Ráiléigh,* not given.

Rawra, *ramhra,* thick.

Rawre, *reamhar,* round.

Ray, *ráithe, ráith, ráth, rath,* a fort or ring fort.

Ray, *réidh,* level.

Ray, *riach,* grey.

Raymeen, *reidhe-mhíne,* smooth moorland plain.

Raymond, *Réamainn,* Réamann, a personal or family name.

Raymond, *Réamoinn,* not given.

Raymunterdoney, *ráith*(sic), not given.

Re, *reidhleach,* réidh, *reidh,* a coarse mountain flat or plain.

Re, *ráth,* a fort.

Rea, peatland.

Rea, *ré, réithigh,* not given.

Rea, *rea,* a boggy flat.

Rea, *réidh,* a clearing.

Rea, *réidh,* smooth, untilled or open.

Rea, *reidhe,* moorland.

Rea, *reidhleach,* réidh, *reidh,* a coarse mountain flat or plain.

Rea, *reidg*(sic), a flat mountain or plain.

Rea, *ria,* red coloured.

Rea, *Riabhaigh,* Rea, a personal or family name.

Rea, *riach, reagh, riabhach,* grey.

Rea, *riabh, riaghadh,* executions.

Readoty, *an-ré-dhóithe,* not given.

Ready, *an-Riadaigh,* an-Riadach, not given.

Ready, *Uí-Riada,* O'Reidy, a personal or family name.

Readypenny, *Cillín-Cúile,* not given.

Reag, *reigh,* smooth.

Reagh, bridled(sic).

Reagh, *riabhach,* brindled(sic).

Reagh, *fhíona,* wine.

Reagh, *Rí,* king.

Reagh, *riabhach,* striped, speckled or grey.

Reagh, *riach,* grey.

Reagh, *riach, reagh, riabhach,* grey.

Reaghan, from *riabhach,* little grey spot of land.

Reaghan, *riacháin,* not given.

Reaghfa, *réidhfa,* level fields.

Reaghya, *rath-a'…,* fort of the…

Reagrove, *rath-groighe,* fortress of the horses.

Reague, *reigh, réidh, reidh,* smooth, clear or level.

Reague, *riabhach,* grey.

Realin, *raithleann,* not given.

Reamlach, *ramalach,* stagnant water.

Reamon, *Réamoinn,* Raimond, a personal or family name.

Rean, *raithin, Rían,* not given.

Rean, *Riáin,* Ryan, a family name.

Rean, *riain,* the track.

Reana, *ráe/rae-na…,* field of the…

Reana, *reidh-na, réidh-na,* marshy or mountain flat of the…., level plain of the …., clearing of the…

Reana, *reidh-na…,* level plain of the ….

Reana, *ré-na…,* level ground of the…

Reane, *Réin,* not given.

Rear (cross), *rae, an-rae,* the level spot.

Rear, *rae,* the level spot or plain.

Reardnogy, *ré-fhearnóige,* not given.

Reardnogy, *reidh-fhearnoige,* moor of the alders.

Reardon, *Uí-Riabhardáin,* O'Riordan, a family name.

Rearke, *radhairc,* not given.

Rearke, *radharc,* the prospect, view.

Rearour, *ré-ramhar, réidh-reamhar,* not given.

Rearowr, *reidh-reamhair,* fat plain.

Reary, *raerin,* the name of an ancient palace.

Reary, *Raoire,* not given.

Reas, *riasc,* not given.

Reash, *Réis,* not given.

Reask, *réisc,* not given.

Reask, *riasc, reusc, rusg, riacsa,* marsh, marshy or marshes.

Reask, *riasg, riasc,* a moor marsh or fen.

Reaska, *riasc-an/a'…,* marsh of the…

Reaskaun, *riasgán,* little marsh.

Reatagh, *reidhtach,* a woody shrubby place or a place overgrown with underwood.

Reatagh, *réiteach,* not given.

Reave, *ruibh,* sulphur.

Reavillin, *reidh-mhillín,* the flat or smooth hillock.

Reavouler, *reidh-Bhalldair,* Baldar's (a personal or a family name) plain.

Reavy, *riabhaigh,* grey.

Reban, *fásach-réaban,* a flat white place on a hill.

Rebane, *ráith-bhán,* not given.

Reboge, *réabóg,* rough broken land.

Reboge, *réabóige,* not given.

Recess, *sraith-salach,* dirty holm.

Redchair, *reed-sheard,* (old west English, not Irish) red gap.

Redcow, *lios-bhaile-Uí-Réigín,* not given.

Reddan, *readán,* reeds.

Reddan, *Rodán,* O'Reddan, a family name.

Redding, *Thréidín,* Tredin, a personal or family name.

Reddy, *roide,* not given.

Reddy, *ruide,* iron scum.

Redeen, *ruidín,* a small piece of land or a little townland.

Rodeen, *roidín,* a place red myrtle.

Redmond, *Mhic-Réamainn,* not given.

Redmond, *Reamon,* Redmond, a personal or family name.

Reduff, *ráith-dhubh,* not given.

Ree, *fhraeigh,* calves.

Ree, *fhraoigh,* heath or heather.

Ree, *fraeigh,* heath.

Ree, grey lake.

Ree, *Raidhe,* name of the grandson of ancient King Felimy.

Ree, *raidhe, raeidhe,* a race of people.

Ree, *Raoidhe,* not given.

Ree, *Réidhe,* not given.

Ree, *Rí, Righ,* king.

Ree, *ria, riaghaidh,* executions.

Ree, *riabhach,* grey or striped.

Ree, *raibhaige,* shallow.

Ree, *Riach,* not given.

Ree, *riaigh,* gallows.

Ree, *Ríbh, Ribh,* Ribh, a personal or family name.

Ree, *righe,* plunder.

Ree, *riogh,* not given.

Reebart, *Righbaird,* not given.

Reedaun, *Raodáin,* not given.

Reedeen, *róidín, róidin,* a little road.

Reeha, *roidheidh,* contending.

Reehan, *Riachain,* Reaghan, a male name.

Reekil, *St Richill,* the virgin Saint.

Reekill, *Rícill,* St Richil, Ricil.

Reeks, ridges or crests.

Reel, *Fhrithil,* Freel, a personal or family name.

Reel, *Riaghla,* St Riaghal.

Reel, *Uí-Fhirghil,* O'Freel, a family name.

Reelan, (river) *an-Raoileann,* not given.

Reelan, *Rairinn,* Reelan, the name of an ancient mound over the grave of King Rairu in Kildare.

Reelin, *Raerin,* the name of an ancient royal palace.

Reelin, *Ríleann,* not given.

Reelion, *raoileann,* not given.

Reelyon, *Righ-Laighen,* the King of leinster.

Reemig, *riamaigh,* victory.

Reen, *Rí-an…,* King of…

Reen, *rinn,* a point of land, a promontory or a headland.

Reen, *rinn, rinne,* a headland.

Reen, *Roighean,* Roighin, not given.

Reena, *rinn-an/a'…,* the point or level place of the…

Reena, *rioghna,* a Queen.

Reenagh, *dhraighneach,* not given.

Reenagh, *raithnighe,* ferns.

Reenda, *rinn-da…,* point of the two…

Reendowney, *Righ-an-Domhnaigh,* King of sunday

Reene, *rioghna,* a Queen.

Reenlanig, *Rinnleanagh,* Ringland, a personal or family name.

Reenna, *ré-na…,* not given.

Reenna, *rinn-na…,* point of the…

Reens, *roighne,* plural of the 'choicest part' or the 'best place'.

Reeny, *raithnighe,* ferns.

Reenydonagan, O'Donagan's point.

Reeoge, *Rioc,* St Rioc.

Reer, *righ-fhir,* the royal man.

Reera, *reimhre,* sea swell.

Reerasta, *riaráiste,* arrears or rearage.

Reesh, *Feargus, Fhearghaois,* Fergus, a male name.

Reeshig, *Risigh, Rísigh,* Rice, a family name.

Reesk, *riasca,* a morass.

Reesode, *Ríosóid, Ríosóid,* not given.

Reeva, *riabhach,* grey.

Reevanagh, *ré-mheanach,* not given.

Reeves, *rubha,* a place of the herb 'rue'.

Refadda, *réidh-fhada,* a long mountain flat or plain.

Regaile, *ré-Ghaeil,* not given.

Regaile, *reidh-Gáedhail,* Irish level mountain flat.

Regan, *Cargan,* not given.

Regan, *Drecon,* a male name.

Regan, Regan, a personal or family name.

Regan, *Riagáin,* Ó Riagain(sic), a family name.

Regan, *Riagáin,* Riagán, a personal or family name.

Regan, *Uí-Riagáin, Réagáin,* Ó Riagáin or O'Regan, a family name.

Regane, *Riagain,* Regan, a male name.

Reglesia, *Réigleasa,* not given.

Reha, *reithe,* rams.

Reher, *righfhear,* royal men.

Rehil, *réid-choill,* open or level topped wood.

Rehili, *réidh-choill, a* smooth, clear, open, easily transversed or passable wood.

Rehill, *réchoill,* not given.

Rehill, *réidhchoill, réidh-choill,* a smooth, clear, passable wood.

Rehins, *raithíní,* ferns.

Rehins, *raithíní,* small forts.

Rehy, *reig,* mountain flats.

Rehy, *reithe,* rams.

Reig, *reidh,* open or easily passable.

Reigh, *reitigh,* smooth or even.

Reigh, *riach,* grey or tan coloured.

Reilly, *airbelaig,* the eastern pass.

Reilly, *Railgheach,* not given.

Reilly, *Uí-Raghallaigh,* O'Reilly, a personal or family name.

Reiny, *Ríoghnaighe,* not given.

Reirk, *radhairc,* view, prospect, vista or outlook.

Reiry, *Ruairí,* not given.

Reisc, *riasc,* a sedgy place.

Reisk, *riasc, reusc, rusg, riasg,* a marsh, a marshy place, a moor or a fen.

Reisk, *riasg, riasc,* a moor marsh or fen.

Reiska, *riasg,* a marsh, marshy.

Reisky, *riasg,* a marsh, marshy.

Reitagh, *réiteach,* not given.

Relagh, a flat part of a mountain.

Relagh, *reidhleach,* a little level place.

Relagh, *reidhleach, reidh,* a coarse mountain flat or plain.

Relessy, *reidh-leasa,* moor of the fort.

Relia, *railgheach,* a place of oaks.

Relick, *reilig,* a Church.

Relick, *roilig, relig,* a cemetery.

Relig, *reilig,* a Churchyard.

Relig, *reilig,* graveyard.

Rella, *Riaghla,* St Riaghla.

Rella, *Riala, Riail,* a personal or family name.

Rellig, *reilig,* graveyard.

Reloagh, *ráth-locha,* fort of the lake.

Remaher, *sraith-Meathair,* Mahers holm/ river island.

Remeen, *ráth-mín,* not given.

Remeen, *reidh-mín,* smooth plain.

Remeen, *reidh-mhín-dhubh,* a smooth high flat of dark-soil.

Remon, *Réamainn, Reamoinn,* Reamon or Redmond, a personal or family name.

Remon, *Réamoinn,* Raimond, a personal or family name.

Remony, *ré-mónaigh,* not given.

Ren, *rinn,* a headland or point.

Rena, *mhargaidh,* the market.

Rena, *rae-na…,* level place of the…

Rena, *reidh-na…*, flat moor of the…

Rena, *Rioghna*, the Queen.

Renagh, *raithneach*, a ferny place.

Renagh, *raonach*, paths.

Renaghan, *raithneachán*, fern shrubbery.

Renan, *Uí-Raonain*, Renan or Renehan, a personal or family name.

Rendoney, *righ-an-domhnaigh*, King of Sunday.

Reneen, *raithnighe*, ferns.

Renny, *raithní*, not given.

Renny, *rannaigh*, a portion.

Renny, *rannaigh*, a portion.

Renny, *rathain, raithnighe*, a place of ferns.

Renvyle, *rinn-Mhaoile/Mhíl*, not given.

Rerin, *réidhinn*, not given.

Rerk, *radhairc*, view or prospect.

Rerrin, *raerainn*, not given.

Rerrin, *reidh-rinn*, level headland.

Resk, *riasc, reusc, rusg, riasg*, a marsh, a marshy place or a morass.

Reska, *riasc-an…*, marsh of the…

Retagh, *réidhteach*, cleared land.

Rev, *ruibh*, sulphur.

Revagh, *riabhach*, the colour grey or a grey field.

Revallagh, *reidh-bealach*, a clear open road or pass.

Revan, *riabháin*, a small stripe.

Revan, *chríocháin*, a small district.

Revanagh, *reidh-mheánach*, middle high flat.

Revlin, *ruibh-linn*, a sulphur pool/stream.

Revog, *riabhóg*, pipits(sic).

Revogagh, *riabhógach*, abounding in tit-larks.

Revogue, *réidhe-bhuige*, a soft plain.

Revy, *riabhach*, grey or grey field.

Rew, *ruaidhe*, red.

Rewy, *riabhach*, grey.

Rey, *reidh*, a coarse mountain flat/plain.

Reynagh, *Cill-Ríonaí/Reaghnaighe*, not given.

Reynard, *Raghnairt*, Raghnart, not given.

Rhehargonogue, *reidh-fhearnóige*, alder plain.

Rhode, *ród*, route.

Rhue, a place where the plant 'Rue' grows.

Rhyne, *roinn*, a division.

Riach, *Riach*, not given.

Riada, *riad*, travelling by chariot or horse or chariot driving.

Riada, *Riata, Riata*, a personal or family name.

Riagh, *riabhach*, grey.

Rian, *rian*, a track.

Riark, *radhairc*, a view.

Ribbeen, *Roibín, Roibín*, Robin, a male name.

Ribben, *Roibín*, not given.

Riblicane, *ribleacan*, sorrel/s.

Riblihane, *ribleacháin, ribleachain*, sorrel.

Riblecane, *ribleacan*, sorrell(sic).

Rickard, *Riocaird, Risteird*, not given.

Richchair, reed-sheard, (old west English, not Irish) red gap.

Rick, *nDaróg*, small oaks.

Rickane, *Riocain*, Rickan, a family name.

Rickard, *Risteird, Riocaird*, not given.

Rickeen, *Ricín*, little Rickard/Dick (a male name).

Ricken, *Ricín*, little Richard, a male name.

Rickin, *Ricín*, not given.

Rickle, *Rícill*, not given.

Riddera, *ridire*, a Knight.

Ridderra, *ridire*, a Knight.

Riddery, *ridire*, a Knight.

Riddia, from *rod, ruide*, iron scum.

Riddig, *roidigh*, a red mire.

Riddy, *roide*, not given.

Riddy, *ruide*, (reddish) scum.

Rider, *Ridire*, a Knight.

Riesk, *riasc, reusc, rusg, riasg*, sedgy land, a marsh, marshy, a moor or fen.

Riff, *roibhe*, not given.

Riff, *roimhe*, brimstone.

Riffet, *Ruiféad*, not given.

Riffit, *Riféad, Rifead*, Riphat, Riphad, a male name.

Riffith, *Riféad, Rifead*, Riphat, Riphad, a male name.

Rig, a corruption of *luig*, a hollow.

Riggin, *Roigin*, not given.

Righ, *Righ*, King.

Rigney, *Raigne*, a male name.

Rigrour, *reamhar*, thick.

Rihen, *airchinn*, the border.

Rihy, *Riche*, not given.

Riland, *Raoileann*, not given.

Riland, *Raoirenn,* Raoire, the name of a royal residence.

Rillig, *reilig,* graveyard.

Rim, *dhruim,* ridge/s.

Rimmaddera, *dhroma-madradh,* dogs ridge.

Rin, *rann,* a promontory.

Rin, *rinn,* a point or a point of land.

Rina, *rinn-na...,* point of the...

Rina, *Rioghna,* Queen.

Rinagh, *draigheanach,* blackthorns.

Rinagh, *raithneach,* a place of ferns.

Rinaha, *rineatán,* ferns.

Rinahan, *Rinneacháin,* not given.

Rinanagh, *rinneanach,* not given.

Rinanagh, *rinn-eanaigh,* the point of the marsh.

Rine, *rinn,* a point of land, a headland.

Rineanna, *rinn-eanaigh,* the point or headland of the marsh.

Rineen, *rennín,* a small point of land.

Rineore, *an-rinn-rua,* not given.

Ring, *rinn,* a point of land.

Ringa, *rinn/rinn-an...,* point of...

Ringabella, *rinn-a'bhile,* promontory of the ancient tree.

Ringarogy, *rinn-gearróige,* point of the little portion.

Ringarogy, *rinn-róige,* not given.

Ringrogy, *rinn-róige,* not given.

Ringsend, (bi-lingual) 'rinn's end', the end of (an-rinn) the point. Another Irish name is *droichead-na-carraige,* bridge of the rock.

Ringsend, *rinn-muirbhthean, droichead-na-carraige-Móirne,* not given.

Ringville, *an-rinn,* not given.

Ringville, *tigh-na-roinne,* house of the point of land.

Rinihan, *rineatán,* ferns.

Rink, *rinceadh,* dancing.

Rinka, *rinceadh, raince,* dancing.

Rinky, *rinceadh,* dancing.

Rinn, (river) *an-Réin,* not given.

Rinn, *rinn,* a point of land.

Rinn, *roinn,* a division.

Rinna, *rann-na...,* not given.

Rinna, *rinn-na...,* point of the...

Rinne, *rinne,* a headland.

Rinne, *roinn-an...,* divison of the...

Rinneen, *rennin, rennin,* a little point of land.

Rinneen, *rinnín,* a little headland.

Rinneen, *roinnín,* little division of land.

Rinneny, *roinne-Eithne,* Enna's (a personal or a family name) division.

Rinville, *rinn-Mhil,* Mil's (a Firbolg chief) point.

Riordane, *Uí-Riobhardáin,* O'Riordan, a family name.

Riordane, *Ui-Ríordáin,* not given.

Riree, *Rudhraighe, Uí-Ruaidhri,* Rory, Rury or Roger, a male name.

Riry, *Rudhraighe, Uí-Ruaidhri,* Rory, Rury or Roger, a male name.

Ris, *ros,* a promontory.

Risheen, *ruisín,* a little ross or wood.

Rishteen, *Ristín,* not given.

Risk, *riasc, riascach, reusc, rusg, riasg,* a marsh, marshy, a moor or fen.

Risode, *disert,* a secluded retreat.

Risteen, *Ghristín,* not given.

Risteen, *Rishteen, Ristín,* little Richard, a male name.

Riverstick, *áth-na-Mhaide,* not given.

Riverstown, *baile-roisín,* town of the little wood.

Rivory, *reigh-Mhóire,* Mór's (a female name) mountain flat.

Ro, *rath,* a fort.

Roach(on its own), *dún-gall,* not given.

Roach, *Róistigh,* Roche, a family name.

Road, *Rada, Rodaigh,* not given.

Road, *ramh-fhada, ramhfhoda,* long rowing(sic).

Road, *roid,ród,* a road.

Road, *róid,* the route.

Road, *ruadh,* red.

Roagh, *riabhach, riach,* grey.

Roagh, *ruadh,* red.

Roal, *Róil,* not given.

Roan, *Eoghain,* Owen, a male name.

Roan, *róinne,* not given.

Roan, *rón, ron,* a marine seal.

Roan, *rón,* the hairy man.

Roan, *Ruadháin,* Rothe or Ruffus a surname.

Roan, *ruadhán,* a wet spongy place.

Roan, *ruadhán,* reddish land.

Roan, *Ruadhán,* Ruadan, Rowan or Roan, a male name.

Roan, Ruadhan, Ruadhain, Uí-Ruadhain, Rowan, O'Ruan or O'Roan a family name.

Roan, ruadhán, ruáin, ruadhain, the red haired man.

Roan, Ruadhan, St Ruadhan.

Roan, Ruáin, Rúan, a personal or family name.

Roan, ruán, red patches.

Roans, rath-Eoghain, Owen's rath.

Roanty, reinte, marine seals.

Roarty, Uí-Rabhartaigh, not given.

Roarty, Rabhartaigh, not given.

Roasty, Roache, a family name.

Robbin, Roibín, Robin, a male name.

Robe, an-Ródgbha/Róba, the river 'Róba', not given.

Robe, ródhbha, not given.

Robert, Riobaird, Robert, a male name.

Robin, roibin, bearded or long rough grass.

Robin, Roibín, Robin or Robert, a male name.

Roche, (river) abhainn-na-Róistighe, not given.

Roche, dú-gall, Róiste, not given.

Roche, roche, a rock.

Rockabill, carraig-dhá-bheola, two lips rock.

Rockabill, cloch-Dhábhiolla, carraig-Dabiolla/Dhabhiolla, Dabhiolla's (a legendary dog) rock.

Rockabill, Rock-dha-bille/Da-bille, two rocks.

Rockabill, Uaibh-Dabille, not given.

Rockady, rocadach, furrowed.

Rockan, rocán, not given.

Rockcorry, an-chribe/ghribe, not given.

Rockcorry, buíochar, yellow land.

Rocker, Rocar, not given.

Rocklow, cnoc-baile-Uí-Mheachair, not given.

Rockshire, scair-na-carraige, not given.

Rockwell, carn-tobar, not given.

Rod, ród, a road.

Rodain, Rodáin, not given.

Rodan, Rodáin, Rodán, the name of a Church founder in Limeirick.

Rodane, Rodáin, not given.

Rodaun, rórain, ruadhán, red land.

Rodda, ruide, iron scum.

Roddan, Rodáin, not given.

Rodden, Rodáin, Rodan, a personal or family name.

Roddenagh, roideánach, (place of?) bog-myrtle.

Roddy, Rodaighe, Roddy, a male name and a family name.

Roddy, Uí-Rodaigh, O'Roddy or Roddy, a family name.

Rode, from ród, roads.

Rodeen, róidín, roidín, ródín, a little road.

Roden, róidín, ródín, róidin, a little road.

Rodus, róda, ródas, not given.

Roe, reddish brown or russet.

Roe, reó, frost.

Roe, rú, the plant 'rue'.

Roe, rua, Ró, Reo, an-Róigh/Roigh, an-Róch, not given.

Roe, rua, red, or red land/place.

Roe, ruadh, ruadha, red.

Roe, ruadh, the red haired persons.

Roe, ruaidh, a red man or red haired man.

Roe, Ruaidh, Rowe, a personal or family name.

Roebuck, reabóg, not given.

Roechrow, ruadh-chro, the red glen.

Roegarraun, ruagharrán, not given.

Roelough, an-rualach, not given.

Roemore, rahemore, big or great fort.

Roes, ruadha, red spots of land.

Rogary, ruagharraí, red garden.

Rogary, ruadhghaire, reddish land.

Roger, Ruairí, not given.

Rogue, ruadh, red.

Rogue, ruaige, the rout.

Rogy, ruadh, red.

Rohan, Uí-Rócháin, O'Roughan, a personal name.

Rohane, Crócháin, Cróchán or Crochan, a personal or family name.

Rohane, ruachain, a beacon.

Rohane, ruacháin, not given.

Rohane, ruachán, ruacháin, not given.

Rohane, ruadhain, moorland.

Rohaun, srutháin, a stream.

Roher, ruathair, ruathar, an attack, invasion or foray

Roher, urchair, a missile.

Rokeby, Rokeby(sic), not given.

Rolach, rua-loch, not given.

Rolagh, ruaidh-tach, reddish spots of land.

Rollagh, *raileach, rálach,* place of oaks.
Roman, *Remoinn,* Redmond, a male name.
Rome, *Róm,* Rome.
Rome, *Ruaime,* not given.
Ronagh, *rónach,* the seal.
Ronagh, *ruadhrach*(sic), not given.
Ronagh, *ruaineach,* feathery.
Ronagh, *rúaineach, ruaidh-eanaigh,* a red morass.
Ronagh, *ruanach,* not given.
Ronagh, *ruanagh,* ruddy, reddish.
Ronan, *Rónáin, Ronáin, Ronain, Rónán,* Ronan, a male name and the name of at least 12 Irish saints.
Ronan, *Uí-Rónán, Uí-Rónáin, Uí-Ronain,* Ó Rónáin, O'Ronan or O'Rónán, a family name and means the descendants of Rónán.
Ronane, *Ronain,* Ronan, a male name and the name of at least 12 Irish saints.
Ronane, *Ronain,* Ronan, a personal or family name.
Roncarrig, *ron-carraig,* seal rock.
Rone, *róin, roin,* a seal.
Rone, *Ruadháin,* Ruadhan, a personal or family name.
Rone, *Ruadhain,* a reddish colour and the male name Ruadhán or Ruadhan.
Rone, *Ruáin, Ruán,* a personal or family name.
Roney, *Uí-Ruanaí,* Ó Ruanaí or O'Roney, a family name and means the descendants of Ruanaí.
Roney, *Uí-Ruanaidhe,* O'Runai, O'Rooney, a family name.
Ronnagh, from *roinn,* divisions.
Rontia, *rón,* seals.
Roo, *Rú,* not given.
Roo, *rua, ruadh,* red.
Roo, *Ruaidh,* Hugh, a male name.
Roo, *rubha,* the plant/herb 'rue'.
Rooa, *rúadh, ruadh,* red bog.
Rooa, *ruaidh, ruadh,* red.
Rooan, *rúadh, rúadhan,* red.
Rooan, *Ruadhain,* Rooan or Rodan, a male name and the name of 4 Irish Saints, It also means the red haired man.
Rooan, *rúadhan,* a plant used for its red dye also the plant called 'rue'.
Rooaun, *an-Ruán,* not given.

Rooaun, *rórain, ruadhán,* red, reddish land.
Rooaun, *ruadhain,* the red haired man.
Rooaun, *ruadhán,* a reddish or heathery place.
Rooaun, *Uí-Ruadhain,* Rowan or O'Ruan, a family name.
Rooaun, *Uí-Ruaidhin,* O'Rooin, a family name.
Rooauna, *ruadhán-a'...,* reddish land of the...
Rooey, *ruaidh,* the red man.
Rooey, *rubha,* a point of land.
Rooey, *rudhaigh, rubha,* where the plant 'rue' grows.
Roog, *ruadh,* red.
Roog, *ruag,* not given.
Roog, *ruaige,* a rout.
Rooga, *ruadh,* red.
Rooga, *ruaige,* a rout.
Roogagh, *an-ruagach,* not given.
Rooghan, *rórain, ruadhán,* red, reddish land.
Rooghann, *ruadhán,* reddish coloured spot of land.
Rooghaun, *rórain, ruadhán,* red, reddish land.
Rooghill, *Ruachaill,* not given.
Rooghill, *rubha-choille,* rue-wood.
Roolagh, *ruaidh-tach,* reddish spots of land.
Roolagh, *rualach,* red lake.
Roon, red or russet.
Roon, *ruadhan,* the red stripe.
Roon, *ruain,* a red-dye plant.
Roon, *Uí-Ruadhain,* Rowan, a personal or family name.
Roon, *Uí-Ruaidhin,* O'Rooin, a family name.
Roonagh Point, *rú/rubha-an-átha,* not given.
Rooni, *rubha-na...,* promontory of the......
Roos, *rubha,* the plant 'rue'.
Roosca, *rúscach,* not given.
Roosca, *rusgach, rusgaidh,* a marsh.
Roose, *rubha,* a place where the herb 'rue' grows.
Roosk, *rúisc,* the bark(sic).
Roosk, *rúsc,* marshes.
Roosk, *rusg,* a morass, marsh or marshy.
Rooska, *riasgach,* a moory place.
Rooska, *ruscach,* marshy.
Rooska, *rúsg,* a skirmish(sic).

Rooskagh, *rúscach, rusgach,* marsh or marshy.

Rooskagh, *rusgach, rusgaidh,* a moor, marsh or marshy,

Roosky, *rúsc, rúscach, rúscaigh, rúscaighe, rusgach, rusgaidh,* a marsh or marshy.

Roosky, *rúscaí,* crusts(sic).

Roosky, *rúscaí,* not given.

Root, *rua, ruadh,* russet or red.

Root, *ruaidh,* red soil.

Rootagh, *ruaiteach, ruaidh-tibh,* reddish land.

Rootiagh, *ruaidh-tibh,* reddish spots of land.

Rootiagh, *ruaiteach,* red bog.

Roovehaghs, *ruadh-bheitheacha,* not given.

Rooves, *ruaidhtibh, ruaidh-tibh,* reddish land.

Rorach, *Ruadhraigh, Ruadhraighe, Ruadhrach,* Rory, a male name.

Roragh, *Rórach,* not given.

Roran, *rórán,* not given.

Roran, *ruadhbharán, rórain,* red, reddish land.

Roranna, *Ruaranna,* not given.

Rorard, *Rórard,* Rorard, a male name.

Rory, *Ruairí, Ruaidhrí,* not given.

Rory, *Rudhaidhe, Rudhraighe, Uí-Ruaidhri*(sic), Rory, Rury or Roger, a male name.

Rory, *Rudh-Raidhe,* Rory, a male name.

Ros, *rás,* a race.

Ros, *ros,* a shrubbery or a high place.

Ros, *ros, ruis,* a wood, grove, copse, headland, point of land or a peninsula.

Ros, rushy(sic).

Rosahane, *rosachán,* underwood, brushwood or a little wood.

Rosanna, *rubha/ros-Seanaigh,* not given.

Rosapenna, *machaire-loiscthe,* the burnt plain.

Rosapenna, *machaire-loist,* not given.

Roscommon, *ros-Comáin,* St Comans wood, grove.

Rose, *ros, ruis,* a wood.

Rosegreen, *cnocán-an-teampuill,* not given.

Rosegreen, *faithche-Ró,* Roe's (a personal or family name) exercise green.

Roselick, *rosrelick,* the point of the graveyard/cemetery.

Rosenallis, *ros-fhionnghlaise,* grove of the bright stream or wood of the clear stream.

Rosenallis, *rosfinglas,* wood of the bright chystal rivulet.

Rosepenna, *machaire-loiscthe,* not given.

Roshin, *roisín,* not given.

Roshin, *ruisín,* a little wood or peninsula.

Roskeda, *ros-Cíde,* not given.

Rosna, *ros-na...,* wood/headland of the...

Ross, *rois,* a grove.

Ross, *ros, ruis,* a wood, shrubbery, underwood, grove, copse, point, headland, promontory, point of land or peninsula.

Ross, *Rosa,* not given.

Ross, *rubha,* a promontory.

Ross, *ruis,* a point.

Rossa, *rosa,* a meadow(sic).

Rossa, *ros-an/a'...,* headland/peninsula or wood of the...

Rossagh, *rosach,* a place of underwood.

Rossalia, *ros-áille,* beautiful wood.

Rossalia, *ros-saile,* sea meadow(sic).,

Rossalia, *ros-sáille,* wood of the brine.

Rossan, *rosán,* a small shrubbery or tree grove.

Rossan, *rosan,* a small wood/shrubbery.

Rossan, *rosán,* the rosses(sic).

Rossan, *ros-an...,* point of the...

Rossanarra, *an-uaine-mór,* the big green(sic).

Rossane, *rosán,* not given.

Rossane, *rossán,* brushwood or underwood.

Rossanty, *Rosanta,* St Rosanta/Roxentius.

Rossary, *ros-an-fhraoigh,* not given.

Rossary, *ross-a'Righ,* wood of the King.

Rossawn, *rosán,* shrubbery or underwood.

Rossen, *ros-an...,* wood or point of the...

Rossenty, *rosanta,* woody or shrubby.

Rosserk, *ros-Serce,* Serce's (a female name) wood.

Rosses, *na-rosa,* headlands or peninsulas.

Rosses, *ros-Ceithe,* not given.

Rossilly, *ros-Uillidhe,* point of the angles or corners.

Rossin, *roisín,* a little wood.

Rossinan, *ros-Séanáin/Seanán,* not given.

Rossinan, *ros-Sheanáin,* the wood or land point of St Synan.

Rosslare, *ros-Láir,* not given.

Rossna, *ros-na...,* wood of the...

Rossolus, *ros-solas,* not given.

Rossrehill, *an-ros*(sic), not given.

Rossroe, *an-ros*(sic), not given.

Rostellan, *ros-Tialláin/Stialláin*, not given.

Rostig, *Róistíg, Roistigh*, Roche, a family name.

Rostrevor, *carraig-an-bhrághad*, not given.

Rosty, *ros-tighe*, not given.

Rotate, *táte-Rú*, not given.

Rothery, *ridire*, a knight.

Rotton, *ruppa, ropaire*, a robber.

Rouga, *ruag, ruaige*, a battle-rout.

Rouge, *ruaige*, a rout.

Rough, *corrach*, rugged.

Rough, *rough*, a rout or defeat.

Rough, *ruaidhe, ruadh*, red.

Rougha, *ruaige*, a rout.

Rougham, *orc-cam*, crooked hollow.

Roughan, *rabhacán*, a beacon fire.

Roughan, *ruachán*, not given.

Roughan, *ruadhán, ruhán*, red land.

Roughan, *Ua-Rabhacáin, Ruadhachain*, O'Roughan, a family name.

Rougher, *uachtair*, not given.

Rougher, *urchair*, a missile, cast or throw.

Roughil, *urchail*, spancil.

Rought, *Ruachtaighe*, not given.

Roughty, *Ruachtach, O'Ruachtann*, belonging to O'Rouchtan or O'Ruaghtan (a family name).

Roughty, *ruathtach*, destructive (river).

Roundstone, (bi-lingial) 'róinte-stone', the stone of the (marine) seals.

Rour, *ramhar*, thick.

Rour, *reamhair, reamhar*, fat, round, bulky or thick.

Rour, *reamhar*, round.

Rourke, *Uí-Ruairc*, O'Rourke, a family name.

Roury, *Uí-Ruadhri*, O'Rory, a family name.

Rousca, *rusgach, rusgaidh*, a marsh.

Rousk, *rúsc*, marsh.

Rousky, *riasc, reusc, rusg, riasg, rúscaigh, rusgach, rusgaidh*, a marsh or marshy.

Routagh, *ruaidh-tibh*, reddish spots of land.

Routagh, *ruaiteach*, red bog.

Route, *Riada*, son of King Conary, II.

Route, *rúta*, not given.

Rovaddy, *ruadh-mhadaigh*, red dog.

Rovanagh, *Rómhánach*, not given.

Rovanagh, *Romhánach, Romhanach*, the Roman/s.

Rovar, *reamhar*, not given.

Rover, *reamhar*, thick.

Rover, *robhar, ruadbhair, ruadhbhar*, reddish land.

Row, *Rabhaidh*, not given.

Row, *rogha*, choice.

Row, *rua, ruadh*, red.

Row, *rubha*, the plant 'rue'.

Rowan, *ruadhán*, reddish coloured spot of land.

Rowans, from *ruadhán*, reddish coloured spot of land.

Rowarty, Rowarty or Raverty, a personal or family name.

Rowe, *rubha*, the plant 'rue'.

Rower, *ramhar*, not given.

Rower, *reamhar*, fat or thick.

Rower, *robhar*, flood.

Rower, *robhar*, the red land.

Rower, *ruadhbhar*, red.

Rowl, *urchaill*, not given.

Rowlagh, *ruaidh-tach*, reddish spots of land.

Rowley, *Rothláin*, Rowley, a personal or family name.

Rowr, *eamhar*, thick.

Rowragh, *Ruarach*, not given.

Rowragh, *Ruadhrach*, Rury, a personal or family name.

Roxton, *creag-an-bhran*, rocky land of the raven.

Roy, (island), *abhraidhe, abhraidh, aimhréidh*, the prisoner, another version of this island name is *oileán-an-bhráighe*, not given.

Roy, *raith, rath*, fort.

Roy, *ráthadh*, not given.

Roy, *ruadh, rua*, red.

Roya, *ruaidhe*, the red cow.

Royan, *Rhuadhain*, Ruadan, a male name.

Royey, *ruaidh*, the red haired men.

Ru, *rubha*, a clearing.

Ruacan, *racán*, tumult, revelry or fighting.

Ruag, *ruaige*, a defeat or rout.

Ruan, *ruadháin*, a moory place.

Ruan, *ruadhain*, the red haired man.

Ruan, *ruadhán*, a place of the plant 'Ruan'.

Ruan, *ruadhan*, red bog.

Ruan, *ruadhán, ruán, ruhán*, red land.

Ruan, *an-ruáin,* the mystery.
Ruan, *ruáin,* not given.
Ruan, *ruan, ruabhan,* alders.
Ruane, *Romhanach,* Romans.
Ruane, *ruadhain,* red land.
Ruane, *Ruadháin,* St Rodanus/Ruan/ Rodan.
Ruane, *ruadhain,* the red haired man.
Ruane, *Ruadhan,* Rowan, a family name.
Ruane, *ruáin,* red place.
Ruane, *Ruáin,* Ruán, a personal or family name.
Ruane, *t-sruthain,* a small river.
Ruanes, from *ruadhán,* reddish coloured spots of land.
Ruaun, *ruadhán,* reddish coloured spots of land.
Ruaun, *ruadhán,* the red haired man.
Rub, *rubha,* the brake or thicket.
Rubane, *rubha-bán,* white clearing.
Rubble, *earball,* a tail.
Rubble, *rubaill,* not given.
Rud, *ród,* a road.
Rud, *roid, rod, ruide, rud,* iron scum or rust.
Rudane, *roideain,* red water.
Rudda, *roda,* not given.
Rudda, *rúdha,* ...by the wood(sic).
Rudda, *ruide,* iron scum.
Ruddan, *Rodáin,* Roddan, a personal or family name.
Ruddan, *Ruadháin,* Rowan, a personal or family name.
Ruddee, from *rod, ruide,* red iron scum.
Ruddera, *Ridire,* a Knight.
Rudderagh, *ridire,* a knight.
Ruddery, *ridire,* a Knight.
Ruddery, *rothaire, ruairí,* vagrants or wanderers.
Ruddery, *Ruairí,* Ruairí, a male name.
Ruddig, *rodaig, rodach, ruide,* iron scum.
Ruddy, from *rod/ruide,* iron scum.
Rude, *ruide,* rusty, reddish colour.
Rude, *rúide,* not given.
Rue, *rua,* red coloured.
Rue, *rubha,* a clearing.
Rue, *rubha,* the herb 'rue'.
Rue, a promontory or point.
Ruena, *Rubha-na...,* promontory of the......
Ruff, *ruibhe,* sulphur.

Ruid, *rod,* not given.
Ruid, *rud,* red iron scum or mire.
Ruin, *Riúin,* not given.
Ruin, *Uí-Ruaidhin,* O'Rooin, a family name.
Rum, *dhroma, dhruim,* a ridge, a long hill.
Runaniree, *réidh-na-nDoirí,* not given.
Rundle, a round object/burial mound etc.
Rune, *Riúin,* Riún, not given.
Rune, *Uí-Ruaidhin,* O'Rooin, a family name.
Rung, *rinn,* a point of land.
Runinch, *rinn-inse,* point of the river holm or island.
Runna, *roinn-an/na...,* portion or division of the...
Runniaght, *cruithneacht,* wheat.
Runta, *rúnta,* not given.
Runtha, *Rúnta,* not given.
Runtagh, *ronntach,* divisions.
Ruogy, *ruaige,* a rout or pursuit.
Ruogy, *ruaige,* the rout.
Rup, *rop, ropaire,* robbers.
Rup, *ropa,* not given.
Rupla, bad land.
Ruppa, *ropach,* a place of marauders..
Ruppa, *ropuigh, ropaigh,* plundering.
Ruppera, *ropaire,* rapparee.
Ruppla, *raplach,* not given.
Ruppulagh, *Roplach,* not given.
Rus, *iorras,* a peninsula.
Rus, *ruis, ros,* a peninsula or a wood.
Rusco, *rúscach,* moory.
Rush, *Fhearghuis,* Fergus, a male name.
Rush, *iorrais,* a headland.
Rush, *rois,* a headland, meadow, wood, land-point or grove.
Rush, *rois,* a meadow or wood.
Rush, *ros, ruis,* a wood, clearing or peninsula.
Rush, *ros-eó,* peninsula of the yew trees.
Rushane, *ruiseain,* a little wood or grove.
Rushanes, *ruiseán, ruiseain,* little woods or groves.
Rushaun, *rosán,* small arable place.
Rushaun, *ruiseain,* a little wood or grove.
Rusheen, *roisín, rúisín, ruisín,* a little wood, point, copse or peninsula.
Rusheena, *roisín-na...,* little point of the...
Rusheenna, *roisín/ruisín-na...,* little point of the...

Rusheens, *na-roisíní,* not given.

Rusheeny, *ruisinídhe,* little woods.

Rusheenyvulligan, *roisín-an-Bholgáin,* not given.

Rushen, *ruisín, ruisen,* the little wood or point.

Rushin, *roisín,* not given.

Rusk, *riasc, roisc, ruisc,* a marsh.

Rusk, *rosc,* not given.

Rusk, *rusc,* fleeces.

Rusk, *rusg,* a morass.

Ruskey, *rúscach,* not given.

Ruskey, *rúscaigh,* a morass.

Ruskin, *ruiscin,* a marsh.

Ruskin, *rusclainn,* bark.

Rusky, *riasc, reusc, rusg, riasg,* a morass, a marsh or marshy.

Rusky, *rusgach, rusgaidh,* a marsh.

Rusley, *Ruiséalach,* Russelagh, a male name.

Russa, promontories or woods.

Russa, *rosach,* woody.

Russagh, *rosach,* woody.

Russagh, *ros-each,* wood of the horses.

Russagh, *rúscach, rosach-na-Ríoghnaidhe,* not given.

Russaun, *rosán,* underwood or a little wood.

Russel, *Ruiséalach,* Russelagh, a male name.

Russel, *Ruiséalaigh,* not given.

Russel, *ruisen,* little wood.

Russell, *Ruiséalaigh,* Russell, a personal or family name.

Rutagh, *Ruatach,* not given.

Ruther, *Ridire,* a Knight.

Rutland, (island), named after the Duke of Rutland (Charles Manners) in the 18th cent. The Irish name is *Inis-Mhic-an-Doirn,* Mac an Doirn's island.

Ruttery, *Ridire,* a Knight.

Ruttery, *Ridire,* a Knight.

Ruyr, *ramhair,* thick.

Ry, …*rach,* as an ending to a word can sometimes mean, a place of…. or abounding in…

Ryan, *Riáin,* Rián, a personal or family name.

Ryan, *rian,* the track.

Ryane, *rian,* the track.

Ryark, *radharc,* the prospect, **view.**

Rye, *riabhach,* not given.

Rye, *Righ,* King.

Ryelanes, *na-réileáin,* not given.

Rylaan, *reighleán,* exercise ground.

Ryland, *raoileann,* not given.

Rylane, plural of *reidhleán,* sports greens or dancing greens.

Rylane, *reidhleain, reidhleán, reidhlean,* a sports green or dancing green.

Rylane, *réidhleán-an-ringce,* not given.

Rylane, *reighleán,* a green field for sports and festivities.

Rylane, *réileán,* the level land/s or meadow/s.

Rylanes, *na-réileáin,* the level tracts.

Rylanes, *reidhleán,* a sporting green.

Ryn, *rin, rinn,* a point of land.

Rynn, *Réin,* not given.

Rynn, *rinn,* a headland or point.

Ryrke, *rhadharc,* prospect/s.

Ryrke, *rhadharc,* prospect/s.

S

Sack, *mhalá,* sack or bag.
Sadare, *eas-dara,* oak cataract/waterfall.
Safagh, *safach,* spade handles.
Safagh, *samhthach,* polearm shafts or spear handles.
Sagcart(sic), *sagart,* the preist.
Saggart, in Dublin, originally called **Tassagard,** *Teach-Sagard, Sagra, Sacra,* the house of St Sacra, Sagra (7th cent).
Saggart, *sagart,* land of the clergy, priest or priests.
Saharn, *Sabhrainn,* Saurin, a personal or family name.
Saharn, *Sathairn, tSathairn,* Saturday.
Saharn, *Sorachain,* Sorohan, a personal or family name.
Sahrin, *Sabhrainn,* Saurin, a personal or family name.
Sahrin, *Sorachain,* Sorohan, a personal or family name.
Saint, *samh,* sorrel.
Saintlour, *San-Lobhar,* not given.
Saintlour, *slórtha, slabarta, chains.*
Saivnose, *Samhas,* where savin grows.
Saivnose, *saobhnós,* not given.
Sakeely, *easa-caoile,* narrow cataract/waterfall.
Sakeery, *easa-caerach,* not given.
Sakeery, *easa-caoile*(sic), *easa-caoire,* narrow cataract/waterfall.
Sakeery, *easa-caoire,* berry waterfall.
Sala, *sáile,* not given.
Salagh, *saileach,* willows.
Sale, *sáile, t-saile, tSáile, saile,* brine, the sea.
Saleen, a small estuary or creek.
Saleen, *sáileáin,* a little arm of the sea.
Saleen, *sáilín,* not given.
Saley, *tSáile, saile,* brine, the sea.

Salia, *sáile,* brine, sea or salt water.
Salla, *saile,* not given.
Salla, *salach,* dirty.
Sallach, *salach,* miry.
Sallagh, *saileach, saileóg, sáileach,* sallows, willows.
Sallagh, *salac, salach,* filthy, muddy, miry, dirty or unclean.
Sallagh, *salach,* sticky soil(sic).
Sallagh, *tSalach, shaileach,* not given.
Sallaghan, *shalcáin,* place of sallows, willows.
Sallaghan, *saileachan,* a place of willows.
Sallagher, *salachair,* the miry or dirty place.
Sallaghill, *sal-choill,* wood of sallow trees.
Sallaghy, from *sail,* place of sallows or willows.
Sallahig, *saileáin,* a place of willows.
Sallahig, *salachuig,* the miry or dirty spot.
Sallem, *sailm,* psalms.
Sallem, *salm,* not given.
Salley, *sailigh,* sally trees
Sallins, *na-solláin/saileán,* the place of willows or willow groves.
Sallins, *ráth-Sollain,* not given.
Sallough, *salach,* dirty.
Sallow, *saileóg,* willows, sallow trees.
Sallow, *salach,* dirty.
Sally Gap, *bearnas-na-diallaite,* the saddle gap.
Sally, *saile,* brine, the sea.
Sally, *sailigh,* underwood, shrubbery and can also be a gallows(sic).
Sally, *sailighe, saileach,* sallows.
Sallygap, *srath-na-muc/muice,* not given.
Salon, *tSalainn,* salt.
Salough, *saileach,* not given.
Salrock, *sal-Roc,* not given.
Salrock, St Roc's briny inlet.
Salruck, *oileáin-an-tSáile, /tsaile,* sea islands.
Salry, *salruighe,* the sally plantation.
Salt, *salt,* leap.
Salt, *Sálta,* not given.
Saltee, bi-lingual, English and Scandanavian, *salt-ee/ei,* salt island.
Saltee, *na-sailtí,* the salt islands.
Saltee, *tSalainn,* salt (island)
Samer, *camhar,* the morning star.
Samer, *Samhair, Samer,* a female name.

Samney, *samhain, shamhuin,* a pagan festival on Nov 1st for the end of summer and is usually held on hills.

Samsonagh, *samhsonagh,* abounding in sorrel.

Sanaghan, *sabhnachán,* wild juniper.

Sancer, *sasair*(sic),*sansair,* tradesmen.

Sandle, *Sandail,* Sandal, a personal or family name.

Sangyny, *seanganach,* abounding in ants.

Sansaw, *San-sá,* not given.

Santry, *sen-trabh, sen-trebh, sean-truibh, sean-trabh, sentreibh,* the old tribe/dwelling.

Santry, the old petty kingdom.

Sany, *Saithne,* not given.

Sany, *Samhnaí,* Samhnach, a personal or family name.

Sapperton, *baile-Mhic-Sheonaic/Sheonaigh,* not given.

Sara, *Sarain,* Saran, a personal or family name.

Sara, *Sarain,* Saran, a personal or family name.

Saran, parsnips.

Saran, *Saráin, Sáráin, Sarain,* St Saran.

Saran, *Sáran,* not given.

Sarcon, *Árcoin,* Árcon, a personal or family name and the name of a Church founder.

Sare, *saor,* not given.

Sarehan, *Sabhrainn,* Saurin, a personal or family name.

Sarehan, *Sorachain,* Sorohan, a personal or family name.

Sarlaght, *Sarlachta,* St Sarlaght.

Sarn, *Sarn,* a personal or family name.

Sarnaght, *sár-nocht,* very naked, bare or exposed hill.

Sart, *Sáirt,* not given.

Sart, *suí-ard,* the high mound(sic).

Sarue, *samhadh-rubha,* brake, thicket or sorrel.

Sasonagh, *Sassonach,* Saxons or Englishmen.

Sasseragh, *sasaraá(sic), sheisreach,* ploughland.

Sasseragh, *seisreach,* not given.

Sassonagh, *Sasanach,* not given.

Sassonagh, *Sassonach,* Saxons, protestants or Englishmen.

Sast, *sosta,* a retreat or rest and tranquillity.

Sastry, *seisreach,* ploughland.

Sate, *saighead,* arrows.

Satookeen, *a'stuaicín,* of the pinnacle.

Saul, *sabhail, sabhall,* a barn.

Saul, *sabhaill,* not given.

Saul, *sabhall,* a Church.

Saul, *sál,* a heel.

Sauran, *Samhradháin,* Samradan or Sauran, a personal name.

Sause, *sas, sás,* nets or engines.

Savage, MacTavish or Savage, a family name.

Savagh, *samhas,* place producing sorrel.

Saval, *sabhall,* a barn.

Saval, *sabhall,* a Church.

Savane, *Sabháin,* Savan, a personal or family name.

Savane, *Samháin,* not given.

Savaun, *samhán,* a puppy.

Savaun, Savaunagh, the name of a Co Clare castle, the meaning is unclear.

Save, *sabh,* not given.

Savoge, *samhog,* sorrel.

Sawal, *sabhall,* a Church.

Sawel, a barn.

Sawel, *samhail,* the apparition.

Sawna, *Samhna, Samhuin, samh-fhuin,* a pagan festival on Nov 1st for the end of summer and is usually held on hills.

Sawnagh, *samhnach,* a place of sorrel.

Sawny, *samhain,* a pagan festival on Nov 1st for the end of summer and is usually held on hills.

Sawry, *samhradh,* summer.

Sax, *Saghais,* Seix, Seyse, a family name.

Sax, *Sax,* not given.

Saxon, Englishman/men.

Saxon, *Sacsan,* a Saxon.

Sca, *scáth,* a shade or shelter.

Scabail, *scabail,* shoulder guard.

Scaddaman, *sceadamán,* spotted land.

Scaddan, *scadán, scatan,* herrings.

Scaddane, *scadan, scadán, scatan,* herrings.

Scaddy, *sceadach,* not given.

Scaddy, *sceadaigh,* spotted.

Scagh, *sgeach,* briars.

Scahroome, *scaghtroum, sceach-erom,* stooping bush.

Scalaheen, *scallaichín,* not given.

Scalaheen, *scáth-Láithín,* Lahin's (a family name) shade or shelter.

Scale, *sgéal,* stories.

Scale, *scaile,* shade or shadow.

Scalia, Scalia, the name of the daughter of Mannanan MacLir.

Scalkill, *scallchoill,* not given.

Scall, *scáil,* shade.

Scall, *scáile,* not given.

Scallan, *Scalláin,* not given.

Scallon, *sceallan,* acorns, kernels or seeds.

Scally, *Uí-Scealaighe,* O'Scally, a family name.

Scalp, *scailp,* a cleft, chasm or shelters.

Scalp, *scalp, schailp,* a cattle shed.

Scalp, *scealp,* a cleft, cliff, chasm or split.

Scalty, *scoilte,* a cleft or split rock.

Scamph, *sceamh,* wall ferns (polypodium vulgare).

Scanavan, *Sceanbháin,* not given.

Scandal, *Uí-Scannail,* O'Scannel, a family name.

Scanlan, *Ua-Scanláin,* O'Scanlan, a family name.

Scanlan, *Uí-Scannlain,* O'Scanlon, Scanlon a family name.

Scanlan, *Uí-Scannláin, Uí-Scanlain,* O'Scanlon, O'Scanlan, a family name.

Scannel, *Scannail,* Scannal, the name of a Church founder in Limerick.

Scannel, *Uí-Scannail,* O'Scannel, a family name.

Scannell, *Scannail,* the name of a Church founder in Limerick.

Scar, *scarách, scairbhe, scirbh, scairbh,* a shallow, a rough river crossing place or a rugged shallow ford.

Scar, *scearr,* sharp rocks.

Scar, *sceir, sceire,* sea rocks.

Scara, *scairbh,* shallow water.

Scaragh, *an-scarbhach,* not given.

Scaral(sic), *scairbh,* a shallow.

Scaraugh, *scairbheach,* shallow ford.

Scarawalsh, *scairbh-sholuis,* not given.

Scardan, *scardán,* a little cascade of water.

Scardans, from *scardán,* little cascades of water.

Scardaun, *scardán,* a little cascade of water or cataract.

Scardaune, *scardán,* a very small waterfall.

Scariff, *scarbh,* a shallow ford.

Scarna, *scairbh-na…,* not given.

Scarna, *scarbh-na…,* shallow ford of the…

Scarr, *sceir, scor,* a sharp rock.

Scarra, *sgairbh-a'…,* the shallow ford of….

Scarragh, *scarách, scairbhe, scirbh, scairbh,* a shallow, a rough river crossing place or a rugged shallow ford.

Scarragh, *scarbhach,* not given.

Scarriff, *an-scairbh,* the shallow or shallow ford.

Scarriff, *scarách, scairbhe, scirbh, scairbh,* a shallow, a rough river crossing place or a rugged shallow ford.

Scarrive, *scarbh,* cormorants.

Scarrouga, *scarach, scarbach,* a shallow ford.

Scarrough, *scarách, scairbhe, scairbh,* a shallow, a rough river crossing place or a rugged shallow ford.

Scarrough, *scarbhach,* not given.

Scarrow, *scarách, scairbhe, scirbh, scairbh,* a shallow, a rough river crossing place, a rugged shallow ford.

Scarrs, clefts or gullies.

Scarry, *scarách, scairbhe, scirbh, scairbh,* a shallow ford, a rough river crossing place or a rugged shallow ford.

Scart, *scairte, scairt, scart,* a thicket, shrubbery or cluster.

Scart, *scart,* caves or shelters.

Scart, *scartach, scairt-an-bhailtín,* not given.

Scart, *screag,* rocky land.

Scarta, *scáirde,* (of the) spurting.

Scarta, *scairt-an…,* not given.

Scarta, *scairte, scairt, scart,* a thicket, a cluster.

Scarta, *scairte,* shrubs or whitethorn.

Scarta, *scairteach,* a thicket or grove.

Scarta, *scairteach-an…,* thicket of the…

Scartagh, *scartach,* a thicket.

Scartana, *scartánaigh, scartánach,* not given.

Scarteen, *scairtín,* a little thicket or shrubbery.

Scarthy, *scairte,* a thicket or shrubbery.

Scartna, *scairt-na…,* thicket of the…

Scartore, *scairt-an-Óraigh,* not given.

Scartore, *scairteóir,* Hore's (a personal or family name) thicket.

Scarty, *scairte, scairt, scart,* a shrubbery, thicket or a cluster.

Scarva, *scairbhe,* a rough shallow ford.

Scarva, *scairbhigh, an-scarbhachadh-dubh,* not given.

Scarva, *scarách, scairbhe, scairbh,* a shallow, a rough river crossing place or a rugged shallow ford.

Scarva, *scarbhach,* a place of shallow fords.

Scarva, *scarbhach,* a rough place.

Scarva, *scarbhach,* a shallow.

Scarvy, *scarách, scairbhe, scirbh, scairbh,* a shallow, a rough river crossing place or a rugged shallow ford.

Scary, *scragán,* rocky.

Scary, *scarach,* spreading.

Scatternagh, from *sceach,* a place of briars.

Scattery, *inis-Cathaigh,* the island of Cathach (the name of a mighty demoniac monster who lived there). The monster, a snake, was banished by St Senán.

Scaugh, *sceach,* a bush.

Scaul, *scáil,* the hero or phantom.

Scaul, *scál,* heroes.

Scaula, *scálaigh,* not given.

Scauley, *scaile, scáile,* shadow.

Scaw, *scáth,* shadow.

Scecour, *sceach-cumhra,* fragrant bush.

Schoolhill, *scumhall,* not given.

Schull, *an-scoil,* the school.

Schull, *scoil,* splinters(sic).

Schull, *Scoil-Mhuire,* St Mary's school, (West Cork).

Schull, *scolb,* a place of scolbs (thatching rods).

Schull, *scumhaill, scumhall,* not given.

Schull, *scumhal,* a cliff.

Scilly, *saillighe,* willow.

Sco, *scoth,* a reef or point.

Scoba, *scuaba,* brooms.

Scobaun, *scoth-bhan,* white reef.

Scobe, *scuab,* brooms.

Scobin, *Scuaibín,* not given.

Scoffagh, *scothach,* flowers.

Scoffin, *Scoithín, Scoithin,* St Scoithin.

Scogh, *an-sceach,* not given.

Scohagh, *scothach,* a flowery place.

Scohanach, *scothanach,* a flowery place.

Scohanagh, *Scothana, Scoithin,* a personal or family name.

Scoheen, *Scotina, Scota,* a male name.

Scolban, *Scolbáin,* not given.

Scoll, *na-Scol,* not given.

Scolloge, *sciolóige,* not given.

Scollop, *scolb,* a bent twig used in thatching.

Scolly, *scoile,* school.

Scolta, *scoilte,* split.

Scoltia, *scoilte,* not given.

Sconce, *an-sconsa,* not given.

Scooba, *scuaibe,* not given.

Scooby, *scuaibe,* broom or brushwood.

Scooby, *sgúabaidh,* a sheaf or broom.

Scool, *scumhail, scamhal, scamhail,* a precipice, steep hill or a sharp slope.

Scoola, *scúlaigh,* not given.

Scoola, *scumhail, scamhail,* a precipice, steep hill or a sharp slope.

Scor, *scar,* the split.

Scor, *scart,* not given.

Scordaun, *scardán,* a little cataract.

Scornagh, *scórnach,* a gorge.

Scorney, *scórnach,* a gorge.

Scorney, *scornaí,* throats.

Scorny, *scórnad,* the gullet.

Scort, *scairt,* a thicket.

Scotha, *scothaidh,* not given.

Scotha, *scotha,* a land or field projection.

Scott, *Scot,* Scot, a personal or family name.

Scotty, *scairt,* a thicket.

Scoul, *scamhall,* not given.

Scoul, *scumhail, scamhail,* a precipice, steep hill or a sharp slope.

Scouse, *sceamhais,* polybody or wallfern (the herb).

Scovane, from *sceamh,* wall ferns (polypodium vulgare).

Scrabbagh, *scrabach,* not given.

Scrabbagh, *screabach,* bad/rough land.

Scrabby, *scrabaigh,* not given.

Scrabby, *screabach,* bad/rough land.

Scrabo, from *sgraithe,* sward of the cows.

Scrabo, *scrábach,* rough land.

Scrabo, *screabach,* crusted or crusted place.

Scradadaun, little grassy sward.

Scradaun, *screadáin,* not given.

Scradaun, *sceardáin,* a ravine.

Scragaun, *scragán,* rocky.

Scrageen, *scraigín, screagín,* little rocky land.

Scragg, *scraig,* not given.

Scragg, *screag,* a rock or rocky land.

Scraggane, *an-scragán,* not given.

Scraggane, *screagán,* little rock or rocky land.

Scraggaun, *screagán*, little rock or rocky land.

Scraggeen, *scraigín*, *screagín*, little rocky land.

Scragh, *screech*, screeching.

Scragh, *sgraithe*, green swards, sods or grassy surfaces.

Scraghan, *srathán*, the sward.

Scraghy, a grassy or boggy place.

Scrah, *scráth*, a grassy surface-bog.

Scrahan, *srathan*, a little sward.

Scrahan, *sráthán*, grassy surface-bog or sward.

Scrahan, *sreathan*, a stony slope or coarse land.

Scrahan, *sreathan*, coarse land.

Scrahan, *sreathan*, *sreathain*, a stony slope.

Scrahana, *sráthan*, sward of bones(sic).

Scrahana, *sreathanna*, poor soiled/light fields.

Scrahana, *sreathan-na…*, scree(sic) of the…

Scrahana, sward of the…

Scrahane, *srathan*, a little sward.

Scrahans, *an-sreathan*, rocky place of briars.

Scramoge, *scramóg*, not given.

Scramoge, *screamóg*, a excrescence(sic).

Scrathans, from *srathan*, little swards.

Scraw, *scráth*, a grassy surface-bog.

Scraw, *sgraithe*, green swards, sods or grassy surfaces.

Screagan, from *screige*, little rocks.

Screchoge, *screachóg*, screech owls.

Screeb, *scríb*, *scríob*, the furrow or track.

Screebe, *scríbe*, not given.

Screeboge, *scríobóg*, rugged or furrowed land.

Screeby, *scríobóg*, rugged or furrowed land.

Screen, *scrín*, *scríne*, a shrine.

Screen, *sraon*(sic), not given.

Screena, *scrine*, *scríne*, a shrine.

Screeny, *scríne*, *scrín*, *srine*, a shrine or Chapel built over a shrine.

Screer, a furrow.

Screevagh, *scríobóg*, rugged or furrowed land.

Scregg, *screag*, a rock or rocky land.

Scregg, *screige*, a cliff.

Scregg, *screig*, not given.

Scregga, *screige*, the rock.

Screggagh, *screagach*, rocky land.

Screggan, *an-screagán*, the rough ground/place.

Screggan, from *screag*, a rock or rocky land.

Screggawn, *scragán*, rocky hill.

Screghog, *screachog*, a screech owl.

Screhan, *scráthán*, grassy surface-bog or sward.

Screhan, *sreathan*, a stony slope.

Screhane, *sreatháin*, the shallow sod.

Screhaun, *sreachán*, a stony place or scree.

Scribbagh, poor meadow land.

Scribbagh, *scríobach*, furrowed or rugged land.

Scribbagh, *scriobach*, the crusted place.

Scribby, furrowed or striped land.

Scribly, furrowed or striped land.

Scriboge, *scríobóg*, furrowed or rugged land.

Scriboge, *scríobóg*, *sriobóg*, furrowed or rugged land.

Scribogue, *scríobóg*, *scriobhóg*, furrowed or rugged land.

Scridlin, screaming.

Scriggan, *screagán*, little rock or rocky land.

Scrivoge, *scriobhóg*, furrowed or rugged land.

Scroghill, *scráth-choill*, sward hill.

Scrona, *scrath/scraith-na…*, sward of the…

Scrothea, *scrabhtae*, not given.

Scrothea, *scraghtae*, *sraith-taeibh*, sward-side.

Scrow, *scrah*, *scráth*, a grassy surfaced-bog or sward.

Scrow, *tSrúibh*, *srúibhe*, *screabha*, not given.

Scubbig, *sciobaidh*, the grab.

Scuddan, *scadán*, *scatan*, herrings.

Scuddane, *scádán*, herrings.

Scufa, *scotha*, fences formed with bushes and brambles,

Scufaboy, *scotha-buidhe*, yellow fences.

Scull, *scol*, schools.

Scull, *scol*, shouting or schools.

Scull, scolbs or thatching sticks.

Scullaboge, *scolbóg*, a place producing twigs or scallops (used in thatching).

Scullib, *scolb*, can mean wattles, a skirmish or a battle.

Scullibeen, *scoilbín*, not given.

Scullihy, *scoilighthe*, split or fractured.

Scullion, *Uí-Scoláin*, O'Scollan, a family name.

Scullog, *scullog, scológ,* farmers.

Sculloge, *scológ,* a small, petty farmer or farm servants.

Scullogue, *sculloag, scológ,* farmers.

Scully, *scoile,* the school.

Scully, *Uí-Scolaidhe,* O'Scully, a family name.

Scur, horse stud.

Scur, *scuir,* the camp.

Scur, *scor,* a rock pinnacle.

Scurlock, a family name.

Scurlogs, *Scorlóg,* Scurlog's, not given.

Scurlogue, *sciorlach,* barren land.

Scurlogue, Scurlock, Scurlogue, a family name.

Scythe, *saigit, saighead,* arrows.

Sea, *sáeth,* diseases.

Sea, *suí, suidhe,* seat.

Seacon, *suidhe-Con,* Con's (a male name) seat.

Seacor, *suí-cor,* not given.

Seagoe, *sidh-gCóbha,* not given.

Seagoe, *teach-Daghobha,* Daghabha's (a personal or family name) house.

Seagoe, the seat of St Gobha.

Sear, *saer,* artisans, carpenters or artificers.

Searhagh, *saorthach,* freeholders.

Seark, *Sadhairc,* not given.

Searkin, *Sadhaircín,* not given.

Seaveagh, *suí-Bheac,* not given.

Seavickna, *suidhe-mhic-na…,* seat of the son of the…

Seavaughan, *baile-sebac-an*(sic), town of the hawk.

Secane, *siocán,* frost birds or field-fares.

Sedagh, *Séadach,* not given.

Sedan, *Shéideáin,* not given.

Sedy, *Saighde,* not given.

See, *saoi,* learned men.

See, *suí, suidhe,* a seat or resting place.

Seeaghan, *suidheachán,* little seats.

Seebohilla, *suidhe-bhuachalla,* the cowboys seat.

Seechon, *suídheachan,* the seat.

Seecon, *suidhe-Con,* Con's (a male name) seat.

Seecrin, *suí-croinn,* not given.

Seecrin, *suidhe-crainn,* residence near or of the tree.

Seed, *saigit, saighead,* arrows.

Seed, *soighead,* arrows or darts.

Seeda, *Uí-Shíoda, Síoda,* O'Sheedy, a family name.

Seedan, *séideáin,* squally.

Seedy, *Uí-Sioda,* O'Sheedy, a family name.

Seefin, *suidhe-Finn,* Fionn/Finn MacCumhail's seat or resting place.

Seefin, *suidhe-Finn,* not given however it is a common name around Ireland for a mountain with a cairn on it.

Seegane, from *suidheachán,* little seats.

Seegane, *suidheachán,* little seat.

Seehanes, *suidheachain,* seats.

Seekery, *easa-caoile,* a narrow cataract or waterfall.

Seeoge, *suidhóg,* the little seat.

Seeola, *suí-Eola,* not given.

Seeoran, *seidhe-Odhráin,* not given.

Seer, *saer,* a carpenter, builder or artificer.

Seer, *saera,* free.

Seer, *saoir,* craftsman or craftsmen.

Seer, *saor,* a craftsman.

Seer, *saor,* free(sic).

Seer, *saor,* artificers, tradesmen, carpenters or builder/s.

Seer, *tSaeir,* carpenter.

Seera, *saoire,* freedom or freehold.

Seera, *saorach,* freemen.

Seeragh, *saothrach,* not given.

Seerin, *sírin,* cherries.

Seersha, *saoirse, saeirse,* freehold land.

Seershin, *an-tSaoirsin,* not given.

Seershin, *saeirse,* freehold.

Seev, *saobh,* bad.

Seevnis, *saobh-inis,* bad river holm or island.

Segard, *sagart,* the priest.

Seily, *Sailleach,* the name of a County Clare saint.

Seir, *saighir,* the name of an ancient fountain.

Seixeslough, *loch-an-Tsaghasaigh,* not given.

Selerna, *Sailearna,* not given.

Selherny, *sailleach, sailchearnaigh, sailchearnach,* a place of sallows or an osier plantation.

Sell, *sail,* a sally tree.

Sell, *saille,* not given.

Sella, *saileach, saileog,* sally trees.

Sella, *saille,* not given.

Sellagh, *saileach,* willows or sally trees.

Sellan, *saileáin,* place of sallows/willows.

Sellernaun, *sailearnán,* little sallow land.

Selloo, *sail-Lugha,* Lugh (a personal or family name) tree.

Selloo, *suí-Lú,* not given.

Selloo, *suí-Lua,* Lua's (a personal or family name) seat.

Selsana, *soillsean,* illuminations.

Selsana, *soilseánach,* not given.

Selshan, *soillsean,* illuminations.

Seltan, *sailtean,* sallies, a place of sallies/sallows.

Seltanna, *sailtean-na…,* sallow plantation of the…

Semanus, *sidhe-Manuis,* Manus's (a male name) fairy mount.

Senaw, *San-Sáth,* St Saw/Saviour.

Senlis, the old fort.

Sentry, *Uí-Ursainte,* not given.

Seoltia, *scoilte,* torn.

Serges, *Saerghusa,* Saerghus, a male name.

Serges, *Searghusa,* St Seargus.

Seripont, *Seiripuin,* Jerry's or Jerimia's (mens names) bridge.

Serse, *saeirse,* freehold.

Sershin, *seirsin,* warbling of birds.

Ses, *seisíoch,* a sixth part (a land measure).

Sescenn, *sescenn, seisceann* a marsh, bog.

Sesk, *seisce,* sedge.

Seskan, *sescenn, seisceann* a marsh, bog.

Seskanore, *seisceann-mhór,* the big marsh.

Seskanore, *seisceann-odhar,* pale coloured marsh.

Seskilgreen, *seisceann-Ghréine,* not given.

Seskilgreen, *seisíoch-chill-ghréine,* plot of the Church of the sun.

Seskilgreen, *seisíoch-chill-Ghrianna,* the Church of the Grianna, not given.

Seskin, *seiscinn, sescenn, seisceann,* a marsh.

Seskinan, *Seisceanán, Seisceannán,* not given.

Seskinane, *Sescnean,* St Sescnenus/Sescnen.

Seskinore, *seisceann-mhór,* the big marsh.

Sesragh, *sesragh,* a measure of one sixth of land.

Sess, *seiseadh,* a sixth.

Sessagh, *seiseadhach,* sixths (measures of land).

Sessia, *seiseadh,* a sixth.

Sessiagh, *seiseadh,* a sixth.

Sessiagh, *seisíoch, seisiach,* not given.

Sessnagh, a sixth part.

Sessuegilroy, *seiseadh-Mhic-Giollaruaidh,* MacGilroy's (a family name) one sixth measure of land.

Sessy, *seisidh,* a sixth (measure of land).

Severick, *Sobhairce,* Sobhairce, a male name.

Sgeagh, *sceach,* white thorn bushes.

Shaan, *Sheághan,* John.

Shade, *séad,* jewels.

Shade, *sed,* jewels.

Shaen, *sidheán,* a fairy hill.

Shaggy, *seagaidh,* cormorants.

Shagh, *…seach,* as an ending to a word can sometimes mean, a place of…. or abounding in…. It can also indicate feminine.

Shaghra, *Shéafra,* not given.

Shaghry, Geoffrey, a male name.

Shaghtena, *seachtmhuine,* the week.

Shal, *íseal,* low.

Shall, *íseal,* low.

Shallany, *sealan,* the hangmans rope or gallows.

Shallee, from *sailighe,* sallows or willows.

Shallee, *sealaí,* not given.

Shallee, *sealaibh,* timber cutting and lopping.

Shallog, *sealga, sealg,* the chase or hunt.

Shalloghan, *an-sealgán,* not given.

Shallon, *sealan,* the hangmans rope or gallows.

Shallon, *Sealann,* not given.

Shaloge, *sealg,* the hunt or chase.

Shalvy, *Sealbhaigh, Sealbach,* Shalvy, a personal name or a family name and the name of the founder of the Church of Kilshalvy in Sligo.

Shalwy, *Sealbhai,* not given.

Shalwy, *sealbhuidhe,* possessions.

Shambo, *seanbhoth,* the old hut/s.

Shammer, *seamar,* shamrock, clover or trefoils.

Shamoge, *samóg,* sorrel.

Shamroge, *seamroige, seamróige, seamróg,* shamrock.

Shamrogue, *seamrog, seamróg,* shamrock.

Shamsoge, *shamsoge,* shamrocks.

Shan, *sean, tSean,* old.

Shana, *siodhanach...,* the place of the mounds of...

Shana, *sionnach,* foxe/s.

Shana, *srath-na...,* holm of the...

Shana, *tSean, sean, seana,* old.

Shana, *tSean, seanadh,* not given.

Shanagh, *seanachaidh, sean-achadh,* the old field.

Shanagh, *seancha,* not given.

Shanagh, *sionnach,* a fox.

Shanahea, *sanachaidh,* not given.

Shanahoe, *seanchua,* the old hollow.

Shanakiel, the old wood, the original name was *caill-na-sindach,* wood of the foxes.

Shanally, *Sanaile,* not given.

Shanamore, *seanmóir,* sermon/s.

Shananagh, *seangánach,* abounding in pismires or ants.

Shanavogh, *sean-bhoithe,* the old hut.

Shanbo (Templeshanbo), Church of Sin's (a male name) hut.

Shanbo, *seanbhó,* the old cow.

Shanbo, *seanbhoth, sean-both,* the old hut/tent.

Shanboe, *seanbhoithe,* not given.

Shanboe, *sean-both,* the old hut/tent.

Shanchoe, *seanchua, seanchuaiche,* the old hollow.

Shanco, *seanchua,* the old hollow.

Shanco, *seanchuach,* not given.

Shandeny, *sheandoine,* not given.

Shandeny, *tSeanduine,* the old man.

Shandon, *seandún, seandun,* old fort.

Shandra, *seanrátha, sean-ratha,* the old fort or old ring fort.

Shandragh, the old ruin.

Shandree, *seandruadh,* the old druids.

Shandree, *sean-drui,* old druids.

Shane, *Seáin,* Shane, John, a personal or family name.

Shane, *sean,* old.

Shane, *seangán,* ants.

Shane, *tSeáin, Sheáin,* not given.

Shane, *sían,* storm/s.

Shane, *sidheain,* not given.

Shane, *tSiain,* a fairy fort.

Shane, *tSiáin, siadhán, sidheán,* a fairy mount.

Shanedehey, *Sheoin-de-Hae,* not given.

Shanes, fairy mounts.

Shangan, *seangan, seangán,* ants or pismires.

Shanganagh, *seanchonach, ráth-salchan,* not given.

Shanganagh, *seangánach,* abounding in pismires or ants.

Shangane, *seangán,* not given.

Shanganny, *seangánach,* abounding in pismires or ants.

Shanho, *seanchua,* the old hollow.

Shania, *seanad,* a synod.

Shanid, *seanaid,* a place where meetings are held.

Shanker, *seanchraobh,* the old trees.

Shankill, *seincheall,* old Church.

Shankill, *tSeanchoill, seanchill, an-tSeanchill,* not given.

Shanmore, *seanmora,* the sermon.

Shanna, *seannach, shinnagh*(sic), the fox.

Shanna, the old land.

Shanna, *tSean, seanadh,* not given.

Shannagh, *duibh-leacht-a'tsionnaigh,* black stone monument of the fox.

Shannagh, *sean-ath,* not given.

Shannagh, *sionnaigh, seancha, seannach, seanach, sionnach,* a fox or foxes.

Shannakae, *seanachae,* not given.

Shannaunna, *seanán-an...,* old land of the...

Shannawona, *seanabhán,* not given.

Shannera, *seanaire,* old land.

Shannig, *seanach, seanaigh,* wise/prudent.

Shannig, *Seanaigh,* St Seanach.

Shannoge, *Sheáinóig,* Shaneoge or young John.

Shannon, *an-tSionna, Sionainne, Sionnain, Sionna,* the old one. This river was called Senus, Sena and Saecana-flumen-Senese in the old days.

Shannon, *an-tSionnainn,* not given.

Shannon, from *Seanach,* a male name.

Shannon, Seanach, a personal or family name.

Shannon, *seanaidh,* a hillside or slope.

Shannon, *seanaidh, seanaigh,* not given.

Shannon, *Seanáin,* a personal name meaning 'the old one'.

Shannon, *Seanáin,* St Senan.

Shannon, *seandun,* old fort.

Shannon, *Sionainn,* the ancient goddess.

Shannow, old river.
Shanny, *Seanach, Seanaigh,* a male name.
Shanny, *Seanaigh, Sheanaigh,* St Seanach.
Shanny, *seannach,* a fox.
Shanny, *Seannaigh, sionnach,* not given.
Shanog, *seanog,* hooded.
Shanoge, *Seaghain-óig,* young John.
Shanona, *sean-dumhnach,* old Church.
Shanoon, *seanuaimh,* old cave.
Shanore, *seanóir,* the old man.
Shanow, old river.
Shanowen, old river.
Shanroon, *Siarthúin,* Geoffry, a male name.
Shantony, *seantuinne,* the old woman.
Shanvaus, *seanmhás,* not given.
Shanville, *seanmhaoil,* the bald old man.
Shanvo, *seanbhotha, sean-both/bhoith,* the old hut/tent.
Shanvo, *sean-mho,* the old man.
Shanwee, *sean-mhuighe,* the old plain.
Shara, *searadh,* a pasture.
Sharavoge, *searbhóg,* land producing dandelions.
Sharavogue, *searbhóg, an-tSearbhóg,* the bitter place.
Shark, *searc,* sharks.
Sharough, *siorach, searac, searrach,* foals.
Sharra, *an-tSaor,* bitter.
Sharragh, *siorach, searac, searach, searrach,* foals.
Sharriv, *searbh,* bitter.
Sharrold, *Searúill, Searúll,* not given.
Sharrold, *Seathrún,* not given.
Sharry, *searrach,* a foal.
Sharvan, *searbhán,* dandelion/s.
Sharvoge, *searbhóg,* bitter grass or a place producing dandelions.
Sharvoges, *searbhóg,* land producing dandelions.
Shas, *seas,* a sea, bank or bench.
Shask, *seasg,* barren.
Shask, *seisce, seasg, seasc,* sedge grass.
Shaska, *seasc, seascaigh, seascaich,* sedge grass or a sedgy place.
Shaskin, *seisceann,* a marsh.
Shasky, *seascaich, seascaigh,* sedge grass.
Shass, *seas,* a seat, bank or bench.
Shaughlin, *Seachnaill, Sechnaill, Sechlann, Seachlainn,* Seachnall or Secundinus, the name of an ancient Bishop and Saint.

Shaughnessy, *Ua-Seachneasadh,* O'Shaughnessy, a family name.
Shavoy, *seanmhaoil,* not given.
Shawn, *Eoin,* John.
She, *suidhe,* sitting.
Shea, *Uí-Shéaghdha/Seadha,* O'Shea, a family name.
Shea, *Uí-Shé, Seithe,* not given.
Sheafield, *gort-na-bPunann,* field of sheaves.
Shean, *séadhan,* a fairy mount.
Shean, *sean,* old.
Shean, *Sián,* not given.
Shean, *síodhán, sídhean, sidhean,* a fairy mount, hill or knoll.
Sheane, *Séann,* not given.
Sheane, *siadhain,* a fairy mount.
Shear, *siar,* western aspect.
Shearoon, *Séathrúin,* not given.
Shearoon, *Shearoon,* Geoffrey, a male name.
Shearsane, *searsean,* foraging.
Sheaver, *siabhra,* a fairy.
Shedoge, *Shéideog,* not given.
Shee, *seisidh,* not given.
Shee, *sí,* fairy hill or a mound.
Shee, *sidhe, sidh,* fairies, a fairy palace, hill, mound or dwelling.
Sheean, *sián, sídheán, sidheán, siodhán,* a fairy hill or mound.
Sheean, *sidh,* the fairies.
Sheeana, *sidhne,* fairy hills.
Sheeana, *síodhán,* a fairy mound or prehistoric tumulus.
Sheeana, *síodhánach,* place of the fairy mound.
Sheeaun, *an-Sián,* not given.
Sheeaun, *siadháin, siadhain, sidheán,* a fairy mount, fort.
Sheeaun, *tSíodhán,* pagan festivals(sic).
Sheeaun, *sidhean, siothán,* a fairy mound or hillock.
Sheeda, *Shíoda, Síoda,* a personal or family name.
Sheeda, *Sioda,* Sheedy, a family name.
Sheeda, *sioda,* silken.
Sheeda, *Uí-Sioda,* O'Sheedy, a family name.
Sheedy, *Shíodha, Síoda,* not given.
Sheedy, *Uí-Sioda,* O'Sheedy, a family name.
Sheeffry, of the fairy mansion.

Sheefry, *Shiofra,* Siofra, a personal or family name.

Sheega, *síge,* fairies.

Sheega, *síge,* stack or streak.

Sheega, *síoga,* not given.

Sheeghary, *sioth-chaire,* fairies wood.

Sheegy's, fairy hills.

Sheehane, *sidheán,* a fairy mount.

Sheehaun, *sidheán,* a fairy mount.

Sheehy, *na-sithe,* fairy hills.

Sheehy, *síthe,* a fairy hill.

Sheehys, *na-síthe,* not given.

Sheel, *siol...,* the seed or descendants of...

Sheela, *Shialaigh, Sighile,* Sheela, a female name.

Sheela, *Síolaidh, saileogach,* not given.

Sheela, *tSile,* Celia.

Sheelagh, *Sighiles,* Sheela, Sheila, a female name.

Sheelan, *Síleann,* withies(sic).

Sheelan, *Síoláin, tSíoláin, tSioláin,* St Síolán/Selanus/Sillan.

Sheelane, *Síolain,* Siolán, a personal or family name.

Sheelavarra, *Shile-Bharra,* Sheila Barry's crossroads.

Sheelin, *sidhe-linn,* fairy stream.

Sheelin, *sighleann, saileann,* not given.

Sheelin, *Síleann,* Sileann, not given.

Sheelin, *Síoláin,* St Siolan.

Sheelin, *sithleann,* the fairies.

Sheeman, *Shiomain,* Simon, a male name.

Sheeman, *síománaigh,* not given.

Sheen, *Oisín,* O'Oisín, a family name.

Sheena, *sidhne,* fairy hills.

Sheenaghan, *Sionacháin,* Sheenaghan, a family name.

Sheenoge, *Sinigh-óige,* the virgin Sineach (a personal or family name).

Sheeny, *sidhnidhe, sidhne,* fairy hills.

Sheeny, *sionnaigh,* not given.

Sheeoge, *sidheóg,* fairies or fairy place/s.

Sheer, *siur,* sisters.

Sheeran, Sheeran, a family name.

Sheerea, *siaráidh,* western.

Sheeroe, *sidh-ruadh,* not given.

Sheestown, *baile-an-fhásaigh,* a place of lush grass.

Sheevar, *siabhra,* a fairy.

Sheever, *siabhra,* a fairy.

Sheffin, *simhne,* bulrushes.

Sheffin, *tigh-Fachna,* not given.

Shegle, *seagal,* rye field.

Shehy, *seagha,* elk.

Shehy, *seithe,* fairies.

Shehy, *seithe,* hide/s or the pelt.

Sheil, *Siadhail,* Shiel, a family or a persons name.

Shel, *siol,* the seed, generation, posterity or descendants of...

Shelagh, *sceirde,* a storm.

Shelbourne, *ais-láir,* not given.

Shelbourne, *siol-Brain,* the progeny of Bran, a personal or family name.

Shelbourne, *síol-Broin,* the seed/posterity or descendants of Broin (a personal or family name).

Shelburne, *síol-mBrian,* descendants of Bran (a personal or family name).

Shelferty, *siolfartaí,* not given.

Shelin, *Ui-Shleibhleachain,* O'Shleibhlachan, a family name.

Shellig, *sealg,* the chase.

Shellistragh, *felestar,* flaggers.

Shellums, *Sheallaim,* belonging to Shellum or Sholdum, a personal or family name.

Shelton, named after an English place name, the Irish name is *teach-na-gCanónach,* house of the canons.

Shelvins, *na-sealbha*(sic), not given.

Shenane, *tSeanáin,* not given.

Shendony, the old man.

Sheorie, *siodh-bruig,* a fairy mansion.

Shepeal, *Seipeal,* a Chapel.

Shera, Geoffrey, a male name.

Shercock, *searcóg,* sweetheart.

Sherick, *Séaraic,* not given.

Sherkin, (island) *inis-Arcáin/Oircín,* not given.

Sherkin, *seirgh, seirg,* trefoil.

Sherky, (island) *Oirce,* not given.

Sherky, *seirce,* love.

Shermeen, *Searmín,* Jermyn, a male name.

Sherrick, *Séaraic,* not given.

Sherron, *Shearoon,* Geoffrey.

Sherry, *sceir, sceire,* sea rocks.

Shersheen, *soirsín,* a freehold.

Shershin, *seirsin,* warbling of birds.

Shesh, *seiseadh,* a sixth or ploughland.

Shesharoe(sic), *tSeisreach-rua,* not given.

Sheshera, *seisreac, seisheragh,* ploughland.

Shesheroe, *seisreac, seisheragh,* ploughland.

Sheshery, *seisrighe,* a plough team.

Sheshiv, *seiseamh,* a sixth part.

Sheshive, *seiseadh,* a ploughland.

Sheshure, *seisiúr,* six.

Shesk, from seasc, *seasg,* sedge grass.

Shesk, *seisc,* sedges.

Shesk, *seisce, samhairce,* not given.

Sheskeen, *seiscín,* a marsh.

Sheskeragh, *hEiscreach,* a sand hill.

Sheskin, *seascain*(sic), quagmire.

Sheskin, *seisceann, seascann, tSeascainn,* not given.

Sheskin, *seiscinn,* sedgy bog.

Sheskin, *seiscinn, sescenn,* a marsh.

Sheskina, *seascann-an…,* not given.

Sheskina, *seisceann-an…,* swamp of the…

Sheskinshule, *seisceann-siúil,* moving marsh.

Shesko, from *seasg,* sedge grass.

Shesy, *seiseadh,* a ploughland.

Shevrie, *siodhbhruigh, siodh-bruigh,* a fairy mansion.

Shevry, *seithe-Bhreighe,* not given.

Shevry, *siodhbhruigh, siodh bruigh,* a fairy mansion.

Shigagh, *uiseannach,* a place of ash trees.

Shigo, *uiseannach,* a place of ash trees.

Shigowna, *sidh-Una,* Una's fairy palace.

Shigowna, *sí-ghabhna, sidhe-Eabhna,* not given.

Shileshawn, *soillseán,* a light or place of lights.

Shill, *siol,* the seed or descendants of…

Shillane, *silleáin,* trickling.

Shilleeny, *silíní, silínidhe,* cherries.

Shillelagh, *síol-Éalaigh,* the descendants of Éláthach, Elach, Ealach or Éalach (9th cent hero).

Shillelogher, *síol-Fhaolchair/Fhaelchair,* not given.

Shillelogher, *síol-Uí-Luachra,* decendants of Luachair, a personal name.

Shillida, *seilide,* snails.

Shilloge, *sciollóg,* waste eyeless potato slices that are no use for planting.

Shilly, *sileadh,* oozing or trickling.

Shimna, *simhne,* bulrushes.

Shimna, *simin,* not given.

Shin, *sin,* the elder.

Shin, *suide..,* a seat (of power) of…

Shinagh, *sionnach,* the fox.

Shinagh, *soillsean,* illuminations.

Shinahan, *Sheanachain,* St Shanahan.

Shinanagh, *seangánach,* a place of pismires.

Shinawn, *Sionain,* St Senen.

Shindilla, *seindile,* the beetle.

Shine, *Sinche,* St Sinech, the virgin Saint.

Shingan, *seangán,* pismires.

Shinganagh, *seangánach,* a place of pismires.

Shinganagh, *seangánach,* abounding in pismires or ants.

Shingane, *seangán, seangan,* ants, pishmires.

Shingaun, (Lough Coumshingaun) *chom/com-seangáin/seangán,* the lake of the hollow of the narrows(sic) and the lake of the valley of the hollow of the narrows(sic).

Shingaun, *seangáin, seangán,* pismires or ants.

Shingaunagh, *seangánach,* abounding in pismires or ants.

Shinglis, *seanlis, seanlios, sean-lios,* the old fort.

Shinnagh, *seangánach,* abounding in pismires or ants.

Shinnagh, *sinneach, sionnaigh, sionnach,* a fox, foxes or a resort of foxes.

Shinnaun, *Seanáin,* not given.

Shinnaun, Shinnog or Jennet, a male name.

Shinnaun, *Sionan,* St Seanan.

Shinnawn, *seangan,* pismires.

Shinny, *Sinche,* St Sinech, the virgin saint.

Shinny, *Siní, Sineach,* a personal or family name.

Shinny, *sionnach,* a fox or a foxes tail.

Shinrone, *suí/suide-an-Róin,* the seat of Róin, the seal of the hairy man (*Rón*) or the seat of the seal.

Shinshame, *sin-Sheamus,* James the elder.

Shintilla, *seindile,* the beetle.

Shiplough, *cluain-na-loinge,* the plain(sic) containing a rock shaped like a ship.

Shire, *siabhra,* the phantom.

Shire, *siar,* western.

Shivane, *Shiobháin,* Johanna, a womans name.

Shivdelagh, *seimhdile,* an instrument for bettling (while washing) clothes.

Shivdella, *seimhdile,* the beetle.

Shivdellaugh, *seimhdile,* the beetle.

Shivdilla, *seimhdile,* the beetle.

Shiven, *simhin,* not given.

Shiven, *simhne,* bulrushes.

Shivey, *sithbhe,* a fairy fort.

Shivna, *simhne,* bulrushes.

Shlea, *shleibhe, sliabh,* mountain.

Shligan, *slightheán,* a little road.

Shoal, *seól, seol,* a sail.

Shock, *seabhaic, seabhac, seboc,* a hawk.

Shock, *seac,* not given.

Shoggy, *seagaidh,* cormorants.

Shoke, *seabhaic, seabhac, seboc,* a hawk.

Shone, *Seoin,* not given.

Shone, *Seón, Seóin,* John.

Shoneen, *Seoinín, Sheonín, Sheoinin, Shoneen, Seainín, tSeoinín,* Shoneen, little John (a male name) or Jennings, a family name.

Shonick, *Sheonaich,* young John, a male name.

Shonickbane, *Sheoinic-Bháin,* Seoinic Bán, not given.

Shonikeen, *Seoinicín,* little John, a male name.

Shonikin, *Seoinicín, Seónógín,* little young John.

Shonikin, *Sheoinicín,* not given.

Shonock, *Shaunóg, Sheonaich, Seáinóig,* Shaunoge or young John, a male name.

Shonock, *Sheonaic(sic),* not given.

Shonog, little John, a mans name.

Shooey, *samhaidh,* sorrel.

Shouk, *seabhac,* hawks.

Shouks, *seabhac,* hawks.

Shournagh, *sabhrainneach,* not given.

Shower, *seabhair,* not given.

Shower, *seamhar, seamar,* clover.

Shragh, *sraith,* a river holm, an island on a river.

Shragh, *srath,* a holm.

Shraheens, *na-sraithíní,* not given.

Shraleagh, *srath-lia,* grey holm.

Shree, *srae, sraeth,* a millrace.

Shreelane, *sraoilleán,* not given.

Shreelane, *s-ruithlean,* a place of streamlets.

Shrewan, *srutháin,* a rivulet.

Shrewly, *sruillidhe,* a stream.

Shroghan, *t-srotháin,* a stream.

Shron, *sron,* a nose, a snout, a rock, a hill, a projecting point or a promontory.

Shron, *srón,* a snout.

Shrona, *srón-na…,* point of the …

Shrone, *srón,* a nose, point of land, a rock, a hill, a beak or a pointed hill.

Shronell, *srónaill,* not given.

Shronell, *srónchoill,* not given.

Shrough, *sruth,* a stream.

Shrough, *srut-na-gamhnaighe,* (stream of the) calves.

Shroughan, *sruthán,* a stream.

Shroul, from *sruthair, sruill',* a stream.

Shrove, *srubh-Brain,* not given.

Shrove, *srúibh,* a snout.

Shrue, *sidh-ruadh,* red fairy hill.

Shruel, from *sruthair, sruill',* a stream.

Shruel, *sroohil,* a stream.

Shrule, *shruthla,* a stream.

Shrule, *srúille,* not given.

Shrule, *sruthail, sruthair, sruthra, sruill,* a stream.

Shrura, from *sruthair, sruill',* a stream.

Shrura, *sruthair,* a stream.

Shule, *siúil,* moving.

Shunna, *chuna,* firewood.

Shunsoge, *sionnsoige,* wood sorrel.

Shurdane, *Shurdane,* Jordan, a personal or family name.

Shy, *…seach,* as an ending to a word can sometimes mean, a place of…. or abounding in…. It can also indicate feminine.

Shyane, *an-Sián,* not given.

Shyne, *t-sidheaín,* a fairy mount.

Siberia, *sliabh-ruadh,* not given.

Siddan, Sodan, a personal name.

Siddoge, *sudóg,* wild ducks.

Side, *soighead,* arrows or darts.

Sig, *fhásaig,* wilderness.

Sigh, *saighe,* a bitch or greyhound.

Sigha, *saíghe,* a bitch.

Sileshaun, *soillseán, soillsean,* illuminations, lightsome or shining.

Sileshaun, *soilseán,* brightness.

Silk, Sioda, Sheedy, a personal or family name.

Sill, *saileach,* willow trees.

Silla, *saileach, saileóg, sáileach,* sallows or willows.

Silla, *tSileach,* (of the) dripping.

Sillagh, *tSaileach, saileach, saileóg, sáileach,* sallows or sally trees.

Sillagh, *saileach,* osiers, swallows(sic).

Sillaheens, *sailchín,* not given.

Sillaheens, *sailichín,* not given.

Sillaheens, *saillithín,* a place of willow growing.

Sillahertane, *saileachartan, saileachartán,* a plantation of willows, sallies or osiers.

Sillahy, *sailighthe,* willows.

Sillan, *saileann,* not given.

Sillan, *sileachán, saileán,* willow groves.

Sillane, *saileán, sailean,* (plantation of) sallows, willows.

Sillees, (river), *abhainn-na-sailíre,* not given.

Sillerna, *sailchearnach,* not given.

Sillihy, *saileacha,* sallows.

Sillis, *sailis,* not given.

Sillis, *silleadh,* dropping or oozing, watery land.

Sillish, *soluis,* light.

Silloga, *saileach, saileóg, sáileach,* sallows.

Silloga, *saileogach,* willows.

Silloga, *shaileogach,* not given.

Sillogagh, *saileógach, shaileach,* sallows.

Sillogagh, *shaileogach,* not given.

Silloge, *an-tSaileog,* not given.

Silloge, *saileach, saileóg, sáileach,* sallows.

Silloge, *sailóg,* osier or sallow bearing land.

Silly, *saileach,* not given.

Silly, *sailigh, saillighe,* sally trees or willows.

Silly, *sailigh,* underwood, shrubbery and can also be a gallows.

Silvia, *coille*(sic), the wood.

Simon, *Mhic-Shíomoin,* not given.

Simon, *Síomoin, Shiomain, Síomon* or Simon, a male name.

Sine, *saighne,* attack.

Sineirl, *suí-an-Iarla,* the earls seat.

Sineirl, *suidhe-an-Iarla,* not given.

Singland, *saingeal,* not given.

Singland, *sangal, sain-aingel,* a different angel.

Single, *Singil,* not given.

Single, *singil,* single, one.

Sink, *Since, Sineach,* a personal or family name.

Sink, *Sinche,* not given.

Sinnot, *Seanaid,* not given.

Sinnot, *sinead,* the synod.

Siol, *siol…,* the seed or descendants of…

Sion, *Sióin, Sión, suidhe-Fhinn, Séadhan,* not given.

Sion, *síodhán, tSiáin, sidhean, sidheán,* a fairy mount/mound or hill.

Siselly, *Siosala,* of the Cecils, a personal or family name.

Sissala, *Siosala,* of the Cecils, a personal or family name.

Sissala, *Siosalach,* not given.

Sistra, *seisreach,* ploughland.

Sitrick, *Sitric,* a Danish personal name.

Siveen, *Saidhbhín, Sadhbh,* Sabina or Siveen, a female name.

Sivey, *sithbhe,* not given.

Sivney, *Suibhne,* Sweeny, a family name.

Size, *Saghais,* Seix, Seyse, a family name.

Skagh, *scátha, sceitheanach, sceitnánagh, sceach, sceiche, sgeach*(sic), white thorn, a place of white thorns or brambles.

Skagh, *sceach,* hawthorn.

Skagh, *sceach, sgiat, sgeach,* bushes.

Skagh, *sceach,* thorn bushes.

Skagh, *sceach-Connla,* not given.

Skaghard, *sceach-ard,* the high white thorn bush.

Skah, *Esce,* Eskin, a male name.

Skahanagh, *sceachanach,* a place of whitethorn.

Skahanagh, *scechanach, sceitheanach, sceit-nánagh, sceach, sceiche,* white thorn, a place of white thorns or brambles.

Skahard, *sceach-ard,* high hawthorn.

Skahies, *scátha,* shades or shadows.

Skally, *Scallaigh,* Skally, a personal or family name.

Skana, *sceach na…,* thicket of the …

Skane, (river) *an-scéin,* not given.

Skannelane, *Uí-Scannlain,* Scanlon, a family name.

Skannive, *scainimh, scainnimh,* not given.

Skarragh, *scairbheach,* the shallow ford.

Skaw, *scátha,* not given.

Skaw, shade, shadow.

Ske, *sceach,* white thorn, haw trees or thorn bushes.

Ske, *skeagh,* a bush.

Skea, *sceach,* hawthorn.

Skea, *sceiche,* the thorn or lone bush.

Skea, *scéithe, sciath,* the shield.

Skea, *scéithe,* the shield.

Skea, *sceitheach, sciadh, sciath, sciach,* not given.

Skea, *sceitheanach, sceitnánagh, sceach, sceiche,* white thorn, a place of white thorns or brambles.

Skea, *sgiat, sgeach,* bushes.

Skeaf, *sceach,* whitethorn or a bush.

Skeagh, *sceach,* thorn bush, whitethorn or hawthorn.

Skeagh, *sgiath,* briers(sic).

Skeagh, *sceiche, sceach,* thorn/s.

Skeagh, *scéithe, sciath,* shields.

Skeagh, *Sceithe,* the virgin Saint Sciath.

Skeagh, *sceitheach, na-sceitheach, an-sceitheog,* not given.

Skeagh, *sceitheanach, sceitnánagh, sceiche,* whitethorn, a place of whitethorns or brambles.

Skeagh, *scia, sgiat, sgeach,* bushes.

Skeagh, *sciach,* whitethorns.

Skeagh, *sciath,* shield.

Skeagh, *sgiathóg,* hawthorns.

Skeagha, *sceach-an/a'…,* (whitethorn)bush of the…

Skeaghorn, *sceach-chairn,* thornbush of the carn (a monumental heap of stones or a grave pile).

Skeaghorn, *sceach-Theorann,* not given.

Skealy, *sceallaidh,* not given.

Skealy, *sceulaidhe,* the story teller.

Skeam, *inis-Ceim/Cein,* Cian's (a male name) island.

Skean, *scine, scéine,* not given.

Skeana, *sceach-na…,* thornbush of the…

Skeana, *sciath-na…,* not given.

Skeard, *scéird,* a bleak hill.

Skeard, *sceird,* not given.

Skeatry, *scéatraigh,* not given.

Skeatry, *sceithre,* spewy wet land.

Skee, *sceithe,* the whitethorn bush.

Skeehan, *sciathain, sciathan,* wings.

Skeelta, *scaoilte,* a cleft.

Skeeny, *scíne,* the knife blade.

Skeer, *Scíre, Scire,* St Scíre, Scire, the virgin saint.

Skeery, *ease*(sic)*-caoire,* the narrow waterfall.

Skeery, *Scíre,* St Scire.

Skeewaun, from *sceamh,* wall ferns (polypodium vulgare).

Skeg, *sceach,* white thorn.

Skeg, *sceitheog,* a bush, a thornbush or whitethorn.

Skeg, *sceitheog,* a little bush.

Skeg, *sciachóg,* not given.

Skeh, *sceitheanach, sceitnánagh, sceach, sceiche,* white thorn, a place of white thorns or brambles.

Skeha, from *sceitheanach, sceitnánagh, sceach, sceiche,* white thorn, a place of white thorns or brambles.

Skeha, *sceach,* hawthorn.

Skeha, *sceitheanach, sceitnánagh, sceach, sceiche,* white thorn, a place of white thorns or brambles.

Skehacrine, *sceach-an-chrainn,* not given.

Skehana, *sceachánach,* not given.

Skehana, *sgeitheánach, sceitheánach,* bushes or briars.

Skehanagh, *sceachánach,* (a place of) hawthorns.

Skehanagh, *sceicheanach,* not given.

Skehanagh, *sgeachanach, sgeitheánach, sceitheánach,* bushes or briars, a bushy place.

Skehancrine, *sceach-a-chrainn,* whitethorn bush by or of, the tree.

Skehane, *Sgéatáin,* O'Skehan, a family name.

Skehane, *sceachánach,* a place of thorn bushes.

Skeharoe, *sceiche-rua,* not given.

Skeharoe, *sceithe-ruaidhe,* the red thornbush.

Skehaun, *sciotháin,* the wing.

Skeheen, little bushy place/brake.

Skeheen, *sceichín, sceichin, sceachín,* little white thorn bush.

Skeheen, *sceithín,* the little whitethorn bush.

Skeheenaranky(sic), *sceichín-an-rince,* not given.

Skeheenarinky, *sceith-a'raince,* the little bush of the dancing.

Skeherny, from *sceach,* bushes.

Skehil, *sceachail,* a lump or knob.

Skehil, *sceach-choill,* whitethorn wood.

Skehy, *sceiche, sceach,* white thorn.
Skela, *scéalach,* story tellers.
Skela, *sceimhle, scéalaidhe,* not given.
Skeldragh, *scealdrach,* rocky.
Skelgagh, from *sceilig,* a place of rocks, rocky land.
Skellan, *sceallan,* small nuts or kernels.
Skellan, Skellan or Skillin, a family or a persons name.
Skellig, *sceilge,* the crag.
Skellig, *sceilig,* a rocky pinnacle, a splinter or crag.
Skellig, *sceilig, scillic,* a rock or sea rock.
Skelligs, *na-scealaga,* the splinters.
Skelligs, *sceilg,* not given.
Skelligs, *sceillig, sceallaga, scillic,* rocks, sea rocks.
Skelpy, from *scealp,* full of splits, clefts or chasms.
Skelt, *scoilte, scoilte,* a cleft or split.
Skemolin, *sceithe-Mholing,* St Moling's bush.
Sken, *sceach,* hawthorn.
Skena, *sceach-na…,* bush of the…
Skeoge, from *sceach,* a place of thorn bushes.
Skeoge, *sceicheóg,* not given.
Skeogh, *sceach,* white thorn bush.
Skeour, *sceabhrach,* sloping land.
Sker, *sceire,* a rock or a sharp rock.
Skerd, *sceird,* not given.
Skerdagh, *scardach,* a cataract or waterfall.
Skerdane, *scardán,* cataracts or cascades of water.
Skerdeen, *Sceirdín,* Sceirdín, not given.
Skerkin, *inis-Arcáin,* Arcán's (a male name) island.
Skerkinis, Arcan's (a male name) island.
Skernaghan, *sceirnechán,* not given.
Skernaghan, *sceireachán*(sic), place of the reef.
Skerrick, *sceiric,* a rocky place.
Skerrick, *sceirig,* not given.
Skerries, *na-sceirí,* the reefs or reef islands.
Skerries, *sceirí, sceire,* sea rocks.
Skerriff, *scarách, scairbhe, scirbh, scairbh,* a shallow, a rough river crossing place or a rugged shallow ford.
Skerrig, *sceiric,* a rocky place.
Skerry, (Owenskerry), a rough shallow ford.

Skerry, *sceir, sceire,* a rock, sea rocks.
Skerry, *sceire,* the sharp rock.
Skerry, *sceiridh,* not given.
Skervan, *scearbhán,* not given.
Sketrick, (island) *scathdearg,* not given.
Skevanish, *scéim-an-ois,* not given.
Skevanish, *sceimh-fhainchis,* projecting edge of the fox cover or lair.
Skew, *sceach,* white thorn, haw trees or thorn bushes.
Skew, *sciadh,* not given.
Skey, from *sceitheanach, sceitnánagh, sceach, sceiche,* white thorn, a place of white thorns or brambles.
Skeyan, *sceachán,* bushy.
Skibbereen, *an-sgibirín,* not given.
Skibbereen, *sciobairín,* little boat harbour or place of the little boats.
Skibbereen, *sciobairín, scibirín,* a place frequented by 'scib's' or boats.
Skibbol, *an-scioból,* not given.
Skibbole, *sciobóil, sciobol, scioból,* a barn or granary.
Skibole, *sgioból,* a barn.
Skiddernagh, *sciodarnach,* a place of puddles.
Skiddy, *Scide,* not given.
Skiddy, *Scidígh, Scídigh, Scidigh,* Skiddy, a personal or family name.
Skidoo, *sceach-dubh,* a black or blackish bush.
Skiertaun, many legged insects(sic).
Skiha, *sceach,* white thorn.
Skillane, Skillane, a family name.
Skillane, *Uí-Chilleáin,* not given.
Skilloge, *sceallóg,* not given.
Skilloge, *sciollóg,* waste eyeless potato slices that are no use for planting.
Skilloge, *sgiollóg,* sliced potatoes.
Skin, *scian,* a knife.
Skin, *scime,* misty.
Skineen, *Uí-Sgingín,* O'Sgingín, a family name.
Skinlahane, *sceinmneachan,* people on watch/alert.
Skinna, *sceach-na…,* bush of the…
Skinna, *sceith-na…,* not given.
Skinny, *sceine,* not given.
Skinny, *scine,* a knife.
Skiog, *sgiathóg,* hawthorns.

Skirk, *sceirc, scathdearc,* not given.
Skirra-go-hiffirn, slipping to hell, the name of a waterfall in Mayo.
Skirtaun, *sciortán,* a type of small fish.
Skirteen, *scairtín,* a little thicket.
Skit, *scairte,* a thicket.
Skool, *sciúil, sciúl,* not given.
Skool, *scumhail, scamhail,* a precipice, steep hill or a sharp slope.
Skoolhill(sic), *cnoc-Sciúil,* not given.
Skough, *sgeach, sceach,* bushes, briars.
Skreen, *scrín, scrín,* a shrine containing relics.
Skreena, *scríne,* a shrine.
Skreeny, from *scrín,* a shrine.
Skreg, *screag,* rocky ground.
Skregg, *scraig,* rock.
Skrillagh, *screallach,* not given.
Skrine, *scrín,* a shrine containing relics.
Skuddal, *scudal,* a fishing basket.
Skul, *scoil,* school.
Skull (Cork), *Sancta Maria de Scholia* (Latin) St Mary of the school, (Irish) *scol,* schools.
Skull, *scoltadh,* a cleft.
Skull, *scumhal,* a precipice.
Skullihy, *scaoilte, scoilighthe,* split.
Skyre, *Scíre,* St Scire.
Slabooley, *salach-búaile,* muddy milking place.
Sladagh, *sladach, sládach,* glen.
Sladdy, *sladaidhe,* not given.
Sladdy, *sladaí,* robbers.
Sladdy, *sladaighe,* the robber.
Slade, *slade, slád,* a stream running in a mountain valley or between two hills.
Slade, *slaed,* dray cars, cars without wheels or slide cars.
Slade, *slaod,* a glen, sloping ground or fall away of ground(sic).
Sladoo, *slád-dubh,* black valley.
Slagh, *leacht,* a sepulchral monument, grave.
Slagh, *saileach,* willows.
Slagh, *slach, salach,* filthy, dirty, unclean.
Slaght, *leacht,* a sepulchral monument, grave.
Slaght, *sleacht,* not given.
Slaghty, *leacht,* a sepulchral monument, grave.
Slanan, *slanan,* health giving.

Slane, *shláine,* fullness.
Slane, *Shleáin, Shléain, Shláinge,* not given.
Slane, *Slaine, Shláine,* Slane, a personal or family name.
Slane, *slán,* health, healing.
Slane, *sleamhain,* a sleek place.
Slanes, *sleamhan,* a place of elms.
Slaney, *sír-buan-Sláne,* the everlasting Slaney.
Slaney, *sláinge-Garman, abha-na-slinne/sléine,* not given.
Slaney, *sleamhain,* a sleek place.
Slanore, modern version of the ancient
Snawlugher, *Snamh-Luthir,* the swimming ford of Luthir, a personal or family name.
Slany, *Slaine,* a male name.
Slapragh, *slaprach,* bad rough land.
Slat, *slat,* a rod or rods.
Slatt, *slat,* a rod or rods.
Slattagh, *slattach,* abounding in twigs, rods or osiers.
Slatteen, *slaitín,* the little rod or rods.
Slattery, *Ua-Slataradh,* O'Slattery, a family name.
Slattinagh, *slattnach,* abounding in twigs, rods or osiers.
Slatty, *slaite,* the rod or twigs.
Slatty, *slataí,* twigs or rods.
Slaud, *slade, slád,* a stream running in a mountain valley or between two hills.
Slaught, *leacht,* a grave.
Slaun, *sláin, slán,* health, healing.
Slauntia, *sláinte,* health.
Slavan, *shleamháin,* not given.
Slavin, *sleamhain, sleamhán,* elm/s.
Slavog, *slabhóg,* the mire.
Slavog, *sleamhóg,* not given.
Slawin, *sleamhain,* elm wood or a place of elms.
Slay, *sleibh,* a mountain.
Sle, *sléibhte, shleibhe, sliabh, tSleibhe,* mountain.
Slea, *shléibhte, shleibhe, sléibhe, sliabh,* mountain.
Slea, *slighe,* not given.
Sleade, *sláid,* robbery or slaughter.
Sleade, *slaod,* small hollows.
Sleady, *carraig-shlaodh, currach-na-slaodaighe,* not given.
Sleady, *slaodaí,* not given.

Sleady, *slaodaighe,* sliding.

Sleana, *sliabh-na...,* mountain of the...

Sleans from *sleamhain,* elm woods or a place of elms.

Sleaty, near the hills.

Sleaty, *shléibhte,* of the mountain.

Sleaty, *shléibhte, sleibhte,* mountains.

Slee, *slí,* a path or highway.

Slee, *sligheadh, slighe,* a pass or main road.

Slee, *sluighe,* the slaughter.

Sleed, *slaed,* dray cars, cars without wheels, slide cars.

Sleeghan, *an-sloitheán,* not given.

Sleehan, from *slighe,* a little road.

Sleehaun, from *slighe,* a little road.

Sleek, *slig,* shells.

Sleen, *slinn,* slate.

Sleesit, *sliasad,* the ledge.

Sleeve, *slaidheamh,* slaughters.

Sleeve, *sliabh,* not given.

Sleeveen, *sléibhín,* little mountain.

Sleggaun, *sliogán,* small flat stones.

Sleiga, *slige,* not given.

Sleivin, *sleamhain,* not given.

Slemish, *Sliabh-Mis,* mountain of Mis, a female name.

Sletty, *sléibhte,* not given.

Slevan, *sleamhain,* elm/s.

Sleveen, *sléibhín, sleibhín,* a little mountain or a mound.

Sleveen, *sliabhín,* a little mountain.

Sleven, *sleibhin,* little mountain.

Slevin, *sleamha,* not given.

Slevin, *Sleibhin,* Slevin, a personal or family name.

Slevin, *sleibhín,* a little mountain.

Slevoir, *sliabh-Mhaghair,* not given.

Sli, *sliabh,* a mountain.

Sli, *slighe,* a road.

Slieva, *sliabh-an...,* mountain of the...

Slievaduff, *sliabh-a-duibh,* mountain of the black bog dye (for colouring wool).

Slievaduff, *sliabh-an-daimh,* mountain of the ox.

Slieve Mish, *Sliabh-Mis,* mountain of Mis, a female name.

Slieve, *sliabh,* a mountain.

Slievean, *slíabh-an...,* mountain of the...

Slievena, *sliabh-na...,* mountain of the...

Slievenagh, *sliabhnach,* a mountainous place.

Slievenaghy, *sliabh-an-achaidh,* mountain of the field.

Slievenamon, *sliabh-na-mban,* the mountain of the women (shortened name).

Slievenamon, *sliabh-na-mban-Feimhinn,* the mountain of the women of Feimhenn (an ancient territory).

Slievenamon, *sliabh-na-mban-fionn,* the mountain of the fair haired women.

Slievera, *Sliabh-iarach,* western moorland.

Slievin, *sleibhín,* a little mountain.

Slig, *slige,* shells.

Slig, *sliog,* not given.

Slig, *slioga,* shell.

Sliganagh, *sligeanach,* shelly land.

Sligaunagh, *sligeanach,* shelly land.

Sligaunagh, *sliogánach,* soil abounding in slate or shells.

Slige, *slige,* not given.

Sligeen, *sligín,* little shells/slates.

Sligga, *sliogach,* shelly or slatey.

Sliggan, *sliogán,* thin slatey stones or shells

Sliggaun, *sligeán,* flat little stones.

Sliggeen, *sligín,* little shells or small flat slatey stones.

Sligo, *sligeach,* abounding in shells, the shelly river or the shelly place.

Sligo, *sligigh,* not given.

Sligo, *sligighe,* shells.

Sliguff, *sliabh-dhubh,* not given.

Sliguff, *slighe-dhubh,* black road.

Slihaun, *slighteán,* the little pass.

Slihaun, *slinneán,* the shoulder blade.

Slin, *slinn,* slates.

Slina, *sline,* slates.

Sling, *sleimhne,* not given.

Sling, *slinne, slinn,* shingle, flat stones or slates.

Slinn, *slinn,* slates.

Slinna, *slinn,* slates.

Slinnaun, *slineán,* the shoulder blade.

Sliogan, *sliogain,* spoon shaped.

Slip, *fanan,* a slip for boats.

Slis, a slice of land or a side.

Slish, *slis,* beetles.

Slisheen, *slisne,* the smooth beetle.

Sliss, a slice of land or a side.

Sloakan, *sleabhacán,* the marine plant 'porphyra vulgaris'.

Sloake, *sleabhacán,* the marine plant 'porphyra vulgaris'.

Sloakna, pit of the…

Sloe, hosting.

Sloe, *slua,* not given.

Sloe, *sluagh,* hosts or armies.

Sloe, *sluagh, sluaighe, sluaigheadh,* gatherings, hostings or hosts.

Sloe, *sluaighe,* the gathering.

Slooeen, *sluaighean,* hosts or armies.

Slough, *saileach,* willow/s.

Slough, *slach, salach,* filthy, dirty, miry or unclean.

Sloura, *slabhra,* the chain.

Sluastia, *sluaiste,* the shovel.

Slug, *slogha,* not given.

Slug, the swallow, (not the bird).

Slugera, *slugaire, slogaire,* a swallow hole.

Sluggan, *slogán,* a swallow hole.

Sluggary, *slogaire,* a quagmire, a sunken surface or a swallow hole.

Sluggawn, *slogán,* a little swallow hole.

Sluggayea, *slugaire, slogaire,* a swallow hole.

Sluggera, *slugaire, slogaire,* a swallow hole.

Sluggera, *slugaire, slogaire,* a swallow hole.

Sluke, *sleabhacán,* the marine plant 'porphyra vulgaris'.

Slut, *sliocht,* breed or descendants

Slyne, *ceinn-léime, ceann-leama, ceann-léime,* the head or headland of the leap/jump.

Smaghraan, *smeachrán,* a point or stripe of land.

Smaghran, *smeachrán,* a point or stripe of land.

Small, *smail,* ashes.

Small, *smáil,* the mire.

Smarmore, *smearamair, smioramar,* not given.

Smarra, *smeara,* the marrow.

Smarra, *smeartha,* grassy.

Smaula, *smála,* the mire.

Smear, *sméar, smear, smeire,* berries or blackberries.

Smeare, *sméar,* blackberries.

Smearlagh, *sméarlach,* blackberry producing river.

Smeesta, *smíste, smiste,* a schemer or evil doer.

Smerlagh, (river) *sméirleach,* not given.

Smerwick, *árd/ard-na-caithne,* height of the arbutus wood.

Smoil, *smól, smóil, smolách,* thrush/s.

Smolagh, *smólach,* thrushes.

Smole, *smoil,* evidence of burning.

Smole, *smóil,* not given.

Smole, *smól, smolách,* thrush/es.

Smoor, *smúr,* embers, rubbish or a cindery dusty spot.

Smoorane, *smurain,* ashes.

Smoran, *smuran,* burnt land.

Smorane, *smúrán,* a cindery dusty spot.

Smulgedon, *smuilgeadan,* the collar bone.

Smut, *smot,* tree stumps.

Smut, *smut,* stocks, trunks of trees.

Smuth, *smut,* stocks of trees.

Smuttan, *smotáin,* a bog-deal stump.

Smuttan, *smotáin,* a place full of tree stumps, tree trunks or stakes.

Smuttan, *smutain,* not given.

Smuttan, *smután,* built with logs or tree stumps.

Smuttanagh, *smotáin,* a place full of tree stumps.

Smuttann, *smotáin,* a stump.

Smuttaun, *smutáin,* not given.

Smuttaun, *smután,* stakes or tree stumps.

Smuttawn, *smotan,* stocks or stumps of trees.

Smutternagh, *smuternach,* a place of old tree trunks.

Sna, *snamha, snámh, snamh,* swimming or swimming place.

Snaa, *sionnach,* foxes.

Snachtig, *sneachtaidh,* snow.

Snade, *snaithaide,* the needle.

Snade, *snaithad,* needles.

Snag, *snaig,* the woodpecker.

Snagadan, *shnagadáin,* not given.

Snagadan, *snagadáin,* a place of cats courtship or fawning.

Snaght, *shneachta,* not given.

Snaght, *sneachta, sneacht,* snow.

Snaghta, *sneacht, snechta,* snow.

Snaghta, *tSneachtaidh,* not given.

Snaghten, *sneachta,* snow.

Snaghtig, *sneachtaig, sneachtaidh,* snow.

Snahida, *snáthad,* the needle.

Snakeel, *snámh-caol,* narrow swimming place or narrow swim.

Snamh, *snamh,* swimming.

Snat, *sneacht, snechta,* snow.

Snaty, *ins-na-áite,* on the eminences or high hills(sic).

Snaty, *snaidhte,* setarated.

Snauv, *snamh…,* swimming place of the…

Snauv, *snámha,* not given.

Snave, *snámh, snamh,* swimming or swimming place.

Snaw, *snamh,* swim, swimming.

Sneem, *an-tSnaidhm, snaidhm,* the knot (from a rock in the river just below the bridge).

Sneem, *an-tSnaidhm,* the knot, joining or junction.

Sneeoge, *sniodhóg,* the small stream.

Snim, *snaidhm,* the knot.

Snimna, *snaidhm-na…,* the knot of…

Snow, *snamh,* swimming.

Soarn, *sórn,* a kiln.

Sob, *subh,* berries.

Sock, *soc,* a snout, beak or point.

Sock, *soc,* ploughshares.

Sockar, *socair,* open level land.

Sockna, *soc-na…,* snout or point of the…

Socks, from *soc,* snouts, beaks or points.

Sod, (island) *oileán-dubhach,* sad island.

Sodan, *sodan,* a type of duck known locally (near Tuam) as 'dumpy or dumpies'.

Sodden, *Sodáin,* Sodan, a personal or family name.

Soerneog, the kiln.

Sogher, *sochar,* produce or profit.

Soghly, *Sachaille,* Sachaille, Sochaille, a personal or family name.

Soheen, *sóin,* a place of pleasure or rest.

Soheen, *soithín,* a small vessel.

Soilshaun, *shoillséain,* luminous.

Soilshawn, *soillseán,* lights.

Solais, *solas,* light.

Soldad, *sulchoid,* a sallow or willow wood.

Sole, *solas,* light/s.

Sollas, *solas,* a light.

Sollis, *solais,* light.

Sollis, *tSolais, solus,* not given.

Sollis, *tSoluis,* brightness.

Sollish, *solais,* not given.

Sollish, *soluis,* the light.

Solloghod, *tSulchóid, sulchóid, sulchoid, salchoit,* a sallow, willow wood.

Sollus, *solas,* a light.

Sologhod, *sulchóid,* not given.

Soluis, *soluis,* not given.

Soluis, *solais,* light.

Solus, *solas,* light/s.

Son, *sonn,* ramparts.

Sona, *sonna,* a mound or rampart.

Sonna, *suidhe-Adhamhnán,* not given.

Sonnagh, *tSonnach, sonagh, sonnach, sonnaidh, sonaidh,* a defensive rampart, fortification, mound or palisade.

Sonvolaun, *sanúlan,* not given.

Soo, *sú, sumhaigh,* not given.

Soo, *subhán, subh,* berries.

Soo, *sugh,* strawberries or raspberries.

Soodry, *súdaire,* tanners.

Soodry, *súdairí,* not given.

Sooey, *samhaidh,* sorrel.

Sooey, *Súmhaí,* not given.

Soogaun, *súgan,* a rope.

Sool, *súl, sul, suil,* eye/s.

Soolagh, *subhallach,* religious people.

Soolmoy, *súl-mBuí/mBuidhe,* not given.

Soon, *sonn,* stakes or palisades.

Soon, wild strawberries.

Sooreeny, *siuirínidhe,* little sisters.

Sooska, *samhaisce,* heifers.

Sop, *sop,* wisps (of straw).

Soppoge, from *sop,* the little wisp or wispy grass.

Sopwell, *coill-na-lathach,* not given.

Soran, *sorn,* a kiln or a place for making lime.

Sorcha, a male name.

Sore, *ore,* a Danish word for a sandy point.

Sore, *sratha,* not given.

Sorn, *sorn,* a kiln.

Sorne *sorn,* a kiln.

Sorrel, *samhach,* sorrel, a herb.

Sorrel, *Saorghail,* O'Sorrel, a family name.

Sorrel, *Sharail,* not given.

Sough, *samhach,* sorrel.

Soughane, *suidheachán,* a residence or seat.

Soughly, *Sachaille,* not given.

Souna, *Samhna, Samhuin, samh-fhuin,* a pagan festival on Nov 1st for the end of summer and is usually held on hills.

Sour, *shamhar,* not given.

Sov, *subh,* berries.

Sow, (river) *siomha,* not given.

Sow, *samha, samhaidh,* sorrel.

Sowna, *sabhna,* savin (a plant).

Sowna, *samhain,* summer.

Sowna, *shamhuin,* a pagan festival on Nov 1st for the end of summer and is usually held on hills.

Spa, *an-spá,* not given.

Spaddagh, *spadach,* heavy wet land.

Spaddan, heavy poor land.

Spaddaun, *spadán,* lazy or poor land.

Spallan, *Uí-Spealláin,* O'Spellan or Spillane, a family name.

Spancel Hill, *cnoc-urchoille,* not given.

Spancelhill, *cnoc-an-urchaill,* hill of the spancel (a cow–tether).

Spancillhill, *cnoc-fhuarcoill/fuarchoill/urchaill,* hill of the cold wood.

Spar, *spárr,* a military gateway.

Spar, spars or rafters.

Sparr, *sparr,* a gate.

Sparraun, *sparáin,* the purse.

Sparrograda, *speara-greadhtha,* a place of shamrocks.

Spaug, *spag,* not given.

Spaunig, *Spainnigh,* a Spaniard.

Speara, *spiara,* not given.

Speck, *speice,* a spike of rock.

Spedogue, *spideóige, spideóg,* red breasts.

Speeg, *spiog,* spikes.

Speek, *spéice,* the spike.

Speenan, *spionán,* gooseberry places.

Speenoge, *spíonóg, spionán,* gooseberry place/s.

Speenoge, *spionóg,* spoon.

Spelga, *speilge,* the pointed rock.

Spellan, *Uí-Spealláin,* O'Spellan or Spillane, a family name.

Spellane, *Uí-Speallain,* O'Spillane, a family name.

Spellane, *Uí-Spoláin,* not given.

Spellickanee, *speilg-an-fhiaigh,* not given.

Sperrin, *speirín,* pointed.

Sperrin, *speirin,* points or pointed.

Spick, *spic, easpuig,* a Bishop.

Spickoen, *easpog-Eóin,* not given.

Spicktarvin, *easpog-Tairbhin,* not given.

Spiddal, *spidéal,* a hospital.

Spiddale, *spidéal,* a hospital.

Spiddle, *spidéal, spital,* a hospital.

Spiddoge, *spideóg,* the robin redbreast.

Spiddogy, *spidoige,* the robin.

Spidogy, *spidoige, spideóige,* the robin redbreast.

Spig, *spic, easpuig,* a Bishop.

Spike (Island), *inis-Picht,* island of the Picts.

Spike, (island) *inis-Píc,* not given.

Spillane, *Uí-Spealláin/Spealáin,* O'Spellan or Spillane, a family name and means the descendants of Spealán.

Spinans, *spíonáin,* thorns or gooseberry bushes.

Spinans, *spionán,* gooseberry places.

Spindle, a personal or family name.

Spindle, *spíonóg,* gooseberry.

Spink, *spinc,* a point of rock, a pointed rock, a pinnacle or an overhanging cliff.

Spink, *spuinnc,* coltsfoot.

Spinkaun, *spincán,* a little pinnacle.

Spinnell, *spannla,* the shank.

Spital, *spidéil,* not given.

Spittal, *spital,* a hospital.

Spittle, *spidéil, spidéal, spideil,* hospital.

Splane, *Spealain,* McSpillane, a family name.

Spol, *spall,* fallow burning.

Spoo, *speó,* not given.

Spoug, *spág,* a club-foot or a long ugly foot.

Spout, *spuit,* a spout.

Spreireoige, *spreireoige,* the sparrowhawk.

Springan, *spionáin, sprionán,* gooseberries or gooseberry places.

Sprinka, *spínce,* projecting rock.

Spruceshay, *garraí-an-Sprúisigh,* not given.

Sprucheshay, *garraí-Sprúis,* Spruce's (a personal or family name) thicket or shaw(sic). Also known by *goirtín-Sprúis,* not given.

Sprunane, *sprionán,* gooseberry places.

Spuag, *spág,* shaped like a long ugly foot.

Spunkane, from *spunc,* the herb 'coltsfoot'.

Spur, *spor,* a spur or spur shape.

Spurree, *sporaí-cloch,* not given.

Spurree, *sporaidhe,* spurs or pointed rocks.

Squillib, *scoilb,* not given.

Squillib, *scuilb,* a scollop (used in thatching).

Squire, *scuir,* a camp.

Squllop, *scolb,* a bent twig used in thatching.

Sra, *sraith,* not given.

Sra, *sratha, srath,* a river holm.

Srabra, *srath-breagh,* the fine river holm.

Sragh, a river meadow.
Sragh, *sratha,* a fen.
Sragh, *srath,* a river holm.
Sraghan, *srathán, srathín,* little river holm.
Sraghoe, *srath-abha,* river holm.
Srah, *an-tSraith, srath,* a river holm or riverside meadow.
Srah, *srath,* a river valley(sic).
Srah, *sraithe,* not given.
Sraha, *sraith-an...,* not given.
Sraha, *srath-an/a'...,* river holm of the...
Sraha, *srutha,* a stream.
Srahan, *srathán, srathín,* little river holm.
Srahan, *sruthán, sruhan,* a streamlet.
Srahane, *srathán,* little river holm.
Sraharla, from *srathar,* the pack saddle river holm.
Srahaun, *srathán, srathín,* little river holm.
Sraheen, *sraithín, srathán, srathín,* little river holm or riverside meadow.
Sraheens, *na-sraithíní,* the small holms.
Srahna, *sraith/srath-na...,* river holm or riverside meadow of the...
Srahy, *sraithe,* a river holm.
Sraid, *sráid,* little field hamlets(sic).
Srana, *srath-na...,* holm of the...
Srana, *sruthan-na...,* streamlet of the...
Srananny, *srian-eanaigh,* not given.
Sranure, *sraith-an-iúir,* not given.
Srath, *srath,* a river holm.
Sraud, *sráid, sraid,* a street.
Sreane, *srian,* bridle/s.
Sreelane, *sraoilleán,* not given.
Sreenty, *na-srianta,* not given.
Sreenty, *sriantaidhe,* bridles.
Sriff, *sruibh,* a stream.
Srim, *Srian,* not given.
Sroan, *sron,* the nose.
Sron, *sron,* a nose or promontory.
Sronagh, *srónach,* nosy or snouted.
Srone, *sróna, srona,* the nose.
Sroohil, *sruthra, sruill,* a stream.
Sroohill, *sruill,* a stream.
Sroohill, *sruthail,* rushing of water.
Sroolane, *srúilleán,* not given.
Sroolane, *sruthlán, sruthain,* a streamlet.
Srooleen, *sruthain,* a streamlet.
Sroove, *srúbh, srubh, sruibh,* a stream.
Srough, *sruthair,* a stream.
Sroughan, *sruthain,* a streamlet.

Sroughan, *sruthan,* a brook or dirty stream.
Sru, *srath,* not given.
Sru, *sruth, srotha,* a stream.
Srue, *sruth,* a stream.
Sruell, *an-tSruthail,* not given.
Sruell, *sruthair,* a stream.
Sruffane, *sruthán,* a little stream.
Sruffaun, *sruthán,* a little stream.
Srugha, *sruth-an...,* stream of the...
Srughawn, *shruthan,* a small stream.
Sruh, *sruth,* a stream.
Sruhaan, *sruthán,* the little stream.
Sruhagh, *sruthach,* a place of streams.
Sruhan, *an-sruthán,* not given.
Sruhanagh, *sruthanach,* a place of streams.
Sruhane, *sruthán,* the little stream.
Sruhaun, *srothrán,* a purling, voiceful or babbling brook.
Sruhaun, *sruthán,* streamlets.
Sruher, (river) *sruthair,* not given.
Sruthair, *sruthair,* a stream.
Sruwaddacon, *sruth-Mhada-Con,* not given.
Sta, *steach,* a fort.
Sta, *tigh, steach, teach,* house.
Staad, *stáid,* not given.
Stabannan, *tigh-Beannáin,* not given.
Stabla, a stable.
Stack, *stac,* not given.
Stack, *stigh, steach, teach,* a house.
Stackallen, *stigh/steach-Colláin, teach-Collan/Collain,* Collán's or Collan's (a male name) house.
Stackan, *stacáin, stácain,* a stump, stake, standing stone or little peak.
Stackan, *stacán,* not given.
Stackarnagh, *stacadharnach,* a place of stakes or tree trunks.
Stackaun, *stacáin,* not given.
Stackin, *staicín,* the stake.
Stael, *stéill, stael,* not given.
Stagh, *teach,* house.
Stagholmog, St Colmoc's or Mocholmoc's house.
Stagonil, *teach-Conaill,* not given.
Stags, rocks.
Stah, *teach,* house.
Staholmog, *teach-Cholmóg,* Colmog's house.
Staholmog, *tigh-Colmóg,* not given.
Staig, *stéidhg,* the stripe.

Staig, *stéig,* not given.

Staigue, *stéidhe,* the stripe.

Staigue, *stéig,* a strip of land or a rocky ledge.

Staigue, *stéighe,* not given.

Stakally, *stá-Chaile,* Caile's (a personal or family name) house.

Stakarnagh, *staicearnach,* abounding in posts or stakes.

Stal, *Stáhail,* Státhal or Stathel, a personal or family name.

Stal, *Stáil, Státhail,* not given.

Stalla, *stalach,* a stallion.

Stamullen, *tach-Meallán,* not given.

Stan, *an-stanna,* not given.

Stan, *stainge,* a stang (measure of land).

Stang, *stang,* a measure of land equal to a rood.

Stangaun, *stangán,* little measure of land.

Stangs, *na-stanga,* measures of land.

Stangs, *stangaí,* a place of small fields.

Stanly, *Stónlailigh,* not given.

Stash, *staitse,* a platform crossing.

Steage, *Stáige,* a personal name.

Steage, *Steig,* not given.

Steage, *steidhg,* a land measurment.

Steague, *Stéige,* not given.

Steal, *stíall,* a strip.

Steales, *na-stialla,* not given.

Steals, from *stíall,* strips.

Steel, *stíall,* a strip.

Steelagh, *stiallach,* striped.

Steelaun, *stíallán, stialláin,* the little stripe.

Steen, *Aistín, Stibhín,* not given.

Steen, *Stáon,* lying in an oblique direction.

Steen, *Stiabhna,* Stiabhna or Istiadhan, a personal name.

Steen, *Uí-Istiadhain,* O'Istiadhan, O'Isteen or Steen, a family name.

Steen, *Uístín,* Uístín, not given.

Steena, *an-Stiabhnaigh/Stiabhnach,* not given.

Steil, *stíall, stiall, a* strip of land.

Steill *stialla,* a strip.

Stephana, *Stefanach,* Stephen, a male name.

Ster, as a word ending, Danish for a ford or a place.

Stereame, *steirím,* not given.

Sterkin, *stuircin,* a little sturk(sic).

Sterkin, *stuiricin,* a small pinnacle.

Sthaneel, *Stanaolaigh,* Stanly, a male name.

Sthucan, projecting rock pinnacles.

Sthukeen, *móintín,* little bog.

Stiallas, *staillas,* the stripe.

Stick, *stíoc,* not given.

Stick, *Stoic,* Sticks, a family name.

Stick, *stuic,* a stake.

Stickan, *stacáin,* little peak.

Stickane, *stacáin,* not given.

Stickane, *stiocáin,* the stake.

Sticken, *stuican,* a pinnacle.

Stickillin, *tigh-Cillín,* not given.

Stifyans, *tigh-Phaghain,* not given.

Stil, *teach,* house.

Stile, *stíall, stiall,* a strip of land.

Stiles, from *stíall,* strips.

Still, *stialláin,* not given.

Stillan, *stiallán,* the little stripe.

Stillimitty, *an-stiall/stíall/stiall,* a stripe or long narrow piece of land.

Stillimity, *stíall, stiall,* the stripe.

Stillimity, *stiall-an-Fhaoitigh,* not given.

Stillorgan, house of St Lorcan.

Stillorgan, *steach-Lorcán,* not given.

Stillorgan, *stigh/steach-Lorgan, tig/teach-Lorcáin,* Lorcan's (the name of a 12th cent Bishop) house.

Stiloga, *stíall-óga,* little stripes.

Stira, *staighre,* stairs.

Stiree, *staighrí,* stairs.

Stirue, *tigh-Rú,* not given.

Stock, *stoc,* a tree trunk or stake.

Stockan, *stocan,* a crag.

Stockan, *stocán,* stakes or tree trunks.

Stockens, from *stocáin,* tree trunks.

Stocks, from *stoc,* stakes.

Stoe, *stuaighe,* not given.

Stokane, *stuacán,* a stook (little bundle of sheaves).

Stokaun, *stocán, stócán, stuacán,* a slittle stake, tree stumps, a prominent rock or rock stumps.

Stokaun, *stócán, stuacán,* a slittle stake or a prominent rock.

Stollar, *stualaire,* a peak or sharp prominence.

Stollar, *stualaire,* a peak.

Stoller, *stollaire, stualaire,* not given.

Stona, *an-Stónaigh, an-Stónach,* not given.

Stone, *stúin, stang,* a measurment of land.
Stonecarthy, *stúin-Chárthaigh,* Carthach's
(a personal or family name) stang or
measure of land.
Stoneen, *an-stúinín,* not given.
Stoneen, *staingín,* a little stang (measur-
ment of land).
Stonehouse, *Stónús,* not given.
Stong, *stang,* a measurment of land.
Stonga, *stang-a'...,* measurment of land of
the...
Stongaluggaun, *stang-an-logáin,* not given.
Stooagh, *stuadh,* a prominent hill or pin-
nacle.
Stook, *stuac,* not given.
Stook, *stuaic,* a pointed rock.
Stook, *stúic,* pinnacles.
Stooka, *stuaic, stuaice,* a peak, a pinnacle or
pointed hill.
Stookah, from *stuac,* pinnacles or pointed
hills.
Stookan, *stuaicán,* a little pointed rock.
Stookauns, from *stuaicán,* little pointed
rocks.
Stookeen, *stoicín,* a hillock.
Stookeen, *stuaicán,* a little pointed rock or
height.
Stookeen, *stuaicín,* a little pinnacle.
Stookeens, *stuaicíní,* little pointed rocks.
Stoops, an English word for gate posts or
piers.
Stoops, *stupaidhe,* round hills.
Stouke, *stoc,* a tree trunk or stake.
Stouke, *stuaic,* a pinnacle, a height.
Stow, *stuaidh,* a pinnacle or a prominent
hill.
Stowry, *storaidh, storaid,* sheep storage, stor-
age.
Stowry, *stóraigh,* not given.
Stra, *sruth,* not given.
Stra, *tSraith, srath,* a river holm or riverside
land.
Strad, *sráid, sraid,* a street.
Strad, *srath,* a river holm.
Stradbally, *sradbhaile,* street town.
Stradbally, *sráidbhaile,* not given.
Strade, *tSráid, sraide, sraid,* the street.
Stradeen, *sráidín, sraidín,* little street.
Stradone, *sraith-an-domhain,* riverside land
of the deep place.

Stradone, *srath-Domhain,* not given.
Straffan, *sruthán,* a little stream.
Straffan, *teach-Srafáin, tigh-Srafan,* not
given.
Straghan, *srathán, srathín,* little river holm.
Stragolan, the sandy bottomed fork.
Strahart, *sraith/srath-Airt,* not given.
Straid, *tSráid, sráid, sraid,* a street.
Straidarran, O'Aran's (a family name)
village.
Strain, *srian,* not given.
Stramackilmartin, *srath-Máirtín*(sic), not
given.
Strameen, *straimín,* not given.
Stran, *shrón, srón, srone,* a nose.
Stran, *srath,* a river holm.
Stran, *srath-na...,* the holm or river bank
of the....
Stran, *sruthan,* a little stream.
Strana, *srath-na...,* river holm of the...
Strane, *srathan,* streamlets.
Straness, *srath-an easa,* holm of the
waterfall.
Strang, a stream.
Strangford, *Strang Fjorthr,* (Danish, Norse)
strong ford or violent inlet. The Irish
is *baile-loch/locha-cuan,* town of 'haven
lake'..
Stranooden, *sraith-Nuadáin,* Nuadán's (a
personal or family name) riverside land.
Stratford-on-Slaney, named after the
second Earl of Aldborough, Edward
Stratford. The Irish name is *áth-na-sráide,*
ford of the street.
Straugh, *srath,* a river holm.
Straw, *sratha,* riverside land.
Straw, *sratha, srath,* a river holm.
Strawley, *straoilaigh,* straggling.
Strawoaghter, *an srath-uachtair,* not given.
Streame, *stoiracim,* a stream.
Strean, *srathan,* streamlets.
Strean, *sriain, srían,* a bridle.
Streedagh, *srídeach,* a stripe of land.
Streefe, *sraobh,* a mill stream.
Streeve, *sraobh,* a mill stream.
Streile, *straoile,* a slut or steel.
Strekaun, *stríochán,* not given.
Strekaun, *striocán,* strips of land.
Strella, *streille,* a carpet or mat.
Strew, from *sruth,* streams.

Strew, *sruth,* a stream.

Strickeen, *strícín,* little line or stroke.

Strig, *screige*(sic), not given.

Strike, *stréic,* not given.

Stripe, *an-straidhp,* not given.

Stripes, *na-stialla,* not given.

Stroan, *sruthán, sruthain,* a streamlet.

Strogue, *starróg, sreathóg,* not given.

Strogue, *stróg, sturróg,* the top of a hill.

Stroke, *stróic,* a stripe.

Strokes, *na-mBuillí,* the strokes or blows.

Stron, a point.

Stroove, *an-tSrúibh,* not given.

Stroove, *srubh, sruibh,* a stream.

Strowry, *sruthra,* streams.

Strowry, *tSruthair, sruill,* a stream.

Struaun, *sruthán, sruthain,* a streamlet.

Strudder, *sruthair,* stream.

Struel, *srúill, sruill, sruthail,* a stream.

Struell, *sruthail, srúill,* a stream.

Strule, *sruthra,* a stream.

Stuake, *stuaic,* a pinnacle.

Stuc, *stoc,* a tree trunk.

Stucan, *stuacáin,* a stack.

Stucan, *stuaicán,* a little pointed rock.

Stuccolane, *stocolán,* not given.

Stuck, *stoc,* a tree trunk or stake.

Stuck, *stuaic, stuc,* rock promontories, a projecting rock.

Stuck, *stúca,* a point.

Stuck, *stuca,* not given.

Stuckane, *stiocáin,* the stake.

Stuckaun, *stúcáin,* a little cone shaped rock.

Stuckaun, *stacán,* stakes.

Stuckeen, *stoicín,* a little tree trunk or stake.

Stughan, *stuacan,* a little point.

Stuic, *stuaic, stuc,* rock promontories or a projecting rock.

Stumpa, *an-stumpa,* not given.

Stumpa, *stúmpa,* a stock, tree trunk or post.

Sturgan, from *stur,* little peak or hilltop.

Sturkeen, *stuiricín,* the peak.

Sturrakeen, from *stur,* little peak or hilltop.

Sturrall, the pinnacle.

Sturrel, from *stur,* little peak or hilltop.

Sturrin, from *stur,* little peak or hilltop.

Styx, *mhaide,* the stick or sticks.

Subulter, *sabaltair,* a pagan or plague graveyard.

Subulter, *sobaltair,* not given.

Suck, (river) *an-tSúca, Suca,* not given.

Sudder, *súdair,* a tanner.

Suddery, *súdaire, súdairighe,* tanners.

Suddery, *súdairí,* not given.

Sudry, *súdairighe,* tanners.

Suel, *suil,* an eye.

Suerla, *suidhe-Iarla,* seat or residence of the Earl.

Suff, *subh,* berries or strawberries.

Sugagh, *sugach,* merry.

Sugh, *sruh,* a stream.

Suil, *suile, súl,* eye/s.

Suir, *an-tSiúir/siúire/siúr,* the sister.

Suirville, *tigh-an Siúir,* not given.

Sullahaun, *salachain,* a dirty person.

Sullane, (river) *an-sullán,* not given.

Sullas, *solas,* a light.

Sullen, *saileann,* a sallow plantation.

Sullen, *sailean,* willows.

Sullish, *solais,* light.

Sullivan, *Sullivan,* a family name.

Sullus, *soluis,* light.

Sultan, *sailteann,* a sallow plantation.

Sumaghan, *Uí-Somacháin,* O'Summaghan, a family name.

Sundrivan, *Suindreabhain,* Sundrivan, a personal or family name.

Sunglen, *an-spidéal,* not given.

Sunnagh, *sonnach,* a defensive rampart, fortification or mound.

Sunnagh, *sonnach,* a milking place(sic).

Sup, *sop,* a bog-deal torch.

Suppeen, *soipín,* a little wisp or miserable looking person.

Sur, *soir, east,* eastern.

Surahane, *sruthán,* a streamlet.

Sure, *siúr,* the sisters.

Surgeview, *tóin-na-hOlltaí,* not given.

Surhanleanantawey, *sruthán-léana-an-tSamhaidh,* stream of the meadow of sorrel.

Surn, *sorn,* a kiln or furnace.

Sussa, *sosadh,* a resting place.

Sutton, *Cill-Fhionntan,* not given.

Sutton, *suí-Fhionntain, Fhionáin,* St Fintan's seat.

Sutton, *Suí-Fhiontain,* seat of St Fiontan.

Sutton, *tSutúnaigh,* not given.

Swanlinbar, *an-muileann-iarainn,* not given.

Swatragh, *suaithreach,* not given.

Swatragh, *suaitreach,* a soldier.

Swatragh, *suaitreach,* the billeted soldier.

Swihane, *suidheachán,* a residence or seat

Swilly, *an-tSuileach,* not given.

Swilly, *súileach,* clear-seeing.

Swilly, *súilí, súileach,* abounding in eyes or whirlpools.

Swinford, *béal-átha-na-muice,* the ford mouth of the pig.

Swords, *soird, suardair, sórd-Cholmcille,* not given.

Swords, *sord,* sward(sic).

Swords, *sord,* well.

Swords, *sórd-Cholaim-Chille,* St Colmcille's sword.

Swords, *sord-Choluimcille,* St Columkilles well.

Sy, *suidhe,* seat.

Sybil Head, *ceann-Sibil,* not given.

Sybil, (head), *Shibbeal,* named after Isabel Ferriter.

Syddan, *sidhéan,* not given.

Sydenham, *suideanam,* not given.

Sylaun, *saighleán,* not given.

Sylaun, *shaileach, sailaun, sailigh,* sallies, a place of sallies or sallows.

Synone, *sidhean-Eoghain, sídh-Neóin,* Owen's fairy mount or hill.

Synone, *suí-nEoin,* not given.

Syon, *sidhean,* a fairy hill.

Syonee, *sidhean-Aodha,* Hugh's or Aodh's (a male name) fairy hill.

Sythe, *saigit, saighead,* arrows.

T

Ta, *tigh, teach*, house.
Taafe, *Tífe, táthaigh*, not given.
Taaffe, *Tífe*, not given.
Taash, *tais*, moist land.
Taash, *táis*, not given.
Taboe, *teach-bo*, the cow house.
Tach, *teach*, house.
Tachne, *teach-na…*, not given.
Tacka, *tSeaca*, frost.
Tacken, *taicin*, a stake or trunk.
Tacker, *tacair*, a gathering or a collecting heap of something.
Tacker, *tacair*, artificial.
Tacky, *taca*, near at hand.
Taclade, *tochlaidh*, a dug out pit.
Tacum, *Dacoma*, St Dachoma.
Tacumshane, (lake) *loch-Sáile*, not given.
Tacumshane, St Coimshin's house.
Tacumshane, *teach-Coimsín*, Coimsín's (a personal name) house.
Tacumshane, *teach-Cuimsean*, not given.
Tacumshin, *teach-Cuimsin*, Cuimsin's (a personal or family name) house.
Tadavnet, *tigh-Damhnata*, not given.
Tadder, *teadar*, between.
Taff, *chatha*, a battle.
Taffe, *Teá*, Taafe, a family name.
Taffy, *Taffaigh*, Taafe, a family name.
Taggart, *tSagairt*, a priest or clergy.
Taggle, *T'sheagal, T'seagal, tSeagail*, rye.
Tagh, *…tach*, as an ending to a word can sometimes mean, a place of…. or abounding in…
Tagh, *tigh, teach*, house.
Taghadoe, *teach-Tua/Tuae*, house of St Tua.
Taghart, *tachairt*, the skirmish.

Taghart, *tóchair, thachairt, tachar*, not given.
Tagheen, *teach-chaein*, beautiful house.
Tagheen, *teach-chaoin*, pleasant house.
Tagheen, *teach-Dhuinn*, not given.
Taghmon, *tech/teach-Munna*, house of St Munna.
Taghna, *teach-na…*, house of the…
Taglin, *teachlainn*, a stable.
Tagoat, *teach-Cóg*, Cóg's (a personal name) house.
Tagoat, *teach-Gót*, Gót or St Cod's house.
Tagoat, *tigh-Guit*, not given.
Taggart(sic), *tSagart*, the priest.
Tagtoe, *teach-Tua*, not given.
Taha, *tSaithe*, a swarm of bees.
Tahar, *tachair*, the fight.
Taharn, *tSathairn*, Saturday.
Taher, *tachair*, the fight.
Tahilla, *taithille, tathuile*, not given.
Tailltenn, *Taillte, Tailltenn*, the fair of 'Taillte' a Spanish princess and also a place that was named after her.
Tain, *tSéin*, not given.
Tain, *tSíain*, foxgloves.
Tain, *tSiadhain*, a fairy mount or palace.
Taise, *Taisie-taoibhgeal, Taise of the white cheeks, the name of a princess.*
Taite, *tate, tath*, a measurment of land (60 acres).
Tale, *sáile, saile*, brine, the sea.
Tale, *tSiadhail*, St Sedulius.
Tall, *Táil*, Tal, a personal or family name.
Talla, *talamh, Deala*, not given.
Talla, *t-salach*, sallows.
Talla, *tulach*, not given.
Tallagh, *tamlagth*, a plague grave/monument.
Tallagh, *teallaigh, talach*, not given.
Tallagh, *tSaileach, tSailigh, tSailighe*, sally trees.
Tallagh, *tSalach*, dirty.
Tallagh, *tulach*, a hill.
Tallagh, *tulcha*, a knoll.
Tallaghan, *tSaileacháin*, a place of sallows.
Tallaght, (in Dublin) *taimhleacht-Mhuintire-Parthaloin*, the plague grave of Parthalons people.
Tallaght, *taimhleachta*, a plague cemetery.

Tallaght, *tamhlachta*, not given.

Tallan, *tSalainn*, salt.

Tallan, *tSalainn*, salty.

Tallavna, *talamh-na…*, earth or land of the…

Tallel, *tSinill*, not given.

Tallen, *tSalainn*, salty.

Tallin, *tSalainn*, salt.

Talliv, *talamh*, earth or land.

Tallon, *talmhan*, of the earth.

Tallon, *tSalainn*, salt.

Talloon, *talmhan, talún*, of the earth/land.

Talloon, *Tolamhan*, not given.

Tallow, *talamh*, ground, land.

Tallow, *tealach, tulach*, a hill or hillock.

Tallow, *tulach*, a mound or summit.

Tallow, *tulaig/tulach-an-Iarainn*, (Waterford) hillock of (the) iron.

Tally, *talamh*, land.

Tally, *daile, tSalainn*, not given.

Tally, *tulach*, a hill.

Talt, *tailt*, not given.

Talura, *táilliura*, a tailor.

Talure, a tailor.

Tamagh, a groom field.

Tamagh, descendants of Laoch, a personal or family name.

Tamhnagh, *tamhnach*, a green field which produces fresh sweet grass.

Tamlacht, *tamlacht*, a plague burial ground.

Tamlaght, *taimhleacht*, a plague monument or cemetery.

Tamlaght, *tamhlacht*, a burial place.

Tamlaght, *tamhlacht, tamlacht*, a pagan burial place.

Tamlaghta, *tamhlacht-an…, taimh-leacht-a'…*, the plague monument or cemetery of the…

Tamlat, *taimhleacht*, a plague monument.

Tamlat, *taimhleachta*, a plague grave, cemetery.

Tamlat, *tamhlacht*, not given.

Tamlet, *taimhleacht*, a plague monument.

Tammy, *tamhnaigh*, a grassy field.

Tamna, *tamhnaigh, tamhnach*, a green field which produces fresh sweet grass.

Tamnagh, *tamhnach*, a cultivated spot.

Tamney, an arable place in a less fertile district.

Tamney, *an-tamhnach*, not given.

Tamney, *tamhnaigh*, a cultivated spot or green field.

Tamny, *tamhnach*, a green field which produces fresh sweet grass.

Tamny, *tamhnaigh*, a green spot or groom field.

Tampauns, *dTeampán*, round boulders.

Tample, *teampull, teampuill*, Church.

Tampul, *teampull, teampuill*, Church.

Tamry, *tSamhraidh*, summer.

Tamur, *teamhair*, a conspicuous high residence.

Tamy, *tamhain*, not given.

Tamy, *tSamhaidh*, sorrel.

Tan, *tamhnach*, not given.

Tan, *ton*, backside, rear end or posterior.

Tan, *tSean…*, the old…

Tana, *tSeana/tSean…*, the old…

Tanagh, *tanaí*, shallow.

Tanagh, *tamhnach*, a mound(sic).

Tanahee, *t-seanchaidhe*, storyteller.

Tanaknock, *tSeana-chnuic*, the old hill.

Tanavally, *tSeanbhaile*, not given.

Tanderagee, leeward or back to the wind.

Tandragee, *tón-le-gaoith, tóin/toin-re-gaoith*, backside to the wind or leeward.

Tane, *tamhnach*, a green field which produces fresh sweet grass.

Tane, *t-siain, tSiain*, foxglove.

Taney, *tigh-Naithí*, not given.

Tang, *teanga*, a tongue.

Tangaveane, *an-tSeanga-mheáin*, not given.

Tangin, tongue of the…

Taniheen, *tSionaichín*, a little fox.

Tankard, *Tancardaigh*, not given.

Tankin, *Taincín*, Tankin, a personal or family name.

Tankin, *Tancín*, a male name.

Tankin, *tSaincín*, not given.

Tanlis, *tSeanleasa*, the old fort.

Tanna, *t-seana*, blessing or denial.

Tanna, *tSeanach*, Seanach, not given

Tanna, *tSeanaigh*, not given.

Tannagh, *tamhnach*, a fertile green field.

Tannagh, *tamhnach*, a mound(sic).

Tanner, *tineúra*, a tanner.

Tannig, *t-Seanaigh*, Shannagh, a personal or family name.

Tannig, *tSeanaigh,* St Senach, Seanach.

Tannig, *tSeanaigh, t-seanaigh,* a fox.

Tanny, *Tanaí,* not given.

Tanny, *tSionnaigh,* the fox.

Tanon, *tSenain,* St Senan.

Tanrego, *toin-re-go,* backside to the sea.

Tanty, *tSeantí,* not given.

Tanty, *tSean-tighe/toighe,* the old house.

Tanvally, *tSeanbhaile,* the old town.

Tap, *tap,* a lump or mass.

Taplagh, *taplach,* a place of lumps or masses however locals call it 'the place of rubbish'.

Tappaghan, *tapachán, tappadan,* a round hill or a little lumpy hill.

Tappaghan, *tapadan,* not given.

Tar, (river) *abha-an-tSearraigh,* not given.

Tar, *teara,* not given.

Tar, *tír,* country.

Tara, *tarbh,* bulls.

Tara, *dá-tharbh,* not given.

Tara, *teamhair,* a residence on an elevated spot commanding an extensive prospect/view, a lofty place or a conspicuous place.

Tara, *Teamh-air,* the wall of Tea (wife of Heremon).

Tara, *teamhair-na-Ríogh,* not given.

Tara, *teamhrach,* not given.

Tara, the assembly place.

Taraglin, *targlainn,* not given.

Taravan, *tSearbhán,* dandelion/s.

Tarbert, *tairbeart,* an isthmus or a neck of land.

Tarbert, *tairbert, tairbheirt,* the peninsula or isthmus.

Tardree, *taimhreidh,* rough land.

Tardree, *t-ard-fraeigh,* the height of the heather.

Tarf, *tarbh,* bulls.

Tarf, *thairbh, tarbh, tairbh,* a bull.

Tariff, *tarbh,* the bull.

Tarkin, *torcain,* a young boar.

Tarmin, *tearmainn,* sanctuary or glebe land.

Tarmon, *tearmon, tearmann,* Church/glebe land, a refuge or sanctuary.

Tarramud, *tearmand,* Church land.

Tarrif, *tairbh,* the bull.

Tarrif, *thairbh, tarbh, tairbh,* a bull.

Tarriff, *tairbh,* the bull or bulls.

Tarriv, *tarbh,* the bull.

Tarry, *thairbh, tarbh, tairbh,* a bull.

Tarsaghaun, from *tarsainn,* the the little threshold.

Tarsaghaun, *tarsachán,* not given.

Tarsan, *tarsainn,* the threshold.

Tarsany, *tarsna,* a cross in land or crossroads.

Tarsna, *tarsna, across,* across, a cross in land or crossroads.

Tarsney, *tarsna, across,* transverse, a cross in land or crossroads.

Tart, *tart,* the place or house site.

Tartan, *Tartain,* St Tartan.

Tartan, *tortán,* a small knoll, tummock or high turf bank.

Tartan, *tuartain,* a knoll.

Tartaraghan, *tartrachán,* not given.

Tartna, *tart-na...,* site of the...

Tarve, *tairbh,* the bull.

Tarve, *tarbh,* bulls.

Tasha, *taise,* a ghost.

Tashinny, *teach-Sinche,* not given.

Tashinny, *teach-Sinigh,* St Shineach's Church.

Task, *tSeasc,* not given.

Task, *tSeisce,* sedge or coarse grass.

Taska, *teasgadh,* tree felling.

Taskin, *tSeiscinn,* a marsh.

Tass, *teas,* southern.

Tassagard, *teach-Sacra,* Sarca's house.

Tassagh, *teasach,* the cataract.

Tassagh, *teasach-thriúcha,* not given.

Tassan, *t-assan,* little cataract waterfall.

Tassan, *tEasán,* not given.

Tassona, *tSasanaig, tSasanaigh,* protestants or Englishmen.

Tassonig, *t-sasanaigh, t-assonaig,* Englishman/men or Protestant/s.

Tassonig, *tSasanaigh,* the Englishman.

Tat, *tate, tath,* a measurment of land (60 acres).

Tate, *táite,* not given.

Tate, *tate,* a measurment of land.

Tateetragh, *an-táite-íochtarach,* not given.

Tath, *tate, tath,* a measurment of land (60 acres).

Tatna, *táite/taite-na...,* land

Tattena, *taite-na...*, land measurment of the...measurment of the...

Tattin, *táite-an...*, not given.

Tattina, *taite-na...*, land measurment of the...

Tattina, *taite-na...*, not given.

Tattraconnaghty, *tait-raith-Chonnachtaigh*, land measurment of the rath of the Connaughtman.

Tatty, *táite, tate, tath*, a measurment of land (60 acres).

Tatty, *tate, taite, tath*, a measurment of land (60 acres).

Tattyna, *taite-na...*, measurment of the...

Taudurie, *t-saighdura*, soldiers.

Taugh, *teach, tech*, a house.

Taugh, territory.

Taula, St Tola.

Taun, *táin*, herds.

Taun, *tamhnach*, a green field which produces fresh sweet grass.

Taun, *tSeáin*, not given.

Taur, *teamhair*, a conspicusus place.

Taur, *teamhair*, a residence on an elevated spot commanding an extensive prospect/view.

Taur, *tura, teamhair-luachra/Éireann*, not given.

Taura, *teamhrach*, a high wide viewing station or a high fort.

Tava, *tSamha, tSamhaidh, tSamhaigh*, sorrel.

Tavan, *tamhain*, the trunk, stock or pole.

Tavana, *tamhnaigh*, a green field.

Tavana, *taobh-na...*, not given.

Tavanagh, *tamhnach*, a green field which produces fresh sweet grass.

Tavenahy, *tamhnach*, a green field.

Tavish, *tSamhais*, sorrel.

Tavna, *tamhnach*, a field.

Tavna, *tamhnaigh*, a green field.

Tavnagh, *tamhnach*, a field.

Tavnagh, *tamhnach*, a green field which produces fresh sweet grass.

Tavnaghan, *tamhnachán, tamhnachan*, little green or fertile field.

Tavnauchan, *tamhnachán*, little green field.

Tavnaugh, *tamhnach*, a field.

Tavnaughan, *tamhnachán*, little green field.

Tavney, *tamhnach*, a field.

Tavran, from *teamhair*, a little residence on an elevated spot commanding an extensive prospect/view.

Tavraun, from *teamhair*, a little residence on an elevated spot commanding an extensive prospect/view.

Tavraun, *tSamhráin*, Samhran or Samhran, a personal or family name.

Tavy, *a'tsamhaidh*, the sorrel.

Tavy, *tamhnach*, a green field.

Taw, *tSamhaigh, tSamhaidh*, sorrel.

Tawa, *tSamhaidh, tSamha, samhadh*, sorrel.

Tawan, *tamhan, tamhain*, a block or tree trunk.

Tawen, *tamhain*, a stake, trunk or stock.

Tawin, *tamhain*, the stump.

Tawlaght, *tamhlacht, tamlagth, taimhleacht*, a plague grave, monument or burial ground.

Tawly, *tamhlaght*, a plague grave.

Tawna, *tamhain-na...*, not given.

Tawna, *tamhnach-na...*, field of the...

Tawna, *tamhnaigh, tamhnach*, a green field which produces fresh sweet grass.

Tawnagh, *an-tamhnaigh*, not given.

Tawnagh, *tamhnach*, a cultivated spot.

Tawnagh, *tamhnach*, a green field which produces fresh sweet grass.

Tawnana, *tamhnach-na...*, field of the...

Tawnana, *tamhnaigh-na...*, not given.

Tawnies, *tamhnaighe*, green fields.

Tawnies, tamhnach, a fertile spot in bad land or a green field.

Tawny, *tamhnaí*, not given.

Tawny, *tannach*(sic)-*a'...*, field of the...

Tawny, *tamhnaigh*, a field, green field or a cultivated spot.

Tawny, *tamhnaigh, tamhnach*, a green field that produces fresh sweet grass.

Tawny, *tamhnaigh...*, cultivated spot of the... or clearing of the...

Tawnyna, *tamhnaigh-na...*, field of the...

Tawragh, *teamhair*, a residence on an elevated spot commanding an extensive prospect/view.

Tawragh, *teamhrach*, a conspicuous residence on a hill.

Tawran, from *teamhair,* a little residence on an elevated spot commanding an extensive prospect/view.

Tawy, *tSamhaidh, tSamhaid, tSamha, samhadh,* sorrel.

Tay, *Taoi, tae, téig, téa,* not given.

Tay, *te, té,* tea.

Tay, *toe,* the silent one.

Taylor, *táilliúra,* the tailor.

Te, *teach, tigh,* a house.

Tea, *tín,* little.

Tead, *teide,* a flat topped hill.

Teadies, from *teide,* flat topped hills.

Teadies, *teadaí,* not given.

Tealy, St Sheila.

Tealy, *Téile, Tíle, Tíl* or St Síle.

Tealy, *tSíle, Síle,* a personal name.

Tean, *tSiadhain,* foxglove.

Tean, *tSiadhean,* a fairy mount.

Teana, *tSeánaigh,* not given.

Teane, *tSidheáin, tSiadháin, a fairy mount/hill or palace.*

Teane, *tSiain, a fairy mound.*

Teane, *tSiain, tSidheáin, foxglove/s also known as fairy thimbles.*

Teangue, *a long strip or tongue.*

Tearaght, *an-tiaracht, the buttock.*

Teaun, *tSiadhain, tSiadhain, a fairy mount, hill or palace.*

Tebrien, *tíghe Bhriain,* Brian's house.

Tecolm, St Colm's house.

Teconet, house of the Connaught settler.

Tedagh, *teideach,* a flat topped hill.

Tedane, *seidán,* quick sand.

Tedane, *téadáin, tSéideáin,* not given.

Tedane, *t-séadáin,* puffing or blowing.

Tedaun, *tSéideáin,* breeze or breezy.

Tedavnet, *tigh-Damhnata, teach-Damhnat,* not given.

Tedd, *teide,* a flat topped hill.

Tedery, *tSudaire,* tanners.

Tee, a fairy hill.

Tee, *taobh,* the side.

Tee, *taobh, tigh, tígh,* a house.

Tee, *tí,* marking(sic).

Tee, *Tiúigh, Tighe, an-tSí,* not given.

Teeaan(sic), *tSiadhain,* foxglove.

Teean, *tSiadhain, tSiáin, tSiain,* foxglove.

Teean, *tSiodháin, tSiodhain, a fairy mount, hill.*

Teeaun, *tSiadhain, tSiáin, tSiadháin, a fairy mount, hill or palace.*

Teeaun, *tSidheáin,* not given.

Teedan, *tSéideán,* gusts.

Teehill, *cnoc-an-tí,* not given.

Teel, *t-Siadhail, Siadhail, Shiel, a male name.*

Teel, *tSiail, Shaohal or Sial, a personal or family name.*

Teel, *tSíle, St Síle,* Sheila.

Teelin, *teileann,* a dish.

Teelin, *teilann,* not given.

Teely, *Tíle, Tíl, a personal or family name and the founder of a Church in Limerick.*

Teely, *tSíle, Síle, a personal name.*

Teemore, *tighe-móir,* the great house.

Teen, *tigh-na,* at a beginning of a word means the house of....

Teen, *tSiadain,* the foxglove.

Teen, *tín,* little.

Teen, *(Gorteenteen) tinn,* sore.

Teena, *tigh-na...,* house of the...

Teenah, *taoidhne, a mill stream or pond.*

Teenoe, *tí/tigh-nua,* new house.

Teenoe, *tSiadhain, a fairy mount or palace.*

Teentallin, *tighe-an-tsailainn, house of the salt.*

Teeny, *tiní,* little.

Teer, *saer,* a carpenter, builder.

Teer, *tír,* land, country, territory or district.

Teer, *tSaeir,* a carpenter.

Teer, *tSaoir,* a craftsman.

Teera, *Tiaraigh,* not given.

Teera, *tiara,* the back part(sic).

Teera, *tír-a'..., district of the...*

Teera, *tire,* the land.

Teeragh, *tíreachas,* colonization.

Teeran, *tír-an...,* district of the...

Teeranea, *tír-an-fhia,* not given.

Teeranearagh, *trian(sic)-iartach,* not given.

Teeravane, *tíorabháin,* not given.

Teere, *tíre,* not given.

Teerna, *tigherna,* belonging to the chieftain.

Teerna, *tír-na...,* land, district or territory of the...

Teernacreeve, *tír-da-craebh,* district of the two sacred trees.

Teernea, *tír-néidh,* windy district.

Teeronan, *tír-tónán,* western land or back land.

Teery, *tire,* the district.

Teeskagh, *teasgadh,* cutting trees.

Teev, *taebh,* a side of a hill.

Teeva, *taobh-an…,* not given.

Teevan, *taobháin,* not given.

Teevaun, *taobháin,* a side of a hill.

Teeve, *taebh,* a side of a hill.

Teevena, *taobh-na…,* a side of the…

Teevna, *taobh-na…,* a side of the…

Teevoge, *Taebhóg,* St Taobhohg-Ni-Duibheannaigh, the virgin saint.

Teevogue, *Taobhóg,* not given.

Teevy, *taoibhe,* a hillside.

Teeworker, *taobh-urchair,* side of the cast.

Tegall, *tSeagail,* not given.

Tegan, *Tadhgain, Tagan,* a male name.

Tegan, *Tadhgáin, Tegan,* a personal or family name.

Tegan, *Tagáin,* Tecan, a contemporary of St Patrick.

Tegan, *Taidhgín,* little Teige or Tegan, a personal name.

Tegan, *Téagáin,* St Téagán, Tegan.

Tegan, *Téagáin, Tagáin, not given.*

Teggal, *tSeagail,* rye.

Teggart, *an-sagairt,* of the priest.

Teggle, *tSeagail,* rye.

Tegin, *Taidhgín,* not given.

Tehelly, *tech-Thelle,* house of St Telle.

Teia, *Théighe,* not given.

Teia, *tSeighe,* wild deer.

Teig, *Tadhg,* Tague, not given.

Teige, *dTadhg,* Tiege, a nickname of the west Cork Sullivans.

Teige, *mhic-Thaidhg,* a personal or family name.

Teige, *Taidhg, Thaidhg,* Taidg, a mans name.

Teige, Teige or Timothy, a male name.

Teige, *Thaidhg,* Teague, a personal name.

Teige, *tigh,* a house.

Teige, *Uí-Thaidhg/Teige,* Teige, Ó Taidhg or O'Teige, a family name.

Teigeroe, Red Teige or Timothy, a male name.

Teigh, *te, tae,* tea.

Telawn, *tulláin,* a hillock.

Telaydan, *tigh-Léadáin,* not given.

Tell, Shaohal, a personal or family name.

Tella, *tola, tulach,* a hill, sometimes a small hill.

Tellan, *Diolain,* Dillon, a personal or family name.

Tellan, *Teileáin,* not given.

Tellan, *Tialláin,* Tillán, a personal or family name.

Tellian, *Tealláin,* Teallán, Tealláin or Teallan, a personal name.

Telton, *Taílltenn,* Tailltenn, a female name.

Teltown, *Tailltenn,* the fair of 'Taillte' a Spanish princess and also a place that was named after her.

Teltown, *Tailtean,* Taillte's (see above) place.

Teltown, *Tailtin, Tailteann,* not given.

Temora, *Temora,* not given.

Tempan, *tiompain,* a standing stone or a tall round hill.

Tempan, *tiompan,* a hillock.

Tempanroe, *tiompan-roe,* red hillock.

Tempin, *tiompan,* a small abrupt hill, a hillock or a standing stone.

Templan, *tSeampláin,* Semplán, the name of a Church founder in Limerick.

Templastragh, *teampall-Lasrach,* Lasair's Church.

Temple, *teampuill, teampall, teampaill, teampoll, teampull,* a Church.

Templeastragh, *teampull-Lasrach,* St Laisre's Church.

Templena, *teampall/teampull-na…,* Church of the…

Templeogue, *teach-Mealóg*(sic), St Maolog's Church.

Templeogue, *teach-Mealóg/Maológ,* Maológ's (a personal or family name) house.

Templeogue, *tigh-Mallóg,* not given.

Templeusque, *teampull-loiscthe,* burnt Church.

Tempo, *an-tIompódh-deisil,* not given.

Tempo, *t-iompodh, tIompú, tIompó,* turning.

Tempo, *tIompu, tiompú (deiseal),* a right handed turn.

Ten, *tigh-na,* the house of…

Tena, *tigh-na,* the house of…

Tenagh, *teanach,* a hill.

Tenan, *síonán,* a breeze.

Tenan, *tSenain, tSeanáin,* Seanán, a male name.

Tenanlea, *Senán-liath,* St Senán.

Tenanlea, *Senán-liath, tSenain-leith,* St Senán/Senan the hoary.

Tenant, *teannail,* ceremonial.

Tendry, *tSeandruadh,* the old druid.

Teneh, *tigh-na,* the house of the….

Teneil, *teine-aoil,* a lime kiln.

Teneil, *teiníl,* not given.

Tenna, *tigh-na…,* house of the…

Tennell, *Senchill, tSinchill,* St Sinchill, Sinchell.

Tenny, *teine,* fire.

Tenny, *toinne,* not given.

Tenny, *tuine,* flood.

Tent, *teinte,* fires.

Tentore, *tigh-an-tuair,* house of the nleach green.

Tentore, *teach-an-túr,* tower house.

Tents, *dTeine,* fires.

Ter, *tir,* land.

Teragh, *tirach…,* district of the…

Teraverty, *tír-Raifeartaigh,* not given.

Terenure, *tir-an-iubhair, tír-an-Iúir,* land, territory of the yew.

Terenure, *tor-Fhionnabhra,* not given.

Terin, *tSoirn,* not given.

Terman, *tearmann,* Church land.

Termon, *tarmon, tearmainn, tearmann,* Church land, santuary or sanctuary land.

Termon, *tearmonn,* not given.

Tern, *turainn,* not given.

Terna, *tighearna,* landlord.

Terna, *tir-na…,* district of …

Ternan, *tearmann,* a sanctuary.

Ternan, *Thiarnáin, Tiarnáin,* St Tiarnáin/ Tiarnán/Tiarnan.

Terr, *tír,* land or territory.

Terra, *doire,* oaks.

Terra, *t-siorragh, searrach,* foal/s.

Terra, *tSiorraigh,* a colt.

Terrela, *Toirdhealbhach,* Turlogh, a male name.

Terrif, *tairbh,* a bull.

Terriff, *thairbh, tarbh, tairbh,* a bull.

Terrila, Turlogh or Terlagh, a male name.

Terry, *doire,* an oak wood.

Terry, *thairbh, tarbh, tairbh,* a bull.

Terry, *tír, tir,* land.

Terry, *tír-na…,* land of the…

Terry, *tir-da…,* territory of the two…...

Terry, *tir-dhá/da…,* the land of the two…...

Terry, *tSiorraigh, tSearraigh,* the foal.

Terryglass, *tír/tír-dhá-ghlas,* land, territory of the two streams.

Terryland, *tír-oileáin,* not given.

Terrysstang(sic), *stang-an-Tiaraigh,* not given.

Tervoe, *tír-Bhú,* land of Bú, not given.

Tervoe, *tir-bhugha,* district of the blue plant 'bugh'.

Tervoe, *tír-mhaighe,* not given.

Teskill, *tSoisgeil,* the Gospel.

Teskin, *sescenn, t-scescenn,* a marsh/morass.

Teskin, *t-seiscin,* marsh grass.

Teskin, *tSeiscinn, tSeiscenn, tSeiscin,* not given.

Teskin, *t-uisce-finn,* clear water.

Teskinny, *tSeiscine,* the marsh.

Tethmoy, *tuath-da-mhagh,* district of the two plains.

Tetoppa, *taobh-tapach,* not given.

Tevane, *taobhain,* a stave or beam.

Tevdilla, *tSeimhdile,* the beetle.

Tevraun, from *Teamhair,* a little residence on an elevated spot commanding an extensive prospect/view.

Tevrin, *teamhairín,* a little hill.

Tevrin, *teamhrín,* a little residence on an elevated spot commanding an extensive prospect, view or a conspicuous hillock.

Thabowel, *Tiobóld,* Theobald, a male name.

Thaneel, *tine-aoileach,* a lime kiln.

Thawrla, *teamhair,* high spot commanding a wide view.

Thee, *dTigheadh,* houses.

Thee, *Tuí,* not given.

Thee, *tuighe,* straw or sedge.

They, *teitheadh,* fleeing/flight.

Thina, *tine,* fire.

Thirigy, *tSioraig,* the foal.

Thirigy, *tSiorraidh,* a blast or cold appearance.

Thogill, *t-seagail*, rye.

Thomond, *Thuamhan*, not given.

Thomond, *tuadh–Mumain*, north Munster.

Thonlagee, *tóin-le-gaoith*, not given.

Thonoge, *tonóg*, little hole.

Thonuv, *t-sonnbha*, the paling.

Thoo, *tuat, tuaith*, a district.

Thoohill, *tuathail*, left handed.

Thorpen, *torpain*, a cluster.

Thoul, *thuathail*, not given.

Thoumona, *tuaim-móna*, tumulus of the bog.

Thoumpol, *teampull*, a Church.

Thoun, *ton*, wave.

Thour, *tuar*, a bleach green.

Thoureen, *tóirthín*, a little tower.

Thoureen, *tuarín*, little bleach green.

Thread, *troid*, a battle or fight.

Threan, *trian*, a third.

Thubbrid, *tubraid*, a well.

Thule, *Tuathail*, Thoohal, Tuathal or Toole, a male name.

Thullaun, *tulan*, a small hill.

Thum, *tom*, a thicket.

Thunna, *t-sonaigh*, a rampart.

Thunna, *tSonnaigh*, entrenchments.

Thur, *dur*, strong.

Thur, *tor*, a bush.

Thur, *túr*, a tower.

Thurfune, *túrfion*, white tower.

Thurles, *durlias, durlais, durlas-Éile*, not given.

Thurles, *durlas, dur-lios*, the strong fort.

Thurles, *durlas*, the stronghold(sic).

Thurlisk, *thurluisc*, oak.

Thurliss, *Durlas, dur-lios*, the strong fort.

Thying, *doimhin*, deep.

Ti, *teach, tigh*, a house.

Tia, *teach, tigh*, a house.

Tiagh, ...*tach*, (as an ending to a word) a place of.... or abounding in...

Tian, *tSiain, foxglove*.

Tiaquin, *teach-Dáchonna, tigh-Dáchonna/ Dachonna*, house of St Dáchonna/ Dachonna.

Tibber, *tobar*, a spring, well.

Tibbera, *tiobraid*, a spring.

Tibberaghny, *tiobraid-Fhachtna*, St Fachtna's (a personal or family name) well.

Tibberaghny, *tigh-Braichne*, House of st Braichne.

Tibberaghny, *tiobra-Fhachna*, not given.

Tibberedoge, *tiobraid-óg*, the little well.

Tibbot, *Tiobóid*, Tibbot, a personal or family name.

Tibohine, *tigh-Baoithín*, St Baoithín/ Baothan's Church or house.

Tibret, *tiobrad, tiobrat*, a spring, well.

Tic, *teach, tigh*, a house.

Ticall, *tighe-Cathail*, Cahill's (a personal or family name) house.

Ticarbat, *feadha-car-bait*, chariot wood.

Tick, *tine*, bones(sic).

Tick, *tigh*, a house.

Ticknick, *tigh-chnuic*, house of the hill.

Ticknock, *tigh-an-chnuic*, not given.

Ticknock, *tigh-chnuic*, house of the hill.

Ticlare, *tighe-cléire*, the priests house.

Ticor, *tigh-Corr*, not given.

Tier, *tír*, land, territory or district.

Tier, *tuar*, a bleaching green.

Tiere, *tír*, land, territory or district.

Tiermore, *tír-Uí-Mhórdha*, O'Moore's (a personal or family name) country.

Tierna, *Tiarna*, St Tiarnach.

Tierna, *tiarna*, not given.

Tierna, *Tighearnaigh, Tierna, Tigernach*, a 1st cent Ulster King.

Tierna, *tigherna, tighearna*, a lord.

Tierna, *Tighernach*, St Tierna.

Tierna, *Tighernach, Tigernaigh, Tighernach Tetbannach*, an *ancient King of Munster*.

Tierny, *dTighearnaigh*, lords.

Tieva, *taobh-an*..., not given.

Tieve, *taebh-a'*..., the hillside of the...

Tieve, *taobh, taebh*, the side or the hillside.

Tieve, *taobh*, the side, hillside or district.

Tieve, *taobh-a'*..., side of the...

Tieve, *tuighe*, rushes (for thatching).

Tieveleny, *taobh-an-léana*, not given.

Tievena, *taebh-na*..., the hillside of the...

Tigeen, *Thaidhgín*, little Teige, a male name.

Tiggle, *tSeagail*, rye.

Tigore, *tigh-gabhar*, the goats house.

Tigroe, *tigh-rua*, not given.

Tigue, *Thaidhg,* Thady, a male name.

Tikin, *tigh-chinn…,* house at the head of ….

Tikincor, *tigh-ceann-coradh, tigh-cinn-coraidh/chora,* house at the head of the weir.

Tiknock, *tigh-an-chnoic, tigh-chnuic,* house of the hill.

Tildarg, red land.

Tilister, *tSiolastair,* flaggers.

Tillahan, *tSaileacháin,* a place of sallows.

Tillan, *tulán-na…,* mound of the…

Tillane, *tSaileacháin,* sallows.

Tillane, *tSeithleáin,* a channel.

Tillane, *tSilleáin,* of the dropping/watery sloping land.

Tillane, *tSiolláin,* St Sellan.

Tillaun, *t-Sileáin, tSileáin,* water trickling.

Tillaun, *tSilláin,* watery or water trickling.

Tilleene, *Daitlin,* a male name.

Tillid, *tSeilide,* snails.

Tillida, *tSeilide,* snails.

Tillig, *teilig,* a lime tree.

Tilliha, *Teille,* St Telle.

Tilliha, *Tuilithe,* not given.

Tillister, *tSeileastair, tSoileastair,* not given.

Tilloge, *tSaileóge,* sallows.

Tilly, *teaghlaigh, teaghlach,* household or family.

Tim, *tuaim,* a grave, burial ground.

Timard, *tomard, tuimard,* the high bush.

Timeeighter, *tom-iochtair,* lower mound.

Timeighter, *tuaim-íochtair/iachtair,* lower burial mound.

Timeighter, *tuaim-íochtair,* not given.

Timmon, *Díomáin,* Diomán, a personal or family name.

Timon, *diamáin,* fruitful.

Timon, *Díomáin, Diomain,* Diamain, a personal or family name.

Timon, *Díomain, Diomain,* Dimon, a personal or family name.

Timon, *tSiomóin,* Simon, a male name.

Timoney, *thuaim/tuaim-Eabhna,* not given.

Timoney, *tigh-muine,* the house of the shrubbery.

Timpan, *tiompáin,* not given.

Timpan, *tiompan,* a small abrupt hill, a pointed little hill, a hillock or a standing stone.

Timpany, *tiompanach,* hillocks.

Timpany, *Atimpanaig,* Mc Atimpaney, a personal or family name.

Timpany, *tiompanaigh,* a standing stone or a round peaked hill.

Timpaun, *tiompan,* a small abrupt hill, a hillock or a standing stone.

Timullen, *tigh-an-mhuilinn,* not given.

Tin, *tigh/tigh-an, tighe-an…,* the house of the…

Tin, (Tincashel) *tinne,* a hill.

Tin, *t-sein…,* the old…

Tina, *tigh-an…,* the house of/on/by the…

Tina, *tigh-na…,* house of …

Tinagh, *tSnamh,* swimming.

Tinagh, *tnátha(sic),* not given.

Tinagh, *tuinne,* a shaking bog.

Tinahely, *tigh-na-hÉille,* house of the thong.

Tinahely, *tigh-na-hÉille/hEilighe,* house of the river Ely.

Tinahy, *t-Sinche,* St Sinchea.

Tinan, *Teimhneáin,* not given.

Tinary, *tamhnaigh-Airí,* not given.

Tine, *sidhean,* a fairy mount/hill.

Tine, *taoidhne,* a mill stream or pond.

Tine, *tom, tuaim,* a bush.

Tine, *tSiain,* foxglove.

Tineel, *tiníle,* not given.

Tineel, *tornoige,* a lime kiln.

Tineen, from *teine,* little fire.

Tinehely, *tigh-na-hÉilighe,* house of the little river called 'Ely'.

Tinhea, *Tillithe,* Telle, a male name.

Tinie, *tine,* fire.

Tinlis, *t-sein-lis,* the old fort.

Tinn, *tigh-an…,* the house of the…

Tinna, *tigh-na….* house of/on/by the…

Tinna, *tinne,* a hill.

Tinnahinch, *tuath-Uí-Riagáin,* not given.

Tinne, *tigh-na…,* the house of…

Tinne, *tonnaigh,* a mound.

Tinneel, *tein-aoil, teine-aeil,* a lime kiln.

Tinnenaire, *tigh-na-n-ár,* house of the slaughters.

Tinnick, *tigh-chnuic,* house of the hill.

Tinnies, *d'Teine,* fires.

Tinnig, *tSionnaig,* the fox.

Tinnig, *tSonnaig,* not given.

Tinnole, *tionóil,* the assembly.

Tinnole, *tionóla,* not given.

Tinny, *aiteann,* furze.

Tinny, *taine, teine,* a fire, a fire light from marsh gas/rotten wood or light from a jack-o-the-lantern.

Tinny, *teine, tine,* fire.

Tinny, *tigh-na...,* house of the...

Tinny, *tinne, toinne,* not given.

Tinny, *tSionnaigh,* Sionnach or Fox, a persons name.

Tinny, *tSionnaigh, tSionnach,* a fox.

Tinny, *tuinne,* a quagmire.

Tinnyweel, *teine-aeil,* a lime kiln.

Tinock, *tigh-an-chnoic,* not given.

Tinode, *tigh-an-fhóid,* not given.

Tinshera, *tSinnsir,* the ancestor.

Tintagh, *teinnteach,* not given.

Tintagh, *teinteach,* a place of fires.

Tinteragh, *teinntreach,* not given.

Tintern, *cinn-eich,* not given.

Tintern, named after Tintern abbey in Wales, the Irish name is *mainister-chinn-eich,* monastery of the horses head.

Tintin, from *teine,* little fire.

Tintine, *tigh-an-toim,* not given.

Tintine, *tigh-tinn,* the sick house.

Tintore, *tigh-an-tuair,* house of the bleach green.

Tinty, *teintrighe,* lightning.

Tinty, *tinte, teinte, d'Teine,* fires.

Tinure, *tigh-an-iúir,* not given.

Tinvane, *tigh-an-mheáin,* not given.

Tioge, *Teog, Teog/Teoc,* a personal or family name.

Tioge, *Tíog, Teoc,* Tiog, Teoc or Tioc, a male name.

Tiogue, *Téog,* not given.

Tipper, *tiobraid, tobar,* a well or spring.

Tipper, *tiopar,* not given.

Tipperary, *tiobraid-Árainn, thiobraid-Arainn,* house of the well of Ara(sic).

Tipperary, *tiobraid-Árann, tiobraidh-arann,* the well of Ara, an ancient territory.

Tir, *tir, tír,* district, land or territory.

Tira, *tír-an/a'...,* district of the...

Tirahan, *tír-athan,* not given.

Tiran, *tir-an...,* district of the...

Tiranascragh, *tír-chinn-eascrach,* land of the head of the esker.

Tiraun, *torán, tireán,* not given.

Tiravera, *tír-ramhar,* not given.

Tiravray, *tír-Bhreithimh,* not given.

Tiredigan, *tír-Roideagáin,* not given.

Tireragh, *tír/tir-Fhiachrach,* Fiachra's district.

Tireragh, *tír-Fhiachraigh,* land or territory of chieftain Fiachra O'Dowd.

Tirerill, *tír-Ailealla,* not given.

Tirerril, *Tir-Oliolla,* Olioll's district.

Tirgan, *torgan,* a small tower.

Tirinchinan, *tír-na-hIníne*(sic), not given...., not given.

Tirkeeran, *tir-mic-Caerthainn,* territory of Caerthann.

Tirm, *tirim,* dried.

Tirna, *tír/tir-na...,* territory, district or land of the...

Tirnahinch, *tír-Choininse*(sic), not given.

Tirnamona, *tír-Ó-Mónáin*(sic), not given.

Tirnanneill, *tír-Ní-Néill,* not given.

Tirnea, *tir-nDeaghaidh,* Dea's (a personal or family name) district.

Tiroe, *tí-rua, tigh-rua/ruadh,* red house.

Tironaun, *tir-O-nDán,* O'Daon's or O'Dan's (family names) district.

Tiroory, Rory's house.

Tirra, *tuireadh,* towers.

Tirriff, *tairbh,* the bull.

Tirrig, *t-siorraidh,* a blast, breeze.

Tirrig, *tSiorraigh,* the foal.

Tirriv, *tairbh,* the bull.

Tirrough, *tigh-ruadh,* red house.

Tirry, *tSiorragh, searrach,* foal/s.

Tirur, *tir-ur,* green or fresh land.

Tisaran, *tigh-Sarain,* the house of St Saran.

Tishaughlin, *thí-Seachlainn*(sic), not given.

Tithewer, *tigh-an-tuair,* house of the bleach green.

Titoppy, *taobh-Tapaigh,* not given.

Titoppy, *tighe-Tapaigh,* Toppy's (a personal or a family name) house.

Tivannagh, *taobhanna,* not given.

Tivna, *taobh-na…,* side of the…

Tivna, *tSuibhne,* Sweeney, a personal or family name and also the name of the founder of the Church of Kiltivna in Galway.

Tivnan, *Uí-Tiomhnain,* O'Tivnan, a family name.

Tivoli, *tigh-Folaigh,* not given.

Tivrin, *Tibhrinn,* not given.

Tlaba, *tSlabaigh,* Slabhach, not given.

Tlaghtan, *slochdán,* a hole or pit.

Tlavan, *tSleamháin,* not given.

Tlavin, *tSleamhain,* elms.

Tlea, *tle*(sic), a mountainside.

Tlea, *tSléibhe, tSleibhe,* a mountain.

Tleave, *tSléibhe,* a mountain.

Tleva, *tSleibhe,* a mountain.

Tleva, *tSléibhe,* not given.

Tlevy, *tSleibhe,* a mountain.

Tlieve, *t-sléibhe,* moorland(sic).

Tlieve, *tSléibhe, tSleibhe,* a mountain.

Tlisny, *tSlisnigh,* not given.

Tlisny, *tSlisnighe, tSlisne,* the beetle.

Tloe, *t'sluagh,* an army.

Tloe, *tSluaigh,* the host.

Tlooig, *tSlauig,* the host or army.

Tloukan, *tSleabhacán,* the marine plant 'porphyra vulgaris'.

Tloukane, *tSleabcáin,* an edible seaweed.

Tloukaun, *tSleabhacán,* the marine plant 'porphyra vulgaris'

Tloura, *tSlabhra,* the chain.

Tlowig, *tSluaigh,* assembly, hosting or the host.

Tloy, *tSluaigh,* the host.

Tlucky, *tSlogaidhe,* a swallow hole.

Tluggera, *…a-tSlugaure/tSlogaire,* …of the swallow hole.

Tluggig, *tSlogaidhe,* a swallow hole.

Tnaght, *tSnechta,* snow.

Tnave, *t-snamha,* of the swimming.

Tnaw, *t-snaith,* a narrow path.

Toames, *tuaim,* a mound.

Toames, *tuamacha,* not given.

Toan, *tóin,* back, rear.

Toanragee, *tóin-re-gaoith,* bottom to the wind.

Tobarna, *tobar-na…,* well of the…

Tobber, *tobar, tobhar,* a well.

Tobbers, *toibreacha,* wells.

Tobeen, *Tóibin,* Tobin, a personal or family name.

Tobeen, *Tóibínigh,* not given.

Tober, *tobair, tiobrad, tobar,* a well.

Tobera, *tobar-a'/an…,* well of the…

Toberadora, *tiobraid-an-fheorainn*(sic), not given.

Toberadora, *tiobrad-an-deóra,* well of the tear or teardrop.

Toberadora,

Toberaheena, *tobar-Thaoine,* not given.

Toberan, *tobar-an…,* well of the…

Toberanashig, *tobar-na-bhFaoiteac,* the vomiting well.

Toberdan, *tobardán,* the little well.

Tobereen, *tobairín,* little well.

Tobereen, *tobar-Rí-an…,* well of the King of…

Toberna, *tobar-na…,* well of the…

Tobernafauna(sic), *tobar-Afána,* not given.

Tobernea, *tobar-an-fhiadh/Naithi,* not given.

Toberreen, *tobar-Righ-an…* well of the king of…

Tobet, *Tioboid,* Theobald, a personal name.

Tobin, *tóba,* burdock.

Tobin, *Tóibínigh,* not given.

Tobit, *Tioboid,* Theobald or Tibbot, a personal name.

Tobradan, *tobardán,* the little well.

Tobran, *tobar-an…* well of the…

Tocher, a causeway.

Tocker, *tacair,* of the pickings.

Toe, *Teo, tuaithe,* not given.

Toe, *Tó, Tó,* a personal or family name.

Toe, *tuaith,* north.

Toem, *tuaim, tóm,* a mound.

Togan, *Tógán,* not given.

Toggurt, *t-sagairt,* priest.

Togh, *teach,* a house.

Togher, *tachar,* a battle or skirmish.

Togher, *tóchar, tóchair, tóchuir, togher,* a causeway or a path-through a bog.

Toghereen, *tocharín,* a little causeway.

Togherna, *tochar-na…,* causeway of the…

Toghill, *Uí-Thuathail,* Ó Tuathal, a family name.

Tighter, *tochair,* a causeway.

Togle, *thógála,* a tomb.

Toher, *tóchair,* a causeway.

Tohig, *Eochaidh,* Eochy, a personal or family name.

Tohil, *Uí-Thuathail, Uí-Tuathail,* O'Tohil, O'Tuohill or O'Toole, a family name.

Tohill, *Thuathail, Tuathail,* Tuathal or Toohal, a mans name.

Tohill, *tuáthail,* lying at the left hand side(sic).

Toinnahaha, *tom*(sic)*-na-hAithe,* knoll of the kiln.

Toinriac, the bottom of the marsh.

Toirbirt, *tairbeart,* not given.

Toirc, *toirc,* a bull.

Toke, *tSeabhaic,* the hawk.

Toker, *tóchar, tóchair, togher,* a causeway, a path-through a bog.

Tole, *'tostail,* blundering or bad luck.

Tole, *Tuathail,* Tole, Toole, Tuathal or Tuathail, a family name.

Tole, *tuthail,* the sun(sic).

Tolka, (river) *an-tolca,* not given.

Tollohe, *tulach,* a mound summit.

Tollum, *talamh...,* land of the...

Tollus, *solas,* light/s.

Tolly, *tulaigh,* a hillock, a large hillock or a hill.

Tom, *tom,* a bush.

Tom, *tonn,* a quagmire or a wave.

Tom, *tuaim,* a tumulus, grave.

Toma, *Toma, Toma,* a female name.

Toma, *tom-a'...,* bush of the...

Toma, *tom-an...,* knoll(sic) of the...

Toma, *tuaim-a'...,* the tomb or burial mound of...

Toman, *tuaim-an...,* tomb or burial mound of the...

Tomany, *tomanaighe,* a place of bushes.

Tomany, *tomnaigh,* not given.

Tomanyan, *tomanaighe-an...,* bushy place of the...

Tomb, *tuaim,* a tumulus, grave.

Tombay, *tuama-beith, tuaim-beithe,* tomb or mound of the birch tree.

Tombeagh, *tuaim-beithe,* burial mound of the birch tree.

Tombrickane, *tuaim-Breacáin,* not given.

Tombrickane, *tuaim-Bricéán,* Brecan's/Brickanes tumulus or mound.

Tomcoyle, *tom-cuill,* hazel thicket.

Tomcoyle, *tuaim-coll,* tomb of the hazel.

Tome, *tóm,* a thicket.

Tome, *tuaim,* a burial mound or tumulus.

Tomhaggard, *teach-Moshagard, tigh-Moshagra,* Moshagra's (a personal or family name) house.

Tomhaggard, *teach-Moshagra,* not given.

Tomies, from *tuaim,* tombs.

Tomies, from *tumaidhe,* monumental mounds.

Tomies, the burial mound.

Tomies, *tóimidhe,* not given.

Tomin, *Toimín,* Tomin a personal or family name.

Tomish, *Tomais, Tomáis,* Thomas or Tomas, a male name.

Tomish, *tSómais,* not given.

Tomna, *tuaim-na...,* tomb or burial mound of the...

Tomogrow, *tomóg-rua/ruadh,* small red heath bushes.

Tomona, *tuaim-móinín,* not given.

Tomona, *tuaim-móna,* tumulus of the bog.

Tomulty, *Tomulty,* a personal or family name.

Ton, *tamhnaigh, tamhnach,* not given.

Ton, *tóin,* the bottom, backside, a thick hill or bottom land.

Ton, *tóin, tón,* bottom land.

Ton, *ton,* low lying land.

Tona, *tamhnach, tomhnach,* a field.

Tona, *tóin,* backside, posterior, also means the bottom.

Tona, *tóna, tóin-na...,* not given.

Tona, *tón,* backside.

Tona, *tona,* low ground or the backside of a hill.

Tona, *tón-an/a'...,* bottom or back of the...

Tona, *tón-an...,* western part of the...

Tona, *tuath-na...,* district of the...

Tonacash, *tónacáis,* not given.

Tonagh, *tamhnach,* a green field which produces fresh sweet grass.

Tonagh, *Tomach*(sic), *tSonnach,* not given.

Tonagh, *tonnach*, a quagmire.

Tonagh, *tonnach, tonaigh*, a rampart.

Tonagimsy, *tamhnaigh-Dhíomasaigh*, not given.

Tonagimsy, *tonnach-'ic-Dhiomasaigh*, rampart of the son of Dempsey.

Tonan, *tóin-an…*, back or bottom land of the…

Tone, bottom land.

Tone, *tón, tóna*, low lying land.

Tonea, *tiathan-fhiodhbhaich*, a wood district.

Toneel, *tóin-aoiligh*, bottom land of the lime.

Toneen, *tóinín*, little paddock.

Toneen, *tuinín*, little bottom land.

Tonelegee, *tón-le-ghaoth*, back to the wind.

Tonet, *tonach*, not given.

Tonet, *tonnait*, wavy.

Toney, *tonnaigh*, a srockade.

Tonga, *teanga*, a tongue of land.

Tonicane, *tonacain*, a slippery place.

Tonin, *tamhnaigh-an…*, not given.

Tonin, *tóin-an…*, back or bottom land of the…

Toniscoffy, *tamhnaigh-Scafaí*, not given.

Tonle, *tóin-le…*, not given.

Tonle, *tóin-le-gaoith*, bottom land facing a stretch of water(sic).

Tonle, *tón-le…, ton-le…*, backside to the…

Tonn, *tonn*, waves.

Tonnagh, *tonaigh*, a rampart.

Tonnagh, *tonnach, tSonnach*, a mound or rampart.

Tonny, *tonaigh, an-tEanach*, a rampart.

Tonny, *tSonnaigh*, not given.

Tonragee, *tóin-re-gaoith*, backside to the wind.

Tonregee, *tóin-re-gaoith, ton-re-gaeith*, backside to the wind or leeward.

Tont, *tonnagh*, a mound.

Tonteeheige, *tóin-tí-Thaidhg, tóin-tighe-Thaidh*, bottom of Tadhg's (a mans name) house.

Tony, *tamhnagh*, a clearing or green field.

Tony, *tamhnaigh*, a field.

Tony, *tamhnaigh, tonnaigh, tamhnaigh-an…*, not given.

Tony, *tonaigh*, a rampart.

Tonyfinnigan, *tamhnaigh-Uí-Fhionnagáin*, not given.

Tonyin, *tamhnaigh-Fhinn*, Finn's (a male name) field.

Too, *samhadh, tSamhaidh*, sorrel.

Too, *tuaith*, a district or territory.

Too, *tuaith*, northern.

Too, *tuath*, a field(sic).

Too, *tuain*(sic), a mound.

Tooa, sorrel.

Tooa, *tuaith*, a district or territory.

Tooa, *tuath, tuaidh*, northern.

Tooan, *tSuain*, sleep.

Toocananagh, *tuath-Canánach*, not given.

Tooda, *Túda*, not given.

Tooda, *Túdaig*, Toode, O'Thudaig, a male name and a family name.

Tooder, *tSúdaire*, a cobbler(sic).

Tooder, *tSudaire*, tanners.

Toodry, *tSudaire*, tanner/s.

Tooera, *tuartha*, green fields.

Tooey, *tSamhaigh*, sorrel.

Tooey, *tuaidh*, northern.

Tooey, *tuaidh*, the district.

Tooey, *tuaithe*, not given.

Tooha, *tuaithe*, not given.

Tooha, *tuath*, north.

Toohil, *tuathail*, not given

Toohill, inverted.

Toohy, *tuaithe, túath*, north.

Toohy, *tuatha, tuathaigh*, belonging to lay people.

Tool, a district or petty kingdom.

Toole, *tuathail*, not given.

Toole, *Uí-Thuathail, Uí-Tuathail*, O'Tohil, O'Tuohill or O'Toole, a family name.

Toollone, *tuluain*, lambs hill.

Tooloone, *tulúin, tuluain*, lambs hill.

Toom, *toim*, a funeral mound or fortified hill.

Toom, *Tóma*, Toma, a personal or family name.

Toom, *tuama, tuaim*, a tumulus, mound or burial mound.

Tooma, *tuama*, a tumulus or burial mound.

Tooman, *tuaman*, a small tumulus.

Toome, *Fearthair-tuama*, not given.

Toome, *tuaim,* a tumulus or burial mound.

Toomes, *na-toim,* not given.

Toomies, *Tumaidhe,* burial mounds.

Toomog, *tuama,* a burial mound.

Toomona, *tuaim-mona,* tomb of the bog.

Toomore, *tuaim-da-bhodhar, bhodar,* tomb of the two deaf persons.

Toomore, *tuaim-mhór,* not given.

Toomour, *tuaim-fhobhair,* not given.

Tooms, *tuaim, na-tuamaí,* not given.

Tooms, *tuamacha,* burial mounds or hillocks.

Toomy, *tuaimna,* tombs.

Toomyvara, *tuaim-Uí-Mheára/Mheadhra,* Ó Meára's or O'Maras tumulus or mound.

Toon, *tonn, toinne,* not given.

Toona, *tuarád, tuarad,* bleaching.

Toonagh, *tamhnac,* a green field.

Toonan, *tuathanach,* a farmer.

Tooncane, *tuath-na-n-uan,* district of the stone monuments.

Toor, *tuair,* a cattle field.

Toor, *tuar, tuair,* a bleach green, a drying place.

Toor, *tuar,* wheat producing land, pasture land, lea land, fallow land, a sheep walk, a green spot by a stream, a bleach green, a sheep fold, a cattle field, a bleach green or a night field for cattle.

Toor, *túr,* a tower.

Toora, *na-tuara,* animal enclosures(sic).

Toora, *teamhrach,* a conspicuous residence on a hill.

Toora, *tuara, tuartha,* not given.

Toora, *tuaraidh, tuarádh tuarad,* bleaching.

Toora, *tuar-an…,* bleach green of the…

Toora, *tulach*(sic), a hillock.

Toorala, *tuar-a-lága,* the cattlefield of the hill.

Tooralaw, *tuar-an-lá,* not given.

Tooran, *tuartha-an…,* not given.

Tooranaraheen, *tuar-an-fhairchín, tuartha-an-Airchínn,* not given.

Tooraree, *tulach*(sic)*-fhraoigh,* not given.

Toore, *tuar, tuair,* a bleach green or drying place.

Tooreagh, *tuairiaigh,* grey cattle field.

Tooreagh, *tuar-riabhach,* not given.

Tooreen, *an-torn*(sic)*-mór,* not given.

Tooreen, *tuairín,* a sheep walk or grazing place.

Tooreen, *tuairín,* small animal enclosure(sic).

Tooreen, *tuairín, tuarín,* a little green or a little bleaching green.

Tooreenna, *tuairín-na…,* little bleach green of the….

Tooreenna, *tuarín-na…,* bleaching green or grazing field of….

Tooreens, *na-tuaríní,* not given.

Tooreeny, *na-tuairíní,* not given.

Tooreenyduneen, *tuairín-Uí-Dhuinnín,* not given.

Tooreigh, *tuar-riabhach,* not given.

Toorevagh, *tuar-riabhach,* striped bleach green.

Toories, *na-Tuartha,* not given.

Toorig, *tSamhraig,* summer.

Toorin, *tuairín,* little night field for cattle.

Toorin, *tuirín,* a little tower.

Toorlough, *túrlocha, turlach,* a lake that dries up in summer.

Toorna, *tuar-na…,* field or bleach green of the…

Toort, *tort,* a hill.

Toortane, *tortán,* a small knoll, tummock or high turf bank.

Toortane, *túrtán, tortán,* a little hill.

Toortane, *tortán,* a tree clump.

Toortaun, *tortán,* a little hill.

Toortaun, *tuartán,* a holm(sic).

Toos, *túis,* not given.

Toosan, *tSúsáin,* long grass.

Toosane, *tSúasáin,* long hairy-looking grass.

Toose, *tús,* front.

Toosh, *túis,* not given.

Tooskert, *tuaisceart, tuaiscirt,* north.

Tootagh, *tuadhtach,* land belonging to lay people.

Tootagh, *tuathaigh,* the layman.

Tooterny, *tuatarnaigh, tuatarnach,* a layman or rustic.

Tooterny, *tútarnaigh,* not given.

Tooth, (Mt) *Daod,* not given.

Top, *tap,* a lump, hill or round mass.

Topher, *tóchair, tóchair, tochair,* a causeway.

Topp, *tap,* a lump, hill or round mass.

Toppan, *tapain,* a tradesman who 'hackles' flax.

Toppan, *tapan,* a lump or a round hill.

Topped, from *tap,* a round hill.

Topras, *taparán,* not given.

Tor, *tor,* a towerlike rock, a pointed hill or a tower.

Tor, *tuar,* a cattle field.

Torach, *torach,* abounding in pointing hills.

Toragh, *tuaraigh,* not given.

Toragh, *turach,* a green field.

Torah, *tuath-rátha,* not given.

Toran, *teórann,* a border or boundary.

Toran, *torainn, teorann,* not given.

Torc, *torc,* a boar.

Torcan, *Torcáin,* Torcan, a personal or family name and the name of a Church founder in Derrynahinch parish.

Tore, (from Stratore), *tuair,* manuring(sic).

Tore, *teóra,* not given.

Tore, *tuair, tuar,* a bleach, bleaching green, pasture, a cattle enclosure, grazing field or drying place.

Toreen, *tuarin,* a little bleaching green.

Torges, *Torges,* Turgesius, the name of an ancient Danish tyrant.

Torick, from *teóra,* a border or boundary.

Tormaun, *trommán,* the boor tree or elder tree.

Tormer, *Tormóir,* Tormór, a personal or family name and the founder of a Church in Galway.

Torna, *tor-na...,* pointed hill of the...

Torna, *tuar-na...,* cattle field of the...

Tornan, *Tornáin,* not given.

Tornant, *tor-neanta,* hill of nettles.

Tornora, *tornóra, tornora,* a turner or wheel-wright.

Torny, *tóirnighe,* thunder.

Torny, *tornóige,* a limekiln.

Torpan, *torpan, torpán,* a little knoll.

Torr, *toir,* a pointed hill.

Torrent, (river) *an-torann,* not given.

Torrewa, *tor-riabhaigh,* grey hill tower.

Torr-head, *torbhuirg,* pointed head.

Tort, *tort,* a hill.

Tory, a tower like rock.

Tory, from *tóir,* the persuer or outlaw.

Tory, *toirínis, torach,* island of the tower.

Tory, *toraigh,* the place of towers.

Tory, *toraigh, torach,* abounding in Tors.

Tory, *thoraí,* not given.

Toskerty, *tuaiscertaighe,* north.

Tossy, *ceathrú-an-tSosaidh,* not given.

Tossy, *tosaigh,* first or front.

Tota, *doighte,* burnt.

Tota, *tuata,* rough or coarse.

Tota, *tuathta,* laymen.

Totam, burning.

Totan, *teotáin, teótáin,* burning or the burning.

Totan, *Tóiteáin, Toiteáin,* not given.

Totaun, *teotáin, teotain,* burning.

Totaun, *tóiteáin,* conflagration.

Tothmoy, *tuath-dá-maighe,* not given.

Totmoy, *tuath-dá-maighe,* not given.

Totty, *Totaigh,* Tott, a family name.

Tou, *tuath,* a district.

Toua, *tuath,* a district.

Touaghty, *tuath-aitheachta,* district of the Plebeians.

Toudera, *tSudaire,* tanners.

Tough, *tour-a'...,* paddock of the...

Tough, *tuath,* a tribeland or district.

Toughnane, *tuath-cananach,* district of the canons.

Touhill, *Tuathail,* Tuathal, a personal or family name.

Touhy, *tuaithe, tuatha,* a district or territory.

Touk, *tSeabhaich, tSeabhaic,* a hawk.

Touke, *t-seabhaic,* a hawk.

Touknockane, *tuath-cnocáin,* not given.

Toul, *toll,* a pond.

Toulett, *taimhleacht, tamlagth,* a plague grave or monument.

Touloure, *toll-odhar,* a dun coloured pit or hollow.

Touloure, *toll-odhar,* the dun-coloured pond.

Toumpane, *tiompáin,* a standing stone.

Toumpleen, *Teampull-Aedha,* Hugh's Church.

Toun, from *tonn,* waves, billows.

Tounagha, *tamhnacha,* green fields.

Toung, *tuinne,* a shaking bog.

Tountinna, *tonn-toinne,* not given.

Tountinna, *tultuinne, tul-tuinne,* hill of the wave.

Tour, *teamhair,* not given.

Tour, *tuar,* a bleach green.

Toura, *tuar-a',* bleach, usually a bleaching green.

Touragh, *Teamhair,* a residence on an elevated spot commanding an extensive prospect/view.

Toureen, *tuairín,* a small animal enclosure(sic).

Toureen, *tuarin, tuarín,* a little bleach green, field.

Tourig, (river) *an-tuairigh,* not given.

Tourigh, *teamhrach,* Tara.

Tourin, *tuarín,* little bleach green.

Tourly, Tourly or Turly, a personal or family name.

Tourna, *tuar-na...,* not given.

Tournore, fearann-an-tornóraigh, not given.

Touse, *tSúsa,* a blanket.

Towar, *tuar,* a bleach green.

Towdrie, *tSudaire,* tanners.

Towdry, *tSudaire,* tanners.

Towel, *'tostail,* blundering or bad luck.

Towel, *Tuathal, Tuathail,* Toohal, Tuathal, a male name.

Towel, *tuthail,* the sun(sic).

Tower, *teamhair,* a residence on an elevated spot commanding an extensive prospect/view.

Tower, *tuar,* a cattle field.

Towick, *tSeabhaic,* the hawk.

Towlaght, *taimhleacht,* a plague monument.

Towlerton, *tamhlachtain,* a burial place.

Towloure, *toll-odhar,* a dun coloured pit or hollow.

Town, *tonn,* a quagmire.

Towna, *tamhain-na...,* not given.

Towna, *tamhnach,* a green field.

Townagh, *tamhnach,* a green field.

Townagha, *tamhnacha,* green fields.

Towney, *tamhnaigh,* not given.

Townley, *Tóinligh,* not given.

Townlough, *tonnlocha,* wave of the lake.

Townlough, *tuaim-locha,* not given.

Towy, *tSamhaigh,* not given.

Toy, *tuaighe, tuath,* laity or a layman.

Toy, *tuaithe,* not given.

Toy, *tuiaghe, tuaidh,* north or northern.

Toye, *tuaith,* a territory.

Tra, *...trach,* as an ending to a word can sometimes mean, a place of.... or abounding in...

Tra, *thrá, treagha, trágha,* not given.

Tra, *trádh,* a lance.

Tra, *traigh, tracht,* strand or shore.

Tra, *tSratha,* a holm.

Tracey, *Uí-Treasaigh,* O'Tracy, a family name.

Tracton, *tractu,* a tract.

Trae, *trá,* beach.

Trae, *tSratha,* not given.

Tragalee, *traigh-a'-laoigh,* strand of the calf.

Tragh, *...trach,* as an ending to a word can sometimes mean, a place of.... or abounding in...

Tragh, *traigh,* a strand.

Traght, *tSneachta,* not given.

Traght, *tSnechta,* snow.

Traghta, *dTráchta,* not given.

Traghta, snowy.

Trague, *Tréige,* not given.

Trahane, *sruthán, t-sruthain,* a little stream.

Trahull, *Streachall,* not given.

Trahull, *traigh-holl,* the great strand.

Train, *tréin, tréun,* a strong, brave, mighty, powerful man or a hero.

Train, *tSraein,* not given.

Tralee, strand of Li.

Tralee, *traigh-Lí,* not given.

Tralee, *traigh-Li,* the strand of the Lee (river).

Tramon, *Croman,* Croman, a personal or family name.

Tramon, *Shreamann,* not given.

Tramona, *trágh-móna,* not given.

Trana, *trá-na...,* strand of the...

Trand, *tréann,* a field.

Trane, a place where corn is burned in the ear.

Trane, *torán,* a hillock.

Trannish, *traigh-inis,* shore island.

Trant, *Traint,* Trant, a personal or family name.

Trant, *Treantaigh, Treant,* not given.

Traow, *trágha,* the strand.

Tras, *treas,* a third of land.

Trascan, *treascán,* not given.

Traskernagh, from *treasc*, a place of rough brambles.

Trasna, *trasna, tarsna*, across, oblique or a cross in land, crossroads or lying transversely.

Trasna, *thra sna*(sic), cross.

Trasna, *treasna*, not given.

Trasnagh, *tarsna*, across, a cross in land or crossroads.

Trasnane, *treasnáin*, not given.

Trass, *treas, treasa*, conflict or battle.

Trassa, *treasa*, the conflict or skirmish.

Trassy, *Dreasa*, not given.

Trassy, *Treasa*, St Teresa.

Trat, *tSnechta*, snow.

Trath, *tSraithe, sraith, strath, tSraith*, a river holm.

Traud, *tSráid*, a street.

Trauve, *traigh*, strand.

Trave, *a'tsnamha*, of the swimming.

Travin, *tráighmhín, treabhair*(sic), not given.

Traw, *traigh, tragha, trá, tracht*, strand or shore.

Trawadile, *traigh-an-daill*, dark gloomy strand.

Trawn, *trian*, a division or area.

Trawna, *traigh/tráigh-na…*, strand of the…

Tray, *baile-an-tSratha, trá*, not given.

Tray, *traigh, tracht*, strand or shore.

Tray, *traoth, tSrae, tSraeth*, a millrace.

Trea, *na-trágha*, not given.

Trea, *Tré*, a personal or family name.

Trea, *Trea, Trega*, the virgin St Trea.

Trea, *tréith*, wearied.

Trea, *tSrae, tSraeth*, a millrace.

Tread, *dTréad*, flocks (of cattle).

Treada, *tread*, the drove.

Treagh, *tré*, not given.

Treagh, *treidh*, a third (of land).

Treame, *troím*, alder trees.

Trean, *an-thrian, trian*, one third (a land measurment).

Treana, *trian-na…*, not given.

Treana, *trian-na…*, one third of the….

Treane, *tradhna, tradhnach, treanach*, corcrake/s.

Treane, *triain*, a third (measure of land).

Treane, *tSréin*, not given.

Treanna, *trian-na…*, one third of the….

Treannahow, *tréann-an-abháin*, the field by the river(sic).

Treantagh, *tréantacha*, not given.

Treantagh, *triantach*, a farm made up from thirds.

Treany, *tradhnaigh*, the corncrake.

Treanybrogaun, *trian-Uí-Bhrogáin*, O'Brogan's (a family name) third.

Treasna, *tarsna*, across.

Treat, *tréad*, not given.

Treat, *treada*, the flock.

Treda, *treada*, herds.

Tredida, *traitéadaigh*, not given.

Tree, *dTrí, tri*, three, sometimes three persons.

Treel, *traoile, traoil*, a stripe or strip of land.

Treem, *truim*, a place of alders.

Treen, *trian*, a third part.

Treenearla, *dTrí-nIarla*, the three earls.

Tregaun, *trí-gCam*, not given.

Treguam, *trí-gCom*, three hollows.

Treh, *Troighe*, not given.

Trehy, *Uí-Throithigh*, O'Trihy, a family name.

Trehy, *Uí-Troighthe*, O'Trehy, a family name.

Treila, *tradhlach*, corncrake/s.

Trellane, *tríoláin*, a water-cut track.

Trellane, *tSraoileáin*, not given.

Trellick, *tri-liag*, three piller stones.

Trellig, *tri-lice*, three standing stones.

Tremoge, *tromóg*, a place of elders.

Trenaree, *trian-na-Righ*, the Kings third.

Trench, *trinse*, a hollow.

Trentagh, *triantach*, not given.

Tresk, *traisc*, grain.

Tresk, *triosca*, brewers grains.

Tress, *treas, treasa*, the battle.

Trether, *tSruthar*, a brook.

Trevet, *trefoit, tre-foit*, three sods.

Trevor, *Treabhair*, Treabhar or Trevor a male name.

Trew, *triúch*, not given.

Trien, *thrian, trian*, a third.

Trien, *trian*, good portion or a third.

Trienagh, *draighneach*, blackthorn.

Trieneens, *trinini*, little thirds.

Trigan, *Triagáin, Triagan*, a male name.

Trila, *traoile*, a stripe.

Trillic, *treilic, na-dTreilic,* not given.

Trillick, *treileac,* three flagstones.

Trillick, *treileac, trí-liag,* three flagstones.

Trillick, *treileac, tri-liag,* three piller stones.

Trillick, *treileac, trilic,* three stones.

Trillick, *trilic,* a stone tomb.

Trim, (in Meath), *ath-truim,* the ford of the elder trees/bushes.

Trim, *drum, druim,* a hill ridge.

Trim, *tirim,* dry.

Trim, *troim, truimm,* the elder or boor tree.

Trim, *tromm,* the boor tree.

Trim, *truimm, truim,* elder trees or boor-trees.

Trime, *truim,* elder trees.

Trimegish, *troim-Éigis,* not given.

Trimmer, *tromaire,* where elders grow.

Trimoge, (river) *an-triomóg,* not given.

Trinaree, *train-an*(sic)*-Rí,* the Kings third..

Trinane, *trianain,* a small third.

Tringane, *t-sreangain,* a cable.

Trippal, *triopal,* not given.

Trippul, *triopoll,* a bush cluster.

Trisk, brewers grains.

Trisnane, *Threasnáin,* not given.

Trisnane, *Uí-Treasnáin,* O'Tresnan, a personal or family name.

Trisnane, *Troisneain,* Trusnan, a personal or family name.

Trissaun, *dreasan,* a place of briars, blackthorns.

Tristaun, *trosdan,* a pilgrims staff.

Tristernagh, a place of briars, blackthorns.

Tristia, *troiste,* not given.

Tristle, *disert,* a hermitage.

Troad, *treóit,* not given.

Troar, *Treabhair,* not given.

Troddan, *trodan,* a quarrel or strife.

Trofaun, *tSrotháin,* a little stream.

Troge, *Tórróg,* not given.

Trogue, *Tróg,* Trog, a personal or family name.

Trohanny, *triúch-Eanga,* not given.

Trohaun, *tSrotháin,* the little stream.

Trohy, *Uí-Throighthe,* O'Trehy a family name.

Trolin, *dreóilín,* not given.

Trolin, *Trolainn,* Trolann, a personal name or Troland a family name.

Trom, *trom,* elders trees.

Trom, *trom,* heavy.

Trom, *truim,* elder trees.

Troma, *druim-a'...,* hill ridge of the...

Tromaun, *tromraigh, tromán,* a place of elder bushes.

Tromawna, *tróman,* not given.

Tromera, *tromra,* a place of alders.

Tromery, *tromaire,* elder trees.

Tromman, *tromán,* elder, a place of elders (trees) or a small place of elders.

Trommaun, *tromán,* a small place of elders.

Tromogagh, *trommógach,* abounding in boor trees or elders.

Tromra, *tromán, trommra,* abounding in elder trees or boor trees.

Tromra, *tromra,* not given.

Trone, *sruthain,* a streamlet.

Troor, *tri,* three, sometimes three persons.

Trost, *troste, troist,* a fissure or crack.

Trostan, *trosdan,* a pilgrims staff.

Trostan, *trostán,* a pole.

Troste, *troste, troist,* a fissure or crack.

Trough, *traith,* a holm.

Trough, *tricha, triucha,* a cantred or district and is also the name of a Barony of thirty hundreds of land.

Trough, *triúcha,* a cantred (a land measurment of a hundred).

Trough, *tSrotha, sruth,* a stream.

Trower, *treabhair,* a tillage plot.

Troy, *an-treoigh,* not given.

Truan, *sruthain,* a streamlet.

Truan, *t-srotháin,* a streamlet.

Truce, *truis,* trousered.

Truckle, *Throcail,* not given.

Truckle, *Torcal, Thrucail,* Torcal, Thorgils, Thorkils, Turgesius or Turgeis, the name of an ancient Danish chieftain.

Trudder, *an-tSruthair,* the stream.

Trudders, a 'drundle' or a pass for water.

True, *tri,* three, sometimes three persons.

True, *tricha, triucha,* a cantred or district.

Truer, *tri,* three, sometimes three persons.

Truer, *triúir,* three persons.

Truffaun, *tSrothain, tSrotháin,* the streamlet.

Trughanacmy, *triúc-an-aicme,* not given.

Truhaun, *tSrutháin,* not given.

Truhaun, *t-sruthaun,* the stream.

Trum, *trom,* alders.

Truman, *tromán,* elder, a place of elders (trees or bushes).

Trumenery, *tromraigh,* from *truim,* a place of Elder bushes.

Trumera, *tromaire,* not given.

Trumman, *tromraigh, trommain,* a place of elder or boortrees.

Trummaun, *tromán,* a place of elder trees.

Trummer, *tromaire,* where elders grow.

Trummera, *tromaire,* where elders grow.

Trummery, *tromraigh, tromaire,* a place of Elder bushes.

Trumon, *tromán,* the elder tree.

Trumpa, *trúmpha,* the trumpet.

Trumra, *trommra,* abounding in elder trees or boor trees.

Trumra, *tromra,* not given.

Trusk, *trosc, troisc,* codfish.

Trusk, *troscach,* abounding in codfish.

Truskaunna, *truscaigh-na…,* not given.

Trusklieve, *troisc-shliabh,* hungry mountain.

Trusklieve, *trosc-shliabh,* cod mountain.

Trusky, *troscach,* abounding in codfish.

Trusky, *troscaigh,* not given.

Trusnan, *treasnáin,* the crossing stick.

Trustan, *trosdan,* a pilgrims staff.

Try, *…trach,* as an ending to a word can sometimes mean, a place of…. or abounding in…

Try, *tire,* territory.

Try, *traigh,* a strand.

Try, *trí, tri,* three.

Tryla, *tradhlach,* corncrake/s.

Tryna, *tradhnach, tradhna, treanach,* corncrake/s.

Tryna, *traghna,* not given.

Tslea, *tSleibhe,* a mountain.

Tslochtan, *tSlochtain,* dandelion.

Tu, *tuath,* a district, territory.

Tua, *tuath,* a district, territory.

Tuaimna, *Tuamaidhe,* tombs.

Tuairin, *tuairín,* a green or a night field for cattle.

Tuam, *tuaim,* a tumulus, mound or burial mound.

Tuam, *tuaim-an-dá-ghualainn,* not given.

Tuama, from *tuaim,* burial mounds.

Tuan, *tSeán,* Sean, a male name.

Tuar, *tuar,* a night cattle field.

Tuarig, (river) *an-tuarigh,* not given.

Tuarna, *tuar-na…,* night cattle field of the…

Tubber, *tobair,* a well.

Tubberid, *tobruid, tobar,* a well.

Tubbert, *tiobrad,* a well.

Tubbrid, *dTiobrad, tiobraide, tiobraid, tiobrad, tipra, tiprat, tobruid, tobar, tiprait,* a well.

Tubbrid, *Tiobratan,* not given.

Tubbrit, *tiobraite,* a spring well.

Tubrid, *tiobraid, tobraide,* a well.

Tuckera, *t-siucaíre,* sugar.

Tuckmill, *tocuile,* not given.

Tuckmilltate, *táite-mhuileann-an-Úcaire,* not given.

Tuder, *tSudaire,* a tanner.

Tudor, *tSudaire,* tanners.

Tudra, *tSudaire,* tanners.

Tuke, *tSeabhaic, tSeabhaic,* a hawk.

Tul, *tulach,* a hill or hillock.

Tulach, *tulach,* a hill, a small or gentle hill.

Tulcon, *tullachan,* a small hill.

Tulk, *Tulcha,* not given.

Tull, *tulaigh, tulach,* not given.

Tulla, *tola, tulach,* a hill, a small or gentle hill.

Tulla, *tula,* not given.

Tulla, *ulaidh,* not given.

Tullacawn, *tullachán,* a hill.

Tullach, *tulach,* a hill, a small or gentle hill.

Tullagh, *tulach,* a hill, a small or gentle hill.

Tullagh, *tulach,* hills(sic).

Tullagh, *tulaighe,* not given.

Tullagha, *tulaigh,* not given.

Tullaghan, from *tulán,* a little hills.

Tullaghan, *tulchán, tulchan, tullachán, tulachán,* little hill.

Tullaghanoge, *tulach-Chonóg,* not given.

Tullaghans, from *tulán,* a little hills.

Tullaghaun, *tulachán, tulchan,* little hills.

Tullaghauna, *tulchán-na* , little hill of…

Tullagher, from *tulach,* a hill.

Tullagher, *tulchair, tulachar,* a hilly place.

Tullaghna, *tul-Lachtna,* Lachtna's (a personal or family name) hill.

Tullaghobegley, *tulacha-Beigile, tulach-Ó-Beigfhile,* not given.

Tullaghobegly, *tulachan-Bigli*, Bigli or Begley's (a personal or a family name) little hill.

Tullaghorton, *cúl-an-gharrain*(sic), not given.

Tullaghorton, *tulach-Artáin*, not given.

Tullaha, *na-tulacha*, the hillocks.

Tullahaun, *tulachán*, a little hill.

Tullahedy, *tulach-Éide*, not given.

Tullaher, *tulach-shoir*, eastern hill.

Tullaherin, *an-tulach-thirim*, not given.

Tullahought, *tulchacht*, not given.

Tullahought, *ulaidh-hOchta*, not given.

Tullahought, *tulach-dhocht*, the difficult hill.

Tullamain, *tulach-Mathain*, not given.

Tullamin, *tulach-Maoin*, not given.

Tullamine, *tulach-Máinne, teallach-Diomain*, not given.

Tullan, from *tulán*, a little hills.

Tullan, *tulaigh/tula-an...*, little hill of the...

Tullan, *tulán*, a little hill.

Tullana, *talamh-na...*, land of the...

Tullana, *tulach-na...*, hillock of the...

Tullana, *tulaigh-na...*, not given.

Tullaroan, *tulach-Ruadhán*, hillock of the red complexioned man, also Roan's (a male name) hillock.

Tullaroan, *tulach-Ruáin*, Rowan's (a personal or family name.) hill.

Tullassa, *tulach-asa*, hill by the waterfall.

Tullen, *tulán*, a little hill.

Tullequane, *tulach-Chuáin*, not given.

Tullequane, *tulach-Cuain*, Quans (a family name) hill.

Tullerboy, *Tulach-Orbhaí*, not given.

Tulleroghe, *tulach*, a mound summit.

Tulli, *tulagh*, a hillock.

Tullig, *tuilg*, a small hill.

Tullig, *tulaigh*, a mound, a hill, a small or gentle hill.

Tullin, *tulaigh-an...*, not given.

Tullin, *tulán*, a little hill.

Tullinatrat, *tulaigh-an-tSneachta*, not given.

Tullogher, *tulchair*, not given.

Tulloha, *tulach-átha*, small hill of the ford.

Tullohea, *tulach-Aodha*, Hugh's (a male name) hill summit.

Tullokyne, *tulach-Ó-bhFéidhlimidh, tulaigh-Mhic-Aodháin*, not given.

Tullovin, *tulach/tul' O-bhFinn*, hill of Uí-Fhinn or the O'Finn's (a family name).

Tullow, *tulach*, the hill or hillock.

Tully, *talmhaidhe*, lands.

Tully, *tealach...*, family or household of...

Tully, *tola, tulach*, a hill, a small or gentle hill.

Tully, *tuillighthe*, not given.

Tully, *tulaigh*, a hill.

Tullyco, *tulach-cuach*, not given.

Tullyesker, *tulaigh-an-Choscair*(sic), not given.

Tullyhaw, *teallach-Eachach*, not given.

Tullyhogue, *tulach-óg*, not given.

Tullyhogue, *tulaigh-óg*, small hill of the youths.

Tullyleer, *tulaigh-Mhaoilir*, not given.

Tullymorerahan, *tulaigh-mhaí-raithin*, not given.

Tullyna, *tulach/tulaigh-na...*, hill or hillock of the...

Tullynahinnera, the 'Tully' in this place name is a corruption of *talamh*. The whole name means 'land of the anvil'.

Tullysiddoge, *tulaigh-sudóg*, hill of the wild ducks.

Tullywasnacunagh, Tullywasnecunagh, hill of rabbit holes.

Tulna, *tulach-na...*, not given.

Tulrahan, *tulach-shrutháin*, hill of the stream.

Tulrohan, *tulach-srutháin*, not given.

Tulsk, *tuilsc, tuilsce*, not given.

Tum, *tom*, a bush or a thicket.

Tum, *tuaim*, a burial mound.

Tummery, *t-iomaire*, a ridge.

Tumna, *tom-na...*, not given.

Tumna, *tumna, tuaim-mna*, the womans tomb.

Tumper, *tiomchair*, a carriage.

Tumper, *tiompar*, a trough or trench.

Tumper, *tuimpe*, a hillside or hump.

Tumpher, *tiomchair*, a carriage.

Tuna, *t'shunnach*, a milking place.

Tuney, *sionnach*, ..of the fox.

Tunna, *teanna*, stiff, stout or strong.

Tunna, *tSonnaigh*, a mound or rampart.

Tunnacha, *tonnach*, bog or swamp.

Tunnagh, *tonnach*, a rampart or mound.

Tunns, from *tonn*, waves, billows.

Tunny, *tonnach,* a quagmire.

Tunny, *tonnaigh, tSonnach, tonnach, tonaigh,* a rampart or mound.

Tunny, *tSonnaigh, tamhnaigh,* not given.

Tuo, *tuath,* a district.

Tuogh, *tuath, tuaith,* a district.

Tuohill, *tuathail,* left handed or reversed.

Tuohill, Tuathal, a personal or family name.

Tuohy, *tuath,* territory.

Tuor, *tuar,* a bleach green, a field.

Tuosist, *tuath-Ó-Síosta/Síosta,* territory of the Uí Síosta, a family/clan name.

Tur, *tír,* land of…

Tur, *toir,* not given.

Tur, *torr,* a heap.

Tur, *tuar,* a bleach green, a field.

Tur, *tuir, tor,* a bush or a small round hill.

Tur, *tur,* bushy.

Tura, *tuire,* not given.

Tura, *tuireadh,* towers.

Turagh, *teamhrach,* not given.

Turagh, *t-iubhrach, t-iubhragh,* yew land.

Turavoggan, *tor-an-bhogáin,* not given.

Turbet, *tairbeirt,* not given.

Turbet, *tairbhirt,* not given.

Turbet, *tairbirt,* an isthmus.

Turcher, *turchair,* the shot or cast.

Ture, *tIubhar,* not given.

Ture, *t-Iúr, tIúr,* the yew or yew tree.

Ture, *tuar,* a bleach green/field.

Turick, *Turaig,* Turick, a personal or family name.

Turin, *tuairín,* not given.

Turish, *turais,* a pilgrimage.

Turk, *toirc,* boars.

Turk, *turke*(sic), *tuirc, toirc, torc,* a boar/ swine.

Turkenagh, a place of wild boars.

Turkenagh, *tuar-ceannach,* a market.

Turlagh, *turlach,* a lake that dries up in summer.

Turlaghna, *turlach-na…,* the lake (that dries up in summer) of the…

Turley, *turlaigh,* not given.

Turlinn, *tuirlinn,* a strand full of large stones.

Turlough, *turlach,* a fen.

Turlough, *turlach, turlaigh, turloch,* a dry lake, a half-dried lake or a lake that dries up in summer.

Turly, *tuirléim*(sic), not given.

Turly, *turlaigh,* a fen(sic).

Turly, *turlaigh,* dried or half dried lake.

Turn, *tSoirn,* a kiln.

Turna, *torna…,* bush of the…

Turna, *tur-na…,* round hill of the…

Turnant, *tor/túr-neannta,* fort or tower of nettles.

Turnaun, *tornáin,* a lime kiln.

Turnory, *tornóir,* the turner.

Turnory, *tornóraigh,* not given.

Turnory, *turnóra,* turners.

Turpaun, *turpán,* a small peaked hill.

Turr, *tor,* a bush.

Turra, *thura,* a bush.

Turra, *tor-a'…,* little hill or place of the

Turra, *turra,* not given.

Turraheen, a little peaked hill.

Turraheen, *toirthín,* not given.

Turraun, a little round hill or little bush.

Turraun, *torán,* not given.

Turreagh, *torr-riabhach,* grey heap.

Turreen, a little round hill.

Turreen, *tuirrín,* little bush.

Turris, *turais,* the visit or station.

Turrish, *turais,* a pilgrimage.

Turrock, *an-turrac,* not given.

Turrock, *turóg,* a hillock.

Tursalla, a miry hillock or a miry bush.

Tursallagh, a miry hillock or a miry bush.

Tursker, *torscar,* a rugged rocky shrubby place

Turtane, *tortán,* a small knoll, tummock or high turf bank.

Turtle, *Torcaill,* Torcall or MacTorcaill a family name.

Turton, *Tortain,* Turton, a personal or family name.

Turton, *Tortan,* not given.

Turtulla, *tor-tulaigh,* the bushy hill.

Turtulla, *torclach, thorclaigh, tuar-Tula,* not given.

Turvey, *Thuirbhe, Tuirbhi,* a male name.

Turvey, *tráigh-Tuirbhe,* not given.

Tuskar, rock.

Tuskar, *torscar,* a rugged rocky place.

Tusker, *torscar,* a rugged rocky shrubby place.

Tuskert, *tuaisceart,* not given.

Tuskert, *tuaisceirt, tuaiscirt, tuaiscert,* northern, northern part or direction.

Tuskert, *tuaiscirt,* insulated.

Tussa, *tosaigh, tossaig,* front.

Tweedy, *Uí-tSioda,* O'Tweedy, a family name.

Twenties, *na-fichidhi,* not given.

Twohil, *Thuathail,* not given.

Ty, *tigh,* a house.

Tyanee, *tigh-O'Niaidh,* O'Nee's (a family name) house.

Tydavnet, *tigh-Damhnat,* not given.

Tygore, *tigh-gabhar,* the goats house.

Tymon, *Díomáin,* Díomáin, Dioman, a personal or family name.

Tymon, *Diomán,* not given.

Tymon, *teach-Modhichon,* Modhichon's (a personal or family name) house.

Tymon, *teach-Motháin,* Mothán's (a personal or family name) house.

Tymon, *tech-Munna,* house of Munna.

Tymore, *tighe-moir,* the great house.

Tymore, *tí-mhór,* nettles(sic).

Tyna, *tóin-na…,* bog(sic) of the…

Tyna, tóin-na…, not given.

Tynagh, *toinn-an…,* not given.

Tynagh, *tine, thíne,* not given.

Tynan, *tighneathán,* not given.

Tynan, *tuidhnigha, tuíneán, tuidhidhean,* a watercourse.

Tyone, *tigh-Eoghain/Eóin,* Eoghan's or Johns house.

Tyr, *tir,* land.

Tyrella, *teach-Riala,* St Rial/Riail/Riaghal's house.

Tyrone, *Tír/Tir-Eoghain,* Eogans, Owen's (a male name) district, territory or land.

U

Uaddra, mhadra, dog/s.
Uarach, (river) *an-uarach,* not given.
Ubber, abar, a mire.
Uctough, uchtach, a slope.
Uddy, Odaigh, not given.
Uff, damh, the ox/oxen.
Uge, éige, death.
Uggool, a hollow.
Uggool, ogúil, not given.
Ughera, úcaire, the fuller or napper.
Ught, uchta, ucht, breast.
Uinnseann, fuinnseann, ash trees.
Ukin, Eimhicín, St Eimhicin/Eimhicín/
   Eimhchícín.
Ula, ula, an altar stone.
Ulagh, ullach, proud.
Ulatagh, chodlatach, sleepy.
Ulk, olc, worthless or bad.
Ulk, uilc, badness or evil.
Ulkin, Mhic-Uilcín, MacUlkin or Culkin,
   a family name.
Ull, ulla, úmhall, apples seeds or acorns.
Ulla, abhladh, a orchard.
Ulla, ulla, ulaidh, uladh, an altar tomb or
   penitential station.
Ullaan, ubhalán, apple/s.
Ullagh, uladh, tombs.
Ullagha, ulacha, not given.
Ullagha, uladhcha, prayer stations or altar
   tombs.
Ullan, abhalan, abhálan, an orchard.
Ullanes, from *ulaidh,* little stone altars.
Ullanes, na-hUláim/hUlláin, not given.
Ullanes, ulain, stone altars or stone blocks.
Ullard, abhall-ghort, abhalghort, the orchard
   field.
Ullard, iolard, irirda, irarda-hUlláin, not
   given.

Ullard, iorarda, heights.
Ullard, ulaidh-ard, a high penitential station.
Ullard, ulard, the high place.
Ullauns, from *ulaidh,* little stone altars.
Ullauns, ulán, high penitential stations.
Uller, iolar, iolair, an eagle.
Ullid, iollad, ulaid, not given.
Ullid, uille-fhada, the long angular place.
Ullinagh, uilleannach, with elbows or
   corners.
Ully, ulaidh, hUlaidh, a tomb.
Ulra, iolar, an eagle or eagles.
Ulrith, abhalghort, an orchard.
Ulton, Ulton, St Ultan.
Ulster, Ultaibh, Uladh, not given.
Ulster, Ulaidh, land of the Ulaidh, one of
   the five ancient kingdoms.
Ulster, Ulaidh, cúide-Uladh, land of Ulaid's
   men.
Ult, Ultan, not given.
Ult, Ultán, St Ultan.
Ultagh, Ultach, Oltach, Ulstermen.
Ultan, Ultain, Ultan, a personal name.
Ultan, Ultán, St Ultan.
Ulty, úbhaltadh, apple trees.
Ulty, Ulta, not given.
Ulty, Ultach, an Ulsterman.
Ulty, Ultaigh, Ultach, Oltach, Ulstermen.
Ulusker, uladh, ulaidh-Oscair, Oscar's carn
   or grave pile.
Ulyman, bhladhmainn, boasting.
Umber, umar, amar, amuir, a trough shape or
   hollow.
Umbra, iomaire, a ridge.
Umera, iomaire, a ridge.
Umery, iomaire, a ridge.
Umfin, (island) *iompainn, iomthuinn,* not
   given.
Umgall, umghall, not given.
Umiskin, umascan, not given.
Umlagh, imleach, land bordering a lake or
   a marshy place.
Umma, iomaidh, conflict or contention.
*Umma, iomdha-Chiaráin, iomdaid, móin-na-
   manach,* not given.
Ummer, iomaire, a ridge.
Ummer, nUmar, umar, amar, amuir, a trough
   shape or hollow.
Ummer, umair, not given.
Ummera, an-tIomaire, not given.

Ummera, *iomaire,* a ridge.

Ummeras, *imreas,* controversy.

Ummery, *iomaire,* a ridge.

Ummet, *iomaire,* a ridge.

Ummoon, *Iomún, Umaghadhainn,* not given.

Umna, *omna,* the tree trunk.

Umna, *umna, omna,* oaks.

Umney, *omna,* oak.

Umpher, *umair,* a cup or cup shape.

Umpy, *ionpodh,* turning.

Umragar, *iomaire-gearr,* not given.

Umry, *iomaire,* a ridge.

Umuskan, *Iomascan,* not given.

Ungwee, *ionga-bhuidhe,* not given.

Uniacke (Mount), *cúil-Ó-gCorra,* not given.

Unihy, *gCoincinne, O-gCoinchinn,* the O'Coincinn's, a family name.

Union Hall, *bréantrá,* not given.

Unna, *Onna, Fhionnaigh,* not given.

Unnagher, *Unachair,* St Unachar/Unachair.

Unsaghan, *uinseachan,* ash trees.

Unshaghan, *uinseachan,* ash trees.

Unshin, (river) *an-fhuinnsean,* not given.

Unshin, *fuinnseann, uinsinn,* ash trees.

Unshin, *uinnseann,* not given.

Unshinagh, *fuinnseanach, unseanach, uinseanagh, uinseannach, uinnseannach,* a place of ash trees.

Unshinaghain, *uinseannach,* a place of ash trees.

Unshog, *fuinnseóg,* a place of ash trees.

Upton, *garraí-Thancaird, baile-Hobac, cnoc-an-bhile,* not given.

Ura, *odhardha,* brown or yellow.

Ura, *Úra,* not given.

Uragh, *iurach, iúrach, iubharach, iubhrach,* a place of yews.

Uran, *Odhran, Odhran,* a personal or family name.

Uran, *uarán,* cold springs.

Urane, *iurain, lur,* yew.

Urane, *iúráin,* not given.

Urard, *iúr-ard,* not given.

Urard, *úrárd,* an irriguous height or hill.

Urbal, *iorball,* not given.

Urbal, *urbal, earball, eirball,* a tail.

Urbalreagh, *earball-riabhach,* striped end piece.

Urbalreagh, the grey dell(sic).

Urcher, *an-tUrchar, Urchair,* not given.

Urcher, *urchur,* a (great) throw, cast or shot.

Urd, *Shiuird, Siurd,* not given.

Urd, *Uird, tSuird, suird, sord,* not given.

Ure, *abhair,* a hill-brow.

Ure, *fhobhair,* not given.

Ure, *fhuar, fuar,* cold.

Ure, *iubhair, Iúir,* yew.

Ure, *Odhar,* sallow or weatherbeaten.

Ure, *úr,* a marsh place.

Uregare, *hÚrach-Giorra, Úir Ghearr,* not given.

Uregare, *iubhar-gearr/ghearr,* short yew tree.

Urglin, *Oirchin-linn,* not given.

Urglin, *uir-ghleann,* green or fresh glen.

Urher, *airthear,* east, eastern.

Urhin, *Iorthan,* not given.

Urhin, *oircheann,* the shore end.

Urhur, *airthir,* eastern.

Urin, *iúirín,* not given.

Urkevaush, *urcomháis,* a cave.

Urlagh, *urlaidhe,* slaughter or conflict.

Urlan, from *urla,* long grass.

Urlan, *urlann,* a forecourt.

Urland, from *urla,* long grass.

Urland, *urlainne,* the spear.

Urland, *urlann,* weapon handes.

Urlar, *urlár,* a floor.

Urlar, *urlaur,* a floor

Urlaur, *urlár,* a floor or level place.

Urlee, from *urla,* long grass.

Urlee, *urlaidhe,* not given.

Urlin, *Urlann, Úrlaing,* not given.

Urlingford, *áth/ath-na-nUrlaidhe,* slaughter ford.

Urlingford, *ath-na-nUrlainn,* ford of the forecourts.

Urlingford, *áth-na-nUrlainn,* ford of the shafts.

Urlingford, *áth-na-nDóirling,* ford of the large tones.

Urlish, *uirlis,* not given.

Urly, *urlaí,* not given.

Urly, *urlaidhe,* slaughter or bloody conflict.

Urna, *eórnan,* barley.

Urney, *ernaidhe, urnaí, urnaidhe,* an oratory or prayerhouse.

Urney, *iurnaidhe,* not given.

Urney, *urnaighe,* (of the) praying.

Urny, *urnaidhe,* an oratory, prayerhouse.

Urra, *fhoraidh,* a mound.

Urra, *urra,* a surety.

Urra, *an-urra,* (belonging to the) chief.

Urra, *urradh,* contention or query.

Urraghil, *urchoill, ur-choill,* green or fresh wood.

Urrasaun, from *iorrus,* a little border or peninsula.

Urrasaun, *iorrasán,* not given.

Urrin, *urrainn,* division.

Urris, *iorrus,* a peninsula.

Urros, *iorrus,* a peninsula.

Ursa, *Fhursa,* St Fursa.

Ury, *iubhraigh,* yew.

Ush, *ois,* a doe.

Ushnagh, *uisneach, uisnech,* place of fawns.

Usk, *loisgthe,* burned.

Usk, *uisce,* water or a watery place.

Uskane, from *uisce,* watery land.

Uskane, *uisceán, uscán,* not given.

Uskeane, *uscán,* watery land.

Usker, *Oscair,* not given.

Uskerty, *ioscarta,* not given.

Uskerty, *easc-scartaigh,* marshy land of the shrubbery.

Usky, *uisce,* water.

Usnagh, *uisneach,* not given.

Usnagh, *uisnech,* place of fawns.

Usque, *loiscthe,* burnt.

Ussaun, *easán,* a small waterfall.

Ussaun, *Osán,* not given.

Usty, *aosta,* aged.

Usty, *Osta,* not given.

Va, *Uibh Fhathaigh,* O'Fahy, a family name.

Vaag, *feadh,* bulrushes.

Vaan, *mheáin,* not given.

Vabby, *Mhabaigh,* Mab, a personal or family name.

Vacadane, *Mhac-Adain,* Mac Cadden, a family name.

Vacan, *Bhacáin,* not given.

Vacan, *mheacain,* (wild) parsnip/s.

Vacan, *mheacain,* wild carrot.

Vackagh, *bhacach,* beggars.

Vackan, *bhacáin, bheacháin,* not given.

Vackey, *bhacaigh,* a cripple or beggarman.

Vackey, *Mhic-Aodha,* MacHugh or Mac Kee, a family name.

Vackey, *Uí-Mhacdha,* Mackey, a family name.

Vackney, *Mhic-Nia,* MacNia, a personal or family name.

Vacoos, *bhácúis,* the oven.

Vacoosh, *bhácúis,* the oven.

Vacorneen, *Mhic-Chuirnin,* Courtney, a personal or family name.

Vacorneen, *Mhic-Coirnín,* not given.

Vacullion, *mhaighe-cuilinn,* holly plain.

Vad, *bhaid, bhaid, bháda, bhada,* boat.

Vad, *bhFead,* whistles.

Vad, *fhada,* long.

Vad, *mhadaidh,* not given.

Vada, *bhádaigh,* not given.

Vadagh, *Bhardaigh,* not given.

Vadagh, *Mhéada,* Meade, a male name.

Vadaroe, *mhadhaidh-ruaidh,* the red dog or fox.

Vadaroe, *mhadra-rua,* the fox.

Vadd, *bhaid, Uad,* not given.

Vadd, *bhFad,* distant.

Vadd, *fhada,* long.

Vadda, *maide, mhaide,* the stick.

Vadda, *mhadaidh,* dog.

Vadda, *mhada,* a dog or fox.

Vaddan, *Uí-Mhadadhain,* O'Madden, a family name.

Vadden, *bhaidín,* not given.

Vadden, *Mheadán,* Maden a male name.

Vadden, *Uí-Mhadadhain, Uí-Mhadudhain,* O'Madden, a family name.

Vaddock, *Mhadóg, Mhadoig,* Madóg or Maddock, a personal or family name.

Vaddog, *feadóg,* plovers.

Vaddoge, *bhFeadóg, feadóg,* plovers.

Vaddra, *mhadaidh, mhadra, madadh,* a dog.

Vaddreen, little dog.

Vaddy, *fhada,* long.

Vaddy, *mhada, mhadhaigh, mhadaigh, mhadaidh, madadh,* a dog or dogs.

Vaddy, *Wádaigh,* Waddy, a male name.

Vade, *bháid,* a boat.

Vaden, *Mhardín,* Madan, a personal or family name.

Vaden, *Bhaidín,* Wadding, a personal or family name.

Vadin, *bháidín,* not given.

Vadin, *Uí-Mhaidín/Mhadadhain,* Ó Maidin or O'Madden, a family name.

Vadlea, *Bhadlaigh,* Badley or Bodley, an English personal name.

Vadlea, *bhadléigh,* a booley or dairying place.

Vadlea, *bhaidléigh,* not given.

Vadogue, *b-fiodóg,* plovers.

Vadra, *mhadaidh, madadh,* a dog.

Vadreen, *mhaidrín,* not given.

Vadrin, *mhaidrin, maidrín,* little dog.

Vady, *mhadaidh, madadh,* a dog.

Vagga, *mhaghaidh,* joking, pleasantry or merriment.

Vagga, *mhaghaidh,* not given.

Vagh, *bhFeadh,* rushes.

Vagh, *bhoth,* a hut or tent.

Vagh, *garbh,* rough.

Vagh, *mhacha,* a farmyard.

Vagh, *mhagh,* a plain.

Vagh, *mhaighe,* plains.

Vagha, *mhacha,* farmyard, cattle pens or a milking field.

Vaghan, *Bheachain,* O'Behan a family name.

Vaghan, *mheatháin,* the oak sieve-slit.

Vaghan, *mheitheán,* not given.

Vaghan, O'Hallaban, a family name.

Vaghan, *Uí-Bheacháin,* Ó Beacháin, O'Beahan, a family name.

Vaghera, *mhachaire, machaire,* a plain or field.

Vaghran, *fachran, feachran, bhFachrán, bhFachran,* bogbines.

Vaghrog, *bhFeathrog,* woodbine plants.

Vaghy, *garbh,* rough.

Vaghy, *machaire,* a plain or field.

Vagliair, *magh-gliadhaire,* plain of the warrior/gladiator.

Vagoon, old bacon(sic).

Vague, *mheidhg,* whey.

Vaha, *bheatha,* life or food.

Vaha, *bheithe,* not given.

Vaha, *mhacha,* a farmyard or cattle field.

Vahagh, *athach,* a giant.

Vahagh, *bheathach,* not given.

Vahalig, *mhaigh-shalaigh,* dirty field or plain.

Vahalla, *Uí-Bhachalla,* O'Buckley, a family name.

Vahalla, *Uí-Mhothlaigh,* Mohill or Moakley, a family name.

Vahan, *mheathan, mheatháin,* oak sieve-slit or slits.

Vahaun, *meathan,* the oak sieve-slit.

Vaheen, *Uí-Bheithín,* O'Behin or Behin, a family name.

Vaire, *Mhaire,* Máire, a female name.

Vakeen, *bháicín,* a little arm or winding road.

Vakeen, *Mhic-Caóin,* Mac Keen, a family name.

Vakig, *bhachaigh,* the cripple or beggar.

Val, *mheall,* hummocks or knolls.

Vala, *mhála,* not given.

Valden, *Bhaldain,* not given.

Valden, *Bhaldáin,* Baldwin, a personal or family name.

Valdon, *Bhaldún, Bhalduin,* Baldwin, a family name.

Vale, *béal, bhéil, bhéal,* mouth.

Vale, *bhealaigh, bealach,* the road, way, route or pass.

Vale, *bhFaol,* wolves.

Vale, *ghabhal,* fork.

Vale, *mhéala,* not given.

Valeen, *ghiolla-Fhinn,* not given.

Valeen, *mhala,* rising ground.

Valeen, *mhaoilin,* a bare eminence.

Valencia, *dairbhre,* not given.

Valentia, a Spanish name for the place of oaks.

Valentia, *béal-Inse,* mouth of the island also known by *dairbhre,* place of oaks.

Valentia (Island), *dairbhre,* not given.

Valherring, *bheil-iarthaigh,* western mouth or opening.

Valia, *baile,* town or townland.

Valla, *bhaile, baile,* a town, townland or homestead.

Valla, *bhaile,* see **Bally.**

Valla, *bhalla,* a wall.

Valla, *bhealaigh,* road or pass.

Valla, *bhile,* an ancient tree.

Valla, *mhála,* a sack or bag.

Valla, *mheille,* Melli, Irish calender November 4th.

Vallagh, *bhealaigh, bealach,* a road or pass.

Vallan, *bhalláin,* not given.

Vallan, *mhalainn,* a prominent peak or hill brow.

Vallanane, *bhaile-Fhionnain,* Finnan's (a male name) homestead.

Vallay, *bhealaigh,* a road.

Valleine, *Mhallúnaigh,* Maloon, a personal or family name.

Vallet, *Bhálait,* not given.

Valley, (when not the English word valley), *bhealaigh,* road.

Valley, *bhealaigh,* not given.

Vallican, *Bhailicín,* Wilkins, a family name.

Vallig, *bhealaig, bhealaigh, bealach,* a road, way or pass.

Vallig, *bhealaigh,* a pathway, pass, road or disused road.

Vallig, two roads.

Valliheen, *bhealaichín,* an old road.

Vallikeen, *bhealaichín,* a little passage.

Vallikin, *Bhailicín,* not given.

Vallo, *bhalla,* a wall.

Vallogue, *bhFáinleog,* swallows.

Vallogue, *bh-fheithleóg,* woodbines.

Vallony, *Mhallúnaigh,* Maloon, a personal or family name.

Valloona, *Bhallúnaigh,* not given.

Vally, *an-bhachlaigh,* the shepherd.

Vally, *baile, bhaile,* this can mean a town, townland, place, spot, homestead, enclosure, habitation, residence or situation.

Vally, *bhealaigh,* a road, a main road or a pass.

Vally, *bhuaile,* a booley or summer pasture.

Vally, *bil , bhile, bile,* an ancient tree.

Valode, *Mhealóid,* not given.

Valoon, *Bhaldúin, Bhalduin,* Baldwin, a personal or family name.

Valoona, *Bhaldúna,* not given.

Valoona, *Mhallúnaigh,* Maloon, a personal or family name.

Valtron, *Bhaltairín,* little Walter (a male name).

Vamane(sic)**,** *bhearnáin,* the little gap.

Van, *bhan,* white.

Van, *bheann,* pinnacles or gables.

Vana, *bhána, bhana,* a green field.

Vana, *Mhághúnaigh,* Mághúnach, not given.

Vanagh *mhanaigh,* monks.

Vanagh, *mhéadhonach,* middle.

Vanagh, *mheanaigh,* middle.

Vanagher, *beannchar, beannchor, bheannchair,* horns, pointed hill/s or rocks.

Vanagher, *bheannchair,* peaks.

Vane, *bháin,* a grassy field or lea land.

Vane, *bhán,* white.

Vane, *mheadhain, mheadháin, mheadhoin, mheáin, mheadhon,* middle.

Vane, *mheadhoin,* not given.

Vane, *mheathain,* saplings or twigs.

Vane, *mheathán,* not given.

Vaneen, *bháinín,* little green or grassy field.

Vaneen, *bháinin,* not given.

Vaneen, *Mhainnín,* Mannin, a family name.

Vaneen, *Mhainnín,* Manning, a personal or family name.

Vangour, *bheanna/beanna-gabhar,* pinnacle of the goat or peaks of the goats.

Vangour, *bheanna-gabhar,* peaks of the goats.

Vanig, *mhanaig,* the monk.

Vanig, *mhanaigh, mhanagh,* monks.

Vanish, *Mhaghnuis,* Manus, a personal or family name.

Vanloman, *beann-lomán,* bare peak.

Vanloman, *bheannlomáin,* not given.

Vanlomaun, *bheannlomáin,* not given.

Vanna, *banach,* the fox.

Vanna, *bheanna,* the peak.

Vanna, *mheana,* not given.

Vannagh, *bheannach,* hilly.

Vannagh, *mBeannach,* hilly.

Vannagh, *mhanach,* monks.

Vannagh, *mhéanaigh,* middle (mountain).

Vannagh, *mheanaigh,* middle.

Vannaghan, *beannahán,* little peak.

Vannan, *Mhanannain,* Mannann Mac Lir, a famous chief.

Vannan, *Uí-Bhanain,* O'Bannon, a family name.

Vanneen, *Ua-Mainin,* O'Manning, a family name.

Vannia, *bhainne,* milk.

Vanniha, *beannuighthe,* a blessing.

Vanniha, *bheannaithe,* not given.

Vannog, *bhFeannog, bhFeannóg,* Royston or scald crows.

Vannoge, *bhFeannog, bhFeannóg,* hooded crow/s or scald crows.

Vannogue, *bhFionnóg,* not given.

Vannon, *banadh,* common land.

Vannon, *mheannáin, meanán,* kid goat/s.

Vanny, *bhainne, baine,* milk.

Vanny, *bhainne,* milk.

Vanny, *bheannaighe,* a peak, a headland.

Vanny, *mhanaigh, manach, mhonaigh*(sic)**,** the monk.

Vanny, *mhanaigh,* the monk.

Vanogue, *bFeanog,* a riven or scald crow.

Vanshere, *mhainséir, mhainseir,* a manger or stable.

Vanue, *Mhaghnus, Mhaghnuis,* Manus, a male name.

Vanus, *Mhaghnus, Mhaghnuis,* Manus, a male name.

Vanus, *Mhánais, Mhaonais,* not given.

Var, *bhairr, barr,* top.

Var, *bharr,* not given.

Var, *fir, bhFear, bh-fhear, bfear, feara,* men.

Vara, *bharra,* the top or high spot.

Vara, *bhéara, Mhara,* not given.

Vara, *Mhaire,* St Mary.

Vara, *Mheádhra,* Meara, a family name.

Vara, *Uí-Bhearra,* O'Barra, a family name.

Varaga, *margadh,* a market.

Varagh, *bhanrach*(sic) , not given.

Varagh, *mhanrach,* mangers.

Varaghan, *Bhearchain,* St Berchan.

Varahane, *a-bharracháin,* the tow.

Varahane, *bharacháin,* a tow.

Varahane, *Bhearchain,* St Berchan.

Varahane, *bhoirain,* the pointed stake.

Vardagh, *bhardaigh, an-Bardach,* Ward a family name.

Vardin, *Uí-Bhardain,* O'Bardan, a family name.

Vareen, *Mhoirín,* not given.

Vareen, *Uí-Bhairín,* O'Barreen, a family name.

Varessa, *Mhairéasaigh,* not given.

Vargy, *bhearga,* not given.

Vargy, *marghaidh,* the market.

Variskal, *mharascail,* a marshal.

Varn, *bhFearn, bhFearna, fearna,* alders trees.

Varna, *bhearnach, bhearna, bearna,* a gap or gapped.

Varna, *fearna,* alder trees.

Varness, *bhearnas, bearnas,* a gap.

Varnet, *bearnas,* a gap.

Varnet, *bhearnain,* not given.

Varney, *bearna, bhearna, bearnas,* a gap.

Varnish, *bhearnas,* a gap.

Varnoge, *fearnóg, bhFearnóg, bh-fearnóg,* alder trees.

Varnogue, *fearnóg, bhFearnóg, bh-fearnóg,* alder trees.

Varoge, young men.

Varosig, *Fhearghusaigh,* Farris or Farrisey, a family name.

Varra, *bharra,* a burial mound.

Varra, *bharraigh, barrach,* not given.

Varra, *Bhearra, Bharraigh,* Barry, a personal or family name.

Varra, *bhearradh,* little hill tops.

Varra, *mhara, mara,* the sea.

Varra, *Uí-Bheara, Uí-Bhearra,* O'Barra, a family name.

Varracks, barracks.

Varraga, *fairrge,* waves.

Varraga, *mharagaidh, mhargaidh,* the market.

Varraga, *Uí-Bhearga,* O'Berga, a family name.

Varran, *bhearrthainn,* shaven or shorn.

Varran, *Uí-Bhearrain,* O'Barron, a family name.

Varrella, *an/a'-bharraille,* of the barrel.

Varrella, *an-bharaille,* not given.

Varrid, *barred,* cap/s.

Varrig, *Bharraig,* Barry, a personal or family name.

Varrigane, *Aimheirgin,* Aimheirgin, a personal or family name.

Varrihy, *bheirthe,* boiling.

Varrihy, *mharbhtha,* slaughter.

Varrinane, *fearnáin,* not given.

Varring, *an-bhairínigh,* not given.

Varring, *Bharain,* Warren, a personal or family name.

Varrodig, *Barrode,* Barrett, a family name.

Varry, Barry, a personal or family name.

Varry, *Bharraigh,* not given.

Varry, *Bearbha,* the Barrow river.

Vart, *bhFeart,* graves or miracles.

Vart, *mhairt,* the ox, fat ox, beef or bullock.

Vartley, *Bhartley,* Bartley, a male name.

Vartnogue, *fearnog, bh-fearnóg,* alder trees.

Vartry, *bhFear-tire,* men of the territory, district.

Varty, *feara/fir-tire,* men of the territory.

Vary, *Baircud,* Barcud or Barrett, a personal or family name.

Vary, *bhearaigh,* a heifer.

Vary, *bhearaigh, bearach,* not given.

Vary, *Bhearaigh,* Berragh or Berrie, a personal or family name.

Vary, *garbh,* rough.

Vas, *easa,* a waterfall.

Vas, *mheasa,* fruit or nuts.

Vasa, *bhásaigh,* not given.

Vasa, *Mhasa, Mhasaigh,* Massy, Massey, a family name.

Vaskin, *Bascain,* a male name.

Vaskin, *Bhaiscin,* not given.

Vaskin, *mic-Bhaskin*(sic), Mac Baskin, a family name.

Vass, *meas,* mast fruit (a type of nut tree).

Vassa, *Mhasaigh,* Massy, a family name.

Vasteen, *mhaistín,* not given.

Vaston, *Weston,* a personal or family name.

Vat, *bhata,* a stick.

Vateen, *Bhaitín,* little Batt, a personal name.

Vatheen, *Bhaitín,* Watteen, Watty or little Walter, a personal or family name.

Vatia, *bhaidhte,* not given.

Vatta, *bhata,* the stick.

Vaucoosh(sic), *bhácúis,* not given.

Vaud, *bháid, bhaid,* a boat.

Vaughan, *Uí-Bheacháin, Uí-Bheachain,*
O'Beacháin, O'Beaghan, O'Behan or
Behan a family name and means he
descendants of Behan.
Vaula, *mhala,* the bag.
Vaum, *maidhm,* a high pass.
Vaum, *mháma,* not given.
Vaun, *bhábhúin,* not given.
Vaun, *bhadhúin,* a cattle enclosure.
Vaun, *bháin,* the field.
Vaun, *bhan, bhán,* white/ish.
Vaun, *madhm,* an elevated pass.
Vaunaun, *Uí-Bhánáin,* O'Bannon, a family
name.
Vaunia, *bhFaithnidhe,* warts.
Vaurigh, *Mháire,* Mary.
Vaus, *mhás,* a plain(sic).
Vaus, *mhás,* a thigh or hill.
Vautia, *bhaidhte,* drowned.
Vautia, inundations or a quagmire.
Vave, *Mheidhbhe,* Maive, the name of the
Queen of Connaught.
Vaw, *bhadhthe,* drowning.
Vawn, *bhan,* white.
Vea, *beithe,* birches.
Vea, *bheithe, beithe,* birch.
Vea, *bhFia,* not given.
Vea, *bhFiadh,* deer.
Vea, *mheadha,* mead.
Veagh, *Bheac,* not given.
Veagh, *bheithe, bheathach, bheithigh, beithe,*
bheatha, birch/es.
Veagh, *bheitheach,* a birch plantation.
Veagh, *bheitheach, bheithe, beith,* birch.
Veagh, *bhFiach, bhFiadh, bhFiada, bhFiagh,*
deer.
Veagh, *bhFiach, fiach, bhFiadh fhiaigha,*
ravens.
Veaghane, *Uí-Mhaothagain,* Mehigan, the
name of an ancient Chief.
Veal, *bél,* mouth.
Veal, *bhéal,* not given.
Veal, *maol,* a hillside.
Veal, *mhíl,* not given.
Veala, *Bhialaigh,* Bialach, not given.
Vealawauma, *bhéal-an-mháma,* not given.
Vealawauma, *bhéil-a'-mhadhma,* at or of
the mouth of the mountain pass.
Vealawauma, *mhaoil-an-mháma,* not given.
Veale, *mhíl,* not given.

Veale, *mhil,* the hare.
Vealnaslee, *bhéil-na-slighe,* mouth or open-
ing of the main road or highway.
Vealran, *maol-rán,* pleasant hillside.
Vean, *bhfiann, b-Fiann,* the Fianna.
Veane, *b-Fiann,* the Fianna.
Veane, *bhFiann,* not given.
Veane, *meadhon,* the middle.
Veane, *meathán,* not given.
Veara, *Mhéara,* not given.
Vecane, *an-Deagánaigh,* not given.
Vecane, *Diogánaigh,* the crafty man or the
Deacon.
Vecane, *mhic-Dhéin(sic)/Céin,* MacKane, a
personal or family name.
Vecarrow, *bhiocaire,* the vicar.
Veccan, mushroom.
Ved, *bhFead,* not given.
Veddan, *bhFeadan,* rivulets.
Veddoge, *bhFeadóg, bhFeadog,* plovers.
Veddy, *Mhíde,* Míde, a personal or family
name.
Vedoge, *bhFeadog,* plovers.
Vee, *bfhiagh,* deer.
Vee, *bhuidhe, buidhe,* yellow.
Vee, *mhigh,* not given.
Veedy, *Mhíde,* Mida, a female name.
Veel, *mhaol,* not given.
Veel, *mhíl, moil,* the beast.
Veel, *mhíle,* the mile.
Veel, *mhíol,* not given.
Veela, *mhíle,* a mile.
Veela, *mhíle,* the soldier.
Veelane, *Mhaoláin,* Moylan, a family name.
Veelaun, *bhFaoileán,* not given.
Veelick, *mhílic,* low marshy ground or
marshy land.
Veelish, *Mhíligh,* not given.
Veelish, *Mhílis, Mhilis, Mhilis, Mílis,* Myles,
a male name.
Veelish, *Míligh,* a personal or family name.
Veely, *mhílic,* low ground.
Veely, (Coolaveely) slaughter or blood.
Veema, *bhioma,* a beam or plank.
Veen, *bhFiann,* the Fianna.
Veen, *bhFionn,* white spots.
Veen, *mhín,* a field.
Veen, *mhín,* smooth.
Veeney, *aoibhínn,* beautiful.
Veenog, StVinnog.

Veenoge, *Bhinog,* Winnoc or Benignus, a personal or family name.

Veeny, *bhFiodhnaighe,* woodmen.

Veeny, *mhianaigh,* mine/s.

Veer, *mhaoir,* a steward or agent.

Veera, *Mhéaraigh,* not given.

Veerane, *Uí-Bhíorain,* O'Birrane, a family name.

Veetry, *an-Bhiatra,* not given.

Veey, *Uí-Mheidhigh,* O'Meey, a family name.

Veg, *bheag, beg,* little.

Vegal, *mheigill,* whisker.

Veha, *bheithach, bheithe, beith, beitheach,* birch tree/s.

Vehagh, *bheitheach, beitheach,* birch trees or birch wood.

Veheen, *bheithín,* little birch.

Vehil, *mheitheal,* reapers.

Vehir, *bheither,* a bear.

Vehir, *bheithir,* not given.

Vehy, *beithe, bheithe,* birch.

Vehy, *bheithe, beith,* birch.

Veige, *bhéicach,* shouting.

Veige, *mheidhg,* inefficient or whey.

Veigh, *bhFia,* not given.

Veigh, *bhFiach,* ravens.

Veigh, *bhFiagh, bhFiadh,* deer.

Veigh, *gaoithe,* wind, windy.

Veiloge, *bhFeithleog,* woodbine.

Veiltig, *mheilitigh,* untidy.

Veiltig, *Mhioloidigh,* Mellot, a personal or family name.

Veilty, *mheallta,* deception.

Veilty, *mheilte,* not given.

Velaghan, *bhelachán,* a pathway.

Velaghan, *Uí-Mhaolachain,* O'Mullaghan, a family name.

Velish, *Mhílis,* Miles, a personal or family name.

Vella, *béille,* a caldron.

Vella, *bil , bhile, bile,* an ancient tree.

Vella, *bhile,* the big tree.

Vella, *bhile,* the sacred lone tree.

Vella, *Mheille,* not given.

Vellane, *Mhealláin,* not given.

Vellia, *bheile,* the ancient tree.

Velligan, *Maoileagáin,* Mulligan, a personal or family name.

Vellon, *Mhealdhún,* Melan, Mellon, a personal or family name.

Vellon, *Mhiolúin,* not given.

Velly, *bhealaigh,* a road or pass.

Velly, *bhile,* the ancient tree.

Velly, low ground.

Veloge, *Bhológ,* not given.

Veloge, *feithleoige,* honeysuckle.

Velone, *bhile-Eoghain,* Owen's (a male name) ancient or sacred tree.

Velone, *Uí-Mhaoileóin,* O'Malone, a family name.

Veltig, *mheiltigh,* not given.

Velton, *bealltaine,* a first of May day druidic festival.

Vemnon, *bhile-Bheanáin,* St Benen's (ancient) tree.

Vemnon, *Mheanmnáin,* not given.

Vena, *Mhaonaigh,* Maonach, a personal or family name.

Venagh, *Fhoibhne,* Foibhne, not given.

Venane, *Bheanain,* St Benan.

Vendrum, *Mhíndhroma,* not given.

Venew, *bheannuighthe,* a blessing.

Vennet, *Bheneit,* Bennet, a personal or family name.

Vennon, *Uí-Bheanáin,* O'Bannon, a family name.

Venny, *beanna,* the peak.

Venoge, *bhFeannóg,* not given.

Venoge, *Bhionóg,* Winoc, a personal or family name.

Venooragh, *bhFionnabhrach,* whitish coloured spots or the personal name 'Finnabair'.

Venooragh, *bhFionnúrach, not* given.

Ventry, *ceann-trágha/trá,* strand head.

Ventry, *fionntrá, fionntráigh, fionn-traigh,* white strand.

Ventry, *gaeth, gaiethe, gaeithe, gaoithe, gaoth,* the wind/s.

Ventry, *Venti* (Latin), wind.

Veny, *mhéine,* not given.

Veny, *mhéinne,* company or retinue.

Veny, *mhine,* smoothness.

Veoge, *Veoge,* St Mobheog.

Veone, *mheodhain,* middle.

Vera, *Mhéara,* not given.

Vera, *Mhíre,* O'Meera, a family name.

Verane, *Uí-Bhiorain,* Burn or Birrane, a family name.

Verassa, *Bhriasa,* Bryce, a male name.

Verassa, *Mhairéasaigh,* not given.

Vergan, *Uí-Mheirgin,* O'Mergin, a family name.

Vergan, *Uí-Mhuireagáin,* Ó Muireagán, a family name and the founder of a Church in Leitrim.

Vergin, *mheirge, mheirgin,* signal/s.

Vergin, *Uí-Mheirgin,* O'Mergin, a family name.

Veriga, *mheirge,* mist or fog.

Veril, *Uriel,* Uriel, a personal or family name.

Vern, *bhFearn,* not given.

Vern, *fearna,* alders trees.

Verna, *bhFearnaí,* not given.

Verneen, *Bhéirnín,* Vernon, a personal or family name.

Vernet, *bernet, barnet,* the gap.

Verney, *bhFearnaigh,* alder trees.

Vernock, *bearnas,* a gap.

Veroge, *Uí-Bhearóg,* O'Barrog or Varrock, a family name.

Verroge, *Uí-Bhearóg,* O'Barrog, a family name.

Verry, *Uí-Bhearaigh,* O'Berry, a family name.

Vert, *bhFeart,* graves.

Veskil, *Uí-Mheiscill,* O'Mescall, a family name.

Veskill, *Ua-Mesgil,* O'Mesgill, a family name.

Vesoge, *fhéasóg,* not given.

Vesoge, *pheasóg,* rough coarse growth.

Vet, *bheith,* birches.

Vetty, *Bheitígh,* Betty.

Vevagh, *Mhéabha,* Maeve a female name.

Vevagh, *Mhéibhe, Mheibhe, Mheidhbhe,* Maive or Maeve, a female name.

Vey, *bheith,* birch.

Vey, *bhFiadh,* deer.

Vhara, *Mheadhra,* O'Meara, a family name.

Viary, *mhaor,* a steward or an agent.

Vic. *mhic,* son.

Vicar, *Bhiocáire,* a vicar.

Vicka, *Mhic-an…,* not given.

Vickanease, *Mhic-Aenghuis,* MacAngus or Macaneese, a family name.

Vickarick, *Uí-Mhic-Broic, Uí-Mhic-Broic,* a family name.

Vickarry, *bhiocaire,* the Vicar.

Vickary, *Bhiocáire,* the vicar.

Vickeen, *Mhic-Cianaigh,* not given.

Vickillane, *Mhic-Aoibhleáin/Fhaoileán,* not given.

Vickillane, *Mhicileáin,* Micileán, a personal or family name.

Vickincrow, *Mhic-Inchró,* MacInchroe and Crowe, a family name.

Vicknaheeha, *Mhic-na-hOidhche,* not given.

Vicknaheeha, *Mhic-na-óidhche,* son of the night (a fairy).

Vickoge, *mhucóg,* broom.

Vickteera, *Mhachtíre,* wolf.

Vicleheen, *Mhicleighin,* McLehaen, a family name.

Vicleheen, *Mhic-Léithín,* not given.

Vicnabo, Macnabo, a family name.

Vicnacally, *Mhic-na-caillighe,* not given.

Vicnacally, *Mhic-na-calliagh,* son of the hag.

Vicnaheeha, *Mhic-na-hOidhche,* son of the night.

Vicneill, *Mhic-Neill,* son of Neill, a male name.

Vicnowen, *mac-nEoghain,* sons of Eoghain, a male name.

Vicrune, *Mhic-Riadhain,* Rowan's (a male name) son.

Victeera, *Mhic-Tíre, Mac-Tíre,* correct translation is son of the country but it is also used to denote a wolf.

Victeeree, *Mhic-Tíre,* Mac Tire, a family name.

Victeery, *Mhic-Tíre,* not given.

Viddane, *bhFeadán,* streamlets.

Viddaun, *bhFeadán,* streamlets.

Viddoge, *bhFeadóg, feadóg,* plover/s.

Viddy, *Mhide, bhFide, Bhide,* not given.

Vidoge, *bhFeadóg,* plover.

Vie, *beithe,* birch.

Viegh(sic), *bhFhia,* not given.

Vigane, *Bheagain,* O'Biggan, a family name.

Viggane, *Uí-Bheagáin,* O'Beggan or Biggane, a family name.

Vihoonig, *bhitheamhnaig, bitheamhnach,* the thief or thieves.

Vikillane, *Mhic-Cilleain,* MacKillane, a family name.

Vilcorris, *Mhaolchoráis,* not given.

Vilcorris, *Mhoil/Mhaoil-Corais,*
MacFheorais, MacFeorais, a family
name and the Irish for Birmingham.

Villa, *bhile, bile,* an ancient branchy, large,
ritual or sacred tree.

Villa, *billa,* a branchy tree.

Villa, *Mhill,* not given.

Village, *Bharragh,* Barry, a pesons name.

Villahowe, *bheile-h-abha,* old tree of the river.

Villahowe, *mhaoile-hAbha,* not given.

Villan, *mhuilin,* a mill.

Villane, *Mhealláin,* not given.

Villane, *Uí-Mhilleain,* O'Millan, a family
name.

Villar, *bhiolair,* watercress.

Ville, *bFhille,* poets.

Ville, *bhaile,* town.

Ville, *bhile,* an ancient, large or sacred tree.

Ville, *Mhil,* Mil the name of an ancient chief.

Ville, *mhil, miol,* a great beast or monster.

Ville, *mhil,* the hare or animal.

Ville, *mhullaigh,* summit.

Villeen, *mhillín,* a flat, smooth hillock.

Villeen, *mhillín,* a little knoll.

Viller, *biolair, biolarach, biolaraigh, bhiolair,*
watercress/es.

Villian, *mhuilluin,* mills.

Villish, *Bhailis,* Wallace, a personal or family name.

Villo, *bile,* and ancient tree.

Villy, *bhile,* a ritual tree.

Villy, *bhile, bile,* an ancient tree.

Villy, *bhileach,* not given.

Vilra, *bhiolra,* watercress.

Viltoge, *mioltóg,* midges.

Vin, *bhinne, bhinn,* the peak.

Vin, *mhaoin,* not given.

Vinaan, *mhionnáin,* the kid (goat).

Vinalla, *Bhinealla,* not given.

Vinally, *fionghaile,* fratricide or murder of
a relative.

Vinally, swans.

Vinane, *Bheanain,* St Benan.

Vinane, *mheannáin,* a kid goat.

Vinaun, *mhionáin,* saxifrage.

Vindee, *bhinidí,* rennet.

Vine, *mhaighean,* not given.

Vinegar hill, *cnoc-fiodh-na-gCaor, cnoc-fidh-*
na-gCaer, hill of the wood of the berries.

Viniter, *Mhiniteir,* Miniter, a family name.

Vinlush, *Mhionlais,* not given.

Vinn, *bhFinn,* the fair haired people.

Vinna, *beinna,* a hill summit.

Vinna, *bhinne,* the hillside(sic).

Vinna, *bhinne,* the peak.

Vinna, *mhuine,* a thicket.

Vinnane, *an-mheannáin,* not given.

Vinnane, *meannán, mhionnáin,* the kid
(goat).

Vinnaun, *mhionnain, mhionnáin,* the kid
(goat).

Vinnaun, *mhoinnán, mheannáin,* not given.

Vinnoge, *bhFeannóg, bhFeannog,* scaldcrows
or royston crows.

Vinnoge, *bhFionnóg,* scald crows.

Vinny, *mhuine,* a shrubbery or brake.

Vinoge, *Mhomhéanóg, Mhíonóg,* not given.

Vinogue, *Uíonóg, Bhinog,* St Winnog/
Winnoc/Winnogus, the virgin Saint.

Vinoge, *mo-Sheanog,* St Seanán.

Vinshire, *mhuinséir, mhainséir, mhainseir,* the
manger.

Vio, *béo,* living.

Vionlach, *mhíonlaigh,* the grassy sward.

Vir, *bhiorra,* standing water(sic).

Vir, *bhiorraigh,* not given.

Vir, *bhiorra,* the watery place.

Vira, *an-Mheidhrigh, an-Meidhreach,* not
given.

Virane, *bhiorain,* the little peak.

Virane, *bhiorain,* the point.

Virane, *bhoighreain,* bulrushes.

Virane, *Mheadhráin,* not given.

Virane, *Uí-Bhioráin/Bhíorain,* O'Birrane, a
family name.

Vireen, *Uí-Mhirín,* O'Mireen, O'Mirrin or
O'Mearain, a family name.

Virginia, named after the virgin Queen
Elizabeth I. The Irish name is *achadh-an-*
Iúir, field of the yew.

Virick, *bhiaraic,* not given.

Viron, *bhioráin,* a brooch, pin or small
pointed stake.

Viron, *mhaighreáin,* not given.

Viscaun, *mhioscáin,* a roll of, or shaped
lumps of butter, a cairn shaped like a
butter roll.

Vishteal, *Mhistéala,* Mitchel, a personal or
family name.

Vistea, *Mhistia,* Mistie a family name.

Vistea, *Mhistígh,* not given.

Visteal, *Mhistéil, Mhistéal,* Mitchel or Michael, a personal or family name.

Visteale, *Mhisteil,* Mitchell, a family name.

Vlin, *Bhilín,* not given.

Vlish, *Eibhlíse,* not given.

Vlyman, *Bhladhmainn, Bhladhmain,* not given.

Voam, *mhadhma,* not given.

Voan, *mhóin,* not given.

Voarheen, *bhóithrin,* a little road.

Vock, a buck.

Vocka, *bhacaigh,* the cripple.

Vockaun, *bocán,* a buck goat.

Vockaun, *bhocáin,* a goat.

Vockoge, *Mhacóg,* not given.

Vockogue, *bhacaigh,* a beggar.

Vodane, *Uí-Bhuadain,* Bowden, Boden or O'Boden, a family name.

Vodda, *mhadaigh,* the dog.

Voddagh, *bhodaigh,* a clown or churl.

Voddig, *bhodaigh,* a low bred person.

Voddig, *bodach,* a churl.

Voddock, *bhodaigh,* a bad mannered clown.

Voddy, *bhodaigh,* a churl or bad mannered clown.

Voddy, *mhadaidh,* not given.

Vode, *bhFod,* green sods or patches.

Voden, *Bhaodain,* Boden, a personal or family name.

Vodig, *bodagh, bhodaigh,* a landlord, a churl or a bad mannered clown.

Vodinnaun, *bhoth-Dinneáin,* Dinan's (a male name) hut or booth.

Vodock, *bhodaigh,* a bad mannered clown.

Vodra, *mhadaidh, madadh,* a dog.

Voe, *bho,* cow.

Voe, *Bhoga, Buidhbh, Buaidhbh,* Bove Derg, an ancient chief and Prince.

Voe, *bhoithe,* a hut or cottage.

Voe, *bhugha,* the blue plant 'bugh'.

Voe, *both,* a hovel(sic).

Voe, *mhogha,* a plain.

Voe, *Uí-Bhuadha,* O'Boy, a personal or family name.

Voge, *Uí-Bhuadhaigh,* O'Bogue, a family name.

Voge, *Uí-Bhuadhoig,* O'Boag, a family name.

Vogga, *a'mhaga,* scoffing.

Vogga, *mhagaidh,* merrymaking.

Vogga, *mhaghaidh,* joking, pleasantry.

Voggan, bog, boggy.

Voggy, *bhogaigh,* bog.

Vogh, *bhoithe,* a hut.

Vogh, *both,* a house or hut.

Vogh, *mhagh,* a plain.

Voghan, *Uí-Bheachain,* O'Beaghan, Behan a family name.

Voghan, *Uí-Bhuacháin,* Ó Baucháin, a family name.

Voghil, *buachaill,* the boy.

Voughil, *bhuachail,* boys.

Voghill, *bhuachaill,* boys.

Voghlaun, *Uí-Bhochaláin,* O'Bohalan, a family name.

Vogie, *bhogaigh,* bog.

Vogig, *bhogaigh,* not given.

Vogue, *Dhabhóg,* Dabhóg, a personal or family name.

Vogue, *gheagháin,* the trifle.

Vogue, *Mhaodhóg,* Maodóg, a personal or family name.

Vogue, *Uí-Bhuadhoig,* O'Boag, a family name.

Vogue, *Uí-Bhuaigh,* Ó Buaigh, a family name.

Vogy, *bhogaighe, bhogaigh, bhogaigh,* a quagmire or bog.

Vogy, *bhogáin,* a little bog.

Vohalane, *Uí-Bhochaláin,* O'Bohalan, a family name.

Vohanaun, *bhFothannán,* thistles.

Vohar, *mhothair,* a thicket.

Vohaun, *bhotháin, bhothán,* a hut or cabin for animals.

Vohaun, *mhúcháin,* not given.

Voher, *bothair, bhóthair, bhothair,* a road.

Voher, *mothar, mother, mhothair,* a grove or thicket.

Voher, *mothar,* a ruin.

Vohil, *bhuachalla,* not given.

Vohill, *bhuachalla,* the boy.

Vohill, *mhothail,* a bushy peak.

Vohumogue, *Mathghamhna,* young Mahon, a family name.

Vohy, *bhoithe,* a cattle hut, a booth, tent or hut.

Voige, *Uí-Bhuadgaigh,* O'Bogue, a family name.

Voir, *oighir,* ice.

Voke, *bhuaic,* a pointed hill.

Vokeen, *bhuaicín,* little pinnacle.

Vokig, *bhuacaigh,* bleaching.

Vola, *Bheoláin,* not given.

Vola, *buaile, bhuaile,* a booley or milking place.

Volan, *Uí-Bheóllain,* O'Boland, a family name.

Volan, *Uí-Mhaolain,* O'Molan, O'Mailan or O'Mullane, a family name.

Volane, *an-mhullain,* the little hill.

Volane, *Uí-Mhaolain,* O'Mullane, O'Mailan, O'Mullane or Mullins, a family name.

Volane, *Uí-Mhothlain,* O'Mohalan, a personal or family name.

Volara, *bhéil-a'gheárrtha,* mouth of the cutting.

Voley, *buaile, bhuaile,* a booley or milking place.

Voley, *ghualaigh,* not given.

Volis, *bhoth-loiscthe,* not given.

Volla, *mhullaigh,* the summit.

Vollaboy, *baile-bhuí,* yellow soil(sic)

Vollahane, *bhuaileachain,* milking fields.

Vollane, *Uí-Mhaolain,* O'Molan, O'Mailan or O'Mullane, a family name.

Volley, *bhaile,* see **Bally.**

Volli, *buaile, bhuaile,* a booley or milking place.

Volly, *bhile,* the big tree.

Vologe, *Bhológ,* not given.

Vologe, *Mhaolmuaidh,* Molloy, a family name.

Voloon, *Uí-Mhaoileoin,* O'Malone, a family name.

Volty, *Bhualtaigh,* not given.

Voly, *buaile, bhuaile,* a booley or milking place.

Volyshane, *bhuaile-Sheáin/Sheain,* John's booley/dairying place.

Vonane, *Fionnain,* Finnan, a personal or family name.

Vonavaun, *bonnamhán,* a small family.

Vone, *mhóin, mhoin,* a bog.

Vone, *mhúin,* putrid water.

Vonear, *mhóinéir, mhóinfhéir,* the meadow.

Vonear, *mhóinfhéir,* bog grass or a mountain meadow.

Voneen, *mhóinín, mhonin,* little bog.

Voney, *muine,* a brake or shrubbery.

Voney, *mhóna,* bog.

Voney, *Uí-Mhughmaid,* O'Mooney or O'Meany, a personal or family name.

Vongane, *Uí-Mhongain,* Mongan, a family name.

Vongane, *Uí-Mhongáin,* O'Mongan or O'Mangan, a family name.

Vonnavaun, *Uí-Bhanbhán,* O'Banavan, a family name.

Vonteen, *mhóintín, mhóintin,* the little bog.

Vony, *mhóna,* bog.

Voo, *bhua,* not given.

Voodane, *Uí-Bhuadáin,* Ó Buadáin or O'Boydane, a family name.

Voodaun, *Bhadáin,* Buadan, a personal or family name.

Vool, *Bhúlaigh, Bhúil,* not given.

Voola, *bhuaile,* a cattle yard.

Voola, *buaile, bhuaile,* a booley or milking place.

Voola, *bhuaile,* a cattle yard.

Voolagh, *buáileach,* boolies.

Vooley, *buailidh,* a mountain dairy.

Voolia, *buaile, bhuaile,* a booley or milking place.

Voolin, *bhFaolán,* seagulls.

Voolin, dairying places.

Voolta, *bhuilg,* bellows.

Voolty, *bhuailte,* the striking or battle.

Vooly, *buailidh,* a mountain dairy.

Voon, *mhuin,* putrid water or weeds.

Voon, *mhuin,* urine.

Voon, *Un,* Un, the name of a firbolg chief.

Voone, *mhóin,* bog.

Vooney, *Uí-Mhughmaid,* O'Mooney or O'Meany, a personal or family name.

Voonteen, *mhóintín,* a little bog.

Voor, *mór,* big.

Voord, *bhoird,* the border.

Vooren, *Mhúirín,* not given.

Vora, *Mhaolmhóra,* not given.

Vora, *Uí-Mhórdha,* O'More or O'Moore, a family name.

Voraha, *Mhurchada,* Murrough or Morgan, a family name.

Voran, *bhotháin,* a little hut.

Voran, *moráin,* rushes.

Vorane, *Uí-Mhearain,* Marron, a family name.

Vorane, *Uí-Mhoráin,* O'Moran, a family name.

Vorda, *Ua-Bhorda,* O'Borda, a family name.

Vordy, *....mhor-duibhe,* black Marthas...

Vore, *Mhora,* Mór or Mora, a female name.

Vore, *Mhórda,* Moore, a family name.

Vore, *Mhórdha,* not given.

Vore, *mór, mhór,* big, great.

Vore, *Uí-Mhordha,* Morda or O'Moore, a personal or family name.

Voreada, *bhó-Riada,* not given.

Voreda, *Mhairghreada,* Margaret, a female name.

Voreen, *Mhuirín,* Moreen, a female name.

Voreen, *Mhuirín,* not given.

Vorgal, *mhorghail,* great slaughter.

Vorheen, *bhoithrín, bhóithrin,* little road or boreen.

Vorheen, *bhotharín,* a by-road.

Vorisheen, *Mhuirishín,* Little Maurice, a mans or boys name.

Vorna, *bhoirne,* not given.

Vorna, *bóirne, boirne,* burren, rocks or rocky.

Vorneen, *bhoirnín,* not given.

Vornlavawn, *bheanlomáin,* bare peak.

Vorouna, *mharbhana,* killings.

Vorraga, *mhargaidh, mharga, marga,* market.

Vorrigan, *Muireagan,* Morgan, a personal or family name.

Vortha, *bhFotharta,* Forthians, i.e. people of the Wexford barony of 'Forth'.

Vortha, *bhFotharta,* Fotharts(sic).

Voster, *bhaistidh,* baptism.

Vota, *mhóta, mhota,* a moat or fort.

Votta, *bhata,* a stick.

Vouchane, the hut(sic).

Vouden, *Bhóidín,* not given.

Vougerish, *bhograis,* shaking sod.

Vough, *mhacha,* an enclosure or milking place.

Vougha, *mhacha,* a farmyard, cattle-field or milking place.

Voughalan, *bhuachaláin,* rag-weed.

Voughallan, *Uí-Bhuachalláin,* O'Bohallan or O'Rohallan, a family name.

Voughallan, *Uí-Bhuachalláin,* O'Bohallan, a family name.

Voughan, *Bhéacháin,* O'Behane, a family name.

Vougher, *a'mhacha,* a milking place.

Voughil, *bhuachaill,* a boy, in this case a shepherd boy.

Voughly, *bhachla,* a crozier.

Vought, *bhoicht,* poor.

Vouig, *bhuadhaigh,* victory.

Voula, *buaile, bhuaile,* a booley or milking place.

Vouler, *Bhalldair,* Balldar, a personal or family name.

Voulera, *Bhúlaeraigh,* not given.

Voulera, *Bholaerigh,* Bowler, a personal or family name.

Voultig, *bhuailtigh,* a cattle field.

Voultry, *bhualtraigh,* cow-dung.

Voulty, *bhuailte,* threshing(sic).

Voun, *bheann,* gables.

Vouncough, *banca,* the bank.

Vounkagh, *bh-frangcach,* rats or Frenchmen.

Voura, *bhannraigh,* a pound, pen or enclosure.

Vourk, *bhruaich,* a boundary.

Vourneen, *Mhaíre-Ní,* Mary, a female name.

Vourney, *bhúirne, bhuirne, mhuirnigh, bhoirne,* rocky or stony land.

Vourney, *Mhúirne, Mhuirne,* Murna, a female name.

Vouskill, *Uí-Mheiscill,* Meskill, a family name.

Vow, (The) *an-bhadhbh,* not given.

Vowe, *Uí-Bhogha,* O'Bowe, a family name.

Vownig, *Mhathamhnaigh,* not given.

Voy, *bhagha,* fighting.

Voy, *bhaidhidh,* drowning.

Voy, *bhoidh,* a shaft.

Voy, *Bhoidhe, Buite, Boethius,* a persons name and possibly a Saints name.

Voy, *bhoth,* the hut.

Voy, *bhuaidh,* not given.

Voy, *bhuí, bhuidhe,* yellow.

Voy, *mhá, mhaí, mhagh,* a plain.

Voydan, *Bhaodáin,* St Baedan, Baetan.

Voydan, *Bhoidán,* St Boydaun.

Voyle, *Uí-Bhaoghill/Bhaoill,* Ó Baoill or O'Boyle, a family name and means the descendants of Boyle.

Vraghan, *Uí-Bhracháin,* O'Braghan, a family name.

Vragnosig, *Bhraghnosaigh,* Bragnose, a personal or family name.

Vranneen, *bhranín,* a rookery or rooks.

Vranneen, *Uí-Bhrainín,* O'Brannin, a family name.

Vranner, *bhranair,* a fallow field.

Vrannig, *Bhreathnaig,* Walsh, a family name, can also mean British.

Vranny, *bhreathnaigh,* shallow.

Vrantry, *an-bhruinnteora,* not given.

Vrantry, *bhróinteóra, bhroinnteoraigh, brointeiraigh,* a quern-stone maker.

Vrauca, *bráca,* a harrow.

Vraugher, *bhrathar, m-bráthar,* Friars.

Vrauka, *bhráca,* a harrow.

Vray, *bhFraoch,* heaths.

Vreagh, *bh-fiarach,* rough grounds.

Vreaghaun, *fraochán, bhFraochán,* whortleberries.

Vreaneen, *Bhraoinín,* not given.

Vredth, *Bhrídhge,* Bridget.

Vree, *bhrí,* not given.

Vreeda, *bhraighde,* hostages.

Vreeda, *Bhrighde,* Brigit, a female name.

Vreedig, *bhreadaigh,* an opening or narrow glen.

Vreeghan, *bhFraochán,* whortleberries.

Vreeghaun, *bhFraochán,* not given.

Vreen, *bruighne,* a fairy palace.

Vreen, *Uí-Bhraoin,* O'Breen, a family name.

Vreen, *Uí-Briain,* O'Brien, a family name.

Vreena, *an-Bhrianaigh, an-Brianach,* not given.

Vreena, *braoinigh, bruighean,* a fairy mashion, ford or Inn.

Vreena, from *bruighean,* a fairy mansion.

Vrega, *bhréige,* phantastic(sic) men.

Vrick, *bhruic,* the badger.

Vrick, *Uí-Bhric,* not given.

Vrick, *Uí-Mhic-Broic, Uí-Mhic Broic,* a family name and the name of an ancient tribe.

Vriesta, *bhriste,* broken.

Vrin, *Bhroin,* Bron, a male name.

Vrin, *Bran,* Brin, a male name.

Vrin, Byrne, a personal or family name.

Vrin, *Uí-Bhrin,* O'Brin or O'Byrne, a family name.

Vrin, *Uí-Bhroin,* O'Byrne, a family name.

Vrinsig, *Phroinsigh,* French, a personal or family name.

Vrisk, *Bhriosc,* not given.

Vrislaun, *Uí-Bhreisleáin,* O'Breslin, a family name.

Vrogeen, *bhróigín,* not given.

Vroghaun, *bhruachán,* sloping ground.

Vroghaun, *Uí-Bhruacháin,* O'Brohan, a family name.

Vrokig, *bhrocaigh,* a badger warren.

Vrolla, *bhrollaigh, brollach,* the breast.

Vrona, *Bhrúnaigh,* Browne, a family name.

Vrona, *Bhrúnaigh,* not given.

Vronig, *Bhrunaigh, Bhronaigh,* Brown, a family name.

Vroonig, *Bhrunaigh,* Browne, a family name.

Vroughel, *brothail,* heat.

Vruggy, *bhrogaidh,* a resident of a farmhouse or a farmer.

Vrulla, *bhrollach,* the breast or front.

Vuck, *mhuc, muc,* a pig/pigs.

Vuckane, *bhacáin,* not given.

Vuckee, *mhuicidhe,* pigs.

Vuddig, *bhodaigh,* a clown or churl or labourer.

Vugga, *bhogaigh,* a quagmire.

Vulhane, *Uí-Mhothláin,* Ó Mothláin, a family name.

Vulla, *mhuilin,* a mill.

Vulla, *mullach, mhullaigh,* a summit.

Vullagh, *mhullaigh,* the summit.

Vullan, *Mhalán, Maelain,* Maelán or Maelan, a personal or family name.

Vullan, *Mhaolán,* not given.

Vullane, *bhalláin,* not given.

Vullane, *mhulláin,* little summit.

Vullane, *Uí-Mhaolain,* O'Molan, O'Mailan or O'Mullane, a family name.

Vullar, *bhiolair,* water cresses.

Vullaun, *mhulláin,* little hill or summit.

Vullaun, *mulláin, mhullán, mullán,* a little summit/s.

Vulleen, *maoilín,* a little hill.

Vulleen, *mhaoilín,* a little bare or bald knoll.

Vullen, *mhaolain, mullen,* a hill.

Vullen, *mholainn(sic),* not given.

Vullen, *mhuilinn,* a mill.

Vullig, *bhoilg,* not given.

Vullig, *mhullaigh,* a peak.

Vulligan, *bholgan,* cow pasture.

Vulligan, *Uí-Mhaolagain,* O'Mulligan, a family name.

Vullin, *mhuilaigh,* a summit.

Vullin, mhuilinn, not given.

Vullin, mhuileann, a mill.

Vun, *bun,* bottom (land).

Vunaknick, *bhun-a'chnuic,* bottom of the hill.

Vunatrime, *bun-a'truím,* the bottom of the elder trees.

Vunatrime, *mhóin-an-troim,* not given.

Vune, *bhFionn,* white spots.

Vung, *mhuing, muing,* a sedgy place, a morass.

Vurra, *Bhurra,* Burr, a personal or family name.

Vurra, *Mhuire,* (St?)Mary, a female name.

Vurra, *Mhurchadha,* Murrough, a family name.

Vurrig, *bhuirg,* not given.

Vurrin, *Bhoirn,* not given.

Vurrin, *Muirinn,* Murrin a female name.

Vuscaun, *bhoscáin,* not given.

Vuskig, *Bhoscaigh,* Fox, a family name.

Vyle, *mhaoile,* the bald man.

W

Wack, *bhaic,* the bend or turning.

Wackeen, *bhaicín,* little cripple or beggar.

Wackey, *bhachaigh,* a vagrant or travelling people.

Wadda, *madadh,* a dog.

Wadda, *mhaide,* not given.

Waddera, *mhadra, mhadraidh,* a dog/s.

Waddra, *mhadra,* the dog.

Waddy, *mhadaidh,* fox.

Waddy, *mhadaigh,* dog.

Waddy, *mhada, mhadaigh,* a dog.

Wade, *bháid,* a boat.

Wadra, *mhadra, mhadraidh,* a dog/s.

Wadreen, *maidrín,* the little dog.

Wady, *mhadra, mhadraidh,* a dog/s.

Wahera, *mhachaire,* a plain.

Waine, *Dubhain,* O'Duane a family name.

Waine, white.

Wairy, *mhaoiririgh*(sic), not given.

Wal, *bhaile,* town.

Waleen, *mauleen,* a little bag.

Waleen, *mhailín,* not given.

Walkey, *bhalcoigh,* driving.

Walky, *bhalcaigh,* driving.

Wall, *bhFál,* hedges.

Wall, *bhFal,* fences.

Walla, *báile, baile,* a town/land.

Wallace, *Mhic-Mhalais,* not given.

Wallan, *Mhailín,* not given.

Wallig, *bhealaigh,* road, way route or pass.

Wally, *baile,* a townland/town.

Walsh, *an-Bhreathaigh,* not given.

Walsh, *Bhailise,* Wallace, a personal or family name.

Walsh, *solais, sholuis, sholais,* light.

Walter, *Bháltair, Bhaitéir, Bhaitér, Ualtair,* Walter, a male name.

Walter, *Uaitéir*(sic), *Bhaltuir,* not given.

Waltrin, *Bhaltraim,* not given.

Waltrin, *Ualtairín, Ualtruim,* little Walter, a male name.

Wana, *bán,* lea land.

Wana, *bhána,* white.

Wana, *bhFánadh,* slopes or sloping lands.

Wanna, *mhanaigh,* monks.

Wannagh, *bhFánach,* slopes.

Wannagh, *mhanach,* monks.

Wannia, *bhainne, baine,* milk.

Wannia, *bhFáinne,* rings.

Wanny, *baine,* milk.

Wanny, *bf-faithuidhe,* warts.

War, *bháirr,* high lands.

War, *bháirr,* the top.

War, *bharr,* a top or summit.

Warbera, *Barbera,* Barbara, a personal or family name.

Warble, *earball,* a tail.

Ward, *bard,* a bard or poet.

Ward, *bárda, bháird, bharda,* not given.

Ward, *bhárda,* garrison.

Ward, Ward, a family name.

Ward, *mBard,* bards.

Ward, *Mhic-an-Bhaird,* Macaward, a family name.

Warden, *Uí-Bhardain,* O'Bardan, a family name.

Wardy, *bhardaigh,* not given.

Ware, *mháor,* stewards.

Wargy, *mhargaidh,* the market.

Wark, *mhairc,* boundary.

Warla, *mhárla,* yellow clay.

Warra, *marbhtha,* murder.

Warraga, *mhargaidh,* a market.

Warreela, *Bharrthuisle,* not given.

Warriff, *mharbhtha,* murder or slaying.

Warrig, *bharra,* a burial mound.

Warrig, *Bharraigh,* Barry, a personal or family name.

Warrige, *mhargaidh,* a market.

Warry, *mharaidhe,* the mariner.

Warry, *bhaire,* a contest or game.

Warvaneill, *mharbhtha-Neill,* Neill's (a personal or family name) death or the killing of Neill.

Wary, *bháire,* the winning gap or goal.

Wary, *Mhuireadhaigh,* Murray, a family name.

Wasna, *chuas-na…,* holes of the…

Water, *uachter, uachtair, uachdar, uachtar,* upper.

Wateree, *uachtaraí,* upper fields.

Waterfall, *tobar-an-Iarla,* not given.

Waterford, *Vadrefiord, Vedrefiordr,* a Danish name. The Irish name is *Port Lairge* or lairges (a personal or family name) landing place.

Waterig, *uachtaraigh,* upper.

Watermoy, *uachtar/uachtair-maighe,* upper plain.

Waterville, *an-Coireán,* not given.

Waterway, *uachtar-maí/mhuighe,* the upper plain.

Watia, *baithe,* drowned.

Watree, *uachdaraighe,* upper lands.

Watree, *uatraí,* not given.

Wattick, *Bhattoig,* little Watt, a personal or family name.

Waughter, *uachtar, uachtair,* upper.

Waum, *mhadhma,* a breach or defeat.

Waum, *mhádhma,* a chasm, breach or narrow mountain pass.

Waun, *bhán,* white/ish.

Waun, *bhFán,* slopes.

Waus, *mhás,* a hill.

Way, *both,* an old booth, hut or tent.

Way, *buidhe,* yellow.

Way, *mhaigh, mhuighe,* a plain.

Waystick, *Bostoic,* Bostock, a personal or family name.

Waystick, *istigh,* inner.

Weal, *mheal,* bald or flat.

Wear, *mhaoire, mhaior, mhaeir,* a steward or keeper.

Wear, *Mhéara,* not given.

Wee, *buí, bhuí, bhuidhe, buidhe,* yellow.

Wee, *mael,* hornless cow or cows.

Wee, *mhuighe,* a plain.

Wee, *uaimh,* caves.

Weehill, *maethail,* soft spongy land.

Weel, *mael,* hornless cow/cows.

Weel, *méoel*(sic), low.

Weel, *mhaoil,* a hillock.

Weel, *mhaoil,* the bald (man).

Weel, *mhaol,* bare.

Weelan, *faoileánn,* seagulls.

Weelan, *Mhaoláin,* not given.

Weelan, *Mhoilain,* Moylan, a family name.

Weelan, *Uí-Mhaoileáin,* O'Moylan, a family name.

Weelaun, *bhFaeileán, bhFaoileán, faoileánn, faoiléann, faoileán, faeileán,* seagulls.

Weelaun, *maoilean,* bare knolls.

Weeleen, *maoelín*(sic) a small hillock.

Weeleen, *mhaoilín,* a round hillock.

Weelis, *mhaoil-lis,* the bald or flattened fort.

Weelis, *mhaoilis,* a flat fort.

Weeloge, *faeilóg,* seagulls.

Weema, *mhaoidheama,* spring or eruption.

Weenagh, *Mhuimhneach,* Munstermen.

Weer, *maoir, mhaoir, mhaor, mhaeir,* a steward or keeper.

Weesha, *mhaighe-Seaghdha,* Shea's (a personal or a family name) plain.

Wehichy, *na-bhFaochacha,* not given.

Weir, *Uí-Mhuighir,* O'Moyre, a family name.

Well, *mhaol,* not given.

Wellan, *Uidhilín, Uidhilin,* Hugolin, Uidhilín or Uidhilin, a personal or family name.

Welligan, *Uí-Mhaelagáin,* O'Mulligan, a personal or family name.

Wells, *tobar-Scoilbín,* not given.

Wesnagh, *bhFaistneach,* soothsayers, diviners or fortune tellers.

Westmeath, *an-Iarmhí,* the west part of old Meath.

Westport, *cathair-na-mart,* stone fort of the market.

Wexford, *Weisford,* a Danish name for the West Ford. The Irish name is *loch-Garman,* lake of the river 'Garma'. See **Garma.**

Whack, *bhaic,* an angle, angular space, land or a river turn.

Whealt, *fiodhalt,* wooded cliff.

Wheela, *faill-a'…,* declivity of the…

Wheelion, *bhFaeileán, faeileán,* seagulls.

Wheelion, *faoileann,* not given.

Wheery, *fiodhre, fuidhre, foithre* a wood, forest, underwood or copse.

Wheery, *foíre, fhoíre,* not given.

Whelan, *faoileann, faoilean,* seagulls.

Whelan, *Fhaoláin, Faolán,* a personal or family name.

Wherrew, *foithre,* underwood or copse.

Wherry, *choire,* the cauldron.

Whiddy, *faoide,* bad weather.

Whiddy, *oileann-Faoite,* White's (a family name) island.

Whiggel, *chuigile,* a distaff or professional spinner.

Whillan Rock, *faoileann, daoileann,* not given.

Whinnigan, from *finn,* whitish spot of land.

Whinnoo, *fuineadh,* the limit or end.

Whirry, a whirlpool.

Whirry, *choire,* a cauldren or whirlpool.

Whishogue, *fuiseóg,* skylark/s.

Whissock, *fuiseog,* larks (birds).

White, *fuit,* cold(sic).

Whollart, *abhall-ghort, abhalghort,* the orchard field.

Why, *chuaigh,* cuckoo.

Wick, *bhaic,* not given.

Wickeen, *Macín,* Macken, a personal or family name.

Wicklow, *Vikingr-ló, Wykyngelow, Wkyynglo,* Danish/Norse meaning 'Viking meadow', also known by the anglicized wording **Kilmantan,** *Cill-Mhantáin* 'St Mantans Church'.

Wigna, *uaigneach, uaignighe,* lonely or desolate.

Wik, *mhoilc,* the throng.

Wilder, *Wilder,* Wilder, a personal or family name.

Wilderg, *bhaill-dheirg,* the red spot.

Wilk, *mhoilc,* not given.

Willadoon, *mhaoiledún,* not given.

Willan, *mhuilinn, mhuillin,* a mill.

Willan, *mhuillinn,* a mill.

William, *cuileann,* holly.

William, *Liam, Uilliam,* William, a male name.

William, *raithne,* bracken(sic).

Willian, *mhuilinn,* a mill.

Willigan, *bhFaoileagán,* gulls.

Willigan, O'Mulligan, a family name.

Willin, *buaile-na…,* the milking place of the……

Willin, *mhuilinn, mhuillin, mhuileann, mhuilleann,* a mill.

Willing, *mhuilinn,* a mill.

Willistown, *baile-bhuilí,* not given.

Willow, *bhaile,* a town, townland or homestead.

Willville, *an-corrbhaile,* not given.

Willy, *mhuillinn,* a mill.

Willy, *buailí,* a grazing and milking place.

Willy, *(an)-bhaile,* (of the) homesteads(sic).

Wilt, *mhoilt,* not given.

Wilt, *mhuilt,* a wether.

Wing, *bhán,* white.

Wing, *muing,* a sedgy place, a morass.

Winga, *muinga,* a sedgy place, a morass.

Winna, *bhainne,* milk.

Winna, *mhuine,* a shrubbery.

Winnia, *bhuine,* the herb 'sanicle'.

Winnia, *mhuine,* a brake or shrubbery.

Winny, *bhainne, baine,* milk.

Winny, *bhainne,* milk.

Winny, *fhine,* the race of…, (tribe or people).

Winny, *mhuine,* a brake or shrubbery.

Winny, *Mhuinghin, Fhinghin,* a personal or family name.

Winny, *Mhuinín,* not given.

Winshin, *bhFuinnseann,* ash trees.

Winterrourke, *mhuintir-Ruairc, mhuinter-Uí-Ruairc,* (*muinter, mhuinter*=family of) O'Rourke, a family name.

Wire, *Ghuaire, Guara,* a personal name.

Wire, *Uí-Mhaoighir,* O'Moyre, a family name.

Wirra, *Bhuire,* not given.

Wirra, *Muire, Mhuire,* Mary, a female name.

Wirrinan, *Mhuireanáin,* not given.

Wirrinaun, *Uí-Mhuireannain,* O'Mirrinan or Marrinan, a family name.

Witter, *uachdar,* upper or upper place.

Woaghternerry, *uachtar-neirghe,* upper ground elevation.

Wob, *Bhob,* Bob, a male name.

Wockrish, *mhacruais,* amusement.

Wodeen, *Bhóidín,* a male name.

Woe, *mBó,* cattle.

Woer, *mhaior,* a steward.

Woer, *tuair,* a bleach green.

Wogga, *mhaghaidh,* joking or pleasantry.

Woggaun, *bhogáin,* a quagmire or soft bog.

Wolie, *bhuaile, buaile,* a dairying place.

Wollin, *mhuilinn,* a mill.

Wolly, *mhullaigh,* not given.

Womanagh, (river) *Iomaghanach, Uamna,* not given.

Wonagh, *mhóineach,* boggy.

Woneen, *mhóinín,* a little bog.

Woney, *mhóna, mhona,* bog.

Wongaun, *mongan,* long grass.

Wonny, *baine,* milk.

Woo, *bhFuath,* spectres.

Wooa, *bhFuath,* spectres.

Woodan, *Uí-Bhuadáin,* O'Boydane, a family name.

Woodsgift, *baile-na-lochan,* the place of pools.

Wool, *bhuaile,* a dairying place.

Woolan, *mhulláin,* the small mill.

Woolie, *bhuaile,* cattle enclosure(sic).

Wooly, *buailidh,* a mountain dairy.

Wooraun, *bhFuarán,* cold spring wells.

Woran, *bhFuaran,* cold springs.

Wore, *mhór,* not given.

Worfy, *Mhurchadha,* Murrogh, a personal or family name.

Worgle, *Uí-Mhuireagáin,* Morgan a male name.

Workan, *Uí-Mharcain,* O'Markan, a family name.

Worker, *urchair,* the cast.

Worley, *Mhuirthille,* Murthuile, a male name.

Worly, *Mhuirghioll,* not given.

Worly, *Mhuirghiolla,* Murrel or Morrel, a personal or family name.

Worly, *Mhurthuile,* Murthuile, a male name.

Worna, *Mhoirne,* Moran, a personal or family name.

Worneen, *mhuirnín,* the lover.

Worry, *Bharaigh,* not given.

Worth, *abhnach, amhnach,* marshy, a watery place, a place of rivers.

Worth, *ghuirt, ghort,* a field, garden.

Worth, *iubhair,* yew.

Worth, *uird,* the order.

Worth, *úird,* the ritual.

Woteraghy, *uachtar-achaidh,* upper field.

Wotragh, *uachtrach, uachdar,* upper.

Wuddy, *bhodaigh,* a clown or churl.

Wullaun, *bhulláin,* a small or young bull.

Wullaun, *bullán,* a well in a rock.

Wully, *mhullaigh, mullagh,* a summit.

Wyanteean, *mhagh-an-tsidheáin,* field of the fairy hill.

Wyanurlaur, *mhagh-an-urláir,* field of the level spot.

Wylie, *bhile,* an ancient or sacred tree.

Y

Y, *aigh,* as an ending to a word can sometimes mean, a place of…. or abounding in…

Yagan, *Uí-Ágáin,* not given.

Yalla, *gheala,* white.

Yallaght, *Uí-Allaght,* Ó Allaght, a personal or family name.

Yallia, *Ua-Aille,* O'Healy, a family name.

Yallinan, *Uí-Áilíonáin,* Ó hÁilíonáin, a family name.

Yallinan, *Uí-Áilíonáin/Aileannáin,* not given.

Yallinan, *Uí-Áilleanáin,* Ó Áilleanáin, a personal or family name.

Yallog, *Uí-Mhaoil-Laodhóg,* O'Logue, a family name

Yallogue, *…na-ngealóg, …na geallog,* of the white bellied eels.

Yannan, *Uí-Ghanainn,* not given.

Yanny, *Uí-Annaidh,* not given.

Yanrahan, *Uí-Anracháin,* not given.

Yara, O'Hara, a family name.

Yaran, *iarainn,* not given.

Yaran, *Uí-Áráin, Uí-Árán,* a family name.

Yarkin, *O'Harkin,* a family name.

Yarra, *ghearra,* short.

Yarra, *Uí-hEaghra,* O'Hara, a family name.

Yartella, *Ui-Artaíle,* not given.

Yashea, *Uí-Aisí,* not given.

Ybacon, *Uí-Bhéacáin,* not given.

Ybanaun, *Uí-Bhánáin,* not given.

Ybeggane, *Uí-Bheagáin,* not given.

Ybegraly, *Uí-Mhic-Gréalaigh*(sic), not given.

Yblood, *Ó-mBloid,* not given.

Ybo, *Uí-Bhuaidh,* O'Boy, a personal or family name.

Yboden, *Ui-Bhuadáin,* O'Bodan, a family name.

Yboe, *Uí-Bhuaigh,* not given.

Yboggan, *Uí-Bhogáin, Bhogain,* O'Boggan, a family name.

Yboyland, *Uí-Bheoláin,* not given.

Yboyle, *Uí-Baoill,* not given.

Ybrackan, *Uí-Bhreacáin,* not given.

Ybraddan, *Uí-Bhradain,* O'Braddon, a family name.

Ybrannan, *Ui-Bhraonáin,* not given.

Ybrassil, *Uí-Bhreasail,* not given.

Ybrazil, *Uí-Bhreasail,* O'Brazil, a family name.

Ybreen, *Uí-Bhriain,* not given.

Ybregin, *Uí-Bheirgín,* not given.

Ybregin, *Uí-Bhréigin,* O'Bregan, a personal or family name.

Ybrennan, *Uí-Braonáin,* O'Brennan, a family name.

Ybrennock, *Uí-Bhreannóig,* not given.

Ybressil, *Uí-Breasail,* O'Brassil or O'Brazil, a family name.

Ybrew, *Uí-Bhrúin,* not given.

Ybricken, *Uí-Bhricín,* not given.

Ybrien, *Uí-Bhriain,* O'Brien, O'Brien, a family name.

Ybrigane, *Uí-Bhriagáin,* not given.

Ybrophy, *Uí-Bhróithe,* Ó Bróithe, Brophy, a family name.

Ybur, *Uí-Bhurra,* O'Burr, a family name.

Ybyrne, O'Byrne, a family name.

Ycahalan, *Uí-Chathaláin,* not given.

Ycahane, *Mhic-Eacháin*(sic), not given.

Ycahane, *Uí-Chatháin,* O'Cahane, a personal or family name.

Ycahill, *Uí-Chathail,* not given.

Ycallaghan, *Uí-Cheallacháin/Cheallachain,* not given.

Ycallan, *Uí-Challáin,* not given.

Ycallan, *Ui-Chaoláin,* O'Keelan, a family name.

Ycallinan, *Ua-Callanáin,* O'Callinan, a family name.

Ycanew, *Uí-Chonnmhaí/Chonbhaigh,* not given.

Ycannan, *Uí-Cheannáin,* not given.

Ycannon, *Uí-Chonnáin/Chonáin/Chanann,* not given.

Ycannon, *Uí-Chanáin,* O'Cannon, a family name.

Ycanvan, *Uí-Cheannabháin,* not given.

Ycarna, *Uí-Cearnaigh,* O'Kearney, a family name.

Ycarney, *Uí-Chearnaigh,* descendants of Carney, a personal or family name.

Ycarney, *Uí-Chearnaigh/Chatharnaigh,* not given.

Ycarran, *Uí-Charráin,* O'Carran, a family name..

Ycarrane, *Uí-Charráin/Chorráin,* not given.

Ycarroll, *Uí-Cearbhaill/Chearbhaill,* not given.

Ycasey, *Uí-Cathasach/Chathasaigh,* Ó Cathasaigh or O'Casey, a family name and means the descendants of Cathasach (a personal name).

Ycashin, *Uí-Chaisín,* O'Cashin, a personal or family name.

Ycassidy, *Uí-Chaiside,* not given.

Ycavan, *Uí-Caomhain,* O'Cavan, a family name.

Ychristal, *Mhic-Chriostail,* not given.

Ycleara, *Uí-Chléirigh,* not given.

Yclearig, *Uí-Cleirig,* O'Cleary, a family name.

Ycleary, *Uí-Chléirigh,* not given.

Ycleary, *Uí-Cleirig,* O'Cleary, a family name.

Yclerahan, *Ui-Chléireacháin,* not given.

Yclerihan, *Uí-Chléireacháin/Chleireacháin,* a family name meaning the descendants of Clerahan.

Yclery, *Uí-Chléirigh,* not given.

Yclohassy, *Uí-Chlochasaigh,* not given.

Yclohessy, O'Clohessy, a family name.

Ycloney, *Uí-Chluanaigh,* Clooney(sic), a personal or family name.

Yclovan, *Uí-Chlúmháin,* not given.

Yclovan, *Ui-Chlumháin,* Clifford, a personal or family name.

Ycluvane, *Uí-Chlúmháin,* not given.

Ycoffey, *Uí-Chofaigh,* not given.

Ycogley, *Uí-Choigligh/Chuigle,* not given.

Ycohy, *Uí-Chothaigh,* not given.

Ycolgan, *Mhic-Colgan,* not given.

Ycollin, *Uí-Choileinn, Mhic-Coillín,* not given.

Ycolliton, *Ui-Chollatáin,* not given.

Ycomain, *Uí-Chomain,* O'Common, a family name.

Ycommon, *Uí-Chomáin,* not given.

Yconigan, *Uí-Chonnagáin,* not given.

Yconnelly, *Uí-Chonghaile,* not given.

Yconnery, *Uí-Chonairche,* not given.

Yconnery, *Uí-Chonaire,* O'Connery, a personal or family name.

Yconnigan, *Uí-Choineagain,* O'Cunnigan, a family name.

Yconnor, *Uí-Chonchúir,* not given.

Yconry, *Ua-Chonaire,* O'Conroy, a family name.

Yconry, *Uí-Chonraoi,* not given.

Yconway, *Uí-Chonnmhaigh,* not given.

Yconway, *Uí-Chonbhuidhe,* O'Conway, a personal or family name.

Ycoogan, *Uí-Chuagain,* not given.

Ycormick, *Uí-Chormagáin/Chormaic,* not given.

Ycornane, *Ui-Churnáin,* not given.

Ycorraun, *Uí-Chorráin,* not given.

Ycurreen, *Uí-Chuirrín,* not given.

Ycorrigan, *Uí-Chorragáin,* not given.

Ycosker, *Uí-Choscraigh,* O'Cosgry, a family name.

Ycowan, *Mhic-Comhainn, Uí-Cobháin,* not given.

Ycowan, *Uí-Chomhghain,* O'Cowan, a family name.

Ycrehane, *Uí-Chreacháin,* not given.

Ycrimmeen, *Uí-Chroimín,* not given.

Ycuddihy, *Uí-Chuidithigh,* not given.

Ycuddihy, *Uí-Chuidithe,* O'Cuddihy, a family name.

Ycuddy, *Uí-Chuidithigh,* not given.

Ycue, *Mhic-Aodha,* not given.

Ycuirke, *Uí-Chuirc,* not given.

Yculhane, *Uí-Chathláin,* not given.

Ycullane, *Uí-Chathláin,* Ó Cathláin, a family name.

Ycullane, *Uí-Choileán/Choileáin,* Ó Coileáin, O'Cullane or Collins, a family name.

Ycullane, *Uí-Coilean,* Collins, a personal or family name.

Ycullen, *Uí-Choilín/Choiléin,* not given.

Ycullen, *Uí-Chuilinn,* O'Cullen, a family name.

Ycullin, *Uí-Chuilín,* not given.

Ycurkeen, *Uí-Chuircín,* O'Curkeen, a personal or family name.

Ycurragh, *Mhic-Mhurchú,* not given.

Ycurrane, *Ui-Chiaráin/Chiarain/Chorráin,* not given.

Ycurrany, *Uí-Charáinigh,* not given.

Ycurreen, *Uí-Churraoin,* not given.

Ycurrin, *Uí-Churraoin,* not given.

Ycurrin, *Uí-Chuirrin,* O'Curren, a personal or family name.

Ydaly, *Uí-Dhálaigh,* O'Daly, a family name.

Ydaniel, *Uí-Dhónaill,* O'Donnel, a family name.

Ydelogher, *Uí-Dubhluachra,* not given.

Ydermot, *Mhic-Dhiarmada,* not given.

Ydevet, O'Devitt, a family name.

Ydhuv, *Uí-Dhuibh,* O'Duff, a family name.

Ydine, *Uí-Dhiana,* O'Dyne, a personal or family name.

Ydonagh, *Uí-Dhonnchú,* not given.

Ydonegan, *Uí-Dhonnagáin/Dhonagain,* O'Donegan, a family name.

Ydonnel, *Uí-Dhónaill,* O'Donnell, a family name.

Ydonnell(sic), *Ó-dTomhrair, Uí-Tomhrair,* a family name.

Ydonnell, *Uí-Dhónaill, Dhúlaing*(sic)*/ Dhónaill,* not given.

Ydonnell, *Uí-Domhnaill, Uí-Dhomhnaill,* Ó Dónaill or O'Donnell, a family name.

Ydonnelly, *Uí-Dhonghaile,* not given.

Ydonohoe, *Uí-Dhonnchú,* not given.

Ydoody, *Uí-Dhúda,* not given.

Ydoole, *Uí-Dhúill,* not given.

Ydooley, *Uí-Dhubhlaoich,* not given.

Ydoorty, *Uí-Dhúrtaigh,* not given.

Ydougan, *Uí-Dhubhgáin,* not given.

Ydowan, *Uí-Dhubháin,* O'Dowan, a family name.

Ydowane, *Yí-Dhubháin,* not given.

Ydowda, *Uí-Dhúda,* not given.

Ydowel, *Uí-Dhúill,* not given.

Ydowel, *Uí-Dhubhghaill,* O'Dowel, a family name.

Ydownan, *Uí-Dhúnáin,* not given.

Ydrinan, *Ui-Dhroighneáin,* not given.

Ydrislane, *Uí-Dhrisleáin,* not given.

Yduane, *Uí-Dhubháin,* not given.

Yduff, *Uí-Dhuibh,* O'Duff, a family name.

Yduffy, O'Duffy, a family name.

Yduggan, *Uí-Dhuíginn/Dubhgáin,* not given.

Yduhig, *Uí-Dhúthaigh,* not given.

Ydun, *Uí-Dhuinn,* not given.

Yduneen, *Uí-Dhuinnín,* not given.

Ydurn, *Uí-Dhiornáin,* O'Durran, a personal or family name.

Ydurn, *Uí-Dhoirn,* not given.

Yduvana, *Uí-Dhubhain,* Dubhan or Devane a family name.

Yea, *Uí-Aodha,* O'Hea, a family name.

Yea, *Uí-Eachach,* not given.

Yeala, *Uí-Fhailbhe,* O'Falvey, a family name.

Yeden, *Uí-Éidín,* not given.

Yeden, *Uí-Aodáin,* O'Hayden, a personal or family name.

Yeelinan, *Uí-Oileannáin,* not given.

Yegan, *Uí-Aogáin,* not given.

Yeher, *gheithir, dhoithir,* black, gloomy or a wilderness.

Yelan, *Uí-Faoláin,* O'Phelan, a personal or family name.

Yelan, *Uí-Fhaoláin,* Ó Faoláin, a family name.

Yellinan, *Uí-Oileannáin,* not given.

Yerk, *Uí-Eirc,* not given.

Yermer, *Uí-Dheirmir,* not given.

Yewen, *Eoghan,* Owen, a male name and means 'well born'.

Yewer, *Iubhar,* yew.

Yforan, *Uí-Fhuaradháin,* not given.

Yfowloo, *Uí-Fhoghlú,* not given.

Yfraley, *Uí-Fhreáile,* not given.

Ygaddy, *Ui-Ghadaí, Uí-Aidín*(sic) *fochaire,*

Ygagan, *'ic-Eochagain,* Mageoghegan, a family name.

Ygagin, *Uí-Gháigín/Ghaigín,* O'Gagin, a personal or family name.

Ygaheen, *Uí-Ghaoithín,* not given.

Ygalane, *Uí-Ghiolláin,* not given.

Ygalley, *Uí-Dhálaigh,* not given.

Ygallon, *Uí-Ghiolláin,* O'Giollan, a family name.

Ygalvan, *Ua-Galmhán,* O'Galvan, a family name.

Ygalvan, *Uí-Ghealbháin,* not given.

Ygalvin, *Ui-Ghealbháin,* not given.

Yganavan, *Uí-Ghaineamháin,* not given.

Ygara, O'Gara, a family name.

Ygardra, *Uí-Ghéardra,* O'Gearda, a family name.

Ygarra, *Uí-Ghearraidh,* the cutting(sic).

Ygarvey, *Uí-Ghairbhíth,* not given.

Ygawley, *Uí-Dhálaigh,* not given.

Ygeana, *Uí-Ghéibheannaigh,* not given.

Ygeany, *Uí-Dhíonaighe,* not given.

Ygeela, *Ó gCadhla,* Uí Chadhla, a family name.

Ygeely, *Mhic-Caollaí,* not given.

Ygeerahan, *Mhic-Ghaoirechain,* McGahern, a personal or family name.

Ygegan, *Mhic-Aodhagáin,* Mac Geoghagan, a personal or family name.

Ygillane, *Ui-Ghiolláin,* not given.

Yglasheen, *Uí-Ghlaisín,* not given.

Yglassoon, *Uí-Ghlasún,* not given.

Yglassoon, *glas-uaine,* abounding in green verdue.

Yglooneen, *Uí-Ghlóinín,* O'Gloneen, a family name.

Ygoghlan, *Ó-gCochláin,* not given.

Ygone, *Uí-Ghabhann,* not given.

Ygonnelly, *Uí-Dhonghaile,* not given.

Ygooney, *Uí-Ghamhnaigh,* Gaffney, a personal or family name.

Ygorey, *Uí-Ghuara/Guaire,* not given.

Ygorey, *Uí-Ghuaire,* O'Gorey, a personal or family name.

Ygorman, *Uí-Ghormáin/Ghormain,* a family name.

Ygormican, *Uí-Ghormacáin,* not given.

Ygowan, *Uí-Ghabhann,* O'Gowan, a family name and means descendants of the smith.

Ygowan, *Uí-Ghamhna,* O'Gowna or Gaffney, a family name.

Ygowney, *Uí-Ghamhna,* O'Gaffney, a family name.

Ygreeghan, *Uí-Ghréacháin,* not given.

Ygreek, *Uí-Ghreig,* O'Greig, a family name.

Ygrennan, *Uí-Dhroighneáin/Ghrianáin,* not given.

Ygriffin, *Uí-Ghríofa,* not given.

Ygriffin, *Uí-Ghrifin,* O'Griffin, a family name.

Ygrogan, *Uí-Ghuagáin,* not given.

Ygroman,(sic) *Uí-Ghormáin,* not given.

Yguineen, *Uí-Ghaibhnín,* not given.

Yguiry, *Uí-Ghadhra,* O'Guiry, a personal or family name.

Ygulleen, *Uí-Ghoillín,* not given.

Ygunnigan, *Uí-Chonnagáin,* not given.

Yhagan, *Uí-Éacháin,* not given.

Yhahil, *Uí-Sháithil, dhá-thuile,* not given.

Yhalwick, *Uí-Shealbhaigh,* not given.

Yhamigan, *Uí-Chonnagáin,* not given.

Yhane, *Uí-Cháin,* O'Cane, a personal or family name.

Yhane, *Uí-Fheacháin/Sheáin,* not given.

Yhane, *Uí-Sheagháin,* O'Shane, a family name.

Yhannon, *Uí-hAnnachain,* O'Hannon, a personal or family name.

Yhar, *Ui-Aichir,* not given.

Yharp, *Uí-Thorpa,* not given.

Yharrahan, *Uí-Shearúcháin,* not given.

Yhea, *Uí-Shé,* not given.

Yheadon, *Uí-Éidheáin,* not given.

Yheadon, *Uí-Éidín,* O'Headon or Hayden, a family name.

Yheafy, *Uí-hÉamthaigh,* O'Heafy, a family name.

Yheedy, *Uí-Síoda,* not given.

Yheeny, *Uí-Shuibhne/Ínidh,* not given.

Yheerin, *Uí-Shírín,* not given.

Yheige, *Uí-Thaidhg/Thadhg,* not given.

Yhenan, *Uí-Sheighneáin,* Ó Seighneáin, a family name.

Yhickey, *Uí-Ící,* not given.

Yhickey, *Uí-Icidhe,* O'Hickey, a personal or family name.

Yhogan, *Uí-Ógáin,* not given.

Yhoge, *Uí-Cheog,* not given.

Yhohan, *Uí-Thuacháin,* O'Tuachan, a personal or family name.

Yhohan, *Uí-Thuatháin,* not given.

Yholahan, *Uí-Uallacháin,* not given.

Yhone, *Ui-Eoghain,* not given.

Yhoneen, *Uí-Uaithnín,* not given.

Yhoodane, *Uí-Thuadáin,* not given.

Yhooig, *Uí-Bhuaigh,* not given.

Yhoolihan, *Uí-Uallacháin,* not given.

Yhoolihane, O'Hoolahan, a family name.

Yhooriskey, *Uí-Fhuaruisce,* not given.

Yhorgan, *Uí-Argáin,* not given.

Yhough, *Uí-Eachach,* not given.

Yhourigan, *Uí-Odhragáin,* not given.

Yhowly, *Uí-Amhalghaid,* not given.

Yhugh, *Mhic-Aodha,* not given.

Yhurrow, *Uí-Urchú,* not given.

Ykealy, *Uí-Chaelluiodhe,* O'Kealy, a family name.

Ykealy, *Uí-Chaeluighe,* O'Kelly, a family name.

Ykealy, *Uí-Chaollaí/Chadhla,* not given.

Ykean, *Uí-Chéin,* not given.

Ykeefe, *Uí-Chaoimh,* O'Keeffe, a family name.

Ykeenaghan, *Uí-Choinneacháin,* not given.

Ykelly, *Uí-Cheallaigh/Chealaigh,* O'Kelly, a family name.

Ykenealy, *Uí-Chinnfhailaidh, not* given.

Ykenna, *Uí-Chineá,* not given.

Ykennedy, *Uí-Chinnéide,* not given.

Ykenny, *Uí-Chionaith,* not given.

Ykenny, *Uí-Chionaoith/Chionaith,* not given.

Ykeoghan, *Uí-Cheocháin,* O'Keoghan, a family name.

Ykeoghan, *Uí-Sheocháin,* O'Keoghane, a family name.

Ykeoghane, *Mhic-Eochain,* not given.

Ykeohane, *Mhic-Eocháin,* Mac Eocháin, not given.

Ykeohane, O'Keohane, a family name.

Ykergan, *Uí-Chiaragáin,* not given.

Ykerin, *Uí-Chírín/Chéirín,* O'Kerrin, a family name.

Ykeroge, *Uí-Chiaróg,* not given.

Ykerrin, *Uí-Chéirín,* O'Kerrin, a personal or family name.

Ykerrivan, *Uí-Ciárabháin,* O'Kirwin, a family name.

Ykevan, *Uí-Chiabháin,* not given.

Ykillaboy, *Mhic-Giolla-Bhuí,* not given.

Ykine, *O'Kine or Mackine,* a personal or family name.

Yknaveen, *Uí-Chnaimhín,* O'Knavin, Nevin or Bowen, a family name.

Yknaveen, *Uí-Chnaimhin/ Chnáimhín,* O'Nevin, a family name.

Ylahiff, *Uí-Fhlaitimh,* not given.

Ylahy, *Uí-Laithí,* not given.

Ylane, *Uí-Léin,* not given.

Ylaneen, *Uí-Fhlaithnín/Laithnín,* not given.

Ylangadon, *Uí-Fhlannagáin,* not given.

Ylanigan, O'Lanigan or O'Flanagan, a family name.

Ylanigan, *Uí-Lonnagáin/Fhlannagáin,* not given.

Ylarkin, *Uí-Lorcain,* not given.

Ylarkin, *Uí-Lorcáin,* O'Lorcan, O'Larkin, a family name.

Ylaughnane, *Ui-Lachnáin,* not given.

Yleagh, *Ó-Laoch, Uí-Laoch,* a family name.

Yleahy, *Uí-Laochdha,* Leahy, O'Leahy, a family name.

Yleamy, *Uí-Léime,* not given.

Yleane, *Uí-Liain,* O'Leane, a family name.

Yleary, *Uí-Laoghaire,* O'Leary, a family name.

Yleary, *Uí-Laoire,* not given.

Ylee, *Uí-Laoigh,* not given.

Ylegat, *Uí-Leagáid,* O'Legat, a personal or family name.

Ylehane, *Ui-Lorcain,* not given.

Ylehaun, *Uí-Liatháin,* O'Lehane, a family name..

Ylemon, *Uí-Loimín,* O'Loman, a personal or family name.

Ylenane, *Uí-Leannáin,* not given.

Ylennin, *Ui-Leannáin,* not given.

Ylin, *Uí-Fhloinn, Uí-Fhlaoinn,* a family name.

Ylin, *Uí-Laighin,* not given.

Ylinan, *Uí-Laidhgnéin,* not given.

Ylinane, *Uí-Leannáin,* not given.

Ylinch, *Uí-Loingsigh,* not given.

Yline, *Uí-Fhloinn,* O'Flynn, a family name.

Yline, *Uí-Laighin,* Ó Laighin, a family name.

Ylinnen, *Uí-Lonáin,* not given.

Ylonnan, *Ui-Luanaim,* not given.

Ylooby, *Uí-Lúbaigh,* not given.

Yloughlin, *Uí-Lochlainn,* not given.

Yloughnaan, *Uí-Lachnáin,* not given.

Yloughnane, *Uí-Lachnáin,* not given.

Ylowra, *Uí-Labhra,* not given.

Ylowra, *Uí-Labhraidh,* O'Lowry, a family name.

Ylynan, *Uí-Laigheanáin,* not given.

Ylynch, *Uí-Loingsigh,* not given.

Ylynch, *Uí-Loinsigh,* O'Lynch, a family name.

Ymacaramery, *O'Ramery,* a personal or family name.

Ymacarn, Macarn or Macartan, a personal or family name.

Ymacashel, *Uí-Mhaolchaisil,* not given.

Ymackesy, *Uí-Mhacasa,* not given.

Ymackey, *Uí-Mhacaí,* not given.

Ymadden, Madden or O'Madden, a family name.

Ymadden, *Uí-Mhadaín/Madadhain,* not given.

Ymagauran, *Mic-Shamradháin/ Shamhradhain,* Macauran or MacGouran, a family name.

Ymahon, *Uí-Mhatháin,* not given.

Ymailley, *Uí-Mhaille,* not given.

Ymakeery, *Uí-Mhic-Tíre,* not given.

Ymaleel, *Ui-Mhaolaíola,* not given.

Ymalone, *Uí-Mhaolomhnaigh,* not given.

Ymard, *Ua-mBaird,* O'Ward or Mac-an-ward, a family name.

Ymarly, *Ó-Mearlaigh,* not given.

Ymarran, *Uí-Mhearáin,* not given.

Ymartin, *Uí-Mháirtín,* not given.

Ymassy, *Uí-Mhaoilmheasa,* not given.

Ymitty, *Uí-Mhitigh/Muide,* not given.

Ymoghany, *Ui-Mhochaine,* O'Moghany, not given.

Ymohan, *Ó-mBuacháin,* not given.

Ymonaghan, O'Monaghan, a family name.

Ymongaun, *Uí-Mhongáin,* not given.

Ymooney, *Uí-Mhaonaigh,* not given.

Ymoran, *Uí-Mhórain,* not given.

Ymorran, *Uí-Mhoráin,* not given.

Ymorris, *Uí-Mhuiris,* Ó Muiris, a family name.

Ymoylin, *Uí-Mhaoilín,* not given.

Ymulalla, *Uí-Mhaolalaidh,* not given.

Ymullins, *Uí-Maolfhinne,* not given.

Ymurn, *Ui-Mhurúin,* not given.

Ymurphy, *Uí-Mhurchú/Mhurchadha,* not given.

Ymurragh, *Uí-Mhurchú,* not given.

Ymurraghoo, *Uí-Mhurchadha,* not given.

Ymurray, *Uí-Mhurígh/Mhuireadh,* not given.

Ymurreen, *Amoraoin(sic), Uí-Mhuirín,* not given.

Ynanty, *Uí-Neachtain*(sic), not given.

Ynavin, *Uí-Chnáimhín,* O'Cnavin(sic), a personal or family name.

Yneal, *Uí-Neill/Néill,* O'Neill, a family name.

Yneale, *Uí-Néill,* not given.

Yneilan, *Ua-Nialain,* O'Neylan, a family name.

Yneill, O'Neill, a family name.

Yneill, *Uí-Néill,* not given.

Yneilly, *Uí-Neillighe,* O'Neilly, a family name.

Ynelligan, *Uí-Niallagáin,* O'Nelligan, a family name.

Ynevin, *Uí-Chnáimhín/Chnaimhín,* O'Nevin, a personal or family name.

Ynicole, *Mhic-Niocóil,* not given.

Ynolan, *Ó-Nialláin,* not given.

Ynolan, *Ui-Nualláin,* O'Nolan, a family name.

Ynomasna, *Uí-Lomasna,* O'Lomasny, a personal or family name.

Ynomasna, *Uí-Lomasnaigh,* not given.

Ynoon, *Uí-Nuadhain,* O'Noone, a family name.

Ynough, *Ó-nEachach,* not given.

Yogan, *Uí-Ógain/Ogáin,* not given.

Yogan, *Uí-Ogáin/Hógain,* O'Hogan a family name.

Yogarty, *Uí-Fhógarta,* not given.

Yogarty, *Ui-Fhógartaigh,* O'Fogerty, a family name.

Yohil, *eó-choill,* yew wood.

Yolaghan, *Uí-Uallachain,* not given.

Yonan, *Uí-Mhaonáin,* not given.

Yoogan, *Uí-Dhubhgáin,* O'Duggan, a family name.

Yoolahan, *Ui-Uallacháin,* O'Houlahan, a personal or family name.

Yooloo, *Uí-Fhoghladha,* O'Fouloo or O'Foley, a family name.

Yoreawn, *fheabhrán,* cow-parsnips.

Yorgan, *Uí-Argáin,* not given.

Youghal, *eochaille, eochaill, eo-choill,* yew wood.

Youghalarra, *eochaill*(sic), not given.

Youghalarra, *eóchaill-Ára,* not given.

Youghter, *Uí-Eachtair,* not given.

Youl, *Uí-Áille,* not given.

Youragan, *Uí-Anragáin,* not given.

Youth, *Thiuit,* Tuite, a personal or family name.

Yowla, *abhla, ubhla,* apples or apple trees.

Yowla, *úlla,* hills.

Yowle, *abhla, ubhla,* apples or apple trees.

Yowle, *úlla,* hills.

Yquin, *Uí-Chuinn,* Ó Cuinn, a family name.

Yquin, *Uí-Dhuinn,* not given.

Yquinlevan, *Uí-Chaoinleabháin,* not given.

Yquinn, *Uí-Choinn,* Quinn, a family name and means the descendants of Quinn.

Yquirk, *Uí-Chuirc,* O'Quirk, a family name.

Yrafter, *Uí-Reachtúir,* not given.

Yrafton, *Uí-Reachtain,* not given.

Yrafton, *Ní-Reachtúir*(sic), Rafter, a personal or family name.

Yrahilly, *Uí-Raithile,* not given.

Yready, *Uí-Riada,* O'Reidy, a personal or family name.

Yreddy, *Uí-Rioda,* not given.

Yreddy, *Uí-Riada,* O'Reidy, a family name.

Yreea, *aimhreid,* uneven.

Yreel, *Uí-Fhríl,* not given.

Yreen, *Ua-Rín,* O'Reen, a family name.

Yregan, *Uí-Réigín,* not given.

Yregan, *Uí-Riagáin/Riagain/Riagan,* O'Regan, a family name.

Yreilly, *Uí-Raghallaigh,* not given.

Yrickane, *Uí-Lorcáin/Lorcain*(sic), not given.

Yring, *Uí-Rinn,* a family name.

Yriordane, *Ui-Ríordáin/Ríoghbhardáin,* not given.

Yroddy, *Uí-Rodaighe,* not given.

Yroe, *Uí-Ruaidh,* O'Rowe, a family name.

Yrohan, *Uí-Rócháin,* not given.

Yronan, *Uí-Rónáin,* not given.

Yroney, *Uí-Ruanaidh/Ruanadha,* not given.

Yroney, *Uí-Ruanaí,* O'Rooney, a family name.

Yrourke, *Uí-Ruairc,* not given.

Yroyan, *Uí-Ruadhain,* O'Rowan, a family name.

Yrush, *Uí-Rois,* not given.

Yryan, *Uí-Riain,* not given.

Yscandal, *Uí-Scannail,* O'Scannel, a family name.

Yscanlan, *Uí-Scanláin,* not given.

Yscannel, *Uí-Scannail,* O'Scannel, a family name.

Yscullion, *Uí-Scuilín,* not given.

Yshanny, *Ua-Seannach,* O'Shanny, a family name.

Yshaughnessy, O'Shaughessy(sic) a family name.

Ysheehan, *Uí-Shíocháin,* not given.

Ysheehan, *Uí-Shíothcháin,* O'Sheehan, a personal or family name.

Ysheil, *Uí-Shiail/Shiadhail,* not given.

Ysheilin, *Uí-Shleibhleachain,* O Shleibhleachain, a family name.

Yspellan, *Uí-Spealáin,* not given.

Yspellane, *Uí-Spealáin,* not given.

Yspillane, *Ui-Spalláin,* not given.

Yteige, *Uí-Thaidhg,* not given.

Ytohil, *Uí-Thuathail,* O'Toole, a personal or family name.

Ytrehy, *Uí-Throithigh,* not given.

Yugan, *Uí-Dhubhgáin,* not given.

Yure, *iubhair,* a yew wood.

Yuse, *giumhas, ghiumhais,* fir.

Yvadden, *Uí-Mhadudhain,* O'Madden, a family name.

Yvadin, *Ui-Mhaidín,* Ó Maidin, or O'Madden, a family name.

Yvaghan, *Ui-Bheacháin,* not given.

Yvahane, *Uí-Bheacháin,* not given.

Yvaheen, *Uí-Bheaithín*(sic), not given.

Yvallen, *Uí-Mhaoláin,* a family name.

Yvanran, *Uí-Mhanráin,* not given.

Yvara, *Uí-Mheadhra,* O'Mara, O'Meara.

Yvardan, *Uí-Bhárdán,* O'Bardan, a family name.

Yvarra, *Uí-Bhearra/Mheadhra,* not given.

Yvaughan, *Uí-Mhacháin/Bheacháin,* not given.

Yvelig, *Uí-Bhéilig,* Velick, a personal or family name.

Yvera, *Uí-Mheára,* O'Meara, a family name.

Yvergin, *Uí-Mheirgín,* not given.

Yvernín, *Uí-Bheirnín,* not given.

Yviggane, *Uí-Bheagáin,* not given.

Yvillane, *Ó-bhFaoileáin,* not given.

Yvirane, *Ui-Bhioráin,* not given.

Yvoge, *Uí-Bhuaigh,* not given.

Yvohalane, *Uí-Mhothláin/Mhothlain,* O'Mohalan, a personal or family name.

Yvoige, *Uí-Bhuadháigh,* not given.

Yvolane, *Uí-Mhaolain,* O'Mullane, O'Mailan, O'Mullane or Mullins, a family name.

Yvollane, *Uí-Mhaoláin,* not given.

Yvoodane, *Uí-Bhuadáin,* not given.

Yvoony, *Uí-Mhúnigh,* not given.

Yvoyle, *Uí-Bhaoighill,* not given.

Yvoyle, *Uí-Bhaoill,* not given.

Yvrick, *Ui-Bhric,* O'Bric, a personal or family name.

Yvroe, *Uí-Bhró,* not given.

Yvulhane, *Uí-Mhothláin,* not given.

Yvuragha, *Uí-Mhurchú,* not given.

Yvurrheen, *Uí-Murcháin,* little Murrough(sic), a personal or family name.

Ywanig, *Uí-Bhánach,* O'Bana, a family name.

Yweeaun, *Uí-Bhuíáin,* not given.

Yweelagh, *Uí-Mhulais,* Mulash, a family name.

Ywelligan, *Ui-Mhaolagain,* O'Mulligan, not given.

Ywiheen, *Uí-Bhaoithín,* not given.

Ywilliam, *Mhic-Uilliam,* not given.

Ywire, *Uí-Mhaghair,* not given.

Yworfy, *Uí-Mharchaidh,* not given.

Ywulligan, *Uí-Mhaolagain,* O'Mulligan, a family name.

Tom Burnell, Holycross, Tipperary. AD2006.

museumtom@hotmail.com